8·40

O9-BTL-350

ELITES AGAINST DEMOCRACY

ELITES AGAINST DEMOCRACY

Leadership Ideals in Bourgeois
Political Thought in Germany, 1890–1933

Walter Struve

PRINCETON UNIVERSITY PRESS
PRINCETON, NEW JERSEY

Copyright © 1973 by Princeton University Press

All Rights Reserved

LCC: 72–14034

ISBN: 0–691–07555–7 (Hardcover Edition)

ISBN: 0–691–10020–9 (Limited Paperback Edition)

Library of Congress Cataloging in Publication data will be found on the last printed page of this book

This book has been composed in Linotype Caledonia
Printed in the United States of America
by Princeton University Press

119775

For Adam and Derick

Contents

Contents

Dᴜʀɪɴɢ the past few years American academics have often been asked to be "relevant." I hope and believe that my study of elitism will contribute to our ability to comprehend not only Germany's past— itself a matter of untold "relevance"—but also other societies, including our own.

When I began working on German elitism almost fifteen years ago, I thought I was examining doctrines that had developed mainly in Germany and were not characteristic of most industrial societies. These doctrines insist upon the need for an elite which, however broadly and democratically recruited, rules in an authoritarian fashion. Such ideas seemed to me to be much less in evidence in countries with firmly rooted traditions of political democracy. As the book grew, and as my work on it taught me much about how to examine the United States, I came to realize that the notion of German uniqueness made as little sense as the belief in American exceptionalism. The very sort of elitism that I had studied in a German context describes the realities of the political order in the United States or Britain or France better than the dogmas of political democracy, and much better than the contradictory publications of social scientists acting in a dual role as cheerleaders of the American Century and analysts for the ruling class.

Elitism of a variety familiar to me from this study of Germany is now on the rise in the West. After a century of almost uncontested celebration, the doctrines of democracy appear to be losing their supremacy in the United States. After hearing for so long that the people should and can rule, we are frequently being told that they should not and cannot, that we ought to accept the rule of an elite over which we have little or no control, and that all will be for the best if only the members of this elite are qualified for its tasks or "representative" of the racial and ethnic composition of the nation. We are asked to accept equality of opportunity—on the basis of "merit"—to dominate and exploit others. A similar elitism had a progressive as well as a reactionary thrust in the Germany of the 1890's. Today the advance of such elitism is likely to go hand in hand with reaction.

This book can be read either as a study in the political culture of the German bourgeoisie during the first few decades of the era of imperialism or as an examination of the centrality of a specific type of elitism in bourgeois political thought in Germany. For the purposes of analysis and presentation, I have dealt in depth with almost a dozen elitists. I have sought to make a contribution to the literature on each of them. In my efforts to explain the origins of their elitism, I have drawn upon biography, as well as social, intellectual, political, and economic history. I hope that my method has brought this material together effectively in order to lay bare the sources and development of elitism in Germany during the past three generations. The reader must judge for himself whether I have succeeded and whether my approach can be applied to the study of elitism in other countries.

New York
November 1972

Walter Struve

Acknowledgments

O<small>NE</small> of the disadvantages of a lengthy study undertaken over a long period of time is that the author may have difficulty rendering an accounting of the debts that he has incurred. This difficulty, I trust, I do not face. Time and again, continuation of work on this book was possible only because of the moral and intellectual support of my wife and friends. They will no doubt be happier than I not to have to look at the manuscript for this book any longer. Herman Lebovics of the State University of New York at Stony Brook has been helping me to reduce problems to human proportions since I first began working on German elitism. Emanuel Chill and Martin Waldman, both my colleagues at the City College of the City University of New York, became my patient critics somewhat later.

My other obligations are more diverse. My former teacher, the late Hajo Holborn of Yale, gave much-needed encouragement during some early, trying stages of my work. Karl W. Deutsch, now of Harvard, assisted me with conceptualization in ways that he may no longer recognize. The late Sigmund Neumann of Wesleyan gave me wise advice which, if applied, might have saved me several years of work. So also did Arno J. Mayer of Princeton to whom I also owe a more general intellectual debt acquired at a turning point in my own development.

Sanford G. Thatcher and Lewis Bateman, both of Princeton University Press, have my gratitude for the understanding and good judgment that they have shown in dealing with the manuscript.

This work has been supported by fellowships or grants from Yale University, the German Academic Exchange Service, and the City University of New York.

I am grateful for permission to use portions of my article "Hans Zehrer as a Neoconservative Elite Theorist," *American Historical Review*, LXX (July 1965), 1035–57.

The index was prepared by Charles Decker.

ELITES AGAINST DEMOCRACY

For decades, indeed for more than a century, a perennial concern of historical scholarship has been how Germany differs from other countries. An outgrowth of my interest in this question, the present study examines a striking contrast between bourgeois political thought in Germany and the West during the era of imperialism that began in the late nineteenth century and that we are still living in today. This contrast appears in the answers given to the traditional questions of political and social theory: who should rule, why, how, for whom? In Germany, unlike the West, the notion of what, for the sake of brevity, can be described as an "open-yet-authoritarian elite" became predominant in bourgeois political culture. This type of elitism rests upon three major assumptions. First, a few men always rule and make the crucial decisions in any society. Second, other men can or should play little if any role in formulating these decisions, or in controlling the elite. Third, the recruitment of this elite should not be restricted to any one segment of society, but rather should be open to capable men regardless of their origins, class, status, race, or religion. Containing both democratic and nondemocratic elements, these assumptions permit "democracy of personnel selection," but not of decision making. The establishment of effective popular control over the selection, policies, and activities of the elite is thought undesirable.

A cursory look at the ideas of some advocates of this elitism might easily lead to its confusion with Jacobin or Leninist notions. For the moment, a basic distinction should be kept in mind. To the Jacobin or Leninist the rule of the elite, indeed the very existence of the elite, is only temporary, not perennial. For example, Lenin conceived of the vanguard of the proletarian revolution as undertaking measures that would destroy the conditions that had once necessitated its formation.[1] By contrast, the concept of an open-yet-authoritarian elite obviated the possibility of such measures; its proponents considered authoritarian rulers endemic to, and desirable for, every society.

While the idea of an open-yet-authoritarian elite was being developed in Germany, adherents of political democracy came to dominate

---

[1] See esp. Lenin's *What Is To Be Done?* (1902) (Moscow, n.d.), pp. 197–237; *The State and Revolution* (1917) (Moscow, n.d.), pp. 151–75; *"Left-Wing" Communism, an Infantile Disorder* (1920) (New York, 1940), pp. 9–11, 29–39.

3

bourgeois political culture in Western Europe and North America. Clinging to or seizing upon a tradition of democracy that reached back to the ancient world, they worked within this tradition, elaborating the feasibility and desirability of popular control. Whether paying mere lip-service to democratic ideals or actively committed to their realization, most bourgeois ideologists ignored or rejected the argument that democracy should be practiced only in the selection of leaders, and not in decision making as well.

Unlike many of their German counterparts, these ideologists did not divorce the issue of the recruitment of leaders from that of popular control. Democracy, to paraphrase Clemenceau's remark about the French Revolution, had to be accepted or rejected as a *bloc*.[2] Until the middle of the twentieth century, voices championing an open-yet-authoritarian elite were usually drowned out in the West. Without a sharp break in continuity, nineteenth-century conservatism and liberalism were adapted to or supplanted by the doctrines of political democracy. Despite some equivocation, bourgeois political thinkers responded to the rise of labor and socialist movements during the last decades of the nineteenth century by hailing democratic ideals. In the West, the prevailing elitism was nonauthoritarian, as well as open. In Germany, the growth of Social Democracy posed a challenge that led to the articulation of the notion of democracy of personnel selection rather than decision making.

Throughout Europe, as H. Stuart Hughes has shown, Marxism was largely ignored by non-Socialists until the decade of the 1890's.[3] Beginning in this decade some of the most innovative philosophers and social scientists, mainly in France, Italy, and the German-speaking lands, developed critiques of Marxism—critiques that were central to their own contributions to social and political thought. As Hughes neglects to point out, the confrontation with Marxist theory appeared prominently on the agenda of intellectual discourse in the very areas of Europe where mass movements invoking Marxism had developed. Concerned with establishing the importance of nonrational factors in human behavior, but still seeking to assert its tractibility to rational analysis, intellectual pioneers such as Pareto, Croce, Freud, Durkheim, and Bergson offered rejoinders, if often only implicitly, to Marx, whom they correctly regarded as a rationalist. They faulted him and his intellectual heirs for ignoring the critical role of the irrational in individ-

[2] *Journal officiel de la République française, Débats parlementaires,* Jan. 29, 1891, p. 155.

[3] H. Stuart Hughes, *Consciousness and Society: The Reorientation of European Social Thought, 1890–1930* (New York, 1958), p. 67 and passim.

ual and social behavior, and hence for failing to build a solid foundation for a comprehensive, rational theory of society.

In Central Europe, particularly in Germany, a cognate response to Marxism appeared in the development of the concept of an open-yet-authoritarian elite. Much of this elitism was worked out in the context of criticizing the classical ideals of democracy. The high degree of popular control associated with the notions of political equality, majority rule, popular sovereignty, and government by the people was stigmatized as neither desirable nor practicable. The observation that the central tenets of open-yet-authoritarian elitism emerged largely from an assault upon democratic ideals rather than from sustained, explicit attacks on Marxism suggests that bourgeois political thinkers were troubled more by the growth of a militant, well-organized labor movement than by the corpus of Marxist theoretical writings. The immediate objectives of Social Democracy, demanding as they did the establishment of political democracy, revived issues of democratic theory that the political and economic restructuring of Central Europe during the era of national unification had temporarily pushed aside. The theory of democracy became, as it had been during the middle of the nineteenth century, a focal point of political controversy, but the hackneyed rejoinders supplied by conventional liberals and conservatives could not meet the challenge presented either by the revolutionary or reformist potential of the organized proletariat. Although the reformist's preoccupation with the creation of the institutions of political democracy was, for many a sophisticated bourgeois, a welcome relief from the intransigence of the radical Socialists, his insistence upon reform presented dangers to be averted, as well as opportunities to be exploited.

Outside the ranks of the Social Democratic movement democracy and socialism were taken seriously as intellectual problems in Germany before World War I primarily in some left-liberal circles. Such men as Friedrich Naumann, Theodor Barth, Max Weber, and Hugo Preuss played a major part in the development of the notion of democracy of personnel selection rather than decision making. They sought to present an alternative to the leadership vacuum and incessant chaos that, they warned, would ensue in Germany if either political democracy were instituted or social revolution occurred. As a prophylactic for both of these menaces they prescribed timely alterations in the composition, techniques, and objectives of the nation's political leaders. They assumed that these alterations were more important than—indeed, were alternatives to—swift, radical changes in the social and economic structure. Under the proper leadership, the articulation of a highly complex, well-integrated social structure, now fully adapted to the requirements of imperialism, would be brought to completion. Marxism and democracy would be transcended.

The new German liberal elitist, although often disarmingly frank about his political goals, had a penchant for ascribing them to historical inevitability. He explained that elitist rule was inescapable; society was divided perennially into elite and mass, or elites and masses. Hence the vision of a nonelitist order was myopic, and focusing upon popular control of leaders diverted attention from the critical issues of who constituted the elite and what policies it undertook. Thus in 1891 Hugo Preuss described all mankind as belonging, for political purposes, simply to two groups, a few "leaders of the flock" and a vast majority of "ordinary creatures of the herd." "Always and everywhere," Preuss wrote, "the few command, and the many obey. The situation cannot be otherwise as long as man is a herd animal, the multitude of which needs leadership in order to assert itself in any way whatsoever. All political struggles turn only upon the question who these few are to be."[4]

The new liberal elitist subordinated a class analysis of society and a materialist view of history to an approach that recognized elites as the ultimate agencies of historical change. He directed attention mainly to the occupants of political office, to the formal holders of power in the state; he thereby asserted the primacy of an artificially compartmentalized analysis of politics. For him the term "ruling class" served primarily as a pejorative, not as a tool of analysis. Germany should have "true leaders," a "ruling stratum," or an "aristocracy" appropriate to the nation's advanced industrial development and potential international power; and this elite, whose rule would of necessity be largely unchecked by the populace, must be open to recruitment from every section of society.

No matter how open the elite, the new liberal elitist contended, it would and must exercise virtually complete political control over the nonelite. His conclusion that popular control was impossible and undesirable was telling partly because it could be documented by many accurate observations, past and present, from Germany and other countries. He could argue plausibly that belief in the classical ideals of democracy promoted a lack of concern for leadership, nourished dangerous illusions, and legitimized the rule of inferior leaders. Had he lived in Western Europe or the United States, he might have phrased his elitism in language closer to that of the classical ideals of

[4] Hugo Preuss, "Sozialdemokratie und Parlamentarismus" in his *Staat, Recht und Freiheit: Aus 40 Jahren deutscher Politik und Geschichte*, ed. Theodor Heuss (Tübingen, 1926), pp. 162–63.

democracy. Had he lived in a nation with a consensus, however recently established, favorable to democracy as a cherished if often vague
value, he might have given his formal blessing to these ideals. But his
interpretation of critiques of political life in the West served for him
to confirm the realism that he claimed for his strictures on democracy.

He could rely upon the writings of sympathetic, as well as hostile,
students of Western politics to support his conviction that democracy
was, at best, an occasionally useful fraud. When in October 1918 the
sociologist Alfred Weber summed up the relationship of German intellectuals to democracy, he was referring particularly to liberal elitists
like himself and his brother Max Weber:

> We saw—and we continue to see—that it [Western democracy] is
> certainly a program, but far from a reality; that it [Western democ-
> racy] has not substituted freedom and equality for the old authori-
> ties that it destroyed, but only replaced them with other authorities
> that are of very doubtful value and that it did not itself want. . . .
>
> In Germany we have not simply read Tocqueville, Taine, and Os-
> trogorski, but evaluated them objectively. We have not only under-
> stood Sidney Law's critical studies of English parliamentarianism,
> but fully appreciated them as well.[5]

Although the requirement of an open elite became a matter of principle for the new liberal elitist in Germany, his solicitude for democracy of personnel selection originated in the predicament in which a
substantial segment of the German bourgeoisie found itself. National
unification and the development of the Bismarckian Empire had
effected an accommodation of interests between the large agrarians
and the urban bourgeoisie, particularly the heavy industrialists. Most
of the bourgeoisie acquiesced in the maintenance, through political
means and tariff policies, of institutions that shored up the sagging
material foundations of the large agrarians' power. Initially formed for
mutual self-defense, the social coalition of the bourgeoisie and the
Junkers prevented the achievement of bourgeois hegemony in imperial
Germany. Emboldened by the dissatisfaction of many a bourgeois with
this social coalition, the new liberal elitist contemplated its dissolution.

The proponents of the new elitism were harsh critics of the policies
and political structure of Wilhelminian Germany. Standing outside, if
occasionally close to, official governing circles, they had both the lati-
tude and the incentive to search for daring, innovative schemes that
more conservative liberals found embarrassing and even threatening.
The elitism of the liberal Left became a double-edged weapon, cutting

---

[5] Alfred Weber, "Die Bedeutung der geistigen Führer in Deutschland" in his
Ideen zur Staats- und Kultursoziologie (Karlsruhe, 1927), pp. 108, 111.

on the one side against Social Democracy and on the other against the agrarian-based Right, for the major obstacles to the consolidation of bourgeois society in Germany and the formation of a thoroughly imperialist polity were the weight given by the government to Conservative, Junker requisites and the struggle conducted by Social Democracy, especially the radicals within its fold, against the bourgeoisie and imperialism.

While offering assurances that the entire working class would gain great benefits from the establishment of the preponderance of urban interests, the new liberal elitist framed his appeals to the proletariat with an eye to the labor aristocracy and its exponents. Some few workers and Social Democratic leaders were, in effect, promised entry into the elite. This bait for proletarians, set out with reformists like Georg von Vollmar and Eduard Bernstein in mind, was only somewhat less modest than the tea and cookies served up, as Ralph Abernathy once complained, by white moderates to black civil rights' leaders in the United States.

The new liberal elitist's concessions to democracy of personnel selection were further circumscribed by often subtle restrictions. These restrictions, centering in an insistence upon the possession of certain distinctive qualities by potential members of the elite, reflected his assumption that a bourgeois social order would continue indefinitely. Although the elite might not be drawn entirely or even largely from the ranks of the bourgeoisie, men with these qualities would be predisposed to formulate bourgeois policies.

In France after the first years of the Third Republic, the big bourgeoisie was willing to permit government and administration to be undertaken largely by members of the petty bourgeoisie, or Gambetta's cherished *couches nouvelles sociales*.[6] The political system within which the republican political elite operated helped to prevent the members of this elite from pursuing objectives that posed a radical alternative to bourgeois society; indeed, middle-class politicians provided a political vanguard that served to maintain the position of the big bourgeoisie as the ruling class. During the Wilhelminian period in Germany, the new liberal elitists worked their way, often gropingly, toward the notion of an elite performing similar functions.

But several major differences in approach are suggestive of disparities between bourgeois predilections in the two countries. Germany's new liberal elitists, although more concerned with the inclusion of men identified with the working class in the elite, were less sanguine about the consequences of the big bourgeoisie standing aside from the formal

---

[6] Léon Gambetta, *Discours et plaidoyers politiques de M. Gambetta*, ed. Joseph Reinach (11 vols., Paris, 1881–1885), IV, 155. See also III, 101.

arena of politics; the elite, it was thought, should include men from the urban commercial and industrial segments of the ruling class. Also the German liberal elitists were unwilling, even in the realm of the hypothetical, to sanction effective popular control of the elite.

The social and political institutions of nineteenth-century Germany had fostered the notion of an elite *responsive* to the presumed needs of the populace, but not *responsible* directly to it. The ideologies anchored to major institutions like the state bureaucracy and the landed nobility never tolerated the acceptance of substantial popular control. Similarly, the main current of liberalism in Germany veered away from commitment to direct popular control. Even when nineteenth-century conservatives and liberals came to contemplate broader elite recruitment, they refused to endorse an appreciable measure of popular control. Granting the possibility of membership in the elite seemed an adequate concession to popular aspirations.

As the young German national state underwent a succession of crises arising from tensions between the urban bourgeoisie and the large agrarians, clashes between labor and business, and conflicts over the pursuit of imperialist foreign policies, the new liberal elitist began to search for forms of leadership that would forge a national tradition with broad popular appeal. Somewhere, he felt, something had gone wrong in Germany. The institutions of the Second Empire had failed to capitalize on the nation's assets. Many of the best potential leaders had seemingly been excluded from power. State bureaucracy, army, nobility, and urban self-government had all failed to create a viable national tradition. No German institution had established patterns of behavior emulated by the entire nation, as the aristocracy had presumably done in England. No German social type had come to serve as a model for all Germans. To the liberal elitist the requirements of an imperial polity necessitated the utilization of every national resource, the rationalization of the nation's institutions, and the full integration of the masses into this polity. He recommended an open-yet-authoritarian elite to effect all of these changes, and, above all, to obtain working-class backing for imperialistic objectives.

Another aspect of his approach to politics is, at first glance, bewildering. He tied his elitism to monarchical and great-man doctrines, often in a confused way. This confusion can be seen by comparing his views to those of Mosca and Pareto.[7] Neither a monarch nor a great

[7] There are a number of good, readily available introductions to the elite theories of Mosca and Pareto. Among the best is James Meisel's introduction to a collection of essays by various authors: James H. Meisel, ed., *Pareto and Mosca* (Englewood Cliffs, N.J.: Prentice-Hall paperback, 1965). This collection offers a good sampling of scholarly writing on Pareto and Mosca during the past forty years. Another succinct discussion of Pareto and Mosca can be found in T. B.

leader played an important role in their elitist perspectives. The analytic clarity and economy of their "pure" elitism was not compromised by calls for a single leader to stand "above" the elite. The new German elitist usually succumbed to the subjective satisfactions derived from the widespread belief in Germany in the importance of a single leader. Sustained by the Bismarck myth, by illusions about William II during the early years of his reign,[8] and by the attractiveness of a massive figure whose shadow would obscure the critical role of the ruling class, the liberal elitist clung to impractical notions that his own basic analysis of society contravened. In elite theories he dissected tangible relationships of power within the context of a view of political history that explored the social basis of politics. These theories told him that great men or great monarchs were social myths, not autonomous forces in history.[9] Indeed, he often made—and Max Weber's writings provide prime examples of this tendency—damning criticisms of the faith in the centrality of great men in the historical process. A study of the new elitism in Germany must of necessity contend with its disjointed relationship to this faith.

Developed initially as a weapon against both the Left and the Right, the notion of an open-yet-authoritarian elite was turned primarily against the Left toward the end of World War I. Social revolution in Russia and fears of its eruption in Central Europe led the liberal elitists, whose major objections to Wilhelminian Germany were being rendered obsolete by reforms, and whose hopes of admitting some Social Democrats to high political office were being fulfilled perhaps too abruptly, to concentrate their efforts upon containing the consequences of the German collapse and creating a durable bourgeois order. Their stratagems for stabilizing the state and averting social revolution evinced a much greater solicitude for offsetting the potential power of the organized working class in a political democracy than for destroying the remnants of power held by the large agrarians. The

---

Bottomore, *Elites and Society* (London, 1964), which also provides a short critique of the subsequent use of the elite concept in the social sciences. Similar in scope is Urs Jaeggi, *Die gesellschaftliche Elite: Eine Studie zum Problem der sozialen Macht* (Bern, 1960). Although in many ways pedestrian, Bottomore's book is distinguished from most of the other voluminous recent literature on the elite concept by his ability to cut through many of the behaviorist pretensions of contemporary "elite studies" and pose classic questions of political and social thought. All three of the above books contain good bibliographical leads.

[8] Elisabeth Fehrenbach, *Wandlungen des deutschen Kaisergedankens 1871–1918* (Munich, 1969) helps to fill a major gap in the historical literature on the development of monarchist ideas during the Bismarckian Empire, but she tends to neglect the social sources of these ideas.

[9] For a now classic statement of the case against great-man theories of history see Sidney Hook, *The Hero in History: A Study in Limitation and Possibility* (Boston: Beacon paperback, 1957).

liberals sought to increase the elitist potential inherent in parliamentary government. Men like Friedrich Naumann, Hugo Preuss, Max Weber, and Friedrich Meinecke frequently fell back upon projects to establish a great leader. Walther Rathenau, himself a liberal member of the big bourgeoisie, succeeded in adapting his elitism more creatively to the new situation. But Rathenau's elitist proposals, as well as those of another former left liberal, Leonard Nelson, who became for a short while a Social Democrat, had little perceptible influence in postwar Germany—certainly far less than the impact of the ideas of a Hugo Preuss or Max Weber upon the Weimar Constitution. With Rathenau and Nelson the development of the new liberal elitism in Germany came to a logical, although not historical end. However well suited to counterrevolutionary imperialist needs, the concept of an open-yet-authoritarian elite could not be pursued farther within the framework of liberalism.

One might assume that conservative Social Democrats would have taken up this concept, but even those who publicly distanced themselves from Marxism seem, at least on the plane of theory, not to have espoused authoritarian rule. Many a leading reformist may have tacitly accepted democracy of personnel selection rather than decision making; a close examination of the Social Democrats would probably reveal many adherents of this type of elitism in addition to a major example, that of Leonard Nelson, included in the present study.[10] Yet even during the Weimar Republic the Social Democratic party (SPD), having identified itself intimately with the traditions of political democracy, continued to take official positions hostile toward authoritarianism.

After World War I the concept of an open-yet-authoritarian elite

[10] The history of the political ideas of the Social Democrats has not been thoroughly explored, even for the period before 1914. The most obvious examples of Social Democrats who espoused elitist views similar to those analyzed in the present study are to be found among men who left the party or were expelled by it. Seemingly in a class by themselves are some members of the *Glocke* circle, a group formed during World War I. See, e.g., Johann Plenge's conception of a relationship between *Führer* and *Mannschaft* consonant with the "Ideas of 1914" in his *1789 und 1914: Die symbolischen Jahre in der Geschichte des politischen Geistes* (Berlin, 1916), pp. 144–45. For pertinent discussions of Plenge and the *Glocke* circle see Z.A.B. Zeman and W. B. Scharlau, *The Merchant of Revolution: The Life of Alexander Israel Helphand (Parvus), 1867–1924* (London, 1965), pp. 168–91; Hans Günther, *Der Herren eigner Geist: Die Ideologie des Nationalsozialismus* (Moscow and Leningrad, 1935), p. 65; Klemens von Klemperer, *Germany's New Conservatism: Its History and Dilemma in the Twentieth Century* (Princeton, 1957), pp. 67n., 68–69; and the appropriate sections in Abraham Ascher, "National Solidarity and Imperial Power: The Sources and Early Development of Social Imperialist Thought in Germany, 1871–1914" (Columbia diss., 1957).

was articulated mainly on the Right. Segments of a desperate, but not despairing Right provided the most audacious varieties of it during the Weimar Republic. In these circles, calls for democracy of personnel selection rose to a fever pitch. Similarly, both denial of any prospect for effective popular control and insistence upon the need for unrestricted elite rule far surpassed in intensity and scope those of the liberal elitists, many of whom, as architects of the Weimar Republic, were regarded by the Right as preeminent theorists of democracy. Attacked as midwives of parliamentary government, which had enabled Social Democrats to shape German policy, the liberal elitists were stigmatized as leading representatives of a detestable system marked for destruction.

Many of the modifications in the new elitism after 1917 were linked to shifting expectations about the social strata to which it would appeal. The prewar liberal elitist had regarded as his most likely mass constituency part of the working class, as well as those sections of the middle class (*Mittelstand*) that were still largely impervious to the status anxiety which, originating in the social and economic consequences of the consolidation of large enterprises, was driving much of the "old middle class" of small businessmen, independent artisan producers, and peasant proprietors into the arms of the Right.[11] While the liberal elitist hoped to court free professionals, salaried employees, and small manufacturers in consumer-oriented industries, he generally wrote off the old middle class as an impediment to the extension of capitalism.

The elitists of the postwar Right, although seeking to attract part of the working class, anticipated mass support primarily from the middle class, including the old middle class. The situation of the major strata of the middle class after the war rendered their members particularly susceptible to the allures of open-yet-authoritarian elitism. Status panic spread throughout these strata, which, still recovering from the shock of an aborted social revolution, felt crushed between big labor and big capital.[12] Accelerated by the war, structural changes in the

[11] See the pioneering studies by Hans Rosenberg: "Political and Social Consequences of the Depression of 1873–1896 in Central Europe," *Economic History Review*, XIII (1943), 58–73, and *Grosse Depression und Bismarckzeit: Wirtschaftsablauf, Gesellschaft und Politik in Mitteleuropa* (Berlin, 1967).

[12] See the brief analysis of the position of the middle class during the Weimar Republic in Walter Struve, "Hans Zehrer as a Neoconservative Elite Theorist," *American Historical Review*, LXX (1965), 1037–41, and the more extended treatment in Herman Lebovics, *Social Conservatism and the Middle Classes in Germany, 1914–1933* (Princeton, 1969), pp. 3–48. Excellent material on some portions of the German middle class can be found in a recent monograph by Heinrich August Winkler, *Mittelstand, Demokratie und Nationalsozialismus: Die politische Entwicklung von Handwerk und Kleinhandel in der Weimarer Republik* (Cologne, 1972).

economy continued to undermine the marginal independence of the small businessman, eliminate objective differences between the position of white- and blue-collar workers, and promote overcrowding in the free professions. The impact and pace of these structural changes were further intensified, first by the postwar inflation and later by the great depression, both of which took away the property and reduced the income of broad sectors of the entire middle class.

An expression of the shift in the presumed mass basis of the new elitism appeared in the mining by the Right of a vein of elitist ideas that went back several decades but had been largely ignored by most liberal elitists. These ideas, which might conveniently be labeled as a form of "cultural elitism," can be traced to Herder and romanticism, but the types of interest to us here began to be enunciated by such men as Paul de Lagarde after the middle of the nineteenth century, and particularly during the 1880's and 1890's by Julius Langbehn and others. Although often propounded by men whose personal idiosyncracies contributed to their distress, this cultural elitism reflected the anxieties of sectors of the middle class that were already finding the pressures of industrial capitalism suffocating.[13] Joined on occasion by Nietzsche, the cultural elitists condemned the political and intellectual culture of big business, while denouncing the working class as the champion of materialistic values similar to those of the big bourgeoisie.

Not confining their attacks to plutocracy and proletariat, cultural elitists accused the university and the classical *Gymnasium* of indifference toward the culture of the true German people, the *Volk*. Identified with hearty rustics, painstaking craftsmen, and upright artisan shopkeepers, the *Volk* was admonished not to surrender its soul to the sterile ministrations of those whom Fritz Ringer has dubbed "the German mandarins."[14] The dramatic increase in university enrollments during the second half of the nineteenth century failed to keep pace with the endeavors of members of the sinking old middle class to escape their insecure station in life by mounting the ladder of education.

[13] Fritz Stern, *The Politics of Cultural Despair: A Study in the Rise of the Germanic Ideology* (Berkeley, 1961) has long sections on Lagarde and Langbehn. A broader survey of cultural elitism, and a better, although often skimpy, exploration of its social roots is contained in George L. Mosse, *The Crisis of German Ideology: Intellectual Origins of the Third Reich* (New York, 1964). Much of the same material is dealt with in an unhistorical fashion by Hermann Glaser, *Spiesser-Ideologie: Von der Zerstörung des deutschen Geistes im 19. und 20. Jahrhundert* (Freiburg im Breisgau, 1964). Although Glaser associates cultural elitism with segments of the middle class, he rejects a chronological approach to his subject; for him the *Kleinbürger* is a recurrent human type espousing a timeless potpourri of philistine ideas.

[14] Fritz Ringer, *The Decline of the German Mandarins: The German Academic Community, 1890–1933* (Cambridge, Mass., 1969).

The mandarin was depicted as standing guard over a ladder that was not only too narrow, but all too often led merely to a lifetime of indentured servitude toiling for the new plutocracy. Moreover, as the alma mater of the *Herr Doktor* whom the middle class met almost wherever it came into contact with its social superiors and with the representatives of authority, the university could easily be mistaken as the seminary of the ruling class. Whether in the state bureaucracy, in the school system, or increasingly in industry and commerce, the figure of the *Akademiker* assumed the proportions of a sinister, latter-day St. Christopher who disdainfully refused to come to "the little man's" side of the stream.

Lacking any prospect of becoming a majority rather than remaining a dwindling minority in German society, the old middle class—or better the cultural elitists who spoke to its quandary—searched for battering rams that might be shouldered by the craftsman, the tradesman, and the peasant to smash down the gates manned by bloodless academicians and rapacious plutocrats. The motto in this assault might well have been: "Place not thy trust in the false idols of the proletariat, but in the one true People that is me and thee, for some of us shall yet bring forth a race of saviors." Democracy of personnel selection rather than decision making was presented implicitly as the solution to the problems of a minority that, unwilling to join the proletarian majority in being, sought to shape the destiny of Germany and thereby to secure for itself a niche in society.

The endemic sense of impotence of this minority was manifest in the cultural elitist's invocation of a *deus ex machina*, the great leader. Thus according to Langbehn, a "people's emperor" would take in hand the restoration of the old, true values of the *Volk*. Lacking the intellectual rigor of the new liberal elitist's analysis of German society and politics, the ideas of the cultural elitists were even more muddled about the role of great men; a comparable confusion persisted within the ranks of the postwar Right.

Before World War I the social coalition of Junkers and bourgeois afforded a measure of protection to the status of the middle class. The collapse of the Second Empire disrupted this social coalition, and the economic development of the Republic fostered the increasing social dislocation of the middle class, as the advancing institutions of monopoly capital continued both to lower the status of the old-fashioned clerk by transforming him into one of a myriad of employees of big business and to leave less and less place for the small businessman unless he contracted with large-scale enterprise. The elitists of the Right found in the concept of an open-yet-authoritarian elite a way of expressing their sympathy for the tribulations of the middle class. Although these elitists pressed for the consolidation of the bourgeoisie and the creation of a group of leaders to serve as a vanguard of the ruling class, many of them demonstrated their awareness of the need to gain the acquiescence of the middle class by drawing heavily upon the ideas of the cultural elitists and subscribing to the closely related idealization of preindustrial institutions. For example, Edgar Jung and Count Hermann Keyserling, well suited by their own backgrounds to invoke reactionary, preindustrial ideals, forged a bourgeois elitism decked out in many of the trappings of long-gone eras.

Other elitists of the Right employed a less antiquated vocabulary that signaled their cultivation of white-collar workers and the industrial proletariat. Thus Hans Zehrer, appealing to the former, and particularly Ernst Jünger, appealing to the latter, made little of the tradition of cultural elitism. Whereas Jung and Keyserling became advocates of an open elite that would be careful to include members of the old aristocracy and the old middle class, Zehrer and Jünger presented themselves as men in search of leaders drawn mainly from the lower strata of society produced by the development of industrial capitalism. The elitists of the Right were less frank and often more ambiguous about their commitment to a bourgeois order than the liberal new elitists had been.

Like the liberal new elitist, the conservative assumed that the process of becoming a full-fledged member of the elite would remold the individual; a worker elevated into the elite would have served both as window-dressing to lend credence to the claim that an open elite had been established and as a skillful manipulator of the class from which he had risen.

The crucial issues on which the elitists of the Right disagreed among themselves pivoted on the problem of the relationship between elite and nonelite. Should the masses be permanently available for active mobilization by the elite, or should the basic duty of the general populace consist simply in passive obedience?

Both the stages of World War I in Germany prior to the disintegration of the *Burgfrieden* in 1917 and the entire wartime period in the victorious Western Powers provided examples, frequently cited by bourgeois politicians and writers, of the rich popular resources that might be tapped if the populace actively supported its national leaders; acquired a sense of participation in a common cause; and devoted itself enthusiastically to a great national undertaking. Perhaps even more compelling than distorted recollections of wartime sacrifices freely given, which acquired a legendary character, were popular demands that reached a crescendo at the war's end and during its immediate aftermath. This reassertion of democratic aspirations was encouraged by government-sponsored propaganda aimed at the citizens of neutral states and by the upsurge of radicalism beginning in 1917.

German propaganda about the right of small nations to self-determination, Wilsonian political warfare against the Central Powers, and the successful revolutionary struggle of Russian workers and peasants led many Germans to believe that they must take their destiny into their own hands.[15]

While often hankering for a populace that would complacently accept the rule of an elite, most German proponents of an open-yet-authoritarian elite were unwilling after the war to forgo consideration of the potential advantages of eliciting direct popular support. To be sure, some elitists on the Right preferred the preindustrial, aristocratic perspective in which mass participation in politics was deplorable and presaged disaster, since the masses, once activated, might become an autonomous force or be enlisted by the Left. But even many of the right-wingers who clung to such aristocratic views weighed the use of a temporarily mobilized populace as a stage in the construction of a polity ruled by an authoritarian elite.[16]

Mass activity, however temporary, entailed great dangers, but if carefully controlled, it offered unparalleled opportunities for the exploitation of the energies and enthusiasm of the populace. The new liberal elitists sought to minimize the dangers by calling, as did Naumann and Max Weber, for intermittent and incomplete mobilization within the confines of a political system similar to that existing in the West, or by seeking, as did Rathenau and Nelson, to render nugatory mass participation in politics by subjecting the citizenry to a vast process of bourgeois enlightenment effected by a drastically reformed educational system. Regarding the masses as already mobilized and menacingly active in politics, elitists of the postwar Right like Edgar Jung wished for demobilization, but toyed with the idea of attaining this objective through a *Götterdämmerung* of the masses. The commitment of most of the Right to a vigorous reassertion of German imperialism tended to wreak havoc with such fond hopes. Spengler and, above all, Ernst Jünger took a more consistent position toward the issue of mobilization. For Jünger, permanent, complete mobilization was to be achieved, although ultimately he, too, muddled his proposals by neglecting the use of ideological methods.

---

[15] On the international battle of ideas during World War I and its relationship to diplomacy and domestic politics see Arno J. Mayer, *Political Origins of the New Diplomacy, 1917–1918* (New Haven, 1959), as well as the more summary treatment in Erwin Hölzle, *Die Revolution der zweigeteilten Welt: Eine Geschichte der Mächte 1905–1929* (Reinbek bei Hamburg, Rowohlt paperback, 1963), pp. 60–96.

[16] For an excellent general characterization of aristocratic elitism, as well as a discussion of mass mobilization by elites, see William Kornhauser, *The Politics of Mass Society* (Glencoe, Ill., 1959), pp. 21–73. At an early stage of the present work I found Kornhauser's suggestive distinctions between different types of elite theories of great assistance.

After 1917 the proponents of an open-yet-authoritarian elite expressed a sense of urgency that was absent from the attitudes of the prewar liberal elitist. He had felt confident that although time was growing short the tide of the Left could be reversed, revolution avoided, and a consistent imperialist policy adopted. For example, at the turn of the century Naumann was not apprehensive about basing political calculations on the assumption that the foundations for a new elite would be created gradually and might require a generation or more to complete. Such assurance was rarely found on the postwar Right. The German defeat and the Red scare nurtured a frenzy alien to the mentality of the prewar liberal. The margin of bourgeois power in Germany had almost been erased before the revolutionary tide ebbed, while the setback given to German imperialism by the outcome of the war left little room for optimism about international politics.

The demand for an open elite was thus not only a demagogic maneuver to obtain mass support in the struggle to establish the uncontested hegemony of the bourgeoisie but also a technique for tapping all of the nation's resources, which had now come to appear so finite. The margin of waste in the discovery and cultivation of talent that had been tolerated by the prewar liberal elitist became impermissible. In the new elitist order of the future, everyone would have to be in his proper place, and his assumption of his post could no longer be entrusted largely to the vicissitudes of a free market, whether in the economy or in politics. The exigencies of survival and the demands of monopoly capital were too powerful to permit anything less than the effective rationalization of bourgeois society.

A comparison with the Horatio Alger myth in the United States serves to underline some of the distinctive characteristics of the German conception of democracy of personnel selection rather than decision making. The sudden ascent of Horatio Alger's hero depends upon good luck; the myth emphasizes that the functioning of a free-market economy leads occasionally to extreme instances of social mobility. Although a precondition to the hero's acquisition of wealth and power, his talent and persistence are shared by many who never get the "breaks" that come his way. As developed in Germany, particularly after World War I, the notion of an open-yet-authoritarian elite leaves nothing to chance. The "little man" is told that he may become part of the elite, but only if his unique talents merit his elevation. His entry into the elite cannot be accidental. Either he has the necessary characteristics, or he does not. The postwar new elitist in Germany assumed that the regenerative potential of German imperialism could be realized only through the careful husbanding and application of all of the nation's assets.

Becoming the prevailing theme of bourgeois political culture during the Weimar Republic, the notion of an open-yet-authoritarian elite was espoused, if with racist restrictions, by the National Socialists both before and after 1933. Reference to the appropriation of this notion by the Nazis, who made modest contributions of their own to its development, requires a word of explanation. The present study is not an investigation of the intellectual origins of national socialism. Whatever merit such studies may have—and I am inclined to question the value of most of them because of their implicit assertion of the primacy of ideas in historical causation—I am more interested in examining the political and social roots of ideas. As we shall see in the concluding chapter, the Nazis were drawn toward the concept of democracy of personnel selection rather than decision making because of the attractiveness of this type of elitism to the bourgeoisie and the middle class, and more basically because the Nazis, like other German elitists, confronted German society without having broken with bourgeois perspectives.

Mention of the National Socialists raises inevitably the question of the relationship between racism and elitism in Germany. Racist doctrines played little direct role in the development of the concept of an open-yet-authoritarian elite; to attempt to unravel the knotty problem of racism would overburden the present work without yielding enough compensatory insights. Hence, most of the observations on the relationship between racism and elitism are confined to the concluding chapter.

Of the elitists examined in the chapters that follow, most, perhaps all, believed in white superiority, but in the absence of nonwhites in Germany, this racism did not critically affect their views on the best elite for Germany. As for other forms of racism, none of these elitists was consistently a racial anti-Semite. Even nonracist anti-Semitism was not intrinsically linked to an open-yet-authoritarian elitism.[17]

My work is focused upon nine men whose ideas provide a good sampling of the full range of this elitism. An examination of their ideas reveals not only how widespread the new elitism became but also the scope of controversy among its proponents. How authoritarian should the elite be? Who should be admitted to it, and why? What limits, if any, should be set to its control over the populace? In treating these

---

[17] For valuable discussions of the differences between racist and nonracist anti-Semitism see Hannah Arendt, *The Origins of Totalitarianism* (New York: Meridian paperback, 1958), pp. 83–87; Paul W. Massing, *Rehearsal for Destruction: A Study of Political Anti-Semitism in Imperial Germany* (New York, 1949), pp. 75–98; Peter G. J. Pulzer, *The Rise of Political Anti-Semitism in Germany and Austria* (New York: Wiley paperback, 1964), pp. 49–58.

and other critical issues, liberals contradicted each other, as did conservatives.

All of the nine men were activists as well as theorists. Their readiness to assume both roles may appear strange to those Anglo-Saxons as well as Germans who still make the erroneous assumption that intellectuals in Germany have been simply impractical men of thought. As may be inferred from Fritz Ringer's recent work, this misapprehension owes much of its persistence to the German "mandarins," who found the cultivation of such myths agreeable and useful.[18] None of the nine men chained himself to his armchair or writing desk. Each sought to realize his ideas through direct participation in politics; indeed, some worked out their ideas in the midst of active political careers. An analysis of their writings without reference to their political activities would ignore important clues to the sources of their elitism. Hence I have examined these activities, as well as the social situations of the elitists.

As the last sentence implies, the present work should be considered a study in the social and political context of intellectual history. I have set out to explore how biography becomes social and intellectual history. This approach to history should be contrasted to the efforts of the neo-Freudian school of historical biography that has of late become fashionable in the United States. The nine men have not been selected with the intention of uncovering instances of the origins and espousal of ideas due to the pressure of psychological stresses within the individual. Nor do I believe that the search for the sources of social and political ideas in the interior of the individual can be successful with any object of historical inquiry. The historian can benefit from a reminder provided by Peter Weiss's recent drama *Marat/Sade*. Weiss demonstrates brilliantly that even the pathologist of the ideas of the madhouse must look mainly at society in his effort to locate their roots. Attempting to explain the political and social views of the inhabitants of the sanitarium through the use of most psychiatric theory is as fruitless as an endeavor to attribute the programmatic statements of the American Medical Association to the personal idiosyncrasies of their drafters, or to the "identity crises" that these men have undergone.

I suspect that many a reader will question the choice of elitists. No doubt the names of others who might have been included will occur to him, and he may well wonder whether some of the nine might not have been passed over. I cannot provide an irrefragable reply that would set to rest these doubts; to pretend that I could do so would be pointless. Each of the nine has been selected because the configuration

[18] Ringer, *Decline of the German Mandarins*, pp. 121–23.

of his elitism affords an instance of an important style or type of thought. I have contemplated using many more supplementary examples than I have but the inclusion of them would probably have accomplished little, other than to illustrate again and again the presence of a wide variety of approaches employed by the proponents of an open-yet-authoritarian elite. Moreover, the inclusion of still more examples might have taxed unduly the patience of the reader, and would certainly have exhausted the energies of the author.

My own criticism of my work will, I suspect, be shared by few of my readers. Briefly, it is this: that I have slighted the economic nexus of social history and the impact of the development of the institutions of monopoly capitalism upon bourgeois political and intellectual culture. In view of the uneven state of research on German economic history,[19] a bias toward historical idealism is understandable, but inexcusable.

The organization of this work follows the development of the new elitism. The first chapter traces its precursors. After examining liberals during the prewar, wartime, and immediate postwar years, the study moves on to conservatives during the Weimar Republic and concludes with some reflections on the National Socialist era.

[19] See the Bibliographical Essay.

PART I

Intellectual Traditions

Patterns in the Development of German Elite Theories During the Nineteenth Century

Despite the emergence of some militantly democratic ideas, the concept of an elite subject to little popular control prevailed in Germany during the nineteenth century. As an increasingly large proportion of the population took an active interest in public policy, elite theorists talked more and more about "merit" and "achievement" as qualifications for decision makers. Emphasis upon birth and class decreased. Yet the predominant elite theorists circumvented the issue of popular control by recommending that an elite might accept some individuals, but no direct pressures from below. An effective elite had to select its own members and formulate decisions without external interference.

Conservative Elite Theories

The conflict between the nobility and its opponents during the late eighteenth and early nineteenth century led to the development of modern conservatism as a weapon for the defense of the nobility. The apologists for the nobility employed many arguments which, although often in somewhat different forms, were to remain typical of later German elite theories. Because particularly in Prussia the nobility continued to play a major political role well into the twentieth century, the doctrines of conservatism made significant contributions to the development of other German elite theories.

By the end of the eighteenth century, the nobility no longer occupied an unquestioned place in German society. During the latter part of the Enlightenment, bourgeois opinion became overtly hostile toward the nobility.[1] Despite extensive concessions to the nobility, espe-

---

[1] See Fritz Valjavec, *Die Entstehung der politischen Strömungen in Deutschland* (Munich, 1951), p. 83; Reinhold Aris, *History of Political Thought in Germany from 1789 to 1815* (London, 1936), p. 391; Johanna Schultze, *Die Auseinandersetzung zwischen Adel und Bürgertum in den deutschen Zeitschriften der letzten drei Jahrzehnte des 18. Jahrhunderts (1773–1806)* (Berlin, 1925); Klaus Epstein, *The Genesis of German Conservatism* (Princeton, 1966); Uwe-Jens Heuer,

cially in Frederician Prussia, the absolute state of the eighteenth century exerted a leveling influence upon German society. The virtual destruction of most of the local and provincial diets deprived the nobility of an important channel of political participation. The expanding state administrative apparatus grew partly at the expense of the nobility.[2] Changes in agriculture weakened the material foundations of the nobility. In Prussia, for example, the Junkers, the east Elbian noblemen, were becoming a class of large landowners rather than remaining an estate with specific economic and political privileges. The customary division of society into three estates had lost much of its significance, but until the French Revolution, Germans lacked enticing images of a new social and political order.

Even before the growth in Germany of a strong bourgeoisie, German political thought received a tremendous impetus from the new France, for the work and ideas of the French Revolution went far beyond the mere destruction of the old nobility. The events of the revolutionary period presented a direct threat to the previous conception of nobility, as well as positive alternatives. The initial phases of the Revolution eventuated in a model for an attempt to implement the will of the majority through popularly elected representatives and to construct a constitutional democracy based upon the concepts of popular sovereignty and equal political rights. Shortly thereafter, the rule of the Jacobins provided a model for the temporary dictatorship of a select few, whose own social origins were unimportant and whose task was to raise all men to a similar level. Finally, came the example of Napoleon's institution of a new "nobility of merit." This last example became more potent through its association with the strand in the development of absolutism that culminated in attempts by Enlightened Despots, most notably by Joseph II, to create a new social hierarchy dependent upon the state.

The consequences of Napoleon's victory over Prussia provided still another stimulus to the development of a conservative ideology. The reorganization of Prussia under Stein and Hardenberg, who tried to meet the challenge of a new era by creating a modern administrative state and by providing for popular political participation, provoked the opposition of an important segment of the Prussian nobility. The tenets of what was to become the main stream of German conservatism were forged largely in Prussia in order to defend the position of

---

Allgemeines Landrecht und Klassenkampf: Die Auseinandersetzungen um die Prinzipien des Allgemeinen Landrechts am Ende des 18. Jahrhunderts als Ausdruck der Krise des Feudalsystems in Preussen (Berlin, 1960).

[2] See Hans Rosenberg, *Bureaucracy, Aristocracy, and Autocracy: The Prussian Experience, 1660–1815* (Cambridge, Mass., 1958).

the nobility as an independent estate marked by special, formally recognized privileges.[3]

The close association of romanticism with early conservatism provided conservative elite theories with much of their intellectual embroidery. Novalis, Arnim, Friedrich Schlegel, and other Romantics idealized the role of the nobility in the Middle Ages. Viewing the absolute state as an artificial mechanism and the Revolution's destruction of a corporate society in France as an abomination, Romantic conservatives like Adam Müller searched for the "organic," "natural" bases of society and found them in a hierarchically ordered series of estates, each with its own functions, duties, and privileges. In such a social order, the most important political and military functions belonged solely to the nobility and the prince.

Conservatives strove for a society in which the nobility, acting in concert with the prince, monopolized the processes leading to the formulation of the more important decisions. Although Prussia had tended to produce a nobility whose *raison d'être* lay in service as military officers, conservatives made claims that would have raised the nobility, *as a group*, above all other institutions except the throne. Since many early conservatives were highly critical of the king, his role could often even appear secondary in comparison with that of the nobility. The tendency to characterize the king, in accordance with medieval terminology, simply as *primus inter pares*, further decreased the relative importance of his role. Yet the elite theories of conservatism seldom approached a strict bipartite model with the nobility on one side and all "the people" on the other side. The populace was regarded as consisting of two or more highly differentiated estates.

The concept of a special estate, or stratum, entrusted with political leadership reappeared in most later elite theories. Similarly, the conservative notion of the nobility as mediator between crown and people eventually became that of an elite mediating between a "mass" on one side and a "great leader" on the other side. Indeed, mediation could come to entail primarily the execution of a single leader's decisions.

Of the arguments used by the early conservatives to justify a hierarchically ordered society only some were to be accepted by later, nonconservative elite theorists. Despite the permeation of most German thought since the early nineteenth century by historicism, appeals to tradition and historical privileges exercised only a limited attraction

[3] In the following discussion of conservatism, especially in the period through 1860, I am greatly indebted to Sigmund Neumann's *Die Stufen des preussischen Konservatismus: Ein Beitrag zum Staats- und Gesellschaftsbild Deutschlands im 19. Jahrhundert* (Berlin, 1930).

William Luther Cobb Library
Eckerd College
St. Petersburg, Florida

upon other elite theorists. More important for the future was the conservative's claim to supernatural sanction for his view of society. He could utilize the Lutheran emphasis upon the concept of a divine "calling" and upon the concept of reciprocal privileges and duties among men. Completely secularized versions of such concepts, in the form of the division of labor, later buttressed claims for an elite on functionalist grounds. The functionalist arguments of the early conservative rested upon premises involving organic interdependence; much of later functionalism would assume a mechanistic tone.

Perhaps most important for later developments was the conservative's insistence upon human inequality. The conservative conceived of inequality as permanent and ineradicable. He contended that certain characteristics appeared only in noblemen. Whereas both German neo-humanism and the early liberal-democratic movement emphasized the importance of environment, the conservative emphasized the importance of heredity. As advanced by neo-humanists as divergent as Lessing and Wilhelm von Humboldt, the conception of *Bildung*, of the enormous possibilities for the development of the individual's mind and personality, constituted a serious threat to the claims of uniqueness on the part of the nobility. If the individual could master the process leading to *Bildung*, noble birth had no special significance.[4] Although the neo-humanist conception of the acquisition of *Bildung* involved the cultivation of capacities already present in the individual, the possession of these capacities was not confined to men from any one segment of the population. Even the modest version of the process presented by Goethe in part two of *Wilhelm Meister* asserted the potential of the individual. Realism, not inherent limitations lead Wilhelm to renounce the attempt to develop every aspect of his abilities and to concentrate upon a profession that will provide him both security and satisfaction. The world in which he lives demands specialization, and in any age the true master must establish priorities for himself in his work.

The conservatives countered the neo-humanist position by claiming that only a noble possessed an "inherent" character of the type suitable for political and social leadership. Only a noble could have a "harmonious," "integrated" personality.[5] The Romantic's concern for

---

[4] See Rosenberg, *Bureaucracy, Aristocracy, and Autocracy*, pp. 182–88.

[5] "The fundamental thesis of the declining society of Estates is: *Harmony and Personality belong only to the uppermost social stratum, that is to say, are accessible and peculiar only to the upper and lower nobility.*" Ernst Kohn-Bramstedt, *Aristocracy and the Middle Classes in Germany: Social Types in German Literature, 1830–1900* (London, 1937), p. 29. Bramstedt's italics. A revised edition of this book (Chicago: Phoenix paperback, 1964) was published under the author's anglicized name, Ernest K. Bramsted. The revised edition contains a new preface but few, if any other changes.

individuality and unique traits, for *Eigentümlichkeit* and *Einzigartigkeit,* reinforced the claims of the nobility. To the conservative, the characteristics of nobility could not be acquired. They could be developed only over the course of many generations. Although German conservatives did not resort to the racism of an eighteenth-century defender of the French nobility such as Boulvanvilliers with his thesis of the "two nations" comprising France,[6] their arguments implied the inheritance of acquired characteristics and the hereditary transmission of character traits. German conservatism fostered a pattern of thought in which "inherent" characteristics furnished a precondition for political leadership. Prior to political participation, these characteristics could not be developed through it. Later, such ideas would merge with the concept of the "born leader" and the "political genius." For conservatives, as for many subsequent German elite theorists, "on the job" training for political leadership was inconceivable.

While the conservatives spoke of the desirability for some sort of rapport between the nobility and "the people," their doctrines affirmed a need for "distance" on the part of the nobility. Dignified withdrawal, although not complete isolation, from the people was, the conservative contended, essential to the maintenance of the nobility. In order to perform its role, the nobility had to maintain a high degree of cohesiveness within its ranks, as well as a united front vis-à-vis nonnobles. Family ties, special privileges, and special duties were to ensure the necessary unity of outlook and action. Stress on exclusiveness and solidarity called for an elite effectively insulated from popular pressures. Not only was access to the nobility as an estate to be minimized by virtually excluding outsiders, but also any direct popular influence upon the nobility was deemed highly undesirable. Although cohesiveness as an essential elite attribute would remain a component of most German elite theories, the methods for achieving it would change. Many later elite theorists abandoned the criterion of birth for admission to the elite, but they generally retained the notion of effective insulation from nonelite pressures.

Conservatives rarely excluded the possibility of some reforms in the nobility. Were not the conservatives attempting to create a society on the basis of an idealized version of the past? In addition, the challenge of liberalism and new social forces had, especially by the middle of the nineteenth century, induced some reformist conservatives to make appreciable concessions in an endeavor to reinvigorate the concept of nobility.[7] From the modest suggestions of early conservatives to the

[6] See Hannah Arendt, *The Origins of Totalitarianism* (New York: Meridian paperback, 1958), pp. 165–67.

[7] See Neumann, *Stufen des preussischen Konservatismus,* pp. 33, 43, 45, 55–60, 65.

more demanding proposals of reformist conservatives, the English aristocracy served as a model which inspired many a plan to reform the German nobility.

The projected reforms of early conservatives aimed at strengthening the position of the nobility, but without altering its basic character. Beginning with Ludwig von der Marwitz, the indefatigable Junker opponent of the Stein-Hardenberg reforms, many prominent conservatives agreed on certain practical reforms. They suggested, for example, numerous schemes to retain the landed basis of the nobility. Thus Marwitz demanded that a grant in land accompany every patent of nobility.[8] Although the divisibility of landed estates among all male heirs had contributed to the economic difficulties of the nobility, attempts to introduce primogeniture in Prussia always failed.[9] Nevertheless, the substitution of English practices regarding inheritance remained a favorite project of conservatives. The introduction of primogeniture would have established a definite channel for departure from the nobility. There was also virtual unanimity among conservatives that other provisions for leaving the nobility must be established. By envisioning definite avenues of ascent into and descent from the nobility, conservatives suggested that the superiority of the nobility could not be maintained by preserving it as a castelike institution.

By developing similar proposals still farther, reformist conservatives such as Joseph Maria von Radowitz had, by the middle of the nineteenth century, conceived projects for a new "nobility of merit." Basic to most of these projects was the transformation of the nobility into a "microcosm" of the entire society.[10] The old nobility would have been formally opened to men from other estates or classes. Changes in the structure of German society would thus have found formal recognition. Portions of the upper middle class would have fused with the nobility in order to make the latter more "representative" of the nation as a whole. The nobility would then have been in a better position to reaffirm its claim to occupy a superordinate position and to represent the interests of the community as a whole.

No more than in earlier conservatism were "the people" to exercise any control over the nobility. The reformist conservatives regarded recruitment of the nobility from a larger segment of the population as obviating any need for popular control over the decisions or actions of the nobility. A partially open elite sufficed to permit the rejection of claims for direct controls by the populace. The optimal amount of pop-

[8] Fritz Martiny, *Die Adelsfrage in Preussen vor 1806 als politisches und soziales Problem: Erläutert am Beispiele des kurmärckischen Adels* (Stuttgart, 1938), p. 79.

[9] Neumann, *Stufen des preussischen Konservatismus*, pp. 54–55.

[10] See *ibid.*, pp. 55–60.

ular influence would have entered the nobility through the new nobles. The question of popular control, insofar as adjudged worthy of discussion, had been subsumed under the heading of elite recruitment. Many later German elite theorists would continue to equate a formally open elite with sufficient popular control over the elite.

The views of Paul de Lagarde, a bitter critic of Bismarck and the Bismarckian Reich, provide an excellent example of reformist conservatism during the latter half of the nineteenth century.[11] Lagarde's writings, which were "rediscovered" in the twentieth century, reached the height of their influence during the Weimar Republic. His plans for a "reorganization" of the nobility consisted in a notable admixture of hereditarily transmittable status with an aristocracy of talent. A fervent admirer of the English gentry, he hoped for a social stratum which, although possessing few formally recognized privileges, would conduct the affairs of the nation.[12] Only insofar as necessary for the execution of its duties should the nobility possess special privileges. For "rights always come by themselves when duties are taken seriously."[13] Like the early conservatives, Lagarde regarded duties as an effective check upon the nobility, but he advocated supplementing the individual's sense of duty with external means of enforcing it. He envisioned formal machinery for expelling members of the nobility.

Lagarde laid down detailed admission requirements for newcomers to the nobility.[14] In accordance with the tradition of state service that had taken root in the nobility and sections of the middle class and bourgeoisie, his new nobility would have been open to families with three generations of "direct or indirect service to the state." Military officers, university-educated state officials, clergymen, and teachers together with their entire families would have become eligible for admission to the nobility, if enough of their ancestors had held similar positions.[15] The strong *étatist* element in Lagarde's recommendations was symptomatic of a trend which would eventually prevail in con-

---

[11] See esp. "Konservativ?" (1853) and "Die Reorganisation des Adels" (1881) in *Deutsche Schriften*, Gesamtausgabe letzter Hand, 3. Abdruck (Göttingen, 1892). Fritz Stern's *The Politics of Cultural Despair: A Study in the Rise of the Germanic Ideology* (Berkeley, 1961), pp. 3–94 provides a good historical treatment of Lagarde. Of the other literature on Lagarde, see esp. Jean-Jacques Anstett, "Paul de Lagarde" in *The Third Reich*, ed. Maurice Baumont et al. (New York, 1955); Robert W. Lougee, *Paul de Lagarde, 1827–1891: A Study of Radical Conservatism in Germany* (Cambridge, Mass., 1962).

[12] See "Konservativ?" p. 9.

[13] "Die Reorganisation des Adels," p. 284.

[14] In "Die Reorganisation des Adels," pp. 285–90, he listed fifteen conditions for membership in the nobility.

[15] As employees of the state, teachers and clergymen had the status of state officials in Germany. Lagarde specifically excluded Jews from his proposal.

servative thinking, but in his programs this element was still overshadowed by a concern for the autonomy of family, nobility, and prince.

By suggesting the official opening of the nobility to portions of the middle class, Lagarde recognized claims of merit from significant segments of the nonnoble population. Most conservatives still disapproved of permitting any sizable number of commoners to enter the nobility. On the other hand, Lagarde's traditionalism led him to consider merit as something that developed over the course of generations and appeared only in families. His conception of merit marked the limits of his reformism. Otherwise—and if we also ignore his emphasis upon a *landed* nobility—his proposals manifested a great deal of affinity with certain liberal currents. Many of the ideas of the reformist conservatives formed a bridge to the elite theories of the liberals.

LIBERAL ELITE THEORIES

Although early liberals generally viewed the existing nobility with suspicion and animosity, most German liberals did not reject the notion of an aristocracy acting through constitutionally established institutions.[16] Symptomatic of the liberal position was a remark made by a representative from Rostock during the Frankfurt Assembly's debate on whether to abolish the nobility as an estate: "The present democratic movement is not directed against the originally true and pure nature of the nobility, but rather against its caricature—*Junkertum*."[17] The idea of an open aristocracy of wealth and achievement without any formal privileges occupied a prominent place in liberal thought. Liberals would have diminished the significance of birth and increased the significance of wealth, ability, education, and achievement as criteria for the exercise of political power.

Despite its essentially bourgeois character, liberalism seldom asked for reforms which would have destroyed the economic foundations of

[16] For liberal elite theories, see esp. Joachim H. Knoll, *Führungsauslese in Liberalismus und Demokratie: Zur politischen Geistesgeschichte der letzten 100 Jahre* (Stuttgart, 1957), pp. 42–44, 84–86, and passim; Leonard Krieger, *The German Idea of Freedom: History of a Political Tradition* (Boston, 1957); Kurt Klotzbach, *Das Eliteproblem im politischen Liberalismus: Ein Beitrag zum Staats- und Gesellschaftsbild des 19. Jahrhunderts* (Cologne, 1966).

[17] Kieruff-Rostock quoted in Ferdinand Tönnies, "Deutscher Adel im 19. Jahrhundert," *Neue Rundschau*, XXIII (1912), 1056. The Frankfurt Assembly voted 282 to 167 against abolishing the nobility (*ibid.*, p. 1057). Theodore S. Hamerow's *Restoration, Revolution, Reaction: Economics and Politics in Germany, 1815–1871* (Princeton, 1958), esp. pp. 161-64 brings out clearly the reluctance of most of the liberals in 1848-1849 to destroy the social and economic basis of the nobility. Their fear of popular control is well documented by Gerhard Schilfert, *Sieg und Niederlage des demokratischen Wahlrechts in der deutschen Revolution 1848–49* (Berlin, 1952).

the nobility's power. Even early liberals would have left the nobility as a class of large landowners. The identification of economic power with political power, which characterized so much of nineteenth-century thought, predominated in German liberalism. Liberals argued that economic power *should* result in political power. Although assigning priority to bourgeois claims for political power, liberals could hardly ask for the abolition of the nobility's economic power. After the failure of the liberals in 1848 to create a German national state, they shed much of their earlier antagonism toward the nobility.

The accommodation of liberalism to the Second Reich was greatly facilitated by the development of a positive attitude toward the administrative state. The early liberals had tended to reject the state bureaucracy as one of the strongest props of the existing political order.[18] They assailed bureaucracy for its alleged alienation from the people. After the failure of the Revolution of 1848, and especially after the founding of a constitutional national state satisfying many liberal desires, liberals tended to view bureaucracy as the most important element in any political order. Growing disillusionment with the caliber and effectiveness of the Reichstag in the late nineteenth century strengthened this tendency. The bourgeoisie turned to the bureaucracy to restrain the proletariat at home and to advance imperialist ventures overseas. To later liberals administration became more important than constitutions. A popular German saying assumed more and more significance: "The best constitution is a good administration."

Bureaucratic Elite Theories

Since the eighteenth century, the state bureaucracy had provided one of the most important paths to political power. The size and scope of bureaucracy in Germany promoted the dissemination of a series of ideas that were by no means confined solely to liberalism and had penetrated much of German political thought even before 1871.[19] Most notably in Prussia, the development of an extensive state administrative apparatus preceded the formation of modern representative bodies and was not altered substantially by their appearance. Indeed, the concept of the *Rechtsstaat*, the characteristic ideal of German lib-

[18] Theodor Wilhelm, *Die Idee des Berufsbeamtentums: Ein Beitrag zur Staatslehre des deutschen Frühkonstitutionalismus* (Tübingen, 1933), esp. pp. 8–17.

[19] A history of changing German attitudes toward bureaucracy could make a major contribution to our understanding of modern German history. In addition to Rosenberg's *Aristocracy, Bureaucracy, and Autocracy*, another recent monograph, John R. Gillis, *The Prussian Bureaucracy in Crisis, 1840–1860: Origins of an Administrative Ethos* (Stanford, 1971), would be indispensable to such an undertaking.

eralism, developed partly as a result of the reaction of the bourgeoisie to the state bureaucracy. During the earlier phases in the development of the concept, it was utilized as a standard by means of which the operations of the existing state could be criticized. Eventually and especially after 1871, the ideal of the *Rechtsstaat* was felt to have been realized by the existing state. Bureaucracy seemed to offer an excellent example of the state acting according to fixed laws and within definite areas of competence. Furnished with a set of general norms applicable to every situation, the bureaucracy could presumably follow them without resorting to arbitrary measures.

German theories of the state thus contributed substantially to the image of the state bureaucracy. Except the army, the bureaucracy was the only state institution with which most Germans had any repeated contacts. "The state" frequently became synonymous with the bureaucracy. "The officials are the state" (*Der Staat sind die Beamten*) summed up a widely held conception of the bureaucracy as the most important political institution. Bureaucracy became associated with the conceptions of the state as subject to a special morality, as the mainspring of progress, and as an institution designed to absorb and guarantee all the freedoms and wants of its citizens.[20]

In the latter part of the nineteenth century, many German political thinkers came to regard the state as an end in itself, the main property of which was the acquisition of power. Similarly, they found the essence of politics in the struggle for power.[21] The image of the bureaucracy benefited from these abstract conceptions of the state and politics. The bureaucracy became heir to some of the characteristics that came to be attributed less and less frequently to the state. The function of the bureaucracy was all the more strongly identified with the achievement of the welfare of the entire community. In non-Marxist thought the bureaucracy tended to be considered as the only agency capable of realizing the common good. For example, the "Socialists of the chair" (*Kathedersozialisten*) promised the achievement of social jus-

[20] For the relevant analyses of German conceptions of the state see esp.: Friedrich Meinecke, *Machiavellism: The Doctrine of raison d'état and Its Place in Modern History*, trans. Douglas Scott (New Haven, 1957); Gerhard Ritter, *Die Dämonie der Macht*, 5th rev. ed. of *Machtstaat und Utopie* (Stuttgart, 1947); Leonard Krieger, *The German Idea of Freedom*; John H. Hallowell, *The Decline of Liberalism as an Ideology: With Particular Reference to German Politico-Legal Thought* (Berkeley, 1943); Rupert Emerson, *State and Sovereignty in Modern Germany* (New Haven, 1928); Hajo Holborn, "Der deutsche Idealismus in sozialgeschichtlicher Beleuchtung," *Historische Zeitschrift*, CLXXIV (1952), 359–84; Helmut Plessner, *Schicksal des deutschen Geistes am Ausgang seiner bürgerlichen Epoche* (Zurich, 1935). A new edition of the last work has appeared under the title *Die verspätete Nation* (Stuttgart, 1959).

[21] See Wilhelm Hennis, "Zum Problem der deutschen Staatsanschauung, "*Vierteljahrshefte für Zeitgeschichte*, VII (1959), 1–23.

tice by expanding the state administration. The prince had once been viewed as the educator (*Erzieher*) of the nation; the depersonalization of the state meant that this function was also readily ascribed to the bureaucracy.

The bureaucrat came to represent a distinct type of elite individual.[22] His admission to power did not result from nonadministrative accomplishments. Administration was a full-time, life-long career. Theoretically, success in other fields was both unnecessary and irrelevant. The bureaucrat, like the ideal noble of conservatism, had something very special that set him off from other men. But in bureaucratic elite theories the special ingredient could be acquired—although primarily through the apparatus of the state.[23]

Hegel was one of the most influential nineteenth-century thinkers who became proponents of the state bureaucracy.[24] To Hegel the bureaucracy stood above and apart from the rest of society. The state officials constituted an independent estate (*Stand*). Like the conservatives, he assumed the necessity of a special, relatively homogeneous elite stratum.[25] Acting as an impartial intermediary between people and prince, his bureaucracy performed a neutral role between opposing social forces. Reminiscent of Plato's class of philosophic rulers, Hegel's bureaucrats possessed most of the knowledge and talent of the community. Yet to Hegel and to many other Germans, the bureaucracy acted primarily as the executor of one man's wishes. It supplied the king with information and conceived plans, but he made the final decisions.

Later apologists for the bureaucracy could hardly ignore the pressures exerted by political parties and pressure groups, but the bureaucrat continued to be considered as an impartial technician. His role was assumed to be nonpolitical and above parties. The Prussian minis-

[22] Although the state administrative apparatus as a whole furnished a model for elite theorists, the elite which they usually had in mind consisted of the higher, university-educated officials.

[23] Even the characteristics of the ideal bureaucrat were sometimes thought to be developed best over the course of several generations: "Die Qualitäten eines guten Beamten können durch Züchtung Generationen hindurch unter Umständen zu einer gewissen Höhe gesteigert und befestigt werden. Es handelt sich dabei namentlich um die Ersetzung des natürlichen egoistischen Selbstinteresses durch die aus amtlichem Pflichtgefühl und Ehrgeiz entspringenden Motive." Otto Hintze, *Der Beamtenstand*, Vorträge der Gehe-Stiftung zu Dresden, III (Dresden, 1911), p. 47.

[24] See esp. Hegel's *Grundlinien der Philosophie des Rechts*, pars., 287, 291, 295–97, 300–301. Where applicable, all references to this work include the addenda, which in most recent German editions are not printed separately. I have used the new edition by Johannes Hoffmeister (Berlin, 1956).

[25] His statement that the middle class (*Mittelstand*) would "constitute the major portion" of the state officials (*Philosophie des Rechts*, par. 297) served to underline the element of social homogeneity.

ter of finance from 1910 to 1912, Adolf von Wermuth, penned the classic apologia for the German bureaucrat: "I have never belonged to a political party. I employed all of my abilities to serve, as a loyal official, for the benefit of all."[26]

The bureaucracy together with the king claimed to represent the "real" or hypothetical will of the people.[27] Any counterclaims after 1871 by a parliament that was internally divided by many parties and factions scarcely seemed convincing. To most non-Marxists only the bureaucracy and the monarchy could claim to be working impartially for the best interests of everyone. The economist Werner Sombart voiced a common opinion when he asserted: "In no way do the officials represent any one particular group within a community. Rather, they represent the community as a whole."[28]

Because the predominant stream of German political thought entrusted the state with the fulfillment of the highest and noblest goals of society, the ethos of state service could appear superior to that of all other professions. Having received its classical formulation in German Idealist philosophy, the notion of duty, when applied to bureaucracy, resulted in the image of the self-sacrificing bureaucrat. Employment by the state bureaucracy was felt to be radically different, no matter how high or low the post, from employment in private business. The difference found its symbolic expression in the special oath of allegiance required of the state bureaucrat. His loyalty, directed toward such ideals as "King and Fatherland," was viewed as higher and more complete than that of the private employee. The state official was frequently contrasted to the "money-grubbing businessman." The state official felt superior because he "sacrificed" himself to state and society.[29] His devotion to duty could not, it was maintained, be attenuated. His *Hingabe* had to be complete.[30]

[26] Adolf von Wermuth, *Ein Beamtenleben: Erinnerungen* (Berlin, 1922). Quoted in Maxwell Knight, *The German Executive, 1890–1933* (Stanford, 1952), p. 18.

[27] See Ernst Fraenkel, *Die repräsentative und die plebiszitäre Komponente im demokratischen Verfassungsstaat* (Tübingen, 1958), p. 41 and passim. See also Fraenkel's "Historische Vorbelastungen des deutschen Parlamentarismus," *Vierteljahrshefte für Zeitgeschichte,* viii (1960), 323-40.

[28] Werner Sombart, *Der moderne Kapitalismus,* 3rd ed. (Munich and Leipzig, 1919), ii, 2. Hälfte, p. 1097. Quoted in Hans Gerth, *Die sozialgeschichtliche Lage der bürgerlichen Intelligenz um die Wende des 18. Jahrhunderts: Ein Beitrag zur Soziologie des deutschen Frühliberalismus* (Berlin, 1935), p. 110.

[29] The repeated assertion that state officials were poorly paid should be accepted only with great caution. Particularly in the lowest grades of the bureaucracy the financial remuneration was probably not as great as that which could have been gained by comparable private employment. This disadvantage would have been partly offset by the security of employment afforded by the civil service. Otto Most, *Zur Wirtschafts- und Sozialstatistik der höheren Beamten in Preussen* (Munich, 1916) marshals much evidence in an effort to demonstrate that the salaries

Bureaucratic efficiency was reputed to surpass that of any other type of organization except the military. Hierarchy seemed to furnish the key to success. Prussian military organization acted as a model for civil administration and was itself, in turn, influenced by bureaucratic ideals. The ease with which retired commissioned and noncommissioned officers received posts in the Prussian bureaucracy[31] provided a continual channel for military influence. The unquestioning obedience of the bureaucrat became almost as legendary as that of the soldier. Submission could even become imperative for the individual's equilibrium. In the words of a German aphorism, "he who has to choose bears the anguish" (*Wer die Wahl hat, hat die Qual*). Informal deviations from the hierarchic principle of making and executing decisions were overlooked. To have admitted that bargaining ever occurred within the Prussian bureaucracy would have sounded scandalous.

Somewhat paradoxically, a large measure of independent spirit never ceased to be praised as an attribute of the German bureaucrat. Since bureaucracy seemed to function so well and to accomplish such notable ideals, interference with its operations was often regarded as unnecessary and undesirable. Only from above did interference seem appropriate. Although Hegel's conception of society was markedly pluralist, like later apologists for bureaucracy, he deprecated the desirability or necessity of checks upon the bureaucracy.[32] Later political practice, moreover, hardly went beyond his modest suggestions.

For the eulogizers of a bureaucratic regime, as for many other Germans, politics could readily appear as a "dirty business." "Politics," went a German proverb, "wrecks a man's character." Political parties seemed to interfere with the functioning of an administrative elite. During World War I, Thomas Mann could write thus: "I do not want politics. I want objectivity, order, and propriety."[33] Like the conserva-

---

of higher officials began to fall behind after the middle of the nineteenth century, but to my knowledge no one has completed a reliable and broadly based comparative analysis of salaries. Confined mainly to the twentieth century, Hans Otto Hauck's *Die Problematik des Mittelstandes, dargestellt durch eine Analyse des deutschen Volkseinkommens* (Mannheim diss., 1954) is an impassioned, methodologically questionable study bemoaning the impoverishment of the middle class effected by labor and big capital.

[30] See Talcott Parsons's analysis of the lack of separation in German society between occupational status and the individual's private life. Talcott Parsons, "Democracy and Social Structure in Pre-Nazi Germany" in his *Essays in Sociological Theory*, rev. ed. (Glencoe, Ill., 1954).

[31] See Emil Obermann, *Soldaten, Bürger, Militaristen: Militär und Demokratie in Deutschland* (Stuttgart, 1958), pp. 41, 127.

[32] See *Philosophie des Rechts*, pars. 289, 295, 297, 301.

[33] Thomas Mann, *Betrachtungen eines Unpolitischen*, Stockholmer Gesamtaus-

tives, bureaucratic elite theorists wished their elite to be well protected from popular pressures. Otherwise, its activities would be hampered.

Despite many restrictions in practice, the recruitment of the state bureaucracy became the German version of a *carrière ouverte aux talents*. Theoretically, the bureaucracy was staffed on the basis of education and merit. The Prussian Constitution of 1850 and the Imperial Civil Service Act of 1873 stated that positions in the bureaucracy were open to all citizens according to their abilities. The formal educational qualifications required for the uppermost grades—or first class—of the civil service furthered the notion of it as a technical elite. These same educational qualifications acted as severe restrictions upon the recruitment of the civil service; they effectively prohibited men in the second or third class of the civil service from rising into the first class. Since the precondition to entry into the first class consisted in a university education, only the sons of the affluent, whose families could provide them with a higher education, were usually qualified for admittance. Furthermore, a civil servant in the first class received no salary during the initial years of his employment. By the end of the 1880's, the young judicial official, for example, had to obtain financial support from his family for as long as ten years after completing his stay at the university.[34]

Both admission and advancement depended largely upon cooptation. Since technically no advancements came simply after a fixed period of service, performance and capacity often appeared to be the only criteria for promotions. Rather than utilizing a system of examinations with open competition, promotions hinged upon the impression that the candidate made upon the personnel officer and the information recorded by his superiors in his dossier. The civil service filled its vacancies largely without outside influence.[35]

Other restrictions also operated as serious barriers to a career open to talents. Especially after the so-called Puttkamer reforms in the 1880's, the Prussian bureaucracy maintained obviously discriminatory standards of admission.[36] Jews and Social Democrats were excluded entirely. Conservative political beliefs and affiliations became the only fully acceptable ones. Conservatism displaced a moderate, *étatist* lib-

gabe der Werke von Thomas Mann (Frankfurt am Main, 1956), p. 253. See also esp. pp. 293–95.
[34] Eckart Kehr, "Zur Genesis der preussischen Bürokratie und des Rechtsstaats: Ein Beitrag zum Diktaturproblem," *Die Gesellschaft*, IX (1932), Band 1, p. 119.
[35] Fritz Morstein Marx, "Civil Service in Germany" in Leonard D. White et al., *Civil Service Abroad* (New York, 1935), pp. 227-29.
[36] See Eckart Kehr, "Das soziale System der Reaktion in Preussen unter dem Ministerium Puttkamer," *Die Gesellschaft*, VI (1929), Band 2, pp. 253-74.

eralism as the dominant ideology of the bureaucracy. The king of Prussia publicly demanded that civil servants support government candidates and policies in elections. As demonstrated by the king's dismissal of the so-called Canal Rebels in 1899, even conservatives were occasionally subjected to strong political pressures.[37]

The members of the imperial as well as the Prussian government consisted largely of career bureaucrats.[38] Even most of the highest political offices, those without tenure or educational qualifications, were occupied by career bureaucrats. The king-emperor made appointments to such offices almost exclusively from the ranks of the Prussian and imperial bureaucracies. From 1870 through 1918 three quarters of the Prussian ministers had served in the civil service. During the same period, substantially over two thirds of the imperial secretaries of state had a similar background.[39] The bureaucrat regarded high political appointments as a normal part of a successful administrative career. The usual path to high political posts began with entry into the first class of the civil service.

Although Hegel had still spoken of chance as a factor in appointments to the civil service,[40] many later bureaucratic elite theorists simply identified the higher, university-trained portions of the civil service with the cream of the nation's talent. Nevertheless, in the latter half of the nineteenth century, there were frequent complaints that the bureaucracy was not living up to its ideal. Talent, it was often asserted, was being drawn off into private business. Thus Treitschke, who praised the bureaucracy for having realized the ideal of the Platonic state in the eighteenth century, bemoaned its subsequent decline.[41] Yet he found no serious grounds for alarm and spoke fondly of the bu-

[37] For refusal to vote for the Ems-Weser Canal Bill twenty members of the Prussian House of Representatives were dismissed by royal decree from the high administrative offices which they simultaneously held. Yet it should be noted that most of them were reinstated shortly thereafter.

[38] The higher civil service of the Empire was probably less conservative and less socially homogeneous than that of Prussia. See Rudolf Morsey, *Die oberste Reichsverwaltung unter Bismarck 1867–1890* (Münster, 1957), pp. 262–63.

[39] Computed from statistics in Herman Finer, *The Theory and Practice of Modern Government* (New York, 1932), II, 1082. The actual percentages were 75.8 per cent and 70 per cent. For the period from 1890 to 1914 in Prussia, Knight, *The German Executive*, Table 41, arrives at the figure 64.5 per cent. See the similar figures in Walther Kamm, "Minister und Beruf," *Allgemeines statistisches Archiv*, XVII (1929), 446–49. According to Kamm (p. 446), 70 per cent of the Imperial chancellors and state secretaries had been state officials before appointment to their present posts.

[40] *Philosophie des Rechts*, pars. 291–92.

[41] "Das constitutionelle Königthum in Deutschland" in his *Historische und politische Aufsätze*, 6th ed. (Leipzig, 1903), III, 483, 486–87. For Treitschke see esp. Otto Westphal, "Der Staatsbegriff Heinrich von Treitschkes" in *Deutscher Staat und deutsche Parteien*, ed. Paul Wentzcke (Munich, 1922).

reaucracy as the "ruling class" of Germany. No ruling class in Europe was, he maintained, as open as the German bureaucracy. Furthermore, the "eminent" intellectual and scientific character of the German bureaucracy made it unquestionably the best in the world. In Treitschke's eyes, German bureaucracy represented an admirable synthesis between democracy and aristocracy. Without destroying the monarchical character of the state, it utilized the best talents of both the nobility and the bourgeoisie.[42]

Bureaucracy and nobility were, then, the two institutions that decisively shaped modern German elite theories. Themselves the foci of specific elite theories, the bureaucracy and the nobility continued to leave their stamp upon most German elite theories well into the twentieth century. Of the two, bureaucratic elite theories remained more clearly discernible.

CHANGES IN THE CONCEPT OF INEQUALITY AFTER 1850

More and more in the latter half of the nineteenth century, elite theorists divided society into two distinct parts. On the one side stood the elite; on the other, the "masses." Neither of these categories had much connection with earlier estate or class divisions. The rapidity of urbanization and industrialization, especially notable in Germany after 1850, focused attention upon what was viewed as a bipolarization of society.

The mere magnitude of population increases frequently seemed to have had the effect of creating a traditionless stratum that was not integrated into society. The industrial revolution produced a class of workers, who, living together in large urban centers, appeared far more menacing to the existing order than the peasantry. The proletariat's adoption of a militant democratic and socialist creed threatened a radical transformation of the existing order.

Events outside Germany also stimulated German elite thought. French experiences in the nineteenth century seemed to herald the dangers emanating from the masses. Almost at the moment that German unification was finally achieved, the Paris Commune emerged, and its memory long haunted bourgeois Germany.[43] From de Tocqueville through Taine, Tarde, and Le Bon, one strand of French political thought sought to demonstrate the dangers of "mass phenomena." The

[42] "Der Sozialismus und seine Gönner" in his *Aufsätze, Reden und Briefe*, ed. K. M. Schiller (Meersburg, 1929), IV, 141; *Politik*, 5th ed., ed. Max Cornicelius (Leipzig, 1922), II, 486.

[43] See Günter Grützner, *Die Pariser Kommune: Macht und Karriere einer politischen Legende. Die Auswirkungen auf das politische Denken in Deutschland* (Cologne, 1963), pp. 88–109, 169–77.

observation of "irrational" elements in mass behavior suggested the possibility of their manipulation through the application of appropriate techniques. The era of imperialism added further confirmation for the necessity—or at least desirability—of elites. Colonial administrators and European settlers demonstrated the possibilities of stringent elite rule over large subordinate populations.

Corresponding to the new emphasis upon "the masses," the predominant arguments for the necessity of elites shifted. Tradition, the appeal to "what has always been," now carried less weight. Rather, the incipient revival of cyclical views of history corresponded to the image of an eternal polarization of society into elite and mass. While the concept of the division of labor still occupied a prominent place in elite thought, it too changed.

The implicit rationale for previous conceptions of a hierarchically ordered society had become doubtful. Did not the industrial revolution hold forth the promise of a more than adequate material basis for society? Indeed, Marx and Engels predicated their view of a communist society upon the opportunities for human self-realization brought about by the industrial revolution. Modern means of production, Engels argued, had finally created "the possibility of securing for every member of society . . . an existence not only . . . sufficient from a material point of view, but also . . . warranting . . . the development and exercise of his physical and mental faculties."[44]

One typical reaction to the prospect of such a society countered with a miscellaneous assortment of objections. Heinrich von Treitschke, coiner of the phrase, "no higher culture without servants," denied the possibility of production ever attaining the level suggested by Marx and Engels. But in a society with a rapidly expanding productive capacity, older arguments about the limited quantity of goods or marginal productivity no longer seemed as convincing as they once had, and Treitschke did not mention them. Instead, he asserted that every increase in material goods awakened new material desires and needs in an endless succession. Machines might satisfy mass needs, but they could never replace "lower" personal services. Treitschke's belief in human insatiability ruled out the possibility of a "non-aristocratic" society. "The millions must plow, hammer, and grind, in order that a few thousand can study, paint, and govern." "Hard, dirty, half-bestial labor" was essential for the maintenance of "the achieved state of civilized morals."[45]

Treitschke also employed a series of related arguments involving the

---

[44] Quoted in Karl Popper, *The Open Society and Its Enemies* (Princeton, 1956), p. 297.
[45] *Politik*, i, 50, 53; "Der Sozialismus und seine Gönner," pp. 136–43, 152.

division of labor. Appealing to the Lutheran concept of *Beruf*, he sentimentally praised the virtues of all occupations; work with the hands was certainly not to be despised. The division of labor ensured a harmonious society. The "health of a nation" could not permit too many men who had no material woes, for the nation's thought would become etherealized. Variety was a beautiful thing, and after all someone had to build schoolrooms. There was no point in giving equal opportunities to all; the poor should not be deprived of their last comfort—the feeling that perhaps they really did not deserve their fate.[46]

Of particular interest to us here is another approach employed by Treitschke. In it he manifested the rudiments of a type of thinking that was becoming increasingly common as the final, decisive rejoinder to socialism and democracy. No longer invoking assumptions about a rational division of labor and about social and economic expediency, he postulated the existence of radical, inherent differences between men. Only a minority, he asserted, was ever capable of appreciating fully the "ideal goods" of a civilization. The "masses," on the other hand, would always remain the "masses."[47] Such propositions might have led merely to the conclusion that a cultural elite had to exist. But as we saw earlier, Treitschke equated, in large part, the highly educated with his elite. Moreover, since he emphasized heredity much more than environment, mass and elite were from his point of view largely self-perpetuating.[48]

Similar arguments based upon the assumption of radical and permanent human inequality had become frequent by the end of the nineteenth century. Much of their appeal can only be explained by the apparent ease with which they contradicted both the Marxist and the democratic utopias. Because of the rejection of the secularized natural law tradition by the main body of nineteenth-century German thought, such views asssumed particularly virulent forms in Germany. Ethnic tensions in Central Europe, especially in the Hapsburg Empire, also fostered emphasis upon inequality.

One line of reasoning concentrated upon an inherent faculty for cultural accomplishments. Another accentuated the role of inheritance in making men unequal. Both thus presented updated forms of the old conservative assertion of the uniqueness of the nobility and the inferiority of commoners.

---

[46] "Der Sozialismus und seine Gönner," pp. 142–44; *Politik*, I, 51–53. For a curious restatement of this thesis by a British Laborite see Michael Young, *The Rise of the Meritocracy, 1870–2033: An Essay on Education and Equality* (London, 1958), pp. 12–13, 85–87.

[47] "Der Sozialismus und seine Gönner," pp. 137–38; *Politik*, I, 50.

[48] See *Politik*, I, 304, where, in effect, he accepted the inheritance of acquired characteristics.

CULTURAL ELITE THEORIES

The cultural elite theorist held that the capacity to create or appreciate "higher" culture was confined to a small minority of men. Treitschke did not fully develop this thesis; for him it served only as one in a series of arguments against equality. But it became the primary theme of the cultural elite theorists, many of whom belonged to the so-called cultural opposition to the Second Reich. They denounced the existing order as decadently "materialistic" and already far too democratic. With Treitschke they expressed an increasingly powerful sentiment against the alleged arrogation of power by a plutocracy.

Standing, for the most part, outside the academic establishment, the cultural elitists scorned the universities as well as the *nouveaux riches*. One type of cultural elitist, exemplified by Jacob Burckhardt, viewed the new Germany from a patrician vantage point; he found that the *Bildung* of the highly educated was being attenuated by industrialization and nationalism.[49] Assuming that most men wanted only "material things"—material comfort and power—Burckhardt despaired of any possibility of elevating the masses. Through the growth of egalitarian ideas the masses, who hated the old elites and anything superior to themselves, had become too important in politics. Traditionless and rootless, they would, he predicted, destroy Western civilization. Only elites shielded from popular pressures, as in the *ancien régime*, could maintain and create worthwhile cultural values.

Some of Burckhardt's somber conclusions were difficult to distinguish from the more strident, often nationalistic voices of cultural elitists who spoke to the situation of the lower strata of the old middle class that were immediately and materially menaced by the development of large-scale capitalism. These strata, particularly artisans and small businessmen, had become dependent upon short-lived reprieves in order to maintain their occupations, as the guilds had been granted a new lease on life after the Revolution of 1848, only to find, in the economic institutions of the Bismarckian Empire and the depression of 1873, their death sentence reinstated. Unlike the industrial bourgeoisie, the old middle class derived few if any tangible advantages from the growth of the working class. This growth served as a constant warning that older ways of life were in jeopardy. Fearing descent into the burgeoning ranks of the proletariat, an increasing proportion of the old middle class discovered that routes to escape the insecurity of its own social position were closed off. Few could expect to join the

[49] For Burckhardt see esp. his *Force and Freedom: An Interpretation of History* (New York: Meridian paperback, 1955) and the introduction by James Hastings Nichols.

ranks of big businessmen. Only somewhat greater were the opportunities for most of the old middle class to avail itself of the traditional avenue of social ascent through higher education. Seeking ways to distinguish itself from the proletariat, to justify a title to superior social status, and to obtain weapons with which to compel the university, the state, and the bourgeoisie to render assistance, the old middle class was predisposed to claim for itself the task of preserving German culture. This culture it identified largely with preindustrial conditions. The old middle class was attentive to any suggestion that the state and the university had been captured by men who, lacking any true culture of their own, promoted the materialism of the big bourgeoisie and the proletariat. Although Nietzsche, the most innovative contributor to cultural elitism, frequently voiced contempt for the philistinism of the petty bourgeois, other cultural elitists, disregarding Nietzsche's barbs, expressed less equivocally the fears and aspirations of the old middle class.

By the beginning of the twentieth century, much of the stock of often contradictory ideas propounded by the cultural elitists had been appropriated by spokesmen for the old middle class, and, indeed, increasingly for the middle class as a whole. Not among the predominant bourgeois elite theorists of the nineteenth century, the cultural elitists are important for us primarily as precursors of subsequent developments. Their influence reached its apex only in the years following World War I, when their names and writings were invoked by the Right as part of an elitist tradition that was commonly traced back to Lagarde, or even farther into the past.

The cultural elitists professed to be concerned primarily with the fate of "culture," but the demands that they made in the name of this lofty expression were so great that only a political solution would have sufficed to meet these demands. They fostered the idea of a new elite capable of conceiving values for a German political renewal. While most conservatives had finally become reconciled to a modern administrative state, the cultural elitists believed that the "true" elite existed outside the state and that the special characteristics of its members had no relationship to experiences provided by political activity.

The contempt of many of the cultural elitists for the vast majority of mankind was rarely if ever expressed more forthrightly than by Nietzsche.[50] He envisoned an elite composed of the few men whom he

[50] Of the enormous secondary literature on Nietzsche, see esp. Walter Kaufmann, *Nietzsche: Philosopher, Psychologist, and Antichrist* (New York: Meridian paperback, 1958); and Gisela Deesz, *Die Entwicklung des Nietzsche-Bildes in Deutschland* (Bonn diss., 1933). In what follows I am presenting a view of Nietzsche which takes into account the influential images which his contemporaries and the succeeding generations formed of him. There is one aspect of his conception of an

believed capable of cultural innovations. The masses, worthless in themselves, had to be sacrificed to the few geniuses. The *raison d'être* of Nietzsche's elite lay in the development of its own members. Since the state had not resisted the claims of the masses, it too had to be sacrificed. It and politics were inherently democratic rather than aristocratic. Instead of protecting the elite, the state attempted to realize the common good; but the common good was antithetical to the good of the elite. Through false ideologies the elite had been tricked into becoming the "guardians" rather than the "lords" of the "masses."

Nietzsche's solution involved the complete subordination of the masses to the elite and the isolation of the one from the other. Yet the two sides of his solution were incompatible. If the elite could develop only in isolation from the masses, how would the masses be compelled to accept "a reassertion of hierarchy?" Although he credited the masses with a desire to obey, he never explained fully how this desire could be exploited. In general, Nietzsche emphasized the need for the "pathos of distance" that, he felt, would result from mutual isolation. Above all, the members of the elite had to recognize and assert their own powers. His final admonition to them was: "Go your *own* ways."[51]

In order to realize their own potentialities and not be ensnared by the masses, they had, Nietzsche suggested, to develop their own ideology. His critique of ethical systems led to the conclusion that ethical codes tended to embody the assertive morality of "masters" or the self-denying morality of "slaves." The elite should act upon the basis of an ethic entirely different from that of the nonelite: ". . . Every aristocratic morality springs from a triumphant affirmation of its own demands. . . ."[52]

Both the outrage and the fascination with which Nietzsche's contemporaries received his views were revealing. The extreme formulations of his elitism, such as his belief that the development of the elite should be an end in itself achieved through complete isolation from the masses and a special ideology, were based on logical conclusions from ideas current among other elitists. He pointed up possible responses to the growing organization, self-awareness, and potential political power of the lower classes. Like Machiavelli and Hobbes, he stated directly ideas that many of his contemporaries found intriguing and incisive, but either unnecessarily extreme or unacceptable for public dis-

---

elite which I have ignored because of its irrelevance to the type of elite theories with which the present study is concerned; his work may be interpreted as calling for a pan-European elite.

[51] *Thus Spoke Zarathustra* in *The Viking Portable Nietzsche*, trans. and ed. Walter Kaufmann (New York, 1954), pp. 321–22. Italics Nietzsche's.

[52] *The Genealogy of Morals*, trans. Horace B. Samuel, in *The Philosophy of Nietzsche* (New York: Modern Library, 1937), p. 647.

cussion. His concept of elite rule as a virtual conspiracy which should ignore the common good met, for the moment, few positive echoes.[53] The only notable counterpart in nonracist political thought was the emergence, which we noted earlier, of the concept of the state as an end in itself, but during the Bismarckian Empire this concept was hardly associated with that of an elite like Nietzsche's. Other elite theorists were much more inclined to accuse existing elites of ignoring the common good.

Even among those strongly influenced by Nietzsche, his elite theory was appreciably modified. Some of the other cultural elite theorists felt that the masses could not be left isolated, although they could never be raised to the level of the elite. Julius Langbehn, the author of a bestseller under the pseudonym "the Rembrandt German," was thus more optimistic than either Nietzsche or Burckhardt about the prospect of remolding the masses. Langbehn placed his hopes for a general cultural and political revival in a tiny elite which would penetrate the masses. But first, the new elite had to isolate itself from the rest of society. Only after a period of development in isolation would it go to the masses in order to activate them.[54]

Discussion of the desirability or necessity of mobilizing the masses to accomplish the tasks of the elite became common during the last decades of the nineteenth century. Not confined to some of the cultural elite theorists, this discussion helped to inspire, as we shall see in Chapter Three, Friedrich Naumann's attempt to create a reform party supported by the middle and working classes under the leadership of intellectuals. The notion of mass mobilization was fostered by the search for methods of coping with developments that many elitists viewed as dangerous. The working class was being activated and organized through the growth of the Social Democratic movement; democratic and Socialist ideas, as well as Bismarck's establishment of universal manhood suffrage, legitimized demands for active lower-class participation in government. Mass pressures had become too vigorous to be ignored by the elitist. If nothing else, the acclamation of the populace seemed to be desirable for effective leadership. Elitists sought ways of reducing or preventing any potentially effective mass role in government. Acceptance of some form of mass mobilization often went

---

[53] Many parallels to the extremes of Nietzsche's elitism can be found in the ideas of a Frenchman who lived a hundred years earlier—the Marquis de Sade. See Albert Camus, *The Rebel: Man in Revolt*, trans. Anthony Bower (New York: Vintage Books, 1957), pp. 41–42. For nineteenth-century parallels one must turn to some of the racist breeding schemes found in Social Darwinism.

[54] See *Rembrandt als Erzieher*, ed. H. Kellermann (Weimar, 1943), pp. 32, 142, 159, 250, 280. The first edition appeared in 1890. On Langbehn see esp. Fritz Stern, *Politics of Cultural Despair*, pp. 97–180.

hand in hand with emphasis upon keeping the elite insulated from popular influences and pressures.

At the very end of the nineteenth century and during the early twentieth century two developments strengthened the image of an elite insulated from popular pressures. Although both the Youth Movement and the circle around the poet Stefan George reached the height of their influence after World War I, their stress upon elite cohesiveness had attracted considerable attention earlier,[55] for they actually attempted to create highly cohesive elites shielded from external pressures.

George and his followers developed a more coherent, if always rather ambiguous, body of thought to support their practices. His esoteric poetry, deliberately made as inaccessible as possible to the general public, formed the crystallizing point for his circle. Rituals and rules knowable only to the initiate united the group from within. The selection of members depended upon his "intuition," for only "intuition" could recognize the few men capable of acquiring "the good." Following Nietzsche, George suggested that common morality might be ignored as a hindrance to genius. But within the circle itself, conscious sacrifices and special duties for the good of all members presumably set the tone.

The George Circle conceived of itself as an *Orden* on the model of medieval lay and religious orders. It also contributed to the revival of the *Bund* concept, a term most closely associated with the postwar Youth Movement.[56] *Bund* had long been a vague term with many Romantic associations. Through its application to the George Circle and

[55] No one has published a definitive study of the Youth Movement or the George Circle. Written by participants, who condescendingly assume that a mere outsider can never "understand," most of the numerous works on them are actually memoirs. The surviving participants have almost unanimously rejected, often, it should be noted, with much justification, analyses by nonparticipants. An American participant-observer of the Youth Movement during the 1920's has written a sociological study of the entire Movement: Howard Becker's *German Youth: Bond or Free?* (New York, 1946) brings together a great deal of material and raises most of the important issues. Of the recent general histories of the movement, the best are Harry Pross, *Jugend, Eros, Politik: Die Geschichte der deutschen Jugendverbände* (Bern, 1964) and Walter Z. Laqueur, *Young Germany: A History of the German Youth Movement* (New York, 1962). The more important literature on George and his followers is cited and discussed in Herman Lebovics, *Social Conservatism and the Middle Classes in Germany, 1914–1933* (Princeton, 1969), pp. 80–84.

[56] The classic description of the *Bund* is still Hermann Schmalenbach, "Die soziologische Kategorie des Bundes," *Die Dioskuren: Jahrbuch für Geisteswissenschaften*, I (1922), 35–105. Schmalenbach's attempt to delineate the *Bund* concept as a sociological term was impaired by the deep impression which both the George Circle and the Youth Movement had made upon him. Similar objections apply to Karl Seidelmann's *Bund und Gruppe als Lebensformen deutscher Jugend: Versuch einer Erscheinungskunde des deutschen Jugendlebens in der ersten Hälfte des 20. Jahrhunderts* (Munich, 1955).

the Youth Movement it became even more difficult to define. Its main emphasis now lay upon a small group tightly knit by common emotions and sacrifices with a leader and a lofty mission.

Particularly in the George Circle, this mission consisted in leading the way to a cultural and political "revival." Although, especially prior to World War I, the sense of a cultural mission generally predominated, political elements were always present. For the Georgians a cultural revival constituted the precondition to a political revival. Several important members of the circle, which came to be referred to as "the State" by its members, proudly associated it with the philosophical rulers of Plato. Even to some outsiders, particularly after 1914, the circle seemed to form the core of a new political elite.

Prior to World War I, the Youth Movement manifested a less articulated sense of mission. The participants concentrated upon their own development and expressed little concern for affecting society as a whole. Like the George Circle, they felt that their own development had to be accomplished in isolation from society. Only during and after the war would the Youth Movement become deeply concerned with altering the rest of society. Self-development in isolation then became merely a temporary measure. Many groups within the movement came to believe that they would greatly influence people outside their own ranks and eventually assume the leadership of society. The George Circle, on the other hand, always denied the possibility or desirability of the rest of society achieving anything approaching its level.

The cultural elite theorists supplied a potential weapon against traditional monarchism. They depicted an elite led by a single "hero" or "genius," and this "great leader" did not have to be the legitimate prince. Drawing upon the genius cult promoted by philosophical idealism, by romanticism, and by Carlyle's influence, they could also hark back to the medieval tradition of a *Volkskaiser*. Omission of the legitimate prince avoided one of the contradictions in some earlier elite theories. For example, a latent contradiction existed between Hegel's political philosophy in which the prince headed the elite and his philosophy of history in which a great man acted as the primary agent of the historical process. Cultural elite theories could make the role of the prince superfluous. Indeed, many of the later cultural elite theories both mirrored and reinforced the adulation of Bismarck by broad sectors of the bourgeoisie and middle class.

Social Darwinist Elite Theories

The most significant cultural elite theorists were very dissatisfied with the social and political structure of the Second Empire. The exponents of another major line of thought that insisted upon permanent inequality, the Social Darwinists, served largely as apologists for the existing order. The recourse to heredity as the primary factor in inequality usually accompanied affirmation of the Second Empire or merely mild criticisms of it. Superior heredity had presumably enabled the fittest to survive best. When coupled with a bipolar view of society, this emphasis upon heredity could lead to the notion of virtually self-reproducing elites and masses. In Germany, moreover, Social Darwinism was frequently linked to a revival of interest in the Lamarckian hypothesis of the inheritability of acquired characteristics.

Emphasis upon heredity even appeared in the ideas of some of the cultural elite theorists. Indeed, Nietzsche's conception of biology long provided him with one of the major pseudoscientific props for his elite theory. His belief in the inheritance of acquired characteristics and his fascination by the notion of "sports" or mutants contributed to his plan for a new elite of "supermen." Yet Nietzsche rejected the usual Social Darwinist thesis that "the struggle for existence" and "natural selection" operated in favor of the "best" members of the human species. With the example of plant and animal breeding in mind, he reached his momentous conclusion that the elite of the future could be produced only by protecting it in a "hot house for rare and exceptional plants,"[57] for "species which receive superabundant nourishment, and, in general, a surplus of protection and care, immediately tend in the most marked way to develop variations, and are fertile in prodigies and monstrosities (also in monstrous vices)."[58]

Although Nietzsche could toy with the possibilities of breeding human beings in order to produce a new elite, Langbehn hardly attempted to trace the origins of the genius which he ascribed to his elite. To Langbehn, the elite's special attributes simply appeared spontaneously in certain individuals. He never tired of asserting that these attributes were present from birth (angeboren). Everything aristocratic was inherent or inherited (angeboren). Everything inherent or inherited was "higher, more important, and in every respect more significant" than that which was merely acquired.[59]

To Langbehn and Nietzsche, as to the conservatives, the elite had to have certain characteristics that an individual could hardly acquire. Although Nietzsche's conceptions of the "will to power" and "self-overcoming" often pointed in another direction, the members of his elite always possessed intrinsic elements that made them capable of devel-

[57] *The Will to Power*, trans. A. M. Ludovici, in Oscar Levy, ed., *The Complete Works of Friedrich Nietzsche* (New York, 1924), xv, 328. I have altered the translation to make it conform to contemporary American usage.
[58] *Beyond Good and Evil*, trans. Helen Zimmern, in *The Philosophy of Nietzsche*, p. 584.
[59] *Rembrandt als Erzieher*, p. 34.

opment far beyond the ordinary man. Moreover, Nietzsche's notion of "blood" as largely "spiritual" rather than physical formed one of the most significant links between thoroughgoing racism and essentially nonracist elite theories. From Houston Stewart Chamberlain through Spengler, "blood" could thus be largely stripped of any material causality and appear as a mysterious, nonbiological mark of the elite. Otherwise, the racism so frequently associated with Social Darwinism cannot concern us here.[60]

Nonracist Social Darwinism could be employed to support a number of positions.[61] Applying the concept of the struggle for existence to society, Social Darwinists spoke of a "natural aristocracy" that was present in every society. Human inequality manifested itself in varying degrees of success in "adapting" to society. Every society was by nature aristocratic. As long as the struggle for existence was not interfered with, an aristocracy of achievement and talent appropriate to each society would emerge of its own accord.[62]

Otto Ammon, an anthropologist, thus undertook to demonstrate that the curve of income distribution in Saxony in 1890 corresponded to the distribution of intellect and talent.[63] The scientific character of his work, like every such study, suffered from the assumption that the goal of human evolution lay in the development of certain arbitrarily chosen characteristics. Even Ammon himself implicitly denied the reliability of his results. Like other Social Darwinists, he wished to place specific restrictions upon the struggle for existence in order to favor the type of "natural aristocracy" that he found appropriate to Germany. Rejecting an aristocracy of birth, he argued for an "aristocracy of education." He found the full development of this aristocracy threatened by the power of the masses, especially by the growth of the Social Democratic party.[64]

Indeed, much of Ammon's work stemmed from his desire to combat the Social Democrats. His proposed educational reforms were designed to favor the bourgeoisie and the middle class by segregating their children from those of the lower classes. The application of his

[60] Racist theories, it should be recalled, fall outside the scope of the present study.

[61] For German Social Darwinism see Hedwig Conrad-Martius, *Utopien der Menschenzüchtung: Der Sozialdarwinismus und seine Folgen* (Munich, 1954). An extended monograph on the subject is being undertaken by Hans-Günter Zmarzlik, who has published a disappointing exploratory article, "Der Sozialdarwinismus in Deutschland als geschichtliches Problem," *Vierteljahrshefte für Zeitgeschichte*, XI (1963), 246–73.

[62] See Conrad-Martius, *Utopien der Menschenzüchtung*, pp. 149–51.

[63] See the graphs in his *Die Gesellschaftsordnung und ihre natürlichen Grundlagen* (Jena, 1896), p. 83.

[64] *Ibid.*, pp. 243, 246.

reforms would have tightened the monopoly of the upper classes in higher education.[65] He would have divided society into two major groups: a highly educated elite entrusted with all important political and economic decisions; and the mass of the population held strictly in check.

The class bias so apparent in Ammon's program was present in most German elite theories of the late nineteenth and early twentieth century, but Ammon's lack of subtlety was somewhat exceptional. Many elite theorists had become more sophisticated. Since the end of the eighteenth century, explicit class restrictions on elite recruitment had diminished greatly. Even some of the predominant elite theorists maintained that in principle recruitment should extend to men from all classes. In a sense, a democratic tendency was on the verge of triumph.

Yet the broader pattern within which this tendency had developed hardly suggested democracy. At best, the pattern granted an open elite in lieu of popular control. Only as a member of the elite could an individual affect its decisions or composition. Whether constituting an estate, a class, or simply a group, the elite had to be drawn together by close ties among its members. None of the predominant elite theories suggested that everyone might at sometime become a member of the elite or that the elite might someday disappear. The possibility of an exchange of individuals between elite and nonelite indicated simply that a few of the latter might gain entry into the elite. There was no hint of the Jacobin conception of the member of an elite as a man who is today what all men can become tomorrow. German elite theories perpetuated Lutheran pessimism about human nature and the denial of any hope of establishing the Kingdom of God on earth. The doctrine of two or more kingdoms which could never coincide triumphed over the concept of the priesthood of all believers.

The member of an elite had to possess a special set of characteristics which he could not acquire. For the conservatives and Social Darwinists, as well as for the cultural elite theorists, these characteristics were inherited or innate. For bureaucratic elite theorists, they came only through a special connection with the state.[66] As long as most German

---

[65] See *ibid.*, p. 255.

[66] As a bureaucracy similar in many respects to the state bureaucracy, the Roman Catholic Church might well have provided a model for elite theorists. Although the distinction between priest and layman remained until the end of history, the layman could become a priest after meeting specific qualifications. Association with the Church legitimized his membership in an elite. The layman, like the mere citizen, participated in neither the selection nor the control of the clergy. But none of the elite theorists discussed in this chapter took the Catholic Church as a model. Apparently, the Church did not become the conscious model for many German elite theories until the Weimar Republic. Even then, it was not nearly as important as it had been for a Saint-Simon or Comte in nineteenth-century France.

elite theorists continued to regard the state as a "neutral" institution, whether operating according to the dictates of *raison d'état* or of the "common good," Nietzsche's thesis that the interests of the elite precluded any attempt to promote the welfare of the populace was not accepted. If the elite consisted of the "right people," no one had cause for worry.

A single individual usually stood above the elite. One of its essential functions normally consisted in mediating between him and the populace. The notion of a single leader occupying a position above the remainder of the elite, or above the elite per se, prevented the predominant German elite theorists from developing a "purer" conception of an elite, as the Italians Gaetano Mosca and Vilfredo Pareto had done. For the "antiheroic" Mosca and Pareto the role of a single leader was largely illusory; for many Germans his was the most important of all roles. Although conservative and bureaucratic elite theorists might sometimes make the prince appear dispensable, they did not divest him of the prerogative of making the most important final decisions. Most German elite theories remained monarchical. Potentially, cultural elite theories could sap the vitality of traditional monarchism, but for the moment they reinforced the predominant pattern in German elite theories: an elite free from popular control, recruiting itself from no one segment of the population, and headed by a single leader.

PART II
Liberals in Search of Elites

CHAPTER TWO

The Challenge of the 1890's

THE governance of imperial Germany depended upon a tacit agreement between the Junkers and the bourgeoisie. Worked out after the middle of the nineteenth century, this agreement was a consequence of the bourgeoisie's failure to become the ruling class of Germany through revolutionary means. By contrast, in France the eighteenth-century Revolution established the hegemony of the bourgeoisie, which was confirmed a generation later by the July Revolution; after 1830 the major threats to this hegemony came from the lower classes. The formation of the social coalition of the aristocracy with the bourgeoisie in Germany averted a showdown between the two groups by effecting a mutual accommodation of interests. This accommodation survived Bismarck's chancellorship, but during the 1890's the issue of who should control Germany was brought to the forefront of political discussion by domestic conflicts which, jeopardizing the continuance of the Junker-bourgeois social coalition, seemed to many Germans all the more momentous because for almost two decades the partners in the coalition had successfully muted their differences.

THE SOCIAL COALITION:
JUNKER AND BOURGEOIS IN IMPERIAL GERMANY

The major milestones in the development of the social coalition were the failure of the Revolutions of 1848 and the unification of Germany under Prussian leadership. The outcome of the Revolutions of 1848 weakened the political power and, above all, sapped the political confidence of the bourgeoisie. German unification occurred in a conservative form that realized many of the economic goals of the bourgeoisie while strengthening the position of the nobility, especially that of the Prussian Junkers.[1] Although technically the new German Empire was not highly centralized, Prussia dominated it. Not only did the area,

---

[1] Dealing with many largely neglected social and economic dimensions of German unification, Helmut Böhme's *Deutschlands Weg zur Grossmacht: Studien zum Verhältnis von Wirtschaft und Staat während der Reichsgründungszeit 1848–1881* (Cologne, 1966) makes an invaluable contribution to our understanding of the origins and subsequent vicissitudes of the Junker-bourgeois coalition.

population, and wealth of Prussia greatly exceed those of all of the other German states combined, but also a series of constitutional devices ensured her the political leadership of Germany.

To the king of Prussia went the *praesidium* of the Reich and the title "German Emperor." His constitutional powers included the appointment and dismissal of all imperial officials. By virtue of his office as emperor, the king of Prussia also exercised formal control over German foreign affairs. With certain restrictions, the emperor could declare war and conclude peace. In wartime he was commander-in-chief of all German military forces.

The office of emperor offered great possibilities for the exercise of political control. The extent to which these possibilities were realized depended in part upon the personality and capacities of the emperor. After Bismarck's resignation in 1890, William II tried to utilize the full potential of his position; but by World War I, many setbacks had made his efforts sporadic and generally ineffective.

Just as the emperor had a dual status as both German and Prussian head of state, so one individual usually held the posts of imperial chancellor and Prussian minister president. Although the enactment of legislation and the confirmation of administrative appointments required the signatures of both the chancellor and the emperor, the former's position depended constitutionally upon the emperor. The emperor had sole responsibility for selecting the chancellor. In practice much of the power and authority at the chancellor's disposal hinged upon the chancellor himself, while the structure of German society set limits to the roles of both men.

The constitution stipulated that the chancellor must be one of the delegates to the Federal Council, a legislative organ that represented the princes and states of the Empire. From the founding of the Empire to its demise, the king-emperor never appointed a member of a non-Prussian delegation to the office of chancellor; such a chancellor might have received conflicting instructions. The method of voting and the distribution of votes in the Federal Council furnished Prussia with a *de facto* veto on constitutional changes.

The Federal Council had much more control over the formulation and execution of policy than the Reichstag did. The Federal Council had the right to initiate legislation and to supervise its execution; the Reichstag could only legislate. Not responsible to the Reichstag, the chancellor could also not occupy a seat in it.[2] It was not even customary that the emperor select a former member of the Reichstag. The

[2] By stating that no one could simultaneously be a member of both the Reichstag and the Federal Council, Article IX of the constitution prohibited the chancellor from holding a seat in the Reichstag.

Reichstag exerted little influence over the selection of the chancellor and had no formal process for effecting his resignation. There existed no parliamentary system of government similar to that in France or in Great Britain. Standing outside the parties, the chancellor, for his part, had little opportunity to invoke the support of the Reichstag against other forces such as the emperor, the bureaucracy, and the army. The Reichstag served mainly as a sounding board for imperial policy makers and as a bargaining table at which some of the conflicts within the Junker-bourgeois social coalition were adjudicated. Despite the Reichstag's constitutional power to approve or reject the military budget, effective control of the expanding army lay in the hands of the king of Prussia and the military itself. Even the Prussian and imperial ministries of war, civilian bodies, were deprived of any decisive role in military matters. A Prussian military cabinet was created directly under the king in 1883 to reduce the possibility of non-Prussian and parliamentary interference. The imperial naval cabinet established in 1899 also served the latter function. The three most important political institutions of the Empire thus consisted of the office of emperor, the office of chancellor, and the Federal Council; and all of these institutions lay either in Prussian hands or under Prussian control.

Enlarging the scope of the Empire's activities tended to increase the relative power of Prussia. Throughout the period from 1871 to 1914, a slow increase in centralization occurred largely at the expense of the other German states.[3] Since naval and colonial affairs fell solely within the jurisdiction of the Empire, their rapid development during the reign of William II greatly enhanced its powers. In 1911 the Empire assumed direct control over the previously autonomous social insurance agencies. Although delegating nearly every other aspect of its field administration to the states, which already had fully developed field administrations of their own, the Empire laid down the main features of the policies to be pursued.[4] As the largest state bureaucracy in Germany, the Prussian bureaucracy administered most of the Empire.

The decisive role of Prussia within Germany imparted tremendous significance to the question of who controlled Prussia. The history of the Hohenzollern dynasty consisted in large part of repeated and suc-

[3] Not every aspect of centralization strengthened the position of Prussia. Prussian fears of being submerged in a highly centralized Germany acted as a block to rapid and extensive centralization. Similarly, the particularism of the other German states and the feeling of many specially privileged groups that centralization would lead to parliamentary control of the government promoted the retention of a large measure of autonomy by the individual states.

[4] See Herbert Jacob, *German Administration since Bismarck: Central Authority versus Local Autonomy* (New Haven, 1963), pp. 26–36.

cessful attempts on the part of the crown to find allies against its internal opponents.

The development of Prussian society since the eighteenth century may be viewed as a process whereby various social groups managed to obtain preferential treatment in gaining access to positions of power and privilege within the state. Once having arrived at such positions, each group resisted desires on the part of others to occupy similar positions, but usually only until further resistance seemed to portend revolution. Then the outsiders received enough concessions to placate them without altering radically the character of the existing political order. The newcomers found themselves gradually assimilated to the slowly changing ways and outlook of the older arrivals. The Prussian officer corps and the state bureaucracy provided the major institutions that integrated originally dissident groups into the existing structure of authority. The most important principles that served as criteria for admission to positions of power were birth, wealth, and education (*Herkunft, Besitz,* and *Bildung*). Political institutions and social processes indicated how an elite might broaden the social basis from which it recruited without succumbing to any appreciable popular control. Indeed, they suggested that an elite might expand the basis of its recruitment in order to avoid popular control.

By the end of the eighteenth century, the Prussian state had drawn into service the bulk of an entire social estate. Under Frederick the Great the government committed itself to a policy aimed at preserving the Junkers by discouraging their intermarriage with commoners and by aiding the large estates which provided the economic basis for the Junkers' privileged position.[5] Entrusted to the Junkers, rural administration was to a large extent autonomous. The superordinate social and economic position of the Junkers received official sanction. In exchange, so to speak, for their privileges the Junkers served as officers in the army. The Junkers were formally accorded preference for all governmental posts. The Prussian General Legal Code of 1794 explicitly recognized their special privileges.[6]

What type of person was the typical Junker? Until the latter part of the nineteenth century no other group held him in much esteem. The common image of the Junker did not play a role in Prussian society similar to that of the "gentleman" in the Anglo-Saxon countries or the

[5] See esp. Elsbeth Schwenke, *Friedrich der Grosse und der Adel* (Berlin diss., 1911).

[6] See Uwe-Jens Heurer, *Allgemeines Landrecht und Klassenkampf: Die Auseinandersetzung um die Prinzipien des Allgemeinen Landrechts am Ende des 18. Jahrhunderts als Ausdruck der Krise des Feudalsystems in Preussen* (Berlin, 1960).

"man of letters" in the Latin countries. Since presumably the Junker inherited his most characteristic attributes, how could anyone else really become a Junker? He and the bourgeois failed to find a social type which both could strive to approximate. The Junker lacked the polish supplied by a cosmopolitan court in Vienna or Versailles and the proverbial grace, charm, and *savoir-faire* of a French or Austrian aristocrat. Although by the end of the nineteenth century his spartanism was yielding to a receptive attitude toward conspicuous luxury, the popular notion of the rough, boorish Junker lingered on. Together with self-assertiveness and self-discipline, enormous will power was regarded frequently as an inherent element in the Junker stock. Although essential to the "true lord," an iron will could not simply be acquired or developed. One had to possess it from birth. With it went a strong feeling of independence resulting from the Junker's socioeconomic position.

The development of a tradition of state service diminished his sense of independence. The Junker derived much satisfaction from stressing his devotion to his monarch. The king's position as supreme warlord often appeared more important to the Junker than his position as king. But enough of the Junker sense of independence survived to foster a praetorian guard ideology. The ethos of *travailler pour le Roi de Prusse* had definite limits. In the words of a well-known phrase: "May the king's power be unlimited, as long as he does our will" (*Und der König absolut, wenn er uns den Willen thut*).[7]

Out of a qualified loyalty to the king there thus evolved an ambiguous tradition of state service that included a sense of special personal responsibility and duty. Although the sense of duty might have been considered as a logical corollary to the special privileges of the Junker, often the two were kept in separate compartments. As revealed by Hindenburg's reference to the "right" of the officer "to die before the others," an idealized notion of self-sacrificing duty frequently resulted.[8] The potential irony in such statements passed among Junkers simply as sincerity. The Junker felt that he served a higher cause than himself. If necessary, he could always justify his privileged position by

[7] Similarly, General von York, objecting to projected reforms in the officer corps during the early nineteenth century, had cautioned: "If your majesty deprives me and my children of their rights, upon what basis will yours then rest?" Quoted in Karl Demeter, *Das deutsche Heer und seine Offiziere* (Berlin, 1935), p. 16. A recent edition of this work, published under the title *Das deutsche Offizierkorps in Gesellschaft und Staat 1650–1945* (Frankfurt am Main, 1962), omits some of the material contained in earlier editions.

[8] Quoted in Walter Görlitz, *Die Junker: Adel und Bauern im deutschen Osten: Geschichtliche Bilanz von 7 Jahrhunderten*, 2nd expanded ed. (Glücksburg, 1957), p. 93.

stressing his special duties and responsibilities. His dependence upon the state, directly for employment and indirectly for agricultural subventions, eventuated in a *rentier* mentality. He came to attribute to the state much of the responsibility for maintaining his way of life.

Junkers and other nobles occupied most of the important civilian and military posts in the Prussian state until the collapse of the Empire in 1918. Although the proportion of noblemen in the Prussian officer corps declined substantially even before the mobilization for World War I, the decline was much less pronounced in the higher ranks. In 1860 65 per cent of the entire officer corps consisted of noblemen.[9] By 1899 the percentage had fallen to 40 and by 1913 to 30.[10] In view of the great expansion in the size of the army and the limited number of available noblemen, this decrease was neither precipitous nor indicative of a concomitant decline in the power of the nobility within the officer corps.[11] Among the generals and colonels, the decrease was also marked, but less rapid. In 1860 nobles constituted 86 per cent of these ranks, in 1900 61 per cent, and in 1913 52 per cent.[12] In the highest ranks there was little decline until the very eve of World War I. Thus virtually all of the generals and field marshals in 1909 were noblemen, and almost one third of them belonged to old Junker families.[13] Also suggestive of the continuing power and status of the nobility was the concentration of noblemen in critical posts such as the

[9] Demeter, *Das deutsche Heer*, p. 34. When I use the term nobles, I am referring not only to Junkers but also to noblemen from the Prussian provinces west of the Elbe and noblemen from outside Prussia.

[10] *Ibid.* See also Correlli Barnett, "The Education of Military Elites," *Journal of Contemporary History*, VI (1967), 27.

[11] How much of the decrease can be attributed to the failure of ennoblements of commoners to keep pace with the increase in their numbers in the officer corps is a question seldom raised and never thoroughly explored in the literature on the nobility and the army. A valuable recent study does not deal with the question, but the data provided by it indicate that ennoblements lagged far behind both population growth and the expansion of the army. See Lamar Cecil, "The Creation of Nobles in Prussia, 1871–1918,"*American Historical Review*, LXXV (1970), esp. p. 767.

[12] Demeter, *Das deutsche Heer*, p. 34. As Demeter points out, his figures do not include as nobles any officers ennobled during their careers in the army. If these men were included, the percentages of noblemen would be somewhat higher. For example, in 1913 it would be 56 rather than 52 per cent. For similar statistics on the percentage of noblemen among army officers, see the *Berliner Tageblatt*, XXXIII (1904), No. 41 cited in Robert Michels, *First Lectures in Political Sociology*, trans. Alfred de Grazia (Minneapolis, 1949), p. 71; and Hans Mundt, "Das Offizierkorps des deutschen Heeres von 1918 bis 1935" in *Führungsschicht und Eliteproblem*, Jahrbuch der Ranke-Gesellschaft, III (1957), 115.

[13] Nikolaus von Preradovich, *Die Führungsschichten in Österreich und Preussen 1804–1918* (Wiesbaden, 1955), pp. 142–44, 153. The above figures do not include princes—foreign or German—and members of the higher nobility who held purely honorary ranks.

General Staff and in prestigious branches and regiments such as the cavalry and the guards.[14]

Despite the European arms race, the Prussian Ministry of War undertook no significant expansion in the size of the army during the first decade of the twentieth century. The strategic plans of the General Staff necessitated an expansion, but it would have entailed increasing the proportion of *roturier* officers. The creation of more officers would have outrun the supply of "suitable material" and was hence deemed undesirable by the Prussian military cabinet. Not until 1913 were some of these checks upon the size of the officer corps overcome.[15] Even during World War I the temporary rank of "deputy officer" was created rather than permitting large numbers of "socially unacceptable" non-commissioned officers to enter the officer corps.[16]

The position of the nobility in the civil service was not as prominent as in the officer corps, but again the highest posts contained the highest percentages of nobles. The noblemen preferred the administrative to the more technical judicial branch, and they preferred positions in the Prussian field administration, the Prussian Ministry of the Interior, and, more generally, the Prussian administration to the central Reich offices in Berlin. The major exception was the imperial Foreign Office, where large numbers of noblemen held positions.[17] During the years 1888 to 1914 the Junkers provided between 27 per cent and 38 per cent of the most important Prussian field administrators,[18] and the total per-

---

[14] See Anlagen 1, 2, and 3 in Christian W. Gässler, *Offizier und Offizierkorps der alten Armee in Deutschland als Voraussetzung einer Untersuchung über die Transformation der militärischen Hierarchie* (Heidelberg diss., 1930); Martin Kitchen, *The German Officer Corps, 1890–1914* (Oxford, 1968), pp. 24–25. See also Karl Demeter, "Die militärische Führungsschicht Deutschlands: Eine historisch-soziologische Studie" in *Führungsschicht und Eliteproblem*, p. 103.

[15] See Eckart Kehr, "Klassenkämpfe und Rüstungspolitik im kaiserlichen Deutschland," *Die Gesellschaft*, IX (1932), Band 1, pp. 406–07; Emil Obermann, *Soldaten, Bürger, Militaristen: Militär und Demokratie in Deutschland* (Stuttgart, 1958), p. 78; Fritz Fischer, *Krieg der Illusionen: Die deutsche Politik von 1911 bis 1914* (Düsseldorf, 1969), pp. 251–53. The rapid expansion of the imperial navy after 1898 contributed to the depletion of the pool of "suitable" officer candidates. Gerhard Ritter, *Staatskunst und Kriegshandwerk: Das Problem des "Militarismus" in Deutschland* (Munich, 1954), II, 261–62.

[16] Walter Görlitz, *History of the German General Staff, 1657–1945*, trans. Brian Battershaw (New York, 1957), p. 185.

[17] Lysbeth Walker Muncy, *The Junker in the Prussian Administration under William II, 1888–1914* (Providence, 1944), pp. 43, 70–71; J.C.G. Röhl, "Higher Civil Servants in Germany, 1890-1900," *Journal of Contemporary History*, VI (1967), 116.

[18] Twenty-seven per cent of the *Landräte*, 34 per cent of the *Regierungspräsidenten*, and 38 per cent of the *Oberpräsidenten* were Junkers. Muncy, *The Junker*, p. 191.

centage of nobles was considerably higher.[19] Of the sixteen highest posts in the internal administration in 1903, twelve were filled by members of old noble families, including five from Junker families.[20]

The significance of the nobility becomes even more apparent when we examine the heads of the ministries in Berlin and their administrative policies. The officials in Berlin permitted the field administrator a large measure of autonomy. Since they sought to guide him indirectly rather than directly, he had much leeway in interpreting and executing policy.[21] Of the Prussian ministers between 1888 and 1914, 23 per cent were Junkers, and all together over 70 per cent were nobles.[22] The percentage of nobles among the imperial secretaries of state after Bismarck's dismissal was almost as high.[23]

As in the officer corps, but to a lesser extent, the proportion of Junkers and other older nobles in Prussian ministerial and administrative posts decreased perceptibly in the period from the end of the nineteenth century to World War I.[24] On the basis of the somewhat meager data available, we can discern a general trend beginning in the 1860's toward a higher proportion of newly ennobled individuals, members of recently ennobled families, and nonnobles in the diplomatic service, the higher administration, and the ranks of the generals and field marshals.[25] Although the proportion of Junkers and other representatives of old noble families remained substantial, it decreased significantly, if erratically, from 1806 to 1909.

Outwardly, the political and social position of the Junkers at the beginning of World War I remained intact. Yet due largely to the direct and indirect effects of the Industrial Revolution, the agrarian basis of this position was crumbling. The tremendous alteration in the propor-

[19] Preradovich, *Führungsschichten*, pp. 104–23; Eberhard Pikart, "Preussische Beamtenpolitik 1918–1933," *Vierteljahrshefte für Zeitgeschichte*, vi (1958), 120n.; Walther Kamm, "Minister und Beruf," *Allgemeines statistisches Archiv*, xviii (1929), 450; Röhl, "Higher Civil Servants in Germany," p. 116; Hans-Karl Behrend, "Zur Personalpolitik des preussischen Ministeriums des Innern: Die Besetzung der Landratstellen in den östlichen Provinzen 1919–1933," *Jahrbuch für die Geschichte Mittel- und Ostdeutschlands*, vi (1957), 200.

[20] Of the four men from nonnoble families, one had recently been ennobled. Preradovich, *Führungsschichten*, pp. 120, 122. The individuals involved were: the minister of the interior, the under secretary of the interior, the director of the interior, and 13 *Oberpräsidenten*.

[21] See Jacob, *German Administration since Bismarck*, pp. 48–64.

[22] Muncy, *The Junker*, p. 203.

[23] Altogether 64.5 per cent came from the nobility, including a sizeable proportion from the Junkers. Roughly two thirds of the 64.5 per cent had been born into the nobility, and one third had received ennoblement themselves. Maxwell Knight, *The German Executive, 1890–1933* (Stanford, 1952), p. 28 and table on p. 33.

[24] See Muncy, *The Junker*, p. 232.

[25] See Preradovich, *Führungsschichten*, pp. 100–03, 121–23, 151–53.

tion of rural to urban population and the new urban sources of wealth had diminished the economic power of the Junkers.[26] Despite a series of protective measures, agriculture suffered after 1860. Prussian grain could not compete on the world market with Russian, American, or Canadian grain. By 1900 only one half of the knightly estates (*Rittergüter*) in the eastern provinces of Prussia remained in the possession of nobles.[27] Many Junker families had lost all ties to the land and become nobles whose *raison d'être* now lay in complete dedication to state service in the army or the administration. An increasing number of Junkers also took up pursuits, such as art and scholarship, which they had traditionally shunned.[28] Here and there, other indications of an incipient *embourgeoisement* of the Junkers also became apparent. Some of the Junkers remaining on the land made the successful transition to large landed agrarian capitalists, but they often defended their interests in feudal, patriarchal terms more appropriate to their position and functions in the past than in the present.[29]

As an estate and even as a class, the Junkers were slowly disintegrating. Although the substance of many of their old privileges remained intact, the Prussian Constitution of 1850 had formally abolished all noble privileges. In defending the Junkers against their critics, the historian Otto Hintze had to admit in 1914 that "the great period of the Junkers lies in the past" and consequently "people no longer realize the measure of the Junkers' historical contribution."[30]

The Junkers never formed a true caste. Throughout the eighteenth and nineteenth century they intermarried frequently with German and non-German immigrant nobles, as well as with untitled Prussians. During periods of agrarian distress, many commoners acquired Junker estates, received titles of nobility, and were assimilated by the Junkers.[31]

---

[26] See Ferdinand Tönnies, "Deutscher Adel im 19. Jahrhundert," *Neue Rundschau*, xxiii (1912), 1041–63; Alexander Gerschenkron, *Bread and Democracy in Germany* (Berkeley, 1943), pp. 43–49 and passim.

[27] Görlitz, *Die Junker*, pp. 303–04.   [28] *Ibid.*, p. 308.

[29] Muncy, *The Junker*, pp. 41, 55–56.

[30] Otto Hintze, "Die Hohenzollern und der Adel," *Historische Zeitschrift*, cxii (1914), 494.

[31] Görlitz, *Die Junker*, pp. 159, 161–64, 173–74, 186; Schwenke, *Friedrich der Grosse und der Adel*, pp. 26–27, 42–44; Fritz Martiny, *Die Adelsfrage in Preussen vor 1806 als politisches und soziales Problem: Erläutert am Beispiele des kurmärckischen Adels* (Stuttgart, 1938), p. 38; Hans Rosenberg, "Die 'Demokratisierung' der Rittergutsbesitzerklasse" in *Zur Geschichte und Problematik der Demokratie: Festgabe für Hans Herzfeld*, ed. Wilhelm Berges and Carl Hinrichs (Berlin, 1958). Of one sample consisting of the males of 13 "typical" Junker families with 681 members living between 1888 and 1914 almost 30 per cent married nonnobles. Muncy, *The Junker*, p. 221. I do not understand why Muncy considers 30 per cent indicative of a low rate of intermarriage.

The edicts of the Prussian reform period laid the legal foundation for the separation of nobility from the possession of large landholdings. Thereafter, the ennoblement of bourgeois estate owners no longer took place almost automatically. As noted earlier, only about one half of the estates east of the Elbe remained under Junkers by the end of the nineteenth century. Yet it would be erroneous to assume that because a new owner of an estate did not receive a patent of nobility he kept aloof from his Junker neighbors. On the contrary, he usually identified himself with them and tried to adopt the Junker pattern.

By the last decades of the nineteenth century, not only he but also the entire bourgeoisie stood under the pervasive influence of the Junkers and their ideals.[32] The "feudalization" of the bourgeoisie was well underway. A sizable segment of the Junkers was fusing directly with part of the bourgeoisie to form a new upper class; and the bourgeois sought feverishly to emulate the Junker. While the prestige of the Junker rose, an independent bourgeois tradition declined.

The "refeudalization" of Prusso-German society stemmed indirectly from the consequences of the failure of the Revolution of 1848. More basically, the conservative influence of participation in the Prussian bureaucracy, fear of the industrial proletariat, and assimilation to the Junker pattern through the officer corps undermined bourgeois ideals. The rapid disintegration of these ideals began in the latter half of the nineteenth century.

We can distinguish two major groups within the bourgeoisie before the Industrial Revolution. Apparently, they were rather well separated. Two distinct lines of social ascent existed: one through wealth derived from commerce, and another through higher education.[33]

---

[32] See Werner Sombart, *Die deutsche Volkswirtschaft im 19. Jahrhundert und im Anfang des 20. Jahrhunderts*, 7th ed. (Berlin, 1927), pp. 469–70; Rosenberg, "Die 'Demokratisierung' der Rittergutsbesitzerklasse," pp. 471–72; Ritter, *Staatskunst und Kriegshandwerk*, II, 117–31; Richard Lewinsohn (Morus), *Das Geld in der Politik*, 5.–7., Aufl. (Berlin, 1931), pp. 25–30.

[33] The data available are admittedly insufficient to warrant any more than what appear to be reasonable hypotheses. On the separation of the educated from the rest of the bourgeoisie see Svend Riemer's résumé of a study of Württemberg: "Sozialer Aufstieg und Klassenschichtung," *Archiv für Sozialwissenschaft und Sozialpolitik*, LXVII (1932), 549. Aspects of this separation during the first half of the nineteenth century are the subject of Lenore O'Boyle's "Klassische Bildung und soziale Struktur in Deutschland zwischen 1800 und 1848," *Historische Zeitschrift*, CCVII (1968), 584–608. The persistence into the twentieth century of a clearly delineated group of the university-educated with its own distinctive status and ideology is one of the themes of Fritz K. Ringer, *The Decline of the German Mandarins: The German Academic Community, 1890–1933* (Cambridge, Mass., 1969). See also Ringer's "Higher Education in Germany in the Nineteenth Century," *Journal of Contemporary History*, VI (1967), 123–38, and Reinhard Koselleck, *Preussen zwischen Reform und Revolution: Allgemeines Landrecht, Verwaltung und soziale Bewegung von 1791 bis 1848* (Stuttgart, 1967), pp. 78–115.

Many of the university-trained individuals entered the state administration. Often they or their descendants climbed to high positions. Indeed, the Prussian bureaucracy of the eighteenth century has been
termed the "representation of the middle class."[34] The successful commoners and their noble colleagues provided the administrative elite.
Together with the Junkers and the monarch, the successful middle-
class bureaucrats were the most important political force in Prussia.
Often the commoners received patents of nobility.[35]

With the appearance of a large industrial bourgeoisie in the second
half of the nineteenth century, the stage was set for the incorporation
of a still larger segment of the bourgeoisie into a highly favored position. Most liberals accepted national unity as a tacit *quid pro quo* for
moderating other objectives. The bourgeoisie achieved some of its domestic goals, including new commercial legislation and social stability,
but only by working through the existing order. The wars of unification fostered a favorable attitude toward the military and nobility.[36]
Bourgeois literature, previously often hostile toward the nobleman,
began to portray him sympathetically.[37] Status symbols with an aristocratic flavor, created especially for the wealthy bourgeois such as the
title, Privy Councillor of Commerce (*Geheimer Kommerzienrat*), assumed renewed significance as devices to assuage the craving of the
bourgeoisie to emulate the nobility. "Title brokers," usually impov-
erished noblemen boasting of their excellent connections at court, did
a flourishing business helping eager bourgeois acquire patents of nobility.[38] For the less affluent bourgeois and for the state official, there
was a plethora of titles, decorations, and other honors.

The basis of the Prussian army shifted during the last decades of the
nineteenth century. Peasants left the countryside for the new urban
industrial centers and added to the rapidly swelling ranks of the proletariat. The industrial revolution transformed much of the peasantry,
esteemed in conservative legend for its subservience, into an industrial
working force, whose turbulence was manifest. The Social Democrat

[34] Fritz Morstein Marx, "Civil Service in Germany" in Leonard D. White et al.,
Civil Service Abroad (New York, 1935), p. 179.

[35] See Hans Rosenberg, *Bureaucracy, Aristocracy, and Autocracy: The Prussian
Experience, 1660–1815* (Cambridge, Mass., 1958); Eckart Kehr, "Zur Genesis der
preussischen Bürokratie und des Rechtsstaats: Ein Beitrag zum Diktaturproblem,"
Die Gesellschaft, ix (1932), Band 1, pp. 103–14.

[36] See Felix Priebatsch, *Geschichte des preussischen Offizierkorps* (Breslau,
1919), p. 52.

[37] See Ernst Kohn-Bramstedt, *Aristocracy and the Middle Classes in Germany:
Social Types in German Literature, 1830–1900* (London, 1937), pp. 228–33 and
passim.

[38] Lewinsohn, *Geld in der Politik*, pp. 25–30. A recent study supports, although
not explicitly, most of Lewinsohn's charges about "title brokers." See Cecil, "Creation of Nobles in Prussia," p. 784.

appeared as a threat to the positions of both the Junker officer and the bourgeois industrialist. Mutual fear of the proletariat helped to unite industrialist and Junker. The Junkers made enough concessions to the bourgeoisie to gain a new ally. Imperial tariffs on iron and grain in 1879 marked the drawing together of the interests of the landed nobility and those of heavy industry.

The introduction of the reserve officer system facilitated the incorporation of the bourgeoisie into the existing order.[39] The reserve officer system offered the bourgeoisie a junior partnership in the army. A young man who had completed his secondary education could apply for a reserve commission. Only the son of a father with a marked socioeconomic superiority over the mass of citizens was admitted to candidacy. If the father owned a business, but waited on customers, then the son was ineligible.

Possession of a reserve commission became an eagerly sought social distinction. Often a civil servant's career depended upon his ability to identify himself with the military. The number of openings in the reserve never sufficed to meet the demand, and students of law and state administration (*Juristen*), who usually entered the civil service, were given preference.[40]

William II gave a characteristically erratic impetus to the feudalization of the bourgeoisie. His decree of March 29, 1890 presumed to herald a new era: "In these days the nobility of birth can no longer claim the exclusive privilege of supplying the army with its officers. Rather, the nobility of character, which has always animated the officer corps, should and must be preserved for it unchanged." In addition to nobles, sons of officers, and sons of officials, William asked that the active officer corps of the future also include the sons of "honorable bourgeois families in which the love of King and Fatherland, a warm feeling of affection for the profession of arms, and a Christian outlook are implanted and cultivated."[41]

From 1888 to 1914 the percentage of sons of men who had attended a university among the cadets doubled. The percentage of sons of businessmen and industrialists also increased markedly, as did the sons of bourgeois agriculturalists (*Gutspächter* and *Gutsverwalter*).[42] Wealthy commoners entering the officer corps tried to associate them-

[39] See Eckart Kehr, "Zur Genesis des königlichen preussischen Reserveoffiziers," *Die Gesellschaft*, v (1928), Band 2, pp. 492–502.

[40] F. C. Endres, "The Social Structure and Corresponding Ideologies of the German Officer Corps before the World War," trans. S. Ellison, issued by State Department of Social Welfare and Department of Social Science of Columbia University ([New York], 1937), mimeo., p. 26a. Endres' statement that, as a rule, only *Juristen* were accepted requires qualification.

[41] Quoted in Demeter, *Das deutsche Heer*, pp. 28–29.

[42] *Ibid.*, pp. 30–32; Demeter, "Die militärische Führungsschicht," pp. 101–02.

selves with the nobles rather than with less affluent commoners.[43] Sons of the *nouveaux riches* even managed to gain access to the most exclusive regiments.[44]

Service in the highest civil and military posts had long been a path to ennoblement. Under William II the practice of granting nobility increased, although not as greatly as many of his critics came to believe. Wealthy men not occupying state offices received patents of nobility more often than previously. Whereas most earlier ennoblements had involved families that either had or subsequently acquired landed estates, the ennoblements of the late nineteenth and early twentieth century included a larger proportion of families that did not receive or acquire landed estates.[45]

By the 1890's a new upper class was emerging. Although well under way by the end of the Empire, the process was still incomplete.[46] The incipient new upper class consisted of two major strata: a small group of very wealthy noblemen, who although they had extensive landholdings and were successful agrarian capitalists, often derived much of their income from mining, lumbering, the processing of raw materials, and urban investments; and a larger group of urban commercial and industrial capitalists, many of whom had ties to the land through the acquisition of country estates and intermarriage with landed noblemen and many of whom received patents of nobility. Many big industrial families like the Stumms, the Haniels, and the Hoesches were ennobled and intermarried with the older nobility.[47] The poorer of the Junkers could gain a place for themselves and their families within the incipient new upper class only by capitalizing on their social position and political power, but Junker influences tended to predominate throughout the highest reaches of society.

Socially, then, Prussia and the German Empire in turn rested upon a tacit alliance among the Junkers, the industrial and commercial bourgeoisie, and the administrative middle class. This alliance enabled the nobility to retain the highest status in society. Birth, as symbolized by

[43] Endres, "Social Structure and Corresponding Ideologies of the German Officer Corps," pp. 25–26.

[44] Obermann, *Soldaten, Bürger, Militaristen*, pp. 82, 98; Demeter, *Das deutsche Heer*, pp. 210–18; Gässler, *Offizier und Offizierkorps*, p. 17.

[45] Görlitz, *Die Junker*, p. 302. The shift in the patterns of ennoblements with the accession of William II was probably less dramatic than has generally been thought. See Cecil, "Creation of Nobles in Prussia."

[46] Cf. John R. Gillis, "Aristocracy and Bureaucracy in Nineteenth-Century Prussia," *Past and Present*, No. 41 (Dec. 1968), pp. 105–29. Perhaps because his focal point is the first half of the nineteenth century, Gillis regards the process as completed by the end of the century.

[47] For a lively popular treatment of the wealthy in imperial Germany see Lewinsohn, *Geld in der Politik*, esp. pp. 21–23.

the Junkers, education as symbolized by the administrative middle class, and wealth as symbolized by the commercial and industrial bourgeoisie—these were the factors regulating access to positions of power. The political and social *rapprochement* of these groups provided a strong community of interest and sentiment among them.

Unlike the administrative middle class and the Junkers, the industrial bourgeoisie did not have to enter the professional civil or military service in order to make its weight felt. Through the press, trade associations, political organizations, personal contacts, and the movement of some high state officials from the bureaucracy to private business and often back to the bureaucracy, big businessmen were able to exert their influence. Even after 1890, when state and private business policy became increasingly interdependent, big businessmen who entered government service usually did so only for short periods, an indication of the directness of their function as spokesmen for their interests in governmental circles.[48] Although a myth persists that German businessmen shunned active participation in politics, the number of industrialists holding seats in the Reichstag and Prussian House of Representatives began to rise substantially after the turn of the century. At the end of World War I, the increase was to be even more marked.[49]

The situation in the non-Prussian states of the Empire manifested many similarities to that in Prussia. Although the power and type of the Junker were unique, the remainder of the German nobility, especially in northern Germany, played a somewhat analogous role. In southern Germany and the Hanseatic cities the bourgeoisie, especially the urban patriciate, occupied the decisive position. In the officer corps of Bavaria and Württemberg, for example, the bourgeoisie set the tone.[50] On the other hand, the Bavarian nobility entered into far fewer morganatic marriages than the Junkers. In Bavaria little fusion occurred between the small industrial bourgeoisie and the nobility.[51]

[48] See Eugene N. and Pauline R. Anderson, *Political Institutions and Social Change in Continental Europe in the Nineteenth Century* (Berkeley, 1967), p. 194; Röhl, "Higher Civil Servants in Germany," p. 114.

[49] Hans Jaeger, "Unternehmer und Politik im Wilhelminischen Deutschland," *Tradition: Zeitschrift für Firmengeschichte und Unternehmerbiographie*, XIII (1968), 4–6.

[50] See Demeter, "Die militärische Führungsschicht," p. 103 and *Das deutsche Heer*, pp. 41–56; Obermann, *Soldaten, Bürger, Militaristen*, p. 84.

[51] See Preradovich, *Führungsschichten*, p. 168; Hanns Hubert Hofmann, *Adelige Herrschaft und souveräner Staat: Studien über Staat und Gesellschaft in Franken und Bayern im 18. und 19. Jahrhundert* (Munich, 1962); Walter Schärl, *Die Zusammensetzung der bayerischen Beamtenschaft von 1806 bis 1918* (Kallmünz, 1955).

TOWARD A NEW LIBERAL ELITISM

Although intermarriage and joint business ventures furthered the consolidation of a cohesive German upper class, the persistence of discord among commercial, industrial, and agrarian interests impeded this consolidation. During the 1890's the rise of acute tensions within the dominant social coalition was promoted, but not initiated by the survival of old resentments and animosities between aristocrat and bourgeois. The primary sources of these tensions were struggles that centered in commercial and tariff issues and became entangled with other questions of foreign and domestic policy such as the building of a fleet, the commitment of the Reich to an intensified pursuit of overseas imperialism, and the treatment of the labor movement. Steps in the direction of free trade taken under Caprivi's chancellorship (1890–1894) led disgruntled large agrarians to threaten the dissolution of the social coalition, while some segments of the bourgeoisie, desiring further reductions in tariffs, were emboldened to contemplate the launching of a sustained assault upon the prerogatives of the Junkers. Never securely within the social coalition, large commercial interests in the North German Hanseatic cities of Hamburg and Bremen joined some of the big banks and important segments of light industry in leading the battle for more liberal trade policies. The free traders could count upon a measure of support from the new chemical, electrical, and machine-building industries. Even some of the heavy industrialists, traditionally protectionist in outlook, were now unhappy with the extent and consequences of the agrarian protectionism of their Junker allies.[52]

[52] Among the other issues that aggravated relations between the partners in the social coalition were the new bourse law, the rural government act, taxation bills, and army bills. Important aspects of the relationship of political to social and economic developments during the 1890's, especially the conflicts among large commercial, industrial, and agrarian interests, are discussed in Gerschenkron, *Bread and Democracy*, pp. 48–58; Eckart Kehr, *Schlachtflottenbau und Parteipolitik 1894–1901: Versuch eines Querschnitts durch die innenpolitischen, sozialen und ideologischen Voraussetzungen des deutschen Imperialismus* (Berlin, 1930); J. A. Nichols, *Germany after Bismarck: The Caprivi Era, 1890–1894* (New York: Norton paperback, 1968), esp. pp. 141–53, 217–19, 258, 278, 287–98, 302–07; Peter Gilg, *Die Erneuerung des demokratischen Denkens im Wilhelminischen Deutschland: Eine ideengeschichtliche Studie zur Wende vom 19. zum 20. Jahrhundert* (Wiesbaden, 1965), pp. 26–51; Helmut Kaelble, *Industrielle Interessenpolitik in der Wilhelminischen Gesellschaft: Centralverband Deutscher Industrieller 1895–1914* (Berlin, 1967), esp. pp. 52–53; Hans-Jürgen Puhle, *Agrarische Interessenpolitik und der preussische Konservatismus im Wilhelminischen Reich (1893–1914): Ein Beitrag zur Analyse des Nationalismus in Deutschland am Beispiel des Bundes der Landwirte und der Deutsch-Konservativen Partei* (Hannover, 1967), esp. pp. 156–60; Dirk Stegmann, *Die Erben Bismarcks: Parteien und Verbände in der Spätphase des Wilhelminischen Deutschlands. Sammlungspolitik 1897–1918* (Cologne and Berlin, 1970), esp. pp. 59–130.

Largely on the basis of the conflicts over commercial and tariff policies, there developed a bitter debate between intellectuals favoring and intellectuals opposing protectionist policies for agriculture. Those espousing agrarian protectionism pointed to the imminent danger of Germany's transformation into an "industrial state"; their opponents touted the benefits of a state oriented mainly toward the needs of modern industry.[53] While many of the "industrializers" sought to gain mass support by emphasizing the desirability of extending social legislation designed for the industrial working force, the "agrarians" favored legislation intended to protect the status of the old middle class (*Mittelstand*). The agrarians looked upon the artisan, the peasant proprietor, and the small merchant as suitable allies.

At the beginning of the twentieth century, a compromise was finally hammered out by the bourgeoisie and the large agrarians. In exchange for the maintenance of agricultural tariffs, the bourgeoisie secured a commitment to an accelerated program of naval building and to an intensified policy of overseas imperialism.[54] Although the worst fissures

[53] For a summary of the *Agrar- oder Industriestaat* debate and a skillful attempt to place it in historical context see Herman Lebovics, " 'Agrarians' versus 'Industrializers,' " *International Review of Social History*, XII (1967), Part 1, esp. 43–56. See also Kenneth D. Barkin, *The Controversy over German Industrialization, 1890–1902* (Chicago, 1970).

[54] See Kehr, *Schlachtflottenbau und Parteipolitik*, pp. 203–05, 247–77, and passim; Gerschenkron, *Bread and Democracy*, pp. 58–59, 62. That a real compromise was effected is often disputed. Puhle, *Agrarische Interessenpolitik*, p. 158, n. 94 suggests that the crisis in relations between agrarians and industrialists was not resolved by the tariff bill of 1902. To support his position he points to the Conservative vote in the Reichstag against the new tariff. He neglects to examine the tactical reasons for this negative vote, which, it should be emphasized, did not prevent passage of the bill. The inability of the Conservatives to alter the outcome of the voting seems to have been predictable. Puhle confuses the inevitable presence of tensions within the social coalition with the continuation of a serious rupture. Lebovics' assessment of the outcome and consequences of the crisis is more defensible, although unacceptable. Neglecting the building of the high seas' fleet and omitting any direct reference to the pursuit of *Weltpolitik*, he asserts that the agrarians "won the great intellectual and policy debate . . . , for the agrarian myth was not swept from the field and Germany was committed to the pursuit of an agrarian policy in its industrial age" (Lebovics, " 'Agrarians' versus 'Industrializers,' " p. 63). Lebovics in the same article justly criticizes Gerschenkron for overemphasizing the role of the Junkers in the nineteenth and twentieth centuries (p. 32, n. 1), but his own conclusions reflect a similar error. The fleet appears prominently in Röhl's analysis of the politics of the 1890's, but its significance is distorted. He attributes Admiral Tirpitz' naval propaganda as well as German foreign policy during the last years of the nineteenth century to efforts on the part of high officials to rally mass support for the sagging prestige of the monarchy. See J.C.G. Röhl, *Germany without Bismarck: The Crisis of Government in the Second Reich, 1890–1900* (Berkeley, 1967), pp. 10, 241, 251–58. Röhl does not attempt to come to grips with Kehr's thesis that the initiative for the fleet came primarily from outside government circles, from the bourgeoisie, and that mass support for the navy had to be built up (Kehr, pp.

in the social coalition were patched over, others remained. Some commercial and light industrial interests railed at the terms of the compromise, as did some of the agrarians and their allies. More importantly, the debate of the 1890's had raised political questions that a number of bourgeois politicians and writers continued to dwell upon.

Among these men was a new type of German elite theorist, whose basic political perspectives were delineated in the course of his participation in this debate on the side of the industrializers. Three major aspects of the new liberal elitist's position set him apart from other liberals. First, he insisted, often aggressively, upon the formation of a political elite that would actively recruit members from all strata of society. Second, he gave serious consideration to the advantages of increasing popular control over policy making. Although ultimately he emphasized the disadvantages of effective popular control, the close attention that he gave to this question and that of an open elite frequently made him appear as a "democrat" in the eyes of other liberals, as well as those of conservatives. Third, unlike a few left liberals who expressed, however ambiguously, a commitment to democratic slogans calling for popular control, the new liberal elitist rejected these slogans as empty rhetoric.

Among the foremost initiators of the new liberal elitism were Friedrich Naumann and Max Weber. During the last decade of the nineteenth century, they developed an extensive critique of the existing political elites, of the Empire's foreign and domestic policies, and of the social, political, and economic role of the large agrarians. Naumann, Weber, and other new liberal elitists became impatient with the Junkers' exploitation of their position in state and society to block timely alterations in policy and institutions. Observing major changes in German society, the new liberal elitists demanded a drastic reduction in the power of the Junkers and called for both new leadership and new policies. A new elite was not only desirable but also necessary if one accepted their conception of the magnitude and significance of the changes underway in German society.

The new liberal elitists were sensitive observers of these changes, examining the dramatic increase in tensions within the Junker-bourgeois social coalition as well as the rapid progress of the working-class movement. Social Democracy continued to grow vigorously whether repression was relaxed or intensified, and even when repressive measures against the Social Democratic party were combined with conciliatory gestures toward the industrial working force as a whole. Although

---

168–69, 208–247). Since Röhl's argument constitutes an implicit rejection of Kehr's position, Röhl has an obligation to destroy the credibility of his evidence or the logic of his presentation. Yet Röhl does neither.

finding cause for grave concern in the expansion of Social Democracy, the new liberal elitists were encouraged in their hopes for social and political realignments by the emergence of what soon would be called the Revisionist controversy.

Not all of the new liberal elitists were associated closely with a single political party; many of them switched their party affiliations frequently during the coming decades. By the end of World War I, the number of prominent politicians and intellectuals embracing the new liberal elitism had increased dramatically. By then the views of the surviving initiators of this elitism had undergone many an alteration, but there was an underlying continuity in their views during the quarter century from the early 1890's through the opening years of the Weimar Republic. This continuity is particularly apparent in the ideas of Naumann and Max Weber, who were eventually joined by Theodor Barth and Hugo Preuss, and, still later, by somewhat more conservative men like Ernst Troeltsch and Friedrich Meinecke.

As young men, Naumann (born in 1860) and Weber (born in 1864) were less bound than many of their elders to the clichés of the political traditions in which they had been raised. Naumann came from a conservative family of Protestant pastors; Weber from a family of liberal political notables, politically engaged professors, and small manufacturers. The dissension mounting within the Junker-bourgeois social coalition led Naumann and Weber to work out a position on the conflict. Their concern about the continued rise of the Social Democratic party (SPD) and their interest in methods of harnessing it for nonrevolutionary purposes ensured that their position afforded a comprehensive view of German society and politics. While the new liberal elitists looked with enthusiasm upon the commencement of a true *Weltpolitik*, they considered the price paid for it, especially the renewed submission to the tariff requisites of the Junkers, as exorbitant and unnecessary. Sniping at the agrarians, the new liberal elitists gained some sympathy from other "industrializers," whose attitude toward the compromise was more equivocal.

Naumann and Weber objected not only to the price but also to the extent of the commitment to *Weltpolitik* as inadequate. Despite the accommodation of the agrarians to imperialism and the tangible rewards they derived from it, the new liberal elitists considered the Junkers unreliable and their influence on policy deplorable. The entrenched political and social position of the agrarians seemed to block the pursuit of a consistent *Weltpolitik*.

Thus the new liberal elitists retained a great interest in the Social Democrats, who were clearly within the camp of the industrializers, although not that of the imperialists. The first government bill that the

Social Democrats in the Reichstag voted for was one of Caprivi's bilateral trade treaties in 1891. Two years later Social Democratic support was crucial to the passage of another bilateral trade treaty.[55] More discriminating in assessing the revolutionary potential of the SPD than most bourgeois politicians and political writers, the new liberal elitists foresaw the possibility of an anti-Junker political coalition that would unite much of the bourgeoisie with reformist Social Democrats. In high governmental circles some perceptive political analysts arrived at a similarly cool, reasoned, and optimistic evaluation of the future of Social Democracy. For example, in the midst of heated discussion over the need for a new anti-Socialist law in 1894, the former head of Reich Press Affairs published in the official press a reassuring article on the SPD. Arguing that numerical increases in Socialist strength were misleading since the program and tactics of the party were becoming less revolutionary, he called for universal and equal suffrage to replace the three-class system of voting for the Prussian House of Representatives.[56] Similarly, from 1895 to 1896 the Prussian Minister of Trade, Count Berlepsch, believed that the government could widen the breach between reformists and radicals within the SPD by continuing social welfare programs and favoring trade unions.[57] The new liberal elitists hoped that a segment of the working class might be induced to abandon the Social Democratic policy of opposition to imperialism and, under the leadership of reformist leaders, actively support imperialism. Despite the dimming during the early years of the twentieth century of the immediate prospects for the development of an anti-Junker political alliance, Naumann and Weber clung to the hope that eventually the SPD could be transformed into a frankly reformist party and that in the meantime the existence of the party would strengthen the hand of bourgeois critics of the Junker-bourgeois social coalition.

The new liberal elitists sought to resolve the conflict within the social coalition not simply in favor of the bourgeoisie, but especially to the benefit of its less "feudalized" elements. Such a resolution of the conflict presupposed the destruction of the social status and political power of the large agrarians, and, crucially, the status and power of the Junkers in Prussia. The heavy industrial allies of the Junkers would

[55] See Nichols, *Germany after Bismarck*, p. 295. As Kehr, *Schlachtflottenbau und Parteipolitik*, p. 127 and others have pointed out there were two tendencies within the SPD on the question of imperialism. One tendency wanted to struggle against every aspect of imperialism. The other regarded imperialism as a preliminary stage enroute to socialism. The development of the latter tendency greatly encouraged the new liberal elitists.

[56] Nichols, *Germany after Bismarck*, p. 336.

[57] Röhl, *Germany without Bismarck*, pp. 150–51.

then be compelled to cooperate more closely with other sectors of the bourgeoisie. In terms of party politics, the Conservative parties and the Catholic Center would be destroyed, transformed, or drastically weakened. Because of the prominence within the Center party of large agrarian interests and of peasants following their lead, the Catholic Center was almost as much of an enemy as the Conservatives. The frequent collaboration of the Center with the Conservatives brought down upon it the wrath of the new liberal elitists. This animosity was reinforced by the hostility of the secularly oriented new liberal elitists toward the clericalism of the Catholic Centrists.

The new liberal elitists coupled a positive goal to the largely negative objective of weakening, destroying, or transforming the Conservatives and the Center. They wanted to install political leaders appropriate to a bourgeois industrial society. Although during the last decade before World War I Naumann moderated his opposition to the Conservatives and the Center, older liberals like Theodor Barth and younger liberals like Rudolf Breitscheid, both of whom had worked closely with Naumann, pursued both objectives with increasing militancy,[58] and the ranks of steadfast liberal opponents of the Junkers swelled temporarily following the elections of 1912. Toward the end of World War I, Naumann regained the leading role among the new liberal elitists that he had forfeited a decade earlier.

The new liberal elitists criticized the political leadership of the Empire as consisting of egocentric agrarians determined to artificially maintain their position in German society, spineless bureaucrats who served the narrow interests of the administrative hierarchy, and "feudalized" bourgeois who kowtowed to the Junkers and yielded to the clumsy authoritarianism of heavy industry. The new liberal elitists found that the maintenance of the Junkers' position in German society resulted in poor leadership and vacillating policies for the Empire. However, the new liberal elitists failed to make clear that the inconsistent, zigzag policies followed by the Reich were often due primarily to conflicts within the bourgeoisie itself. Thus, under William II, abrupt shifts in policy toward Britain occurred as a consequence of the disequilibrium produced by struggles between pro- and anti-British interests among German businessmen. For example, in the crises leading up to the Boer War, one of the great German banks, the *Deutsche*

---

[58] See Ludwig Elm, *Zwischen Fortschritt und Reaktion: Geschichte der Parteien der liberalen Bourgeoisie in Deutschland 1893–1918* (Berlin, 1968), pp. 103–09, 229–35; Konstanze Wegner, *Theodor Barth und die Freisinnige Vereinigung: Studien zur Geschichte des Linksliberalismus im Wilhelminischen Deutschland 1893–1910* (Tübingen, 1968).

Bank, and its allies tended to seek an accommodation with Britain, while another of the great banks, the *Disconto Gesellschaft,* favored a more hostile policy. Rooted in different relationships with British business interests and divergent assessments of the gains obtainable from alternative policies, the battle between these two German banking groups played a major role in Anglo-German relations at the turn of the century.[59]

The tendency of the new liberal elitists to minimize or ignore the part played in German foreign policy by struggles within the bourgeoisie is easier to understand during the 1890's at the height of the struggles threatening to disrupt the Junker-bourgeois social coalition than a few years later. With the recementing of the social coalition at the turn of the century, there was less reason to continue to blame the twistings and turnings of German policy on the large agrarians. Yet this is what the new liberal elitists persisted in doing, even as they found another convenient scapegoat in the person of William II. Rather than probing fully the conflicts within the big bourgeoisie itself, they were inclined to discover other culprits to whom to attribute German failings as measured by the standard of a consistent policy of overseas imperialism.

The new liberal elitists regarded Britain as a model for Germany. They were fond of comparing developments in the two countries, suggesting that Germany was going through a period analogous to that which led to the repeal of the British Corn Laws in 1846. At the turn of the century, Naumann confidently predicted that as the English had taken the final step to an "industrial state" in 1846, the Germans would at last follow during the coming quarter of a century.[60] Both he and Max Weber were taken with the possibility that, as in England after the repeal of the Corn Laws, the development of a "labor aristocracy" would provide indispensable mass support for imperialism. Implicitly, they regarded chartism as analogous to German Social Democracy. If the power of the large agrarians could be broken in Germany, as it had been in England during the period from the passage of the Reform Bill of 1832 to the virtual elimination of agricultural protectionism in 1846,

---

[59] See A. S. Jerussalimski, "Der deutsche Imperialismus und der Ausbruch des Burenkrieges" in his *Der deutsche Imperialismus: Geschichte und Gegenwart,* trans. Joachim Böhm et al. (Berlin, 1968). Numerous examples of the importance of conflicts among contending groups within the bourgeoisie may be found in G.W.F. Hallgarten, *Imperialismus vor 1914: Die soziologischen Grundlagen der Aussenpolitik europäischer Grossmächte vor dem ersten Weltkrieg,* 2nd ed. (2 vols., Munich, 1963).

[60] Naumann, "Nationaler und internationaler Sozialismus" (1901) in his *Werke,* ed. Walter Uhsadel, Theodor Schieder, and Heinz Ladendorf (6 vols., Cologne, 1964–1969), v, 279–80.

the working class might become less susceptible to revolutionary rhetoric and split into two groups: well-organized labor aristocrats supporting imperialism; and poorly organized radicals ineffectively attacking imperialism.

The destruction of the position of the Junkers necessitated in the eyes of the new liberal elitists either cooperation with a Social Democracy in which the most moderate of the reformist had gained the ascendancy, or the absorption of the reformists by another party. The anti-Junker, proimperialist bourgeoisie would then be able to rely on the Left for mass support. This support would be essential to pushing forward the more cowardly bourgeois who hesitated to disrupt the social coalition with the Junkers. Working-class followers would be all the more important since the liberal parties had found their adherents attracted increasingly to the Right or the Left. On the Right, the Conservatives and their allies were enlisting stronger and stronger backing from small businessmen, independent craftsmen, and white-collar workers. On the Left, the Social Democrats were making substantial inroads into some of the same groups. A bourgeois-proletarian alliance would have the further advantage of destroying at last the revolutionary stance of many Social Democrats—a stance that Naumann and Weber regarded as at best romantic and at worst an obstacle to broadly based working-class support for the nation-state and imperialism. Naumann repeatedly belittled any expectation of a German revolution as an illusion; a revolution, he announced confidently, could not take place in a society that had firmly begun to tread the path toward the "industrial state." Weber dealt with the same issue in a characteristically different way. To him, bureaucratic structures had become such an integral, permanent, and indestructible part of economic and political life that they could not be swept aside; he too concluded that revolution was out of the question. Naumann, in his more optimistic moments, may even have believed that the mere threat of the formation of a bourgeois-proletarian political coalition would bring the large agrarians to their knees, compelling them to give up voluntarily most of their prerogatives.

The new liberal elitists realized that the disruption of the old social coalition and the social and political realignments that they sought would entail a broader recruitment of political leaders. They welcomed broader recruitment as both desirable and necessary. Although Weber analyzed more clearly the consequences and implications of this broader recruitment, he was, as we shall see in Chapter Four, much more ambivalent toward it. In the midst of the postwar German revolution, he was even to favor a type of leader, for the highest offices, who had of necessity to be affluent. During the same time, Naumann was pushing forward plans for an educational institution that would promote the development of the new elite type on which he and Weber had earlier agreed. Despite differences in their approaches, the two men assumed from the 1890's onward that cooperation between the bourgeoisie and the proletariat necessitated the rise of individual workers and working-class leaders to positions of national leadership. In contrast to many conservatives and liberals, who did not begin to discover a need for including working-class leaders in any national elite until World War I, until 1917, or even until 1918–1919, and who then frantically appealed for new leaders from the entire people, Weber and Naumann approached the subject calmly. They assumed that the bourgeoisie could win valuable allies among its proclaimed enemies, the Social Democrats.

Meeting at the First Evangelical Social Congress in 1890, Naumann and Weber cooperated closely for several years during the middle and later years of the decade. During the 1890's they exerted a strong influence on each other's political development, and even thereafter, although their relationship became less intimate, they continued to influence each other. The writings and speeches of the one often complemented those of the other; the two men provided what can be seen as commentaries on each other's political ideas.

Weber's biographers have generally depicted the relationship as if he exerted a decisive influence upon Naumann's political development and as if Naumann had no influence upon Weber's political development. These biographers credit Weber with having opened Naumann's eyes to the importance of the national state. Thus Marianne Weber, Max Weber's wife and foremost biographer, asserts that, when the two first met, Weber approached problems from the point of view of the nation-state, whereas Naumann approached them from the point of view of the social question.[61] But this contrast is incorrect for several reasons. Naumann's early writings, in the period before he met Weber, and before Weber had published little other than scholarly works on the ancient and medieval world, express not only pronounced social concerns but also an equally tenacious solicitude for the strength of the national state. Weber's influence on Naumann was of a different sort. Weber was one of several academicians and other acquaintances with

[61] Marianne Weber, *Max Weber: Ein Lebensbild* (Tübingen, 1926), pp. 143, 231–32. Despite many criticisms of her work, Wolfgang J. Mommsen, *Max Weber und die deutsche Politik 1890–1920* (Tübingen, 1959), pp. 78–80, 102, 139–41 accepts her basic assessment of the relationship between Weber and Naumann. Although Martin Wenck, *Geschichte der Nationalsozialen von 1895 bis 1903* (Berlin, 1905), p. 33 made similar assertions, later studies of Naumann have been more cautious. See, e.g., Wilhelm Happ, *Das Staatsdenken Friedrich Naumanns*, Schriften zur Rechtslehre und Politik, LVII (Bonn, 1968), 61.

whom Naumann associated in the 1890's who convinced him that the fundamental issue was whether to align oneself with the Junkers or with the bourgeoisie and that expectations about the imminent development of a non-Marxian socialism were both impossible and undesirable. Symptomatically, Naumann seems for several years to have clung to the faint hope that the National Social Association, which he founded in 1896, would be able to win over large numbers of Social Democrats and thereby transform or destroy the SPD. There is no evidence that Weber, who despite his frequent criticisms of the National Socials supported them from their founding until the turn of the century, ever expected them to succeed in these objectives. Thus, in 1903, when Naumann publicly admitted that the National Socials had failed, he moved closer to Weber's position.

Despite broad areas of agreement between the two men, they came from different traditions, occasionally became involved with contending if partly overlapping factions, and generally approached secondary issues differently. Not only a less imaginative and innovative political thinker, Naumann was also less inclined to attempt to forge a synthesis acceptable to the bourgeoisie as a whole. His ideas became more closely identified than Weber's with specific segments of the bourgeoisie, especially with some banking and industrial circles. With some exceptions during the 1890's, Weber confronted problems as a theoretician and long-range strategist less concerned with immediate issues and tactical needs. Naumann was the political practitioner more involved with the immediate implementation of concepts and the day-to-day consequences of political positions. His style was much more popular than Weber's. Naumann had a broader public for his writings and speeches, both of which were beautifully crafted for his audience. Despite the frequent use of an earthy word or a slashing phrase, Weber never broke decisively with the cumbersome expressions and intricate syntax that he employed in his scholarly writings. Appropriately, it was Naumann the politician rather than Weber the social scientist who had the broader and larger audience. Only during a short period in 1917–1918, when Weber wrote frequently for one of Germany's great liberal dailies, the *Frankfurter Zeitung*, and attracted much attention among many who had probably never before heard his name, did he perhaps become as well known as Naumann.

Naumann clung tenaciously to a belief that Weber regarded as an illusion—the belief that the highly and largely university-educated (*Gebildeten*) could play a crucial role as political leaders. This difference in judgment was of less significance after Naumann concluded in 1903 that the National Socials should merge with one of the left-liberal parties. In 1918-1919 a similar difference would emerge again, although in an altered context.

An important divergence of views came during World War I. Naumann became caught up in the celebration of Germandom that many German intellectuals and propagandists proclaimed during the war. Temporarily, he emphasized the insurmountable differences in development that had led and continued to lead Germany to take a different path of political development from England. Although Weber's enthusiasm for the war was perhaps even more intense than Naumann's, and although Weber supported imperialistic war aims, he did not participate in the celebration of German uniqueness undertaken by Naumann and others espousing the "Ideas of 1914." In this respect Hugo Preuss stood much closer to Weber than Naumann did. Only after the Bolshevik Revolution and especially in late 1918 were Preuss and Weber rejoined by Naumann. At the same time, Meinecke and Troeltsch, who, like Naumann, had embraced the "Ideas of 1914," joined the camp of the new liberal elitists.

Weber manifested more confidence in the validity of the new liberal elitists' analysis of Wilhelminian Germany when, during the immediate postwar period, he appeared less worried than Naumann and Preuss by the threat of social revolution. Naumann seems to have panicked momentarily. After regaining his equilibrium, he adopted a stance once again similar to Weber's. In the short time remaining before Naumann's death in late 1919, he and Weber agreed not only on basic issues but also on almost every specific detail.

In examining the new elitism of Naumann and Weber, we shall turn first to Naumann since both the wording and substance of his writings long remained more oriented toward the past.

CHAPTER THREE

Friedrich Naumann: From Social Monarchy to Liberal Democracy

N AUMANN developed a fully articulated elite theory slowly during the decade and a half from the late 1880's to the early 1900's. During the earliest part of this period, his elitism was more implicit than explicit. He saw no need for a new elite. He saw only a need for new attitudes on the part of both rulers and ruled. He attempted to act as a mediator between the lower and upper classes. Concerned with what the nineteenth century euphemistically called "the social question," he struggled to get the Protestant churches to take a more active hand in promoting the enactment of legislation to ameliorate the condition of the working class. He conceived of his role as ascertaining the legitimate grievances of the working class and helping the high and well-born rediscover their social consciences. This rediscovery of conscience would lead, he believed, to a reassertion of the tradition of *noblesse oblige* with the state now footing the bill.

THE SOCIAL AND POLITICAL SOURCES OF NAUMANN'S ELITISM

While studying for the ministry, Naumann worked in the *Rauhe Haus*, a small orphanage and school near Hamburg. In 1885 he began his pastorate in a Saxon village whose economy depended heavily upon cottage textile industry. Gaining a reputation as "the poor people's parson,"[1] he began to write on the social question. He became closely associated with, although not formally a member of, Court Chaplain Adolf Stöcker's Christian Social party. Stöcker founded the party in 1878 to wean the working class from Social Democracy, but his entreaties had little effect, and he soon dropped the word workers, which was included in the party's original name. The party acted as an ally of the Conservatives and had moderate success among the middle class. The Christian Socials retained a strong interest in the working class even after Stöcker became resigned to his inability to compete

[1] Adolf Damaschke, *Aus meinem Leben* (2 vols., Leipzig and Zurich, 1924–1925), II, 68.

effectively with the Social Democrats for the souls and votes of workers. Naumann framed appeals to the working class similar to those issued largely in vain by Stöcker.[2]

Naumann became known as one of the dynamic younger Christian Socials who, unlike Stöcker, harbored much sympathy for the Social Democrats. In an early pamphlet Naumann praised the Social Democrats for compelling the state to come seriously to grips with the social question, but he hastened to tell the worker that he had "no better and more willing friend than his pastor."[3] Want, Naumann argued, would always exist, but a more equitable division of earthly pleasures and pains could be created. He complained that the struggle between the bourgeoisie and the working class was upsetting the entire nation; both classes should obtain their goals through mutual love.[4] Advocating the expansion of the Bismarckian social legislation, he sought to continue the development of what he depicted as a new form of property that would eventually become more important than private property—"social property" in the form of inalienable personal rights to sickness insurance, old age insurance, and factory legislation. The gradual extension of these and similar measures he conceived of as constituting socialism.[5]

As his early faith in the concept of a social monarchy became more reasoned, and as he and many Christian Socials came into conflict with Stöcker's policies, they founded their own party, the National Social Association, in late 1896. The National Socials were to push for social legislation while acting as rivals to the Social Democrats. If successful, the National Socials would have provided a large part of the working class with an organization headed by bourgeois intellectuals like Naumann. He would have given the existing political elite a transfusion of socially minded intellectuals.

The deepening of the concerns that led to the founding of the National Social Association further altered his ideas. The liberal elitism of the mature Naumann was forged both as an offensive weapon against the large agrarians—to promote the development of the bourgeoisie and an imperialistic nation-state—and as a defensive weapon against radicalism on the Left. Originally a reaction to political extremes, Naumann's elitism became, during the period 1917–1919, a

[2] See Walter Frank, *Hofprediger Adolf Stöcker und die christlichsoziale Bewegung* (Berlin, 1928), p. 39 and passim.

[3] *Arbeiterkatechismus, oder der wahre Sozialismus: Seinen arbeitenden Brüdern dargebracht* (Calw, 1889), pp. 2, 62.

[4] *Ibid.*, pp. 7, 49. See also "Die Zukunft der Inneren Mission" (1888) in his *Werke*, ed. Walter Uhsadel, Theodor Schieder, and Heinz Ladendorf (6 vols., Cologne, 1964–1969), I.

[5] See *Arbeiterkatechismus*, pp. 7, 26–35; "Zukunft der Inneren Mission," p. 100.

conservative weapon that he used largely against radicals. Since the basic pattern of his thought was cut in response to the political and social struggles of the 1890's, an examination of his elitism must focus upon his political views as they emerged during the first half of William II's reign.

Only gradually did Naumann come to accept the conclusion that Max Weber had reached by the mid-1890's—that the basic struggle in the German Empire was between the bourgeoisie and the large agrarians and that one must take sides in this struggle. For a number of years Naumann believed that the promotion of solutions to the social problem did not require a clearcut choice. He still seems to have anticipated the conversion of the emperor and the entire ruling class to the Christian Social position and the entry of men like himself into positions of power.[6] He shied away from a commitment to increasing popular control. Naumann expressed this aversion to popular control in an implicit rejection of parliamentary government under German circumstances during the mid-1890's: "I still prefer to see one half of the nation's power remain in the hands of a government whose present representatives are unfortunately attacking the working class [Arbeiterstand] than . . . to entrust all of this power to changing, coming and going, rising and falling [parliamentary] deputies."[7]

Despite Naumann's persisting faith in the monarchy, his writings and other activities brought him increasingly into conflict with the Conservatives and their allies. In 1889 the Protestant Consistory censured him for his Arbeiterkatechismus. During the same year his support for a major miners' strike put him at odds with the more conservative Christian Socials, who were oriented toward agrarian and Mittelstand interests. By the early 1890's a full-scale struggle between his and Stöcker's wing of the party was developing. The limitations imposed by Stöcker's alliance with the Conservatives were becoming intolerable to Naumann and his compatriots. Rejecting Stöcker's conception of the Christian Socials as drummers for the Conservative party, they wanted to pursue an independent policy.

Stöcker found himself in a difficult position. In order to patch up his often uneasy relationship with the Conservatives, he had to distance himself from the more independent of the Christian Socials.[8] In 1890 he had been forced to resign his position as court chaplain and to promise to withdraw from the political arena. He may have regarded the Evangelical Social Congress, which he helped to found during the

---

[6] See, e.g., "Soziale Briefe an reiche Leute" (1894) in Werke, v, 169–70.

[7] "Zum sozialdemokratischen Landprogramm" (1895) in Werke, v, 148.

[8] See Paul W. Massing, Rehearsal for Destruction: A Study of Political Anti-Semitism in Imperial Germany (New York, 1949), pp. 120–22.

same year, as an appropriate way of deflecting the attacks of his enemies. Soon Naumann and other younger Christian Socials were using
both Christian Social publications and the annual meetings of the
Evangelical Social Congress to attack the agrarian interests that
Stöcker was seeking to placate.

Underlying the growing split between the Stöcker and Naumann
factions during the early 1890's were the renewal of aggravated tensions within the Junker-bourgeois social coalition and the continued
rise of the Social Democratic party after the expiration of the anti-
Socialist laws in 1890. For the Christian Socials these developments
posed two urgent problems—the question of their party's relationship
to the agrarian problem and the question of their policy toward the
Social Democrats. Stöcker's position did not entail changes in the existing political order. He was satisfied if much of the political elite continued to be drawn from the ranks of the Junkers. Although not enunciated clearly, the position of the Naumann faction required political
changes, and it conflicted with Stöcker's promotion, within the Conservative party and in legislative bodies, of the interests of the old
middle class.

The agrarian question, which had been simmering for several years,
confronted the Christian Socials directly at the Evangelical Social Congress in 1894. Max Weber and Paul Göhre, a young Christian Social
pastor whose name had been made by a book on his experiences for a
few months as a factory worker,[9] presented a report on the condition
of agricultural laborers in the eastern provinces of Prussia. Weber
and Göhre sided with the agricultural laborers against the large
agrarians.[10] Naumann aligned himself with Weber and Göhre. At first
implicitly and before long explicitly, Naumann and his friends were
calling for a substantial displacement of power within the social coalition to the disadvantage of the Junkers and the large agrarian
interests.

The attack on the Junkers came as Stöcker was aligning himself with
the hard-pressed, less affluent Junkers and attempting to gain support
from their wing of the Conservative party. These Junkers tolerated or
even advocated social reform as long as it affected industry rather than
their own agrarian interests. The wealthier large agrarians, who were
in the process of gaining control of the recently founded League of
Agriculturalists (*Bund der Landwirte*), an organization that would

[9] Paul Göhre, *Drei Monate Fabrikarbeiter* (Leipzig, 1891).
[10] See Paul Göhre and Max Weber, "Referat über die deutschen Landarbeiter"
in *Bericht über die Verhandlungen des 5. evangelisch-sozialen Kongresses abgehal-
ten zu Frankfurt am Main am 16. und 17. Mai 1894* (Berlin, 1894), esp. p. 60
of Göhre's presentation and pp. 78–79 of Weber's presentation.

eventually supplant the Christian Socials as an ally of the Conservative party with a mass membership, resented the Christian Socials' meddling in the social question. This segment of the Conservative party was closely linked politically to large industrial interests. It sought to jeopardize Stöcker's already shaky relationship to the Conservatives by attacking the sympathy of the Naumann faction for workers and Social Democrats.[11] Naumann had become a severe liability to Stöcker's efforts to regain power in the Conservative party. Support for the agricultural worker in the East offended Conservatives, especially the poorer Junkers. Vigorous support for reform in industry offended the heavy industrial wing of the Conservative party and furnished it with ammunition with which to wage its intraparty struggle against the smaller Junkers.

The ramifications of the agrarian question touched upon the issue of policy toward the SPD. After the expiration of the anti-Socialist laws, the Social Democrats considered adopting an agricultural program designed to win peasant support. The Socialists' previous failure to attract peasant support in most areas of the Empire gave some leverage to South German Social Democrats like Georg von Vollmar who were attempting, with a good measure of success, to win peasant votes. Many Social Democrats wanted to remedy what they regarded as a major gap in their program. For several months in 1894 and 1895, there seemed to be a good chance that the party would adopt an agrarian program attractive to many peasants.[12]

During the late 1880's and the early 1890's, elections in the countryside brought the peasant question to the fore. Radical, racist anti-Semites achieved much success in several agrarian electoral districts, partly by attacking the Conservatives and offering a program that included an assault upon the party couched in anti-Semitic terms. Some of these anti-Semites arraigned Stöcker both for the moderation of his

[11] See Massing, *Rehearsal for Destruction*, p. 68; Hartmut Kaelble, *Industrielle Interessenpolitik in der Wilhelminischen Gesellschaft: Centralverband Deutscher Industrieller 1895–1914* (Berlin, 1967), p. 202; Hans-Jürgen Puhle, *Agrarische Interessenpolitik und preussischer Konservatismus im Wilhelminischen Reich (1893–1914): Ein Beitrag zur Analyse des Nationalismus in Deutschland am Beispiel des Bundes der Landwirte und der Deutsch-Konservativen Partei* (Hannover, 1967), pp. 120–21, 136; Martin Wenck, *Geschichte der Nationalsozialen von 1895 bis 1903* (Berlin, 1905), p. 9; Peter Molt, *Der Reichstag vor der improvisierten Revolution* (Cologne, 1963), p. 112.

[12] See H. G. Lehmann, *Die Agrarfrage in der Theorie und Praxis der deutschen und internationalen Sozialdemokratie: Vom Marxismus zum Revisionismus und Bolschewismus* (Tübingen, 1970), pp. 142–202. Naumann's "Zum sozialdemokratischen Landprogramm" (1895) in *Werke*, v, 102–50, assumes that the SPD would adopt the draft program presented to the party congress in 1895.

anti-Semitism and for his relationship to the Conservatives.[13] The success of the radical anti-Semites demonstrated the potential of an aggressive program of reform appealing to the peasantry.

Stöcker did not seek to compete with either the radical anti-Semites or the anticipated agricultural program of the Social Democrats. Naumann wished to compete with both. He rejected the assertions of the League of Agriculturalists that peasant interests were identical with those of the large agrarians. He sought to commit the Christian Socials to a strongly reformist agrarian program. His advocacy of peasants and workers had led him to alienate both the agrarian and the industrial wings of the Conservative party. Although he had thereby contributed to the polarization of Christian Social forces, he still clung to the hope that Stöcker's party could be steered into a new course.

Soon the attack mounted by Conservatives against the Christian Socials gave Stöcker little choice except to risk an exodus of the Naumann faction from his party. After the conflict over the agrarian question at the Evangelical Social Congress in 1894, Naumann and his friends founded a periodical, *Die Hilfe*, to provide them with their own mouthpiece. In 1895 the Christian Social party congress became the occasion for a bitter battle over the party's program. The same year one of Germany's foremost heavy industrialists, "King" Stumm of the Saar, launched a vigorous public campaign against Naumann, the Christian Socials, and the *Kathedersozialisten*. Both the major organization of German heavy industry, the *Centralverband der Industriellen*, and the Protestant Consistory joined the campaign.[14] Naumann's resignation from the ministry made him more vulnerable to the charge that he was a Red. The break with Stöcker came at a time when the elder man's relationship to the Conservatives had reached its nadir. In January 1896 Stöcker was expelled from the Executive Committee of the Conservative party. In an apparent attempt to regain support within the Conservative party, Stöcker purged the "Naumannites" from the Christian Social organ *Das Volk*, and he had Naumann barred from the Christian Social convention. Late in 1896 Naumann and his compatriots founded the National Social Association.

[13] Massing, *Rehearsal for Destruction*, pp. 89–91, 118; Peter G. J. Pulzer, *The Rise of Political Anti-Semitism in Germany and Austria* (New York: Wiley paperback, 1964), pp. 109–14; Molt, *Der Reichstag vor der improvisierten Revolution*, pp. 125–26; Puhle, *Agrarische Interessenpolitik und preussischer Konservatismus*, pp. 136–37.
[14] Massing, *Rehearsal for Destruction*, p. 124; Theodor Heuss, *Friedrich Naumann: Der Mann, das Werk*, 2nd ed. (Stuttgart, 1949), p. 93. The biography by Heuss, who served as Naumann's secretary before World War I, is indispensable, but tantalizingly laconic on many important points. I have not yet seen Dieter Düding, *Der Nationalsoziale Verein 1896–1903* (Munich, 1972).

Issues involving anti-Semitism had helped increasingly to divide the Christian Socials among themselves. Unlike Stöcker, Naumann was not committed to anti-Semitism, which he would eventually reject decisively,[15] and Naumann rejected any orientation that would gain followers from the old middle class of artisans and small businessmen at the risk of sacrificing potential working-class support. More interested in winning over industrial and white-collar workers than in catering to the grievances of the old middle class against large-scale capitalism, he rejected the formulas that had helped Stöcker to obtain a modicum of success and to achieve for several years a position of prominence within the Conservative party.[16] In 1894 Naumann strongly criticized a political orientation that would appeal to the artisan segment of the old middle class:

> The artisan is not as ripe for Christian Socialism as many of our friends believe. He is less concerned with social reforms that would benefit even the poorest [citizens] than with the preservation of his little bit of independence. . . . Only if the artisan perceives the necessity for social change, i.e., when he descends to the level of cottage industry (tailor, shoemaker), will he become susceptible to the Christian-Social conception of things, provided that he wants to remain a Christian.[17]

Naumann's criticism of the artisan anticipated his formulation of a position on capitalism that would postpone the emergence of socialism to the distant future and welcome the general development of large-scale capitalism while maintaining a critical attitude toward the social and political policies of heavy industry. In a series of reflections on the Christian Social program in 1895, Naumann defined his outlook succinctly:

> In the *growing concentration of capital in fewer hands* [italics Naumann's] we find a severe economic abuse. The abuse is not that a few people direct large enterprises, for direction by many people has proven completely impracticable in many areas. The superordination and subordination of men resulting from the division of labor cannot be abolished. The problem is merely to eliminate as far as possible the dangers of the abuse of this superordination and subordination *vis-à-vis* the nondirectors. *Insofar as big industry is promoted*

[15] See, e.g., Naumann, *Demokratie und Kaisertum: Ein Handbuch für innere Politik*, 4th ed. (Berlin-Schöneberg, 1905), p. 106: "Es gibt keine bequemere, aber auch keine unfruchtbarere politische Grundformel als den Antisemitismus." Hereafter this work will be cited as *DuK*.

[16] See Molt, *Der Reichstag vor der improvisierten Revolution*, pp. 214–15.

[17] "Was heisst Christlich-Sozial?" (1894) in *Werke*, I, 365.

by the progress of technology we recognize it as a necessity [My
italics].[18]

Naumann's increasingly positive attitude toward a vigorous policy
of overseas imperialism played no direct role in the break with
Stöcker. The wing of the Conservative party to which Stöcker belonged adopted an antifleet position that reflected a general hostility
to German imperialism. Only later did this wing of the party adopt a
positive position toward imperialism.[19]

Divergences in theology and church policy accentuated the split between Naumann and Stöcker. The consistory's condemnation of Naumann in 1895 included a denunciation of the liberal theology with
which he was identified. Stöcker was more acceptable to the theological orthodoxy of the day. Partly under the influence of the theologian
Rudolf Sohm, Naumann would soon take the position that Christianity
had no clear social message for the modern world.[20]

Significant for the development of Naumann's positive attitude toward big industry and the *haute bourgeoisie* were his political and intellectual associations from the early 1890's onward. The contacts that
he began to develop were, with a partial exception, to remain typical
of his subsequent career. By the mid-1890's the pastors and socially
minded Protestant women like Max Weber's mother and aunt
Ida Baumgarten, who helped to finance Naumann's first, unsuccessful
campaign for the Reichstag in 1898,[21] had become less important to his
career as he established close contacts with businessmen and academicians. Among the former, men in light industry, in commerce, and
in high finance predominated. Among the academicians, scholars favoring industry over agriculture and hostile toward the Junkers prevailed. The men of intellect as well as those of business shared a desire
to propel Germany on a domestic- and foreign-policy course similar to
that of the United States and the parliamentary states of Western Europe. After the turn of the century, especially after the outbreak of
World War I, Naumann became well acquainted with many high state

[18] "Gedanken zum christlich-sozialen Programm" (1895) in *Werke*, v, 66.
[19] See Eckart Kehr, *Schlachtflottenbau und Parteipolitik 1894–1901: Versuch
eines Querschnitts durch die innenpolitischen, sozialen und ideologischen Voraussetzungen des deutschen Imperialismus* (Berlin, 1930), pp. 20–22.
[20] See William O. Shanahan, "Friedrich Naumann, a Mirror of Wilhelmian Germany," *Review of Politics*, xiii (1951), 278–89; Richard Nürnberger, "Imperialismus, Sozialismus und Christentum bei Friedrich Naumann," *Historische Zeitschrift*, clxx (1950), 530–33; Werner Conze, "Friedrich Naumann: Grundlagen
und Ansatz seiner Politik in der nationalsozialen Zeit (1895 bis 1903)" in Walther
Hubatsch, ed., *Schicksalswege deutscher Vergangenheit: Beiträge zur geschichtlichen Deutung der letzten 150 Jahre* (Düsseldorf, 1950), p. 383.
[21] See Marianne Weber, *Max Weber: Ein Lebensbild* (Tübingen, 1926), p. 235.

officials, but these acquaintanceships were not crucial to his development as an elite theorist.

From 1890 to 1894 Naumann served as a pastor for the *Innere Mission*, a Protestant organization concerned with charitable and welfare
activities, in Frankfurt am Main. In Frankfurt he became acquainted
with a German-American banker, Charles L. Hallgarten, who helped
to pull him away from both the Right and the Left and toward left
liberalism. One of Germany's greatest philanthropists, Hallgarten was
very selective in choosing beneficiaries. Among those who came into
contact with him, there is general agreement that he usually gave
money for specific purposes and that he wished to remain in the
background.[22] He was especially interested in supporting non-Zionist
Jewish charities, self-help organizations for Jewish immigrants from
Eastern Europe, certain types of liberal political organizations, and
independent (anti-Socialist) trade unions. He contributed to the
Freisinnige Vereinigung, the left-liberal party that Naumann and
many of his followers joined after the dissolution of the National Socials in 1903. Hallgarten gave Naumann some financial backing and
probably helped him to shed his mild anti-Semitism.[23] When the two

[22] See Hellmut von Gerlach, *Von Rechts nach Links*, ed. Emil Ludwig (Zurich,
1937), p. 117; Adolf Damaschke, *Aus meinem Leben* (2 vols., Leipzig and Zurich,
1924–25), II, 409–17.

[23] Gertrud Theodor, *Friedrich Naumann oder der Prophet des Profits: Ein biographischer Beitrag zur Geschichte des frühen deutschen Imperialismus* (Berlin,
1957) attributes the decisive change in Naumann's political development to his
relationship with Hallgarten. Due to Naumann's financial dependence upon him,
she regards Naumann as having become, as early as 1894, a representative of the
American-oriented wing of German finance capital. These financiers had close
business associations with the United States and favored cooperation between the
two nations in foreign policy; more important, they favored liberalization rather
than repression as a method of dealing with the Social Democrats (Theodor, pp.
19, 44–48). Although Naumann's association with a wealthy liberal like Hallgarten was important for his future development and symptomatic of the direction
in which he was moving, I have not found any evidence to support Theodor's
assertion (p. 69) that Naumann, like the left liberals Theodor Barth and Heinrich
Rickert, became an agent of the *Deutsche Bank*. Theodor speculates about a
Korruptionsfonds that Hallgarten presumably managed (Theodor, p. 46). Heuss's
Naumann scarcely mentions Hallgarten—perhaps because the first edition appeared during the Nazi period, when Naumann's relationship to a Jewish banker
might have appeared sinister. Detailed evidence on the relationship may exist in
twelve surviving letters written by Naumann to Hallgarten. These letters, which
Hallgarten's grandson, the historian George W. F. Hallgarten, loaned to Heuss in
the 1920's, were long thought to have been lost or destroyed during World War
II (letter of Oct. 25, 1967 to me from George W. F. Hallgarten). However, a recent East German monograph on German left liberalism cites three letters, all from
the early twentieth century, written by Naumann to Charles L. Hallgarten: Ludwig Elm, *Zwischen Fortschritt und Reaktion: Geschichte der Parteien der liberalen
Bourgeoisie in Deutschland 1893–1918* (Berlin, 1968), pp. 107, 117, 196. Thus
it is possible that at least some of the missing twelve letters are now in the Naumann *Nachlass* in the Potsdam archives. Elm's references to the letters tell us

men first met, they had some common concerns. Like Naumann, Hallgarten favored social legislation, supported a powerful German military establishment, and sought to promote non-Socialist trade unions— unions that would be "nonpartisan."[24] Naumann always maintained a strong interest in this type of union, which, in the German political context, had of necessity to propagandize against Social Democracy. Soon he came to share Hallgarten's enthusiasm for the building of a high seas fleet and his involvement in left-liberal politics.

During the early years of Naumann's political career, most of his relationships with industrialists were of less importance. The closer of these relationships seem to have been with light industrialists interested in left-liberal politics and social reform. During his unsuccessful bid for a Reichstag seat from Jena-Neustadt, he may well have first met Ernst Abbé of the Zeiss optical works. Abbé was active in left-liberal circles in Jena. Both Abbé and another of Naumann's early friends, Heinrich Freese, were pioneers in German industrial relations. A manufacturer of window blinds and other wooden products, Freese instituted a works' council, a profit-sharing plan for employees, and the eight-hour day in his factory. Naumann's friendship with Robert Bosch, one of the most important entrepreneurs in the German electrical industry, developed somewhat later and deepened on the eve of World War I.[25]

Among Naumann's most significant academic contacts were those with economists and sociologists. He maintained a long and occasionally troubled relationship with a number of scholars. Although often very critical of Naumann's position on specific issues, men like Werner Sombart, Hans Delbrück, and Gerhart von Schulze-Gävernitz as well as Max Weber assisted him with his writings and other activities dur-

---

little more than could be inferred from other evidence. After leaving Frankfurt, Naumann continued to remain in touch with Hallgarten and they discussed in detail left-liberal tactics. Although Elm cites Gertrud Theodor without offering any criticism of her work, his inquiry into the social, political, and economic roots of left liberalism is much more incisive. Other literature dealing with Hallgarten also provides no information to document many of Theodor's assertions. For example, Alfred Vagts, *Deutsch-Amerikanische Rückwanderung*, Jahrbuch für Amerikastudien, Beiheft 6 (Heidelberg, 1960), p. 81, n. 106 mentions that Anton Erkelenz (a non-Socialist labor leader and a friend of Naumann) supplied information on Hallgarten's financial support for Naumann, but does not elaborate.

[24] See Gerlach, *Von Rechts nach Links*, pp. 116–17; Robert Hallgarten, *Charles L. Hallgarten* (Frankfurt am Main, 1915), pp. 32–33, 36.

[25] Heuss, *Naumann*, p. 195; Heuss, *Robert Bosch: Leben und Leistung* (Stuttgart, 1948), p. 275. Although Heuss stresses the closeness of the friendships with Abbé, Freese, and Bosch, he provides few details. For a discussion of Freese and his "constitutional factory" see Hans Jürgen Teuteberg, *Geschichte der industriellen Mitbestimmung in Deutschland: Ursprung und Entwicklung ihrer Vorläufer im Denken und in der Wirklichkeit des 19. Jahrhunderts* (Tübingen, 1961), pp. 261–64.

ing the earlier part of his career. In addition to the relationship with Weber, the most fruitful of these early academic associations were those with Rudolf Sohm, a prominent Protestant church historian, and Lujo Brentano, a prominent Anglophile economist. Symptomatically, the friendship with Brentano developed only when Naumann's political position had become similar to that of many left liberals.[26]

Two other types of contacts were indicative of Naumann's development during the earlier part of his career. First, he came to know personally many right-wing Social Democrats.[27] Second, he worked together with political publicists of imperialism, the most famous of whom was probably Paul Rohrbach, a Baltic German Russophobe who eventually became German colonial minister.[28]

Despite criticism from some of his friends, Naumann clung for some time after the organization of the National Social Association in 1896 to the belief that academically educated intellectuals could take over the leadership of the working-class movement and play a decisive role in politics.[29] At the founding convention of the National Socials, Weber pointed to the lack of a potential mass basis for the party except among the very lowest strata of the population. Weber argued that the National Socials would become the party of the "wretched and downtrodden," "a haven for malcontents from the Right and the Left," and repellent to all members of rising social strata, including part of the working class. He criticized the party's program for failing to take a stand clearly favorable to the bourgeoisie and against the large agrarians.[30] In an essay two years earlier, Weber had made a similar point by referring to himself and Christian Socials like Naumann as "we bourgeois."[31]

Probably typical of Naumann's thinking and that of most of the National Socials was an address given at the founding convention by Rudolf Sohm. The theme of Sohm's speech was the duty of the Nation-

[26] See James J. Sheehan, *The Career of Lujo Brentano: A Study of Liberalism and Social Reform in Imperial Germany* (Chicago, 1966), pp. 143–44.

[27] Gertrud Theodor, *Friedrich Naumann*, p. 59 suggests that he met many Revisionists at Hallgarten's home.

[28] In the preface to his *Neudeutsche Wirtschaftspolitik* (Berlin-Schöneberg, [1906]), p. iv, Naumann stated that he regarded his book as complementing Rohrbach's *Deutschland unter den Weltvölkern* and that the two works formed a single whole. For a brief discussion of the relationship between the two men see Heuss, *Naumann*, p. 184.

[29] For an early, unreflective form of this emphasis on intellectuals see "Die geistliche Not unserer Universitäten" (1887) in *Werke*, i, 31.

[30] For Weber's remarks see Wenck, *Geschichte der Nationalsozialen*, pp. 63–64; and Weber, "Zur Gründung einer national-sozialen Partei" (1896) in his *Gesammelte politische Schriften*, 2nd ed., ed. Johannes Winckelmann (Tübingen, 1958), pp. 27–28.

[31] Wolfgang J. Mommsen, *Max Weber und die deutsche Politik 1890–1920* (Tübingen, 1959), p. 139.

al Socials to elevate (*erziehen*) the Fourth Estate. Sohm asserted that it was essential "that we, the educated, get the leadership of the Fourth Estate into our hands, that we displace the Social Democratic leaders from their leadership roles. Otherwise we shall never be able to overcome Social Democracy." In the debate that followed Weber's rejection of this point of view, Sohm became even more precise as to his objective: "We want to replace the Social Democratic leadership. If possible we want to put ourselves at the head of the working-class movement."[32] Despite Naumann's lack of success in promoting a Protestant trade-union movement, he held to a similar conception of the bourgeois intellectual as late as 1897 and possibly a bit longer. Asking rhetorically whether "the intellectuals" were *an sich* representatives of the class struggle, he replied, "No, they are representatives of the idea of the state, of justice, and of the common good. Simply because they are not in a position to come forward themselves as a party, they can represent unreservedly the interests of the whole."[33]

By 1907, when Naumann devoted an entire pamphlet to the subject of the role of the intellectual in politics, his views had changed decisively. As had often become his wont, he did not repudiate his earlier ideas. Rather, he implicitly moderated his old objectives and postponed indefinitely even the achievement of these modified goals. Attributing the political abstention that he found prevalent among German intellectuals to the peculiarities of German history and especially to the influence of Bismarck, he predicted that eventually the intellectual would play an important political role in Germany.[34]

As Werner Conze has pointed out, Naumann's assessment of the German constitution long remained unclear and contradictory.[35] Although calling for the extension of the Reichstag suffrage to elections for representative bodies within the individual German states, he did not think in terms of a fundamental alteration of the constitution.

Before the obvious failure of the National Socials to become a major political force demonstrated the inefficacy of his conception of the intellectual, Naumann had articulated his own version of the new liberal elitism. Thus the dissolution of the National Socials in 1903 did not mark a major turning point in the development of his political

---

[32] Quoted in Wenck, *Geschichte der Nationalsozialen*, pp. 42, 66.

[33] "National-sozialer Katechismus" (1897) in *Werke*, v, 223. See also the less explicit passage in a work published two years later in which he defined National Socialism as "the union of workers and the educated." "Weshalb nennen wir uns Sozialisten?" (1899) in *Werke*, v, 270.

[34] See "Die Stellung der Gebildeten im politischen Leben" in *Patria: Jahrbuch der "Hilfe" 1907* (Berlin-Schöneberg, 1907), pp. 80-93 and passim. See also Naumann's comments on the failure of the National Socials in his preface (1905) to Wenck's *Geschichte der Nationalsozialen*, p. iii.

[35] Conze, "Friedrich Naumann," p. 378.

ideas, although he led most of his followers into one of the small left-liberal parties, the *Freisinnige Vereinigung*. His mature views were expressed in *Demokratie und Kaisertum* and other works at the turn of the century. His elite theory, later elaborated further in writings that were influenced by the tactical political requirements of the day, underwent little change after the early twentieth century; even the destruction of the monarchy in 1918 did not lead to basic modifications in it.

The Elitism of the Mature Naumann

Naumann's basic objective was to secure leaders who, in cooperation with the emperor, would steer Germany through and beyond a great transformation that would complete the nation's modernization. In addition to the pursuit of an extensive policy of imperialism, this transformation entailed the completion of the transition to an industrially organized state, the slow development of a parliamentary monarchy similar to England's, and the elimination of the "new feudalism" in industry. Little of his earlier criticism of capitalism remained except pleas for flexibility in dealing with the Social Democrats and for a vigorous policy of social reform. He saved most of his venom for the large agrarians. Even the "new feudalism" of heavy industry did not disturb him as much as both the political possibilities that seemed to be blocked by heavy industry's cooperation with the large agrarians and the political advantages over commerce and light industry that heavy industry obtained through this cooperation.[36] He was convinced that sooner or later big business would come to the conclusion that compromise with the Conservatives was more costly than compromise with the Left. He distinguished two major wings of German business: on the one side, the producers of raw materials and semifinished products (mining, foundries, and spinning); on the other, the producers of finished products (machine tools, weaving, furniture, luxury goods). The first wing could cooperate more readily with the large agrarians, and the second with "democracy."[37] Identifying himself with the most dynamic elements in capitalism, Naumann cautioned against attempts to restrict their development; such attempts would impede progress. With the proper political guidance, capitalism could be made to serve the interests of everyone.[38]

The merger of the National Socials with the *Freisinnige Vereinigung*

[36] See "Die politischen Aufgaben im Industrie-Zeitalter" (1904) in *Werke*, iii, 18.
[37] *DuK*, pp. 110–19.
[38] "Was ist Kapitalismus?" *Süddeutsche Monatshefte*, ii (1905), 509.

brought them together with a small left-liberal party that was committed to free trade and that represented many large commercial, export, shipping, and banking interests. Unlike other left-liberal groups, the *Freisinnige Vereinigung* had been identified since its founding in the early 1890's with a flexible policy toward Social Democracy, support for the military budget, and enthusiasm for *Weltpolitik*. The party's following was predominantly urban. Many of its adherents were university graduates and elementary school teachers.[39] Both the *Freisinnige Vereinigung* and the union of left-liberal parties that it entered in 1910, the *Fortschrittliche Volkspartei*, combined a largely middle-class basis with decisive backing from the sectors of the bourgeoisie that were most critical of the social coalition with the Junkers. Indicative of the dimensions of this backing was the major role that newer industries, above all the electrical and chemical industries, played in the *Fortschrittliche Volkspartei*.[40]

The political elite that Naumann envisioned was appropriate to a bourgeois-dominated state functioning largely within the political framework of the Second Empire. A member of the major associations pressing for the expansion of the high seas fleet and the acquisition of overseas colonies, he argued that Germany, like every other large state, must either expand or stagnate and decay.[41] The fleet and imperialism were essential to Germany's economic, political, and social development and stability. The opposition of the SPD to the building of the high seas fleet compelled Naumann to stress the economic value of a world empire to the working class. The good standard of living of the English worker rested primarily, he asserted, upon England's position as a world capitalist power.[42] Time and again, he emphasized that the German fleet would provide for the needs of the masses as well as enhancing the profits of the capitalist.[43] In a revealing passage, he invoked the image of thousands of faithful natives in distant Ger-

[39] Thomas Nipperdey, *Die Organisation der deutschen Parteien vor 1918* (Düsseldorf, 1961), p. 185; Walter Tormin, *Geschichte der deutschen Parteien seit 1848* (Stuttgart, [1966?]), p. 113; Elm, *Zwischen Fortschritt und Reaktion*, pp. 4, 21–22, 44; Molt, *Der Reichstag vor der improvisierten Revolution*, pp. 195, 200. Molt fails to make clear that his study deals with the proportion of the parties' Reichstag deputies occupied in the different professions and businesses, not with the actual influence of an institution or a group. For example, he studied the proportion of bankers among the deputies of each party, not the influence of bankers or banks.

[40] Tormin, *Geschichte der deutschen Parteien*, p. 115; Molt, *Der Reichstag vor der improvisierten Revolution*, p. 195; Elm, *Zwischen Fortschritt und Reaktion*, pp. 210–17, 237.

[41] "Politik der Gegenwart" (1905) in *Werke*, iv, 46–47.

[42] *DuK*, p. 215. For a succinct discussion, focused on Naumann, of the arguments employed by liberal imperialists in their efforts to win working-class support for the fleet see Kehr, *Schlachtflottenbau und Parteipolitik*, pp. 437–41.

[43] See, e.g., "Politik der Gegenwart," p. 55.

man colonies toiling dutifully to benefit the citizens of the Father-land: "Somewhere on the surface of the earth we need land that will be cultivated for us, land where, beneath men's sweating brows, at least a third of our bread will grow; we need tropical land where someone will cultivate and prepare tropical fruits, coffee, rice, and cotton for us; we need foreign steppes where wool and leather will be prepared for us."[44]

During the war Naumann added another consideration that had been implicit in his earlier writings—a theme often associated with Rudyard Kipling and other propagandists of British imperialism,[45] and a theme that was one of the refrains in Hans Grimm's enormous post-war political tract thinly disguised as a novel.[46] Praising the advantages of a colonial empire for the spirit and character of a nation, Naumann portrayed colonies as havens for the restless and adventurous who might cause trouble at home, but who would blossom overseas: "In our homeland, which is regulated by strict laws, we always have a number of able men incapable of wandering in narrow corridors without bumping into something. We have young people full of fantasy and energy who want to make a new beginning for themselves somewhere in the world and who would like to go where they can see their neighbor's smoke only on the horizon."[47]

Having abandoned his earlier hope of destroying or completely transforming the SPD, Naumann sought to encourage the party's reformists, discourage its radicals, and push its center of gravity to the right. Like his friends Lujo Brentano and Max Weber, he was fond of invoking parallels with England to support his belief in the possibility of fostering a nonrevolutionary working class. Ironically, during the same period that the new liberals still relied heavily on these parallels, working-class militancy of the type that they consigned to the dustbin of history was rising throughout Europe, certainly as visibly in England as in Germany. Whereas the lockout of 1913 in the steel industry of the Ruhr marked the nadir of naked class struggle in prewar Germany, the threat of a general strike hung over Britain during the summer of 1914.[48]

[44] *Ibid.*, p. 48.
[45] See Hannah Arendt, *The Origins of Totalitarianism* (New York: Meridian paperback, 1958), pp. 210–11.
[46] Hans Grimm, *Volk ohne Raum* (Munich, 1931). The first edition appeared in 1926. For a brief pedestrian discussion of Grimm and the novel see Francis L. Carsten, "'Volk ohne Raum': A Note on Hans Grimm," *Journal of Contemporary History*, v (1967), 213–19.
[47] "Deutsche Kolonialpolitik" (an address given to the meeting of the *Deutsche Kolonialgesellschaft* in Berlin in July 1916) in *Werke*, iv, 849.
[48] See George Dangerfield, *The Strange Death of Liberal England, 1910–1914* (New York: Capricorn paperback, 1961); Ronald V. Sires, "Labor Unrest in Eng-

Naumann argued, as had been his wont since the beginning of his political career, that the era of revolution had passed in advanced industrial societies like England and Germany. He offered a broad array of examples and data to support his conclusion. One of his favorite arguments was that "revolution is a phenomenon [characteristic] of the transitional stage from an agrarian state to a liberal industrial state. Once a state has passed through this stage, it is immune to revolution. We have outgrown the era in which revolution is possible, and yet we atavistically drag along the old ways of thinking and the old phrases [in the SPD]."[49] Like Weber, Brentano, and other perspective bourgeois students of the labor movement, Naumann felt encouraged by the apparent diversification within the working class. He suggested that the locus of revolutionary rhetoric was among the lower strata of the working class, among the unskilled workers not affected by trade unionism. The better paid and more highly skilled worker had been educated by the trade unions to adopt more realistic expectations.[50]

In studying the SPD, Naumann and other new liberals combined careful observation with wishful thinking. Both at the time and subsequently, in Germany and elsewhere, Naumann's generalization about the outlook and behavior of "higher" and "lower" strata within the working class has proven untenable. Often the "higher" have been more revolutionary than the "lower." Similarly, his assertion in 1905 that Bernstein and the Revisionists were in control of the SPD cannot be supported.[51]

Another of Naumann's arguments against the possibility of revolution appears to have been derived directly from Max Weber. Naumann embraced the view—without sharing Weber's ambivalent attitude toward it—that modern technology and bureaucratic organization precluded the possibility of a successful revolution. According to

---

land, 1910–1914," *Journal of Economic History*, xv (1955), 246–66. More subtle than the comparison of developments in the labor movements of the two countries is the question whether the prewar political crisis was not actually more severe in Germany than in Britain. Of the recent literature on Germany see esp. Kurt Stenkewitz, *Gegen Bajonett und Dividende: Die politische Krise in Deutschland am Vorabend des 1. Weltkrieges* (Berlin, 1960); chap. 5 in Fritz Klein, *Deutschland von 1897/98 bis 1917* (Berlin, 1961); H. Pogge-von Strandmann and Imanuel Geiss, *Die Erforderlichkeit des Unmöglichen: Deutschland am Vorabend des ersten Weltkrieges* (Frankfurt am Main, [1965?]); Fritz Fischer, *Krieg der Illusionen: Die deutsche Politik von 1911 bis 1914* (Düsseldorf, 1969).

[49] "Die revolutionäre Phrase" (1902) in *Werke*, iv, 337.

[50] See *ibid.*, p. 338; "Die inneren Wandlungen der Sozialdemokratie" (1906) in *Werke*, iv, 347. See also "Der Niedergang des Liberalismus" (1901) in *Werke*, iv, 230; "Politik der Gegenwart" (1904–1905) in *Werke*, iv, 40, 83; *DuK*, p. 23; "Das Schicksal des Marxismus" (1908) in *Werke*, iv, 371.

[51] *DuK*, p. 3. For an acute analysis of the forces at work within the SPD see Carl E. Schorske, *German Social Democracy, 1905–1917: The Development of the Great Schism* (Cambridge, Mass., 1955).

Naumann, the integration of the workers into the national economy, the organization of big business, and the vulnerability of the modern metropolis to blockades ruled out any realistic belief in revolution. Only Romantics could continue to think in revolutionary terms.[52]

To effect political changes, Naumann pressed for the eventual conclusion of an "alliance" between a transformed Social Democracy and a reinvigorated liberalism. The notion of such an alliance was popularized with the aid of a slogan calling for the formation of a bloc "from Bassermann to Bebel" (from the National Liberals to the Social Democrats). In the social terms in which Naumann was fond of expressing the same proposal, the social coalition of the Junkers with the bourgeoisie would be supplanted by a coalition of the bourgeoisie with the upper strata of the working class. He often used phrases almost identical to Weber's in predicting that the monarchy could not indefinitely rest upon groups that were losing economic and political significance.[53]

Was the appeal for a bourgeois-proletarian alliance against the Junkers and the Catholic Center a sincere proposal, or was it, as one historian has argued, merely a device to manipulate the Social Democrats by encouraging the reformists in the party?[54] Certainly Naumann's suggestion was designed to draw the SPD toward the right, but at the turn of the century, when he first made the proposal in a concrete form, he seems to have believed that it might soon be realized. A few years later he no longer took seriously the prospects for a speedy conclusion of the projected alliance, especially after he accepted the formation of the Bülow bloc, which, under the leadership of Chancellor Bülow, began in 1906–1907 as a parliamentary alliance of almost all of the non-Socialist parties except the Catholic Center, and from the beginning had the character of a "patriotic" coalition directed against Social Democracy. Even at the turn of the century, a major consideration in Naumann's suggestion was the need of the liberal bourgeoisie to secure the assistance of the Social Democratic masses in a struggle for bourgeois objectives against the agrarian conservatism of the Junkers and the clericalism of the Catholic Center. As he occasionally described the battle for new German policies, it depended upon the coordination of the infantry of Social Democracy with the cavalry of

[52] "Die psychologischen Naturbedingungen des Sozialismus" (1902) in *Werke*, IV, 334; "Die revolutionäre Phrase," p. 337; "Das Schicksal des Marxismus," pp. 366–68; "Demokratie und Monarchie" (1912) in *Werke*, II, 442.

[53] See, e.g., "National-sozialer Katechismus: Erklärung der Grundlinien des National-sozialen Vereins" (1897) in *Werke*, V, 211; "Politik der Gegenwart," p. 40; *DuK*, p. 156; *Neudeutsche Wirtschaftspolitik*, pp. 10, 411.

[54] Gertrud Theodor, *Friedrich Naumann*, pp. 81, 208.

finance and the artillery of industry.[55] The core of Naumann's proposal was that the economic and political liberalism of the dynamic sectors of German commerce, finance, and light industry should play the decisive role in German politics in cooperation with the monarchy and reformist working-class leaders. The residue of his early political development and his early sympathy for the plight of the worker combined with tactical considerations determined by his mature political perspective to lead him to hold forth new political and social possibilities for much of the working class, especially for the less militant leaders of working-class organizations.

These hopes were encouraged first by groups of young liberals at the turn of the century and by similar groups a few years later. The Young Liberals (*Jungliberalen*) created an organization in 1898. Its founding was a tacit act of protest against the constant reliance of the National Liberal party and its leadership on the Conservatives. Critical of big industry and sympathetic toward social legislation, the Young Liberals favored imperialism. The movement became identified with the slogan "from Bassermann to Bebel."[56]

Naumann helped to inspire an attempt to unite all liberals. In 1906 he called for the spiritual and organizational renewal of liberalism. After a meeting of representatives of liberal groups in Bavaria, where an intense struggle against the Catholic Center served to draw all liberals together, a new, nonpartisan liberal organization for the entire Reich was founded. The National Association for a Liberal Germany (*Nationalverein für das liberale Deutschland*) played on the notion of a new period of liberal renewal comparable to that marked by the creation of the *Nationalverein* in 1859. Like Naumann, the founders of the new *Nationalverein* emphasized the need for liberalism to win working-class support. Although the new *Nationalverein* succeeded in promoting cooperation among Bavarian liberals and in winning support from organizations of liberal industrial and white-collar workers, it failed to achieve any major success in the Reich as a whole.[57] Due partly to the formation of the Bülow bloc, Naumann soon lost interest in it. As we shall see in Chapter Six, the *Nationalverein* had much greater significance for Leonard Nelson than for Naumann.

Alongside the existing monarchy, Naumann hoped for the develop-

---

[55] "Politik der Gegenwart," pp. 73, 86.

[56] Nipperdey, *Organisation der deutschen Parteien vor 1918*, pp. 95–96, 128; Tormin, *Geschichte der deutschen Parteien*, p. 109.

[57] See Werner Link, "Das Nationalverein für das liberale Deutschland (1907–1918)," *Politische Vierteljahresschrift*, v (1964), 422–44. During the first three months of its existence the name of the organization was the *Nationalverein für das Deutsche Reich*.

ment of a political elite composed largely of professional politicians. In the face of the widespread belief in Germany that political parties were a sign of decadence, Naumann stressed their potential role in the formation of a viable political elite. His conception of this role was based on his understanding of the functions of a two-party system of the British or American type and his expectations about the future development of German parties. He described the essential characteristics of a political party as "an organization of voters (coming together) for the purpose of winning a majority." Such an organization required a permanent apparatus and hence professional politicians.[58] Relying on the work of Weber and Robert Michels, Naumann became a vigorous proponent of an extensive political organization.

Like most parties in mid-nineteenth–century Europe, the early German parties had been loose organizations of individuals. The parties were activated primarily at election time; their parliamentary representatives, who were usually men well known for nonpolitical accomplishments, so-called notables, provided most of the fragmentary organization remaining between elections. In the Frankfurt Assembly of 1848 and in parliamentary bodies shortly after the middle of the nineteenth century, civil servants, the university educated, and aristocrats predominated.[59]

With the development of mass politics after the founding of the Empire, and especially during the 1880's and early 1890's, the character of the parties, most notably the Catholic Center, the Socialists, and the Conservatives, began to change markedly. The parties and the interest groups allied with them developed large permanent organizations and staffs that functioned after as well as during elections; the notables were replaced by men who held, and often continued to hold, paid positions in the parties, the interest groups, or the press. After a period from the late 1860's through the early 1880's during which each party, with the exception of the Catholic Centrists, restricted its appeal at the polls to a narrow social basis—even to a few strata within a single class —the parties made many successful attempts to acquire wider support. This diversification of the social bases of the parties was scarcely apparent in both the Catholic Center, which from its origins had been more a confessional than a class party, and in the liberal parties, which found many of their previous supporters attracted to Social Democracy or the Conservatives. By the beginning of the twentieth century

[58] *DuK*, pp. 52–53.

[59] See Günther Franz, "Der Parlamentarismus" in *Führungsschicht und Eliteproblem*, Jahrbuch der Ranke-Gesellschaft, III, 87–88; Karl Demeter, "Die soziale Schichtung des deutschen Parlaments seit 1848: Ein Spiegelbild der Strukturwandlung des Volkes," *Vierteljahresschrift für Sozial- und Wirtschaftsgeschichte*, XXXIX (1952), 6–16.

the Social Democrats, once a proletarian party with little appeal out-side the industrial working class and some lower-middle–class groups, drew 20 to 25 per cent of their votes from outside working-class circles.[60]

The trend toward the formation of large permanent organizations and the rise of professional politicians had extensive social and politi-cal consequences. Men who devoted their lives to interest group and party affairs became the typical parliamentary representatives of the Center, Conservative, and Social Democratic parties. Although many a noble estate-owner continued to occupy a Conservative seat, often he could obtain a place on the party's electoral lists only if the League of Agriculturalists supported him.[61] A well-known example of how the trend to professionalization affected, if to a lesser extent, the liberal parties is the prewar career of Gustav Stresemann. An official of the League of Saxon Industrialists, he entered the Reichstag as a National Liberal deputy. Especially for Social Democrats and more generally for workers and members of the lower strata of the middle class, party politics came to offer a frequently traveled path to social ascent.[62] Of the eighty-one Socialist Reichstag seats in 1903, only thirteen were oc-cupied by men with nonproletarian backgrounds, but few, if any, of the Socialist deputies could still be classified as workers. Most of them held party offices or wrote for party newspapers.[63] In 1905 the Social Democrats created a permanent party bureaucracy. The party for-mally acquired a pronounced hierarchical structure. Decisions came to be made more and more at the regional and national levels.[64]

Understandably, then, Robert Michels's now classic study of politi-

[60] Sigmund Neumann, *Die deutschen Parteien: Wesen und Wandel nach dem Kriege* (Berlin, 1932), p. 29; Nipperdey, *Organisation der deutschen Parteien vor 1918*, pp. 320–21. This trend was especially marked in the large cities. See Rudolf Schlesinger, *Central European Democracy and its Backgrounds: Economic and Political Group Organization* (London, 1953), p. 29.

[61] See Molt, *Der Reichstag vor der improvisierten Revolution*, pp. 46–48, 336–37, 349–51. For a review of recent literature on the professionalization of Reich-stag deputies, see James J. Sheehan, "Political Leadership in the German *Reichstag*, 1871–1918," *American Historical Review*, LXXIV (1968), 511–28.

[62] See Bavarian Statistisches Landesamt, *Soziales Auf- und Abstieg im deutschen Volke* [by Josef Nothaas], Beiträge zur Statistik Bayerns, Heft 117 (Munich, 1930), p. 117; Leopold von Wiese, "Social Stratification and Social Ascent as Problems" in Reinhard Bendix and S. M. Lipset, eds., *Class, Status, and Power* (Glencoe, Ill., 1953), p. 590; Wolfgang Zapf, *Wandlungen der deutschen Elite: Ein Zirkulationsmodell deutscher Führungsgruppen 1919–1961* (Munich, [1965?]), pp. 45–48.

[63] Robert Michels, "Proletariat und Bourgeoisie in der sozialistischen Bewegung Italiens," *Archiv für Sozialwissenschaft und Sozialpolitik*, XXI (1905), 579, and *Political Parties: A Sociological Study of the Oligarchical Tendencies of Modern Democracy*, trans. Eden and Cedar Paul (Glencoe, Ill., 1949), pp. 278–79.

[64] See Schorske, *German Social Democracy*, pp. 118–28; Nipperdey, *Organisa-tion der deutschen Parteien vor 1918*, pp. 351–86.

cal parties used the Socialists as its primary model. Published in 1911 as the work of a disillusioned Social Democrat, his *Political Parties* called attention to what he believed to be an inherent tendency in any organization—"the iron law of oligarchy."[65] From his studies, as well as from his personal experiences, Michels had become convinced that no "democratically organized" party could survive. No matter how firmly committed to democracy, which, he assumed, involved a high degree of popular control over political leadership and a high degree of popular participation, any highly organized party would be controlled by a few individuals. The disposition of all essential party affairs would lie in the hands of a small minority of active members who occupied key positions and filled vacancies in their ranks through cooptation.

What Michels regarded as a perennial law governing the development of social and political organizations, Naumann regarded as an enduring tendency in any maturing and mature industrial society. Naumann hoped that the formation of a new German political elite could be furthered by exploiting this tendency. He complained that German liberals did not comprehend the need for highly developed party structures and for professional politicians. After describing politics as a "business enterprise" in "all states furnished with parliamentary institutions," he went on to compare the liberals unfavorably with the agrarians and the Social Democrats: "The transformation of the will of the citizen into parliamentary influence has become a skilled trade that does not arise spontaneously. The agrarians and the Social Democrats have long known that, but we have still not learned it."[66]

It would be tempting to find an irony of fate in the gap between Naumann's forceful admonition to his fellow liberals and the bromides that he dispensed to them on the methods of party organization. Naumann, whose speeches were skilfully constructed, beautifully tailored to his audience, and according to contemporary reports masterfully delivered, could speak much more compellingly on the art of speechmaking than on the techniques of organization.[67] This discrepancy can be attributed partly to his own lack of experience in a large mass

[65] Previously, Michels had written several articles on the German Social Democratic party. Published in the *Archiv für Sozialwissenschaft und Sozialpolitik*, a journal of which his friend Max Weber was an editor, these articles contained some of the material which Michels later employed in his *Political Parties*.

[66] "Die Erneuerung des Liberalismus" (1906) in *Werke*, IV, 281. See also "Klassenpolitik des Liberalismus" (1904) in *Werke*, IV, 256.

[67] See "Vier Reden an junge Freunde" (1918) in *Werke*, V. For an excellent description of Naumann as orator see the memoirs of the Christian trade unionist official August Springer, *Der Andere, das bist Du: Lebensgeschichte eines reichen armen Mannes* (Tübingen, 1957), pp. 91–96.

party. He and other former National Socials played a decisive role in the reorganization of the *Freisinnige Vereinigung*; they brought with them skills and organizational concepts that helped to reinvigorate it;[68] but despite their concerted efforts, the party remained small, as did the merger of left-liberal parties that it joined in 1910. A decade later, in 1918, Naumann was still recommending that liberals could best inform themselves about an electoral district by studying the *Parteiberichte* of the SPD, together with the reports of the Catholic People's Association (*Katholischer Volksverein*) and the League of Agriculturalists.[69]

Yet his conception of the proper functions and characteristics of political leaders in Wilhelminian Germany served as a greater impediment to his articulation of organizational techniques than his lack of experience in a large party. Participation in grass-roots political activity was for Naumann primarily a means to acquire a better understanding of how best to gain mass support for those segments of the bourgeoisie with which he had identified himself.

He desired political technicians who would serve as power brokers, both among the representatives of organized interest groups and between these groups and what he found to be the ultimate political power in Germany—the Prussian monarchy. Acting as the political vanguard of the bourgeoisie, these political technicians would eventually have reduced the monarch to little more than a figurehead. An important attribute of this vanguard would be its ability to control and manipulate its followers. Even shortly after the turn of the century, Naumann assumed that the leaders he desired would promote the basic interests of the bourgeoisie, especially its financial, commercial, and light industrial elements. But in the earlier years of the century, he put this assumption in negative rather than positive terms, underscoring the need to displace the large agrarians as the ruling class. With a phrase similar to one used a few years earlier by Max Weber, he cautioned his readers to remember that "only through the rule of a class that has material interests of its own in democracy will the democratic spirit triumph in the life of any state. No liberal era will dawn unless a new class throws an old one out of the saddle."[70] In the last few years before the war, when he became deeply involved in organizations like the *Hansabund*, which, supported heavily by commercial, financial, and light-industrial interests, sought to create

[68] See Tormin, *Geschichte der deutschen Parteien*, pp. 113–14; Nipperdey, *Organisation der deutschen Parteien vor 1918*, p. 185; Molt, *Der Reichstag vor der improvisierten Revolution*, p. 271.
[69] "Vier Reden an junge Freunde," (1918) p. 727.
[70] "Klassenpolitik des Liberalismus" (1904), pp. 256–57.

a solid liberal bloc,[71] he was even franker about his goals. He defined the German "industrial state" that he looked forward to as "a future condition in which the industrial upper stratum will, through its organization and its will to power, take into its own hands the governmental apparatus as well as parliamentary leadership."[72]

Like Weber, he complained that too few businessmen participated in politics. Although Weber's strictures on the deleterious political influence of Bismarck on the German bourgeoisie must still have been much in Naumann's mind, he often appeared sanguine about the future role of businessmen. Interjecting barbs about the maladroitness of heavy industrialists, Naumann argued that industry must provide political leaders "who have not only business experience and business sense, but above all a feeling for political power and not for raw and brutal power; for industrial masses who have gone through the German school will not permit themselves to be treated like the Russian people. . . ."[73]

Naumann assumed that most of the effective political leaders that he sought would originate in the middle class or in the upper strata of the working class. But he made no attempt to exclude other men from political leadership as long as they shared his view of politics as a business. After the completion of Germany's transformation to an industrial state and the defeat of the large agrarians, German aristocrats would, he predicted, play a role similar to that of the aristocracy in Britain. The Junker, like his British counterpart, would then be able to serve the nation state effectively.[74] What Naumann had in mind in making this prediction is unclear. Presumably, the Junkers, many of whom would continue to hold high political offices, would be loyal helpmates of the urban bourgeoisie, becoming simply a status group within the administrative middle class or completing their transition to an agrarian section within the incipient new upper class. Less speculative is the inference that Naumann wished to allay Junker anxieties about the consequences of the completion of bourgeois hegemony in Germany and to indicate that this process need not occur in a revolutionary fashion.

As important to his elitism as the ways in which he circumscribed

---

[71] See Hans Jaeger, *Unternehmer in der deutschen Politik 1890–1918* (Bonn, 1967), pp. 153–55; Schorske, *German Social Democracy*, p. 153; Molt, *Der Reichstag vor der improvisierten Revolution*, p. 292. For a general discussion of the *Hansabund* and its specific problems during the election campaign of 1912 see Jürgen Bertram, *Die Wahlen zum Deutschen Reichstag vom Jahre 1912: Parteien und Verbände in der Innenpolitik des Wilhelminischen Reiches* (Düsseldorf, 1965), pp. 102–07; Fritz Fischer, *Krieg der Illusionen*, pp. 56–61, 145–67.

[72] "Der Industriestaat," *Neue Rundschau*, xx (1909), 1392.

[73] "Politik der Gegenwart" (1904–1905), p. 42.

[74] *Neudeutsche Wirtschaftspolitik*, p. 405.

elite recruitment were the restrictions that he placed upon popular control. Never far below the surface of his writings lurked a fear of popular demands and hence of popular control. This apprehension reflected his desire to enlist broad working-class support in order to terminate, or renegotiate, the Junker-bourgeois social coalition and to divert, once and for all, the Socialists from radical paths. He limited popular control by his position on the suffrage question, by his conception of a two-party system, and by his theory of the emergence of new types of political and economic structures.

At the time of the founding of the National Socials, Naumann and the new party committed themselves to work for the extension of the Reichstag electoral law to other elected bodies in Germany.[75] The National Socials stood for universal and equal manhood suffrage, but like many, if not all, of his left-liberal comrades after the turn of the century, he was reluctant to insist upon it unequivocally. His friend Hellmut von Gerlach, scion of an old Junker family, was among the few who clung to the demand that the *Freisinnige Vereinigung* maintain a steadfast commitment to the extension of the Reichstag suffrage. In 1908 the issue was among those that led Gerlach and some of Naumann's other close associates to bolt the *Freisinnige Vereinigung* and found a new left-liberal organization, the *Demokratische Vereinigung*.[76] Naumann's old political associate Adolf Damaschke recounts an incident that reveals Naumann's changing stance during this period. Having gone together for an outing, the two friends were rowing in a boat when Naumann abruptly asked Damaschke what he now thought of direct, equal, and secret universal suffrage. Damaschke replied that the question was a curious one since each of them had done his part in seeking to bring about this very type of franchise. "Of course," said Naumann, "it goes without saying that I am for it, but things are somewhat different [now]. Today I am for it only because everything else is even worse."[77]

The tactical requirements of party politics reinforced Naumann's tendency to become more skeptical about universal manhood suffrage. His support for the Bülow bloc, as well as his desire to continue to cooperate with the National Liberals after this bloc fell apart in 1909,

[75] The original National Social Program of 1896 is reproduced in Wenck, *Geschichte der Nationalsozialen*, pp. 57–58.

[76] See Walter Gagel, *Die Wahlrechtsfrage in der Geschichte der deutschen liberalen Parteien 1848–1918* (Düsseldorf, 1958), p. 167; Elm, *Zwischen Fortschritt und Reaktion*, pp. 197–205.

[77] Damaschke, *Aus meinem Leben*, II, 455. Naumann abandoned his early hostility to women's suffrage (see Wilhelm Happ, *Das Staatsdenken Friedrich Naumanns* [Bonn, 1968], p. 156), but without adopting a clear, consistent position on it before 1918. See, e.g., "Das alte Recht der Frau" (1913) in *Werke*, v, 486–87.

served to restrict his public utterances on the subject. During World War I he long held loyally to the *Burgfrieden,* the domestic political truce under which even the most forthright proponents of electoral reform were supposed to remain silent for the duration of the war. The enforcement of this silence was aided by the perhaps incorrect belief in left-liberal circles that electoral reforms would affect their strength at the polls even more adversely than that of the other non-Socialist parties.[78]

Tactical political considerations could also lead Naumann to minimize the impact of universal suffrage. In order to convince reluctant liberals to accept electoral reform and to counter the fears played upon by conservatives, he denied that abandonment of the three-class electoral system in Prussia would usher in revolution. Yet the way in which Naumann chose to allay these fears indicated much about his own attitude, and he accepted the formidable arguments developed by Weber and Michels to demonstrate that minorities would always rule. In 1904 he belittled the charge that universal suffrage would put the state in the hands of the Socialist leader August Bebel. The most that would happen would be that the Social Democrats would, in Naumann's ambiguous phrase, "participate in government [*Mitwirkung an der Regierung*]."[79] In a work published two years later, he defined the essence of a democratic organization negatively as one in which "no party member is entirely without influence on the party's leadership."[80] At least until the later stages of World War I, Naumann thought majority government in Germany would take years to develop.[81] Since his more theoretical arguments against the possibility of extensive popular control were similar to, but not as acute as Weber's, we shall not examine them here.[82] Particularly revealing, however, is a review that Naumann wrote when Michels's *Political Parties* first appeared in 1911. Naumann treated Michels condescendingly as a *Hans naivus* with little to tell anyone active in politics: ". . . All those involved in the affairs of any organization will find absolutely nothing new in Michels, but simply a frank discussion of matters difficult to discuss for anyone in-

---

[78] Compare the discussion in Hellmuth Weber, *Ludendorff und die Monopole: Deutsche Kriegspolitik 1916–1918* (Berlin, 1966), pp. 84–90 with that in Reinhard Patemann, *Der Kampf um die preussische Wahlreform im 1. Weltkrieg* (Düsseldorf, 1964), p. 253 and Molt, *Der Reichstag vor der improvisierten Revolution,* p. 56.

[79] "Das allgemeine Wahlrecht" (1904) in *Werke,* v, 339.

[80] "Die Erneuerung des Liberalismus" (1906) in *Werke,* iv, 279.

[81] See, e.g., "Umgestaltung der deutschen Reichsverfassung" (1908) in *Werke,* ii, 385; "Deutscher Liberalismus" (1909) in *Werke,* iv, 319; "Erziehung zur Politik" (1914) in *Werke,* v, 708.

[82] See, e.g., *DuK,* pp. 80–81; "Die psychologischen Naturbedingungen des Sozialismus" (1902) in *Werke,* iv, 332–33; "Wahlrechtsfragen" (1905), pp. 530–31; "Der Gesellschaftsvertrag" (1912) in *Werke,* v, 485.

volved in public activity." Naumann went on to dispute the conception of democracy that he found underlying Michels's book. It was false, Naumann complained, to describe the essence of democracy as a social order without leaders: "Democracy is merely the replacement of hereditary rights by suffrage rights."[83]

Naumann's conception of a two-party system—an institution that he hoped to see develop in Germany—revealed another aspect of his resistance to the notion of popular control. Although skeptical about the possibility of a two-party system developing in the near future, he anticipated that the polarization of German politics around the issues of an agrarian versus an industrial state, and protectionism versus free trade, would lead to the emergence of two blocs—a step in the direction of a two-party system.[84] Soon if not from the beginning, his admiration for a two-party system stemmed primarily from its potential for discouraging radical alternatives. He sought to achieve a state of near equilibrium in which each of the two parties or blocs would seek to win power for itself by calling out "the mass of unpolitical people (those who simply have the vote)." Shifts of this mass from one party or bloc to the other would determine the outcome of elections.[85] During the immediate postwar period, he returned to this conception of a two-party system. Looking wistfully at England, he declared that in a two-party system the dissatisfied would go from one party to the other "like molasses in a ship's hold."[86] He assumed that a two-party system would effectively restrict the meaningful options open to the voter. The ship might shift from side to side, but it would remain afloat and its basic structure would not change. Naumann invoked also the familiar argument that a system of two parties alternating in office helped to moderate the criticism of "the outs."[87]

Perhaps the most severe limitations on popular control imposed by Naumann stemmed from his conception of a rapidly emerging "new monarchism." He employed this term as a catchall for several developments that he sought to promote. He had in mind the political structure of both monarchies and nonmonarchies as well as the hierarchical organization of large business enterprises and of industrial society generally. Like Weber, he foresaw a continuing concentration of power at the apex of expanding, bureaucratic organizations. Since Naumann's discussions of the "new monarchy" ran parallel to Weber's more discriminating analysis of both bureaucracy and plebiscitarian leadership, only a few crucial aspects of these discussions will be considered.

[83] "Demokratie und Herrschaft" in *Werke*, v, 454.
[84] See, e.g., *DuK*, pp. 42–43.
[85] "Von wem werden wir regiert?" (1909) in *Werke*, ii, 393–95.
[86] "Demokratie als Staatsgrundlage" (Mar. 1919) in *Werke*, ii, 569–70.
[87] *Ibid.*, p. 570.

In a long programmatic work written shortly after the turn of the century, Naumann explained how the Hohenzollerns would complete the transition to a "new monarchy" in Germany. Absolute monarchy was, he contended, as impossible in the modern world as "absolute democracy." The "new monarchy" must rest on the will of "the masses." The complexities of the modern technological world required an assertion of strong leadership, and the direction of foreign policy must not become entangled in party strife. Until the Left abandoned its opposition to the army and the fleet, the emperor would have to conduct his military policy with the support of the Right, and his economic policy with the support of the Left. If the Social Democrats were clever, Naumann asserted, they would support the emperor and permit him thereby to abandon the Right.[88] Eventually, the emperor would lead the nation "as the dictator of the new industry. When he does this, however, he will need the masses—democracy."[89] By "new industry" Naumann was referring in this context not simply to industrial entrepreneurs, but more generally to everyone involved in the industrial sector of society. This failure to distinguish employees from employers recalls the more ingenuous use of the term *les industrielles* by the Saint-Simonians in nineteenth-century France to denote entrepreneurs, technicians, scientists, and workers.

Naumann found no great difficulty in maintaining the principle of hereditary succession in the German monarchy. Indeed, he found advantages in this principle when it was applied to the state. He invoked the natural sciences to support his assertion that an hereditary monarchy was preferable to an elective one. Inherited wisdom (*Erbweisheit*) made a hereditary monarch superior to an elected one.[90] As late as the early fall of 1918, Naumann was still employing similar arguments: like a queen bee, the future monarch was prepared for his office; although more gifted men might be resentful, the hereditary monarch had the training and assurance to act as a mediator between high officials.[91]

The *Daily Telegraph* incident of 1908 led Naumann to become rather skeptical about the political astuteness of William II, but produced no basic alteration in his views on the "new monarchy." Naumann was still content to see the emperor retain broad powers.

[88] *DuK*, pp. 180–92. For a good discussion of Naumann's conception of the potential of the emperor's role see William O. Shanahan, "Friedrich Naumann: A German View of Power and Nationalism" in E. M. Earle, ed., *Nationalism and Internationalism: Essays Inscribed to Carlton J. H. Hayes* (New York, 1950), pp. 389–90.

[89] *DuK*, p. 181. See also pp. 148–49.

[90] *DuK*, p. 142.

[91] "Der Kaiser im Volksstaat" in *Werke*, II, 493–96.

Although frequently predicting the development, over a long period of time, of a parliamentary monarchy similar to England's, Naumann shared an exaggeration of the British monarch's role that was common in German liberal circles.[92]

The continuity in Naumann's ideas can be seen clearly in an article on kingship published in 1909. He failed to come to grips with the contradiction in his assertion that both the president of the United States and the German emperor were "new monarchs."[93] He admitted that the predominance of the characteristics of a new monarchy in the office of German emperor was partly obscured by his position as king of Prussia. Naumann assumed that, as "new monarchs," both the president and the emperor should establish the general lines of policy and invoke popular support to overcome resistance to it. Yet this assumption neglected the ease with which the American president could claim that his election gave him a mandate from the people. To be sure, the emperor might also claim a similar mandate if he identified himself with a victorious party or coalition, but in the essay on kingship, as in earlier programmatic works, Naumann often, if not consistently, cautioned against the political involvement of the emperor. Some of these difficulties in Naumann's ideas, as in Weber's, were to be removed by the departure of William II in 1918.

In 1909 Naumann was still intent upon marshaling arguments for the monarchy, even though his essay on kingship reads, unintentionally, like a brief for the abandonment of hereditary monarchy. Monarchism in Germany was strengthened, he argued, by the "character" of the German people. German national character and Germany's peculiar historical development became for him further arguments against popular control.[94] He went on to explain that the old monarchism was impersonal; the new monarchism was very personal. In the old form of monarchism, special achievements were not required of the monarch. They could scarcely be expected in a hereditary system. The new type of monarch, whether in politics or business, relied heavily upon the advice of experts; he did not pretend that he knew everything necessary to perform his duties. Naumann followed these obvious admonitions to William II with a general evaluation of the potential development of the office of emperor in Germany. As long as the emperor had a strong personality and a hearty appetite for hard work, there was lit-

[92] See "Die Umgestaltung der deutschen Reichsverfassung" (1908) in *Werke*, II, 385, 388; "Das Königtum" (1909) in *Werke*, II, 437; "Deutscher Liberalismus" (1909) in *Werke*, IV, 319; "Erziehung zur Politik" (1914) in *Werke*, V, 708. For another assessment of the impact of the *Daily Telegraph* incident on Naumann's thinking, see Heuss, *Naumann*, pp. 258, 260.
[93] "Das Königtum" (1909) in *Werke*, II, 421.
[94] *Ibid.*, p. 409.

tle possibility of much control over him being exercised from below. If his personality were weaker or if he were inclined to view himself as the mere exponent of others, a period of temporary decentralization would ensue, and he would exercise much less power. Naumann suggested that the power of the emperor was expanding and would continue to expand, as long as the number of state officials increased. In an aside directed to the Social Democrats and anyone else who might believe in the possibility of arresting or destroying the growth of centralized power in the hands of monarchs and businessmen, Naumann asserted that the erection of a Socialist state would not reverse this basic tendency toward the concentration of power.[95]

Although accepting the belief of the nineteenth-century liberal that political could be distinguished from economic power, Naumann suggested that the two were increasingly becoming interlocked. He based his hopes for the demise of the *Herr-im-Hause* type of industrialist and the flourishing of the "new monarchism" in business on the development of this interlocking relationship. The former, his old opponents in heavy industry, he continued to castigate until World War I as exponents of a "new feudalism."[96] Consistency might have dictated that he rename them "old monarchs," but Naumann was now more concerned with demonstrating the virtues of new forms of capitalist enterprise. Implicitly accepting much of his friend Eduard Bernstein's analysis of modern capitalism, he discerned a tendency toward the separation of ownership from control in large undertakings.[97] Economic leadership was being taken from the producers and assumed by economic associations, by cartels, and by the state. As a consequence, "the number of economic leaders becomes smaller and smaller."[98]

Weber accepted this proposition as unalterable but regarded some of the consequences with misgivings; Naumann accepted it sanguinely. He wished simply to tinker a bit with its consequences. His acquaintance the ancient historian Ludwig Curtius, who was more conservative than Naumann, has provided a good insight into the nature of his optimism:

> Naumann, who had put aside all Christian romance, who kept his faith locked up in the innermost secret reaches of his heart, wanted to be a completely modern man. Perhaps his only cruelty lay in the relentlessness of the logic with which he enumerated for us the consequences of modern life in the age of the masses, the machine, the

[95] *Ibid.*, p. 435.
[96] See, e.g., "Die politischen Aufgaben im Industrie-Zeitalter" (1904) in *Werke*, III, 18; *Neudeutsche Wirtschaftspolitik*, 2nd ed. (Berlin-Schöneberg, 1907), p. 330.
[97] *Neudeutsche Wirtschaftspolitik*, p. 268.
[98] *Ibid.*, p. 28. Naumann italicized the entire passage. See also "Das Königtum" (1909) in *Werke*, II, 435.

department store, and steel buildings—an era in which the column was obsolete and in which no angel or winged goddess of victory was possible because physiology had long ago taught us that wings cannot grow on human shoulders.[99]

Despite his belief in the interdependence of economic and political power, Naumann confined proposals for reforms affecting employees to refining the institutions of the "new monarchy" in business. He endorsed plans that would create an atmosphere in which employees would appear to have a voice in management. Some form of "constitutionalism" instituted in business enterprises would, he hoped, help to promote the integration of workers into the existing order and undercut radicalism.[100] He could be optimistic about the possibility of the widespread establishment of "industrial parliaments" because he was more concerned with their form than their substance. Some type of popular representation of the employees in large enterprises would, he believed, suffice to bring about a less disharmonious relationship between big business and its employees. As Hans Jürgen Teuteberg has pointed out, Naumann did not want employee representatives to play an active role in determining profits, wages, and most business expenditures.[101] Seeking to convince the Socialists to divert their energies into a struggle over what would later be termed codetermination, he warned that socialization was coming in a form very different from that anticipated by the Social Democrats. Rather than coming from below in response to the threat of the proletariat, socialization was coming from above due to a concern for dividends and for a lightening of the tasks of the entrepreneur. The SPD must see to it that socialization did not take place at the expense of the employees, that socialization did not become a strait jacket worse than the old guilds. Rather than asking with the Social Democrats how the anarchy of free competition could be overcome, the workers, both salaried and unsalaried, must ask how they could overcome the pressure of a centralized social order on them.[102]

During World War I Naumann argued that industry had been brought under the control of the state and subjected to the common good of the body politic.[103] In line with his acceptance of the *Burg-*

[99] Ludwig Curtius, *Deutsche und antike Welt: Lebenserinnerungen* (Stuttgart, 1950), p. 162.

[100] See "Politik der Gegenwart" (1905), pp. 93–98; *Neudeutsche Wirtschaftspolitik*, pp. 430–31; Naumann's comments on Lujo Brentano's paper on "Das Arbeitsverhältnis in den privaten Riesenbetrieben" at the meeting of the Verein für Sozialpolitik in 1905 in *Schriften des Vereins für Sozialpolitik*, cxvi (Leipzig, 1906), pp. 188–90.

[101] Teuteberg, *Geschichte der industriellen Mitbestimmung*, pp. 487–88.

[102] *Die politischen Parteien* (Berlin-Schöneberg, 1911), pp. 108–09.

[103] *Mitteleuropa* (Berlin, 1915), pp. 140–43.

frieden[104] and his participation in the ideological battle against the Entente, he argued that the drive toward what he termed "state socialism" existed in other nations, but that it had matured more among the Germans. He professed to see tangible evidence of a reconciliation between "national bourgeois and socialist conceptions of the economy."[105]

Throughout most of the war, he relied heavily upon arguments concerning German uniqueness to undergird his support for the status quo in Germany and his criticism of the political system of the Western Powers. He was a founder and supporter of societies promoting propaganda for the German cause at home and abroad. He contributed to the wave of Teutonism that served to cement the domestic political truce. Yet his major wartime publication and his most famous work, *Mitteleuropa*, invoked fewer arguments about German uniqueness than most of his other wartime writings. Perhaps Naumann's hope that a Central European customs union might eventually include most of the continent led him to avoid using such arguments. Certainly his inclusion of the Hapsburg Empire in his plans for Central Europe and his courting of the Magyars would have made Teutonic arguments implausible if not offensive. He did not give up his advocacy of a German world empire; his proposals for Central Europe were sufficiently flexible to provide for the contingency that the war went poorly for Germany and to secure the potential basis for a large-scale policy of overseas imperialism.[106] As recent research has demonstrated, the conception of a Central European union advanced by Naumann was neither a romantic fantasy shared by a few idealists nor a stopgap proposal advanced suddenly in the midst of the war, but rather a program, which, conceived in its major outlines in government and business circles before the war, offered a broad basis of compromise for many big business interests during the war.[107]

ELITE VERSUS REVOLUTION

During the last months of the war and the first months after the armistice, Naumann devoted much of his energy to the battle against

[104] See Heuss, *Naumann*, pp. 352, 362.

[105] *Mitteleuropa*, p. 143.

[106] See "Deutsche Kolonialpolitik" (1916) in *Werke*, IV, 851. See also Theodor Schieder's comments in *Werke*, IV, 388; Theodor Heuss, "Friedrich Naumann als politischer Pädagoge" in Ernst Jäckh, ed., *Politik als Wissenschaft: Zehn Jahre Deutsche Hochschule für Politik* (Berlin, 1930), p. 121.

[107] Cf. the interpretations of Henry Cord Meyer, *Central Europe in German Thought and Action, 1815–1945* (The Hague, 1955), esp. pp. 194–217 and Jacques Droz, *L'Europe centrale: évolution historique de l'idée de "Mitteleuropa"* (Paris, 1960), esp. pp. 207–22 with Fritz Fischer, *Krieg der Illusionen*, esp. pp. 34–39, 368–69, 739–74.

social revolution, which he, like many other opponents of revolution, termed bolshevism. Writing under the impact of both the Bolshevik Revolution and the strike wave that touched most of Germany and Austria-Hungary in January 1918, he began to warn against the danger of revolution, a danger that he had always dismissed in his writings. He sought to discredit the Bolshevik Revolution by dismissing it as the work of a few men; he inveighed against the assumption of power by a minority, even though he had long been an advocate of the "realistic" view that majorities could only support and never make the crucial decisions. Now he alluded somberly to the possibility that "a minority—a proletarian minority—can push its way into control of the state."[108] The war and the Russian Revolution were, he feared, reviving questions that had long been settled outside Russia: "Because Russia is starting from the beginning, we too shall relive old pains and reconduct outmoded debates; we shall have to concern ourselves seriously with the problem of revolution, which we have already overcome for ourselves." In Germany the problem was especially serious, for "in the older [sic] democracies the receptivity to notions of revolution" was not as great as in Germany. "There the belief in the majority is firmer than in our country; [there] it is an article of popular faith." Naumann sought to gain some sign of reform from above to convince the Germans that the doctrines of majority rule and popular sovereignty were being implemented in their country. No drastic steps were necessary: "Even if our parliamentarism has flaws and anachronisms, it is not so ineffective that it has to be replaced by a workers' and soldiers' council."[109] Already Naumann was rapidly shedding the remnants of his wartime Teutonism in the face of a revolution that he wanted to confine to Russia.

By the end of the war, he had returned to his earlier position that the West, especially England and the United States, provided general models for Germany to follow. Now that the establishment of political democracy similar to that of the West seemed to offer a method of circumventing revolution, he referred to democracy as the most suitable form of political organization for Germany. He argued that after a lost war the vanquished were subject to pressure from without to adopt the political system of the victors.[110]

The German defeat provided an opportunity for the realization of Naumann's prewar political ideas, although in a context that he had

[108] "Europäische Revolution?" (Feb. 9, 1918) in *Werke*, v, 604.

[109] *Ibid.*, pp. 607–08.

[110] See, e.g., "Die Demokratie in der Nationalversammlung" (Speech of Feb. 19, 1919 to the National Assembly) in *Werke*, ii, 545–46; "Demokratie als Staatsgrundlage" (Speech of Mar. 4, 1919 in Jena) in *Werke*, ii, 562.

not foreseen. Under the pressures of the upheavals in Central Europe and increasingly handicapped by illness, he had neither the time nor the energy to adapt his elitism to the new situation as creatively as Weber. Often he simply echoed Weber. At other times he gave temporary support to schemes that had little direct relationship to his own elitism but that promised to help stave off social revolution. While lending tacit support to the Ebert-Scheidemann provisional government as it pursued a counterrevolutionary policy that led the Minority Socialists to withdraw their support and while encouraging it to move farther and farther from the radicals on the Left,[111] he supported Eduard Stadtler's Anti-Bolshevik League. This league was the most important organization in North Germany coordinating propaganda and armed activities against social revolutionaries. Stadtler, an army officer returned from a Russian prisoner of war camp, received financial assistance from Naumann, and, more important, through Naumann was introduced to many of the prominent bankers and industrialists who underwrote the Anti-Bolshevik League.[112] Stadtler succeeded temporarily in gaining the support of big business interests that were often at odds, as, for example, Naumann's "new monarchists" in the electrical industry and "new feudalists" in heavy industry. Stadtler called for new leaders drawn mainly from the lower strata of society and for a popularly supported dictatorship that would establish a "national socialism" in Germany. While he was denouncing parliamentary institutions and all elected bodies in late 1918 and early 1919, Naumann was publicly taking a strong stand in favor of parliamentary democracy.[113]

[111] See "Deutsche Einheit" (1918), *Werke*, v, 646–47. See also Heuss, *Naumann*, pp. 444, 452.

[112] A monograph on the Anti-Bolshevik League and Stadtler's activities is sorely needed. (Some suggestions for research on the general problem of the subsidization of elitists by business organizations and other groups will be found in Section II of the Bibliographical Essay.) Discussions of the Anti-Bolshevik League rely largely, often exclusively, upon one volume of Stadtler's memoirs: Eduard Stadtler, *Als Antibolschewist 1918–19* (Düsseldorf, [1935]), esp. pp. 8–131. Written from opposing points of view, but in agreement on most details are Jürgen Kuczynski, *Studien zur Geschichte des deutschen Imperialismus*, II: *Propagandaorganisationen des Monopolkapitalismus* (Berlin, 1950), pp. 261–309, and Hans-Joachim Schwierskott, *Arthur Moeller van den Bruck und der revolutionäre Nationalismus in der Weimarer Republik* (Göttingen, [1962?]), pp. 46–54. Briefer, but still useful for the league and Naumann's relationship to Stadtler are: Heuss, *Naumann*, pp. 453–54, 500–01; George W. F. Hallgarten, *Hitler, Reichswehr und Industrie* (Frankfurt am Main, 1962), pp. 86–87; Klemens von Klemperer, *Germany's New Conservatism: Its History and Dilemma in the Twentieth Century* (Princeton, 1957), pp. 34–37; Ernst Nolte, *Die faschistischen Bewegungen: Die Krise des liberalen Systems und die Entwicklung der Faschismen* (Munich, 1966), pp. 33–34.

[113] According to Heuss, Naumann finally broke, privately, with Stadtler in March 1919. Heuss attributes the break to Naumann's distaste for a manifesto

Active in the new Democratic party and serving in the National Assembly, Naumann supported the formation of the Weimar coalition of Majority Socialists, Democrats, and Catholic Centrists. This moderate coalition he identified with his old notion of a "left coalition." The splitting up of the Social Democrats had accomplished one of his major prewar goals, and the shift in power within the Catholic Center party opened up possibilities that he had scarcely alluded to before the war. Like most supporters of the Democratic party, Naumann found in it a useful device in the battle to ward off revolution.[114] In a speech to the National Assembly in Weimar in February 1919, he professed to see no other viable possibility than the assumption of leadership by a "union of Majority Socialism with the democratic parts of the bourgeoisie. If these groups come together, they can easily agree among themselves on questions of democracy. A truly complete bourgeois transformation, which Germany has failed to undergo previously, is now possible. . . ."[115]

Seemingly discarding any reservations about an open elite, he began to extol the destruction of all limitations on the development of individual abilities. In a draft bill of rights that he submitted for the new German constitution, he stressed the need of education to provide a vehicle for the talented to develop their abilities.[116] As happened frequently during the last year of his life, Naumann either found no opportunity or had no wish to elaborate further. Nelson and Rathenau would find both the time and the will to do so. Typical of Naumann's vague emphasis upon a fully open elite was a passage in a public speech that he gave in March 1919: "A growing movement of millions of people, especially in an industrial nation, can be nothing other than a democratic movement. When it has grown even greater, it says to the state: 'The state of privilege has come to an end; hereditary powers no

favoring a dictatorship issued by Stadtler. Heuss, *Naumann*, pp. 500–01. This explanation of the break is unconvincing since Stadtler had been calling for dictatorship since the previous fall. Heuss fails to note that Stadtler lost much of his big business backing during the same month that Naumann turned against him. The causes of the break seem to have consisted mainly in the falling apart of the big business coalition that had backed Stadtler and Naumann's belief that Stadtler's type of propaganda was no longer opportune.

[114] See Bruce B. Frye, "The German Democratic Party, 1918–1930," *Western Political Quarterly*, xvi (1963), 168–69; Ernst Portner, "Der Ansatz zur demokratischen Massenpartei im deutschen Linksliberalismus," *Vierteljahrshefte für Zeitgeschichte*, xiii (1965), 155, n. 41.

[115] "Die Demokratie in der Nationalversammlung" (speech of Feb. 19, 1919 to the National Assembly) in *Werke*, ii, 540.

[116] One of the catch phrases used by Naumann in the article on education for a draft of the bill of rights was "freie Bahn dem Tüchtigen!" "Versuch volksverständlicher Grundrechte" (1919) in *Werke*, ii, 576.

longer exist; every little child must have the possibility of ascent, even a child of the masses.' "[117]

A logical consequence of Naumann's emphasis upon an open elite was the founding of a school for the education of political leaders and the study of politics. For a decade, the notion of such a school had been bandied about in left-liberal circles; most of the discussion had centered in the creation of a party school that would serve one or more of the liberal parties.[118] Both the circumstances of the school's founding and the form it took were symptomatic of the changing moods among the new liberals. It appears likely that until 1917 not only was the financial backing for the realization of the idea lacking, but also Naumann himself did not regard the need as sufficiently pressing. Both the sense of urgency and the financial backing came when he and other liberals began to fear the possibility of an impending social revolution.[119] A gift from his friend the industrialist Robert Bosch enabled the opening in mid-1918 of the precursor to the *Deutsche Hochschule für Politik*, an institution that flourished during the Weimar Republic.

Although more closely linked to the Democratic party than to any other political group, the school was not, as in most of the early sketches of it, simply an institution for liberals. The staff included a wide range of scholars and practicing politicians. Presumably, the school stood above parties and partisan politics, although Communists were excluded from the ranks of both its permanent and visiting faculty. In imperial Germany academic careers had been difficult for Jews and virtually impossible for Socialists. The *Hochschule für Politik* set up no impediments for the first group, but, by excluding Communists, left standing a barrier to the second.

The basic functions of the school remained those that Naumann had envisioned. It provided a training center for future political leaders and their staffs, served to subsidize the careers of the politicians who became temporary members of its faculty, and offered a forum for the interchange of knowledge between scholar and politician. The school's first director, Ernst Jäckh, found not only a parallel, but also a direct influence in the *École libre des sciences politiques* founded after the

[117] "Demokratie als Staatsgrundlage" (Mar. 4, 1919) in *Werke*, II, 561.
[118] See Ernst Jäckh, "Zur Gründung und Entwicklung der Deutschen Hochschule für Politik" in Ernst Jäckh, ed., *Politik als Wissenschaft: Zehn Jahre Deutsche Hochschule für Politik* (Berlin, 1930), pp. 176–77; Joachim Heinrich Knoll, *Führungsauslese in Liberalismus und Demokratie: Zur politischen Geistesgeschichte der lezten 100 Jahre* (Stuttgart, 1957), p. 139.
[119] Heuss suggests that during the last stages of the war Naumann was struck by the politicization of the entire populace—the civilians as well as the men at the front. Heuss, *Naumann*, pp. 411–12, and "Naumann als politischer Erzieher," p. 123.

Franco-Prussian War in Paris. Both schools, he explained, were intended to promote national revival after a lost war.[120]

While Naumann was stressing the need to make training for political leadership widely available and to create an open elite, he was restricting the possibility of establishing democracy in personnel selection. What he gave with the one hand he took back with the other. In the course of a series of addresses on politics delivered during the last months of the war, he raised the question whether politics could be taught and learned. Falling back upon the notion of politics as an art, he told his youthful audience that although effective political activity always needed acquired knowledge, mere knowledge never sufficed. The pursuit of politics depended upon impulses originating deep in a man's nature. As an art, politics depended upon "an inherent [*angeborenen*], but unclear drive" that only some men possessed.[121] Thus Naumann left open the possibility of making membership in the elite contingent upon factors not subject to rational analysis. As we shall see in Chapter Four, a similar, potentially arbitrary method of restricting entrance to the elite occupied a much more prominent place in Weber's elite theory.

Indicative of the continuity in Naumann's elitism was a severe limitation that he placed on popular control after the war. His conception of the office of the new German presidency was little more than an updated version of the new monarch that he had worked out at the turn of the century.[122] Perhaps because Weber was bolder, more innovative, and less closely involved with day-to-day political realities—or perhaps because he was not plagued by illness as was Naumann, who died in August 1919—Weber worked out his plans for the presidency in greater detail and related them to his elite theory more creatively. Naumann ended his life as a practicing politician with strong authoritarian reservations willing to work within the framework of parliamentary democracy, but unable to provide a comprehensive theoretical justification for his position. Although Weber died less than a year after Naumann, he responded more coherently on a theoretical level to the collapse of the monarchy.

[120] Jäckh, "Zur Gründung der Deutschen Hochschule für Politik," pp. 180–83. A rewarding comparative study might be done on the two schools and similar institutions, such as the Woodrow Wilson School for International Affairs at Princeton University.

[121] "Vier Reden an junge Freunde" (1918) in *Werke*, v, 709–15.

[122] See, e.g., "Demokratie als Staatsgrundlage" (Mar. 1919) in *Werke*, ii, 566–67.

CHAPTER FOUR

Max Weber: Great Men, Elites, and Democracy

Unlike most German academicians before 1918, Max Weber frequently identified his political views with democracy. Although regarding the realization of the classical ideals of democracy as impossible, he considered the political institutions of the Western Powers as models with much relevance for Germany. At the end of World War I, he was one of the few Germans to have developed an elaborate elite theory that presupposed political institutions resembling those in the West. Yet his refusal to engage in the anti-Western diatribes of many of his contemporaries obscured his relationship to democracy. Upon the institutions of modern democracy, he imposed many of the patterns associated with the predominant non-Socialist German elite theories. He viewed open elites and any increase in popular control as devices to promote the development of a state that would pursue a consistent policy of imperialism tapping fully the resources of the entire nation.

Weber's Basic Political Concerns

Esteemed by scholars for his brilliance as a social scientist, Weber became more widely known as one of the most prominent non-Marxist critics of the Wilhelminian era.[1] Even before the *Daily Telegraph* epi-

---

[1] For biographical details see esp. the biography by his wife, Marianne Weber, *Max Weber: Ein Lebensbild* (Tübingen, 1926). Wolfgang J. Mommsen's *Max Weber und die deutsche Politik 1890–1920* (Tübingen, 1959), the best and most detailed general study of Weber as a political figure and thinker, provides a useful supplement and, at times, corrective to her work. The most rewarding concise sketch of Weber's life and thought is the introduction by Hans Gerth and C. Wright Mills to their volume (hereafter referred to as Gerth and Mills) *From Max Weber: Essays in Sociology* (New York: Galaxy paperback, 1958). Arthur Mitzman's *The Iron Cage: An Historical Interpretation of Max Weber* (New York, 1970) pulls together coherently a wealth of biographical material, most of it pertaining to the 1880's and 1890's, for a psychoanalytic study. Distinguished by a sound grasp of psychoanalytic theory and a familiarity with the social history of Imperial Germany, Mitzman's work constitutes a prime example of the failure of contemporary psychoanalytically oriented biographical studies to explain the origins and espousal of social and political ideas. Examining Weber's politics during the 1890's in terms of his relationship to his parents, Mitzman suggests that the conflicts between Junker and bourgeois, as well as within the bourgeoisie itself, were basically subjective in origin. The application of the hypothesis that the

sode of 1908 he seems to have had a much greater sense of urgency than Naumann about the consequences of the failings of William II, but the plans that Weber drew up to deal with the situation were not published and have not survived.[2] His public strictures against what he viewed as Germany's political ills culminated in feverish activities toward the end of World War I. Although he focused much of his criticism directly upon William II, like Naumann, Weber wanted to retain some type of monarchy as long as the Hohenzollerns remained. Even after the Kaiser's departure, Weber would have liked a plebiscite to choose between a monarchy and a republic. But with less difficulty than Naumann, he accommodated his thinking to the absence of a monarchy. By serving on the committee entrusted with the drafting of

---

development of a man's social and political views is determined by tensions arising from psychic relations among father, son, and mother poses some fruitful questions about the degree of continuity in Weber's thought, but these questions are not dependent upon this hypothesis and cannot be answered with its assistance, as becomes only too patent in the latter half of Mitzman's book, which deals with Weber after the turn of the century. Mitzman's attempt to relativize Weber the social scientist may provide an antidote of sorts to the naive, unhistorical enthusiasm displayed by many current admirers of Weberian sociology in Western Europe and the United States, who have adopted Weber's concepts without understanding, often without questioning, the historical situation in which they were formulated. More likely, however, Mitzman's study will deflect attention from the relationship between Weber's thought and the social and political context in which Weber worked and thereby obscure the similarities between Imperial Germany and today's bourgeois societies that predispose many bourgeois scholars to embrace Weber's sociology.

[2] See Mommsen, *Max Weber*, pp. 191–92. Mommsen's book has helped to provoke a lively discussion of Weber's political thought. In 1961 the *Kölner Zeitschrift für Soziologie und Sozialpsychologie*, XIII (1961), 258–89 carried a discussion of Mommsen's book by Reinhard Bendix, Paul Honigsheim, and Karl Loewenstein. They failed to adduce any telling criticisms of Mommsen's work. For example, Loewenstein and Honigsheim, who knew Weber personally, added nothing of significance to the existing body of memoir literature on Weber. For the most part they retold incidents that had been recounted years earlier, including incidents mentioned by Honigsheim in his article "Der Max-Weber-Kreis in Heidelberg," *Kölner Vierteljahrshefte für Soziologie*, v (1926), 270–87. Much of the debate over Mommsen's book narrowed down to the question of the relationship between National Socialism and Weber's concept of plebiscitarian leadership. See esp. René König and Johannes Winckelmann, eds., *Max Weber zum Gedächtnis: Materialien und Dokumente zur Bewertung von Werk und Persönlichkeit, Kölner Zeitschrift für Soziologie und Sozialpsychologie*, Sonderheft 7 (Cologne and Opladen, 1963); Ernst Nolte, "Max Weber vor dem Faschismus," *Der Staat*, II (1963), 1–24; Eduard Baumgarten, ed., *Max Weber, Werk und Person: Dokumente* (Tübingen, 1964); Otto Stammer, ed., *Max Weber und die Soziologie heute, Verhandlungen des 15. deutschen Soziologentages* (Tübingen, 1965); Karl Loewenstein, *Max Webers staatspolitische Anschauungen in der Sicht unserer Zeit* (Frankfurt am Main, 1965). Mommsen's defense against the attacks of his critics has been uninspired: "Zum Begriff der 'plebiszitären Führerdemokratie' bei Max Weber," *Kölner Zeitschrift für Soziologie und Sozialpsychologie*, XV (1963), 295–322; "Universalgeschichtliches und politisches Denken bei Max Weber," *Historische Zeitschrift*, CCI (1965), 557–612.

the new constitution, Weber became one of the "founding fathers" of the Weimar Republic.

Throughout most of his mature years, he moved gradually leftward. Although no party held his allegiance for long, he was closely associated with liberalism. After the armistice in 1918, he almost obtained a nomination from the new Democratic party to the National Assembly at Weimar.

Partly as a result of changes in his position, his writings contained many incongruous elements. He usually took a clear stand on specific issues, but he never integrated his political ideas into a harmonious system.[3] His distress over many tendencies in modern society often left him without clearcut solutions.

He was acutely aware of the ambivalent attitude of the bourgeoisie toward an increase in the amount of popular control over government. Dread of the consequences of disrupting the alliance with the Junkers for most bourgeois outweighed any thought of the advantages. Some of the same attitude affected Weber. He worried about it, and he sought increasingly to overcome it in himself and in others. He tried to convince the bourgeoisie that democracy need involve only a slight increase in popular control—an increase that would harm no one except the Junkers and some bureaucrats.

His passionate interest in politics prompted him to draw a clear line between scientific knowledge and personal opinions. He distinguished scientific conclusions, or "value-free judgments," from partisan conclusions, or "value judgments." With this distinction he hoped to avoid the partisanship exhibited by many of his academic colleagues who identified their personal views with scholarly impartiality. At the same time, he implicitly prepared for a separation of the "impartial expert" from the political decision maker: either the "man of knowledge" acted solely in an advisory capacity, or he relinquished any claim to impartiality.

---

[3] The thin volume bearing his name on the title page and edited by Johannes Winckelmann, *Staatssoziologie* (Berlin, 1956), cannot substitute for a work which Weber never wrote. Winckelmann simply selected passages from Weber's published writings and arranged them in a logical order. Of Weber's works, I have relied most heavily upon the second edition of his collected political essays, *Gesammelte politische Schriften*, ed. Johannes Winckelmann (Tübingen, 1958), and his political letters, which, at present, are contained only in the first edition of the *Gesammelte politische Schriften*, [ed. Marianne Weber] (Munich, 1921). Hereafter the second edition will be cited as *GpS*. Whenever followed by only a page reference, a letter will be found in the first edition. I have also drawn heavily upon his posthumously published *magnum opus*, *Wirtschaft und Gesellschaft*, Abteilung III of *Grundriss der Sozialökonomik* (Tübingen, 1921–1922). Hereafter this work will be cited as *WuG*. Other collections of Weber's essays which will be cited by abbreviations are: *Gesammelte Aufsätze zur Soziologie und Sozialpolitik* (Tübingen, 1924) (*GAzSuSp*); and *Gesammelte Aufsätze zur Wissenschaftslehre* (Tübingen, 1922) (*GAzWl*).

A science free from value judgments involved merely the investigation of causes and effects.[4] Such a science could not tell anyone whether to adopt one value in preference to another. A value-free science could only indicate what the consequences would be if he tried to effect a value of his choice.[5] Although the choice had to be a personal one, it seemed sensible to Weber to adopt values capable of realization.[6]

The significance of the debate provoked among German academicians by his conception of science has usually been lost. Most interpretations have stressed Weber's fear of professors like Heinrich von Treitschke using the lectern for political purposes while posing as objective scholars.[7] While directed against the celebration of the existing order under the guise of impartiality, Weber's concept of a value-free science was also directed against the Socialist Left. Weber and other proponents of a value-free science staked out a claim to impartiality even though they were opting for a bourgeois order. At the same time, they were making a covert plea for their own indispensability as men of science.

There appears never to have been any serious doubt in Weber's mind about his own primary values. He committed himself to the ideal of the national state.[8] Deliberately exploring some of the ramifications of this commitment, which many of his contemporaries, both in Germany and elsewhere, preferred to take for granted, he indicated that history had reached a stage in which the national state was a desirable historical necessity and that consequently the individual should act through and for the national state.

Intellectually, his acceptance of the national state entailed not simply, or even primarily, an allegiance to German culture or the German

[4] H. Stuart Hughes, *Consciousness and Society: The Reorientation of European Social Thought, 1890–1930* (New York, 1958), esp. pp. 300–10 places Weber's attempt to create the basis for a value-free science within the general context of European intellectual history.

[5] For a highly critical and stimulating discussion of Weber's position see Eric Voegelin, *The New Science of Politics* (Chicago, 1952), pp. 14–18.

[6] See "Die 'Objektivität' sozialwissenschaftlicher und sozialpolitischer Erkenntnis" in *GAzWl*, esp. p. 151. For the final statement of Weber's position see the popularized and simplified version in "Wissenschaft als Beruf" in *GAzWl*.

[7] Mommsen, *Max Weber*, p. 41 still clings to this interpretation, as does Fritz K. Ringer, *The Decline of the German Mandarins: The German Academic Community, 1890–1933* (Cambridge, Mass., 1969), esp. pp. 354–55. Ringer discusses cogently Weber's views on a value-free science as "modernist" criticisms of German academic traditions raised by a man who still stood partly within these traditions. This interpretation fails to take into account other dimensions of the historical context of Weber's position. Thus Ringer does not ask whether Weber's demand for value-free science was offered as a challenge not only to conservatives within the "mandarin" tradition but also to radicals outside it.

[8] For an indication of how conscious Weber was of his elevation of the national state to the place of an ultimate value see "Der Sinn der 'Wertfreiheit' der soziologischen und ökonomischen Wissenschaften" in *GAzWl*, p. 501.

people. Rather, it involved dedication to "the state" as an abstraction. The "needs" and "progress" of "the state" should, he felt, take precedence over those of class and even of the people as a whole. Like many liberals of the generation which grew up immediately before and after the founding of the Bismarckian Empire, Weber believed that "the state" should function according to laws operating within itself. He viewed the "national power-state [*Machtstaat*]" as an institution with an existence partly independent of the society surrounding it and animated by the desire for more power. In 1907 he spoke of national power as his "final and ultimate value."[9] Before the full elaboration of his conception of science, he had even made this commitment appear inevitable.[10]

Repeatedly, he urged that Germany pursue power politics on a worldwide scale. He shared the feeling, common in the German bourgeoisie and middle class, that Germany should assume its "rightful" place alongside the older colonial powers.[11] As in many other respects, England and the British Empire supplied his model. From 1893 to 1899 he was a member of the Pan-German League, one of the major organizations that advocated German expansion both in Europe and overseas and agitated for the construction of a large fleet.[12] Until World War I and even during it, Weber tended to favor a strategy of cooperation with England in the pursuit of overseas imperialism. Unlike Naumann, who as early as 1899 seems to have considered war with England inevitable, Weber was usually much more responsive to the possibility of imperialistic cooperation with the British.[13] Weber's hopes may have contributed to his reluctance to become involved with the concept of Central European union during the war, although he agreed to join the Working Committee for Central Europe (*Arbeitsausschuss für Mitteleuropa*) founded by Naumann and the banker Felix Somary.

Often Weber introduced transcendental imperatives into his nationalism and imperialism. In a speech in the middle of the war, for

[9] "Diskussionsrede" at the 1907 meeting of the Verein für Sozialpolitik in *GAzSuSp*, p. 416. Hereafter cited as "Diskussionsrede" 1907.

[10] See "Der Nationalstaat und die Volkswirtschaftspolitik" in *GpS*, pp. 13–14.

[11] See Ludwig Dehio, "Thoughts on Germany's Mission, 1900–1918" in his *Germany and World Politics in the Twentieth Century*, trans. Dieter Pevsner (London, 1959), esp. pp. 86–91, 94–96.

[12] For samples of the types of criticism to which Weber's nationalism and imperialism have been subjected see: J. P. Mayer, *Max Weber and German Politics: A Study in Political Sociology* (London, 1944); Georg Lukács, *Die Zerstörung der Vernunft* (Berlin, 1955), pp. 481, 488; Hans Kohn, *The Mind of Germany: The Education of a Nation* (New York, 1960), pp. 278–87.

[13] See Mommsen, *Max Weber*, pp. 156, 215, 230–31.

example, he emphasized that he had always viewed politics, whether foreign or domestic, from a national point of view and went on to speak of Germany's "responsibility" and "duty" to "history" to assert its national power.[14]

The Allied victory in 1918 filled him with despair, but he still hoped for the eventual resurgence of Germany as a world power.[15] While he recognized a need to limit the scope of German foreign policy in the immediate postwar period, he stressed the "necessity" of preserving the integrity of German territory. At the end of 1918 and the beginning of 1919 he publicly proposed a popular uprising to prevent the separation of any territory in the East.[16] Shortly after the armistice he justified the creation of a republic as the surest means of settling the Greater German problem: "We must favor *that* form of state which makes possible the union of the largest possible number of Germans in one body."[17]

To his last days there is no evidence that he altered his standpoint. Despite his awareness that his nationalism was a product of his times, he made no apologies for it. The strength of the German nation-state and its effectiveness in world politics provided him with the ultimate standard by which to assess all political activity in Germany.

Like Naumann, Weber was perturbed during the 1890's by the failure of the Social Democrats to support imperialism but heartened by the rise of reformism in the party. Although less sanguine than Naumann about the possibility of gaining massive working-class support for imperialism, he regarded this support as essential to the construction of an adequate social basis for imperialism: "For us it is a question of life or death whether there awakens in the broad masses of our people a consciousness that in the long run only the expansion of German power can create employment at home and the possibility of further ascent. The fate of replacements from below is indissolubly linked to the rise of Germany to the position of a political and economic world

[14] Speech delivered at the end of October 1916. Quoted in Marianne Weber, *Max Weber*, pp. 590–91.

[15] See Letter of Nov. 24, 1918, to Friedrich Crusius (a professor of classical philology at Munich), p. 484. A few lines before (p. 483) Weber had been far more pessimistic, referring to the passing of Germany's role in world politics and the commencement of Anglo-Saxon world domination.

[16] In December 1918, he even urged a student gathering to make certain that the first Polish official entering Danzig be assassinated. Marianne Weber, *Max Weber*, pp. 643–44.

[17] "Deutschlands künftige Staatsform" in *GpS*, p. 441. Weber's italics. Hereafter cited as "DkS." For similar evidence of Weber's views after the armistice see Mommsen, *Max Weber*, pp. 304–14; Gustav Stolper, *This Age of Fable* (New York, 1942), p. 318n.; René König, "Max Weber" in *Die Grossen Deutschen*.

power, to the power and greatness of the Fatherland."[18] The objective of German social policy should be "the *social unification* of the nation, which modern economic development has destroyed, in order to wage the difficult battles of the future."[19] Weber expected that social policies favoring one group of workers over another would promote the development of a labor aristocracy. Despite his hope for a labor aristocracy that would support imperialism, after 1907 he became more pessimistic than Naumann about the possibility of political cooperation between the Social Democrats and the liberals.[20]

Nationalism and imperialism helped to shape his elite theory from the beginning. He felt that Germany lacked political leaders capable of conceiving and implementing policies appropriate to a world power. Again and again, he bemoaned the absence of effective political leaders. In his eyes German domestic and foreign policies after 1890 came to appear as a long series of failures, blunders, and missed opportunities.

The first generation of political leaders in the Second Reich had largely disappeared from the political scene. To Weber and many of his contemporaries, no replacements of equal stature had appeared. Above all, these Germans missed Bismarck, the man who had often seemed to be the sole director of Germany's political course. Even during the Iron Chancellor's period of office his political abilities had become legendary. Fed by the uncritical hero-worship of the middle class, the Bismarck legend assumed increasing proportions after his death. The notion of political genius as personified in Bismarck was fusing with the cult of the hero and made a deep impression upon Weber's generation. Dissatisfaction with William II helped to erode faith in dynasticism. Weber realized that a longing for protection against the proletariat underlay much of the widespread hero-worship, but the potentialities of great men intrigued him.

Although he adopted a highly critical attitude toward Bismarck's postunification policies, he shared the current assumption that Bismarck had possessed virtual omnipotence in German politics. Weber was convinced that a great leader who, unlike Bismarck, pursued a vigorous policy of overseas expansion could help to execute the major "tasks" that Germany "should" fulfill. Ultimately, he believed, single individuals formulated all "great decisions."[21] His liberal background

[18] Discussion of Hans Delbrück's paper on "Arbeitslosigkeit und das Recht auf Arbeit," *Bericht über die Verhandlungen des 7. evangelisch-sozialen Kongresses* (Berlin, 1896), p. 123.

[19] "Der Nationalstaat," p. 23. Weber's italics.

[20] See the evidence from Weber's *Nachlass* cited in Mommsen, *Max Weber*, pp. 102 n. 1, 115 n. 3, 127 n. 2.

[21] "Parlament und Regierung im neugeordneten Deutschland" in *GpS*, p. 383. Hereafter cited as "PuR."

and his individualism supplied the intellectual background for his rejection of collective decision making, and in his sociology he took special pains to demonstrate its inefficiency.[22]

On the other hand, he harbored much skepticism about "great leaders." A great man of Bismarck's type, he complained, left a nation accustomed to almost complete reliance upon him and inclined to helplessness after his departure.[23] Still more importantly, Weber felt pessimistic about the possibility of such a leader appearing in the near future. Only once in centuries, he cautioned, could one expect a true "political genius."[24] Implicitly, he asked what Germany would do in the centuries between Bismarcks. In the meantime leadership had to come from somewhere, if Germany were to overcome what Weber viewed as her present leadership vacuum. He sought ways to ensure a steady succession of leaders capable of conducting German *Weltpolitik*.

ELITES AND SOCIETY

Social conflict, a recurrent theme in his sociology, supplied one of the presuppositions of Weber's elite theory. Reworking some of the basic ideas of liberalism, Social Darwinism,[25] and Marxism, he viewed social conflict as ineradicable. He found conflict not only inevitable but also desirable. Whether involving nations, classes, groups, or simply individuals, conflict was for Weber an integral part of all human existence. By and large, he accepted the liberal notion of conflict as beneficial to all concerned. Unlike Marxists and many popular German social thinkers, he did not desire the establishment of a society free from conflicts. At the same time, he rejected any exclusively economic interpretation of social struggles.

In his sociological works, he examined in great detail the institutions, ideas, and sentiments that, despite conflicts, held a society together. His studies in the sociology of religion began with the implicit assumption that societies were composites of positively and negatively privileged status groups (*Stände*). By seeking exclusiveness and attempting to monopolize economic and political opportunities, each status group endeavored to preserve or enhance its "style of life." Each status group stood in a condition of endemic conflict with the others,

[22] See *WuG*, esp. pp. 128, 162–63.

[23] "PuR," pp. 307–08. For a short period during the early 1890's Weber took a more balanced view of Bismarck's political impact (see Mommsen, *Max Weber*, p. 98), but he did not follow through on the questions that he raised.

[24] "PuR," p. 324.

[25] Weber's reliance upon Social Darwinist concepts appeared clearly in his early work. See, e.g., "Der Nationalstaat" (1895), pp. 2, 9 n. 1; "Zur Gründung einer national-sozialen Partei" (1896) in *GpS*, p. 29.

but society did not necessarily exhibit continual instability. One status group, like the Confucian literati or the Brahmin priests, might eventually become the dominant "bearer of culture," set the tone of social relations by its ideas and style of life, and give great stability to society.[26] Weber's conception of society might well be characterized as a "delicate balance" of opposing forces.[27]

The effective exercise of political control always lay, he argued, in the hands of a few men. They made all of the important political decisions. No matter what the form of state, all decisive political action emanated from a small number of individuals: "*Everywhere*, whether within or outside democracies, politics is made *by the few*."[28] "The *demos* itself, in the sense of an inarticulate mass, never 'governs' larger associations; rather it is governed. . . ."[29]

Convinced of the advantages of a very limited number of decision makers, Weber referred to a "principle of small numbers."[30] Decisions could be made best and most readily by a few individuals. The few would be relatively unaffected by the "emotional factors" operative in the masses.[31] They could rapidly reach an understanding and initiate the action necessary to preserve their position. Responsibility for decisions would be clear, and secrets could be well guarded. Weber viewed secrecy as an essential element in all political rule.[32]

Weber believed that modern industrial society tended to concentrate important decisions in fewer hands. Bryce, Ostrogorski, and other critics of the Western democracies helped to confirm his image of the realities of political life in a democracy. He accepted their conclusion that even in the existing democracies small groups of men dominated all important political activities. When his friend Robert Michels arrived at similar conclusions about political parties, he lent support and encouragement.[33] Never having committed himself to the

[26] Reinhard Bendix, *Max Weber: An Intellectual Portrait* (Garden City, 1960), pp. 266–75.

[27] The phrase is that of Talcott Parsons in the introduction to his and A. M. Henderson's translation of Part 1 of *Wirtschaft und Gesellschaft* under the title *The Theory of Social and Economic Organization* (Glencoe, Ill., 1947), pp. 31–32. Hereafter this translation will be cited as Parsons and Henderson.

[28] "Die Lehren der deutschen Kanzlerkrisis" in *GpS*, pp. 214–15. Weber's italics. See also "PuR," p. 344; "Politik als Beruf" in *GpS* (hereafter cited as "PaB"), pp. 516–17; *WuG*, p. 667.

[29] *WuG*, p. 667. When an English translation of a quotation is available, I have usually used it as the basis of my translation. Often I have made substantial changes in the existing translation, and I shall do so without further indication.

[30] See, e.g., "PuR," p. 332.

[31] "Wahlrecht und Demokratie" in *GpS* (hereafter abbreviated as "WuD"), p. 258; "PuR," pp. 336, 392; "DkS," pp. 452–53; *WuG*, p. 610.

[32] See *WuG*, pp. 671–72.

[33] Michels served as a go-between, bringing Weber into touch with the ideas of Mosca and Pareto. Weber read and respected Mosca, but knew of Pareto only

classical ideals of democracy, Weber did not share the disillusionment of men such as Michels or Bryce. He simply integrated many of their findings into his own political thought.

Emphasizing the economic foundations of rule by a few, Weber revealed himself as strongly influenced by Marx, as well as by the German Historical School of Economics in which he had received his academic training. As long as economic inequalities existed—and Weber found no sign of their diminishing—the economically privileged would possess a disproportionate influence upon the formation of policy. Direct democratic administration, he argued, always fell into the hands of those with both the wealth and leisure for politics.[34] Most people were merely "occasional politicians." They were usually content to leave the management of politics to others.[35] Thus basically Weber did not recognize hereditary differences as decisive factors in differential participation in the exercise of power. The decisive factors were the products of an individual's socioeconomic position, and to Weber education and technical training assumed an increasingly important place as determinants of socioeconomic differentiation in modern society.[36]

His conception of society sometimes resembled the bipolar views of many late nineteenth-century elite theorists. He thought in terms of a "mass" which for political purposes remained largely undifferentiated. With popular exponents of "mass psychology" like Gustave Le Bon, he regarded men in larger groups as irrational. While Weber claimed to dismiss "mass rule" as an absurd impossibility, he still felt compelled to warn against its dangers: "The 'mass' as such (no matter which so-

---

indirectly. Robert Michels, *Bedeutende Männer* (Leipzig, 1927), pp. 113–14. Cf. the recent assessment of the intellectual relationship between Weber and Michels in Reinhard Bendix and Guenther Roth, *Scholarship and Partisanship: Essays on Max Weber* (Berkeley, 1971), pp. 246–52. On the whole, this collection of essays is disappointing.

[34] *WuG*, pp. 608–09.

[35] "PaB," pp. 500, 517.

[36] "WuD," p. 254; "PaB," pp. 508–09; *WuG*, p. 610. During the 1890's Weber assumed that inherited racial differences might play an important role in political and economic struggles (see, e.g., the second sentence in "Der Nationalstaat," p. 2). Although recognizing the anti-Socialist thrust involved in the work of bourgeois Social Darwinists like Otto Ammon, Weber suggested that their work deserved more scholarly attention than it had received (*ibid.*, p. 9 n. 1). Later Weber took a very skeptical view of the role of race in social and political development. See, e.g., his remarks at sessions of the *Deutsche Gesellschaft für Soziologie* devoted to the question of race in 1910 and 1912: *Schriften der Deutschen Gesellschaft für Soziologie*, Series 1: *Verhandlungen des . . . Deutschen Soziologentages . . .*, vol. 1 (Tübingen, 1911), pp. 151–64 and vol. 2 (Tübingen, 1913), pp. 50, 74, 188. While leaning over backward to dissociate the mature Weber from the taint of racism, Ernst Moritz Manasse discusses perceptively the development of Weber's attitudes toward race: "Max Weber on Race," *Social Research*, v (1947), 191–221.

cial strata comprise it) thinks only as far as tomorrow."[37] Most men, he argued, lacked the knowledge and techniques to participate actively in politics. Concluding some observations on the "fictitious concept of the popular will," he once complained: "It is as if one were to speak of a will of shoe consumers which should determine the technology of shoemaking! Of course the shoe consumers know where the shoe pinches, but they never know how it can be improved."[38]

The type of leaders in a society was of the utmost importance to Weber. He did not view leadership traits as identical throughout history. He stressed the importance of a society's institutions and social structure for the type of leadership which emerged: ". . . Every type of social order, without exception, must, if one wishes to *evaluate* it, be examined with reference to the opportunities which it affords to *certain types of persons* to rise to positions of superiority through the operation of the various objective and subjective selective factors."[39]

Weber held forth hope of a change in the type of leadership by altering the German political structure. But his pragmatic attitude toward political institutions as simply means for fostering leadership conflicted with some of his other attitudes. As a sociologist, he thought that the socioeconomic structure exerted a powerful influence on the type of leadership; as an observer of contemporary German politics, he tended to relegate socioeconomic structure to the background.[40] He retained much of the classical liberal's belief in the possibility of treating political institutions separately. Without any substantial alteration in the German social structure, through the modification of political institutions, he hoped to produce a new type of political leadership. He was interested primarily in changes, which by weakening the political and social power of the Junkers would permit the development of political institutions fully suited to an imperialistic nation-state.

A German Aristocracy?

Particularly in his earlier years, Weber had a readily discernible yearning for a new, politically mature and active "aristocracy." Although he never fully shared the "inferiority complex of the German

[37] "PuR," pp. 391–92.

[38] Letter of Apr. 8, 1908, to Robert Michels, a copy of which is in the Weber *Nachlass*. Quoted in Mommsen, *Max Weber*, pp. 892–93. See also "PaB," pp. 508–09.

[39] "Sinn der Wertfreiheit," pp. 479–80. The translation is that found in *Max Weber on the Methodology of the Social Sciences*, trans. and ed. E. A. Shils and H. A. Finch (Glencoe, Ill., 1949), p. 27. Weber's italics.

[40] See, e.g., "PuR," p. 238.

middle classes,"[41] he saw many advantages in a largely hereditary class to supply political leadership.

His attitude was linked to the disillusionment of many liberals in the latter half of the nineteenth century. During his youth and his student days, family connections brought him into contact with such discontented and pessimistic old liberals as the historians Theodor Mommsen and Hermann Baumgarten. Both Mommsen and Baumgarten had come to consider the tragic fault of German political life to lie in an absence of leaders and in the "political immaturity" of the nation. They dreamed of a special group of political leaders who would dedicate their lives to politics. Baumgarten had even decided that the "great tasks" of politics could only be solved by a nobility.[42] Weber never abandoned their idea of a special group of political leaders.

Viewing aristocracies as recurrent historical phenomena,[43] he predicted the rise of a nobility "in form, though probably not in fact" in the United States.[44] An aristocracy could, he felt, offer numerous advantages. A nation's "political sense" could be concentrated in an aristocracy, for in normal times the political instincts of the lower classes became unconscious: "At such times it is the specific function of the leading economic and political strata to act as the bearers of political consciousness—the *sole* political justification for their existence."[45]

With the English gentry and nobility in mind, Weber stressed that a "true" aristocracy might form an entire nation in accordance with its social ideals. Even the lowest classes could be attracted to this ideal and be molded by it. As a bearer of a political tradition, an aristocracy could never be surpassed. From its members one might expect calm, rational action. An aristocracy combined "the advantages of firm tradition and broad social horizons with the advantage of 'small numbers'" and could thus attain "highly valued political successes as the director of a state."[46]

Although Weber recognized the great power wielded by the Junkers,[47] they failed to measure up to his conception of a class capable of leading Germany. Agricultural income, which he regarded as the

[41] The phrase is that of Heinz Gollwitzer, *Die Standesherren: Die politische und gesellschaftliche Stellung der Mediatisierten 1815–1918: Ein Beitrag zur deutschen Sozialgeschichte* (Stuttgart, 1957), p. 334.

[42] *Ibid.*, pp. 333–34; Mommsen, *Max Weber*, pp. 12–13.

[43] See esp. "Zur Lage der bürgerlichen Demokratie in Russland" in *GpS*, p. 60.

[44] "Capitalism and Rural Society" in Gerth and Mills, p. 383.

[45] "Der Nationalstaat," p. 19. Weber's italics.

[46] "WuD," p. 258. See also pp. 265, 270; and *WuG*, p. 600.

[47] See, e.g., his *Die Verhältnisse der Landarbeiter im ostelbischen Deutschland, Schriften des Vereins für Sozialpolitik*, LV (Berlin, 1892), p. 796; his *Referat* "Über die deutschen Landarbeiter" in *Verhandlungen des 5. evangelisch-sozialen Kongresses* (Berlin, 1894), p. 70; "Capitalism and Rural Society," p. 373; "PuR," pp. 329–30, 400.

economic basis of every true aristocracy, had decreased markedly.[48] In order to furnish effective political leadership, an aristocracy, he argued, had to possess "unearned income." Its members needed leisure to engage in politics. They had to be able to devote their lives to politics, rather than living simply "from" the state. The Junkers, on the other hand, could be maintained as a class only by economic subventions from the state.[49] The solution of Germany's present political "tasks" could not depend upon the Junkers.[50] As early as 1895, he warned: "It is dangerous and in the long run incompatible with the interests of the nation when an economically descending class retains political domination in its hands."[51] Throughout most of his life, he waged a public battle against economic policies favoring the Junkers.

Weber could never have been satisfied with the domination of Germany by individuals closely linked to agrarian interests. The economic position of the Junkers did not lead them to favor imperialism. Almost as serious was the importation of Slavic agricultural laborers by the Junkers. He feared that the eastern provinces of Prussia were undergoing de-Germanization.[52] To protest the Pan-German League's support for the use of foreign workers in the eastern provinces, he renounced his membership in it. He desired a strong German agriculture, but he believed that it could be best maintained by small, landholding peasants.[53] Germany's future lay, he felt, in industrialization that would supply the economic underpinning for world politics.

He also deplored the failure of the Junkers to provide social forms suitable to mold the whole of German society. Without employing the term itself, Weber bemoaned the "feudalization" of the German bourgeoisie. Attempts to imitate the nobility angered him. Despite his own social background, he saw little hope in direct political rule by the bourgeoisie. The bourgeois had not asserted his independence from the nobleman, and the former's fear of Social Democrats Weber found reprehensible. He repeated his warning about the relationship between

[48] "Capitalism and Rural Society," p. 369; "WuD," p. 265.
[49] See Weber's reply to the critics of his *Referat* "Über die deutschen Landarbeiter" in *Verhandlungen des 5. evangelisch-sozialen Kongresses*, p. 92; "Capitalism and Rural Society," p. 369; "WuD," p. 260.
[50] "Der Nationalstaat," p. 19. Weber's frequent use of terms like "tasks [*Aufgaben*]" introduced transcendental imperatives stemming primarily from his nationalism and imperialism.
[51] "Der Nationalstaat," p. 19. See also "WuD," p. 265.
[52] See, e.g., *Die Verhältnisse der Landarbeiter im ostelbischen Deutschland*, p. 795; Weber's *Referat* "Über die ländliche Arbeitsverfassung" in *Verhandlungen des Vereins für Sozialpolitik, Schriften des Vereins für Sozialpolitik*, LVIII (Leipzig, 1893), p. 73.
[53] In this respect Weber maintained a life-long devotion to the ideals of Georg Knapp's school of economics. See, e.g., Weber's *Referat* "Über die deutschen Landarbeiter" in *Verhandlungen des 5. evangelisch-sozialen Kongresses*, pp. 78–79.

economic and political power by referring to the dangers encountered when "classes, to which economic power is accruing and which thus become candidates for political rule, are not yet politically mature enough for the leadership of the state."[54]

German workers also failed to meet his stringent demands. They were more immature than the bourgeoisie and the middle class. The workers lacked "the highly developed instincts for power of a class summoned to political leadership."[55] Basically, he did not trust them to pursue an active policy of imperialism. He compared them unfavorably with British workers, who, as citizens of a great imperial power, had become accustomed to thinking in terms of world politics.[56]

No single social class could provide the leadership he sought. His basic assumptions, his own background, and his strongest sensibilities prompted him to regard the bourgeoisie as the class that should be ruling Germany.[57] Although convinced during the 1890's that the basic domestic choice was between the large agrarians and the bourgeoisie, he did not believe that the German bourgeoisie was capable of supplying enough satisfactory political leaders. He found few militant and capable anti-Junker bourgeois. Much of the haute bourgeoisie had permitted itself to be "feudalized," and the remainder of the bourgeoisie was hopelessly provincial and narrow-minded. In 1894 Weber asserted:

> The greatest danger to our political life in Germany is that we fall under the rule of philistines, the petty bourgeoisie. And the typical traits of the philistine—the lack of developed instincts for national power, the limitation of political endeavors to material goals or even the interests of one's own generation, the lack of any consciousness of the measure of responsibility vis-à-vis our heirs—that is what also continues to divide us from the Social Democratic movement. It [the Social Democratic movement], too, is in large part a product of German philistinism.[58]

He hoped that the bourgeoisie would be able to enlist the support of a working class fully integrated into German society, but his disappointment over the inadequacies of the bourgeoisie often brought him

---

[54] "Der Nationalstaat," p. 19. See also *Verhältnisse der Landarbeiter im ostelbischen Deutschland*, p. 776; Weber's comments on Karl Oldenberg's *Referat* "Über Deutschland als Industriestaat" in *Verhandlungen des 8. evangelisch-sozialen Kongresses* (Göttingen, 1897), p. 110; "WuD," pp. 270–72; "PuR," p. 429.

[55] "Der Nationalstaat," p. 22.

[56] *Ibid.*, p. 23.

[57] During the 1890's Weber often made a point of referring to himself publicly as a bourgeois. See, e.g., "Über die deutschen Landarbeiter" in *Verhandlungen des 5. evangelisch-sozialen Kongresses*, p. 77; "Der Nationalstaat," p. 20.

[58] "Über die deutschen Landarbeiter," p. 81.

to despair. He grew increasingly skeptical about its political potentialities. To satisfy him, any future elite would have to draw upon all social classes. He always assumed that it would recruit most heavily from the bourgeoisie and the middle class, once the bourgeoisie had asserted its independence from the Junkers. Crucial to Weber was neither a prospective leader's social origins nor his present position in society, but the framing of policies to promote the national state and German imperialism.

BUREAUCRACY—THE IDEAL ELITE?

What of the state bureaucracy? Could not it supply the leadership which Weber sought? In many respects it would have seemed so. A bureaucratic administration offered, he believed, numerous advantages as a method of exercising governmental authority: "If a technically flawless administration, a precise and exact solution of concrete problems, is taken as the highest and only goal, then one can only say to hell with everything except a hierarchy of bureaucrats. . . ."[59]

Weber devoted much of his sociology to a theoretical analysis of bureaucracy. Basing his analysis largely, if by no means exclusively, upon his knowledge of the Prussian bureaucracy, he abstracted certain elements from reality and developed them into a logically precise concept —into one of his famous "ideal types."[60] To Weber bureaucracy denoted an organization characterized by a more or less firmly ordered system of superordination. Each unit or individual in the system supervised a lower unit or individual, which in turn supervised the one below it. Each unit had fixed jurisdictional areas ordered by rules for which it was responsible and the limits of which it could not exceed. The organization conducted its affairs on the basis of written documents and kept extensive records.

In Weber's "ideal type," bureaucratic officials were freely selected on the basis of their technical qualifications. The bureaucrat received certain rights in exchange, so to speak, for his loyalty. He could resign, but normally he could not be dismissed. He had the opportunity to advance in the hierarchy and to receive salary increases in accordance with a fixed pattern. His obedience was impersonal. He obeyed rules and commands simply because they were rules or commands. Similarly, the people outside the bureaucracy obeyed it in an impersonal manner. They obeyed "the law," not an individual.

Weber attributed the superiority of bureaucratic administration primarily to its capacity to store and utilize information. The compil-

[59] "Diskussionsrede" at the Verein für Sozialpolitik in 1909 (hereafter cited as "Diskussionsrede" 1909) in GAzSuSp, p. 413.
[60] See esp. WuG, pp.124–28, 650–55.

ing of written records furnished means for ruling a society on the basis of knowledge. Bureaucracy provided, Weber believed, the most rational form of administration known to man. Bureaucracy could operate in a uniform manner without regard for personal matters and with the lowest possible material and personnel costs.

Weber's conception of the superiority of bureaucracy revealed a strong faith in the efficacy of hierarchy. Like Germans of almost every political point of view, he was profoundly impressed by the methods and accomplishments of the Prussian-German administration and army. Despite many reservations, he admired their discipline and effectiveness. As a young officer's candidate, he had complained about the "incredible waste of time required to domesticate thinking beings into machines responding to commands with automatic precision." But he found himself admitting that the human body worked more precisely when all thinking was eliminated.[61] The state socialism of the "Socialists of the chair," with whom he had many contacts, rested upon the assumption of the advantages of a hierarchic administration. His general assessment of the importance of bureaucracy agreed with the bureaucratic elite theorists.

Because of its technical superiorities, bureaucratic organization became, he believed, increasingly important in the modern world. For the daily management of government and everyday administration, no nation could afford to do without a bureaucracy. "Dilettantism" was the only alternative he could envision.[62] He assumed that the pursuit of an imperialistic German foreign policy depended upon a highly developed bureaucracy. He even discerned a direct relationship between the capacity of a state to expand and the degree of its bureaucratization.[63] The outward form of a country's government made little difference. Only a tiny democracy had a choice between "self-government administered by local notables and bureaucratization."[64] Bureaucracy manifested an inherent tendency to expand, and once established, it assumed a high degree of permanence.[65] Bureaucracy was triumphing over all other forms of organization.

Weber had two basic reservations about the Prussian-German civil service, both of which affected his assessment of the role of any bureaucratic organization. The significance of the first reservation has usually been overlooked by students of Weber's thought. He disliked

[61] Letter quoted in Marianne Weber, *Max Weber*, p. 77.
[62] "PaB," pp. 508–09; "PuR," p. 308. See also *WuG*, p. 128.
[63] See *WuG*, p. 659.
[64] *WuG*, p. 666. See also "Der Sozialismus" in *GAzSuSp*, pp. 494–97.
[65] "PuR," p. 320; "Agrarverhältnisse im Altertum" in *Gesammelte Aufsätze zur Sozial- und Wirtschaftsgeschichte* (Tübingen, 1924), pp. 277–78; *WuG*, pp. 669–70.

the preference given to Junkers in the recruitment of the Prussian-German civil service and its framing of policies acceptable to the Junkers whose influence might be reduced by recruiting fewer of them or by restricting the prerogatives of the bureaucracy. Increasingly, Weber inclined toward the latter solution, perhaps because he grew pessimistic about the possibility of limiting drastically the recruitment of Junkers and because he realized that the crucial question was not who occupied state offices, but in whose interest policies were framed. The relationship between the Junkers and the state bureaucracy helped to feed if not initiate Weber's more general misgivings about bureaucracy.

He identified the extension of bureaucracy with broader tendencies at work in modern society. For Weber bureaucratization constituted simply one aspect of a larger process, rationalization, which was affecting almost every aspect of modern life. Science and the scientific method, systematization, specialization, and standardization had become predominant.[66] Even music, art, and religion had undergone rationalization. Rational, logical explanations had removed the mystery from life. Capitalism, itself partly an outgrowth of forces other than those of rationalization, was becoming more and more highly rationalized as it refined the techniques of economic calculation.

Despite his fundamental commitment to rationalization, Weber viewed its advance with suspicion.[67] He dreaded the thought of a world filled with "little cogs," "little men clinging to little jobs and striving for bigger ones."[68] His commitment to the liberal ideal of the free development of the individual's personality made him fear rationalization and its accompanying bureaucratization. Implicitly, he evaluated rationalization by a standard that appeared to him as its opposite—the freedom of an individual to make his own decisions and to act accordingly. He hoped to provide a few policy makers with some of the freedom which presumably all men had once possessed. Indirectly, he added another argument for his "principle of small numbers."

His own conception of rationality also cast doubts upon many consequences of rationalization. For Weber the highest form of rationality consisted in "purposive rationality [*Zweckrationalität*]." Purposive rationality involved a choice among several ends and the selection of

[66] See esp. *The Protestant Ethic and the Spirit of Capitalism*, trans. Talcott Parsons (New York: Scribner's paperback, 1958), pp. 13–14, and "Die bürgerliche Demokratie in Russland," p. 61.

[67] My analysis of Weber's attitude toward rationalization has benefited greatly from Karl Löwith, "Max Weber und Karl Marx," *Archiv für Sozialwissenschaft und Sozialpolitik*, LXVII (1932), esp. 77–96.

[68] "Diskussionsrede" 1909, p. 414.

means suited to the attainment of the selected end. In choosing between ends, the individual had to consider the availability of appropriate means. Someone whose actions could be viewed as purposively
rational would not therefore commit himself to a goal incapable of
realization.

Weber contrasted purposive rationality with "rational orientation to
an absolute value [*Wertrationalität*]."[69] In the choice of means, the
practitioner of *Wertrationalität* proceeded in much the same way as
the practitioner of purposive rationality. The difference lay in the failure of the former to choose among ends. An absolute value was
adopted without considering its chances of realization. From the
standpoint of purposive rationality, *Wertrationalität* was irrational.
The more an absolute value was stressed, the less the consequences of
actions to achieve it were weighed.[70]

In the process of rationalization, Weber discerned a reversal of ends
and means which horrified him. Rationalization, which should have
been simply the means to an end, had become an end in itself. Instead
of creating conditions permitting men more choice, it had restricted
the area of freedom. The institutions and practices of modern civilization had become so rationalized that they determined the men who
had constructed them. Rationalization had engendered frightening
new forms of irrationality. In the secularization of the "Protestant
ethic," Weber discovered one of the clearest examples of the inversion
of means and ends. The acquisition of more and more money had become an end in itself rather than a way of serving God. Capitalism had
once been a light cloak which the "saint" could throw aside at any
time, "but fate decreed that the cloak should become an iron cage."[71]
Similarly, bureaucracy had become an "iron cage."

To Weber the problem of bureaucratization was not how one could
halt it. That was impossible. Bureaucratization had become an irre-
versible historical process. The real problem consisted in determining
the undesirable results of bureaucratization and devising suitable
means to combat them. His skepticism about bureaucracy was held in
check by his belief that both modern capitalism and the modern state
required large bureaucratic apparatuses in order to function properly.
In order to maintain a sphere of freedom, Weber sanctioned diametri-
cally opposed forces. Although he personally felt that purposive rationality represented the most rational and desirable form of action,
he could still admire *Wertrationalität*. At times *Wertrationalität* could
act as a counterweight to bureaucratization: "In a sense, successful po-

[69] I have employed Talcott Parsons' translation of the term.
[70] *WuG*, pp. 12–13.
[71] *The Protestant Ethic*, pp. 181, 182.

litical action is always the 'art of the possible.' Nonetheless, the possible is often reached only by striving to attain the impossible that lies beyond it."[72]

Weber rejected bureaucratic elite theories that assigned to the state bureaucracy the role of the most important elite in society. German society had, he felt, succumbed to many of the most unhealthy aspects of bureaucratization. As usual he was particularly critical of the bourgeoisie. The antagonism between bourgeois and worker, together with the resulting "cowardice" of the former toward democracy, had strengthened the bureaucratic domination of Germany.[73]

In the political rule of bureaucrats, Weber found the main source of German political failures. No monarch by himself could control a modern bureaucracy. Even if it were possible, William II was particularly unsuited for the task. The superiority of the bureaucracy over the emperor rested upon its specialized knowledge and its familiarity with administrative affairs. The emperor could interfere and attempt to control the bureaucracy, but only as a "dilettante." Germany swung from "dilettantism," when William II intervened in the bureaucracy, to complete bureaucratic domination, when he did not intervene. The resulting instability, Weber was convinced, had prevented Germany from pursuing a "realistic" foreign policy. Effective world politics had been impossible. The German system enabled a good bureaucrat without any talent as a political leader to possess a high political office, until some intrigue led to his replacement by another bureaucrat. The emperor and the bureaucracy could cover up their errors by hiding behind each other.[74]

Unlike the bureaucratic elite theorists, Weber made a sharp theoretical distinction between the bureaucrat and the political leader or politician. The ideal administrator performed his functions without scorn or bias (*sine ira et studio*). His task consisted in administering impartially in conformity to definite rules. His honor rested upon self-denial and complete obedience to his superior. The bureaucrat had to execute orders as if they agreed with his own convictions. He could protest or even resign, but as long as he remained at his post, he had to obey.[75]

Although this image of the bureaucrat agreed in large part with that

[72] "Sinn der 'Wertfreiheit,' " p. 476. The translation is that of Shils and Finch in *Max Weber on the Methodology of the Social Sciences*, pp. 23–24.

[73] "Diskussionsrede" at the Verein für Sozialpolitik in 1905 in *GAzSuSp*, pp. 395–96; "Zur Lage der bürgerlichen Demokratie," p. 61; "Agrarverhältnisse im Altertum," p. 278; "Diskussionsrede" 1909, p. 414; "WuD," p. 233.

[74] "PuR," pp. 240, 325–26, 308, 366–67; Letter of Nov. 12, 1908, to Friedrich Naumann, p. 456; Letter of Apr. 16, 1917, to Prof. Hans Ehrenberg, pp. 469–70.

[75] "PaB," p. 512; "PuR," p. 323.

of the bureaucratic elite theorists, Weber did not share the conclusions that they drew from it. To him the bureaucrat was hardly a sacrosanct individual to be contrasted with an inferior politician. As long as the bureaucrat remained in his proper sphere, Weber did not object. The bureaucratic type had its place. But since the departure of Bismarck, Weber never tired of repeating, Germany had been ruled by bureaucrats. Bismarck had promoted the bureaucratic type of docile obedience in order to secure the execution of his policies. Now, with Bismarck gone, the bureaucrats had taken over the government. They occupied what should be *political*, not bureaucratic offices.[76] Weber denounced the prevailing German practice of placing a bureaucrat at the head of a bureaucracy. A minister or secretary of state needed political skills that most bureaucrats had not acquired. Every bureaucracy should, Weber urged, be commanded by a nonbureaucrat—or at least by a bureaucrat with political talents foreign to most bureaucrats.[77]

He never proposed any concrete plans to broaden the social basis from which the bureaucracy recruited its members. He simply noted some of the ways in which the recruitment policies favored the wealthy. Largely in the interests of efficiency, he desired to minimize the tendency toward bureaucratic exclusiveness. He found some utility in the ideology of democracy when it worked against legal inequalities and against a caste of officials.[78] Although previous German experiences with bureaucracy certainly could give him little cause for optimism, he hoped that egalitarian sentiments might combat some of the less desirable consequences of bureaucratization. But he did not rely upon what he regarded as the quixotic attitudes of unrealistic democrats.

Weber wanted to retain a highly organized bureaucracy, but only as an efficient tool of government. The integrity and efficiency of officialdom in Germany were, he contended, unsurpassed anywhere else in the world;[79] any attempt to dispense with the mechanism of bureaucracy would lead to "dilettantism."[80] He rejected any suggestion of the popular election of administrative officials. The official appointed by a chief normally functioned more exactly and efficiently since purely functional considerations and personal qualifications would be more likely to determine his career. For Weber American

[76] See, e.g., "Bismarcks Erbe in der Reichsverfassung" in *GpS*, p. 232; "PuR," p. 323; "WuD," p. 233.

[77] See *WuG*, p. 127.

[78] See "Sozialismus," p. 494; *WuG*, pp. 666–67.

[79] "Diskussionsrede" 1909, pp. 415–16; "PaB," p. 529.

[80] See his letter published in the *Frankfurter Zeitung* of Apr. 14, 1919 (1st ed. of *GpS*, p. 486). See also *WuG*, p. 128.

experiences with the election of administrative officials had proved highly unsatisfactory.[81] Popular election disrupted the bureaucratic mechanism and weakened the hierarchic principle. Bureaucracy had to be controlled from without, but only from the top and by political leaders. The bureaucrat's area of competence did not extend beyond providing advice. Someone else had to make the important decisions.

For Weber the bureaucracy's primary functions should consist in the conduct of routine administration, the collection and evaluation of information, and the execution of decisions made by political leaders. The central question of German politics was, then, how to get the proper type of political leaders into positions from which they could control the state bureaucracy.

THE ROLE OF PARLIAMENT

During most of his life, Weber believed that increasing the power of Germany's parliamentary institutions would reduce the power of the bureaucracy and mitigate the nation's leadership problems. Although he perceived that the core of his solution required changes in the political structure of Prussia, by World War I his hopes of beginning there had faded. He began to concentrate most of his energies on reforming the Empire. Prussia would, he believed, be forced to follow.

As long as the Hohenzollerns remained, he advocated a greatly strengthened Reichstag.[82] A strong Reichstag and a strong Prussian House of Representatives could, he predicted, act as counterweights to bureaucracy and supply a reservoir of trained and experienced political leaders to hold the highest political posts. Where a hereditary monarch occupied a position as the formal head of a bureaucracy, a vigorous parliament was a necessity.[83]

Weber demanded parliamentary powers of investigation. To aid in controlling the bureaucracy, the Reichstag needed the right to examine the workings of the latter.[84] Indeed, Weber's demand was eventually adopted in the Weimar Constitution. In the liberal tradition, he viewed the budgetary powers of parliament as decisive.[85] Yet he hesitated before the full consequences of a parliamentary system modeled on England's.[86] His overestimation of the powers of the English mon-

---

[81] "DkS," p. 466; WuG, pp. 653–54; "PuR," pp. 337, 386.

[82] In 1917–1918 Weber developed plans for the conversion of the Federal Council (Bundesrat) into a parliamentary body that would adequately express the powers of the states comprising the Empire, but both then and in 1919 developments passed by all such plans. See Mommsen, Max Weber, pp. 190–92.

[83] "WuD," p. 277.   [84] "PuR," pp. 343, 428.   [85] "PuR," p. 327.

[86] See Mommsen, Max Weber, pp. 196–200.

arch confirmed his distaste for a monarch who would be a figurehead. He also saw no signs of a two-party system developing in Germany, and he rejected as unstable the French system of combining a weak head of state with a multiparty system. His primary recommendation was that the chancellor and secretaries of state be made more dependent upon the Reichstag. The emperor would still have the right to appoint them. Either they should be chosen from the Reichstag, or their continuance in office should depend upon the maintenance of parliamentary confidence.[87] Presumably the emperor would then have to consider the composition of the Reichstag very carefully and appoint a member of a strong party to the chancellorship.

If the Reichstag had more than semifictitious powers, Weber expected better leaders to emerge from it. Because German parliamentary institutions were weak and lacked popular respect, they did not, he asserted, attract potential political leaders. Such men went instead into private business.[88] The prospect of "real power" in exercising control over the bureaucracy and in the opportunity for men to become ministers while retaining their seats in the Reichstag would attract and develop capable leaders. The party struggles within the Reichstag would provide excellent leadership training and ensure a constant supply of able leaders to fill the top governmental posts. Men trained in a powerful Reichstag would learn how to make themselves masters of the bureaucracy and use it as a tool. Even then patience would be necessary; the Reichstag had been virtually powerless for so long that leaders could not be expected to appear in it overnight.[89]

The Characteristics of Political Leaders

With Nietzsche's phrase, Weber referred to the "will to power" as the most essential drive animating the political leader. Both the bureaucrat and the political leader had a well-developed desire for power. But whereas the bureaucrat might desire power, a strong "instinct for power" was essential to the effective political leader. The political leader strove egoistically for power and patronage for himself and his followers. Only party and parliamentary struggles focused upon winning political offices would bring to the fore the kind of leader who had a strong instinct for power.[90]

To Weber, politics consisted essentially in striving to share power and to participate in its distribution, for "he who is active in politics

[87] "PuR," pp. 328, 356; Letter of June 16, 1917, to Prof. E. J. Lesser, p. 473.
[88] "PuR," pp. 334-35.
[89] Letter of June 16, 1917, to Prof. E. J. Lesser, p. 473; "PuR," pp. 328-29, 356, 428; "Kanzlerkrisis," p. 213.
[90] "PuR," pp. 329, 338.

strives for power either as a means of serving other aims, ideal or egoistic, or as 'power for power's sake,' that is, to enjoy the feeling of prestige that power gives."[91] Every political struggle was an implicit struggle for personal power, as well as a struggle for "essential differences."[92] Among the rewards of politics was the satisfaction derived from a feeling of power, from "the knowledge of influencing men, of participating in power over them, and above all, the feeling of holding in one's hands a nerve fiber of historically important events."[93]

Weber's earlier desire for an aristocracy was expressed in his concern for a special group of professional political leaders. He wanted political leaders who would devote all of their energies to political activity. Politics should be the center of the political leader's existence: "He who lives 'for' politics makes politics his life in an internal sense. Either he enjoys the naked possession of the power that he exerts, or else he nourishes his inner balance and his feeling of self-reliance from the consciousness that his life has *meaning* in the service of a 'cause.' "[94]

One of the preconditions to living "for" politics consisted in a secure economic existence which permitted a man to devote his full working days to politics. Weber preferred the man of independent economic means to the individual who had to derive the bulk of his income from politics. Only the man of independent means could become a political leader "on a grand style."[95] Weber realized that his emphasis upon men who lived "for" politics involved a "plutocratic recruitment" of political leaders. Of course, if the political leader really lived "for" politics, the extent to which he lived "from" politics had relatively little significance. But Weber justified his emphasis upon economic independence by arguing that the advantages outweighed the disadvantages. The individual of means was far less likely to be greedy than the one without income or property: "All the preaching in the world cannot change the fact that 'political character' is cheaper for a wealthy man."[96]

This last statement reveals how strongly Weber clung to the desire to recruit the political elite largely from the bourgeoisie and from *grand seigneurs* among the nobility. He could not conceive of an upheaval in Germany in which men without money might have more "political character" than those with money. He looked for socially secure men who could calmly formulate policy without calculating directly

[91] "PaB," p. 495. For a recent criticism of Weber's conception of politics, see Wilhelm Hennis, "Zum Problem der deutschen Staatsanschauung," *Vierteljahreshefte für Zeitgeschichte*, vii (1959), 19–22.
[92] "PuR," p. 328. [93] "PaB," p. 533.
[94] "PaB," p. 501. Weber's italics. [95] "PuR," p. 352.
[96] "WuD," p. 263.

their own immediate interest in these policies and without feeling threatened from below. As Wolfgang Mommsen has pointed out, Weber was unwilling fully to accept the logical consequences of his own argument that the character of parliamentary bodies changed with the replacement of parties of notables by mass parties.[97]

Because the private practice of law permitted an individual to devote most of his energies to politics, Weber called for a larger proportion of lawyers in German political life.[98] Impressed by the large numbers of politically active lawyers in Western Europe and America, he valued a legal practice as an education for politics. Unlike the business executive or industrialist, the lawyer could place the burden of his work upon the shoulders of subordinates. The lawyer's constant presence in his office was not essential to the operation of his firm. He could still derive an income from his profession. His legal staff could double as the political staff which a modern politician needed. Moreover, the lawyer's training in verbal battles provided an excellent apprenticeship for political activity.[99]

Unlike most German scholars, Weber also respected journalists. He commended them for their sense of responsibility and their familiarity with a wide range of problems. He would have welcomed more active participation in politics by journalists. But for the present, as well as the immediate future, he foresaw few possibilities for them to participate except in the Social Democratic party. The need to write frequent articles was like "lead" on the journalist's feet. His profession did not allow him sufficient time to engage in active politics.[100]

Weber's hope to see more lawyers and journalists become parliamentary deputies is somewhat perplexing. For he assumed that in Germany, as compared to the West, few deputies came from these professions. Subsequent studies have demonstrated a trend after 1890 toward more Reichstag deputies from both professions.[101] Also, although

[97] Mommsen, *Max Weber*, p. 202.
[98] See "PaB," pp. 501–02; "PuR," pp. 376–77, 351–52.
[99] "WuD," pp. 260–61; "PaB," pp. 511–12.
[100] See "PaB," pp. 513–16.
[101] See Günther Franz, "Der Parlamentarismus" in *Führungsschicht und Eliteproblem, Jahrbuch der Rankegesellschaft*, III (Frankfurt am Main, 1957), pp. 87–88; Karl Demeter, "Die soziale Schichtung des deutschen Parlaments seit 1848: Ein Spiegelbild der Strukturwandlung des Volkes," *Vierteljahrschrift für Sozial- und Wirtschaftsgeschichte*, XXIX (1952), 14–16; Peter Molt, *Der Reichstag vor der improvisierten Revolution* (Cologne, 1963), pp. 40–41, 176–82. The statement by James J. Sheehan, "Political Leadership in the German *Reichstag*, 1871–1918," *American Historical Review*, LXXIV (1968), 520, that the proportion of lawyers remained roughly the same during the period covered by his review article is highly misleading. During the 1870's and 1880's the proportion fell markedly, but thereafter it rose markedly. By 1913 it had almost reached the level of 1871 (see Demeter, pp. 14–15). More important, we can probably assume that whereas the

extensive comparative research on the occupations of members of parliamentary bodies is sorely needed, the low status of journalists appears, contrary to Weber's assertions, to have been common elsewhere on the Continent except in France.[102] Perhaps Weber's desire for lawyers and journalists stemmed more directly than is readily discernible from his search for more politicians from the bourgeoisie and, if necessary, from the upper strata of the middle class. Similarly, his preference for lawyers over journalists may have been largely a function of the size in Germany of the Social Democratic press, which, although promoting the *embourgeoisement* of the staffs and harboring reformists, provided employment for many a radical.

There was little place for effective popular control in Weber's conception of leadership. After becoming "impassioned" and taking a stand, the political leader had to assume exclusive personal responsibility for his decisions and actions. Without rejecting or passing on responsibility, as the bureaucrat could, the political leader had to act according to his own judgment. The bureaucrat had to answer to a master; once in office, the political leader should have to answer to no one except himself. The only time an elected leader should have to answer to his electorate was at election time.

Unlike most German liberals, Weber fully accepted universal suffrage.[103] Even though he did not consider popular elections as an important factor in selecting or controlling the members of elites, he endorsed universal suffrage for elections to German parliaments.[104] A sense of participation in the selection of political leaders would, he thought, be an educational experience for the average German. Political immaturity ensued from the effects of uncontrolled bureaucratic domination, for the citizen felt no sense of personal responsibility for the acts of his governors.[105] If the populace felt responsible for choosing its leaders, it would follow them more willingly and energetically. Thus Weber considered formal participation of most citizens in some stages in the selection of political leaders as the most important char-

---

lawyer serving as a Reichstag deputy in 1871 was a local notable, the lawyer serving as a Reichstag deputy in 1913 was likely to be an employee of a business association or a man active in the local organization of a party.

[102] See Eugene N. and Pauline R. Anderson, *Political Institutions and Social Change in Continental Europe in the Nineteenth Century* (Berkeley, 1967), p. 383.

[103] In his writings he failed to distinguish between male suffrage and universal suffrage; but from our knowledge of his personal life, it hardly seems possible that he objected to female suffrage. His wife was an active feminist. In this endeavor she seems to have had his full support. Although he never held an elective office, she was elected to the Baden parliament in 1919. See Marianne Weber, *Lebenserinnerungen* (Bremen, 1948), pp. 82–83.

[104] "WuD," p. 254.   [105] "PuR," p. 429.

acteristic of modern democracies. The existence of democracy altered "only the way in which the executive leaders are selected and the measure of influence which the *demos,* or better, which groups of people from its midst, are able to exert upon the content and direction of administrative activities by supplementing what is called 'public opinion.' "[106]

Weber rejected any attempt, whether by referendum or recall, to bind the representative to the "expressed or presumed" "will of the electors."[107] The leader, during his tenure of office, should act entirely according to his own judgment. He should not act as if he had received any sort of specific mandate. Similarly, a political leader who was appointed instead of elected should act according to his own judgment. If he were bound to specific, unalterable instructions, he could not compromise. He should be free to bargain and to make compromises.[108]

The actions of the political leader, Weber insisted, should be guided by an "ethic of responsibility," not by an "ethic of conscience."[109] The basis of this contrast lay in Weber's distinction between purposive rationality and *Wertrationalität.* The political leader had to give himself the opportunity to choose among several goals, assess the probable results, decide upon a desirable one capable of realization, and then implement it. The effective political leader could not accept a goal solely on faith and proceed to implement it regardless of the consequences. The practitioner of an ethic of responsibility had to realize that evil could result from good and good from evil.[110] He had to take the means *and* their consequences into consideration.

Weber's political leader was largely immune to popular pressures. Checked at first by internal restraints, he was restrained externally by bureaucracy and by competition from other political leaders. Weber wanted leaders chosen upon the basis of personal qualities, and not because of their adherence to definite programs.

The final element in his conception of the ideal political leader reinforced the image of a highly independent leader. First applied in his studies in the sociology of religion at the beginning of the twentieth century, "charisma" denoted for Weber a peculiar, partly inexplicable element in the personalities of some religious leaders that attracted followers who gave their allegiance primarily to a person, not to his

[106] *WuG,* p. 667.

[107] *WuG,* pp. 766–67; "Die drei reinen Typen der legitimen Herrschaft," *Preussische Jahrbücher,* clxxxvii (1922), 12; "PuR," p. 323; "DkS," pp. 462–63.

[108] "PaB," pp. 512, 535–42; "PuR," pp. 323, 365–66, 410, 412; "DkS," pp. 462–63; *WuG,* pp. 766–67; "Die drei reinen Typen der legitimen Herrschaft," p. 12.

[109] "PaB," pp. 536–42.   [110] "PaB," pp. 541–42.

ideas or goals.[111] In his political writings, Weber usually employed "plebiscitarian" or "caesaristic" to indicate the secularized and diluted type of charisma which he found in modern political life.

Weber's ideal of the highest type of political leader was that of a man recognized by his followers as an "innerly called leader of men." Some quality of the leader's personality exercised an almost irresistible attraction upon his followers: "Men do not obey him by virtue of tradition or statute, but because they believe in him. The devotion of his followers is oriented toward his person and its qualities."[112] Weber constructed the political leader on the model of a Hebrew prophet who flayed the people, but because he was endowed with exceptional virtues was still accepted as their chief.[113]

Weber tended to view modern history largely as the product of the conflicting forces of charisma and bureaucratization. At present, charisma had generally receded into the background, or been "castrated," as he was wont to say. Charisma inevitably became "routinized." It became submerged, but he considered a reassertion of charisma essential. He regarded charisma as the "specifically 'creative' power in history."[114] Bureaucracy simply transformed society from without; charisma harnessed tremendous emotional forces and transformed society from within. Bureaucratic order merely replaced the belief in tradition by substituting other types of rules; the highest forms of charisma shattered all rules and traditions. Charisma compelled the inner subordination of men to a vision of "what's not yet been," the absolutely unique.[115]

Through the concept of charisma, Weber applied to his ideal leader criteria of behavior similar to those of the "ethic of conscience" of which he was so critical. In order to accomplish an objective, a leader often had to pursue a goal far beyond it—a goal that was actually unattainable. Believing that all political leadership contained some charismatic elements, Weber wished to strengthen them, and thereby prevent total bureaucratization. He assigned a positive function to ac-

[111] Weber originally took over the expression from his and Naumann's friend the church historian Rudolf Sohm. The term, often employed by sociologists and other scholars who claim to follow Weber's usage, has become fashionable in broad circles in the United States. For some telling arguments against the usefulness of Weber's concept see Carl J. Friedrich, "Political Leadership and the Problem of Charismatic Power," *Journal of Politics*, xxiii (1961), 15–16.

[112] "PaB," pp. 495–96.

[113] Raymond Aron, *German Sociology*, trans. Mary and Thomas Bottomore (Glencoe, Ill., 1957), p. 90. As Aron and others have pointed out, Weber was strongly drawn to the Hebrew prophets, whom in many respects he would have liked to imitate.

[114] *WuG*, p. 759.

[115] *WuG*, pp. 758–59.

tions which, from his own standpoint, were nonrational. Leaders with sufficient charisma could mobilize the social forces necessary to achieve the objectives he had set for German policies.

In the concept of charisma, Weber found a way of enlisting people for aims to which they would not otherwise be attracted. Charisma assisted the leader in manipulating the populace, in imposing upon it objectives that would be unpalatable without charismatic appeal. The concept of charisma may have been so attractive to Weber because it offered a way of avoiding, when one wished to do so, the classic question *cui bono*—whose interests are served by the leaders' policies? A leader with charisma could ignore Socialist criticisms of the irrationality of bourgeois society and of proletarian support for imperialism. Charisma could veil the existence of social conflicts that prevented agreement on policy objectives.

Despite his essentially institutional approach to leadership and his belief in the possibility of training leaders through political institutions, Weber's concern for a charismatic element in leadership entailed emphasis upon inherent, unacquirable personal characteristics. Weber could speak of "born leaders."[116] His charismatic leader possessed an undefinable set of personality traits which an individual could not acquire simply through political activities. Weber thus continued one of the prevalent themes in earlier German elite theories. Similarly, political leadership remained for him a highly specialized function. He did not indicate that charisma was to be found largely or entirely in one class or stratum. He welcomed charisma, wherever it originated, if he found the possessor of it useful, but clearly he expected charisma to appear most frequently among those who could afford to live "for" rather than "from" politics.

Political Parties as Elites

For Weber one of the most important functions of modern political parties consisted in their capacity to act as followings for a charismatic leader. He considered the charismatic tendencies in German parties as far too severely checked by countertendencies. With the partial exceptions of the Social Democrats and the Catholic Center, German parties were, he complained, still essentially collections of notables. Most bitter about the bourgeois parties, he charged them with being animated by a spirit similar to that of a medieval guild.[117] The notables formed a clique interested primarily in preserving their own po-

[116] "PuR," pp. 334–35.
[117] See, e.g., "Kanzlerkrisis," pp. 214–15; "PuR," p. 344; "PaB," p. 530.

litical positions and therefore fearful of any extraordinary leadership. No one individual could emerge who would take clear responsibility for making decisions.

Even in Germany, Weber believed, the notable was finally yielding to a type of bureaucrat—the party official. As the significance of the party apparatus increased, the role of the notables declined; soon their era would pass forever.[118] The most highly developed forms of the bureaucratically organized party, like the two major parties in the United States, had no fixed program. The platform was designed simply to attract the largest possible number of voters. A paid bureaucracy ensured a strong party organization with strict discipline.[119] Yet the party official, as a man who lived "from" politics, did not gain Weber's full respect.

Despite Weber's sympathy for some of the criticism of highly organized parties, his functional attitude toward them overcame most of his misgivings. He viewed the "bureaucratic" party described by Michels as an effective mode of organizing large numbers of people. Highly structured and disciplined parties would eliminate the "demagoguery" of men like Admiral Tirpitz and the Catholic Centrist Matthias Erzberger, for "only the organized leadership of the masses by responsible politicians [can] destroy the disorderly domination of the street and the leadership of occasional demagogues."[120] In his political writings, Weber failed to distinguish demagogic from charismatic traits. Tending to equate the two, he made a distinction between "irresponsible" and "responsible" demagoguery. He believed that democracy, in the sense of independent leadership receiving popular backing, would serve to hold the masses in check and gain their support for the rise of strong leaders. Since a small minority usually determined a party's program, activities, and candidates, mass influences could be held in check much better by a bureaucratically organized party than by one under the domination of notables.[121] Weber relied upon the political organization of the masses to reduce direct popular pressures to a minimum.

[118] "PuR," pp. 372–73; WuG, p. 769.
[119] "PuR," pp. 314–15. Weber's characterization of the two major American parties as the best examples of bureaucratization can be partly understood by recalling his concept of an "ideal type." A specific phenomenon did not necessarily contain every element of the ideal type. Nevertheless, he apparently misunderstood the structure of American parties in the late nineteenth and early twentieth century, regarding electoral machines like Tammany Hall's and Boise Penrose's as more bureaucratic than the apparatus of the Social Democratic party in his own country.
[120] "WuD," p. 245. See also "PuR," p. 381.
[121] "Diskussionsrede" at the First German Soziologentag (1910) in GAzSuSp, p. 444; "PuR," pp. 312–13; "PaB," p. 520.

He looked upon a bureaucratically organized party as susceptible to strong charismatic influences. In a mixture of charismatic and bureaucratic tendencies, he found his ideal party: "Because all attempts to influence the masses necessarily involve certain 'charismatic' elements, the increasing bureaucratization of parties and of the electoral process can, in the very moment when it attains its peak, be harnessed through a sudden eruption of charismatic hero-worship."[122]

Usually, Weber complained, the party officials struggled to keep themselves free from the charismatic leader who would be independent of the party organization. Only too often the "party regulars" succeeded in "castrating" charisma. On the other hand, a party frequently needed forceful personalities to win votes. Temporarily, the party officials had to swallow their resentment toward an outsider.[123] The bureaucratically organized party and the charismatic leader could supplement one another. At times, a party needed a charismatic leader who, like Lincoln, could carry it on to victory.[124] The party supplied a permanent stage on which occasional charismatic leaders could exercise their charms in order to gain power for themselves and consequently for the party bureaucracy as well. From the competition among highly bureaucratized political parties, Weber expected the emergence of a few political leaders of the charismatic type.

Believing that a party bureaucracy was a technical necessity for an effective modern party, Weber saw a choice only between "leaderless democracy without a machine" and "leadership democracy with a machine."[125] Winning the trust and faith of the masses through "responsible demagoguery," the charismatic leader could exercise great power over them, for his election was no ordinary election. It was the "profession of 'belief' in the call to leadership of the person who claims this acclamation."[126] Insofar as possible, Weber wished to see German parties organized as followings for charismatic leaders.[127]

His belief in the superiority of hierarchy as a principle of social and political organization led him to stress the necessity for complete subservience and "blind obedience" on the part of the followers.[128] In doing so, he minimized the differences between a charismatic following and a bureaucratic organization. Like the bureaucrat, the follower of the charismatic leader felt that he had to obey his master. The essential difference consisted in the degree of obedience. Charismatic obedience was unquestioning. The bureaucrat might question a command before obeying it; the follower of a charismatic leader either

---

[122] *WuG*, p. 768.
[123] "PuR," pp. 390–91; "PaB," pp. 521, 532. See also *WuG*, pp. 769–70.
[124] "PaB," pp. 521, 528, 532.   [125] "DkS," p. 443; "PaB," p. 532.
[126] "PuR," p. 382.   [127] "Kanzlerkrisis," pp. 214–15.
[128] "PuR," p. 336.

obeyed unhesitatingly or ceased to believe in the charisma. As long as the charismatic leader had success, his following would obey him "blindly."[129] The nonmaterial rewards of the followers consisted in the personal satisfaction of working with loyal devotion for a man, and not merely for "the program of a party consisting of mediocrities."[130]

Weber did not find the consequences of charisma entirely pleasant, but he considered them necessary: "The plebiscitarian leadership of parties entails the 'soullessness' of the following, their intellectual proletarianization, one might say. In order to be a useful apparatus, a machine in the American sense—undisturbed by the vanity of notables or pretensions to independent views—the following of such a leader must obey him blindly. . . . This is simply the price paid for guidance by leaders."[131]

For Weber, most members of an elite, whether in a bureaucracy or a charismatic following, should act largely as intermediaries between a supreme leader and the populace. The main functions of most elite individuals were to conduct routine business and to provide an apparatus to assist him. Weber designed techniques to further the rise of single great leaders who would make all important political decisions. Even though he foresaw little chance for a great leader of Bismarck's caliber in the near future, Weber still hoped that "born leaders" might emerge from political democracy in Germany.

Although favoring reforms, Weber was wary of the rising strength of the Left during the last year and a half of World War I. He began to fear the possibility of radical changes occurring in Germany. But until the fall of 1918, this fear appears to have been much weaker than Naumann's. Weber's belief in the stability of bureaucratic structures and his skepticism about the possibility of much spontaneity in mass movements predisposed him to underestimate the likelihood of social revolution occurring in Europe, even in Russia. He had difficulty in grasping the possibility of spontaneous mass movements arising.[132]

In the months immediately after Germany's November revolution, he employed some of the stratagems frequently used in this period by those seeking to avert social revolution. On the one hand, he unjustifiably identified himself with socialism, professed a commitment to a Socialist Germany, but argued against radical measures as impediments to the realization of socialism. On the other hand, he rejected some radical measures with the argument that Germany would not be able to deal with the Allies if these measures were adopted. His self-identification with socialism went so far that in early 1919 he is reported to have said in the course of a speech for the Democratic party

[129] *Ibid.*
[131] "PaB," p. 532.
[130] "PaB," p. 521.
[132] See Mommsen, *Max Weber*, p. 275.

in Berlin: "I stand so close to the Independent Socialists as to be indistinguishable from them."[133] In late 1918 and early 1919, he argued that measures for immediate socialization would be catastrophic for Germany. Only with the assistance of experienced entrepreneurs would Germany rise again economically. Only bourgeois businessmen could obtain the credits from the Allies necessary for reconstruction. Strong bourgeois participation in the provisional government was essential to the conclusion of peace with the Allies and to the success of the German revolution.[134]

An incident recounted by a Munich student of the period reveals much about Weber's attitudes. The young man wrote to Weber in early 1919, inviting him to give a talk on politics to a student audience. Weber tried to beg off and proposed Friedrich Naumann as a substitute. When poor health prevented Naumann's acceptance, Weber still refused to give the lecture himself. The student then wrote that some radical colleagues were leaning toward Kurt Eisner, the Bavarian Independent Socialist, as a substitute. Weber finally agreed to give the lecture, apparently to prevent Eisner from winning a student audience.[135]

The President of the Weimar Republic as a Great Leader

After examining the charismatic elements in Weber's elite thought, we should not be surprised to learn that he was an adamant proponent of a "plebiscitarian" president for the Weimar Republic. Indeed, he was one of the authors of the clauses in the new constitution that provided for far-reaching presidential powers and for popular instead of parliamentary election of the president.[136] Although many of the most important aspects of Weber's conception of the president were not embodied in the Weimar Constitution, his conception of the office was

[133] Quoted in Baumgarten, *Max Weber*, p. 607n. Baumgarten holds that this statement was sincere, but he quotes material from Weber's personal papers in his possession that suggests tactical purposes led Weber to make the remark.

[134] See Mommsen, *Max Weber*, pp. 294–98. For an assessment of the usefulness of these and similar arguments in consolidating the position of the provisional government both at home and vis-à-vis the Allies see Arno J. Mayer, *Politics and Diplomacy of Peacemaking: Containment and Counterrevolution at Versailles, 1918–1919* (New York, 1967), pp. 101–03 and passim.

[135] Immanuel Birnbaum, "Erinnerungen an Max Weber" in König and Winckelmann, *Max Weber zum Gedächtnis*, pp. 19–21. The lecture that Weber presented was published as "Wissenschaft als Beruf."

[136] Gerhard Schulz's *Zwischen Demokratie und Diktatur: Verfassungspolitik und Reichsreform in der Weimarer Republik*, Vol. 1: *Die Periode der Konsolidierung und der Revision des Bismarckschen Reichsaufbaus 1919–1930* (Berlin, 1963) provides a good synthetic treatment of the origins of the Weimar constitution and pays close attention to Weber's role in its drafting.

symptomatic of his basic position as well as his specific fears of the Left in 1918–1919.

Since William II had left the country, Weber felt free to create his own conception of a modern monarch's position. He no longer had to take into consideration the personal failings of William II. Beginning in November 1918, Weber concentrated much of his energy upon the creation of an office which could be occupied by a great leader. He gladly gave the holder of this office far more power than he would ever have entrusted to a Hohenzollern. He developed a theory of presidential leadership that overcame the problems that, especially since the time of the *Daily Telegraph* affair, had plagued Naumann's "new monarchism" and the ideas of the liberal new elitists generally. Through his sociology, which subsumed under new analytic headings aspects of the traditional concept of monarchy, Weber had already provided the theoretical basis that he now applied to the drafting of a new German constitution.

His proposals for the constitution were probably influenced greatly by his observation of the dictatorial powers assumed by the wartime governments of the Western Powers, especially by the French Premier Clemenceau and the British Prime Minister Lloyd George.[137] Weber assumed that a popularly elected president provided with dictatorial powers could help to stem the tide of revolution, as Lloyd George and Clemenceau had presumably been able to contribute to social and political stability.

Through the popular election of the president, Weber hoped also to find a charismatic individual who, while restraining both party and state bureaucracies,[138] would act as a counterweight to the Reichstag and the Federal Council. A president with the power to dissolve the

[137] See Gustav Schmidt, *Deutscher Historismus und der Übergang zur parlamentarischen Demokratie: Untersuchungen zu den politischen Gedanken von Meinecke, Troeltsch, Max Weber* (Lübeck, 1964), pp. 269–70, 277, 292. While stressing the importance of English models in Weber's thinking, Schmidt tends to ignore the importance of French models. Schmidt's attempt to show a similarity between Weber's political thought and that of A. D. Lindsay is more convincing than the conclusion that this similarity indicates that Weber succeeded in reconciling the political approach of German Historicism with parliamentary democracy (see Schmidt, pp. 280–81, 291–92, 305–08, 317–20). Since government leaders provided with dictatorial powers, claiming to act with popular support, and legitimized by appeals to popular sovereignty were attractive to antirevolutionary forces in the Western Powers as well as in Germany, Schmidt's conclusion contains a core of validity; but he does not come to grips with the break in the tradition of parliamentary government that these leaders represented in the West.

[138] Karl Loewenstein's argument that Weber did not conceive of the president of the new German republic as someone who must have charisma is unconvincing. "Max Weber als 'Ahnherr' des plebiszitären Führerstaats," *Kölner Zeitschrift für Soziologie und Sozialpsychologie*, XIII (1961), 281–82. For Weber every effective political leader needed a modicum of charisma.

Reichstag and to appoint the chancellor would help to supply the leadership Weber had been seeking. He wanted the president to be provided with enough constitutional powers to enable him to exercise a strong, independent role. Distrustful of the bureaucratic type of politician, he felt that the popular election of the president would supply a "safety valve" for leadership to rise to the top.[139] Weber was certain that the Reichstag alone would supply a more than ample check upon the president.[140]

Yet he did not simply overestimate the power of the Reichstag. His conception of the presidency resembled that of a temporarily elected, constitutional dictator. "The much discussed dictatorship of the masses," he wrote, "necessitates a 'dictator'—an elected individual possessing the confidence of the masses and to whom the masses subordinate themselves as long as he retains their confidence. . . ."[141]

Through his activities Weber helped to prepare for a change in the political system of the Bismarckian Empire. He sought to free the bourgeoisie from its undue dependence on the Junkers and the bureaucracy. In his double role as political journalist and social scientist, he worked out a program for parliamentary democracy in Germany. With some success he took an active part in shaping the institutions of the Weimar Republic. His writings, many of which were published or republished shortly after his death, had a great influence on his own and subsequent generations. He presented German intellectuals with a complex, sophisticated view of politics. He told them what to expect from democracy. To those who feared that it would entail a high degree of popular control he said: "Your fears are largely baseless." To those who advocated a high degree of popular control he said: "You are very naive."

Seeking new leadership, he advocated a political system outwardly very different from that of Wilhelminian Germany, but he scarcely wished to increase the amount of popular control. His desire for heroic, charismatic leadership helped him to abandon his allegiance to monarchism. The same desire led him to retain the notion of inher-

---

[139] See "PaB," p. 532. See also "Der Reichspräsident," in *GpS*, p. 487.

[140] "Der Reichspräsident," pp. 486–89.

[141] *Ibid.*, p. 487. In an informal conversation with General Ludendorff, Weber expressed similar ideas more colorfully: "In a democracy the people choose a leader in whom they trust. Then the chosen leader says, 'Now shut up and obey me [*parieren*].' People and party are no longer free to interfere with him. . . . Afterwards the people can sit in judgment. If the leader has made mistakes—to the gallows with him!" Quoted (from Weber's notes of the meeting) in Marianne Weber, *Max Weber*, p. 665. Gerth and Mills, p. 42. The meeting took place in 1919, apparently in the spring of the year. Significantly, in his *magnum opus* Weber noted a direct connection between imperialism and a charismatic leader in the ancient as well as in the modern world. See *WuG*, pp. 620–21.

ent leadership qualities, even though he usually linked the development of leadership to experiences gained in party and parliament. Weber remained more closely attached to the existing social order than he realized. Despite his stress upon the importance of education in modern society, he never suggested expanding the narrow social basis of German secondary and higher education. Both Rathenau and Nelson regarded the resolution of this problem as crucial to the realization of their views on political leadership.

CHAPTER FIVE

Walther Rathenau: Toward a New Society?

In a memorial address following Walther Rathenau's assassination in 1922, an admiring acquaintance, the philosopher and sociologist Max Scheler, asked that Rathenau be viewed as a pathfinder for every German, especially for students. Scheler went on to explain why Rathenau, despite his service to the Weimar Republic, should not be regarded as a martyr for democracy: "I have never personally known anyone more convinced that the history of mankind is propelled solely by *tiny elites* [Scheler's italics] and that the masses always provide only the material and the obstacles for the constructive political and economic spirit and will of these elites."[1] Rathenau was much bolder than Naumann or Weber in devising elitist alternatives to the Second Empire. Describing institutions that would make Germany a model for every other nation, Rathenau brought up to date the optimistic nineteenth-century liberal faith in the development of a social order in which everyone would rise to a position commensurate with his abilities.

From his birth in 1867 to his death in 1922, events led Rathenau to shift from capricious expressions of this faith to detailed proclamations in which he envisioned a "new society" that would improve upon both bourgeois society and Marxian socialism. He came to believe that the revolutionary potential of the working class, the growing discontent of the middle class, and the persistent conflicts between the bourgeoisie and the nobility could no longer be contained by the outmoded institutions of Wilhelminian Germany. Although apprehensive lest the German revolution of 1918 get out of hand, he found in it an opportunity to enact reforms that he had long pondered. Presenting these reforms as the benevolent product of his imagination, he may never have perceived how closely this imagination was dependent upon his experiences as one of Germany's foremost industrialists.

THE PRECARIOUS SECURITY OF A WILHELMINIAN TYCOON

Rathenau's life gave him many good vantage points from which to observe malfunctions in German society. His mother came from an old

[1] Walther Rathenau, "Eine Würdigung zu seinem Gedächtnis" in Max Scheler, *Gesammelte Werke,* ed. Maria Scheler (Bern and Munich, 1954–   ), VI, 370.

cultured and wealthy family; his father, Emil, from a less pretentious and less affluent background. Emil Rathenau became an entrepreneur of great skill, whose major accomplishment was the organization of the German General Electric Company (AEG).[2] The AEG became one of the two German giants in a field that developed during the era of cartelization beginning in the 1880's and 1890's. The working force of the AEG, which included many white-collar workers, was highly stratified. The electrical industry employed a much higher proportion of technicians and skilled workers than heavy industry. Like many branches of light, consumer-oriented industry, the AEG adopted a policy less hostile and more flexible than that of heavy industry toward trade unions. Walther Rathenau weighed possibilities that a Stumm or Krupp rejected out of hand.

In the period before World War I, he clung to the belief that most business leaders were the men best qualified for the positions that they held. As the son of a millionaire, he was vulnerable to the charge that he had attained his own position of eminence through his father's assistance. Attacks from both the Right and the Left exploited this vulnerability. In a personal apologia written shortly after the war, he took great pains to demonstrate that he had worked his way up in business and that his own success in the AEG and in its great banking ally, the *Berliner Handelsgesellschaft,* was due solely to his own talent and persistence. He tried to give the impression that he had put in a grueling apprenticeship that deprived him of the amenities of cosmopolitan life and that his achievements had nothing to do with his father's position.[3] Perhaps credible about his first job, a position as an engineer in a small aluminum factory in Switzerland, this impression was false about the second, which he described as managing a small, remote electrochemical plant. A subsidiary of the AEG, this plant was located in Bitterfeld near Leipzig, less than seventy miles on the main rail line to Berlin. A close friend of his family reports that while living in Bitterfeld

---

For a brief discussion of why, as an elitist, Scheler found Rathenau so attractive see John R. Staude, *Max Scheler, 1874–1928: An Intellectual Portrait* (New York, 1967), pp. 125–26.

[2] On the early history of the AEG see esp. Felix Pinner, *Emil Rathenau und das elektrische Zeitalter* (Leipzig, 1918). Much of the surviving archival material pertaining to the AEG before 1945 is now located in East Germany, but a recent study by an East German scholar is disappointingly brief and sketchy: Hans Radandt, *AEG: Ein typischer Konzern* (Berlin, 1958). Although confined to the period after 1918 Peter Czada, *Die Berliner Elektroindustrie in der Weimarer Zeit: Eine regionalstatistisch-wirtschaftshistorische Untersuchung* (Berlin, 1969) deals with aspects of the AEG.

[3] See "Apologie" (1919) in *Gesammelte Schriften* (6 vols., Berlin, 1925–1929), vi, 422–24. Hereafter the *Gesammelte Schriften* will be cited as *GS*.

Rathenau frequently visited Berlin.[4] Rathenau felt uneasy about his rapid ascent in business. Although himself heir to a vast fortune, he was sufficiently candid to admit that inherited wealth could interfere with the operation of a system based on individual talents. Without referring directly to his own fortune, he often called for restrictions upon inheritances.

A usually latent, but occasionally overt conflict with his father contributed to his desire to become successful in his own right. For years his father regarded him as a dreamer who could not really make a go of it in business.[5] Rathenau proved his father wrong, but only by subordinating a part of himself that regarded the world of business with contempt.

Although Rathenau liked to portray himself as a modestly living white-collar worker or technician,[6] he was a member of the *grande bourgeoisie* and owned at least two aristocratic villas, including a former royal estate. Several years before his father's death, Rathenau's personal fortune was estimated at two million marks, and his annual income at three hundred thousand marks. He was associated with scores of enormous concerns as a managing director or as a member of the supervisory board.[7]

Although he tended to think of himself as a Christian in his fundamental beliefs,[8] he was never baptized. Often both Rathenau himself

[4] Hans Fürstenberg, "Erinnerung an Walther Rathenau: Ein Kommentar" in Harry Graf Kessler, *Walther Rathenau: Sein Leben und sein Werk* (Wiesbaden, [1962?]), pp. 388, 434. The essay by Fürstenberg, whose father was one of the founders of the *Berliner Handelsgesellschaft* and who knew Rathenau more intimately than Kessler did, is not contained in earlier editions of Kessler's indispensable biography. Subsequent references to Kessler's work will be to the English edition: *Walther Rathenau: His Life and Work*, trans. W. D. Robson-Scott and Lawrence Hyde (New York, 1930). Among the other extended studies of Rathenau, Peter Berglar's *Walther Rathenau: Seine Zeit, sein Werk, seine Persönlichkeit* (Bremen, 1970) is particularly noteworthy, mainly for its up-to-date bibliography. Although Berglar examined much unpublished material, most of it was available to Kessler, and Berglar adds little that is new, either in interpretation or details, to the large body of literature on Rathenau.

[5] See James Joll, "Walther Rathenau: Prophet without a Cause" in Joll's *Three Intellectuals in Politics* (New York, 1965), pp. 62–63. This essay is the best brief treatment of Rathenau's life and thought.

[6] "Mein eigner Aufwand aber ist nicht gross. Er . . . bewegt sich etwa in den Grenzen, die für jüngere Prokuristen industrieller Werke gelten." "Apologie," p. 435.

[7] For the estimates of his wealth see Walther Rathenau, *Tagebuch 1907–1922*, ed. Hartmut Pogge-von Strandmann (Düsseldorf, 1967), p. 118. In an appendix (pp. 287–88) Pogge lists 68 concerns on whose supervisory boards Rathenau sat during the period 1907 to 1922. According to Kessler, *Walther Rathenau*, p. 117, he was a managing director or member of the supervisory board of 84 concerns in 1909.

[8] See Kessler, *Walther Rathenau*, p. 51. Robert A. Pois, "Walther Rathenau's Jewish Quandary." *Leo Baeck Institute Yearbook*, XIII (1968), 129 remarks ap-

and other Germans regarded him as a Jew.[9] As a bourgeois he shared much of the ambivalence of the bourgeoisie toward the nobility. His Jewish origins and his membership in a *nouveau riche* family compounded his disabilities as a bourgeois. He reacted to this situation by adopting a haughty air, and like Disraeli he often sought to exploit his status as a partial outsider. As Rathenau's best biographer observes, he tried to play the part of an exotic oriental prince who did not really belong to German society.[10] Publicly he always affected a disinterest in titles and honors, but privately he made strenuous efforts to gain royal medals, and his persistence may have helped to ensure him several awards.[11]

It is difficult, but occasionally possible to distinguish the disabilities that he incurred as a Jew from those he incurred as a bourgeois. He did his military service as a one-year volunteer when his father's fame and fortune were only beginning to be established. Although able to enter one of the most exclusive units in the Prussian army, Walther Rathenau failed to receive a commission as a reserve officer upon completion of his training, most likely because he was unbaptized.[12] On the

---

propriately that "Rathenau was in actuality a Jew neither in the cultural nor the spiritual sense. For the nonracist observer, he was a Jew only by birth." But Pois goes on to draw a more questionable conclusion: "For himself, he was a Jew in an economic, social, and probably intellectual setting."

[9] Joll divorces this aspect of Rathenau's make-up from its full social context when he argues that "this German Jew's [Rathenau's] cult of Prussian traditions and his attempts to combine the Jewish and Prussian elements both in the German Empire and his own nature is the key to his character and actions. . . ." Joll, "Walther Rathenau," pp. 60-61.

[10] Kessler, *Walther Rathenau*, p. 53. See also Alfred Kerr, *Walther Rathenau: Erinnerungen eines Freundes* (Amsterdam, 1935), pp. 129–30. Some of the most perceptive characterizations of Rathenau's personality, as well as his ideas, appear in Robert Musil's great novel *Der Mann ohne Eigenschaften* (ed., Adolf Frisé), (Hamburg, [1953]). Musil intended one of the leading characters, Arnheim, to represent Rathenau, whom he first met shortly before World War I (see Frisé's postscript, p. 1661). Arnheim appears unpredictably throughout the work, which is set in Vienna. Before long Viennese society is buzzing with rumors that Arnheim is at least partly Jewish, if only by descent (see p. 110). On occasion he is termed a "nabob" (p. 188), and Musil describes his relationships with the highest social circles in a way that brings out Arnheim's consummate skill in turning disadvantages into advantages. Thus in intercourse with "Personen, deren Sonderfach der Geburtsadel war," Arnheim "dämpfte seine eigene Vornehmheit ab und beschränkte sich so bescheiden auf Geistesadel, der seine Vorzüge und Grenzen kennt, dass nach einer Weile die Träger hochadeliger Namen neben ihm wirkten, als hätten sie vom Tragen dieser Last einen gekrümmten Arbeiterrücken" (p. 200).

[11] See *Tagebuch*, pp. 74, 100–01, 118. See also the biting remarks by Rathenau's off-again-on-again friend and enemy Maximilian Harden quoted in Harry F. Young, *Maximilian Harden, censor germaniae: The Critic in Opposition from Bismarck to the Rise of Nazism* (The Hague, 1959), p. 244.

[12] See letter of Dec. 12, 1917 to Frau von Hindenburg in Walther Rathenau, *Ein preussischer Europäer: Briefe*, ed. Margaret von Eynern (Berlin, 1955), p. 243. (Frau von Hindenburg, née Sophie Gräfin zu Münster, was a close friend of

other hand, his limited access to the highest levels of the court was largely a consequence of his status as a bourgeois. He preferred—or perhaps reconciled himself to—less restrictive social circles embracing cultivated *haute-bourgeois*, artists, writers, and an occasional aristocrat. In these circles, his desire to be the center of attention posed fewer problems.

Despite his criticisms of the influence of the Prussian Junkers in the Empire, he revered many of their characteristics and traditions. When he felt that one of his intimate friends had insulted him, Rathenau proposed a duel.[13] His relationship to the bourgeoisie was similar. He developed a pronounced *Hassliebe* for the typical bourgeois, an ambivalence that he shared with many other Wilhelminian intellectuals. This ambivalence was reinforced by his penchant for scrutinizing society as an iconoclastic technician.

An Elite for Wilhelminian Germany?

Like Naumann and Max Weber, Rathenau was committed to the establishment of the uncontested hegemony of the bourgeoisie, but his views on prewar Germany were even more ambiguous than Naumann's became after the turn of the century. The primary source of Rathenau's ambiguity was his hope that the social coalition of the bourgeoisie with the Junkers would dissolve only very slowly and in a way that would preserve many Prussian traditions. This commitment to a gradual rather than an abrupt assertion of the bourgeoisie was both expressed in and reinforced by his fondness for aristocratic forms of life, even for many of the inelegant practices of the Junkers.

At times he minced no words in attributing to the Junkers the failures of political leadership in Wilhelminian Germany. In earlier centuries, he once observed, the Prussian nobility had been able to provide effective political leadership, but it had not developed the skills necessary for the management of a twentieth-century state.[14] He complained that other countries, mainly England and France, had developed effective procedures for selecting leaders. Although differing greatly from country to country, these methods, he believed, brought forward men who were by nature suited to political responsibility. Making clear his regret that there was not in Germany, as in

Rathenau's family and not the wife of her famous contemporary Marshal Paul von Hindenburg.) Rathenau's assertions in this letter are supported, if only with circumstantial evidence, by Martin Kitchen, *The German Officer Corps, 1890–1914* (Oxford, 1968), pp. 37–44.

[13] Emil Ludwig, *Führer Europas nach der Natur gezeichnet* (Amsterdam, 1934), p. 118.

[14] "Zur Kritik der Zeit" (1912) in *GS*, I, 120, 124–25.

many other nations, some type of party government to supply continuity and tradition, he expressed the common complaint that the Germans had lacked political leadership since the days of Bismarck.[15]

Rathenau found superior principles operative in the selection of business leaders. As late as 1912, he made the revealing assertion that economic life was open to everyone; the unqualified were excluded in accordance with a single standard—success.[16] In an earlier essay, he expressed obliquely his belief in the rule of the bourgeoisie through the musings of an imaginary Russian financier: "The most bearable and therefore most worthwhile form of plutocracy to strive for seems to me to be reached . . . when the hardest working, most capable, and most conscientious are the propertied."[17] Both the legal institutions and the popular will of every country were, according to this Russian financier, groping toward such a system of "euplutism." Why, the financier asked, should not this goal be pursued candidly and with appropriate means?[18]

Although as we shall see Rathenau was critical of the bourgeoisie for raising obstacles to the selection of the most capable businessmen, he became much more severe when alluding to the Junkers. Thus he denounced monopolies in land as the most unjust form of monopoly.[19] In a letter to a diplomat, he complained more openly: "What concerns me is not so much the fact that government posts are occupied by aristocrats as the absence of an independent method of selection. It is a matter of complete indifference to me from what social stratum competent people are recruited. But what is necessary is that there should be some guarantee that only the fittest—and these in the largest possible number—be entrusted with responsibility."[20]

In these forthright words about the Junkers, there appears a disclaimer, often interjected by Rathenau, of concern for the social origins of leaders. This sort of disclaimer might be interpreted as evidence of confidence that the interests served by the policy maker, not his origins, were crucial. Yet these disclaimers were also indicative of Rathenau's willingness to tolerate indefinitely the domination of part of the state apparatus by the Junkers. Thus, in an essay published in 1912, he denounced the quality of German political leaders, but went on to remark that the only organ of state in Prussia in which effective

[15] *Ibid.*, pp. 121–23.

[16] "Politische Auslese" (1912) in *GS*, II, 226.

[17] "Zur Physiologie der Geschäfte" (1901) in *GS*, IV, 333.

[18] *Ibid.*, p. 333.

[19] "Vom wirtschaftlichen Gleichgewicht" (1908) in *GS*, IV, 296–97.

[20] Letter of June 1, 1912 to von Lucius in *Briefe* (3 vols., Dresden, 1930), I, 102. The translation is, with slight modifications, that provided in Kessler, *Walther Rathenau*, p. 129.

methods of leadership selection still operated was the army. The best officers were selected from hundreds of candidates after extensive observation and testing: "As long as a man is educated, of honorable origins, not a cripple or a Jew, he is admitted to the professional [military] service."[21] In another work, he explicitly left open the possibility that the Junkers and some other groups might retain certain privileges, even when ability gained in importance as a criterion for the pursuit of every vocation. The community, he explained, had an interest in securing inheritance rights insofar as they served to preserve several "castes": warriors, officials, and husbandmen.[22]

Rathenau's criticisms of prewar Germany fluctuated between moralizing and class analysis. Was the lack of political leadership due to the absence of men with certain abstract qualities in high office, or was it a consequence of the social and political power of the Junkers? Rathenau delighted in drawing banal contrasts such as that between "men of courage" and "men of purpose." The men of courage were the noblemen; the men of purpose he identified with capitalism and with what he termed "mechanization," a concept similar to Weber's "rationalization." Several years earlier he had made a similar, if more jejune, comparison of the "race of the instinctive" with the "race of the intellectuals." The instinctive, the noblemen, were "proud, courageous, passionate, principled, cruel, nervous, magnanimous, beautiful, spiritual, indolent, and imaginative." The intellectuals, the bourgeois, were "cold, feeble, clever, witty, energetic, unimaginative, good hearted, phlegmatic, slanderous, and unprincipled." Rathenau indicated that although many of his own sympathies were with the instinctive, only a mixture of the two races produced genius.[23]

He propounded an elaborate theory that expressed both his sympathies for the nobility and his commitment to the ultimate triumph of a society similar to that envisioned by the classical liberals of the nineteenth century. This theory embodied his longing for the emergence of a homogeneous upper class that would result from the fusion of part of the bourgeoisie with part of the nobility and that would be the major recruiting ground for an open political elite. The theory rested on the idea that true culture is always the work of an aristocracy, or elite. He never completely abandoned this turn-of-the-century intellectual creation in which his receptivity to the rhetoric of Nietzsche, Darwinism, racism, and recent anthropology were evident.

[21] "Politische Auslese," p. 229.
[22] "Vom wirtschaftlichen Gleichgewicht," pp. 296–97.
[23] *Zur Mechanik des Geistes, oder vom Reich der Seele* (1913) in *GS*, II, 26, 57; "Astern und Georginen" (written ca. 1900) in *Nachgelassene Schriften* (2 vols., Berlin, 1928), II, 170. Hereafter the *Nachgelassene Schriften* will be cited as *NS*.

These influences served to provide illustrative material and fashionable buttresses for age-old notions that Rathenau found appealing because they appeared relevant to the social situation in Germany.

Even the early versions of his cultural elite theory were very repetitious, a general characteristic of Rathenau's work. A comment that his close friend, the one-time Prussian General Staff officer Gustav Steinbömer, makes about Rathenau as a conversationalist applies to his writings as well. After a few encounters with Rathenau, Steinbömer began to realize that the man repeated, often word for word, the same "lectures" to all of his acquaintances. Why, Steinbömer queries satirically, should Rathenau have bothered altering his text once he had hit upon the best possible choice of words?[24]

Rathenau argued that throughout history three basic forms of societies had existed. The first type he found in areas like China and ancient Egypt. This type contained only peoples of "common racial descent or well-fused racial elements."[25] Homogeneous and unstratified, these civilizations changed little, even over the course of centuries.

Disliking static societies, Rathenau found much more attractive a second type of civilization, which he found examples of in pre-Periclean Athens and medieval Europe. A creative group formed a ruling caste physically different from the uncreative populace over which it ruled. The two groups—or races, as Rathenau sometimes called them —did not interbreed, and they had little contact with each other. Rathenau believed that this sort of society could not survive for long. It could develop a high culture, but eventually the barriers between the two castes or races would crumble.[26]

The crumbling of these barriers led to the third type of society. "Nature," Rathenau wrote, "was never satisfied with the formation of an elite [*Auslese*]. As rulers, the elect had to spread out among the lower peoples in order to lead them, to train them, to implant new forces in them, in order to awaken the dormant."[27] After fulfilling these tasks, the members of the former elite dispersed throughout the rest of the population. In Western Europe, Rathenau explained, the most recent phase of this process of intermixture had proceeded much farther than in Central Europe. Thus, when a Prussian regiment marched by, a bystander could still readily distinguish two different races if he compared the men with their officers.[28]

Rathenau believed that Germany had already benefited from one

[24] Gustav Steinbömer [pseud. Gustav Hillard], *Herren und Narren der Welt* (Munich, 1954), pp. 224–25.

[25] "Kritik der Zeit," p. 25.   [26] *Ibid.*, pp. 23–26.

[27] *Ibid.*, p. 147.   [28] *Ibid.*, pp. 29–30.

period of tremendous creativity as the result of the intermingling of two races, or strata, and he looked forward to a second great creative era. The first had reached its highpoint with the cultural achievements of Goethe and Germany's classical period in the late eighteenth and early nineteenth century. These achievements were the product of fruitful cooperation between the two strata: "The upper stratum still has so much legitimacy and potency that its purer and freer ideals dominate the spirit of the whole; the lower stratum still has so much belief and respect that it places its ability, its traditional craftsmanship, and its artistic skill in the service of these ideals." The process of intermingling became more and more rapid and intense: "Now some of the gifted in the upper stratum descend from the sphere of the rulers into the multitudes of ruled; now the more important members of the lower stratum ascend into the circle of the rulers. . . ."[29] After this period of creativity came to an end, a "baroque" era of decay, materialism, and skepticism set in. The lower stratum, more numerous than the upper, placed its stamp on society, as the last traces of the energy produced by the intermingling of the two original strata disappeared.

Rathenau furnished few clues to his dating of this baroque era in recent German history. Perhaps he thought of it as spanning most of the second third of the nineteenth century. If so, the basis for a new cycle of creativity would have been laid by the unification of Germany under Prussia that, he seems to have believed, constituted the conquest of one race by another. Hence, the initial intermingling of the two races would have been the collaboration of the Junkers with the industrial bourgeoisie.

In an early elaboration of his often contrived and confusing cultural elite theory, Rathenau expressed the hope that the amalgamation of the two races or strata would take place in such a way as to preserve much that was valuable in the nobility. Although, he explained, the nobility's chances of being inundated were great, there was a good possibility that a historically unique process might occur "if the national spirit is resolute and the national will can preserve the old values."[30] This sort of attempt to reconcile his conflicting attitudes toward the Junkers and the bourgeoisie appeared with a different emphasis in a later work, some sections of which provided the rudiments of a coherent explanation of the contradictions of Wilhelminian society. He suggested that two opposing systems of social stratification existed side by side in the Germany of his day. The first was a remnant of feudalism; the second a product of capitalism. Although the first

[29] *Ibid.*, p. 25.
[30] "Zur Kritik der Moral" (1903) in *GS*, IV, 261.

was still decisive in the political and military spheres, the second would inevitably overturn it. The feudal system of stratification had persisted because it had remained closely linked to the soil and thereby benefited from the development of capitalism (*Mechanisierung*) in the countryside during the past century and because a number of European dynasties whose existence was threatened by the emergence of the industrial bourgeoisie had remained closely allied with feudal elements. Feudally anchored dynasties still survived in Central Europe.[31]

Rathenau pointed to foreign policy as the area most seriously affected by the lack of appropriate leadership in Germany.[32] Like Naumann and Weber, he was committed deeply to the pursuit of an active, consistent policy of overseas imperialism, but he was more directly involved in German colonies through his business activities.[33] He was among the most prominent members of the entourage of businessmen, journalists, and state officials accompanying Colonial Secretary Bernhard Dernburg on extended African trips in 1907 and 1908. Both privately and publicly Rathenau stressed the economic need for colonies.[34] Like many German imperialists, he was convinced that sooner or later there would be a redivision of colonial spoils among the Great Powers. Germany, he complained, had acquired little overseas territory, but in the future every scrap would be of value. Even the smallest possession might have some raw material; if a territory had no direct use, it could be exchanged.[35] In the memoranda that he drew up for the German government after his visits to Africa, he cited the lack of a German gentry similar to England's and the consequent absence of leadership qualities among the German bourgeoisie as an explanation for Germany's weakness as a colonial power.[36]

The racism that appeared often in his prewar writings, most notoriously in one of his earliest essays "Höre Israel!" (1897),[37] soon came

[31] "Kritik der Zeit," pp. 75–76.   [32] *Ibid.*, p. 122.

[33] See the memoirs of his associate at the *Berliner Handelsgesellschaft*, Carl Fürstenberg, *Die Lebensgeschichte eines deutschen Bankiers*, ed. Hans Fürstenberg (Wiesbaden, [1961?]), pp. 468–69; and Pogge's notes in *Tagebuch*, pp. 93, n. 33; 94, n. 34; 98, n. 62.

[34] See "Erwägungen über die Erschliessung des Deutsch-Ostafrikanischen Schutzgebietes" (first published in 1908) and "Denkschrift über den Stand des Südwestafrikanischen Schutzgebietes" (written in 1908 but first published posthumously) in *NS*, II. See also "Deutsche Gefahren und neue Ziele" (1913) in *GS*, I, 269.

[35] See "Deutsche Gefahren und neue Ziele," pp. 269–72; "Erwägungen über die Erschliessung des Deutsch-Ostafrikanischen Schutzgebietes," p. 12.

[36] See, e.g., "Erwägungen über die Erschliessung des Deutsch-Ostafrikanischen Schutzgebietes," pp. 16, 72.

[37] First published, under a pseudonym, in Maximilian Harden's periodical *Die Zukunft*, Mar. 6, 1897. The essay is reprinted in Walther Rathenau, *Schriften*, ed. Arnold Harttung et al. (Berlin, 1965).

to serve mainly foreign-policy purposes. His often quoted phrases lamenting the fate of the blond nordic,[38] gave way to an increasingly vague, inconsistent, and when he dealt with imperialism, peripheral racism. Although retaining a materialistic undertone perceptible in his allusions to cultural characteristics resulting from sexual unions between members of different races, his use of the expression "race" became similar to that which we shall encounter in Spengler's work. As Rathenau's interest in overseas imperialism became pronounced, he expressed a firm belief in the superiority of whites over blacks, but only lingering traces of his former emphasis upon the importance of racial differences among Europeans.[39] His belief in the inferiority of Negroes came to provide a major prop for his justification of overseas imperialism.[40]

The waning of Rathenau's belief in the significance of racial differences among Germans did not lead him to abandon his related notion of "genius." He continued to assert that some men possessed inherent qualities which could not be developed through education or training. These qualities made a man capable of becoming an outstanding leader: "What is the real meaning of business or political genius? To me, nothing more than that in the *camera obscura* of the mind an image of the world is formed that unconsciously reflects all essential relationships and laws of reality and that therefore may at any time be, to a degree, projected experimentally so that within human limits it reveals the future. This process of forming an image of the world is intuitive. . . ."[41]

[38] See, e.g., the study, first published in 1926, by the future National Socialist minister of agriculture: R. Walther Darré, *Walther Rathenau und das Problem des nordischen Menschen* (Munich, 1933). Darré quotes extensively from Rathenau's *Reflexionen* (1908), which is reprinted in GS, IV.

[39] Now and then he still used racist terminology in referring to whites. See, e.g., "Kritik der Zeit" (1912), p. 92, where he bemoans the de-Germanization of Europe, and *Zur Mechanik des Geistes*, pp. 137-38, where he employs the notions of higher and lower races in a materialist fashion. Among similar evidence a letter of 1917 might be mentioned. In this letter Rathenau offered the following explanation of the failure of "two thirds" of the Jews in Germany to be completely assimilated, or "regenerated": ". . . Es lassen sich bei einem Stamm nicht in Geschwindigkeit neue Eigenschaften züchten, sondern nur die ursprünglichen wieder hervorholen." Letter of July 11, 1917 to Gottlieb von Jagow in *Briefe*, III, 231.

[40] See esp. the memorandum that he prepared for the German government after his first visit to Africa. In one passage he discussed the inability of the Negro to think abstractly and concluded: "Deshalb wird eine festgegründete geistige Entwicklung des Negers für alle absehbare Zeit ein frommer Wunsch bleiben; wollte man sie forcieren, so konnte leicht durch missverstandene Nachahmung okzidentalen Wesens ein ähnliches Zerrbild hervorgerufen werden, wie es der amerikanischer Neger bietet." "Erwägungen über die Erschliessung des Deutsch-Ostafrikanischen Schutzgebietes," p. 25.

[41] "Politik, Humor und Abrüstung" (1911) in GS, I, 174. For an earlier statement on genius see "Vom Ziel der Geschäfte" (1902) in GS, IV, 87.

This conception of genius did not seriously restrict the two major methods that Rathenau envisioned to improve the quality of leadership in Germany. The first method consisted of several devices to increase social mobility, and sets off Rathenau's views sharply from those of Weber as well as Naumann in the period before 1918. The second method was the much more familiar one of reforming political institutions and introducing a version of parliamentary government.

The measures to promote social mobility were largely economic. Like the classical liberal of the nineteenth century, Rathenau believed that the spontaneous forces of the market, if permitted free play, would ensure the success of the able. According to Rathenau, the major impediments to the success of the most qualified business leaders were monopolies and large inheritances. Yet he failed to confront the problem that the major restrictions upon the market in his day were imposed by monopoly capitalism, not by remnants of feudalism or mercantilism. As an industrialist with a liberal bent, he exaggerated the magnitude of the obstacles presented to the free exchange of property by institutions such as the entailing of landed estates in the eastern provinces of Prussia. Circumventing the issue of industrial monopolies, he focused upon measures to diminish the advantages given the children of the wealthy. Among his favorite remedies were taxes on inheritances and gifts, a heavy progressive income tax, and limitations on economic concessions granted by the state. As long as a man was able, "through inventiveness, business traditions, or entrepreneurial skills" to move ahead of his competitors, Rathenau wished simply to prevent "too much" concentration of wealth in his hands. When the advantages obtained by the man were passed on to his children, Rathenau became more concerned. He looked forward to restrictions upon wealth and economic activity that would increase the opportunities for economic ascent for individual members of the lower classes and decrease the possibility that incapable members of the upper class would be able to occupy important positions. As he made clear, his goal was not to obtain material equality, but rather to create a dynamic balance within society.[42]

In line with his conception of a more open elite, he advocated measures to make more educational opportunities available to the lower classes. Already in the prewar period his proposals were, if less detailed than his suggestions for economic reforms, as specific as the postwar rhetoric of Naumann. Rathenau proposed the reorganization of the German educational system to provide appropriate schooling for all children of talent regardless of their social origins. In the course

[42] See "Vom wirtschaftlichen Gleichgewicht," pp. 296–97.

of justifying this proposal, he revealed the primary considerations that motivated him. The most glaring stupidity in Germany, he complained, was that thousands of brains were wasted every year. The waste was obnoxious for two reasons. First, it constituted a "violation of humanity." Second, it created "legions of gifted enemies of the community."[43] Elaborating only upon the second reason, he noted a beneficial consequence of expanding educational opportunities. The quality of candidates for positions open to university graduates would improve greatly if the competition became more intense. Rathenau's own position in the business world had certainly alerted him to the advantages gained by employers if there were more competition among university graduates for jobs, for the demand for degree holders held up well until after the war.[44]

Seeking to dispose of criticisms that his educational proposals might encounter, he anticipated one set of objections from the Right and another from the Left. The Right would claim that the worker was happy with his present situation; the Left would complain that if education were made available to everyone on the basis of ability, the proletariat would be deprived of leadership. The most talented proletarians, Rathenau replied to the first objection, were the most discontented. They were so bitter that almost without exception they were demanding the destruction of the existing economic system. Implicitly, Rathenau held forth the prospect of a passive proletariat. His "answer" to the Left depended upon his elitist belief in the paucity of men capable of becoming true leaders. Even if the proletariat were deprived of its most talented members, he argued, champions of its interests would still come forward from other sections of society.[45]

Through the reconstruction of German education coupled with social and economic legislation, he expected the "abolition" of the proletariat. His definition of the proletariat, which avoided Marxist concepts, was crucial to his argument: "a class of the population . . . whose members can not under normal conditions attain independent responsibility and an independent way of life."[46] The greatest injustice suffered by the worker was "the lifelong, indeed hereditary confinement to the fate of a proletarian."[47] The expansion of educational opportunities, the limitation of inherited wealth, and the restriction of

[43] *Ibid.*, pp. 297–98.
[44] Although colored by distress over the postwar surplus of *Akademiker*, Martha Eva Prochownik, *Die wirtschaftliche Lage der geistigen Arbeiter Deutschlands*, Schriften der Deutschen Gesellschaft zur Bekämpfung der Arbeitslosigkeit, vIII (Berlin, 1925) demonstrates how favorable, for them, the job market in Germany was before the war.
[45] "Vom wirtschaftlichen Gleichgewicht," pp. 299–300.
[46] "Kritik der Zeit," p. 77.　　　　　　[47] *Ibid.*, p. 78.

monopolies would all, he explained, contribute to the abolition of the proletariat. The task would take a lifetime, but through slow change it would be accomplished without a world conflagration. Socialism was not the answer because it did not recognize the duality of work—of invention and execution, of direction and performance.[48]

Through the "abolition" of the proletariat, Rathenau would have reduced working-class pressures for radical change, thwarted the development of socialism, and improved the quality of German leadership by establishing an open elite. He wrote confidently that he had found an effective way of destroying socialism, which with a Nietzschean phrase he termed "the resentment of the servile."[49] As Rathenau stated, he sought to promote the fragmentation of the working class into heterogeneous groups.[50]

He thought that the improvements in wages and the extension of social legislation could prevent German trade unions from becoming as powerful as their English counterparts. During a period of increasing militancy among English trade unionists, he complained that their power was destroying English industry.[51] Drawing upon personal experiences in the electrochemical industry, Rathenau suggested that new technology, or what would today be termed automation, had already made possible the erection of one-man plants. Such technological innovations would, he was confident, enable employers to pay better wages. For examples of the consequences of higher wages, he turned to the United States, where, he noted, employers had reaped great advantages from higher wages; the well-paid worker produced more, and his morale improved.[52]

Rathenau was convinced that in some form the capitalist system would last indefinitely.[53] Several months before the outbreak of World War I, he published a newspaper article defending capitalism. After aptly characterizing most criticisms of capitalism merely as objections to large-scale enterprise, he continued: "The economic form to which we owe not only the development of our national well-being, but also a substantial part of our political strength should not be condemned out of hand when one of its unavoidable consequences is a marked concentration of responsibility in the hands of a few."[54]

Rathenau's discussion of his second major remedy for the problems

---

[48] *Ibid.*, pp. 78–79.

[49] Letter of Jan. 29, 1914 to Prof. K. Joël in *Briefe*, III, 201.

[50] See "Kritik der Zeit," p. 79.

[51] "Die neue Ära" (1907) in *NS*, I, 20.

[52] "Anmerkung vom Konsumanteil" (1908) in *GS*, IV, 304–05.

[53] See "Kritik der Zeit," p. 62.

[54] "Die Funktionen des Aufsichtsrats" (first published in the *Vossische Zeitung*, Apr. 20, 1914) in *NS*, I, 184–85.

of Wilhelminian Germany, changes in political institutions, was less explicit than were his proposals to accelerate social mobility. His admiration for England surpassed even Weber's.[55] Taking England's political system as an instructive example, he advocated a more powerful German parliament, but he did not explain in detail how a parliamentary system similar to England's could be developed in Germany. Only one of his prewar writings, a short article, was devoted explicitly to parliamentarism.[56] Using phrases similar to Weber's, he compared the German type of parliament unfavorably with the English and French types: "Nongoverning, merely supervisory and law-giving parliaments are not productive, for no natural organism does more than is asked of it or more than it can make use of. They [nongoverning parliaments] are unproductive because they lack interest, substantive knowledge of issues, and responsibility."[57]

Rathenau voiced vague hopes for the disassociation of the Hohenzollerns from the Junkers. The monarchy's links to the Conservatives and the nobility raised the danger, he noted circumspectly, that the crown would become partisan. In other states, most notably in England, the monarchy had successfully freed itself from the nobility.[58] He denounced as "the most flagrant injustice of our times" that "the most economically capable nation in the world [Germany] is not permitted to regulate or take responsibility for its affairs."[59] "The double injustice and the double danger" to Germany were on the one hand "class rule, manifested by deficient selection [of leaders] and weak policies," and on the other hand "conservative leadership, manifested by unequal burdens."[60]

Before World War I, Rathenau seems to have taken only a desultory interest in attempts to consolidate and extend the power of parliamentary institutions. Almost as apathetic as Weber about the prospects for cooperation between liberals and Social Democrats,[61] he was especially interested in the creation of a movement that would draw upon both the National Liberals and the left-liberal parties. The resulting "bourgeois-national" movement would, he hoped, be able to limit the power of the conservative agrarians:

[55] See, e.g., "Vier Nationen" (1907) in GS, iv, 124; "England und wir" (1912) in GS, i, 212.

[56] "Parliamentarismus" (1913) in GS, i, 233–49.

[57] Ibid., p. 241.

[58] Ibid., p. 246; "Kritik der Zeit," pp. 118–20.

[59] "Das Euminidenopfer" (1913) in GS, i, 259. Rathenau italicized the entire passage.

[60] Ibid., p. 260.

[61] Even as the election of 1912 approached, Rathenau does not appear to have looked beyond electoral cooperation between liberals and Social Democrats. See his entry of Jan. 3, 1911 in Tagebuch, p. 119.

Such a movement would hold on high the constitutional ideas of liberalism, but work positively, as in England, for the national interest, and not along [sterile] antigovernmental lines. It [this movement] would demand, with greater determination than the rightwings of our moderate parties, to participate in the government, and once in the government, it would represent bourgeois interests *vis-à-vis* feudal, one-sidedly agrarian and orthodox interests. Yet [this movement would] not serve simply the wishes of small rentiers and dissatisfied tradesmen, as the present left liberals do. It [this movement] would support the modernization of the state and take a forward-looking approach to the conduct of foreign policy, whether involving colonial issues or the [other] tasks of a great power.[62]

Hoping to promote the "bourgeois-national" movement of his expectations, Rathenau agreed to a proposal from the chairman of the National Liberal party in early 1911 that he run for the Reichstag, but stipulated that he be nominated by the left liberals as well. Since this reservation was unacceptable, the candidacy fell through.[63]

On the eve of World War I, Rathenau's basic position had changed little during the preceding decade. He was still hoping to promote the development of a bourgeois society in which differential opportunities at birth would be reduced, but scarcely eliminated. Despite his nostalgia for many aristocratic ways, he desired modifications in German institutions that would generally have made them more closely resemble those of the democracies of the West, but he manifested no overwhelming desire to obtain these modifications if the price were acute conflict between the conservative agrarians and the liberal bourgeoisie. Perhaps his social and economic position made him more timid than Weber and Naumann—or afforded him a less sanguine view of the delicate balance of Wilhelminian society. Convinced that changes would come about sooner or later, he was more reluctant to impair domestic stability through the creation of a popular anti-Junker coalition. Only his dissatisfaction with Germany's foreign policies, his apprehension about the growth of the Socialist movement, and a general sense of social malaise induced him to demand reforms as vigorously as he had. From these reforms he expected a sounder foreign policy, an improvement in trade relations with other countries through lowered tariffs, the acquisition of a share of the colonial world com-

[62] "Die neue Ära," pp. 20–21.
[63] Kessler, *Walther Rathenau*, pp. 138–39. See also *Tagebuch*, pp. 119, 145–46. In an apparent slip, Kessler refers to the *Freisinnigen* as the party whose nomination Rathenau wished to obtain in addition to that of the National Liberals, but both of the *Freisinnigen* parties were among the three left-liberal groups that merged in 1910 to form the *Fortschrittliche Volkspartei*. Hence Kessler probably has this last party in mind when he writes about Rathenau's prospective candidacy.

mensurate with Germany's legitimate needs and world position, and, eventually, the creation of a European customs union to ward off competition from the United States.[64]

WARTIME VARIATIONS ON OLD THEMES

The war influenced Rathenau's thinking, but not in a dramatic way until 1917. The partial disintegration of the *Burgfrieden*, the intensification of domestic conflicts, the Reichstag peace resolution, and the tipping of the military balance in favor of the Allies alerted him to the peril of Germany's political and social situation. Although he later acquired a somewhat undeserved reputation as the prophet of the inability of Wilhelminian Germany to win the war,[65] he long assumed that there was still time for the German Empire to be reformed from above.

The outbreak of the war turned his attention to the problems of a wartime economy. Together with Wichard von Moellendorff, an engineer employed in a high managerial post by the AEG, he was instrumental in establishing the War Materials Section (KRA, *Kriegsrohstoffsabteilung*) of the War Ministry. Although later Rathenau and Moellendorff emphasized the "Socialist" potential of the institutions created under the auspices of the KRA, recent studies have made clear that such ideological considerations had little if anything to do with the organization and development of the KRA.[66] The primary impetus for the establishment of the KRA came from men who had sufficient foresight to perceive that the organization of the German economy was inadequate, both for the pursuit of a major war and for the future needs of substantial sectors of big business. Within the KRA competing sectors of big business jockeyed for advantage. Major Josef Koeth, the man who succeeded Rathenau as the head of the KRA in April 1915 and who ironically was Rathenau's personal choice for the position, soon became a virtual representative of heavy industry in the government.[67] As we shall see later, Rathenau's experiences with the KRA were to lead to major innovations in his ideas. Perceiving the need for

[64] "Kritik der Zeit," p. 117; "Deutsche Gefahren und neue Ziele" (1913) in *GS*, I, 267–72.

[65] See Joll, "Walther Rathenau," pp. 109–10.

[66] See Alfred Müller, *Die Kriegsrohstoffbewirtschaftung 1914–1918 im Dienste des deutschen Monopolkapitals* (Berlin, 1955); Robert B. Armeson, *Total Warfare and Compulsory Labor: A Study of the Military-Industrial Complex in Germany during World War I* (The Hague, 1964); Hellmuth Weber, *Ludendorff und die Monopole: Deutsche Kriegspolitik 1916–1918* (Berlin, 1966); and esp. Gerald D. Feldman, *Army, Industry, and Labor in Germany, 1914–1918* (Princeton, 1966).

[67] See Feldman, *Army, Industry, and Labor*, pp. 46–52; Hellmuth Weber, *Ludendorff und die Monopole*, p. 29.

monopoly capitalists like himself to play a more direct role in the formulation of state policy, he was to conclude that the war corporations (*Kriegswirtschaftsgesellschaften*) organized under the direction of the KRA could assist in the systematic development of this role, as well as in adjudicating conflicts between diverging groups of big businessmen.

For the moment, however, he focused publicly on other aspects of these war corporations. Thus, in an address in late December 1915 to the *Deutsche Gesellschaft 1914*—the wartime group of businessmen, academicians, and state officials to which Naumann also belonged—he merely implied that the war corporations could become the vehicle for the self-regulation of industry, and then went on to topics that some members of his audience would have found intrinsically attractive as well as useful for the purposes of wartime propaganda. Describing the creation of the war corporations as a decisive step in the direction of state socialism,[68] he played upon notions developed by the "Socialists of the chair" during the latter part of the nineteenth century and subsequently elaborated by the propagandists of the "Ideas of 1914."

Convinced that the war provided an opportunity for the establishment of German economic and political hegemony on the Continent, Rathenau formulated, perhaps even before the creation of the KRA, a plan for the economic integration of Central Europe. A variant of his own and similar prewar proposals for a European customs union, this plan was based on the assumption that Germany's military position would remain favorable. A Central European economic union would, he wrote to a German diplomat, provide a prize of victory far more valuable than the realization of the wildest dreams of the annexationists.[69] If his plan for Central Europe were implemented by the German government, Rathenau had assured Chancellor Bethmann-Hollweg a few weeks earlier, France would soon be induced to conclude a mutually acceptable separate peace, and eventually a settlement could also be reached with England.[70]

Yet Rathenau regarded Naumann's conception of Central Europe as short sighted. Although some of Rathenau's derisive references to Naumann's book *Mitteleuropa* may have been occasioned by doubts about the durability of any political structure that would unite Central Europe,[71] these strictures probably originated in his preference

[68] "Deutschlands Rohstoffversorgung" in *GS*, v, 40.

[69] Letter of Oct. 10, 1914 to Gerhard von Mutius in *Briefe*, ɪ, 165.

[70] See esp. letter of Sept. 7, 1914 to Bethmann-Hollweg in *Politische Briefe* (Dresden, 1929), p. 12; Fritz Fischer, *Griff nach der Weltmacht: Die Kriegszielpolitik des kaiserlichen Deutschland 1914–1918*, 3rd ed. (Düsseldorf, 1964), p. 114; Kessler, *Walther Rathenau*, p. 171; Joll, "Walther Rathenau," p. 91; Pogge's note in *Tagebuch*, pp. 186–87.

[71] See the letter of Oct. 21, 1916 to Wilhelm Schwaner in *Briefe*, ɪ, 224.

for indirect and economic methods of empire building on the Continent. Like his business associate at the *Berliner Handelsgesellschaft* Carl Fürstenberg and like Albert Ballin of the Hamburg-America shipping line, Rathenau was among the German imperialists most leery of policies that gave any hint of suggesting extensive annexations in Europe by Germany.[72] Rathenau may also have feared that Naumann's scheme was too oriented toward Central Europe and would increase protectionism and preclude the formation of a general European customs union, for he remained strongly committed to free trade. Certainly he was anxious not to destroy his prewar hope for a European customs union and to hold open the possibility of forming a joint union with Germany's wartime enemies in Western Europe. Thus he was merely acknowledging the weakness of most of Germany's political warfare during World War I when, shortly before the armistice, he praised the concept of a German-Austrian customs union as "the only great political idea" that the war had helped to mature on the side of the Central Powers.[73]

After resigning from the KRA, he remained in close touch with the highest political and military circles. One of Ludendorff's early promoters, he wrote retrospectively in late 1919 that he had done everything in his power to have Ludendorff appointed to the German High Command: "For a while I too hoped that Ludendorff could be the man who like Frederick [the Great] and Napoleon would unite political and strategic leadership. . . ."[74] Although bolstered by an irrational conception of genius, Rathenau's wishful thinking about Ludendorff's ability to coordinate the direction of military strategy and state policy probably originated in the desire, shared by contending factions within the German ruling class, to find a popular figure who would take responsibility for the burdens imposed upon the populace by the continuation of the war. Ludendorff's military reputation made him a suitable candidate to assume this task in 1916 as the war increasingly divided Germany, largely along social lines, into a war and a peace party.[75] In 1919 Rathenau claimed that he had become disillusioned with Ludendorff as early as mid-1917, when the failure of unlimited submarine warfare became apparent,[76] but Gustav Steinbömer, one of

[72] See Willibald Gutsche, "Zu einigen Fragen der staatsmonopolischen Verflechtung in den ersten Kriegsjahren am Beispiel der Ausplünderung der belgischen Industrie und Zwangsdeportationen von Belgiern" in Fritz Klein, ed., *Politik im Kriege 1914–1918: Studien zur Politik der deutschen herrschenden Klassen im 1. Weltkrieg* (Berlin, 1964), pp. 68–70.

[73] "Der wahre Grund politischer Fehler" (Sept. 1918) in *GS*, vi, 35.

[74] "Schicksalspiel" (Nov. 23, 1919) in *GS*, vi, 460.

[75] See Hellmuth Weber, *Ludendorff und die Monopole*, pp. 31–32, 40.

[76] "Schicksalspiel," p. 468.

Rathenau's close friends, has suggested that only the German request for an armistice on September 29, 1918 finally destroyed his confidence in Ludendorff.[77] Steinbömer may be correct. Certainly Rathenau concluded that Ludendorff's sudden demand in August 1918 that the German government ask for an armistice revealed poor judgment, although as late as October 1918 both men stood on the same side of two critical issues. Ludendorff, having changed his mind, now wished to have the armistice request retracted, and after the receipt of Wilson's reply to the first German note, he began to explore the idea of using a *levée en masse* in order to continue the war—a scheme that was bruited about by Pan-Germans and other right-wingers, as well as by Majority Socialists like Ebert. In a newspaper article of October 7, Rathenau criticized the armistice request as premature and associated himself with the proposals for a *levée en masse*.[78]

As the war developed into a military stalemate on the western front and increased social and economic tensions within Germany, Rathenau became very disturbed about the welfare and attitudes of the middle class. The redistribution of wealth promoted by the German government's methods of financing the war would, he feared, produce great hardships, especially for the highly educated. The supply of men available for university posts, journalism, engineering, and the civil service would decline drastically. He voiced less concern about the difficulties of small businessmen. Indeed, he warned against measures that might protect inefficient small enterprises: "The tasks of the middle class [*Mittelstand*] are great and beautiful and mighty, but they should not be misinterpreted in such a way that we keep legions of hands away from productive work."[79] By 1918, when Rathenau was referring to the domestic consequences of the war as a "social revolution,"[80] he speculated that "the intellectual middle class" might lose its moorings. More severely affected by the war than any other segment of German society, it was, he complained, beginning to sink into the proletariat. He warned that nihilism might flourish among the intelligentsia.[81]

[77] Steinbömer, *Herren und Narren der Welt*, pp. 233–34.

[78] See Hellmuth Weber, *Ludendorff und die Monopole*, pp. 139–45 for an analysis of both the proposals for a *levée en masse* and the discussion in German ruling circles of the armistice request.

[79] "Probleme der Friedenswirtschaft" (Dec. 1916), in *GS*, v, 65, 80–81. See also "Die neue Wirtschaft" (Jan. 1918) in *GS*, v, 186–87.

[80] See "An Deutschlands Jugend" (written July 1918) in *GS*, vi, 162–64.

[81] "Kriegsgewinner" (Sept. 1918) in *GS*, vi, 64–65. A fascinating testament to his interest in the educated middle class is his correspondence with the Protestant theologian Leopold Ziegler. Their correspondence, which began in 1914, was apparently slight until 1917. Ziegler then turned to Rathenau to lament the fate of the middle class and Germany's lack of adequate leadership. See Leopold Ziegler, *Briefe 1901–1958*, ed. Erwin Stein (Munich, 1963), pp. 219, 238. During the

During the last year and a half of the war, Rathenau's writings were dominated by the search for a political and social order that would provide an alternative to both the Western democracies and the Second Empire—a search made more urgent by the fear of revolution fostered by the upheaval in Russia. He participated in the wartime celebration of Germandom only in a circumspect way. While others sang the praises of Germanic values, Rathenau realized that the domestic order in Germany had little to offer other Europeans, especially those in the West. Unlike the wartime exponents of the uniqueness of German merits, Rathenau dispassionately discussed his nation's relationship to the rest of Europe. Dashing cold water on the fiery utterances of the German chauvinists, he found only one critical difference between German society and that of the West—a German weakness: "The failings and injustices of our economic and social structure are the same as in the rest of the world. . . . With one exception: ascent is more difficult in our country than elsewhere; for plutocratic restrictions are joined to those imposed by the feudal, bureaucratic, and military atmosphere."[82] In private correspondence, he was more precise about the deleterious influence of the Junkers and of heavy industry. In a letter to an aristocratic acquaintance, he sought to demonstrate that restrictions on ascent were increasingly incompatible with the development of modern society:

> It is my belief that as time goes on, political and administrative tasks will become more and more complex and difficult and will call for correspondingly higher talents, talents which the hereditary system is less and less able to provide. . . . As I see the matter, talent is not among the privileges of heredity. It must be generated anew continually from the ranks of a healthy people. A lack of suitable talent and an excessive reliance upon inherited qualities have led to the policy of the past thirty years and to the inevitable conflicts resulting from it.[83]

Rathenau offered a "people's state [*Volksstaat*]" as an alternative to the "plutocratic democracies" of the West and the "mixed plutocratic and feudalistic" system of Germany. When he began to use the term "people's state" favorably in his published writings, he made clear that he did not have in mind the classical conception of democracy:

Weimar Republic Ziegler entered public political discussion as a neoconservative proponent of the middle class. He will be mentioned again in connection with Count Hermann Keyserling and Edgar Jung.

[82] "An Deutschlands Jugend," p. 186. See also letter of Apr. 4, 1917 to Dr. Ernst Norlind in *Briefe*, I, 250.

[83] Letter of Apr. 14, 1917 to Rittmeister Freiherr von Müffling in *Briefe*, I, 256. I have altered slightly the translation found in Kessler, *Walther Rathenau*, p. 129.

There has never been true democracy, the rule of the people, except perhaps during a few days of a revolution. . . . Everywhere in the world some [few] men rule, and the only issue is whether they belong to a small, hereditary and not highly capable caste and must be appointed on the recommendation of secret cabinets, or are supposed to be selected from the entire people; whether as a consequence the people is divided politically into perpetual rulers and perpetually ruled; whether an entire series of estate privileges, customs, and pretensions is maintained through this division. The real issue is this: caste state or people's state? The parliaments, of whose narrow-minded verbosity and bombast the world has had enough and more, are necessary evils, required as places of compromise for parties and as schools for statesmen.[84]

Although serving to justify the military dictatorship in Germany, this conception of a "people's state" also incorporated Rathenau's expectations for future reforms. He sought to demonstrate that broad recruitment of the elite was necessary to produce an authoritarian government of the type that he desired. Using democracy as a term that implied, above all, an open elite, he argued that autocracy and democracy were perfectly compatible. Indeed, all government should be autocratic lest it be powerless and incompetent. Only a combination of democracy and autocracy made effective government possible. Democracy, or an open elite, would give the general populace a feeling of trust in its rulers and enable them to make and execute policy without feeling threatened from below: "Governing is an art; it can only be practiced when the creative individuals, undisturbed and unmolested, are supported by trust. Trust makes autocracy possible; democracy makes trust possible."[85]

In private letters, Rathenau sought to convince some of his friends and acquaintances that his proposals were not as radical as they might appear. He explained that he desired not "the rule of the people," but merely "the organic development and selection of men with a calling."[86] Perhaps bending over backward to reassure a Prussian Junker who was *Landesdirektor* of the Province of Brandenburg as well as a Conservative Reichstag deputy, he wrote that for a long time to come those in power had little to fear: "The headstart of the present ruling class is so great and will in the foreseeable future remain so great that only pronounced incapability will be grounds for departure; on the other side, strong popular forces must be tapped to fill the present de-

[84] "Neue Wirtschaft," p. 254.
[85] "An Deutschlands Jugend," pp. 189–90.
[86] Letter of July 7, 1917 to Prof. Dr. J. Landmann in *Briefe*, I, 298–99; letter of Apr. 14, 1917 to Rittmeister Freiherr von Müffling in *Briefe*, I, 255.

ficiency. Not a fawning mien, but tradition, attitude, schooling, and competition will guarantee us the proper selection."[87]

In a letter describing the thrust of his major wartime book, *Von kommenden Dingen*[88] (*Of Things to Come*), Rathenau characterized his position as neither conservative nor purely democratic, but directed toward "the leadership of the able."[89] Rathenau regarded this work, written before the overthrow of the Tsarist autocracy in Russia and the collapse of the *Burgfrieden* in Germany, as a popular exposition of his ideas. He hoped to have the book as widely read as possible. When it was being reprinted in early 1918, he asked his publisher to keep the price as low as feasible so that workers would be able to buy it. He was elated when the Social Democratic unions ordered 500 copies, and the Christian Trade Unions 250.[90]

The major themes of *Von kommenden Dingen* had all been dealt with by Rathenau in his previous works. He elaborated, often more systematically and comprehensively, upon his elitist themes: Germany was ruled by a plutocracy; some type of oligarchy would rule every society; society could be changed and improved by broadening the social basis from which the rulers were recruited; if it were possible for talented men from every quarter of society to enter the oligarchy, a true aristocracy could be created; although the process of "mechanization" affecting the entire world was ineluctable, its positive effects could be strengthened by the creation of this true aristocracy and by new economic structures. Since Rathenau extended and modified these ideas in his last great social and political works in 1918 and 1919, *Von kommenden Dingen* offered a summary of his position before the threat of social revolution began to emerge clearly in 1917.

Based on the expectation that Germany would win the war, the book nevertheless reflects a heightened awareness of the desirability of curtailing the trade in luxury goods. This subject was not a new one for Rathenau, but he pursued it with a fresh tenacity, revealing his apprehensiveness about the resentment that the standard of living of the wealthy had aroused among the lower classes. He realized that wartime shortages, the brunt of which was borne by the lower classes, had fostered much bitterness about the ready availability of food and luxuries to people with the servants to search for them and money to purchase them. Although conceding that the production of luxury goods was not a crucial social issue and that the diversion of resources into

[87] Letter of Apr. 21, 1917 to Joachim von Winterfeldt in *Briefe*, i, 260. For a list of Winterfeldt's major offices at the time of this letter see Peter Molt, *Der Reichstag vor der improvisierten Revolution* (Cologne, 1963), p. 94n.

[88] Reprinted as *GS*, iii.

[89] Letter of Apr. 30, 1918 to Wilhelm Schwaner in *Briefe*, ii, 40.

[90] Letter of Mar. 12, 1918 to S. Fischer in *Briefe*, iii, 244.

them did not cripple Germany's productive capacity, he called for severe restrictions upon their manufacture and consumption.[91] His solutions to the problems of upper-class consumption were indicative of how uninspired his search for palliatives for bourgeois society had become until the Russian Revolution reinvigorated his ruminations.

NEW SOCIETY VERSUS SOCIAL REVOLUTION

The German defeat, the November Revolution, and the continuing threat of social revolution kept Rathenau's fertile imagination busily engaged in the production of drafts for a new elitist order that would be neither capitalist nor Socialist. These efforts culminated in *The New Society*, published in October 1919,[92] and then fell off. Both through his writings and his political activities he devoted himself from 1917 through 1919 mainly to reducing the power of the working class and to the frustration of Marxism whether German or Bolshevik. As the threat of revolution receded and the power of the Left declined, he placed less emphasis upon the need to realize his visions within the foreseeable future.

Like many a German anti-Marxist, Rathenau began to describe his ideas as "socialist" alternatives to Marxism.[93] Before 1917 he occasionally employed the term "socialism" favorably, but always in conjunction with a qualifying word such as *state* socialism. More often he had avoided even this phrase. By late November 1918, he was using the expression "socialism" positively, if a bit gingerly.[94] His denunciation of Marxism, which embodied criticisms he had developed during the previous two decades, continued to be based upon misconceptions and distortions common among non-Marxists in Germany.[95]

[91] *Von kommenden Dingen*, pp. 94–97.

[92] *Die neue Gesellschaft* now in *GS*, v. The English translation by Arthur Windham, *The New Society* (New York, 1921) is generally adequate, but the explanatory notes are poor and often erroneous.

[93] Rathenau is not mentioned in the index to Herman Lebovics, *Social Conservatism and the Middle Classes in Germany, 1914–1933* (Princeton, 1969), which deals with the proponents of a "Germanic socialism" as ideologists of the *Mittelstand*.

[94] The first favorable reference in his published writings is in a political leaflet, "Die Wirtschaft der Zukunft" (dated Nov. 29, 1918), in *NS*, I, 89. In a letter of Nov. 28, 1918 to Dr. Schillo, *Politische Briefe*, p. 222, he was more reserved in his use of the term, speaking of the need to introduce "einen verständigen Sozialismus."

[95] See, e.g., his interpretation of Marx as having recommended that the worker receive all of the surplus value that he produced. On the basis of this erroneous assertion Rathenau justified his dismissal of Marxists as incapable of developing a workable alternative to capitalism: the distribution of this surplus value to the workers would do little to raise the general standard of living. "Sozialisierung und kein Ende: Ein Wort vom Mehrwert" (Feb. 1919) in *GS*, VI, 218–32. For an

Drawing upon his experiences in the War Ministry, Rathenau argued that the era of a free-market economy had come to an end and that the economic system must be centralized and rationalized with the assistance of state planning. These notions, which he developed in his wartime writings and continued to elaborate in his immediate postwar works, especially in a pamphlet entitled *Autonome Wirtschaft* published in September 1919,[96] aimed at the extension and systematization of cartelization.[97] Private enterprise would continue but would serve public objectives. Through the transformation of cartels into public bodies under the guidance of the state, through the extension of these cartel-like organizations to the entire economy, and through the participation of workers and consumers in management, business would presumably come to serve not primarily private profit, but rather the interests of the community. Both during Rathenau's lifetime and subsequently, critics have frequently charged that these economic plans, which were vague on questions such as the form that worker and consumer "consultation" would take, were designed basically to promote the interests of big business, and indeed primarily the complex of highly cartelized undertakings that had developed around the AEG and the *Berliner Handelsgesellschaft*.[98] Responding to the charge of his

ambitious, but uninspired attempt to distinguish Rathenau's "socialism" from Marxism see Ephraim Fuchs, *Das wirtschaftspolitische System Walther Rathenaus* (Jena diss., 1926). See esp. Fuchs' critique (pp. 60–64) of Rathenau's unsuccessful efforts to come to grips with the Marxian theory of surplus value. Berglar, *Walther Rathenau*, pp. 160–61, 218–19 glosses over the muddle to which these efforts led. Like many of Rathenau's admirers, Berglar accepts, if with reservations, the claim that the man possessed prophetic insight into the future. Typical of the work of Rathenau's less critical, earlier admirers is a Marburg dissertation by Hans Vogt, *Das System Walther Rathenaus und der Versuch eines Vergleichs mit dem von Karl Marx* (1927). Many bourgeois intellectuals during the Weimar Republic sought to denigrate Marx by lauding the originality, incisiveness, or human warmth of some other Socialist—often Weitling, Lassalle, or even Engels. Vogt found his "Socialist" hero in Rathenau.

[96] *Autonome Wirtschaft* (Jena, 1919). The title is ambiguous and might be translated *Autonomous Enterprise* as well as *Autonomous Economy* (this pamphlet is not included in *GS*). See also "Die neue Wirtschaft" (Jan. 1918) in *GS*, v.

[97] An excellent brief exposition of these economic plans is the section entitled "Rathenau's Cartel Corporatism" in Ralph H. Bowen's *German Theories of the Corporative State: With Special Reference to the Period, 1870–1919* (New York, 1947), pp. 164–82.

[98] See, e.g., Walther Lambach, *Diktator Rathenau*, 7.–12. Aufl. (Hamburg and Leipzig, 1918); and Pogge's remarks in the epilogue to his edition of Rathenau's *Tagebuch*, pp. 282–84. Lambach (p. 60) argues that Rathenau's economic writings were based on the realization that peace would bring wage struggles of unprecedented severity and that Rathenau sought to organize businessmen to withstand effectively this assault on their profits. Lambach, although a staunch anti-Marxist, was a member of a major white-collar union, the DHV (*Deutschnationaler Handlungsgehilfenverband*). Significantly, although the DHV remained outspokenly anti-Marxist, by the end of World War I it was adopting a qualified

and Leonard Nelson's friend Franz Oppenheimer, a liberal economist and sociologist, that his economic system presupposed an economic dictator, Rathenau avoided the implications of the issue:

> And my "dictator?" He is already here, and you can't get rid of him. For you he is a tyrant and will become a despot; for me he will become a constitutional servant of the state. His name is syndicate, trust, association. . . . The real question is shall we leave him with his power, which you can't take away from him and which is destroying your system [of free enterprise], or do we want to regulate him in the interests of the community? [If we decide to regulate him,] his power must, on the one side, be broadened by [giving him] the right to [pursue] rationalization, and narrowed, on the other side, through accountability, the limitation of prices, and state participation.[99]

Although Rathenau wished to divert the working-class movement into benign cooperation with these plans for a cartelized economy,[100] they were more tailored to the restructuring of monopoly capital accelerated by the war and the consolidation of the role of the monopolists in the formulation of state policy.[101]

Immediately after the overthrow of the monarchy and the creation of a provisional government headed by Social Democrats, Rathenau became involved in a hectic endeavor to establish a new political organization, the Democratic Popular Union (*Volksbund*). Seeking a counterweight to the strength of the organized working class,[102] he

---

class-struggle position that characterized both big business and big (Socialist) labor as foes. On the changes in the DHV see Iris Hamel, *Völkischer Verband und nationale Gewerkschaft: Der Deutschnationale Handlungs-Gehilfenverband 1893–1933* (Frankfurt am Main, 1967), pp. 169–70, 176. See also my forthcoming studies of Walther Lambach and the DHV.

[99] Letter of Mar. 14, 1918 to Franz Oppenheimer in *Briefe*, I, 384. The ellipses are in the published edition.

[100] See, e.g., his letter of Apr. 26, 1917 to Bethmann-Hollweg. Discussing the need to centralize the economy, Rathenau found one of the most important reasons in the need "der sozialistischen, insbesondere gewerkschaftlichen Bewegung ein ihrer Stärke entsprechendes produktives Arbeitsfeld zu geben und sie von reibendem und zerstörendem Leerlauf abzulenken" (*Politische Briefe*, p. 113).

[101] See Hellmuth Weber, *Ludendorff und die Monopole*, pp. 27–28.

[102] Quoting Rathenau, Joll alludes to the *Volksbund* as an organization whose task was "to encourage social idealism in the bourgeoisie and to strengthen it in the working class." Joll, "Walther Rathenau," p. 106. Although this phrase appears in a letter of Nov. 27, 1918 to Robert Bosch, *Politische Briefe*, pp. 220–21, Rathenau was referring not to the *Volksbund*, but to a possible successor. An article on the *Volksbund* by Hans Martin Barth draws upon much of the available material: "Der Demokratische Volksbund: Zu den Anfängen des politischen Engagements der Unternehmer der Berliner Elektrogrossindustrie im November 1918," *Jahrbuch für die Geschichte Mittel- und Ostdeutschlands*, XVI–XVII (1968), 254–66.

made clear that the immediate function of the *Volksbund* was to unite the entire bourgeoisie and to mobilize it against the revolutionary potential of the proletariat. His speech at the founding meeting of this new organization seems alarmist in retrospect. He warned his audience that the apparent calm in Germany could well prove deceptive: a naive observer walking through the streets and seeing the factories still operating might jump to the conclusion that a radical revolution was not going to take place. Rathenau called for a political force to counteract the threat of a dictatorship of the proletariat.[103]

Despite his labors, the *Volksbund* was dissolved less than two weeks after its founding. Its most obvious accomplishment was an appeal, published in several liberal newspapers, to support the new republican state and to demand a National Assembly. Among the signers of this appeal were big businessmen like Felix Deutsch, Carl Friedrich von Siemens, Ernst von Borsig, Robert Bosch, and Hugo Stinnes, as well as Naumann, scholars, artists, right-wing Social Democrats, and Christian Trade Unionists.[104] But Rathenau's endeavor to gain business backing for a bold social program failed. Although, as we saw in Chapter Three, industrialists as divergent politically and temperamentally as Bosch and Stinnes would join to finance Stadtler's Anti-Bolshevik League despite its espousal of some radical-sounding measures, they would provide only covert support for Stadtler. Rathenau, on the other hand, desired to have his name linked publicly to an innovative social program.[105] By giving tacit assistance to the most conservative Social Democrats in their struggle against the reformers and radicals to their left, the *Volksbund* attempted to strengthen the alliance between big business and right-wing Social Democrats that emerged during the war.[106] At the same time, the *Volksbund* promoted the development in the new German Republic of a nonmonarchist, prorepublican opposition on the basis of the demand for a National Assembly entrusted with sovereignty to supplant the Provisional Government.[107]

[103] "Rede in der Versammlung zur Schaffung eines demokratischen Volksbundes" (Nov. 16, 1918) in *Gesammelte Reden* (Berlin, 1924), pp. 29–35.

[104] See Barth, "Der Demokratische Volksbund," pp. 254–55, n. 1.

[105] Barth's conclusion (*ibid.*, p. 262) that Robert Bosch agreed with Rathenau on the need for a "radical" program seems doubtful. Cf. Theodor Heuss, *Robert Bosch: Leben und Leistung* (Stuttgart, 1948), p. 332.

[106] On this aspect of the *Volksbund* see Barth, "Der Demokratische Volksbund," p. 263.

[107] In a letter Rathenau made the revealing statement that a basic purpose of the *Volksbund* was to gain support for the convening of a National Assembly: "Der Grundgedanke des Demokratischen Volksbundes war gesund; es handelte sich einmal darum, die gesamte bürgerliche Intelligenz zu einer gewissen Gemeinschaft der Einstellung zu sammeln, sodann eine eindrucksvolle Kundgebung für die Nationalversammlung zu schaffen." Letter of Nov. 26, 1918 to Carl Friedrich von Siemens in *Politische Briefe*, p. 217.

Together with the Majority Socialists and others hoping to prevent the radicalization of the German political situation, Rathenau continued to call for early elections for the National Assembly.[108] During the next few months, while the fate of revolution in Central Europe still hung in the balance, he spoke frequently of the necessity of maintaining order, production, and work discipline. He cautioned against the precipitous introduction of economic reforms.[109]

After the *Volksbund* collapsed, Rathenau became associated with the newly formed Democratic party. He ran for the National Assembly as a Democrat, but his name had been placed so far down the party's list that he did not obtain a seat. In a leaflet dated November 29, 1918 that he composed for the elections, he defended the November Revolution primarily on the grounds that it had destroyed the grip of "a small hereditary caste."[110] In another leaflet of the same date, he accused Social Democrats of condemning unfairly all private business as capitalistic. With men like himself apparently in mind, he complained: "It [Social Democracy] unjustly casts suspicion on every leader and responsible collaborator in free enterprise as a servant of capitalism and of capitalists."[111] Germany would be lost, he warned, "without the sense of duty, spirit of initiative, and innovative daring of the owners, managers, white-collar workers, and blue-collar workers in industry."[112]

Rathenau's arrogance as well as duplicity are apparent in a letter that he wrote in December to Friedrich Ebert, the right-wing Social Democrat who headed the provisional government. Rathenau described his chagrin at his exclusion from the Socialization Commission without any public announcement of the cause. He presented Ebert with a pretentious justification for his career: "I do not think that there are many men on the bourgeois side who, at the risk of their position with the bourgeoisie and disregarding all the hostility shown, have done what I felt it my task to be and attacked the old system without reserve, opposed the war, and presented a complete, new economic system scientifically based and elaborated. . . ."[113] Even if every one of these statements had been indisputable, the letter might still have appeared to be either the pompous declamations of a vain man or the crude attempts of someone still desperately hoping to be appointed to

[108] See, e.g., his election leaflet, dated November 29, 1919: "Rettet die Revolution!" in *NS*, I, 83.
[109] See, e.g., *ibid.*, pp. 85–86.   [110] *Ibid.*, p. 81.
[111] "Kapitalismus" in *NS*, I, 90–91. Rathenau italicized the entire passage.
[112] *Ibid.*, p. 92. Significantly Rathenau referred ambiguously to the owners of industry as "our Eigentümer."
[113] Letter of Dec. 16, 1918 to Fritz Ebert in *Briefe*, III, 88. The translation is that provided by Joll, "Walther Rathenau," p. 107.

the Socialization Commission. Apparently, Ebert was not able to appoint Rathenau due to opposition from the Independent Socialists, and an announcement to that effect might have hastened the imminent departure of the Independent Socialist members of the provisional government.

During the early days of the Republic, Rathenau attempted both publicly and privately to promote acceptance of his ideas among the trade unions. He indicated in a letter to Robert Bosch that he had gained some influence in the new *Bund der freien Gewerkschaften,* a non-Socialist association. He claimed that the organization had adopted almost without change the program that he sent to it.[114]

While vigorously denouncing the Left, especially the Spartacists,[115] Rathenau began to find a place for bolshevism in his own view of history. Comparing the French Revolution to the Russian Revolution, he argued that the real objective of the latter was the dissolution of Europe's social stratification. Within a century, he predicted, this goal would be realized. The Russian Revolution was thus part of a world revolution that would tap dormant forces in some members of the lower classes. A "vertical migration" from below would reinvigorate the upper strata of society, strata which had become weak and were in need of renewal. The process was irresistible, but it would not occur rapidly.[116]

Emphasizing the danger of a "rebarbarization" of European society if the "vertical migration" were not properly canalized, Rathenau found that the lower strata of society had not developed the desirable traits possessed by the old upper strata. He dismissed as a "mechanistic superstition" the notion that a few lifetimes of schooling could produce characteristics such as "self-discipline, self-denial, responsibility, nobility of soul, inner freedom, and idealism." The upper strata faced a great trial, for they would have to be willing to permit their own expropriation and to share their spiritual possessions in order to retard the advance of the barbarians.[117]

The threat to "culture" posed by the incipient "vertical migration" was one of Rathenau's favorite themes during 1919. By dwelling upon this threat Rathenau sought to foster the apprehensions of his readers about the consequences of revolution. He also attempted to arouse animosity toward the German Left by identifying it with bolshevism and then discrediting bolshevism as a transient expression of conditions in

[114] Letter of Dec. 16, 1918 to Dr. Robert Bosch in *Briefe,* III, 252. See also letter of Jan. 21, 1919 to Dr. Erich Schairer in *Briefe,* II, 113.
[115] See, e.g., "Sozialisierung und kein Ende: Ein Wort vom Mehrwert" (Feb. 1919) in *GS,* VI, 217.
[116] "Der Kaiser: Eine Betrachtung" (Mar. 1919) in *GS,* VI, 333–34.
[117] *Ibid.,* pp. 334–37.

Russia.[118] Referring to the Bolshevik Revolution as a "revolution of rancor," he predicted that it would soon lead to oligarchy and military dictatorship. Although the original and perhaps strongest impetus behind all revolutions was spite and malice, a true revolution must take place gradually. Otherwise the good characteristics of the old ruling stratum would be destroyed, and a "primitive" struggle among social strata would take place. If the Germans were to avoid both a "revolution of the cossacks" (i.e., a counterrevolution) and a Bolshevik-style revolution, the November Revolution had to be followed by a "moral revolution [*Revolution der Gesinnung*]," for true revolutions were decided in the spirit and involved the victory of an idea.[119]

In June 1919 Rathenau found little hope that the German revolution, which had been simply "the general strike of a defeated army," would take such a course. Seeking to discredit the revolutionary Left, he charged that the same mentality that had once justified imperialism, authority, nationalism, and military dictatorship now justified revolution and the dictatorship of the proletariat.[120]

One of the major immediate problems that Rathenau confronted was how to keep German workers on the job and ensure that they did not let up. Recognizing that new techniques would be necessary in order to improve the morale of the labor force, he believed that the workers' and soldiers' councils might be employed to this end. If only the German council movement would avoid the Russian model, it might be harnessed to increase enormously the worker's desire to work.[121] Rathenau suggested also that the councils might be employed as institutions to promote the social ascent of the more capable members of the lower classes.[122] During part of 1919, he advanced the idea that the councils might provide an alternative to parliamentarism on the Western model.[123] A parliamentary system might work in Western Europe, but in Germany, where internal divisions were much more pronounced, it would not function properly. Only a system involving several parliaments arranged in ascending order of importance was suited to Germany.[124]

In 1920 Rathenau was appointed to the second commission con-

[118] See, e.g., "Kritik der dreifachen Revolution" (written in June 1919) in *GS*, VI, 345–46.

[119] *Ibid.*, pp. 346–48, 358, 364, 368–69.

[120] *Ibid.*, p. 341.

[121] See "Arbeit" (dated Mar. 24, 1919) in *GS*, V, 318, 325.

[122] "Kritik der dreifachen Revolution," p. 397.

[123] *Ibid.*, p. 396.

[124] "Der neue Staat" in *GS*, V, 272–73, 286, 289, 291. Published in May 1919, this work was written before the completion of the Weimar Constitution (see *ibid.*, p. 267). For a halting, but often incisive critique of the essay see Berglar, *Walther Rathenau*, esp. pp. 200–08.

vened to discuss the issue of socialization. One might have thought that he would have played a constructive role in view of his public utterances in favor of the partial socialization of German industry. But he devoted most of his activities on the commission to combating the proposals of the Left.[125]

In a speech in October 1920, he argued that some form of "codetermination [*Mitbestimmung*]" must come, but that it must be developed gradually. In the legislation establishing works' councils (*Betriebsräte*) in certain industries, he found a hopeful development. According to Rathenau, this legislation laid the basis for workers and employers to "educate" each other.[126]

Yet he never suggested a specific political framework within which his ideas on "codetermination" would be implemented. Correctly regarding this failure as "the most serious weakness in Rathenau's social and economic thinking," James Joll[127] neglects to relate it to the basic character of Rathenau's writings. By the middle of World War I, Rathenau assumed that his "cartel corporatism" constituted the political as well as economic foundation for the realization of all of his other plans. Preoccupied by endeavors to undermine the potential of movements like the workers' and soldiers' councils to disrupt the development of this "cartel corporatism," he dealt haphazardly with political institutions, whose place in his thinking had by now become peripheral. He was, as we have seen, more interested in providing a vision of the future that would suggest general alternatives to revolution than in exploring the more complex problems of the political structure of monopoly capitalism.

Rathenau excelled in the drafting of social rather than political blueprints for the future. His social imagination was at its peak in his last major work, *The New Society*, which he completed during the latter half of 1919. In this book he still sought to demonstrate that Germany could avoid both bolshevism and the capitalistic democracy of the West. Prewar Germany had, he argued, just begun to develop general affluence, as had the United States. According to Rathenau, the United States was by now so wealthy that the proletarian condition no longer existed, and to clinch his point he misleadingly referred to the daily wages of the American worker as having a purchasing power equal to one hundred German marks. In the United States, he explained, the development of a society of affluence could continue under capitalism,

[125] See letter of Dec. 6, 1920 to Dr. Keck in *Briefe*, II, 278–79; Felix Pinner, *Deutsche Wirtschaftsführer* (Berlin, 1924), pp. 2–4.

[126] "Produktionspolitik" in *Gesammelte Reden*, p. 91. This speech was given on Oct. 26, 1920 at a congress of the *Deutscher Beamtenbund*.

[127] Joll, "Walther Rathenau," p. 100.

but in Germany a similar development had been blocked by the war. Although Germany would have to begin the process anew, it could no longer occur within the framework of capitalism.[128] Having time and again sought to abolish the proletariat with the strokes of his pen, Rathenau now did the same to capitalism.

Much more concretely than in his earlier writings he depicted a social order in which "every accidental and inherited advantage" had been eliminated. Social stratification would depend upon differences in *Bildung*, in education and culture. The hallmark of a completely "socialized" society was, he asserted, the absence of income without work.[129] Yet neglecting to relate this social system coherently to the conception of a mixed capitalist and socialist economy that he had developed in other writings, he ignored the issue of whether his proposals assumed the perpetuation of some form of capitalism.

A society stratified according to education was for Rathenau the only society appropriate to Germany and worthy of her magnificent past. Since this system would eventually predominate throughout the entire world, Germany's adoption of it would put her in the forefront among nations. For the first time in centuries, the Germans would again become conscious that they had a true calling. Their mission would be comparable to the Anglo-American notion of spreading "civilization and democracy" and to the Russian belief in the destiny of the Orthodox Church. The competition among the members of Germany's "new society" would be akin to the noblest rivalries during the Renaissance.[130]

Rathenau's discussion of how differing degrees of education and culture would be determined was vague. There would be no examinations; rather the only test would be in one's work: "Everyone who makes his ability appear at all credible can demand that he be tested, and if he passes [this work test] will receive further education."[131] The various groupings of education and culture would develop spontaneously. They would constitute "levels" within the society, not classes, estates, or castes. Those who performed creative, intellectual work would be entitled to more freedom from cares and to more protection from external disturbances than those performing "repetitive work."[132]

Essential to a great expansion of popular education was what Rathenau called the "interchange of labor." Everyone involved in intellectual activities would be required to devote daily part of his time to physical labor. Everyone engaged in repetitive labor would be able to request that he exchange part of his present work for "appropriate"

---

[128] *Neue Gesellschaft*, pp. 428–29.   [129] *Ibid.*, p. 341.
[130] *Ibid.*, pp. 440, 449–56.   [131] *Ibid.*, p. 430.
[132] *Ibid.*, pp. 430–32.

intellectual tasks. Young men would have to put in a year at physical work. The only exceptions would be if the youth were physically or mentally incompetent and in the "rare" instances when he performed irreplaceable intellectual tasks.[133] Rathenau never indicated how the decision would be made that released someone from part of his physical work or that exempted the rare individuals engaged in irreplaceable mental work. Nor did he explain what institutions would be erected in order to initiate and enforce the principle of the interchange of labor.

From the interchange of labor he expected several important consequences. The "soulless division of labor" would cease to exist. Although seeing no prospect that repetitive work could be anything except "mindless and soulless," he suggested that its burden to some extent could be shared. The interchange of labor would help to destroy the "educational monopoly" possessed by the upper classes.[134]

The interchange of labor constituted an essential element in his conception of a society without class conflict. The principle would, he felt, help to build a bridge between formerly antagonistic elements of society: "A peace of God must be concluded, not between propertied and propertyless, not between proletariat and capitalist, not between so-called educated and uneducated, but among those who are prepared to exchange experiences, to give and take each other's traditions. Not a barter . . . , but an alliance. This [alliance] is possible only if [the pursuit of] class struggle as an end in itself is given up."[135]

Like Fritz Lang's motion picture *Metropolis* a decade later, Rathenau's *New Society* presented an idealistic resolution of the contradictions of bourgeois society. Relief from class warfare promised benefits that might make the interchange of labor palatable to the middle and upper classes. They could hope for exceptions to the rigid enforcement of this principle; they would not be rudely displaced in a revolutionary fashion and would be able to continue many of their accustomed pursuits for a long time to come. By assuming that the higher culture and education of the present had some inherent worth, Rathenau accorded enormous privileges to the middle and upper classes.

Seeking to make the desirability of his proposals more persuasive to both the Right and the Left, he painted a somber picture of the consequences if they were not adopted. Even if the national product were more evenly distributed, he wrote, three or four social strata would remain as distinct entities. Despite their impoverishment, these groups would find ways of preserving themselves. The first group was the

[133] *Ibid.*, pp. 428, 430. [134] *Ibid.*, p. 424.
[135] *Ibid.*, pp. 421–22. Rathenau italicized the entire last sentence.

feudal nobility, or Junkers. Its special fitness for the military profession and for administrative work would continue. Rathenau assumed that its prestige would remain high and that its cohesiveness would increase. Both the feudal nobility and a second group, the bureaucratic nobility, would be favored in the diplomatic corps, for they would still have the financial means and the familiarity with international life necessary for such positions.[136]

The third group consisted of the members of "the presently leading economic and intellectual stratum," or the bourgeoisie and upper middle class. The mood within this stratum would be similar to that of the Huguenots and the aristocratic émigrés during the French Revolution. They would attempt to preserve some remnant from the past, a few paintings, a library, or a musical instrument. They would pinch pennies in order to maintain their level of education and culture. Since these men would not be understood by others, they would distinguish themselves by dress and way of life. Performing a function similar to that of the inhabitants of monasteries during the Middle Ages, they would supply scholars, clergymen, professors, and other "representatives of the most selfless and intellectual professions."[137]

Rathenau alluded to a fourth stratum that would probably also remain, but he did not elaborate save to cast doubt on the effectiveness of the collectivization of agriculture. Independent peasants as well as farmers holding medium-sized estates would continue to exist, he claimed, even if the land were "radically socialized."[138]

According to Rathenau, conditions in parts of the United States and Eastern Europe provided a taste of what could come to pass in Germany. Higher culture would be at the mercy of men who would be very skeptical about its inherent worth. Public opinion would decide "everything." The prevailing atmosphere in Germany would be determined by the "half-Slavic" lower strata of central and northern Germany. Characterizing the gloomy picture of the future that he had painted as "hell," Rathenau implied that only his proposals, such as the interchange of labor, could mitigate its worst aspects.[139] He appealed to the third stratum, the bourgeoisie and upper middle class, to take the lead in creating the new society. This summons to the wealthy and well-educated is reminiscent of Saint-Simonianism. Yet unlike the Saint-Simonians, Rathenau professed to be concerned with the leadership of such men not primarily because of the entrepreneurial and technical skills that they could provide for social and economic development, but rather because of the cultural traditions that they could preserve. The wealthy and well-educated were, he believed, capable

[136] *Ibid.*, pp. 375–76.
[138] *Ibid.*, p. 377.
[137] *Ibid.*, pp. 376–77.
[139] *Ibid.*, pp. 387–93.

of recognizing the significance of the task that he had assigned to them. He deplored the divisions and animosities within the bourgeoisie that prevented it from devoting its energies to the construction of the new society. If the bourgeoisie would make the necessary sacrifices and devote itself to the service of society, it would carry out irreplaceable tasks: ". . . By virtue of its characteristics as the guardian of the heritage of the past, not its characteristics as the holder of wealth, this stratum is called upon, capable of, and essential to the transformation of the German spirit, its deliverance from the bonds of mechanization, and its passage to self-determination."[140]

The Waning of the Spirit

Business and political activity seem to have absorbed most of Rathenau's energies during the last two and a half years of his life. After his service on the second Socialization Commission, he was frequently called upon to serve as an unofficial advisor to the cabinet on economic questions. In 1921 he accepted a cabinet post for the first time in his life when he was named minister of reconstruction. Several months later he became foreign minister, the office that he held when he was assassinated in June 1922.

His murder by right-wing youths from the same middle class that he had warned during the war was losing its moorings has usually been attributed to anti-Semitism. Yet it is a tribute to the forcefulness of his writings and personality that one of the conspirators, Ernst von Salomon, has argued plausibly that the assassins were motivated by fear that Rathenau, for whom they had much admiration, was the only man who might succeed in rescuing a decadent social order. According to Salomon, they believed that he was the "last, ripest fruit" of an era and class whose shallowness he saw through without taking the decisive step of working against, rather than for.[141]

[140] *Ibid.*, p. 400.

[141] Ernst von Salomon, *Die Geächteten* (Berlin, 1931), pp. 302–03. See also pp. 196–98, 266–67, 301, 307, 309–10. There are still many open questions about the assassination, including the issue of whether the youthful murderers were assisted and perhaps even employed by a secret right-wing organization. One of the earliest and still rare scholarly attempts to examine these and similar problems is E. J. Gumbel, *Verschwörer: Beiträge zur Geschichte und Soziologie der deutschen Geheimbünde seit 1918* (Vienna, 1924). Noting a conversation that the principal assassin had with the owner of the garage in which the car used by the murderers was stored, Gumbel seems to suggest that the assassins were hired killers who had run short of money (see p. 48). Nevertheless, many less crucial aspects of Gumbel's interpretation are compatible with Salomon's. In the course of an examination of Rathenau's role in postwar German foreign policy, David Felix presents the customary American version of the assassins as motivated primarily by anti-Semitism. Dismissing cursorily the possibility of any other explanation, Felix

After 1919 Rathenau offered no more grand blueprints for the future. As Klemens von Klemperer has written, "The last chapter of Rathenau's Utopia was written in 1919; it already contained a marked note of resignation."[142] Calling attention to Rathenau's obvious and often stated disillusionment with the German Revolution, Klemperer suggests that Rathenau "withdrew into his other self."[143] For Klemperer, as for many other historians, Rathenau remained to the end of his days an enigma—a visionary reformer, who seeing his proposals come to naught, asserted the other side of his personality, became simply a practical man of action, and embarked on a career as a statesman.

Although superficially convincing, Klemperer's interpretation does not adequately explain the sudden decline in Rathenau's productivity as a writer. As long as there appeared to be a real possibility of social revolution, he continued to write chapters of his utopia. He had long been most creative as a political and social writer during periods of acute crisis. After 1919 his sense of urgency diminished; social revolution had been averted in Central Europe. The man who often liked to depict himself as a humble engineer had achieved one of his greatest successes in spiritualizing the problems posed by the German and Russian Revolutions.[144] The course of the German Revolution helped to dry up the springs of his literary creativity by demonstrating the gap between his ability to dream up utopias and his inability to work out methods for reaching them, for his idea of a "new society" presupposed the spontaneous generation of forces to establish it. Weber and Naumann had provided bridges, however improvised, from the present to the future. Rathenau had few specific methods to offer other than his own claims to an understanding of the forces that would create the new society. His elitism served up fantasies to bolster the morale of the upper classes and fragmentary techniques for bringing to fruition the rule of the big bourgeoisie.

Although beginning from liberal assumptions similar to Rathenau's and placing even more emphasis on education, Leonard Nelson devel-

---

asserts: "Neither the trial . . . nor the other sources . . . suggest that more responsible thoughts or persons were behind the conspiracy." David Felix, *Walther Rathenau and the Weimar Republic: The Politics of Reparations* (Baltimore, 1971), p. 168.

[142] Klemens von Klemperer, *Germany's New Conservatism: Its History and Dilemma in the Twentieth Century* (Princeton, 1957), p. 84.

[143] *Ibid.*

[144] A passage dealing with German-Austrian relations prior to World War I in Musil's *Der Mann ohne Eigenschaften* (p. 337) provides an amusing description of Rathenau's way of beclouding issues: ". . . In seiner [Arnheim's, i.e., Rathenau's] Darstellung wurde es ein gallisch-keltisch-ostisch-thyreologisches Problem, verbunden mit dem der lothringischen Kohlengruben und weiterhin dem der mexikanischen Ölfelder und dem Gegensatz zwischen Englisch- und Lateinamerika."

oped a theory that embodied a much greater insistence upon concrete measures for bringing about a new elitist order. Nelson's elite was intended to be unrestrictedly authoritarian, and it was implicitly designed as a vehicle of the educated middle class rather than the big bourgeoisie.

CHAPTER SIX

Leonard Nelson: The Rule of the Just

In January 1919 the new Prussian minister of education asked Leonard Nelson for advice on how to finance reforms despite the plight of the treasury. Nelson's reply was simple. He proposed closing all state educational institutions from the elementary school through the university. Perhaps he thought that this drastic measure would not only make funds available to underwrite experimental schools like the one he and his friends proposed to establish but also hasten the general transformation of the entire educational system that he considered imperative. He wanted to give every child an opportunity to develop his capabilities regardless of his financial means, to inculcate in him a respect for the rights of others as human beings, and to employ a version of the Socratic method in the classroom. Although Nelson was not primarily a pedagogical theorist, major changes in education were inseparable from his conception of the future political and social organization of Germany. The collapse of the German Empire seemed to offer a propitious moment for a concerted effort to realize the ideas he had developed during the past decade, but the Social Democratic minister of education rejected his proposal.[1]

Nelson did not despise democracy merely because of this rebuff. The liberating educational measures that he advocated were not devised in a democratic spirit. At the time of his conference at the Ministry of Education, he was well on the way to becoming one of the most articulate and active opponents of democracy in twentieth-century

[1] See Nelson's "Über das Landerziehungsheim Walkemühle," *Die Tat*, xvii (1926), Band 2, p. 869; Werner Link, *Die Geschichte des Internationalen Jugend-Bundes (IJB) und des Internationalen Sozialistischen Kampf-Bundes (ISK): Ein Beitrag zur Geschichte der Arbeiterbewegung in der Weimarer Republik und im Dritten Reich*, Marburger Abhandlungen zur Politischen Wissenschaft, i (Meisenheim am Glan, 1964), pp. 108–09. Hereafter Link's work will be cited as *Geschichte*. By the time of Nelson's conference at the Ministry of Education on January 8, 1919 the prospects for immediate educational reforms had been lessened considerably by the resignation from the ministry of the Independent Socialist Adolf Hoffmann. Hoffmann's Majority Socialist colleague, Konrad Haenisch, now stood alone at the head of the ministry. In line with Majority Socialist policy Haenisch sought to postpone reforms until the Prussian National Assembly convened. See Hermann Giesecke, "Zur Schulpolitik der Sozialdemokratie in Preussen und im Reich 1918–19" *Vierteljahrshefte für Zeitgeschichte*, xiii (1965), 162–66.

Germany. He would soon call publicly for the rule of "the wise"—men and women who responded successfully to a rigorous program of ethical and intellectual training. His appeal was taken up mainly by students, teachers, academicians, and other professionals. They joined the left-wing, but non-Marxist opposition to the Republic.

Nelson's Early Politics

Nelson was born into a distinguished Berlin family. The illustrious ancestors on his mother's side included the composer Felix Mendelssohn-Bartholdy and the physiologist Emil Dubois-Reymond. Nelson's father, who was to become one of his disciples, was an attorney. In 1909, at the age of twenty-seven, Nelson began a life-long career as a teacher of philosophy at the University of Göttingen. He devoted much of his early work to epistemology and the philosophy of science. His professional work earned him a significant place in the history of neo-idealism in Germany.[2] The founder of the neo-Friesian School, he revived and continued the work of an almost forgotten pupil of Kant. Among the German academicians of the early nineteenth century, Jakob Friedrich Fries was one of the most active politically until his close association with the *Burschenschaft* led to his suspension from

[2] Much of the literature on Nelson appeared during the Weimar Republic and deals with technical problems in his philosophy. For a brief assessment of his place in modern philosophy see *Friedrich Überwegs Grundriss der Geschichte der Philosophie*, 13th ed., ed. T. K. Österreich (Basel, 1951, IV, 471–76; for a more detailed analysis of his ethical philosophy see Grete Henry-Hermann, "Die Überwindung des Zufalls: Kritische Bemerkungen zu Leonard Nelsons Begründung der Ethik als Wissenschaft" in *Leonard Nelson zum Gedächtnis*, ed. Minna Specht and Willi Eichler (Frankfurt am Main, 1953). Like most of the work on Nelson, this essay was written by one of his disciples; the volume in which it was published was edited by his foremost adherents. The publication of some of Nelson's philosophical works in English translation has helped to stimulate a recent revival of interest in his philosophy. See, e.g., Richard T. De George, "Duties and Ideals in Leonard Nelson's Ethics," *Kant-Studien*, LI (1960), 259–71. Otto Wilhelm von Tegeln's *Leonard Nelsons Rechts- und Staatslehre*, Schriften zur Rechtslehre und Politik, XIII, ed. Ernst von Hippel (Bonn, 1958) provides a short exposition and critique of Nelson's legal and political philosophy, but does not examine it in historical context. More interesting is the attempt by Ludwig Grunebaum, himself strongly influenced by Nelson's personality and philosophy, to criticize Nelson's political views on the basis of the empirical reality of democracy in the contemporary West: "Führerschaft, Demokratie, Ethik: Eine Kritik von Leonard Nelsons 'Demokratie und Führerschaft,' " *Zeitschrift für die gesamte Staatswissenschaft*, CVII (1951), 36–89. Grunebaum seeks to divorce Nelson's political from his ethical philosophy. The only adequate historical study of Nelson and his followers is Link's *Geschichte*. Link focuses on the development of the political groups that Nelson founded. A pupil of Wolfgang Abendroth, Link is very critical of Nelson and his followers from a nonsectarian Marxist point of view. Two thirds of Link's study deals with Nelson's followers after their leader's death in 1927; it is valuable especially for its use of unpublished material, including interviews. Link provides an excellent bibliography.

his university post. Building upon Fries's critique of Kant's epistemology, Nelson constructed a distinctive philosophical system of his own.

Nelson's ambition to apply his philosophy to society began modestly. His prewar political views were similar to those of other militant left liberals. His first essay on politics echoed the old liberal belief that highly educated and cultured men should have "as much influence as possible on the direction of the affairs of state."[3] First published in 1910, this essay was based on a talk given in 1908 shortly after Nelson became involved in the educational activities of a group associated closely with left liberalism, the National Association for a Liberal Germany (*Nationalverein für das liberale Deutschland*).

As we saw in Chapter Three, the founding of the *Nationalverein* in 1906–1907 owed much to Naumann's initiative. Designed to stand aside from partisan struggles among liberals, the association offered a framework within which they could all work together for the renewal of liberalism in Germany. Much of the association's effort went into educational activities, including the political enlightenment of workers. Its publications often asserted the identity of interests between the bourgeoisie and the upper strata of the working class, and the *Nationalverein* received some support from small liberal organizations of industrial and white-collar workers. Although many of its members sought to promote social reforms that might attract more workers, its general rallying cry was merely a demand for political equality directed primarily against the Junkers and the Conservatives.[4]

Apparently Nelson was drawn to the *Nationalverein* by the notion that the future of Germany depended upon an intensive campaign of political education led by militant liberals and aimed at the middle and working classes. He conducted courses sponsored by the association and its affiliates.[5] Welcoming the growing stress in the *Nationalverein* on the development and training of political leaders, he responded enthusiastically to the plan developed by some left liberals for a political academy. The outbreak of World War I led to the indefinite postponement of the academy's opening, but his keen interest in the plan continued.[6]

[3] "Was ist liberal?" in *Die neue Reformation*, I: *Die Reformation der Gesinnung durch Erziehung zum Selbstvertrauen*, 2nd ed. (Leipzig, 1922), p. 232.
[4] Werner Link, "Das Nationalverein für das liberale Deutschland (1907–1918)," *Politische Vierteljahresschrift*, v (1964), 424, 427, 441–42.
[5] He may have gained his first experience in teaching groups of workers several years earlier when a student organization at the University of Berlin began to offer student-conducted courses for workers. See Ekkehard Hieronimus, "Otto Meyerhof" in *Theodor Lessing, Otto Meyerhof, Leonard Nelson: Bedeutende Juden in Niedersachsen* (Hannover, 1961), p. 63.
[6] See the address that Nelson delivered to a meeting of the *Nationalverein* in Munich in January 1917: "Wilhelm Ohr als politischer Erzieher" in *Die Reformation der Gesinnung*.

His other prewar political activities centered also in left-liberal organizations. He worked for the Göttingen branch of Naumann's party, the *Freisinnige Vereinigung*. In 1910 Nelson served as a delegate to the founding convention of the *Fortschrittliche Volkspartei*, the new party formed by the merger of the major left-liberal groups. When he first became active politically, he was very favorably impressed by Naumann. Shortly after the elections of 1907, Nelson wrote to his parents that he was delighted by Naumann's election to the Reichstag. Nelson admired him as "the only politician from whom we can expect anything."[7] Later in 1907 Naumann spoke in Göttingen, and Nelson took the opportunity to meet him and accompany him to a regional meeting of *Freisinnigen* in Hannover.[8] Typically, Nelson criticized Naumann for sacrificing moral principles on the altar of historical determinism. Nelson rejected Naumann's arguments that history demonstrated that large enterprises would triumph over small ones, that the fate of small, weak nations was to be absorbed by large, powerful ones, and that an attempt to stem the tide of history was sentimental and quixotic.[9] Nelson's strictures were based not upon a romantic commitment to the past, but rather upon the conviction that reality must be judged by an absolute standard of justice and that history set no limits to the realization of this standard.

The pivotal period in Nelson's life came with World War I. He began to devote most of his energy to questions of domestic and international politics. Continuing to conceive of matters idealistically, he propounded solutions dependent upon the resolution of ethical problems and the application of organizational techniques. Committed to an international league of sovereign nation-states, he complained in a work published in 1917 that each belligerent had twisted international law to serve its own purposes.[10] He denounced imperialism, the doctrine of the primacy of foreign policy, and the notion of a special German

[7] Letter of Feb. 9, 1907 in Erna Blencke, "Leonard Nelsons Leben und Wirken im Spiegel der Briefe an seine Eltern 1891–1915" in Hellmut Becker, Willi Eichler, and Gustav Heckmann, eds., *Erziehung und Politik: Minna Specht zu ihrem 80. Geburtstag* (Frankfurt am Main, 1960), p. 27.

[8] *Ibid.*, pp. 30–31. For other evidence of Nelson's esteem for Naumann see Hieronimus, "Otto Meyerhof," pp. 68–69.

[9] "Was ist liberal?" in *Die neue Reformation*, 1st ed. (Leipzig, 1917), i, 230. This is the only reference to the first edition of *Die neue Reformation*.

[10] *Die Rechtswissenschaft ohne Recht: Kritische Bemerkungen über die Grundlagen des Staats- und Völkerrechts* (Leipzig, 1917). For Nelson's views, on international affairs see also "Völkerbundideal" in *Handbuch der Politik*, 3rd ed., ed. Gerhard Anschütz et al. (Berlin, 1922), v; *Vorlesungen über die Grundlagen der Ethik*, iii: *System der philosophischen Rechtslehre und Politik* (Leipzig, 1924), pp. 508–49. Hereafter the last work will be cited as *Rechtslehre*. Research on the relationship of elitism to internationalism is sorely needed. See Bibliographical Essay, Section II, B.

mission. If Germans concentrated on the internal development of their own country, a great moral and political reformation could commence.

Even before the war Nelson had attracted a small group of followers, confined, for the most part, to Göttingen. The Fries Society, which he had founded during his student days, contributed adherents, who were joined by other students and acquaintances. In 1912 he wrote proudly to his parents that his classes had become "a kind of pacifist seminar."[11] In July 1914 he reported that he would work with a "left bloc" which was coalescing within the student body.[12] Although he did not participate directly in the Youth Movement, some of his followers were active in it, and he took a keen interest in its educational possibilities.[13] In 1916 he sought to use his influence to persuade it to take a stand on political issues. As the domestic political truce began to disintegrate, the Youth Movement was pressed from both the Right and the Left to enter the political arena.[14] When Nelson's entreaties were rejected, he searched for other vehicles for his educational and political ideas. His disillusionment with the middle-class Youth Movement probably strengthened his interest in reaching working-class youth, but for the moment he had to fall back on his personal following in Göttingen, which during the war consisted largely of female students. Supplemented by friends and acquaintances returning from military service, this group formed the nucleus of the International Youth League (*Internationaler Jugendbund*, or IJB) founded during the last year of the war and devoted to the realization of his ideals.[15]

The bylaws of the IJB called for it to engage in educational and political activities leading to the development of a "Party of Reason among the youth of all peoples."[16] The group's first manifesto, dated February 8, 1919, was addressed to "the Free Youth of all Estates and Nations." The manifesto was signed not only by the IJB's directorate, but also by a *Freundesrat* that included Albert Einstein and Käthe Kollwitz.[17] The attempt to create an international organization miscarried. During the next decade, the IJB and its successor gained few members from other countries. The good wishes of a substantial number of foreign sympathizers, especially in Britain, could not alter the

[11] Letter of Dec. 15, 1912 in Blencke, "Leonard Nelsons Leben und Wirken im Spiegel der Briefe an seine Eltern," p. 49.

[12] Letter of July 24, 1914 in *ibid.*, p. 59.

[13] See esp. the first three essays in *Die Reformation der Gesinnung*.

[14] For the struggle within the Youth Movement see Walter Z. Laqueur, *Young Germany: A History of the German Youth Movement* (New York, 1962), pp. 95–97.

[15] Link, *Geschichte*, pp. 47–48, 51–52.

[16] Quoted in *ibid.*, p. 55.

[17] Hieronimus, "Leonard Nelson" in *Theodor Lessing, Otto Meyerhof, Leonard Nelson*, p. 107.

almost entirely German composition of Nelson's following. The attempt to recruit from every level of society was only a bit more successful. Despite rapid growth in 1919 and 1920, the IJB remained a predominantly middle-class organization. Although it may have begun to attract a sizable number of white-collar workers, it had more success in recruiting among the highly educated strata of the middle class. By the end of 1920, Nelson's several hundred enthusiastic followers included some workers, but many more students, school teachers, and university-educated professionals.[18]

During the November Revolution and the ensuing revolutionary disturbances, the still minuscule IJB seems to have played no active role as an organization. While a few members belonged to the Majority Socialists and the Communists, the IJB became more closely associated with the Independent Socialists, especially with their youth group. For a short time, Nelson himself was a member of the Independent Socialist party. He was probably attracted by the internationalism of the Independents, by their opposition to the Majority Socialists' support for the war, and by their criticism of the Majority Socialists' failure to fight for basic domestic reforms. When the Independents split in 1920 and part of their organization merged with the Communist party, most members of the IJB remained with the minority faction that attempted to maintain the identity of the Independents as an alternative to both the Communists and the Majority Socialists. After the fusion of the remaining Independents with the Majority Socialists in 1922, Nelson led most of his followers into the reunited Social Democratic party.

THE APPEAL OF THE IJB

In prewar Germany the social coalition of the nobility and bourgeoisie provided the middle class with material and psychological protection against the erosion in its economic position and social status. War and revolution ripped away the mask that had concealed the vul-

[18] Link does not attempt to estimate the size of Nelson's following during the early years of the Republic. Willi Eichler, who assumed the leadership of his followers after Nelson's death in 1927, estimates that in 1920 about 500 people were full, associate, and probationary members of the IJB. Eichler thinks that another perhaps 500 people (*Sympathisierende*) were in close touch with it (letter of Aug. 1, 1962 from Willi Eichler to me). Although the first figure is almost certainly a maximum estimate, the second may be close to the mark. A detailed study of the early IJB and its members, for which the available sources are scanty, might provide further clues to its appeal. If Link's tentative conclusions about the social composition of the ISK, the organization that succeeded the IJB in 1926, are correct, the followers of Nelson's doctrines continued to be drawn predominantly from the educated middle class, although the proportion of both workers and less highly educated members of the middle class seems to have increased. Link, *Geschichte*, pp. 142–44.

nerability of the middle class to long-term social and economic changes.[19] Big business grew at the expense of the old middle class of artisans, small businessmen, and peasant proprietors. The impact of the war and of government policy undercut the property relations on which the old middle class depended. From above, the organization of big business employing cartels, monopolies, and similar arrangements became an overt threat to the survival of the old middle class. From below, the visible advance in the power of the working class through trade unionism and the November Revolution became a more humiliating if less potent threat.

The situation of a second major segment of the middle class was different. The employment opportunities of the new middle class of secretaries, foremen, technicians, sales persons, and lower echelon civil servants depended directly upon the expansion of big business. The unionization of the new middle class, which made great strides from 1918 to 1920,[20] served primarily as a device for regulating employer-employee relations, but many white-collar unions contributed to the maintenance of status barriers between the new middle class and the working class. While the new middle class had no overriding interest in preserving the property relations required by the old middle class, the existence of the old middle class stimulated the wish-dream of a road to social and economic independence. The illusion of occupying a middle position between the bourgeoisie and the working class forged another psychological link between the old middle class and the new middle class.

A third section of the middle class stood somewhat apart from both the old and the new middle class. Most of the men and women educated in universities and teacher-training institutes might be regarded as a part of the new middle class.[21] Their relationship to their employ-

[19] See the analysis of the middle class in Walter Struve, "Hans Zehrer as a Neoconservative Elite Theorist," *American Historical Review*, LXX (1965), 1037–41; Herman Lebovics, *Social Conservatism and the Middle Classes in Germany, 1914–1933* (Princeton, 1969), pp. 3–21.

[20] Günter Hartfiel, *Angestellte und Angestelltengewerkschaften in Deutschland: Entwicklung und gegenwärtige Situation von beruflicher Tätigkeit, sozialer Stellung und Verbandswesen der Angestellten in der gewerblichen Wirtschaft* (Berlin, 1961), pp. 146–66.

[21] A number of works on the social history of the educated middle class, especially on students and universities during the Weimar Republic, has appeared since 1945. Most of these works rely heavily upon the wealth of sociological and statistical studies undertaken during the Republic and do not break significant new ground. An important exception to the latter part of this generalization is Fritz K. Ringer, *The Decline of the German Mandarins: The German Academic Community, 1890–1933* (Cambridge, Mass., 1969). Another engaging study, despite its pretentiousness and moralizing, is Jenö Kurucz's brief typology of the intelligentsia: *Struktur und Funktion der Intelligenz während der Weimarer Republik*, Schriften

er was similar; they derived little of their income from the ownership of property. But their possession of educational certificates provided them with a type of property upon which their income and status depended. Their interest in maintaining this type of property linked them to the old middle class, as did family ties and social history. Historically, the formation of a large educated middle class antedated the rapid growth of the new middle class during the last decades of the nineteenth century, for the old middle class had provided the primary social basis for the recruitment of the educated middle class. Although by the end of the nineteenth century the expansion of the educated middle class came to depend primarily upon the proliferation of the new middle class, the old middle class continued to supply a sizable proportion of the students in institutions of higher learning.[22]

Most members of the educated middle class reacted defensively to their new situation in the Republic. They endeavored to preserve their own position, and they identified their fate with that of the middle class as a whole. They sought to maintain the often tenuous distinctions between themselves and the workers. The educated middle class clung to its threatened prestige, fought to reassert its privileges, resisted most educational reforms, and rejected any plan to make higher education accessible to the working class.[23] The intermittent threat of social revolution during the first years after the November Revolution and the financial hardships that became common among university students strengthened this defensive reflex. Perhaps the failure of a

des Instituts für empirische Soziologie in Saarbrücken, III (n. p., 1967). The most useful general treatment is Jürgen Schwarz, *Studenten in der Weimarer Republik: Die deutsche Studentenschaft in der Zeit von 1918 bis 1923 und ihre Stellung zur Politik* (Berlin, 1971). Two excellent recent articles examine student organizations: Thomas Nipperdey, "Die deutsche Studentenschaft in den ersten Jahren der Weimarer Republik" in Adolf Grimme, ed., *Kulturverwaltung der zwanziger Jahre: Alte Dokumente und neue Beiträge* (Stuttgart, 1961); Wolfgang Zorn, "Die politische Entwicklung des deutschen Studententums 1924–1931" in *Ein Leben aus freier Mitte . . . Festschrift für Prof. Dr. Ulrich Noack* (Göttingen, 1961). Although providing a survey of the universities during the entire Republic, Hans Peter Bleuel and Ernst Klinnert, *Deutsche Studenten auf dem Weg ins Dritte Reich: Ideologien, Programme, Aktionen 1918–1935* (Gütersloh, 1969) does not adequately exploit the sources.

[22] Bavarian Statistisches Landesamt, *Soziales Auf- und Abstieg im deutschen Volke*, [by Josef Nothaas], Beiträge zur Statistik Bayerns, CXVII (Munich, 1930), pp. 35, 42, 45; Fritz K. Ringer, "Higher Education in Germany in the Nineteenth Century," *Journal of Contemporary History*, VI (1967), 136–39.

[23] Assessing, after a decade, the political impact of the November Revolution on the universities, the distinguished jurist Rudolf Smend breathed a sigh of relief that the universities had not been transformed into workers' academies. "Hochschule und Parteien" in *Das akademische Deutschland*, ed. Michael Doeberl et al. (Berlin, 1930–1931), III, 153–55. For a general analysis of conservative responses to the prospect of educational reforms see Ringer, *The Decline of the German Mandarins*, pp. 282–95 and passim.

successful social revolution in postwar Germany blocked the way to radical changes in higher education, but the Republic did not initiate major reforms that might still have been possible. Few serious attempts were undertaken to enable a larger number of the offspring of the lower classes to study in universities and secondary schools. As under the Empire, only a tiny proportion of the students came from the lower classes. For example, during the Weimar Republic less than 5 per cent of the students enrolled in universities and other institutions of higher education came from the peasanty and working class.[24]

The programs and organizations most effective in winning adherents from the educated middle class were those that incorporated its defensive concerns into more subtle appeals to the fate of the nation or for the creation of a *Volksgemeinschaft*. The bulk of these programs and organizations were identified with the Right, but symptomatically many of them did not fit neatly into the concepts of Right and Left derived from the nineteenth century.

Most of Nelson's followers belonged to the minority within the educated middle class that was willing to contemplate far-reaching changes in education. They seem to have had little conscious interest in upholding existing institutions. A pamphlet published in 1918 by one of the first members of the IJB invoked the idealism that attracted its author to Nelson by claiming that "the mission of the educated to be spiritual leaders of the people" required the former to forfeit their own interests.[25] During the same year, another of Nelson's early followers lashed out at "false liberalism" and "the economic despotism of our day—capitalism," but went on to distinguish the inherent virtues of capitalism from its abuses and to praise the achievements of Naumann's businessman friend "the noble Ernst Abbé" at the Zeiss Works. Capitalism was "only *accidentally* an enemy of Reason by virtue of the crudity and faulty knowledge of its [capitalism's] practitioners." On the other hand, the Jesuits were inevitably enemies of reason because of their authoritarian educational principles.[26]

The creation of a radical bourgeois republic might have won the support that the IJB denied to the Weimar Republic. Educational re-

[24] See esp. Svend Riemer, "Sozialer Aufstieg und Klassenschichtung," *Archiv für Sozialwissenschaft und Sozialpolitik*, LXVII (1932), 533; R. H. Samuel and R. Hinton Thomas, *Education and Society in Modern Germany* (London, 1949), p. 126.

[25] Friedrich Oehlkers, *Gedanken zur Neuorientierung der Hochschulen: Erläutert an einem Lehrfach der beschreibenden Naturwissenschaften* (Leipzig, 1918), p. 23.

[26] Hans Mühlestein, *Die Herrschaft der Weisen* (Leipzig, 1918), pp. 18, 34, 52. Italics Mühlestein's.

forms, anticlerical policies, and antimonopoly legislation might have given Nelson's followers a sense of participation in a worthwhile new order. While they came to believe that many of their goals were similar to those of the socialist parties, they were not satisfied with either the moderate reformism of many Social Democrats or the militant Marxism of other Socialists.

Nelson's followers might conceive of their political calling as necessitating working with and even within a predominantly working-class party, but they could not envision the proletarian as the bearer of a new order. His lack of culture disturbed them. They had no wish for a dictatorship of the proletariat. They were willing to turn their backs on the middle class, but they did not want to depart without the culture they prized. Nelson's philosophy reinforced his followers' aversion to materialism, while buttressing the belief in the primacy of ideas and education to which their academic vocation predisposed them. He provided them with doctrines to take among the working class. He gave them a mission that entailed a professed willingness to renounce their privileges as members of the educated middle class. At the same time, his political philosophy promised them the likelihood of becoming members of a new elite. Impartial experts acting as dedicated humanitarians would transform society without awaiting the inevitable development of social and economic forces identified with the predominant strand of prewar Marxism, without undergoing a bloody Bolshevik Revolution, and without following the Social Democrats in the seemingly futile task of reform through parliamentary democracy. As late as July 1918, at a training course for Nelson's followers, one of his most active disciples could argue that "one form of the rule of the wise" could be established "without having to overthrow the existing governments."[27] Another of the earliest members of the IJB has recounted vividly the impact of Nelson's ideas:

For me, as for many of my generation, this year [1918] was a turning point. The old world—which we had often questioned, yet never completely rejected—had fallen apart. The foundations of my previous conception of the world were destroyed, and I found myself in a phase of spiritual nihilism. You can imagine what an impression [Nelson's] doctrines must have made upon me. . . . My nebulous social ideals seemed to receive an indestructible foundation. . . . From the beginning we young socialists stood in a two-front war: against the naive faith of the political leaders in a misunderstood parliamentarianism, on the one side; and against a cynical toying

[27] Quoted in Link, *Geschichte*, p. 61.

with dictatorship, on the other side—on the extreme Left. . . . The doctrine of the "rule of the wise" provided terribly convincing arguments against both positions. . . .[28]

JUSTICE, DEMOCRACY, AND LEADERSHIP

Starting from a single principle and moving through a chain of logical deductions, Nelson arrived at his philosophical system, as well as his critique of democracy and his conception of a true elite. He assumed that a universally valid ideal of justice existed. Unlike Kant he argued that this ideal had a specific content independent of human perception. Nelson's belief in an ideal of justice transcending human experience imparted a highly dogmatic air to his thinking. As might be expected from a man who regarded himself as a successor of Kant and Fries, his concept of justice resembled closely that of early German liberalism. According to Nelson, the imperatives of justice called for the full and autonomous development of each individual's capacities up to the point at which the development of the capacities of others began to be restricted. This concept of justice served for Nelson as an implicit standard for ascertaining the common good.

The optimal development of every individual could, he assumed, be attained only if the state constituted a *Rechtsstaat*. Although Nelson thereby associated his views with one of the classical demands of German liberalism, he rejected the dominant trend in German jurisprudence since the latter part of the nineteenth century. Insisting that an ideal of justice existed independently of every state, he attacked the legal positivists.[29]

While firmly committed to the notion of equality before the law, Nelson found crucial differences among men. Neither the notion of justice nor the imperatives arising from it were always clearly perceptible. All men had at least a hazy perception of them, but largely because of education and training, some men perceived them more clearly. Yet as we shall see later, he made an assumption that prevented him from reaching the conclusion that providing everyone with the same education was desirable and that eventually everyone's perception of justice would be identical. Nelson's critique of democracy had direct antecedents in his belief that some men would always have a better perception of justice than others.

He stigmatized democracy as incompatible with the achievement of justice. Nelson regarded the majority principle as the crux of democ-

---

[28] Adolf Lowe [Löwe], "Ein Freundesbrief" in *Leonard Nelson zum Gedächtnis*, p. 148.

[29] See esp. *Die Rechtswissenschaft ohne Recht*.

racy. He anticipated few convergences of the will of the majority with the imperatives of justice. Since the degree of men's ability to perceive justice differed, a minority or even one man would more often have a better perception of justice. In a democracy "pure chance" determined whether the will of the majority was directed toward justice.[30] Speaking before the German Sociological Association in 1926, Nelson expressed, as he had repeatedly in the past, his contempt for the majority principle: ". . . Democracy means the bowing of the individual to the voice of the majority, and for him who must bow, it is a matter of indifference whether he must subject himself to the whim of one man or the whim of the many." Nelson went on to complain that democracy, rather than offering protection against the rise of fascism, provided fertile soil for its growth. The way to prevent the rise of fascism was to erect a power independent of majority decisions, a power "that would stop a fascist from rising up." To illustrate his argument, Nelson took an example from recent German history. Despite his belief that majority rule could not exist in practice, his example took for granted that a German government could express majority will. He contrasted the policy of the Stresemann cabinet in 1923 toward the Right with its policy toward the Left: while a right-wing *Putsch* (Hitler's "Beer Hall" *Putsch*) was executed in Bavaria, the German army marched into Saxony to destroy a left-wing government.[31] Apparently Nelson wished to imply that even though the Hitler *Putsch* had been unsuccessful the Stresemann cabinet had not prevented its occurrence and was more concerned with suppressing the extreme Left than with the extreme Right, but his reasoning may have been difficult for his listeners to follow. Any difficulty would have increased if his audience recalled that Nelson regarded democracy as an unattainable ideal, the crux of which was the majority principle.

Allusions to the Weimar Republic and the use of historical examples were rare in Nelson's writings, nor did he attempt to dissect and refute the classic works on the theory of democracy. He concentrated his attack upon logical inconsistencies in maxims commonly associated with the concept of democracy. Unlike most other left-wing opponents of the Republic, who regarded popular control as possible after basic or revolutionary changes, Nelson deemed popular control an absurd impossibility in any society. He associated democracy with a demand for "leaderlessness." A democracy lacked good leaders because it sought to impose restrictions upon them. The good leader, the man

[30] *Demokratie und Führerschaft*, 2nd ed. (Stuttgart, 1927), p. 13. Hereafter this work will be abbreviated as *DuF*. The first edition appeared in 1919.

[31] *Verhandlungen des 5. Deutschen Soziologentages . . . , Schriften der Deutschen Gesellschaft für Soziologie*, Series 1, v (Tübingen, 1927), 84–85.

with a superior perception of justice, would hardly degrade himself by conforming to the wishes of the majority. As a result, bad leaders came to the fore: "Democracy is not the great arena from which the best men come forth as victors. It is the fools' stage on which the craftiest or best-paid chatterbox gets the better of that nobility of character which relies only upon the goodness of its cause."[32]

Nelson mingled Marxist arguments against bourgeois democracy with right-wing arguments against any form of popular control. He denounced democratic ideals as a façade for the rule of undesirable minorities. Kept on "leading strings" and manipulated like "marionettes," the masses fell victim to unscrupulous leaders. Everything depended upon demagogues, who obtained the votes of the majority through deceit, and upon "capital," which purchased majorities indirectly through control of public communications.[33] The majority principle led to the exploitation of the masses: "The age of democracy is the age without a will. It [the age of democracy] leaves the act of willing to those, who, because they know what they want, take advantage of their contemporaries' lack of will. . . ."[34]

Nelson described faith in democracy as a "shameful superstition." He attributed most of Germany's political difficulties to this superstition. Leaders refused to take any responsibility for their actions. They pretended that the votes of the majority were responsible for their own actions.[35] If throughout the course of history democracy had occasionally functioned fairly well, its successes had depended upon the "fortunate accident" that a good leader had appeared. Normally, democratic ideology barred the development and assertion of good leadership.[36] To illustrate the incompatibility of democracy and leadership, Nelson selected an example that would appeal especially to Germans with experience in the Youth Movement: if a group went on a hike, it would surely want to visit the nicest possible spot; hence the most experienced *Wanderer*, not the majority, should decide where to go.[37]

Sharing the belief of Naumann, Weber, and Rathenau that the classical ideals of democracy were impossible to fulfill, Nelson did not accept the conclusion reached by these elitists and many other supporters of the Weimar Republic that the institutions of parliamentary democracy could provide the basis for leadership. He would not contemplate seriously the view that these ideals might have the pragmatic

[32] *DuF*, p. 18. [33] *DuF*, pp. 15–16, 40, 44, 160.
[34] *DuF*, p. 69.
[35] *DuF*, pp. 19, 160. See also pp. 20, 81, 108, 117.
[36] *Erziehung zum Führer* (Leipzig, 1920), p. 7.
[37] *DuF*, p. 7.

value of legitimizing the actions of effective leaders. His identification of democracy with the absence of leadership was facilitated by the position adopted by a major school of thought among theorists of Weimar democracy. Hans Kelsen, a representative of this school and a legal positivist, was one of the few eminent contemporary political theorists with whom Nelson engaged in an extended public controversy. In this debate Nelson continued his earlier struggle against the positivists, attacking any suggestion that practice might deviate from theory. Kelsen provided an excellent target since he argued that the essence of democracy was the demand for "leaderlessness," but that nevertheless a democratic state was the best hope for the development of good leaders.[38] The triteness and shallowness of Nelson's political theory was no match for his opponents. His insights into the conservative functions of their views of democracy were rendered inconsequential through his inability to do battle other than with the straw men whom he created. In this battle he often did little more than mouth the slogans of the Right.[39]

Nowhere did Nelson find a democracy he could admire. In "the Age of Democracy," even the few superior leaders hesitated to renounce its ideology. By speaking in public as if they believed in democracy, they permitted the majority to influence them. Despite great admiration for Lenin and the Bolsheviks, Nelson criticized them for committing the error of giving lip-service to democracy.[40]

Nelson regarded democracy and higher culture as incompatible. Although lacking the historical pessimism of such prominent cultural elite theorists as Jacob Burckhardt and Friedrich Nietzsche, he expressed many fears similar to theirs. Nelson accused democracy of undermining all worthwhile values. The masses and those ruling in their name respected only material things.[41] He felt confident that a transformation of the German political system that eliminated any possibility of popular control would promote a flourishing of culture.

In place of democracy, he proposed the rule of one man. One man always had a clearer perception of justice than everyone else, and the demands of "reason" required him to make all of the most important

[38] See Hans Kelsen, *Vom Wesen und Wert der Demokratie*, 2nd ed. (Tübingen, 1929), pp. 11–12, 79.

[39] Cf. the sympathetic assessment, by the Communist philosopher Georg Lukács, of the *Zivilcourage* displayed during World War I by Nelson in his *Rechtswissenschaft ohne Recht*: "Das Tragikomische in der Stellung Nelsons zeigt sich aber darin, dass in diesem Gegenüberstehen zwar moralisch alles Recht auf seiner Seite war, dass er aber sachlich mitunter tief unter das Niveau der von ihm Bekämpften sank." Georg Lukács, "Der Nelson-Bund," *Die Internationale*, ix (1926), 158.

[40] *DuF*, p. 144. See also p. 13.

[41] *DuF*, p. 44.

decisions in a society. As might be expected, Nelson associated his own conception of government with Plato's.[42]

Although Nelson was greatly impressed by historical examples of "great men," his faith in the efficacy of a single ruler resulted from a combination of the Enlightenment's conception of the state with some of the prevailing assumptions of recent German jurisprudence. Like the *philosophes* and like Kant, he tended to view enlightened absolutism as the most effective form of government. From recent German jurisprudence, he accepted the notion of the state as characterized by the possession of a monopoly of the means of violence. He conceived of society mechanistically as composed of numerous separate entities, all of which might be strictly controlled if one of them had a monopoly of force at its disposal. Nelson viewed society as subject to laws of nature paralleling the laws of Newtonian physics.[43] If one man exercised a monopoly of force, nothing could prevent the execution of his decisions: "What occurs in a state actually depends only upon what the rulers want." "When the good has triumphed and reforms have been carried out, it was not because an idea itself triumphed. Rather, it was because some of the rulers accepted the idea."[44]

Nelson refused to contemplate any external institutional controls over the actions and policies of the ruler. The erection of institutions to control him would assume that one or more other men had a better perception of justice. If another man had a better perception of justice, he should rule. If not, controls over the ruler would merely restrict his opportunities to realize justice.[45] Since Nelson's ruler acted in the best interests of everyone, popular control was superfluous. The most sensible political attitude that other members of society could adopt was a willingness to leave all significant decisions to him: ". . . It is better that matters be decided with insight and judgment and in a morally responsible fashion. . . . It is better for the interests of the masses. . . . The people have no other right than to allow themselves to be ruled according to the law of justice."[46]

Nelson relied upon the ruler to control himself. The ruler's success in accomplishing his task would result from his devotion to justice and the strength of his character. To ensure that his decisions coincided with the imperatives of justice, he had to be capable of extensive self-

[42] See, e.g., *Rechtslehre*, p. 274; "Der Internationale Jugendbund" in Anschütz, *Handbuch der Politik*, v, 498. Hereafter this article by Nelson will be abbreviated as "IJB."

[43] See *Rechtslehre*, pp. 131–32, 146, 159, 183–84.

[44] *Ibid.*, p. 271; *Führer-Erziehung als Weg zur Vernunftpolitik* (Leipzig, 1922), pp. 10–11. Hereafter cited as *Führer-Erziehung*. See also *Rechtslehre*, p. 159.

[45] *DuF*, p. 23.

[46] *DuF*, p. 40; *Rechtslehre*, pp. 197–98. See also *DuF*, pp. 7–8.

criticism. He could employ force only to the extent necessary to achieve justice. Otherwise, he would establish a private, despotic relationship with individual members of society. But to achieve justice, he had to be willing to appear tyrannical. Nelson referred to will power as "the secret of politics."[47] The ruler had to be able to override the wills of others, and he had to have the will power to remain objective. When public interests conflicted with his own personal interests, he had to summon the inner strength to ignore the latter.[48]

The only external checks upon Nelson's ruler were those reminding him of his duty. The "*moral* power of the public's consciousness of justice" and freedom of scientific inquiry would help the ruler to keep in mind the imperatives of justice. One of his foremost concerns should be guaranteeing freedom of inquiry.[49]

To Nelson the only effective protection against the ruler's misuse of power consisted in the "perfection of methods for the selection and education of leaders."[50] If the ruler were to be entrusted with the stupendous task of establishing justice, everything possible had to be done to ensure that he was truly the man with the best perception of justice. The major practical problems to which Nelson turned were methods to ensure that the most just individual would rule and that suitable successors would be available.

Nelson's discussion of these methods was indicative of the antihistorical cast of his philosophy. He casually plucked practices and institutions from their historical context and held them up as worthy of imitation. He indicated that the ruler should, if possible, be chosen by his predecessor, as the ancient Roman and Chinese emperors had been.[51] Nelson was convinced that this method of selection could be combined with the imperative that the ruler choose the most just individual available to follow him. The just ruler better than anyone else could recognize his worthiest successor. Nelson wished to provide a reservoir of leaders from which the new ruler might be selected. If the old ruler were for some reason unable to choose his own successor, the men in this reservoir would be able to select him. Seeking institutions that would ensure a succession of suitable rulers, Nelson turned to bureaucratic structures. Significantly, the institutions that he found most worthy of emulation were those to which he attributed many of the world's woes, above all the Roman Catholic Church. Despite his virulent anticlericalism, he praised the structure of the Church, "the

[47] *DuF*, pp. 18, 23, 27, 69, 71; *Rechtslehre*, p. 280. See also *Rechtslehre*, p. 18; *Erziehung zum Führer*, pp. 9–11, 23–26.

[48] *Erziehung zum Führer*, pp. 25–26.

[49] *Rechtslehre*, pp. 184–85, 276–77. Nelson's italics.

[50] *DuF*, p. 23.

[51] See *DuF*, pp. 19, 41, 165; *Rechtslehre*, p. 274.

most highly developed social institution in Europe." He distinguished the Church's institutional principles from its ultimate goals. The organization of the Church, especially the institution of the College of Cardinals, "guaranteed" that the man most suited to pursue the goals of Catholicism became pontiff.[52] Similarly, there was no need to rely upon fortune or a *coup d'état* to furnish the best possible successor to a just ruler: ". . . It is possible to create institutions which automatically permit him to ascend to leadership." Through planned leadership education and training, Nelson hoped to dispense with any dependence upon the "accidental" appearance of "political geniuses."[53]

His conception of the "political genius" had little in common with the romantic, racist, and irrational notions prevalent on the Right. Nelson did not regard the genius as radically different from his fellow men. Nelson's emphasis upon educational and environmental influences resembled that of the Enlightenment. Often the genius was no more highly endowed than "the so-called politically gifted individual."[54] Systematic training could develop leaders equal to any "accidental" genius. Presumably because of heredity or chance, some men had more potential than others to become the just ruler, but a reasonably large number of men could develop the necessary characteristics. Since education always had to reckon with "duds," the training had to begin at an early age.[55] Nelson relied upon equal educational opportunities to provide more than enough enlightened men for an unbroken succession of good rulers.[56]

He insisted that justice demanded the opening of educational institutions to everyone according to ability. Public laws must ensure "the same external possibility for everyone to obtain education."[57] Like the nineteenth-century liberal, Nelson regarded education and merit as criteria for admission to the political elite, but he rejected the other criterion on which the nineteenth-century liberal had insisted—property. Although the formal rejection of property as a criterion was common among the left liberals with whom Nelson had worked before World War I, he went a step farther. He sought to sever all the links between social class and educational possibilities. Yet Nelson drew

---

[52] *DuF*, pp. 14, 18–19, 41, 159, 165. Nelson's admiration for the structure of the Catholic Church seems to have stemmed especially from the vast, if malevolent power that he attributed to the Jesuits. One of his closest associates in the *Nationalverein*, Wilhelm Ohr, wrote a study of the Jesuits that Nelson prized for its explanation of the secret of their "imponierenden Organisationskunst." "Wilhelm Ohr als politischer Erzieher" in *Die neue Reformation*, p. 180.

[53] *DuF*, pp. 19, 23; *Erziehung zum Führer*, p. 12; "IJB," p. 498.

[54] *Führer-Erziehung*, p. 24.   [55] *Erziehung zum Führer*, p. 17.

[56] See *Rechtslehre*, pp. 278, 415; *Führer-Erziehung*, p. 25.

[57] *Rechtslehre*, pp. 278, 416.

back before the destruction of social classes. He was more concerned with the encouragement of mobility between classes than with the elimination of classes themselves. He saw no compelling need to destroy the class structure of bourgeois society in order to realize his objectives. Nelson recognized a serious problem in the continuation of this structure only if the class position of the individual depended simply upon factors that he could not influence.[58] In expounding his concept of justice, Nelson took great pains to delineate the acceptable limits of equality. The precepts of justice demanded "not absolute equality and therefore uniformity, i.e., they do not prohibit consideration of differences in men's position (including their individuality)." Nelson explained that justice prohibited the granting of advantages to someone only if they entailed greater disadvantages for another.[59]

By 1920 Nelson's followers directed much of their attention to influencing working-class youth. The author of one of the IJB's publications wrote in 1920 that whoever sought justice must stand shoulder to shoulder with Socialist youth and that the creative forces of the future must come from "the unexpended strata of the working people." As if to reassure herself, the author affirmed that "capable men suited to become leaders are found among the youth of every estate."[60] Despite the political cooperation of Nelson and his followers with working-class organizations, his objective was to educate a select few workers rather than to destroy bourgeois society. Writing for a political encyclopedia published in 1922, he stressed that the members of the IJB were rigidly selected and included people from all classes.[61]

His belief that the elimination of social classes was not essential to the creation of the just society was related to his insistence upon the need for a rigid specialization of labor and for a distinct vocation of political leadership. Nelson objected to the idea of overcoming the division of labor that he identified with Marxism. He complained that the termination of the division of labor would destroy the distinction between rulers and ruled.[62] His favorite example to illustrate the necessity for experts in all areas including politics was that of a hospital. Elaborating on one version of this example, he revealed in a quip a touch of gloom beneath his optimism: "Politically we are all sick. And therefore I say: politically we need a hospital director." The patients,

---

[58] See "Philosophische Vorfragen der Sozialpolitik" in *Wirtschaft und Gesellschaft: Beiträge zur Ökonomik und Soziologie der Gegenwart: Festschrift für Franz Oppenheimer*, ed. Robert Wilbrandt, Adolf Löwe, and Gottfried Salomon (Frankfurt am Main, 1924), pp. 53–55.

[59] *Ibid.*, pp. 29–30.   [60] Quoted in Link, *Geschichte*, p. 59.

[61] "IJB," pp. 498–99.

[62] "Philosophische Vorfragen der Sozialpolitik," p. 74.

Nelson pointed out, did not run a hospital. As in the Catholic Church, the "experts" made the decisions.[63] Through proper education, he expected the development of political experts. He felt that a special education for future members of the elite was as necessary as vocational training for "any other" occupation: "The profession of politics requires more concentration, devotion, and specialized knowledge than a citizen can muster in addition to his own personal vocation."[64]

Nelson limited the political education he had in mind to a few, carefully selected individuals. The aim of this education was "not the harmonious development of all good capacities in all men, but the ethical strengthening and training of a few men, sound in mind and body, to become political leaders."[65] He never explained in detail how the suitable few were to be recognized and selected.

His conception of the education of political leaders, like his pedagogical techniques, combined libertarian and authoritarian perspectives. He relied heavily upon his version of the Socratic method.[66] Part of the instruction took place in the form of a dialogue between pupil and teacher. The teacher's task was not to point directly to the pupil's errors, but to guide the discussion by raising questions that encouraged the pupil to reach the correct conclusions independently. The teacher helped the pupil to free his thought from dogmatism. Although the mind of the pupil must of necessity be influenced by others, he should never accept their conclusions simply on authority, for the goal of education was "rational self-determination, i.e., a condition in which the individual does not permit himself to be determined by external influences, but rather decides and acts on the basis of his own judgment."[67] Nelson believed that the Socratic method worked well only when employed in a highly disciplined setting.

His views on general education, especially that of children, were strongly influenced by the experimental schools of two prominent educational reformers, Gustav Wyneken and Hermann Lietz. On Nelson's recommendation, one of his closest followers, Minna Specht, familiarized herself with Lietz's methods by taking a post at one of his

[63] *DuF*, pp. 42, 39–41, 159. For Nelson's use of similar examples see esp. *DuF*, p. 7; *Erziehung zum Führer*, p. 8.

[64] *Erziehung zum Führer*, p. 7.　　　　[65] "IJB," p. 497.

[66] In a posthumously published essay Nelson offered a clear discussion of his Socratic method: "Sokratische Methode" in Willi Eichler and Martin Hart [pseud. for Willi Eichler?], eds., *Leonard Nelson: Ein Bild seines Lebens und Wirkens: Aus seinen Werken zusammengefügt und erläutert* (Paris, 1938). Originally a lecture given to the *Pädagogische Gesellschaft* in Göttingen, this essay was first published in 1929 in the *Abhandlungen der Fries'schen Schule*.

[67] "Sokratische Methode," p. 426. My translation of this passage differs somewhat from the version in Leonard Nelson, *Socratic Method and Critical Philosophy: Selected Essays*, trans. T. K. Brown (New Haven, 1949), p. 19.

schools.[68] In the general and children's divisions of the Walkemühle, the school that Nelson and his followers opened in 1924 as part of their version of the Platonic Academy, a modified Montessori method was used and antiauthoritarian attitudes were encouraged.[69]

His plans for leadership training put more emphasis upon the teacher's role and rigid discipline. Under the pressure of strict supervision and a strenuous program, the highest capacities of the best students would unfold: "Little by little there will emerge those who, thanks to their ethical, intellectual, and physical capacities, understand better than the others how to use what the training affords." Although like many contemporary American educational theorists Nelson assumed that some individuals would "naturally come to be leaders of their comrades," he stressed the role of the educator rather than that of the peer group.[70] For example, when an unsuitable person became a leader, the educator had to intervene "with a firm hand" and put an end to "the premature ascent."[71]

Despite the tremendous emphasis Nelson placed upon ethical qualities, the elite in his ideal society consisted of the highly educated. His conception of this society had much in common with Rathenau's vision of a "classless" social hierarchy based upon levels of education, but Nelson shared neither Rathenau's concern for the needs of modern industry nor his desire to institute more flexibility in the division of labor. Closer was the similarity between Nelson's utopia and the "paradise" depicted by Kurt Hiller of the independent left-wing periodical the *Weltbühne*.[72] Where Nelson's conclusions were implicit,

---

[68] "Lebensdaten Minna Spechts" in Becker, Eichler, and Heckmann, *Erziehung und Politik*, p. 402; Link, *Geschichte*, p. 57, n. 89. A succinct discussion of the educational ideas of Wyneken and Lietz is contained in George L. Mosse, *The Crisis of German Ideology: Intellectual Origins of the Third Reich* (New York, 1964), pp. 160–68.

[69] See Link, *Geschichte*, pp. 108, n. 35; 109–12. For a suggestive description of the school by one of its former pupils see Alexander Dehms, "Leonard Nelson und die 'Walkemühle'" in *Leonard Nelson zum Gedächtnis*. Two other excellent firsthand accounts deal with conditions at the *Walkemühle* shortly after Nelson's death in 1927: Hanna Bertholet, "Gedanken über die Walkemühle" and René Bertholet, "Die Probleme schreckten uns nicht mehr" in Becker, Eichler, and Heckmann, *Erziehung und Politik*. See also the section on the *Walkemühle* in Jürgen Ziechmann, *Theorie und Praxis der Erziehung bei Leonard Nelson und seinem Bund* (Bad Heilbrunn, 1970), pp. 103–20.

[70] "IJB," p. 498.   [71] *Führer-Erziehung*, p. 25.

[72] See Alf Enseling, *Die Weltbühne: Organ der "intellektuellen Linken"* (Münster, 1962), p. 125; Istvan Deak, *Weimar Germany's Left-Wing Intellectuals: A Political History of the Weltbühne and its Circle* (Berkeley, 1968), pp. 5, 71, 153, 292n. These excellent studies deal with a loose circle of writers, many of whom on occasion cooperated politically with Nelson and his followers. Hiller's admiration for Nelson appears frequently in a volume consisting largely of excerpts from his *Weltbühne* articles: Kurt Hiller, *Köpfe und Tröpfe: Profile aus einem Vierteljahrhundert* (Hamburg, 1950). See also Hiller's memoirs: *Leben gegen die Zeit* (*Logos*) (Reinbek bei Hamburg, 1969), pp. 390–92.

Hiller's were explicit. Hiller's *Logokratie* would be established when intellectuals assumed political leadership. Nelson was much more rigorously logical and consistent than Hiller. Although throughout the early and middle years of the Weimar Republic the *Weltbühne* circle had a strong sympathy for political democracy, Hiller did not ask whether this sympathy could be reconciled with the quest for *Logokratie*. Nelson attempted, if unsuccessfully, to divorce his conception of an elite from notions of the primacy of bourgeois intellectuals such as Hiller and most of the *Weltbühne* circle expressed, and unlike Nelson they did not seek frequent contacts with workers.

Most members of Nelson's elite would never "rule" in his sense of the term. Only a few of them would have the opportunity and capacity to become the ruler. The main activity of the others would have been the production of cultural values. The selection of candidates for the elite would have depended upon the educators. The ruler would have been the headmaster of a vast educational institution comprising the entire society.[73] Perhaps the real rulers would have been the schoolmasters, although Nelson did not himself draw this conclusion from his elite theory. Significantly, however, he regarded the education of teachers as the crucial function of the state: "The training of the teaching profession is . . . the principal business of a state organized on the basis of justice. The development of society can be influenced systematically and on a large scale only by the teaching profession."[74]

Although by 1919 Nelson referred to himself as a Socialist, his economic beliefs had undergone no radical change. They continued to resemble closely those of many European left liberals and American Progressives of the late nineteenth and early twentieth century. He borrowed his economic doctrines largely from his friend the economist and sociologist Franz Oppenheimer and integrated them logically into his own philosophical system.[75] Oppenheimer tended to trace every malfunctioning of capitalism to monopolies, especially to restrictions upon landed property. His "liberal socialism," as he began to call his system after World War I, was a product of prewar left liberalism directed primarily against the landed aristocracy.

[73] See, e.g., the early version of Nelson's ideal society in *Öffentliches Leben*, 3rd unchanged ed. (Göttingen, 1949), esp. pp. 24–39. The first edition appeared in 1918.

[74] *Rechtslehre*, p. 427.

[75] See "Philosophische Vorfragen der Sozialpolitik," p. 23; "Franz Oppenheimer, der Arzt der Gesellschaft" in Eichler and Hart, *Leonard Nelson*, p. 141. The latter essay was first published in 1927. For a brief critique of Oppenheimer's system see Joseph A. Schumpeter, *History of Economic Analysis*, ed. Elizabeth Boody Schumpeter (New York, 1963), pp. 854–55; and for a discussion of the relationship between Oppenheimer's and Nelson's economic doctrines see Link, *Geschichte*, pp. 21–27.

Like the classical liberal, Nelson hoped for the harmonious adjustment of the interests of all members of society, but Nelson had no confidence in an automatic adjustment. He argued that justice required state intervention to ensure equality of opportunity for everyone to engage in work that satisfied his individual needs and to obtain sufficient property to lead a life worthy of a human being. Nelson insisted upon the necessity of maintaining the institution of private property. Although the state might alter drastically the distribution of property, the complete prohibition of private ownership of the means of production infringed upon the individual's interest in his own self-determination.[76]

Nelson's rejection of the Marxian vision of postbourgeois society was clear in his acceptance of Oppenheimer's "liberal socialism," his commitment to the permanent division of society into rulers and ruled, and his disinterest in a classless society. As Nelson noted,[77] his own philosophical idealism was incompatible with Marx's historical materialism. Yet Nelson was no more capable of confronting Marx than he was of coming to grips with theories of political democracy. Nelson's usual windmill-tilting was abetted by the distorted conceptions of Marxism that lay readily at hand. He made the error, commonly made by bourgeois critics of Marxism since the late nineteenth century, of regarding Marxism as economic determinism. He assumed that the major body of Social Democratic theory, the "orthodoxy" of Karl Kautsky and Rudolf Hilferding, was largely identical with Marx's position. Although somewhat misleading, the description of Social Democratic orthodoxy as economic determinism could be defended more easily.[78] As we shall see later, Nelson began to work out a perceptive critique of Social Democracy, but his insights into the context in which orthodoxy had developed did not prompt him to question his identification of this orthodoxy with Marxism. Characteristically, he argued that the necessity of class struggle must be based upon an ethical imperative. Denying categorically the existence of class interest, he claimed that his own philosophy provided, for the first time, a scientific foundation for socialism in the form of his doctrine of justice.[79]

Nelson's identification with socialism was possible for several rea-

[76] See "Philosophische Vorfragen der Sozialpolitik," pp. 29, 33–35, 43, 48, 56–58; "Franz Oppenheimer, der Arzt der Gesellschaft," pp. 140–41; *Rechtslehre*, pp. 375–76.

[77] See esp. "Die bessere Sicherheit: Ketzereien eines revolutionären Revisionisten" in Eichler and Hart, *Leonard Nelson*, pp. 356–57, 362, 370.

[78] See esp. Erich Matthias, "Kautsky und der Kautskyanismus: Die Funktion der Ideologie in der deutschen Sozialdemokratie vor dem 1. Weltkrieg," *Marxismus-studien*, II (1957), 151–97.

[79] "Die bessere Sicherheit," pp. 370–73.

sons. As Werner Link has pointed out, he altered his terminology; what he had earlier described as liberal he now designated socialist.[80] This ingenuous terminological sleight of hand was made easier by the Revisionists' substitution of ethical for historical imperatives, whereby socialism became merely a desirable goal. The war, the Bolshevik Revolution, and the November Revolution increased the confusion among Socialists and about socialism. By the beginning of the Weimar Republic, the word had lost much of the specific content, especially the Marxian content, once identified with it in Germany.[81] Whether through naive enthusiasm or cold calculation, men whose ideological positions and political objectives had little or nothing in common with the Socialist tradition described themselves as Socialists. Finding much to admire in the Socialist parties and no radical bourgeois alternative, Nelson and his little band entered them in order to avoid isolation and to gain more adherents. Intermittent dialogue with Marxists in these parties was not sufficiently intense to alter Nelson's liberal doctrines. The appeal of his philosophy, as well as the social origins and status of Nelson and most of his followers, impeded their efforts to comprehend Marxism.

THE PARTY OF JUSTICE

In his description of the just society, Nelson expressed only one half of his elite theory. Or perhaps we should say that he had two elite theories closely resembling each other; for in conceiving methods to realize the just society, he envisioned a small group of men who, led by a single leader, would destroy parliamentary democracy and become the elite in the new order.

The history of most previous societies, Nelson believed, consisted in a vicious circle that kept a just individual from ruling. Following the theories of his friend Oppenheimer and an earlier sociologist, Ludwig Gumplowicz, he assumed that the state had originated in the imposition by one conquering tribe of its rule upon a subject population. As a result, unjust individuals or groups had, with a few fortuitous exceptions, ruled throughout history. The rulers seldom chose men of wisdom to succeed them. Indeed, since the rulers were rarely interested in the education of just individuals, there were few good men available as potential successors. As long as the unjust ruled, the educational sys-

[80] Link, *Geschichte*, p. 17, n. 56.
[81] For indications of how diversely the term socialism came to be construed in postwar Germany see Lebovics, *Social Conservatism and the Middle Classes in Germany*; Wolfgang Hock, *Deutscher Antikapitalismus: Der ideologische Kampf gegen die freie Wirtschaft im Zeichen der grossen Krise* (Frankfurt am Main, 1960).

tem remained under their control and produced few men with a superior perception of justice.

Despite his faith in education "to ennoble man," Nelson saw no hope of establishing the just society merely through education. Although he expanded the educational activities that he had begun before the war, he believed that "the political struggle should stand in the foreground."[82] The state, he argued, had to be "conquered" before the proper individual could begin his rule. The education of the members of the new elite in isolation from the rest of society could by itself never achieve the goal of justice. They had to have an organization through which they could actively oppose the evils of "capitalism, imperialism, and clericalism."[83] This organization, or the "Party of Justice,"[84] would be organized in the same way as the government of the future. Upon triumphing, the party could become the new government.[85]

Inspired by the example of Fries and the *Burschenschaft*, as well as by the experiences of the early Youth Movement, Nelson's conception of this party was rigidified by the relentless logic of his philosophy and by the intermittent political isolation of his group. Although he referred occasionally to Lenin's ideas on the development of a cadre of professional revolutionaries, these references were perfunctory and superficial.[86] Nelson was unable to relate the vanguard theory to historical circumstances, as Lenin had grounded it in world and Russian social conditions. Nelson made clear that his own admiration for Lenin as a leader was qualified. Lenin had been a great and successful leader of the proletariat who was flawed by his commitment to the deleterious doctrines of Marxism.

Nelson referred to the principle upon which the organization of the party would rest as the "leadership principle [*Prinzip der Führerschaft*]," which entailed the voluntary, but complete subordination of the followers to a single leader. Yet this subordination did not release each follower from responsibility to his own conscience. The leader had no violence at his disposal with which to ensure compliance with his wishes. He could also not use "the authoritarian principle," which

[82] *Führer-Erziehung*, pp. 16–17, 19–20; *Nicht bürgerliche, sondern proletarische Bildungsarbeit: Ein Wort an die sozialistische Arbeiterschaft* (Göttingen, 1931), p. 12. The latter work is the second edition of *Vom Bildungswahn: Ein Wort an die proletarische Jugend. Rede, gehalten vor den Jungsozialisten in Hannover am 20. Mai 1922* (Leipzig, 1923).

[83] "IJB," p. 499.

[84] *Partei des Rechts*. Nelson sometimes referred to it as the "Party of Reason [*Partei der Vernunft*]."

[85] *DuF*, pp. 22–23.

[86] See, e.g., his speech of Jan. 6, 1926 in Eichler and Hart, *Leonard Nelson*, pp. 278, 288; "Über die Russlandreise 1927" in *ibid.*, pp. 400–01.

involved belief in the infallibility of the leader. The leader's greatest resource would be the confidence that his followers had both in him and in his perception of justice. The personal qualities of the leader had to inspire others voluntarily to obey his commands. The relationship between leader and led had to be based upon "loyalty and faith." The leader would be able to expect his followers to make sacrifices joyfully.[87]

Nelson's conception of the relationship between leader and follower resembled Max Weber's analysis of charismatic leadership. The follower subordinated himself gladly to the leader. Yet for Nelson the goal for which the Party of Justice was constituted had to remain primary rather than the personality of the leader. Unlike Weber's charismatic leader, whom men obeyed primarily because of some facet of his personality, Nelson's leader was to be followed to achieve a definite objective—the establishment of the just society. Where Weber found an irrational dynamic, Nelson found only rational forces and apparent paradox:

> It seems paradoxical that an organization having as its goal the achievement of human dignity, the right of every individual to rational self-determination, is revealed as the most forbidding coercive institution that free men might be expected to enter, . . . as an institution which degrades its members to mere instruments. And this occurs simply because the leader, lacking means of compelling obedience, must rely all the more upon the voluntary compliance of the members.[88]

Probably in an attempt to rebut criticism of his leadership principle raised in the name of democratic ideals, Nelson gave in 1926 a detailed description of its application to his group. He denied that his method of making decisions from above was arbitrary, explaining that they were made only after investigation and discussion of the alternative courses of action. A decision was reached in an open atmosphere of freely expressed criticism. Every follower was not merely permitted to speak his mind; he was obligated to speak up. Nelson went so far as to argue that someone who did not participate in the discussion of serious questions should be considered an exploiter. The exploiter profited

[87] "IJB," pp. 495–96; *DuF*, pp. 24–26; *Rechtslehre*, p. 184; *Führer-Erziehung*, p. 26. For a very similar conception of leadership expressed by a woman who, like Nelson, was a left liberal before the war, but who became a prominent member of the Democratic party during the Weimar Republic see Gertrud Bäumer, *Die seelische Krisis*, 2nd ed. (Berlin, 1924), esp. pp. 135–39; *Grundlagen demokratischer Politik* (Karlsruhe, 1928), esp. pp. 9–10.

[88] *DuF*, p. 26.

from the fruits of others' work without contributing anything of his own.[89]

Nelson expected that the Party of Justice would come to power gradually. He never indicated how the last stages of the process would come about, but the import of his proposals was clear. The party would tirelessly educate and train better and better leaders, while at the same time working actively within the existing parliamentary system. Through discipline and devotion the party would eventually become so powerful that it could "seize power."[90]

Despite his lack of clarity in describing how the party would succeed in seizing power, Nelson believed firmly that its victory would be irresistible. Its establishment, and hence its triumph, depended merely upon "a *single* contingency."[91] A person with sufficient comprehension of justice and with the will to realize it, had to overcome the inertia of the existing order. He had to gather around himself a group of followers. Together with them he would either enter one of the existing parties or organize the Party of Justice.

Such an individual, Nelson reasoned, would not be reluctant to begin his task. If he hesitated, he was not the right man; a truly just person would have no fear of appearing autocratic: "He should not hold back even if he lacks the perfection required by the vocation of leadership. . . . A less able leader must begin to search for better successors and do everything in his power to train them."[92] Convinced that this man must first have clarified all the basic problems of instituting a just society, Nelson saw himself as the founder and leader of the nucleus of the Party of Justice.[93] Soon, if not from the beginning, he equated the IJB with the party of his dreams.

THE IJB AND SOCIAL DEMOCRACY

In 1925 the members of the IJB were expelled from all Social Democratic organizations. Nelson's followers had gained pivotal positions

---

[89] Speech of Jan. 6, 1926 in Eichler and Hart, *Leonard Nelson*, p. 289.

[90] *DuF*, p. 5; *Führer-Erziehung*, p. 13.

[91] *Rechtslehre*, p. 608. Nelson's italics.

[92] *DuF*, p. 24. See also p. 21.

[93] See, e.g., the beginning of the quotation from Confucius which Nelson placed directly after the title page of his *Rechtslehre*: "Dsi Lu sprach: 'Der Fürst von We wartet auf den Meister, um die Regierung auszuüben. Was würde der Meister *zuerst* in Angriff nehmen?' Der Meister sprach: 'Sicherlich die Richtigstellung der Begriffe.'" Nelson's italics. In the opening address to an IJB training course in 1924, the year that his *Rechtslehre* was published, Nelson quoted this same passage from Confucius. See the selections from the address in Eichler and Hart, *Leonard Nelson*, p. 252.

in a few of these organizations, above all in a youth group and in the party's Göttingen branch. The IJB's aggressive anticlerical activities included a successful attempt to organize school teachers struggling against the consolidation of the Catholic Church's influence in education. These anticlerical efforts and a tactical alliance with part of the SPD's Marxist-oriented left wing challenged the authority of the party's executive board. The party executive wished to maintain the ability of the SPD to forge political coalitions with the Catholic Center and sought therefore to avoid a battle over the role of religious instruction in the public schools.[94]

The party executive justified its expulsion of Nelson and his followers by denouncing the IJB as undemocratic, a charge that they proudly acknowledged. Both sides in the controversy couched most of their explanations of the expulsion in misleading ideological terms. But two discussions of it should be mentioned for what they reveal about Nelson and his followers.

Seeking to account for the susceptibility of the SPD's rank and file to "revelations" that IJB members sought to advance self-serving purposes of the IJB, Willi Eichler, one of Nelson's foremost adherents, wrote that many Social Democrats could not imagine anyone having "on the basis of pure idealism an interest in the improvement of the working-class movement."[95] Eichler neglected the opportunity to examine the stake that the many teachers among Nelson's followers had in the struggle against the Church.

In a speech, delivered apparently to a group of workers, Nelson presented the most telling account that we have of his reflections on the conflict. He contrasted the triumph of "opportunism" in Social Democracy to the assertion of a principled position by the IJB. Like Marxist critics of opportunism, he argued that its practitioners needed no philosophy; an opportunist would invoke any argument to justify his acceptance of existing reality. Nelson found the basic conflict between the IJB and the party in the question of educating men for socialism. His analysis of the relationship between opportunism and education indicates how effectively he could use his intellectual talents when he confronted a practical issue. He took the party to task for relying upon the educational institutions of bourgeois society and upon workers' institutions modeled on them. Workers exposed to these institutions were alienated from their own class and encouraged to seek personal advancement. Nelson linked his criticisms to an examination of the bureaucratization of the party. Implicitly, he held up his own school

[94] My account of the troubled relationship with the Social Democrats draws heavily upon Link, *Geschichte*, pp. 74–102.
[95] "Über Leonard Nelson" in Eichler and Hart, *Leonard Nelson*, p. xxiv.

as an institution training men to lead and to make higher demands than the followers upon themselves. This training, as well as provisions preventing party functionaries from using the working-class movement as a springboard to their own social ascent, would prevent the appearance of traitors like Kerensky and Noske.[96]

After the expulsion, Nelson and his followers disbanded the IJB, which they reorganized under a more militant name, the International Socialist *Kampfbund* (ISK). This new group was even more rigidly and hierarchically organized than its predecessor. The ISK was designed to function as a political party, but its failure to gain mass support confirmed its character as a partly isolated left-wing sect. It may have begun with fewer than two hundred members. According to a probably conservative estimate, it had three hundred regular members and a circle of sympathizers of six hundred to one thousand at the end of the Weimar Republic. By 1933 the ISK had local groups in some thirty-two German towns.[97] Provisions to equalize the incomes of its members helped to restrict its size. Membership dues were adjusted, so that all personal income above a minimum amount had to be turned over to the organization.

Like the influence of the IJB, that of the ISK extended far beyond the ranks of its members and sympathizers. Its newsletter had an average circulation of five to six thousand and may have approached ten thousand.[98] Nelson's followers continued to be active in some organizations identified with the Socialist parties. The most important of these organizations were the large Association of Freethinkers for Cremation (*Verein der Freidenker für Feuerbestattung*) and the German Workers' Abstinence League (*Deutscher Arbeiter-Abstinenten Bund*). Playing an important role in the national leadership and several local chapters of these organizations, members of the ISK thereby maintained some contacts with the Socialist parties, but failed to gain any significant influence in the trade unions.

In 1927 less than two years after the founding of the ISK, Nelson died. Two of his closet collaborators attempted to fill his shoes. Minna Specht assumed the direction of the ISK's school, and Willi Eichler took over the leadership of the ISK. In the opinion of the only scholar to make a thorough study of the ISK, Nelson's death did not destroy the continuity in the development of the organization that had been so

---

[96] Speech of Jan. 6, 1926 in Eichler and Hart, *Leonard Nelson*, pp. 269–88.

[97] Link, *Geschichte*, pp. 103–07, 139, 141–42. Eichler's estimate of the number of sympathizers and members is much higher. In his letter to me of Aug. 1, 1962 he places the total number of members and sympathizers at roughly 1,000 shortly after ISK's founding, and at 2,000 by the end of the Republic.

[98] The largest of these figures is Eichler's in his letter of Aug. 1, 1962 and is a bit higher than the figure that he mentioned to Link. Link, *Geschichte*, p. 145.

closely identified with him.[99] Part of the ISK's leadership emigrated in early 1933 but remained in touch with their colleagues in Germany. The organization was able to conduct extensive resistance activities. Both its structure and the zeal of its members made it very effective in opposition to the Nazi dictatorship until shortly before World War II, when many of them were arrested. After the war the ISK disbanded, and a number of its former members became active Social Democrats in West Germany. Some came to occupy important party positions. Revising Nelson's philosophy, these influential Nelsonians accommodated themselves to the swing to the Right in postwar West German Social Democracy.[100]

Nelson himself never came to terms with mass politics. The often impressive internal consistency of his position discouraged him and his followers from comprehending the inability of their idealism to explain historical change and to clarify their own role in society. Adherence to his doctrines led them to cut themselves off from every major political camp. Nelson led a group reminiscent of a utopian Socialist sect struggling bravely to apply doctrines incapable of coping with the realities of the twentieth century. He sought an alternative to revolution and counterrevolution in an era when the middle position was occupied largely by proponents of political democracy. Both he and the students, teachers, and other professionals who provided the basis of the IJB were driven into direct action by war and revolution. His elitism—his critique of democracy and his doctrine of the rule of the just—provided a coherent interpretation of the present and an optimistic vision of the future for small, but significant segments of the middle class. Yet his seemingly boundless optimism obscured a strong element of despair. Permanent dictatorship, however enlightened and benevolent, became the only way to reach and secure the liberal goals that he continued to cherish, even when he identified them with socialism after World War I. His elitism ensured the predominance of part of the middle class, but neither he nor his followers found any connection between their own class interests and their spirited attempts to uplift workers through education. Nelson and his group did not recognize that his doctrines provided a method of defending their own position in society and justifying their function in the future. During the last years of the Weimar Republic, Hans Zehrer's concept of a "revolution of the intelligentsia" would serve a similar function, providing a defensive doctrine in a period of crumbling barriers between the mid-

---

[99] Link, *Geschichte*, p. 140.

[100] See *ibid.*, pp. 322–37. Symptomatic of the reinterpretation of Nelson's philosophy is Willi Eichler, "Philosophie und Politik: Zu Leonard Nelsons 80. Geburtstag am 11. Juli 1962," *Geist und Tat*, XVII (1962), 225–30.

dle and working classes for a larger and more politically sophisticated audience whose sympathies tended toward the Right rather than the Left. But Zehrer appealed explicitly to self-interest as well as self-sacrifice. Nelson appealed directly only to self-sacrifice. The historical significance of Nelson's political doctrines consists less in their impact on German society and politics than in the insights they offer into the mentality of the educated middle class during the early years of the Weimar Republic.

PART III

Conservatives in Search of Elites

CHAPTER SEVEN

Conservatives and Neoconservatives

THE collapse of the Bismarckian Empire and the threat of social revolution fostered important changes on the Right. Some of these changes can be seen in declarations of principles published by the parties of the Right in December 1918. Even the most direct successors to the pre-Weimar Conservatives, drawn together by the newly founded Nationalist party (DNVP), tended to stress merit rather than birth as a qualification for political leadership. A manifesto issued by the directorate of the Nationalist party called for the acceptance of parliamentary government on the basis of universal suffrage and the filling of state offices according to ability.[1] The other major new party on the Right, the People's party (DVP), most of whose leaders had been National Liberals, downgraded the previous liberal emphasis upon wealth and social standing, while continuing to stress personal merit. The Peoples' party appealed for "complete equality of rights, in every sphere of public life, for all German citizens without regard for origins, religion, or social position."[2] A similar posture was assumed by the new Bavarian People's party (BVP), a provincial organization of Catholic Centrists that, more conservative than its national counterpart, became the major party of the Right in Bavaria. The program of

---

[1] "Aufruf des Vorstandes der Deutschnationalen Volkspartei" (Dec. 27, 1918) in Felix Salomon, ed., *Die deutschen Parteiprogramme*, 3rd ed. (Leipzig and Berlin, 1920), III, 122. There have been no comprehensive studies of the parties of the Right during the Weimar Republic. On the extent to which the successors to the Conservatives and to the right wing of the National Liberals felt that they had to make "concessions to democracy" in the period from the end of the war to the early years of the Republic, see: Sigmund Neumann, *Die deutschen Parteien: Wesen und Wandel nach dem Kriege* (Berlin, 1932), pp. 61–62; Theodor Eschenburg, *Die improvisierte Demokratie der Weimarer Republik* (Schloss Laupheim, 1952); Walter Gagel, *Die Wahlrechtsfrage in der Geschichte der deutschen liberalen Parteien 1848–1918* (Düsseldorf, 1958), pp. 167–70; Otto-Ernst Schüddekopf, *Die deutsche Innenpolitik im letzten Jahrhundert und der konservative Gedanke* (Braunschweig, 1951), pp. 108–20; Werner Liebe, *Die Deutschnationale Volkspartei 1918–1924* (Düsseldorf, 1956), pp. 18–24; Lewis Hertzman, *DNVP: Right-Wing Opposition in the Weimar Republic* (Lincoln, Nebraska, 1963), pp. 32–60; Wolfgang Hartenstein, *Die Anfänge der Deutschen Volkspartei 1918–1920* (Düsseldorf, 1962); Hans Booms, *Die Deutschkonservative Partei: Preussischer Charakter, Reichsauffassung, Nationalbegriff* (Düsseldorf, 1954), pp. 34–58.

[2] "Aufruf der Deutschen Volkspartei" (Dec. 18, 1918) in Salomon, *Deutsche Parteiprogramme*, III, 87.

the BVP rejected categorically any recognition of "privileges of status or of birth."[3]

Although attenuated and compromised by subsequent party actions and statements, as well as by right-wing writers, the forthright declarations by the new parties of the Right in late 1918 were never formally repudiated. That the merit principle had been abused as a cloak for the corrupt and unfit soon became a standard right-wing complaint, but under conditions of universal and equal suffrage, formal repudiation of these declarations was inexpedient, even when counter-revolutionaries were emboldened by the dissipation of the shock of the Empire's collapse and by the waning of the threat of social revolution. In the Nationalist party, for example, pressure from trade unions with a strong basis among white-collar workers precluded formal repudiation during the 1920's. Hans Bechly, the head of the large German Nationalist Federation of Commercial Employees (the DHV, *Deutschnationaler Handlungsgehilfenverband*), demanded in no uncertain terms that political leaders be recruited from all social classes.[4]

The ranks of right-wingers who clung to the basic concepts of nineteenth-century conservatism and hence took an unequivocally reactionary position dwindled. Few right-wing writers and publicists failed to make frank concessions to the times. Occasionally these concessions entailed little more than a vigorous affirmation of the racist beliefs that the Conservative party had haltingly identified itself with in the late nineteenth century. Thus *Geheimer Hofrat* Ernst Mayer, a professor of law at Würzburg, offered a transmuted version of early nineteenth-century conservatism in which he invoked racism and anti-Semitism to buttress his case for the nobility.[5] More typical was a discourse on "the renewal of leadership" by another professor of law, Friedrich Lent, a man who later became a German Nationalist Reichstag deputy. Lent declared that an aristocracy of birth provided no

[3] "Programm der Bayerischen Volkspartei vom Dezember 1918" in Walter Nimtz, *Die Novemberrevolution 1918 in Deutschland* (Berlin, 1962), p. 198.

[4] Hans Bechly, *Die Führerfrage im neuen Deutschland: Vortrag, gehalten auf dem 18. Deutschen Kaufmannsgehilfentag am 10. Juni 1928 in Dresden* (Hamburg, [1928]), p. 29. Some glimpses of the relationship between the DHV and the DNVP during the 1920's are provided by ch. 4, sec. 1 of Iris Hamel, *Völkischer Verband und nationale Gewerkschaft: Der Deutschnationale Handlungsgehilfen-Verband 1893–1933* (Frankfurt am Main, [1967]). See also my forthcoming study of the DHV.

[5] Ernst Mayer, *Vom Adel*, Schriften zur politischen Bildung, ed. Gesellschaft "Deutscher Staat," . . . *Friedrich Mann's Pädagogisches Magazin*, Heft 914 (Langensalza, 1922), pp. 5–6, 16–18, 22 and passim. Hereafter this series will be cited simply as *Mann's Päd. Magazin*. See also Mayer's *Vom alten und vom kommenden Deutschen Reich: Reformvorschläge, Mann's Päd. Magazin*, Heft 874 (Langensalza, 1922).

solution to the problem of political leadership; true leaders should be welcomed "whether born in a palace or a hut."[6]

With the notable exception of Bavaria during the early 1920's, monarchism failed to remain a potent political force after 1918. Monarchist sentiments and plots were much in evidence, especially during the early years of the Republic, but few men active on the Right worked tenaciously toward the restoration for which the historian Adalbert Wahl provided an elaborate theoretical and historical justification in 1919.[7] Indeed, talk of a restoration raised seemingly insoluble problems. Should the pre-Weimar social coalition be reconstituted, or would the increased bargaining strength of the industrial and commercial bourgeoisie alter beyond recognition the previous relationship between the partners? Should a restoration assume the form of a parliamentary monarchy similar to England's, as some German monarchists suggested, or should a regime modeled on the preabsolutistic dual state be established, as a Göttingen professor of law, Julius Binder, implied?[8] And what of the conundrum of the German dynasties? Would one, some, or all of the more than twenty old thrones be restored? Should the opportunity of a restoration be seized upon to reestablish in Hannover the Guelfs, whom Bismarck had unseated after the Austro-Prussian war of 1866, and whose supporters now gathered in the German-Hannoverian party? Calls to bring back the Hohenzollerns encountered hostility not only from the adherents of other dynasties but also from other traditionally minded Germans, who disapproved of the behavior of some members of Prussia's former ruling house. William II and the Crown Prince had rather thoroughly discredited themselves. Except as a vague sentiment, monarchism came to have little appeal to most Germans outside Bavaria. Even in Bavaria the political organization of the monarchists, the *Königspartei*, collapsed in 1921. Monarchists had no clear, attractive alternative to the Weimar Republic.

The election of Hindenburg as president of the Republic in 1925 un-

---

[6] Friedrich Lent, *Parlamentarismus und Führertum: Die Erneuerung des Führertums in der Gegenwart*, Mann's Päd. Magazin, Heft 1271 (Langensalza, 1929), pp. 71, 78.

[7] Adalbert Wahl, *Das Führertum in der Geschichte*, 2nd ed., Mann's Päd. Magazin, Heft 1270 (Langensalza, 1929). See also Wahl's article in an issue of the *Süddeutsche Monatshefte* devoted to monarchism: Adalbert Wahl, "Die Monarchie in der deutschen Geschichte," *Süddeutsche Monatshefte*, xxv (1929), 849–53. For a general study of the decline of monarchism see Walter H. Kaufmann, *Monarchism in the Weimar Republic* (New York, 1952). See also Hertzman, *DNVP*, pp. 86–88.

[8] Julius Binder, *Führerauslese in der Demokratie*, Mann's Päd. Magazin, Heft 1247 (Langensalza, 1929), esp. pp. 56–59.

expectedly presented even the most devoted monarchists with another quandary from which they never escaped. At first viewed by many Germans as a stadholder for the Hohenzollerns, the new president became an apparently loyal supporter of the Republic. His failure to prepare for a restoration increased the disarray in the ranks of the monarchists.

Among the nationwide parties of the Right the Nationalist party was the one most closely associated with monarchism, but the Nationalists themselves were badly divided on the issue. This division was successfully exploited during the late 1920's by the faction led by Alfred Hugenberg in the course of struggles that eventually split the party. The Hugenberg faction discredited many of its opponents as renegades from the monarchist cause, even though the basic question confronting the party had little to do with monarchism: should the party in which big business interests predominated reduce the weight given to middle-class, peasant, and large agrarian interests? Hugenberg steered a course that made the party into a direct instrument of a group preoccupied by the concerns of heavy industry and that often led to close cooperation with the Nazis. In 1933 Hugenberg, who had sought to establish the Nationalists as the senior partners in this relationship, found their status downgraded precipitously in the Hitler cabinet.

A major landmark in Hugenberg's consolidation of his control over the Nationalist party was the "Lambach incident" in 1928–1929. Walther Lambach, a Nationalist Reichstag deputy and a white-collar trade unionist who served as a representative of the DHV in the party, wrote a brief article on the decline of monarchist sentiment in Germany. He suggested that his party acknowledge publicly that most Germans had abandoned monarchism.[9] The stormy discussion following Lambach's article recalls, if *en miniature*, the controversy over Eduard Bernstein's revisionism among Social Democrats at the turn of the century. Lambach might well have heeded the warning given by a wily comrade reacting to Bernstein's plea that the SPD admit its essentially reformist outlook: "My dear Eddie, you . . . don't *talk* about it, you just *do* it."[10] Neither Bernstein nor Lambach accepted this type

[9] Walther Lambach, "Monarchismus," *Politische Wochenschrift*, IV (1928), 495–97. On the changes in the DNVP see esp. Friedrich Freiherr Hiller von Gaertringen, "Die Deutschnationale Volkspartei" in Erich Matthias and Rudolf Morsey, eds., *Das Ende der Parteien 1933* (Düsseldorf, 1960), pp. 544–53 and passim; Attila Chanady, "The Disintegration of the German National People's Party, 1924–30," *Journal of Modern History*, XXIX (1967), 65–91.

[10] Quoted in Peter Gay, *The Dilemma of Democratic Socialism: Eduard Bernstein's Challenge to Marx* (New York: Collier paperback, 1962), p. 270. Gay's italics. I have altered Gay's translation slightly.

of opportunistic advice, but Bernstein was able to stay within his party and work doggedly for the acceptance of his views. Lambach was less fortunate. He paid for his frankness by expulsion. Although a party court of appeals soon reinstated him, he led a secession at the end of 1929. The controversy over monarchism, as Lambach realized, provided a diversion from the basic issues at stake in Hugenberg's assault on him. In order to break Social Democracy, undercut the power of the organized working class, and lead industry into a sustained struggle against the foreign and domestic policies of the Reich government, Hugenberg undertook joint action with the Nazis against the Young Plan in 1929. The Lambach incident provided simply the pretext for one of several tests of strength between opposing factions of Nationalists that resulted in the decline of the role of white-collar unionists, principled old conservatives, and agrarians in the party. Although some large agrarians continued to work with Hugenberg, before long he even lost the support of many big business interests.[11] Monarchism was a dying although not a dead issue in Germany long before its unceremonious burial by the Nazi regime.

Disenchantment with hereditary monarchy was expressed, if in a thinly veiled form, in the writings of traditionally minded conservatives like Binder, Lent, and Wahl who discoursed at length on the need for "great men" and "ruling strata." The separation of monarchism from devotion to great men, a process that began during the latter part of the nineteenth century, had come close to completion by 1933. The landmarks in the process were registered in school textbooks. While placing great emphasis upon leadership, authority, and "hero-worship," textbooks under the Empire still linked these concepts with monarchism and dynastic traditions. The new textbooks of the Republic stressed similar concepts, but no longer identified them with monarchism.[12]

The most innovative and potent right-wing forces under the Republic derived much intellectual stimulation from the cultural elite theorists of the Second Empire, and thereby maintained a measure of continuity with those forces on the Right that had been highly critical of

[11] Henry A. Turner, Jr., "Big Business and the Rise of Hitler," *American Historical Review*, LXXV (1969), 60 provides no convincing evidence for his puzzling assertion that much of the DNVP's industrial wing left the party in 1930 and that Hugenberg had to rely increasingly upon backing from agrarians.

[12] See Horst Schallenberger, *Untersuchungen zum Geschichtsbild der Wilhelminischen Ära und der Weimarer Zeit: Eine vergleichende Schulbuchanalyse deutscher Schulgeschichtsbücher aus der Zeit von 1888 bis 1933* (Ratingen bei Düsseldorf, 1964), pp. 54, 58, 72, 203, 242; R. H. Samuel and R. Hinton Thomas, *Education and Society in Modern Germany* (London, 1949), pp. 71–81; Helmut König, *Imperialistische und militaristische Erziehung in den Hörsaalen und Schulstuben Deutschlands 1870–1960* (Berlin, 1960), esp. pp. 110–11.

the Wilhelminian era. Although monarchism still played a part in the thinking of some of these adversaries of the Republic, they refused to sanction anything resembling a mere restoration. As one of their sympathetic critics suggested, they tended to regard the Weimar Republic as a continuation of the Wilhelminian state in which the old opposition, the Social Democrats and left liberals, held the reins of power.[13] Since the foes of both the Republic and a restoration were usually thought of, by themselves and others, as standing on the Right, but were critical, often scornful of the views associated with the more traditionally oriented parties of the Right, they frequently came to be known as "neoconservatives," and their goal was described as a "conservative revolution."[14] The phrase conservative revolution, a semantic absurdity that came into vogue during the last years of the Republic[15] and that we shall meet frequently in the following chapters, has fortunately been used little in recent years.

The word "neoconservative" is easier to justify. Like "conservative revolutionary" and the less striking term "new nationalists," it gained currency as a consequence of a strongly felt need to distinguish backward-looking, more traditionally minded conservatives from intellectually far-ranging, usually younger and more flexible men on the Right. Before 1933 all three terms were employed loosely to point up the importance of many men on the Right who looked forward to a future order that was neither a revamped version of the Republic nor

[13] Waldemar Gurian [pseud. Walter Gerhart], *Um des Reiches Zukunft: Nationale Wiedergeburt oder politische Reaktion?* (Freiburg im Breisgau, 1932), pp. 56–57.

[14] See esp. three recent surveys: Armin Mohler, *Die konservative Revolution in Deutschland 1918–1932: Grundriss ihrer Weltanschauungen* (Stuttgart, 1950); Klemens von Klemperer, *Germany's New Conservatism: Its History and Dilemma in the Twentieth Century* (Princeton, 1957); Kurt Sontheimer, *Antidemokratisches Denken in der Weimarer Republik: Die politischen Ideen des deutschen Nationalismus zwischen 1918 und 1933* (Munich, 1962). An indispensable reference work, Mohler's study contains extensive bibliographies. Klemperer provides a much more readable account, and he makes a greater effort to examine the political context of neoconservatism. Sontheimer's work is the least valuable of the three, although he covers some aspects of neoconservatism neglected by Klemperer and dealt with schematically by Mohler. By chastising opponents of the Weimar Republic as wrong-headed intellectuals who should have supported the Weimar Republic, but perversely refused to do so, Sontheimer introduces premature moral judgments that obscure important historical problems.

[15] The origins of the phrase are uncertain. Its vogue began after its use in 1927, in a speech to students in Munich, by Hugo von Hofmannsthal, the Austrian poet best remembered in the United States as the librettist of Richard Strauss's *Rosenkavalier*. Mohler, *Konservative Revolution*, pp. 18–19; Klemperer, *Germany's New Conservatism*, pp. 9–11. Mohler (p. 18, n. 2) points out that the phrase appeared, as early as 1921, in an essay by Thomas Mann. Perhaps the best, if still unconvincing, case for the appropriateness of the term "revolutionary" to describe part of the Right during the Weimar Republic is made by Otto Ernst Schüddekopf, *Linke Leute von rechts: Die nationalrevolutionären Minderheiten und der Kommunismus in der Weimarer Republik* (Stuttgart, 1960), passim.

an updated model of the Second Empire. In addition to the obvious advantages of implying that vigorous, dynamic, forward-looking men existed on the Right, expressions suggesting a new type of conservatism had other political dividends. These expressions distinguished a new Right from an old Right without necessitating incessant tactless references to the latter as "reactionaries." Many neoconservatives were chary of using a pejorative favored by the Reds, although the Nazis were sufficiently churlish as well as astute, to castigate opponents as "reactionaries."

Today it is easy to forget that during the Weimar Republic the Nazis were usually regarded as a part of the new Right. This classification persisted until 1933 and into the Third Reich, despite the development of an increasingly wary, even hostile attitude toward the Nazis on the part of other segments of the new Right. Since the collapse of the Third Reich, the expressions "neoconservative" and "conservative revolutionary" have come to be used mainly to distinguish a portion of the Right from both the Nazis and the old Right.[16] Thus right-wingers who hesitated or refused to identify themselves with a political party and who looked unsympathetically on yearnings to restore the Second Reich are now commonly known as "neoconservatives."

The intensity of the efforts after World War II to distinguish "neoconservatives" from "Nazis" is understandable. During the Third Reich, historians both in Germany and elsewhere had scanned the German past, "from Luther to Hitler,"[17] in search of Nazis and proto-Nazis. In 1955 a prominent conservative historian, Gerhard Ritter, condemned the distortions of Germany's history resulting from this search with the apt remark that "history can never be written by means of quotations from literature."[18] The postwar "denazification" program undertaken by the United States in its zone of occupation demonstrated the lack of historical and moral discrimination exercised in placing Germans into categories labeled "Nazi," "non-Nazi," and

[16] The most important and symptomatic works in this often subtle shift in terminology and conceptualization are Mohler's *Konservative Revolution* and esp. Klemperer's *Germany's New Conservatism*.

[17] The title of a book by W. M. McGovern, *From Luther to Hitler: The History of Fascist-Nazi Political Philosophy* (Boston, 1941). A superior work of the same genre is Rohan d'O. Butler, *The Roots of National Socialism, 1783–1933* (London, 1941). Another study first published in 1941 might also be noted since a revised and enlarged edition has recently been widely disseminated: Peter Viereck, *Metapolitics: The Roots of the Nazi Mind* (New York: Capricorn paperback, 1961). Of the many similar attempts, but with positive rather than negative accents, to find precursors of Nazism, one important study may serve as an example: Christoph Steding, *Das Reich und die Krankheit der europäischen Kultur* (Hamburg, 1938).

[18] Gerhard Ritter, "The Historical Foundations of the Rise of National-Socialism" in Maurice Baumont, et al., *The Third Reich* (New York, 1955), p. 386.

"victim of the Nazis." As we shall see in Chapter Thirteen, the major advantages that United States imperialists derived from applying these categories based upon many an arbitrary factor lasted only briefly.[19] Soon most scholars in the West were using classifications that seemed to them more discerning. These new classifications avoided the term "fascist," once employed, especially on the Left, to refer to Nazis, neo-conservatives in general, and even to Nationalists like Hugenberg.[20] The foremost postwar students of neoconservatism, Armin Mohler and Klemens von Klemperer, who approached their subject sympathetically when not dealing with "Nazis," became absorbed in the problem of ascertaining significant differences between neoconservatives and National Socialists.[21] The sustained attention that has been devoted during the past twenty years to this problem might suggest to the unwary that firm distinctions can be made among conservatives, neoconservatives, and Nazis on the basis of ideas, activities, and personnel. Yet no one has found distinguishing criteria tenable in all, or even

[19] There has not to my knowledge been a systematic, well-documented study to test the hypothesis that the consequences of the American-sponsored denazification program and related measures like the decartelization decrees promoted both American economic penetration of western Germany and imperialistic cooperation between United States and West German monopoly capitalists.

[20] For examples of left-wing writings on fascism published before or shortly after 1933 see the convenient collection of reprints in Wolfgang Abendroth, ed., *Faschismus und Kapitalismus: Theorien über die sozialen Ursprünge und die Funktion des Faschismus* (Frankfurt am Main, [1967?]), which includes contributions by Otto Bauer, Herbert Marcuse, Arthur Rosenberg, and August Thalheimer. See also a usually overlooked work by a Soviet-oriented German Communist, Hans Günther, *Der Herren eigner Geist: Die Ideologie des Nationalsozialismus* (Moscow, 1935). Ernst Nolte's widely discussed work on fascism is symptomatic of the trend among postwar students of the Right, especially in West Germany and the United States, to separate Nazis from neoconservatives. At first sight, Nolte may appear to oppose this trend, for his operational definition of fascism would not confine the term to the Nazis and some groups outside Germany. Yet when discussing fascism in Germany, he focuses almost uninterruptedly upon the Nazi party, indeed upon Adolf Hitler, as if there were few if any other German fascists. See esp. Nolte's major work, *Three Faces of Fascism: Action française, Italian Fascism, National Socialism*, trans. Leila Vennewitz (New York, 1966), as well as his general survey of European fascist movements, *Die faschistischen Bewegungen: Die Krise des liberalen Systems und die Entwicklung der Faschismen* (Munich, 1966). It should be noted, however, that the tendency to confine the term fascist to the Nazis is not as marked in Nolte's selection of interpretive studies of fascism from the past fifty years. See Ernst Nolte, ed., *Theorien über den Faschismus* (Cologne, 1967).

[21] This pitfall is avoided by George L. Mosse, *The Crisis of German Ideology: Intellectual Origins of the Third Reich* (New York, 1964); but impatient to establish the continuity of ideas on the Right, which he regards as dominated by a "Volkish" strand by 1933—perhaps even before the founding of the Nazi party—Mosse glosses over the problem of distinguishing National Socialism from neoconservatism.

most, instances. Studies of neoconservatism run the danger to which an investigation of twentieth-century liberalism is also prone—the error of implying the existence of clear distinctions where there are none, and of obscuring the basic similarities in political positions, which, however divergent in detail, all assert one version or another of bourgeois society. A study designed mainly to contrast these versions may well not do justice to the affinities among them.

What, then, should be done with the expression "neoconservative"? Should it be discarded? No, no more than the terms liberal and conservative need be abandoned. Once the hazards of referring to "neoconservatives" are clearly understood, the word can provide a convenient form of shorthand to denote a broad grouping of diverse men and organizations who, especially during the last years of the Republic, tended to have strong reservations about the Nazi party, as well as about the more traditionally oriented parties of the Right. In view of the diversity of views among both Nazis and neoconservatives before 1933, lack of membership in the Nazi party can not serve as a touchstone, but simply as a rough guide. A somewhat less elusive distinction is the generalization that racism did not play a central role in many neoconservative elite theories, whereas racism occupied a prominent place in most Nazi elite theories.

Our discussion of the relationship among Nazis, neoconservatives, and conservatives has pointed up the critical role of neoconservatism on the Right under Weimar. Neoconservatism embodied tendencies at work throughout the Right, tendencies that increasingly came to the fore. The neoconservatives formed the intellectual vanguard of the Right. Impatient with received ideologies, programs, and techniques, they were favorably disposed to experimentation. If their own predilection for the articulation of ideology had not been so strong, one would be tempted to treat them as the pragmatists of the Right. Many a conservative sat sluggishly on the accumulated refuse of the past, adding occasionally the remains of a choice dish prepared by others. The neoconservative, acting in consonance with the recipes for "organicism" favored by the Right since the time of the French Revolution, added his own concoctions to this garbage heap, and became adept at composting. Perhaps his sensitivity to the persistent threat of the Left made him so desirous of increasing the tempo of fermentation. He adopted formulas symptomatic of the decline of traditional conservatism and liberalism—formulas that many traditionally oriented conservatives came to espouse, although often slowly, usually only in part, and almost always reluctantly. Thus most of the Right could applaud the best-selling novelist Hans Grimm when, in calling for "generational socialism," he pleaded that "every healthy and gifted child win forever anew the possibility of rising into the upper stratum [of society]."[22]

To the Right, the Weimar Republic was the unwanted result of an unexpected defeat. Although in late 1918 and during the first half of 1919 a Republic under the leadership of the counterrevolutionary Social Democrats Friedrich Ebert and Gustav Noske was preferable to social revolution, the stormy honeymoon of the Right with political democracy soon came to an end. Many of the writers who had served during the war in the government-sponsored Germandom propaganda campaign, to which Naumann had contributed, resumed their leading roles in attacking democracy as a non-German, exclusively Western institution. Indeed, with military and business support the Germandom campaign had continued, if in muted and equivocating forms, during the postwar honeymoon. In connection with Naumann, we have already noted the business-sponsored anti-Bolshevik projects of Eduard Stadtler. The young lance-corporal Adolf Hitler might be mentioned as an example of a lower echelon military-supported propagandist at work during the immediate postarmistice period.[23] The postwar phase in the campaign to promote a peculiarly German ideology played upon the circumstances of the Republic's founding, above all the military victory of the Allies, to associate democracy with the West and the imposition of the Treaty of Versailles. Reenlisting in this phase of the campaign, prominent writers joined with paid propagandists in depicting political democracy as an indigestible product imported from the victors in the war. Continuing, if with redoubled efforts, a development that began during the era of the

[22] Hans Grimm, *Von der bürgerlichen Ehre und bürgerlichen Notwendigkeit* (Munich, 1932), p. 33.

[23] See esp. Ernst Deuerlein, "Hitlers Eintritt in die Politik und die Reichswehr," *Vierteljahrshefte für Zeitgeschichte*, VII (1959), 177–227. Although there are excellent studies of Allied propaganda during World War I, there has been little systematic work done on German propaganda, either civilian or military. For an account of the program of "patriotic instruction [*vaterländischer Unterricht*]" introduced into the army in 1917—a program in whose continuation after the war Hitler became involved—see Reinhard Höhn, *Die Armee als Erziehungsschule der Nation: Das Ende einer Idee* (Bad Harzburg, 1963), pp. 517–68. See also the work by the former chief of military intelligence, Walther Nicolai, *Nachrichtendienst, Presse und Volksstimmung im Weltkrieg* (Berlin, 1920), pp. 113–36, 222–26. Recent research in East Germany has attempted with some success to delineate the relationship between parties, government, and business in German wartime propaganda. See, e.g., Karl-Heinz Schädlich, "Der 'Unabhängige Ausschuss für einen Deutschen Frieden' als Zentrum der Annexationspropaganda im 1. Weltkrieg" in Fritz Klein, ed., *Politik im Kriege: Studien zur Politik der deutschen herrschenden Klassen im 1. Weltkrieg* (Berlin, 1964). Two other recent works are indispensable: Kurt Koszyk, *Deutsche Pressepolitik im 1. Weltkrieg* (Düsseldorf, [1968?]); Wilhelm Deist, ed., *Militär und Innenpolitik im Weltkrieg von 1914–1918* (Düsseldorf, 1970).

French Revolution and reached its climax in Nazi Germany, these men scorned the classical ideals of democracy and exposed the sordid reality of modern democracy in practice. The pernicious effects of these same "Western exports" could be found not only in Germany but also in Eastern Europe, where they had presumably been instrumental in creating nation states inimical to the existence of the German Reich and vindictive toward their sizable German-speaking minorities.[24] Although Germans on the Right might speak with favor of a peculiarly "German" or "Germanic" democracy, they contrasted it with the theory and practice of modern political democracy.

Some neoconservatives—and like Stadtler many of the older, more prominent neoconservatives had participated in the wartime and immediate postwar Germandom campaigns—continued these efforts to identify a beneficial form of democracy suited to Germany. Moeller van den Bruck, the author of the widely read book *The Third Reich*, used as a motto for one of his chapters the elusive phrase "Democracy is a nation's sense of identification with its destiny."[25] Another, more concrete definition of democracy compatible with the notion of an authoritarian elite was devised by Edgar Jung. "True democracy," he wrote, "exists when the circle from which the leaders are recruited is as large as possible, not when as many people as possible have a voice in deciding matters."[26] Thus, like so many other German elitists, Jung divorced the notion of popular control from democracy.

Coming to believe that the German collapse of 1918 had cleared the way for a new order, the neoconservatives formulated principles for social, political, and economic institutions that would overcome the failings of the Second Empire, as well as those of the Weimar Republic. The internal and external difficulties of the Republic during its early years, and again during its last years, strengthened the widespread feeling on the Right that a mere reversion to some version of the *status quo ante* would be both undesirable and impracticable. The neoconservative's quest for a new order frequently led him to the conclusion that only the formation of new elites could cope with the problems of modern society of which the Weimar Republic, however noxious, was simply an expression. On the Right, the demand for an elite that would recruit from every level of society was particularly insistent among

[24] Jean F. Neurohr, *Der Mythos vom 3. Reich: Zur Geistesgeschichte des Nationalsozialismus* (Stuttgart, 1957), p. 209.

[25] "Demokratie ist Anteilnahme eines Volkes an seinem Schicksal." Arthur Moeller van den Bruck, *Das dritte Reich*, 3rd ed., ed. Hans Schwarz (Hamburg, 1931), p. 130. The first edition of this work appeared in 1923. The word *Anteilnahme* in Moeller's motto is ambiguous and might also be translated simply as "participation" rather than as "a sense of identification."

[26] Edgar J. Jung, "Volkserhaltung," *Deutsche Rundschau*, ccxxii (1930), 188.

neoconservatives. For example, Spengler appealed for the selection of leaders "in complete disregard for money or origins" in order to ensure that "no one remains in the depths who is born to command by virtue of his capabilities."[27] Neoconservatives refused to accept proposals by more traditionally minded conservatives that a cosmetically altered nobility or ministerial bureaucracy rule Germany. Whether demanding a "new elite," "new nobility," and "new ruling stratum," or simply "new leadership," neoconservatives dismissed plans smacking of a return to Wilhelminian Germany. The elite of the future would assume many of the functions that the Junkers had performed until 1918. It would accept and perhaps welcome individuals from the old elites, but only on the basis of personal qualifications. The equivocations of Moeller van den Bruck marked the outer limits to the indulgence of the neoconservatives toward the ruling class of the Second Empire: "We need leaders, . . . who, whether they *come from* [my italics] the old ruling stratum [*Führerschicht*] or gradually form a new one, are determined to act upon their resolve for the future of the nation. . . ."[28]

The elite theories of neoconservatism were formulated mainly by intellectuals stemming from the middle class. These intellectuals were responding to the protracted crisis of the middle class in writings intended primarily for a middle-class audience, and they believed that their vision of the future offered hope to this audience. But many neoconservative writers were not in any true sense strategists for the socially heterogeneous groups thought of by many Germans as comprising the *Mittelstand*. Although all of the five major elitists still to be treated in the present study except Count Hermann Keyserling are usually known as neoconservatives, only one, Hans Zehrer, can be described as a man who generally gave precedence to the interests of the *Mittelstand* in his elite theory, and he was committed largely to a segment of the new middle class of white-collar workers. The other four elitists, including Keyserling, were very solicitous of the condition of the middle class and took a protective attitude toward it, but they did not work on the assumption made by Zehrer that the *Mittelstand* or part of it could and should establish hegemony in German society. Yet ironically another assumption, which the five men shared, made Zehrer a strategist for them all. Each of the five's hopes for the future presupposed that his own status and that of a few other men who shared his perspectives would improve dramatically with the realization of a

---

[27] Oswald Spengler, *Jahre der Entscheidung: Deutschland und die weltgeschichtliche Entwicklung* (Munich, 1933), p. 161, and "Preussentum und Sozialismus" in *Politische Schriften* (Munich, 1933), p. 104.

[28] Moeller van den Bruck, *Das dritte Reich*, p. 279.

new elitist order. Thus each tied his own personal fortunes directly to the rise and triumph of a new elite.

The chapters on the Right that follow start with Spengler, whose career spanned the years of the Weimar Republic. His writings drew together old threads from the past with new ones from the present in a suggestive, if ambiguous, way that helped to make him one of the most influential political writers in Germany after 1918. Many of his major works appeared and were widely discussed before Jung, Zehrer, or Jünger began to publish. All three were strongly influenced by him, although they disliked many of his ideas, as did Keyserling. Both Keyserling and Jung were oriented more toward the past than Spengler was; the realization of their elitism presupposed fewer changes in the existing order; and they were less interested in the mobilization of the nonelite. But Spengler will be taken up first because of his central role in the history of the postwar Right.

CHAPTER EIGHT

Oswald Spengler: Caesar and Croesus

In 1922 Ernesto Quesada, a distinguished Argentine professor of government and law who had written sympathetically on Oswald Spengler,[1] arrived in Munich, where Spengler was living. As admirers of Spengler's work, both Quesada and his German-born wife were probably looking forward to their stay in Munich as a highpoint in their travels in Germany. When they reached Spengler's apartment, they were confronted by a menacing notice on the door. "Visitors," the sign warned, "are requested to register at least three days in advance." The couple were amusing themselves over the sign when Spengler opened the door. Eying them through his spectacles, he remarked coolly: "I do not have a servile spirit, and it is very irksome to have to be opening the door all the time." Despite this awkward beginning, Spengler and his guests had a good laugh over the situation on the way to his parlor, and the three became life-long friends.[2]

The Argentine lady recounted the story of her first meeting with Spengler after his death in an attempt to modify the prevailing belief that he was a cold, humorless, and imperious *Stubengelehrter*, but she made a contribution of her own to a more vulnerable part of the Spengler legend: the notion that he lived a withdrawn, isolated, even Olympian existence penetrated only by a very few close personal friends. Although fostered assiduously by Spengler and his friends,[3] this tenacious idea is false. He had a wide circle of important, often highly placed friends and acquaintances, and at least intermittently he played an active if largely covert role in German politics.

The Rise of Spengler as a Political Animal

After retiring from secondary-school teaching at the age of thirty in 1910, Spengler did not long remain an obscure private scholar. The

[1] Quesada had already published at least two essays on Spengler as a sociologist. See, e.g., Ernesto Quesada, *La sociologia relativista spengleriana: Curso dada en el año academico de 1921* (Buenos Aires, 1921).

[2] Eleonore Niessen-Dieters de Quesada, "Nachruf" in Oswald Spengler, *Urfragen: Fragmente aus dem Nachlass*, ed. Anton M. Koktanek (Munich, 1965), p. 362.

[3] His editor and close friend August Albers was one of the early contributors to the legend. See August Albers, "Oswald Spengler," *Preussische Jahrbücher*, cxc (1923), 129–37.

Oswald Spengler—233

publication of the first volume of *The Decline of the West* in 1918 brought him fame and put him in a position to cultivate a broad new circle of contacts. His first political work, "Preussentum und Sozialismus"[4] ("Prussiandom and Socialism") published in late 1919, further enhanced his growing renown and led to his lionization in many circles on the Right. Both the intense interest in Spengler and his carefully promoted public reputation as an aloof, unapproachable titan enabled him to exercise great discrimination in his personal relationships. Since he could easily decide with whom and on what terms to associate, his choice of contacts is very revealing. Some of his new friends and acquaintances were scholars and literary figures; others included industrial magnates, army officers, leaders of right-wing paramilitary organizations, large landowners, and well-known political leaders of the Right.[5] Like Spengler himself, most of the scholars with whom he became friendly did not belong to the established academic world of the German university. With a few notable exceptions, includ-

[4] Reprinted in Oswald Spengler, *Politische Schriften, Volksausgabe* (Munich, 1933). Hereafter the *Politische Schriften* will be abbreviated as *PS* and "Preussentum und Sozialismus" will be cited as "Preussentum."

[5] A mine of information about Spengler's contacts can be unearthed from the selection of his surviving correspondence edited by Anton M. Koktanek in collaboration with Manfred Schröter, *Briefe 1913–1936* (Munich, [1963]). Hereafter cited as *Briefe*. Although we are deeply indebted to Koktanek for making available material that supplies massive documentation to refute the Spengler legend, this edition is often disappointing. It affords a suggestive rather than a detailed guide to Spengler's political activities and contacts. Many of the reasons for the failings of the *Briefe* were beyond Koktanek's control. For example, after the Nazis came to power, Spengler or his heirs destroyed part of his correspondence. Some of the other shortcomings of Koktanek's edition must be attributed to the editor himself and perhaps also to the publisher. The index is inadequate, and the explanatory notes are uneven and occasionally inaccurate. The American edition of the *Briefe*, entitled *Letters, 1913–1936*, trans. and ed. Arthur Helps (New York, 1966), should be mentioned only as a specimen of irresponsible publishing. Passages are omitted without any indication, the translations are poor, and the name of the German editor is not given on the title page. The careful reader of the *Briefe* will find surprisingly little new information in Koktanek's *Oswald Spengler in seiner Zeit* (Munich, [1968?]). Koktanek, who has been editing Spengler's *Nachlass* for publication, has written what he seems to regard as a chronicle of sorts rather than an interpretive study, which he plans to publish in the future. Other than some sections of this "chronicle" the most important literature on Spengler's political contacts consists of the "Biographischer Abriss" in the useful study by Ernst Stutz, *Oswald Spengler als politischer Denker* (Bern, 1958), pp. 240–45 and an article by Koktanek, "Spenglers Verhältnis zum Nationalsozialismus in geschichtlicher Entwicklung," *Zeitschrift für Politik*, XIII (1966), 33–35. Stutz's study, a Zurich diss., was published also under the title *Die philosophische und politische Kritik Oswald Spenglers* (1958). Most of the other secondary literature on Spengler has been of little help to me. The best general work, H. Stuart Hughes, *Oswald Spengler: A Critical Estimate* (New York, 1952), is now partly outdated. Of the remaining literature see esp. Theodor W. Adorno, "Spengler nach dem Untergang" in Adorno's *Prismen: Kulturkritik und Gesellschaft* (Berlin, 1955).

ing the great conservative historian of the ancient world Eduard Meyer, who became a personal friend, German academicians delivered hostile judgments on *The Decline of the West*.[6] This rejection of the book increased Spengler's hostility toward "intellectuals" and probably led him to an even higher esteem for "men of action." During the 1920's he addressed several organizations of Ruhr and Rhenish-Westphalian industrialists, commercial groups in Hamburg, the Association of German Nobles, and a national federation of right-wing students (the *Hochschulring deutscher Art*).[7] Although his deepest political relationships were confined largely, almost exclusively to right-wing activists, writers, and industrialists, Spengler's contacts were sufficiently varied to be indicative of the meeting of the old and the new Germany, of the old Right and the new Right, in his elitism. He associated with nobles as well as big businessmen, with prominent right-wing Reichstag deputies as well as with leaders from the shadowy world of right-wing paramilitary groups, with traditionalists as well as with neoconservative critics of the old Right. Spengler was a member of the Munich group of the *Herrenklub* during the 1920's[8] at a time when the club's membership included representatives of a large segment of the Right—traditionally minded conservatives, neoconservatives, politically active noblemen, socially prominent bourgeois, and social-climbing writers.[9] The *Herrenklub* developed out of the June Club (*Juni-Klub*), which began as an even more broadly based discussion group whose spiritual mentors included Eduard Stadtler and Moeller van den Bruck, as well as political moderates like Ernst Troeltsch and Nelson's friend Franz Oppenheimer. Although Spengler was probably not a member of the June Club, he appeared before it as one of its special guests.[10]

Fame brought Spengler a more secure financial basis as well as new contacts. His premature retirement from teaching before the war had been possible only because the death of his mother had left him with a small inheritance.[11] The German defeat of 1918 temporarily dis-

[6] For an account of the initial reception of Spengler's work see Manfred Schröter, *Der Streit um Spengler: Kritik seiner Kritiker* (Munich, 1922). After World War II Schröter issued an expanded edition of this book: *Metaphysik des Untergangs: Eine kulturkritische Studie über Oswald Spengler* (Munich, 1949).

[7] See esp. his *PS* and his *Reden und Aufsätze* (Munich, 1937).

[8] See his letter of July 7, 1925 to Werner von Alvensleben in *Briefe*, p. 396.

[9] On the *Herrenklub* during the 1920's see esp. Hans-Joachim Schwierskott, *Arthur Moeller van den Bruck und der revolutionäre Nationalismus in der Weimarer Republik* (Göttingen, [1962?]), pp. 72–74.

[10] *Ibid.*, pp. 134–35, n. 3; Klemens von Klemperer, *Germany's New Conservatism: Its History and Dilemma in the Twentieth Century* (Princeton, 1957), p. 109.

[11] Armin Baltzer, *Oswald Spenglers Bedeutung für die Gegenwart: Ein bisher uneröffnetes Vermächtnis* (Neheim-Hüsten, [1959]), p. 220. Spengler's friend and admirer Manfred Schröter provided a preface to this tortured attempt, written from

rupted his modest investments and placed him in a precarious financial situation. By the summer of 1919, due to timely loans from a Swiss friend, royalties from *The Decline of the West*, and the recovery of some foreign holdings, Spengler's finances had improved greatly, and he was searching for real estate or a mortgage in which to make a modest investment of 50,000 marks.[12] Thereafter he seems to have managed to live adequately on the income from his investments and royalties. Spengler was a *rentier* who, as we shall see, looked for leadership to the prewar social coalition, especially the heavy industrial interests within it.

Our information about his political views prior to his fame is sketchy, but much can be gleaned from the first volume of *The Decline of the West* and more concretely if less comprehensively from his published correspondence. There is no indication of an abrupt break in the development of his views. Even during the early part of World War I, he was complaining that parliaments were outmoded, denouncing as opportunistic the intellectuals and artists who had suddenly jumped on the war bandwagon, and expressing a strong preference for *Gewaltmenschen*, technicians, military officers, businessmen, and, above all, "self-made men." Indeed, he was already observing approvingly that the new self-made men would take up positions side by side with the old nobility and the old privy councilors. He was looking forward to a new elite in which technicians and businessmen would provide the most dynamic element.[13] In a memorandum found in his papers and apparently drawn up for submission to William II before 1918, he sought to discredit the existing universal manhood suffrage for the Reichstag. Since most of the Reichstag's business concerned economic matters and was conducted behind the scenes, the body should be made into a house of experts: "The Reichstag is . . . the administrative center of the most valuable economic organism in Europe, . . . and I think that even today the best 'Reichstag election' would be if 400 of the foremost representatives of our economic life . . . were brought into [the Reichstag] and the others were thrown out."[14] During most of the war, he maintained an unshaken belief in Germany's

a contemporary West German conservative point of view, to demonstrate the relevance of Spengler's *Weltanschauung* to the present. More recently Baltzer published a modified and expanded version of his economium under the title *Philosoph oder Prophet? Oswald Spenglers Vermächtnis und Voraussagen* (Neheim-Hüsten, 1962).

[12] For Spengler's financial difficulties in 1919 and their apparently satisfactory resolution see *Briefe*, pp. 122, 126, 130, 135, 137, 141–43. See also Koktanek, *Oswald Spengler in seiner Zeit*, p. 252.

[13] *Ibid.*, pp. 30, 42, 47–48. The phrase "self-made-men" (*sic*) appears in English in his letters.

[14] Quoted in Koktanek, "Spenglers Verhältnis zum Nationalsozialismus," p. 36.

military invincibility and domestic stability. He does not seem to have taken seriously his own prediction of December 1914 that an era of "unparalleled social crises" lay ahead.[15] The rising wave of revolution in Europe that began with the March Revolution of 1917 in Russia led him to search for methods of ensuring political and social equilibrium in Germany. Shortly after the Reichstag peace resolution of July 1917, he wrote a long letter to a close personal friend on a question that Spengler considered crucial to the political future of Germany. What would happen to the National Liberal party? The question was pivotal "because here [in the National Liberal party] industry, commerce, and leading intellectuals must cooperate." Spengler described the organization of the National Liberals as woefully inadequate, and he complained that they lacked a reliable press. Yet he had hope for the future. Through adroit new leaders the party could become "a representative of the propertied as a whole and of a large part of the more elevated workers," and thereby play the deciding role in German politics.[16]

Concern for the recementing of the old social coalition and its reinvigoration under energetic, largely bourgeois leadership troubled Spengler throughout the next decade and a half. Shortly after the collapse of the Wilhelminian Empire, he indicated in a letter to his closest friend his hopes for a revitalized conservatism guided by vibrant leaders, "who today are still hidden and nameless among *decent* workers and in the bourgeoisie. Truly, our future lies on the one hand in Prussian conservatism after it has been cleansed of all feudal-agrarian narrowness and on the other hand in the working people after they have freed themselves from the anarchistic-radical . . . 'masses.' "[17] A parallel set of interests led industrialists and right-wing activists to seek out Spengler, especially after the publication of his "Prussiandom and Socialism" in December 1919. Complimenting Spengler on this pamphlet, Admiral Tirpitz expressed the hope that Spengler's views would meet with acceptance "in the workers' circles poisoned by Marxism."[18]

By 1922 Spengler was exercising a behind-the-scenes political role from which he derived great personal gratification. Although not a Bavarian particularist, he had become enmeshed in the baroque intrigues of his adopted state.[19] He acted frequently as a middleman between

[15] *Briefe*, p. 32. For examples of Spengler's optimism about the prospects for a German annexationist victory and his assumption that the social order was not threatened see *ibid.*, pp. 29, 34, 41.

[16] *Ibid.*, p. 83.

[17] Letter of Dec. 27, 1918 to Hans Klöres in *Briefe*, p. 115. Italics Spengler's.

[18] Letter of May 11, 1920 from Alfred von Tirpitz to Spengler in *Briefe*, p. 159.

[19] For a good if somewhat apologetic general survey of Bavarian politics during the Weimar Republic see Karl Schwend, *Bayern zwischen Monarchie und Diktatur:*

paramilitary action leagues (*Kampfbünde*) and right-wing politicians in Bavaria on the one hand and right-wing politicians and industrialists outside Bavaria on the other. For example, he transmitted funds from the Nationalist (DNVP) politician and former Krupp director Alfred Hugenberg to an associate of Georg Escherich, a prominent leader of paramilitary groups in Bavaria.[20]

A forestry official, *Forstrat* Major Dr. Escherich had been the organizer of the Civil Guards (*Einwohnerwehren*) formed during the revolutionary disturbances of 1919 as a weapon against the Left and as a thinly disguised reserve for the Reichswehr. He worked closely with Gustav von Kahr, the dominant figure in Bavarian politics during the early 1920's. Under Kahr's right-wing governments from 1920 to 1921, Escherich was reputed to be the second most powerful man in Bavaria. Despite these close ties to Kahr, who placed himself at the head of the Bavarian monarchists calling for a restoration of the Wittelsbach dynasty and threatening the separation of Bavaria from the Republic, Escherich was neither a separatist nor a zealous monarchist. He was a Bavarian particularist who stood shoulder to shoulder with Kahr in the struggle against the Left and against the Reich government in Berlin. Escherich's power declined when the strength of the separatists, as well as that of the antiparticularistic but less traditionally oriented action leagues, increased after 1921. He lost the leadership of the Civil Guards to another close associate of Kahr's. Yet as the head of *Orgesch* (*Organisation Escherich*), an armed formation that operated openly in Bavaria and maintained clandestine ties to the Reichswehr, Escherich remained an important figure in Bavarian politics.

Beiträge zur bayerischen Frage in der Zeit von 1918 bis 1933 (Munich, 1954). The best introduction in English is still two largely undocumented articles by Carl Landauer, "The Bavarian Problem in the German Republic," *Journal of Modern History*, xvi (1944), 93–115, 205–23.

[20] See letter of Aug. 25, 1923 from Alfred Hugenberg to Spengler in *Briefe*, pp. 263–64. The funds were to go to Major Karl Wäninger, a leader of the *Stahlhelm* in Bavaria. Part or all of the money may have been intended for propaganda activity. According to Koktanek, "Spenglers Verhältnis zum Nationalsozialismus," p. 44, Wäninger introduced Spengler and Escherich to each other in 1922. Stutz, *Oswald Spengler*, p. 244 alludes to Spengler's participation in several campaigns to recruit new members for Escherich's group. Of the extensive literature on the Bavarian and other German paramilitary groups during the Weimar Republic the most relevant and important treatments are found in Schwend, *Bayern zwischen Monarchie und Diktatur*, pp. 159–70; E. J. Gumbel, *Verschwörer: Beiträge zur Geschichte und Soziologie der deutschen nationalistischen Geheimbünde seit 1918* (Vienna, 1924); Ernst H. Posse, *Die politischen Kampfbünde Deutschlands*, 2nd ed. (Berlin, 1931); Robert G. L. Waite, *Vanguard of Nazism: The Free Corps Movement in Postwar Germany, 1918–1923* (New York: Norton paperback, 1969); and Volker R. Berghahn, *Der Stahlhelm, Bund der Frontsoldaten 1918–1935* (Düsseldorf, 1966), esp. pp. 46–47, 50–52.

As the German and Bavarian crises deepened in 1922 and 1923, he seems often to have been caught between the Bavarian monarchist forces led by Kahr and other antiparticularist forces on the Right. Some of the antiparticularists, among them General Ludendorff, who like Spengler was not a native Bavarian, were committed to a restoration of the Hohenzollerns, but hostile to the Wittelsbach dynasty. Other antiparticularists, of whom Hitler has come to be the best known, were also Pan-German in outlook, but not committed to any type of monarchy. Despite ultimately incompatible goals, the right-wing groups in Bavaria shared many immediate objectives, and there was much overlapping in the membership of the score or so of major action leagues. The Right wished to use Bavaria as a base and Bavarian particularism and separatism as a means for effecting a shift in the policies of the Reich. Each faction of the Bavarian Right attempted to use the others and to exploit for its own ends the severely strained relations between Bavaria and Berlin. In 1922 and 1923 the cry of a march on Berlin served as a rallying point for most of the Right in Bavaria.

Through the climax of the Bavarian and German crises in November 1923, Spengler remained deeply involved in Bavarian politics. He seems to have considered Escherich as the most suitable leader of a *Putsch* despite a growing disillusionment with Escherich's abilities.[21] Spengler's recently published correspondence indicates clearly that Spengler regarded himself as a capable intermediary between part of the Bavarian Right and much of the Right elsewhere in Germany. He felt certain that he was a purveyor of reliable intelligence on political conditions in Bavaria to outsiders. In the light of Bavarian developments in 1922 and 1923, Spengler's confidence in his ability to perform this role was well grounded. Although the *dénouement* of the crisis displeased him greatly, he followed it with the eye of an insider. In addition to his ties to Escherich, Kahr, and other Bavarian leaders, he acquired firsthand knowledge of Ludendorff's activities. By the late summer of 1923, Spengler was taking tea occasionally, perhaps frequently, at the Ludendorff's home near Munich.[22] Spengler met frequently with non-Bavarian big businessmen and right-wing politicians like Karl Helfferich of the *Deutsche Bank* and the Nationalist party, Wilhelm Cuno of the Hamburg-Amerika Line, and Albert Vögler of heavy industry and the Peoples' party, but on the basis of the fragmentary evidence provided by Spengler's letters, we may conclude

[21] Cf. Koktanek, "Spenglers Verhältnis zum Nationalsozialismus," p. 46. Koktanek thinks that Spengler wavered between Escherich and Kahr.

[22] See letters of Sept. 3 and Oct. 21, 1923 from Ludendorff to Spengler in *Briefe*, pp. 266, 279. The dating of the second letter is uncertain.

that the most important and closest of his contacts with highly placed and wealthy right-wingers throughout the 1920's was his relationship with *Kommerzienrat* Dr. Paul Reusch.[23]

A German "self-made man," Reusch was the director of the *Gutehoffnungshütte* and a general representative of the enormous industrial holdings of the Haniel family, as well as an officer of important industry associations. He chaired both the "Long-Name Association" (*Verein zur Wahrung der gemeinsamen wirtschaftlichen Interessen in Rheinland und Westfalen*) and the iron and steel sub-group of the *Reichsverband der Deutschen Industrie*. During World War I, he served as representative of industry in the German War Food Office.[24] He was among the early backers of Eduard Stadtler's Anti-Bolshevik League,[25] but unlike fellow businessmen such as Hugenberg, Helfferich, and Hugo Stinnes, Reusch preferred to play an inconspicuous role in politics. The relationship between Reusch and Spengler deepened into a personal friendship. After Spengler's death in 1936, Reusch had privately published a memorial volume edited by one of Spengler's more scholarly friends, Richard Korherr. Reusch also had a monument erected at the site of Spengler's grave.[26] In addition to their common political concerns, the two men shared other interests. Reusch was an art collector who respected Spengler's aesthetic judgment. From time to time, Spengler purchased for him works at auctions in Munich,[27] and Reusch occasionally sent Spengler a much appreciated gift, such as an *objet d'art* or some vintage wine.[28] In an illustrated di-

[23] Although not examining the political significance of the relationship with Reusch, Bodo Herzog, "Die Freundschaft zwischen Oswald Spengler und Paul Reusch" in A. M. Koktanek, ed. *Spengler-Studien: Festgabe für Manfred Schröter zum 85. Geburtstag* (Munich, 1965), pp. 77–97 stresses the intensity of the friendship. Dealing with the more personal aspects of the relationship, Herzog writes in what might be termed the "Goethe-and-his-women" tradition of German biography: a somewhat mysterious affinity draws the two souls closer and closer together; Reusch is dutifully solicitous of the great genius's health, idiosyncrasies, and creative powers; Reusch relies upon Spengler's judgment in aesthetic and intellectual matters, but is reserved toward his incursions into the kitchen (business and politics). The major value to us of Herzog's essay is that it helps to confirm, partly on the basis of unpublished material, many minor details of the friendship between the two men, for Herzog draws upon Reusch's papers in the Historical Archive of the *Gutehoffnungshütte*.
[24] Gerald D. Feldman, *Army, Industry, and Labor in Germany, 1914–1918* (Princeton, 1966), p. 166.
[25] Eduard Stadtler, *Als Antibolschewist 1918–19* (Düsseldorf, 1935), p. 57.
[26] See Koktanek's editorial note on Eleonore Niessen-Dieters de Quesada, "Nachruf" in Spengler, *Urfragen*, p. 361; Herzog, "Die Freundschaft zwischen Spengler und Reusch," p. 91.
[27] See the correspondence between Spengler and Reusch on this subject in *Briefe*, pp. 437–38, 472–73, 598. Koktanek points out (*ibid.*, p. 786, n. 5) that Spengler frequently purchased pictures at auctions for his friends.
[28] See, e.g., *ibid.*, pp. 585, 640.

rectory of German leaders published by the Nazis in 1934, the *Führer-lexikon*, the entry for Reusch is graced not by the usual photograph, but by a reproduction of a portrait, probably an oil.[29] Spengler often sought Reusch's help in personal as well as political dealings with government and business circles. Thus Reusch was instrumental in obtaining for Spengler an invitation to be a guest on the trial flight of a new Zeppelin.[30] Reusch also arranged and perhaps financed vacation trips on which Spengler sometimes combined recreation with the pursuit of political and scholarly interests.[31] On more than one occasion, Spengler provided a pipeline for funds sent by Reusch to right-wing propagandists and activists in Bavaria.[32]

Both men belonged to the *Gäa* Society (*Gäa-Gesellschaft*), an exclusive, secretive right-wing group that included politicians, writers, businessmen, and officers.[33] Similar to and perhaps largely identical with the Munich branches of the June Club and the *Herrenklub*, the *Gäa* provided a forum for the exchange of ideas and the coordination of policies rather than a tightly knit action group. Among the members were Professor Paul Nikolaus Cossmann, the editor of the *Süddeutsche Monatshefte* and the guiding spirit of the *Münchner Neueste Nachrichten*; Karl Haniel, the chairman of the *Gutehoffnungshütte*; Count Josef Maria Soden-Frauenhofen, an aide to Crown Prince Rupprecht of Bavaria; Paul Lettow-Vorbeck, a prominent participant in the Kapp *Putsch* of 1920; General Franz Freiherr von Gebsattel, a leader of the Pan-German League; and Gerhard von Janson, a right-wing propagandist and a former naval officer. The disagreements among the members often became severe. For example, Spengler complained repeatedly to Reusch about Cossmann's editorial policies. Since the Haniel family was involved in the ownership of Cossmann's publications, Spengler hoped that Reusch would be able to effect modifications in these policies.[34]

[29] See *Das deutsche Führerlexikon 1934–35* (Berlin, 1934).

[30] See *Briefe*, pp. 347, 349.

[31] See Herzog, "Die Freundschaft zwischen Spengler und Reusch," p. 83; *Briefe*, esp. p. 551.

[32] See Spengler's letter of Jan. 3, 1923 to Reusch in *Briefe*, pp. 235–36.

[33] I have been able to locate little information on the *Gäa-Gesellschaft*. Probably not an abbreviation, *Gäa* may have referred to the Greek earth goddess Gaea. Richard Hughes's sensitive semifictional reconstruction of the milieu in Bavaria in 1923, *The Fox in the Attic* (New York, 1961), p. 182, mentions the society briefly. A short, apologetic account of the *Gäa* appears in Wolfram Selig, *Paul Nikolaus Cossmann und die Süddeutschen Monatshefte von 1914–1918: Ein Beitrag zur Geschichte der nationalen Publizistik im 1. Weltkrieg* (Osnabrück, 1967), pp. 46–58.

[34] See, e.g., *Briefe*, pp. 293, 603, 604, 606, 609–10, 626–27, 647, 649, 664, 680–81. See also Spengler's reference (p. 290) to his own direct attempts to get Karl Haniel to intervene. Especially after 1923 Spengler seems to have concentrated upon working through Reusch. Haniel was on the board of directors of the

As a man of the pen, Spengler devoted much attention to the press and propaganda in his dealings with businessmen. By the latter part of 1922, he was deeply involved in these matters.[35] Often participating in meetings with industrialists seeking to coordinate press policies, he does not appear to have been satisfied with the scope of the vast communications network that Hugenberg had been developing.[36] One of Spengler's pet projects was the creation of a press network that would provide effective propaganda for big business and that would apparently have included Hugenberg's communications empire.[37] At least through the mid-1920's, Spengler felt that the coordinated network that he envisioned had not been created and that industry's efforts had been woefully inadequate. He took obvious delight in his attempts to play the role of an *eminence grise* in Bavarian and German affairs. He never wearied of offering advice to industrialists on how best to advance their interests. Among his modest triumphs were securing office space for propaganda coordinators in Berlin and Munich. He took personal credit for convincing Hugenberg to make several rooms available in the Scherl publishing house in Berlin.[38] Although seemingly skeptical about some of Spengler's specific proposals, Reusch took the trouble to investigate them.

Two examples of Spengler's less grandiose projects will suffice. In late 1923 he suggested gaining control of the great German magazine of irony and satire, *Simplizissimus*. He wished to see *Simplizissimus* transformed into a reliable organ of the upper classes, and he mentioned the English humor magazine *Punch* as a good model.[39] A year later he joined the board of the DNVP's *Neue Preussische Zeitung*, a newspaper that was the successor to the proud old Conservative *Kreuzzeitung*. Through Reusch he sought to get financial backing from the Ruhr for the reorganized newspaper and to persuade Reusch to

---

Knorr & Hirth, the concern that published the *Süddeutsche Monatshefte* and *Münchner Neueste Nachrichten*. On Cossmann and the policies of these publications, see George W. F. Hallgarten, *Das Schicksal des Imperialismus im 20. Jahrhundert: Drei Abhandlungen über Kriegsursachen in Vergangenheit und Gegenwart* (Frankfurt am Main, [1969?]), esp. pp. 72–77, 83–84; Ernest K. Bramsted, *Goebbels and National Socialist Propaganda, 1925–1945* (n. p.: Michigan State University Press, 1965), pp. xiii–xxxi.

[35] See Hugenberg's letter of Sept. 2, 1922 to Spengler and Spengler's letter of Sept. 5, 1922 to Escherich in *Briefe*, pp. 211–12.

[36] On Spengler's participation in meetings with industrialists on the press in 1922–1923 see, e.g., *Briefe*, pp. 216, 226, 227, 234–35, 239–44, 264, 266–67. On Hugenberg's communications empire see Valeska Dietrich, *Alfred Hugenberg: Ein Manager in der Publizistik* (Free University of Berlin diss., 1960).

[37] See, e.g., *Briefe*, pp. 205, 241–42, 266–67, 276–77, 305, 307, 346.

[38] See Spengler to Gerhard von Janson, Sept. 9, 1923 in *Briefe*, pp. 266–67.

[39] See the exchange of letters between Reusch and Spengler during the period Nov. 4, 1923 to Jan. 4, 1924 in *Briefe*, pp. 285, 293–94, 298.

take his own place on the board. As Spengler explained to Reusch, the position was reserved for "a representative of western industry."[40]

There were persistent rumors during the Weimar Republic that Spengler was the spiritual founder of an important training and indoctrination arm of big industry, the German Institute for Technical Education and Training (DINTA, *Deutsches Institut für Arbeitsschulung*).[41] The prominent industrialist most closely associated with the establishment of DINTA was Spengler's acquaintance Albert Vögler, a founder of the United Steel Trust (*Vereinigte Stahlwerke*) in 1926. Anticipating the program of the Nazis' German Labor Front, DINTA employed special schools, publications, and job-training centers to divert workers from "materialism"—from wage and class struggles— by promoting spiritualism, apolitical amusements, and pride in workmanship. DINTA's publications suggested that businessmen, although now absorbed in management and production details, could still cultivate the lost art of leading their employees. DINTA concentrated much of its effort on the indoctrination of selected working-class children and adults, especially male adolescents. By 1933 its programs had been established in the bulk of Germany's largest industrial corporations. Hugenberg's communications empire worked closely with DINTA. The cooperation was facilitated by the partial interlocking of the leadership of the two organizations. Thus Albert Vögler was in all probability a member of the secret twelve-man board that directed Hugenberg's empire.[42]

Both the creation of DINTA and its cooperation with the "Hugenberg Concern" were certainly measures adopted along the general lines suggested by Spengler, but no evidence has come to light that indicates he played a direct role in the founding and development of DINTA. During the Weimar Republic, the sweeping press coordination envisioned by Spengler never materialized. He tended to underestimate the conflicts among businessmen, even within heavy industry, that prevented the full realization of his dreams. Often he seems to have felt that even Reusch did not respond adequately to his abundant

[40] See *Briefe*, pp. 393–94. In a letter preceding Spengler's appointment to the board, Count Kuno Westarp asked for his support, noting that Spengler had the confidence of Rhenish industry and Hanseatic businessmen. Westarp to Spengler, Jan. 23, 1925, *ibid.*, p. 381.

[41] See Richard Lewinsohn (Morus), *Das Geld in der Politik* (Berlin, 1931), pp. 197–98. For a succinct analysis of the objectives and methods of DINTA see Robert A. Brady, *The Rationalization Movement in German Industry: A Study in the Evolution of Economic Planning* (Berkeley, 1933), pp. 82, 101, 120; and *The Spirit and Structure of German Fascism* (London, 1937), pp. 153–60.

[42] See Dietrich, *Alfred Hugenberg*, p. 37.

advice, and Spengler did not hide his annoyance.[43] Especially during the early 1920's, he followed German politics as if he were the self-appointed watchdog of German heavy industry. He put many of his warnings in unequivocal terms, as in the following alarm sounded shortly after the appointment of the Stresemann cabinet in August 1923: "I regard the situation as very serious. The replacement of Cuno by Stresemann means a defeat for industry."[44]

The culmination of Spengler's personal activities came in the critical year 1923, the year of the French invasion of the Ruhr; the year of the collapse of the German mark through the dizzying acceleration of the wartime and postwar inflation; the year of reintensified left-wing activity, especially in Saxony, Thuringia, Hamburg, and the Ruhr; and the year of feverish right-wing activity marked most dramatically by Hitler's *Putsch* in Munich. Never before had Spengler been as deeply enmeshed in politics, and probably never again would politics engage him as intensely. There is considerable evidence of his extensive participation in the plans developed in some right-wing circles for the establishment of an authoritarian regime for the Reich—a "Directory," in which he might have become the minister of education. In the version Spengler subscribed to, these plans, promoted by men closer to the old than to the new Right, focused on the chief of the Reichswehr, General Hans von Seeckt. Hostility in many political, business, and military quarters to the Stresemann government gave a decided fillip to the plans.[45] Very critical of Stresemann's wing of the People's party

[43] Although there is much evidence of his annoyance in the *Briefe*, this material is obviously very fragmentary and gives perhaps a distorted impression of his feelings, which may, on balance, have been more optimistic. In 1928 Reusch played the central role in the formation of the *Ruhrlade*, a secretive, highly restrictive organization of Rhenish-Westphalian heavy industrialists that sought to develop common, broadly conservative policies toward the government, the press, and political parties. Subsidizing and purchasing newspapers and other periodicals constituted one of the group's major activities, but both the scope of these activities and the limitation of its membership to a narrow section of industry made it at best a promising step in the direction of the more demanding general coordination of the press proposed by Spengler. On the *Ruhrlade* see Henry A. Turner, Jr., "The *Ruhrlade*, Secret Cabinet of Heavy Industry in the Weimar Republic," *Central European History*, III (1970), 195–228.

[44] Letter of Aug. 17, 1923 from Spengler to Reusch in *Briefe*, p. 260.

[45] Spengler's *Briefe* contain frequent allusions to the plans for a *Direktorium* during the period from 1922 to 1924. Koktanek, "Spenglers Verhältnis zum Nationalsozialismus," p. 43 assumes that Spengler would have become minister of education, but presents only inconclusive evidence. Most of the secondary literature on the projected Directory is focused on Seeckt and the role of the military. Of the recent literature, see esp. Eberhard Kessel "Seeckts politisches Programm von 1923" in Konrad Repgen and Stephan Skalweit, eds., *Spiegel der Geschichte: Festgabe fur Max Braubach* (Münster, 1964), esp. pp. 899–914 and Hans Meier-Welcker, *Seeckt* (Frankfurt am Main, 1967), pp. 389–405, 411–16. A broader

(DVP), Spengler regarded the new chancellor as unfriendly toward much of German industry. Spengler joined with others of Stresemann's opponents in encouraging opposition to the chancellor in the right wing of the People's party.[46] Spengler's attempt to reach an understanding with General Seeckt fell through. After a personal meeting with Seeckt, whom he met in 1923 for the first time, Spengler referred frequently to Seeckt as an "opportunist."[47] The "sphinx," as the laconic Seeckt was often nicknamed during the Weimar Republic, seems to have regarded Spengler as an effusive meddler. In a letter to Frau von Seeckt, the General wished that Spengler "had gone under with the West—a political fool."[48] After the Hitler *Putsch*, the two men may have established a more cordial relationship, but there is no significant evidence of this during the period of Spengler's most active political involvement.[49]

During the weeks when there still appeared to be some hope of establishing a Directory, Spengler made a successful, if minor, sally into international diplomacy. Convinced, as were many other Germans, that the Ruhr invasion was widening the breech between the British and the French, he helped to arrange an exchange of views between Stresemann and the South African Prime Minister, Jan Smuts. The exchange led to Smuts's speech in London on October 23 in which he sharply criticized the Ruhr invasion and proposed a new settlement of the reparations question. Stresemann made use of Spengler's good of-

interpretive framework is provided by George W. F. Hallgarten, "Stinnes, Seeckt und Hitler: Material zur Geschichte von Ruhrkampf und Hitlerputsch" in Hallgarten's *Hitler, Reichswehr und Industrie: Zur Geschichte der Jahre 1918–1933* (Frankfurt am Main, 1962). Hallgarten deals with the objectives of the industrialists, whose tactics were often at odds with Seeckt's.

[46] See, e.g., Spengler's letter of Oct. 30, 1923 to Reinhold Quaatz in *Briefe*, pp. 282–83. Quaatz was a prominent Reichstag member from the People's party. An officer of the formidable Essen-Mülheim-Oberhausen Chamber of Commerce, he was a key representative of heavy industry and a leader of the party's right wing. By November 3 this wing had helped to precipitate the break up of Stresemann's "Great Coalition" that led to the reorganization of the cabinet and the withdrawal of the Social Democrats from the government. See Henry A. Turner, Jr., *Stresemann and the Politics of the Weimar Republic* (Princeton, 1963), pp. 71, 94, 133–40. For an account of Spengler's apparently successful behind-the-scenes attempt to promote the press campaign against Stresemann see Spengler's letter of Oct. 5, 1923 to Gerhard von Janson in *Briefe*, p. 273.

[47] See Spengler's letters at the end of Oct. 1923 to Quaatz, Janson, and Reusch in *Briefe*, pp. 282, 283, 284.

[48] Quoted in Meier-Welcker, *Seeckt*, p. 373.

[49] Meier-Welcker, *Seeckt*, p. 410 thinks that Seeckt and Spengler met again on November 16, a week after the *Putsch*, but has found no evidence indicating what they may have discussed. Spengler had given a lecture in the Reichswehr ministry on the fifteenth.

fices as an intermediary, even though Spengler had earlier been certain that neither the chancellor nor the German Foreign Office had the perspicacity to grasp the opportunity.[50]

When the plans for a Directory were shattered both by conflicts among its prospective backers and by the precipitous actions of the Nazis, Spengler was dismayed. He denounced the participants in the Munich *Putsch*, but mainly Ludendorff and the other prominent Rightists who had not successfully exploited the situation and manipulated effectively the Nazis and the paramilitary organizations in Bavaria. Spengler felt especially resentful toward Kahr, Cossmann, and the *Münchner Neueste Nachrichten*. In Spengler's eyes they had failed to restrain the Nazis by providing public criticism of Hitler and his followers. For Spengler the real responsibility for the failure of the Directory lay with the more traditionally oriented Rightists in both Bavaria and elsewhere in Germany. It was their fault that the Nazis' ambitions had gotten out of hand and that Hitler had refused to play his assigned subordinate role.[51]

When the political situation in Germany stabilized after 1924, Spengler seems to have withdrawn from many of his political activities. Bavaria was no longer a nodal point of German politics, but many of the questions that had absorbed much of his attention may have seemed less pressing. While continuing to remain in touch with his friends and acquaintances on the Right, he appears to have provided information and advice less frequently and more haphazardly. The paramilitary action leagues declined in significance, and his Bavarian friends Kahr and Cossmann seemed to have lost part of their usefulness by mishandling the crisis of 1923 and through futile reactionary and clericalist policies. After 1923 Spengler's associations with industry stood therefore in even bolder relief than previously.

Yet it would be incorrect to regard Spengler as a propagandist for

[50] On Spengler's role in the exchange with Smuts see esp. Spengler's letter of Sept. 26, 1923 to Stresemann, as well as Paul von Lettow-Vorbeck's letter of Oct. 28, 1923 to Spengler in *Briefe*, pp. 271–72, 280–81. See also the exchange of letters between Reusch and Spengler, *ibid.*, pp. 267–69, 273–76, 284–85, 286. For a brief discussion of the incident and Spengler's role in it see two works by Karl Dietrich Erdmann, *Adenauer in der Rheinlandpolitik nach dem 1. Weltkrieg* (Stuttgart, [1966?]), pp. 103–04 and *Die Zeit der Weltkriege*, vol. 4 of Bruno Gebhardt, *Handbuch der deutschen Geschichte*, 8th ed., ed. Herbert Grundmann (Stuttgart, 1959), p. 135.

[51] Although apparently much of Spengler's correspondence dealing with the Nazi *Putsch* and the disintegration of the plans for a Directory was destroyed, there is substantial evidence in the *Briefe* of his general assessment of the *Putsch*. See esp. *Briefe*, pp. 289, 291–92, 302, 304, 308, 517. There is now a detailed monograph on the *Putsch* and its political context, Harold J. Gordon, Jr., *Hitler and the Beer Hall Putsch* (Princeton, 1972).

big business in general. His closest ties to business were confined large-ly to the family-controlled wing of heavy industry, a group that was frequently at odds over policy with other segments of big industry and commerce, especially with light industry and the big banks. More im-portantly, he did not regard himself as a proponent merely of big busi-ness. He was concerned with the development of an elitist society that would produce a fusion of interests between all major segments of the upper class. To be sure, he allotted, especially after 1918, the crucial role within this fusion to big industry and export-oriented commercial interests, but he assumed that these interests would have to accept the framework of a cohesive, well-organized upper class within which to operate. Perhaps his broad conservative perspective interfered with his relationships with many of his associates on the Right in postwar Germany. He may have underestimated the extent to which many of his influential friends and acquaintances were capable of looking at political issues from a more general perspective than that suggested by their statements, and he may also not have realized that often these men hoped to use his talents simply to advance some of their own projects of the moment.

Certainly the view of his relationship to heavy industry presented by his acquaintance the conservative nobleman Fritz Reck-Mal-leczewen is a caricature. Reck-Malleczewen's posthumously published diary written during the Nazi period offers biting comments on his contemporaries—comments that include perceptive reflections, gross errors of fact, and subtle distortions. He suggests that Spengler was a brilliant, searching visionary who disintegrated about 1926 when he marched "into the camp of the heavy industrial oligarchy." Spengler's Achilles' heel turns out to have been love of food—"his predilection for the massive dinners that his industrial Maecenases . . . set before him" —and his longing to live the life of a patrician. "It was his [Spengler's] fate that in the middle of his career he fell into dependence on the heavy industrial oligarchy and that this dependence began in time to influence his thinking. . . ."[52] The major fault in this interpretation of his career is neither the peculiar dating of his association with heavy industry nor the more accurate description of his hedonism, but rather the suggestion of a sharp break in his thought and work. As we have already begun to demonstrate, his basic political views remained re-markably consistent. Long before imbibing the industrialists' "full burgundies" of which Reck-Malleczewen speaks, Spengler had devel-oped a position that made him and his industrial patrons mutually sympathetic.

[52] Friedrich Percyval Reck-Malleczewen, *Tagebuch eines Verzweifelten* (Stutt-gart, [1966]), pp. 13–16.

The Necessity and Inevitability of Elites

Much of Spengler's effectiveness as a political writer stemmed from the broad historical foundation he gave to his elite theory. In the years after 1918, he developed his already antidemocratic views into a detailed assault upon the Weimar Republic. Especially to people whose sympathies lay with the Right, an elite theory like Spengler's offered a far more accurate picture of reality than the ideals of democracy. As interpreter of the past, guide to the present, and prophet of the future, he promised that political democracy would not survive in Germany and that a Marxian classless society could not take its place.

Like the neoconservatives, with whom he has often been associated, Spengler did not advocate a return to the Second Reich. Although he believed monarchy to be an integral part of Europe's heritage and the Germans to be a particularly monarchical people, a mere restoration of the Hohenzollerns never formed the core of his proposals. During the first years of the Republic, he may have looked forward to the reestablishment of the monarchy, but he considered the monarch himself as essentially a symbol.[53] He shared much of the Right's highly critical attitude toward William II.[54] In the years after 1924, if not earlier, Spengler concluded that the formal reinstitution of a monarchy was unnecessary.

In his writings he provided an elaborate, three-pronged justification of elites. He maintained (1) that some type of elite was inevitable in every society; (2) that the proper type of elite was necessary in every worthwhile social order; and (3) that the inherent structure of Western civilization or culture (which for him included Germany and the United States) was uniquely elitist. By pursuing, if intermittently, all three lines of thought, he bolstered his elitism with a particular urgency and authority.

If we overlook such typically Spenglerian expressions as the adjective "Faustian" to indicate a peculiarly Western and German need for elites, we encounter most of the same arguments that we met in German elite theories of the latter half of the nineteenth century and the early years of the twentieth. For Spengler every higher culture rested on the work of an elite; government must be entrusted to a few men with unique qualities of leadership; the dynamics of society could not

---

[53] See *Der Untergang des Abendlandes*, Vol. 2: *Welthistorische Perspektiven* 31.–42. Aufl. (Munich, 1922), pp. 215, 217, 220–21, 434, 467–68, 516. Hereafter cited as *Untergang*, II. Vol. 1: *Gestalt und Wirklichkeit*, 33.–42. völlig umgestaltete Aufl. (Munich, 1923), will be cited as *Untergang*, I. See also "Preussentum," p. 97; *Briefe*, p. 114; "Neubau des Deutschen Reiches" (1924) in *PS*, p. 213. Hereafter the last work will be cited as "Neubau."

[54] See "Preussentum," p. 88.

be elucidated through a class analysis; the potential members of a new elite full of vitality were being kept down by the power of the masses; and this vitality, if released, would promote a healthy German economy and a sorely needed expansion of the nation on the Continent as well as overseas.

Although refurbished with the label "Faustian insatiability," the old thesis of the limited supply of material goods reappeared in Spengler's works. He belittled any attempt to interpret the effects of the Industrial Revolution as making an egalitarian society possible. Like Treitschke, he maintained that the "higher" a culture rose, the greater was the demand for "lower" forms of work. Instead of permitting an increasing number of men the free time to engage in "culturally creative" activities, the development of technology had the opposite effect, for "every discovery contains the possibility and *necessity* of new discoveries; . . . every fulfilled desire awakens a thousand others; . . . every triumph over nature stimulates men to still greater ones."[55]

Spengler found a dichotomy between leaders and led in every social process. He assumed that the organization of society was based upon two types of activity. Between work centered in commanding and work centered in obeying, there existed an unbridgeable gulf: ". . . In every process there is a technique of direction and a technique of execution. . . . In every enterprise *planning out* and *carrying out* are distinct elements. . . ."[56] Insisting upon the necessity never to relax this distinction, Spengler looked suspiciously upon the imposition of restrictions upon the prerogatives of the entrepreneur, the man who "performs work of higher quality."[57]

Wishful thinking and reckless rhetoric predominated in Spengler's discussions of society. Naumann and Weber recognized the existence of a working class, as did Rathenau and Nelson, who sought, if partly by terminological sleights of hand, to abolish it. Spengler refused to

[55] *Der Mensch und die Technik: Beitrag zu einer Philosophie des Lebens* (Munich, 1932), pp. 56–57. Hereafter cited as *MuT*. Spengler's italics. See also pp. 72–73 and *Jahre der Entscheidung*, Part 1 (no more published): *Deutschland und die weltgeschichtliche Entwicklung* (Munich, 1933), pp. 114–15. Hereafter cited as *JdE*.

[56] *MuT*, pp. 49–50. Italics Spengler's. See also "Neubau," p. 218. The English version of the above quotation is that found in C. F. Atkinson's translation of *MuT* under the title *Man and Technics: A Contribution to a Philosophy of Life* (New York, 1932), pp. 62–63. Atkinson also translated the *Untergang* as *The Decline of the West* (2 vols., New York, 1926–28), and *JdE* as *The Hour of Decision* (New York, 1934). I shall cite Atkinson's translations simply as "translation" followed by the page reference. I have often modified these translations, and shall do so without further indication.

[57] "Neubau," p. 284.

acknowledge its existence.[58] For him the separation of society into leaders and led was not simply a matter of convenience or efficiency. Rather, it depended ultimately upon two radically different types of human beings. These two types, far more than any tendency inherent in the division of labor, determined a "natural" separation of society into two parts: ". . . Society rests upon the inequality of men. That is a *natural* fact. There are strong and weak natures. . . . *"There are men whose nature is to command and men whose nature is to obey, subjects and objects of the political or economic process in question."*[59]

In justifying the separation of individuals within a society into two basic groups, Spengler drew heavily upon the cultural elite theories of the late nineteenth and early twentieth century. His approach was strongly influenced by Nietzsche. Discussions of Spengler's work often linked his name to Nietzsche's; and Nietzsche's sister, the founder and director of the Nietzsche Archive, was so impressed by Spengler's admiration for her brother's work—and probably so desirous of associating a best-selling author with her crusade to propagate her version of her brother's philosophy—that she saw to it that Spengler was awarded the Nietzsche Archive Prize in 1919 for the first volume of *The Decline of the West*.[60] But Spengler had crucial reservations about Nietzsche's views. These reservations seem to have stemmed largely from Spengler's awareness that for Nietzsche men were divided primarily by culture and that the polarization of society was largely of cultural significance. Nietzsche's distaste for businessmen, an attitude that Spengler seems to have detected in much less equivocal forms in Stefan George, contributed to these reservations.[61] Spengler believed that the lines separating two human types were as clear in political and economic activity as they were in cultural activity.

He deduced the indispensability of an elite also from the doctrine of the primacy of foreign policy, to which he subscribed emphatically. Despite his conception of world history as the history of self-contained cultures, he regarded each nation or political unit within a culture as an almost autonomous entity. The members of one nation could scarcely understand those of another; nations remained in perpetual conflict with each other. Every state was therefore above all *"the inner order-*

[58] See Herman Lebovics, *Social Conservatism and the Middle Classes in Germany, 1914–1933* (Princeton, 1969), pp. 159–60. In Ch. 5 Lebovics offers a good description of Spengler's economic views, but the interpretation suffers from an understandable impatience with the crudity of Spengler's economic views.

[59] *JdE*, p. 66; *MuT*, p. 50. Translation, p. 56. Spengler's italics. See also *MuT*, p. 61.

[60] See *Briefe*, p. 145.

[61] See *ibid.*, esp. pp. 45, 63–64; *Untergang*, I, 478–79.

ing of a people for external purposes."[62] External relations had to determine the internal organization of a society. Because of the inability of most men either to understand men of other nations or to grasp the primacy of foreign policy over domestic policy, only an elite could be depended upon to conduct the affairs of a nation: "Since the ordinary man is not so far-sighted, it is the ruling minority which must possess this quality on behalf of the others. . . ."[63] Like Naumann, Weber, and Rathenau, Spengler thus maintained that the conduct of foreign affairs constituted one of the decisive factors necessitating an elite.

World War I had stimulated and probably confirmed Spengler's belief in the capacity of Germany to pursue an expansionist policy overseas as well as in Europe. In a letter to a close friend in late October 1914, he began to enumerate the present and prospective German gains from the war: "The possession of Belgium, which will certainly remain German, is by itself an enormous gain: 8 million inhabitants, a port on the English channel, giant industries, and an ancient culture. We shall also acquire something else that we need—a colonial empire in Africa."[64] In another letter to the same friend less than two months later Spengler described Germany's world-historical mission as similar to ancient Rome's. By the summer of 1915, he was referring to a future *imperium germanicum.*[65] In May 1918, two months after the signing of the Treaty of Brest-Litovsk, he observed with satisfaction the emergence of a German system in Eastern Europe, and he alluded jubilantly to "the war after the war" that would lead to a *"de facto* German protectorate over the continent (as far as the Urals!)."[66]

As many writers on Spengler have pointed out, his reputation as a pessimist, derived largely from the title of *The Decline of the West,* is somewhat unwarranted. Indeed, the translation of the word *Untergang* as "decline" rather than "fall" came closer to his intentions than the German title. He long considered using other, less ominous, titles, of which one was "The *Vollendung* (maturation or fulfillment) of the West," and in an essay published in 1921 he defended himself from the charge that he was a pessimist and implied that *Vollendung* might have been a better term since it did not suggest the notion of a catastrophe.[67] The preface to the original edition of the first volume of *The Decline,* dated December 1917, anticipated a German victory. Spengler explained that the *Untergang* of the West was "a world-historical phase lasting several centuries, at the beginning of which we now

[62] *MuT,* p. 53. Spengler's italics. See also *Untergang,* II, 203–06; "Neubau," p. 236; *JdE,* p. 24; "Das heutige Verhältnis zwischen Weltwirtschaft und Weltpolitik" in *PS,* p. 316.

[63] *Untergang,* II, 560. Translation, p. 448. See also "Neubau," p. 209.

[64] *Briefe,* p. 29.

[65] *Ibid.,* pp. 33, 44. See also p. 54.

[66] *Ibid.,* p. 97.

[67] "Pessimismus?" in *PS,* p. 63.

stand."[68] He seems to have believed that the "Fulfillment" or "Decline" of the West would include a German era. A letter that he wrote in 1915 provides illuminating evidence of this belief; he referred to the Russians as the people—perhaps in new forms beginning along the Volga and in Turkestan—to whom the next thousand years belonged after the Germans had a few centuries for themselves.[69]

The outcome of the war made his optimism more guarded, but hardly altered his basic assessment of Germany's potential. A year after the signing of the Treaty of Versailles he referred in a letter to a mere "pause for breath" in the World War,[70] and in 1924, in the introduction to an issue of the *Süddeutsche Monatshefte* devoted to the World War, he played upon the same notion.[71] Foreseeing an era of increasing imperialistic expansion, he did not conceal his hope that Germany would lead the way. He continued to base his writings on the assumption that a German era would precede the historical demise of the West.[72] His last political work, published in 1933, emphasized the "threat" to Western civilization by the "nonwhite peoples" and the necessity for cooperation among the "white" nations, but he still felt that Germany was "destined" to establish hegemony in Europe.[73] He cautioned that during the "coming period of global wars" victory would go to the nation possessing the most capable leading stratum (*führende Schicht*).[74]

His qualified optimism about the possibility of a coming German epoch was compatible with his pessimistic view of universal history. As he pointed out, a true pessimist would see no more tasks to be undertaken, whereas he saw so many tasks that he feared there was neither time nor men for them.[75] Spengler's real pessimism lay in his rejection of the concept of historical progress, his belief in the ultimate triviality of human endeavors, and his conception of nature as the only persistent reality. His pessimism was of a deeper sort than that of those nineteenth-century conservatives who saw the march of history as relentlessly destroying their world and sighed for more time. He purported to find in the future no threat of a social order hostile toward

[68] *Untergang*, Vol. 1, 15.–22. unveränderte Aufl. (Munich, 1920), p. vii. This is the only reference to this edition of the *Untergang*. As indicated earlier, all other references to the first volume of the *Untergang* are to the revised edition of 1923.

[69] *Briefe*, p. 38. Even at the end of his life Spengler made a similar prediction about Russia. See his letter of May 3, 1936 to Wahrhold Drascher, *ibid.*, p. 776.

[70] *Ibid.*, p. 165. See also p. 130.

[71] "Zum 4. August," *Süddeutsche Monatshefte*, xxi (1924), 229.

[72] See "Neue Formen der Weltpolitik" in *PS*, pp. 159–60; *Untergang*, i, 501, and ii, 529, 129; "Einführung zu einem Aufsatz Richard Korherrs über den Geburtenrückgang" in *Reden und Aufsätze*, pp. 135–37; "Aufgaben des Adels," pp. 91–95.

[73] *JdE*, esp. p. 102. [74] "Aufgaben des Adels," p. 91.

[75] "Pessimismus?" p. 75.

his own values. His view of history suggested that both the classical liberal and the Marxian concepts of historical progress rested upon a complete misunderstanding of history. His stoicism was thoroughly bourgeois; he found alternatives in Western history to bourgeois society only in the past. Although he regarded all political programs as merely provisional, he depicted liberal and Marxist programs as having no effective historical role to perform.

THE HISTORICAL SIGNIFICANCE OF MODERN DEMOCRACY

Spengler's cyclical view of history suggested that the essence of history consisted in recurrent series of elites. With one exception, which we shall discuss shortly, all significant history occurred within and through elites. They supplied the primary driving force of the historical process. The activities of the nonelite provided either a mere backdrop to the activities of the elite or simply fuel for the realization of the elite's goals. Every culture and each nation within a culture had a predetermined life-cycle similar to that of a living organism. In each phase of the cycle, a particular type of elite predominated. During the "spring" phase, a nobility acted as the political elite. The nobility as an estate or class ruled and stood above the state. A culture reached its highpoint when, as in the period of royal absolutism in Europe, the nobility and the prince ruled in the name of the state. Although the nobility then became simply the first of several estates, it furnished the core of the political elite.[76]

Even more strongly than Weber, Spengler linked the function of elites to great men. For Spengler the relative importance of the two varied from one historical period to another. In the "springtime" of a culture, the nobility distrusted great men, and the vigor of the nobility usually obviated the need for a great man.[77] Thereafter, great men became more and more important. As usual, Spengler supported his thesis with references to the unique characteristics of Western culture.[78]

He also discerned a special German need for a great leader. He thus added his voice to the cries, particularly strong on the Right, for a great leader to alleviate the sufferings of the German people and overcome internal conflicts: "No other nation today needs a leader so much in order to be something, even to be able to believe in itself. No other

[76] *Untergang*, II, 113, 206–07, 413–18, 353, 457–58, 479, 599. I have found no evidence to support the assertion, which Klemens von Klemperer, *Germany's New Conservatism*, p. 178 mistakenly attributes to H. Stuart Hughes, that Pareto influenced Spengler.

[77] *Untergang*, II, 417.   [78] *Ibid.*, I, 190.

nation can offer a great leader so much. In the proper hands almost all of [the German nation's] defects will become advantages. What might then transpire departs from the realm of customary political speculation."[79]

Although Spengler predicted a coming era of great men, he joined other German elite theorists in cautioning against placing "excessive" hopes in great men, because a great man always needed followers to execute his decisions,[80] and as "a divine spark," genius appeared "suddenly and mysteriously."[81] The German situation was particularly precarious: "In our political and geographical position we cannot afford to depend upon the *fortuitous* appearance of a Bismarck or a Napoleon."[82]

In the Spenglerian pattern of history, the present epoch in European history represented a transition from an era of well-ordered rule by the nobility to an era dominated by great men. Utilizing the analogy of the Roman Empire, Spengler designated the latter era that of "Caesarism." He also adapted the frequent contrast made by Germans between "culture" and "civilization" to serve his purposes. As an age of incipient "civilization" that had begun with the French Revolution, the present period was witnessing the end of the possibilities for the extensive development of the distinctive features of Western culture. All its truly creative potentialities had already been realized, and Western culture was nearing its end. With the full development of Caesarism, it would relapse into the "historyless" and "die." But Spengler graciously predicted that the age of complete Caesarism, the last phase of civilization, was still many decades away.[83] Anything he liked he branded an inevitable aspect of the transition to Caesarism. Anything he disliked he dismissed as another indication of the decline of Western culture during the era of democracy. By democracy he understood the dispersion of unified, capable elites and their replacement by a proliferation of nonunified, destructive elites. Divorced from the traditions of the culture, the new elites could neither develop the culture farther nor create a viable political order. Continual chaos and repeated crises ensued.

Spengler helped to popularize a conception of democracy that became widespread on the Right. He suggested that democracy consisted in an alliance of the urban masses, cosmopolitan intellectuals, and finance capitalists. Spurred on by the meaningless slogans of

[79] "Vom deutschen Volkscharakter" in *Reden und Aufsätze*, p. 134. See also, e.g., "Politische Pflichten der deutschen Jugend" in *PS*, p. 145.
[80] See *Untergang*, ii, 457.   [81] *MuT*, p. 51.
[82] "Aufgaben des Adels," p. 90. My italics.
[83] See, e.g., *Untergang*, i, 42–55, 460–63; ii, 541–46.

democracy, the urban masses had risen against the domination of the old elites. But the masses could only act negatively. Their "revolt"—to use the term popularized by Ortega y Gasset, who made his admiration for Spengler manifest[84]—lacked any positive force. The masses could never create a new order. Powerless and helpless as they had always been, the masses, Spengler never tired of repeating, were manipulated by the intelligentsia, the press, and the parties.[85]

Hostile to the traditions of the culture, the intelligentsia represented abstract intelligence, not wisdom and feeling. With other exponents of antiintellectualism and "Vitalism" such as Ludwig Klages, Spengler posited a radical duality between thought and action. Reason and reflection hindered action. Tearing away the veil of authority that had once covered the rule of suitable elites, the intelligentsia had coined the abstract catchwords of democratic ideology; then the masses had rejected the old elites. The intelligentsia had discredited the authority of any true elite.

Behind the press, which manipulated the masses on the basis of slogans furnished by the intelligentsia, stood "abstract" finance capital. For Spengler the real controlling group in a democracy consisted of the finance capitalists. Slyly and deceitfully, they exploited the institutions of democracy: "The mobile fortunes, which stand behind the banks, corporations, and individual enterprises, have, to an extent undreamed of by the public, brought under their influence the political institutions, parties, governments, press, and public opinion."[86]

Around the finance capitalists Spengler constructed a conspiracy theory, which, in its lack of analysis or proof, vied with the simplicity of the anti-Semitic "Protocols of the Elders of Zion." Similar conspiracy theories, whether taking as their subjects Jews, Freemasons, Jesuits, Bolsheviks, or financiers, flourished during the Weimar Republic. The upheavals of the war and postwar years were made really comprehensible by attributing them all to one central guiding force. Spengler used three key notions involved in such conspiracy theories. He attributed a diabolical cleverness to the finance capitalists; he portrayed them as parasites who lived from the labors of others; and he charged them with being international and therefore opposed to the interests of the German nation.[87]

[84] See José Ortega y Gasset, *The Revolt of the Masses* (New York, 1957), pp. 19, 83. See also *Briefe*, p. 186.

[85] *Untergang*, II, 444; "Preussentum," p. 13; *MuT*, pp. 74, 82–84; *JdE*, pp. 63, 120, 127–34, 147, 164; "Weltwirtschaft und Weltpolitik," p. 324.

[86] "Politische Pflichten," p. 141.

[87] The concept of finance capital to which, often indirectly, many discussions and claims like Spengler's were indebted, was worked out by the Social Democratic theoretician Rudolf Hilferding shortly after the turn of the century. As Franz

He set up a target for all those who felt defenseless since the collapse of the old social coalition in 1918. While resembling the sensationalism of popular Marxism, his nebulous references to "finance capital" appealed directly to the vague anticapitalistic mentality of large segments of the middle class. He diverted animosity from the industrialists and other big businessmen, and he also appealed directly to them. Together with many non-Marxist writers of the period, Spengler distinguished between "good," "creative" capital and "bad," "parasitical" capital. The latter recognized no fatherland and destroyed every national economy. "Bad" capital plotted to control the entire world for the sake of ever-increasing profits.

Spengler's polemic against finance capital remained largely in the realm of mere assertions. Where his arguments seemed paradoxical, he assumed an underlying identity of interests between seemingly antagonistic forces. By attacking the traditions of the culture, even the most radical anticapitalist party created, he charged, a situation favorable to finance capital. Every political party, including the Communists, thus operated in the interests of finance capital.[88]

From Spengler's point of view, belief in democracy promoted a deceptive myth. It permitted the masses to think that they ruled themselves. Yet "the 'sovereignty of the people' only expresses the fact that the ruling power has assumed the title of the leader of the people. The method of governing is scarcely altered thereby, and the position of the governed not at all."[89]

His conception of the structure of political parties closely resembled that of Weber and Michels. Without specifically mentioning either man, Spengler accepted the validity of the "iron law of oligarchy." He spoke of "a few men who, due to their experience, superior will, and

Neumann points out, Hilferding's belief that the big banks controlled industry was becoming outmoded when Hilferding published his *Finanzkapital* in 1910 and was invalid by the 1920's. See Franz Neumann, *Behemoth: The Structure and Practice of National Socialism, 1933–1944* (New York, 1963), pp. 321–26. A history of the roots of European and American theories about the sinister role of international financiers commencing with the French Revolution would make a fascinating study. Fragmentary and often brilliant beginnings of such a study can be found in Parts 1 and 2 of Hannah Arendt's *The Origins of Totalitarianism* (New York: Meridian paperback, 1958). The most recent historical investigation of the often allied myth of the "Elders of Zion" succumbs to a problem that Arendt succeeds partly in overcoming. Norman Cohn's *Warrant for Genocide: The Myth of the Jewish World-Conspiracy and the Protocols of the Elders of Zion* (New York, 1969) fails to provide a historical analysis of either the position of Jewish members of the bourgeoisie or the functions of financiers. For a discussion of some related problems for further research see Section II of the Bibliographical Essay.

[88] *Untergang*, II, 501, 512–13, 582.
[89] *Untergang*, II, 550. Translation, pp. 441–42.

tactical ability," ruled a party "with dictatorial powers."[90] He greeted oligarchical tendencies in the parties as a sign of their decline. Weber had disliked the type of party functionary, but viewed him as a functional necessity; Spengler heaped scorn upon "groups of professional politicians, office seekers, and self-appointed leaders of the people who all want to live from rather than for politics."[91] Only in England, Spengler believed, had political parties served a useful purpose. But England had realized the ideals of democracy no more than any other country had. Within each of the two parties stood a controlling group or "privy council" ready to govern the country if its party were elected. The emergence of a third party, the decreasing influence of the nobility, and the power wielded by demagogues like Lloyd George presaged the end of political parties even in England. Everywhere, the parliamentary system was rapidly disintegrating.[92]

FOLLOWINGS FOR GREAT LEADERS

Spengler linked the decline of parties to the development of "Caesarism." In August Bebel, the prewar leader of the Social Democrats, and especially in Lenin and Mussolini, he found examples of the dictatorial possibilities in the combination of a forceful personality with a rigidly organized party. Instead of the extensive analysis devoted by Weber to assessing the opportunities provided for a great leader by a party organization, Spengler simply alluded to historical necessity: ". . . The form of the ruling minority *develops steadily from that of the estate through that of the individual's following.* . . . A tendency that has organized itself in the people has already *ipso facto* become the tool of the organization, and continues steadily along the same path until the organization becomes in turn the tool of the leader."[93]

Such an organization would act merely as the obedient following of a single individual. The party oligarchies would be supplanted by great men, who, like Weber's charismatic leader, would be obeyed because of their personal qualities. Party programs would disappear. The personal wishes and programs of great men would take their place. Like the Hegelian great man, the Caesar of the future would, however, only create that which was in some indiscernible fashion historically necessary.[94]

[90] "Preussentum," p. 59.
[91] "Politische Pflichten," p. 144. See also "Preussentum," p. 9; "Geburtenrückgang," p. 136; *JdE*, p. 104.
[92] "Preussentum," pp. 17, 65n., 70–71; *Untergang*, ıı, 502, 519–21; "Neubau," p. 206.
[93] *Untergang*, ıı, 565–66. Translation, p. 452. Spengler's italics.
[94] *Untergang*, ıı, 558–59; "Preussentum," pp. 22, 70; "Neubau," pp. 295–96.

Yet Spengler seldom had much confidence in the possibility of any of the established parties providing a springboard to Caesarism. Rather, in the militant, extraparliamentary organizations many of the same elements he found in the disintegration of traditional party forms appeared to Spengler more advanced. The bellicose attitudes, enthusiasm for a common cause, rigid selection of members, and willingness to employ violence—all were quite pronounced in many of the organizations standing outside the parties. Only in organizations willing to resort to physical violence for the sake of their goals or leaders did Spengler find suitable vehicles for the transition to Caesarism: "The Caesarism of the future will triumph by force, not by convincing people."[95] Above all, the uncompromising loyalty and obedience to a single leader of such groups impressed him: ". . . The masses, the majorities, and the parties provide no [true] followings. They only want [personal] advantages. They leave the leader in the lurch the moment he demands sacrifices."[96]

Like some other observers of military affairs, Spengler concluded that the war had forced the development of mass armies to its logical, but unsatisfactory conclusion. Although the mass army had been perfected, it no longer provided an effective instrument of policy. Attempts by both the Central Powers and the Allies to circumvent the limitations of trench warfare through the use of small, highly mobile commando units probably seemed to corroborate his judgment. Moreover, largely on the basis of the war-weariness manifested by the bulk of European soldiers and civilians during the last stages of the war, he apparently thought that the futility of universal military service had been proven beyond a doubt. The masses, he asserted, would not respond adequately to a general mobilization. Small military—or militarily organized—groups would have to take their place. Only "an appeal to those who are voluntarily prepared to work for a cause," especially to young men, would provide units suited to the internal and external struggles of the future.[97] His rejection of universal military service resulted more from political than military considerations: a belief that disillusionment with the war had rendered the ideal of the nation in arms useless and that the placing of weapons in the citizen's hands during a period of incipient civil war had become dangerous. He found the Free Corps, as well as the private militias, and other paramilitary groups, better suited than the Reichswehr to the development of Caesarism.

Composed largely of volunteers from the demobilized army after

---

[95] *JdE*, p. 133.

[96] *JdE*, p. 145. See also *Untergang*, ii, 525; "Politische Pflichten," pp. 133–34.

[97] "Politische Pflichten," p. 133. See also the preface to *PS*, p. ix.

World War I and supplemented by younger men, the Free Corps fought in the internal and border upheavals during the first years of the Republic.[98] They frequently operated in conjunction with the government and generally had the support of the Reichswehr, but they did not have the status of official government troops. In the confusing reversals of sides and issues during this period, the Free Corps developed a high degree of independence from official government policies. Even in the battles on Germany's eastern frontiers after the armistice on the western front, the concept of defending the sacred soil of the Fatherland became blurred. The internal disorders of the early years of the Republic supplied few clear issues. Employed largely, almost exclusively, against the Left, the members of the Free Corps often came to feel a close sense of kinship to the "Reds" and "Bolsheviks" whom they were fighting and a strong feeling of contempt for the *Bürger* whom they were defending. Rather than immobilizing the Free Corps or promoting mass defections from their ranks, these experiences increased their effectiveness as terroristic instruments of civil war. The application of violence irrespective of concrete goals became often an end in itself for the Free Corps and the paramilitary groups that succeeded them. At the same time, the traditional military hierarchy with its close correlation to the prewar social hierarchy tended to disintegrate in the Free Corps and their successors. The old canons of social and military deference lost much of their sanction. Even one of the most conservative of the paramilitary groups, the *Stahlhelm*, which stood close to the Nationalist party and was the largest organization of war veterans in Germany, was affected by the need to appear flexible. At an encampment of veterans in 1922 Franz Seldte, the leader of the *Stahlhelm* and one of Spengler's closer acquaintances, proclaimed: "We say to hell with rank and status. . . . We look only at the man himself. Only character should count."[99]

The experiences of the front army in the war and of the Free Corps in the postwar struggles promoted the notion of mutual self-sacrifice and of a group of men held tightly together by common sentiments and experiences. The Free Corps crystallized around single leaders to whom obedience often seemed more important than the policies pursued. It was especially the devotion to a leader from which Spengler expected so much: ". . . On the soil of Europe *tiny* armies will reappear —armies in which *the individual's personal convictions or veneration*

[98] For the Free Corps, see esp. Waite, *Vanguard of Nazism*.

[99] Quoted in Kurt Finker, "Die militaristischen Wehrverbände in der Weimarer Republik: Ein Beitrag zur Strategie und Taktik der deutschen Grossbourgeoisie," *Zeitschrift für Geschichtswissenschaft*, xiv (1966), 362.

for a leader is decisive."[100] Spengler sought to harness for long-range objectives the hero-worship and the violence of the successors of the Free Corps. During the 1920's, when he was assisting Escherich's para-military group, he implored it and other right-wing organizations to maintain an uncompromising hostility toward the Republic. Any tend-ency to compromise disturbed him. Writing shortly before the advent of the Third Reich, he denounced the Nazis for participating in par-liament; they might provide the "party system" with a new lease on life. Before long the action leagues (*Kampfbünde*) would demolish parliamentary democracy, and the parties would vanish: "The masks from the transitional period will fall. Attempts to fetter the future in parties will soon be forgotten."[101]

The Ideal German Elite

One might logically conclude that Spengler conceived of a *Bund*-like following for a great leader as the type of elite most appropriate to the present age. Spengler certainly wanted to encourage the development of such elites, but he had an ambivalent attitude toward them. He hesi-tated before the logical inferences from his own scheme of history. He looked upon the various types of *Bünde* primarily as the means to an end. Until the full establishment of Caesarism, the future Caesar could not dispense with his following, but eventually he had to turn against it: "Every revolutionary movement triumphs with an *avant-garde* of praetorians, who then lose their usefulness and become dangerous. The real master reveals himself in the manner in which he takes his leave of them. Ruthlessly and ungratefully, he concentrates upon his goal, for which he now has to, and knows how to, find the right men."[102]

In this and similar statements, Spengler's inclination toward an old conservative position is manifest. He tended to consider the demobili-zation of the masses as essential to a viable polity, and he regarded most if not all of the "*avant-garde* of praetorians" as members of the masses. The aid of this *avant-garde* was to be enlisted in order to cre-ate conditions that would strip most of the praetorians of all power and influence. Symptomatic of Spengler's attitude was his view of the

---

[100] "Politische Pflichten," p. 133. Spengler's italics. For an attempt to elaborate upon Spengler's conception of the impact of World War I on military organization and its political implications see Heinz-Erich Fick, *Der deutsche Militarismus der Vorkriegszeit: Ein Beitrag zur Soziologie des Militarismus* (Potsdam, 1932).

[101] *JdE*, p. 165.

[102] *JdE*, p. 135. Spengler's italics. See also "Neue Formen der Weltpolitik," p. 181.

role of the Nazis and many of the paramilitary groups in 1922–1923. While welcoming their existence, he deplored their impulsiveness and hoped to see them used by other less plebian men. Yet as we shall see later, Spengler realized that the old conservative dream of demobilizing the masses was both unrealistic and undesirable, even though this dream had a strong attraction for him.

While the contenders for the role of Caesar and their followings were struggling for supremacy, another elite, Spengler reasoned, could reduce the chaos of the transitional period. This second type of elite was by far the more important for him. The victorious Caesar would have to rely upon it after freeing himself from his followers. It would provide continuity in the disorders that lay ahead, and it would eventually become the appropriate agent of a Caesar.

In selecting his models for the ideal German elite of the future, Spengler turned to the past. Only by salvaging elements from Germany's nonparliamentary institutions and traditions could the ideal elite be created. Caesarism might "grow on the soil of democracy," but "its roots spread deeply into the underground."[103] As a result, Spengler spoke of the "immense superiority of states which manage to retain a tradition longer than others."[104]

He bemoaned the lack of a unified German political tradition and a predominant type of elite. He agreed with many of his countrymen in finding Germany deficient in comparison with the nations of the West, especially England. But Spengler found a positive advantage in the German deficiency. In accordance with the notion—associated with Moeller van den Bruck and especially prevalent among neoconservatives—of Germany as one of the "young nations," he argued that at least she had not become senile and inflexible as the Western European nations had. Germany still possessed enough youthful vigor to create the type of elite best suited to her, as well as to the new era.[105]

In the bureaucracy, officer corps, and Junkers, as all three had existed before 1918, Spengler found the most important models for his elite. From the combination of their traditions and practices, he expected great successes similar to those he attributed to the English nobility and gentry.[106] He wanted to reconstitute the pre-Weimar social coalition in a new form. He envisioned a streamlined version of the Second Reich in which the Hohenzollerns would be supplanted by a great leader. Elements from the nobility, bourgeoisie, and administrative upper middle class would fuse.[107] The new elite would safeguard

[103] *Untergang*, ıı, 583. Translation, p. 464.
[104] *Untergang*, ıı, 505. Translation, p. 405. See also *JdE*, p. 165.
[105] *JdE*, pp. x, xii.   [106] "Neubau," p. 214.
[107] Koktanek, "Spenglers Verhältnis zum Nationalsozialismus," p. 33, asserts that Spengler wanted not a new elite, but rather the *Umerziehung* of the Prussian

the *Mittelstand* and accept some of its members. Indeed, technically no one would be excluded on principle.

Insofar as possible, Spengler wanted his elite to constitute what would have become a single social class. Only such an elite could overcome what he viewed as the chaos engendered by the discordant elites of the Republic. The elite would have to be formally recognized as a class entrusted with all significant political and economic decisions. Spengler based his ideal elite upon the complete centralization of all significant decision making in Germany. The most important of the pre-Weimar hierarchies would be merged into a single, inclusive hierarchy. Weber had considered such a merger as the probable result of the complete bureaucratization of society and had searched for means to combat it. Spengler searched for means to advance it.

He wanted flexible relations among the members of the elite. His criticism of the state bureaucracy agreed largely with Weber's: inside a strictly ordered hierarchy, no place existed for the great man. But what Weber viewed as the inevitable attribute of every bureaucracy, Spengler dismissed as an avoidable aberration. Within the elite there would be no fixed positions, no permanent hierarchy, and no automatic advancements.[108] Ultimately, then, the hierarchy within the elite would depend upon a great leader who appeared either in its midst or from outside it.

Except Nelson, none of our other elite theorists talked as much about an open elite. Spengler considered an open elite as the one worthwhile, or "Prussian," aspect of democracy: *"In England democracy indicates the possibility for everyone to become rich; in Prussia, the possibility to attain every existing rank. . . ."*[109] With great enthusiasm he referred to the "hidden talent" waiting to be uncovered in Germany.[110] He conceived detailed programs to ensure democracy of

---

nobility, which would act as the elite of the future. It is difficult to understand how Koktanek can make this assertion; he probably has in mind an address, "Aufgaben des Adels," which Spengler delivered in 1924 to the Annual Meeting of the German Nobility (*Deutscher Adelstag*) in Breslau. This address, Spengler's most sympathetic evaluation of the contemporary nobility, stops short of the conclusion that German noblemen by themselves could serve as the elite in the future. In analyzing the address not only Spengler's obvious desire to please most of his audience but also his discussion of the nobility in his other works must be kept in mind. A better understanding of Spengler's views on the nobility was manifested in a pamphlet published in 1926 by a nobleman. See Claus von Eickstedt, *Der soziale Beruf wahren Adels*, Schriften zur politischen Bildung, ed. Gesellschaft "Deutscher Staat," . . . *Friedrich Mann's Pädagogisches Magazin*, Heft 1108 (Langensalza, 1926), esp. p. 21.
[108] "Neubau," pp. 217–27.
[109] "Preussentum," p. 45. Spengler's italics. See also pp. 46, 96–97, 104; and *JdE*, p. 138.
[110] "Neubau," p. 226.

personnel selection by making every career open to talents, but these programs were pale and warmed-over versions of some of Rathenau's ideas, of often-discussed projects for educational reform, and other more modest schemes. For example, Spengler called for the institution of a special educational certificate (*Reifeprüfung*) for autodidacts, for the poor, for "late developers," and for nonconformists who could not endure the conventional educational system. Most of Spengler's proposals were intended to promote the development of a labor aristocracy that would doggedly accept the new elite.[111] Like the new liberal elite theorists, he hoped to open the elite to an occasional exceptional individual from the lower classes, but Spengler gave the impression of being more concerned than they were with the abandonment of wealth, origins, and formal education as criteria for recruitment.

Upon closer examination, Spengler's emphasis upon an open elite becomes even more illusory. His elite was to be *formally* open. It was certainly not to be a caste, for he identified castes with the "posthistorical" phase of a culture.[112] And yet he introduced so many restrictions upon elite recruitment that his elite would have been to a large extent self-reproducing.

More than any of the liberal elite theorists whom we have discussed, he limited elite recruitment by basing it upon the presence of characteristics which could hardly be acquired by most men. Although he spoke frequently of the development of elite characteristics through "training," the process would not succeed with most individuals. Its success depended upon the presence of inherent attributes possessed by few men. Some of these attributes might appear in the nonelite, but their appearance there would be purely fortuitous. In general, they would appear only in the progeny of the elite. Through the proper training and institutions, they could be developed, but normally over a long period of time.

For all practical purposes, Spengler believed in the inheritability of acquired characteristics.[113] He discussed the elite characteristic that he considered most important—a strong will—as if it were inherited. Like the strong will of the Junker myth, Spengler's "inherited will" appeared in "every strong race," in every well-established elite, "with the force of a natural phenomenon."[114]

Even if we accept his own assertions that his conception of the production and transmission of elite characteristics was not biological,

[111] *Ibid.*, pp. 237–38, 281–86. See also *Briefe*, p. 160.

[112] See *Untergang*, II, 411.

[113] See, e.g.: "Preussentum," 34–35; *Untergang*, II, 341, 408, 413–21, 505; "Pessimismus?" in *Reden und Aufsätze*, p. 57; "Politische Pflichten," pp. 142–43.

[114] *Untergang*, II, 467.

Spengler still left the details of the process in a cloud of mystery. He referred repeatedly to characteristics "lying in the blood," and yet to blood as something "nonmaterial." The origin of the "race traits" necessary for the elite could not be investigated.[115] Like Nietzsche and the cultural elite theorists, he held that now and then the appropriate characteristics simply appeared in a nonelite individual. Normally, these characteristics would then have to be strengthened by training.

Spengler's type of training could usually function properly only with the progeny of the elite. His usual terms for training (*Zucht* and *Züchtung*) suggested a type of supervision and discipline which would achieve its effects over the course of generations. Despite his criticism of Nietzsche for succumbing to Darwinism,[116] he used much the same terminology used by Nietzsche and the Social Darwinists. Spengler never fully dissociated *Züchtung* from breeding in the biological sense. His elite training had to refine inherent traits: ". . . Everything that . . . we call diplomatic and social tact—including strategic and business flair, the collector's eye for precious things, and the subtle insight of the judge of men—everything that one has and does not learn . . . is nothing but a particular case of the same cosmic and dreamlike certainty which is visibly expressed in the circlings of a flock of birds or the controlled movements of a thoroughbred horse."[117] Since "training influences" consisted primarily in contacts with the elite,[118] the progeny of the elite itself would be those who would usually replenish the elite.

Spengler considered the possession of wealth as one of the foundations of his elite, for "wealth gathered together in a few hands and in ruling classes [*führenden Schichten*] is, together with other factors, a precondition for raising generations of leading men."[119] He attacked contemporary taxation policies for threatening to eliminate this precondition. "Taxation bolshevism," in which he included most forms of direct taxation, and especially progressive income taxes, benefited no one except the mysterious finance capitalists. He contemplated no significant changes in the existing economic order: "Like other countries Germany possesses a highly bred stratum which through its upbringing, station, and culture has for generations acquired something immaterial, something incapable of description: an inward rank. . . . This stratum exists only under the precondition that enough of the national product and of its own inherited wealth remains in its hands to continue and reinforce its training and tradition."[120]

---

[115] See *ibid.*, I, 386, II, 198. [116] See esp. "Pessimismus?" p. 65.
[117] *Untergang*, II, 420–21. Translation, p. 340.
[118] *Untergang*, II, 408. [119] *JdE*, p. 73.
[120] "Politische Pflichten," p. 142. See also "Neubau," pp. 273–79; "Das Verhältnis von Wirtschaft und Steuerpolitik seit 1750" in *PS*, esp. pp. 299–310; *JdE*,

An Uncontrolled Elite

Spengler denied to the nonelite any role in determining the composition of the elite. The elite itself would choose its future members. As in the Prussian bureaucracy and officer corps, cooptation would be the principal method of recruitment.[121] Any form of popular election, Spengler rejected as utterly inappropriate. The German people had never become accustomed to "this form of 'participation [*Mitarbeiten*]' which is so foreign to it."[122]

He indicated no possibility or desirability that any members of the elite act as "representatives" or "agents" of the nonelite. New arrivals had no choice other than complete assimilation to the patterns of the elite. Their identification with the older members had to be complete.[123] If the traditions of an elite were strong and its training effective, it could absorb new men completely: "It matters little if many of the big men come out of the 'people' . . . into the ruling stratum [*leitende Schicht*], or even if they are the only ones left to occupy it. The great tide of tradition takes charge of them all unwitting, forms their intellect and practical conduct, and rules their methods."[124] Spengler thus expressed special admiration for the Roman Catholic Church as an organization with traditions so powerful that they counteracted the undesirable effects of the open recruitment of the priesthood.[125]

To prevent any popular influence, Spengler provided his elite with a special ethos. Although he accused Nietzsche of having confused the question of elite ethics,[126] his own formulations followed Nietzsche's quite closely. For Spengler the essence of elite ethics consisted in the willingness to utilize every method possible to strengthen and extend its domination over the nonelite. Like Nietzsche, he sanctioned any measure that furthered the development of the elite. Without hesitation the elite should exercise its "will to power over other men's

---

pp. 73–75, 125–26. Two sharply worded statements in Spengler's posthumously published notes for the second volume of *JdE* express similar views even more bluntly: "Privatwirtschaft ist die Wirtschaft selbst. Risiko, Unternehmen, Kampf—das ist abendländisch—nordisch. Eigentum ist *Schalten können* in Freiheit." "Der Hass gegen den Kapitalismus ist ein Hass gegen die *Kultur*. Zerstören kann man die *Blüte* des Kapitalismus, *nicht* die Form." Hildegard Kornhardt, ed., " 'Deutschland in Gefahr:' Fragmente zum 2. Band der 'Jahre der Entscheidung' von Oswald Spengler," *Echo der Woche: Unabhängige Wochenzeitung* (Munich), Sept. 17, 1948, p. 6. Spengler's italics.

[121] *Untergang*, ɪɪ, 555. [122] "Preussentum," p. 66.

[123] See *JdE*, p. 65; *Untergang*, ɪɪ, 29, 555–56.

[124] *Untergang*, ɪɪ, 418. Translation, pp. 338–39.

[125] *Untergang*, ɪɪ, 565n.; *JdE*, p. 161.

[126] *Untergang*, ɪ, 443, 449, 478–79; "Nietzsche und sein Jahrhundert" in *Reden und Aufsätze*, p. 122.

destinies."[127] Characteristically, Spengler rephrased Kant's categorical imperative to read: "Act as if the maxims that you practice *should become, by your will, the law for all.*"[128]

The elite, Spengler cautioned, must never attempt to justify its actions. If it began to doubt its superiority, it would no longer be able to assert itself vis-à-vis the nonelite. The members of the elite had to look upon themselves as "born and called to be masters."[129] Their attitude had to be one of contempt for everything beneath them.[130]

Spengler wanted to combat the envy which, like Nietzsche, he attributed to the nonelite by providing it with its own ideology. This ideology, which he found developed to its highest point in Prussia, would maximize the energies of the nonelite, in order to achieve the goals of the elite. Although such an ideology was implicit in many earlier German elite theories, not even Nietzsche had developed it explicitly. Despite its partial derivation from the Protestant conception of vocation and from the values of capitalistic society, it offered the nonelite no rationale for the demands imposed by the elite.

The masses, Spengler proposed, should believe that they were working for the sake of work. Work as an end in itself should be the guiding principle of their thoughts. Just as the elite was never to doubt that its function was to command and decide, the nonelite was never to doubt that its duty was to work and obey.[131] Through work the nonelite was to be given a feeling of participating in the affairs of the nation.[132] Hopelessly muddling Marx's concept of work, Spengler assailed Marxism for its doctrine of work as a "commodity," rather than a "duty."[133]

Spengler conceived of the attitude of the nonelite toward the elite as similar to that of a well-trained dog toward its master. Complete trust was essential to the unhindered activities of the elite. As long as the members of the elite were capable and did not question their right to rule, the nonelite would hardly become presumptuous:

> . . . The courage of a troop depends upon its confidence in the leadership, and confidence means instinctive renunciation of criticism. . . . *Political talent in a people is nothing but confidence in its leadership.* What appears as a lack of feeling of certainty in the ruled is really lack of leadership talent in the ruling class [*herrschenden*

[127] *Untergang*, I, 450.
[128] *Ibid.*, I, 466. Translation, p. 362. Spengler's italics.
[129] *JdE*, pp. 41–42.
[130] *MuT*, pp. 58–59; *JdE*, p. 145.
[131] *Untergang*, I, 466–67. Translation, p. 362. Spengler's italics.
[132] For a prewar attempt by one of the members of the George Circle to formulate a similar ideology see Friedrich Wolters, *Herrschaft und Dienst*, 3rd ed. (Berlin, 1932).
[133] "Preussentum," pp. 79–82.

Schicht] which generates that sort of uninstinctive and meddlesome criticism which by its very existence shows that a people has gotten "out of condition."[134]

Although Spengler identified the principle of "complete confidence" as the formula for the successes of the English "ruling class," his model was far more, as is apparent from the analogy in the above quotation, a hierarchical military system. Whereas Weber viewed hierarchy as the most efficient, if not always the most desirable, method of decision making, Spengler considered hierarchy as the only practicable and desirable method: ". . . A nation cannot rule itself any more than an army can lead itself. It has to be ruled, and as long as it possesses healthy instincts it wants to be ruled."[135]

In Spengler's elite theory, as in Nietzsche's, the development of the elite frequently appeared as an end in itself. Effectively insulated from nonelite pressures, the elite concerned itself primarily with the pursuit of its own goals. The nonelite and its energies stood completely at the disposal of the elite. History had meaning only in and through the elite and the great man. With the exception of the times when a great man appeared and utilized the elite for the accomplishment of his own purposes, the elite stood in the center of the historical process.

Yet the logical conclusion of his proposals dissatisfied Spengler. From the bureaucratic elite theories and his own conception of the Prussian bureaucracy, he retained the concept of an impartial elite capable of realizing the common good.

The establishment of the Weimar Republic reinforced the role played by bureaucratic elite theories in German political thought. Many right-wingers viewed parliamentary democracy as inimical to the old bureaucratic ethos of "disinterested service." To them, political patronage, which they condemned as a systematic innovation of the Republic, threatened the "neutrality" of the bureaucracy. As a result, they portrayed the bureaucrat as an impartial expert who selflessly employed his skills for the benefit of the community.[136]

---

[134] *Untergang*, ii, 551–52. Translation, p. 442. Italics Spengler's. See also *JdE*, p. 66. For an example of Spengler's application of the principle of "complete confidence" to destroy a parliamentary system see "Neubau," pp. 210–12.

[135] *JdE*, p. 26. See also "Neubau," p. 206: "Es gibt nur ein Volksrecht: das auf der Leistungen derer, welche regieren."

[136] Clear expressions of such tendencies may be found in the works of political scientists and philosophers of law such as Heinrich Triepel, Carl Schmitt, Hans Nawiasky, Arnold Köttgen, and Friedrich Lent. For the first three men, as well as for a general discussion of the literature on bureaucracy during the Weimar Republic, see Bracher, *Die Auflösung der Weimarer Republik*, pp. 39–44, 175–98. For Schmitt see also Jürgen Fijalkowski, *Die Wendung zum Führerstaat: Ideologische Komponente in der politischen Philosophie Carl Schmitts* (Cologne, 1958), esp. pp. 77–80. For Köttgen see his *Das deutsche Berufsbeamtentum und die*

The actual composition of the various state bureaucracies underwent no drastic change. Both in the upper and lower levels almost all of the personnel remained from the previous regime. Especially in the uppermost levels, political patronage assumed more overt and systematic forms than it had before, but the bureaucracies remained largely self-recruiting, cooptative bodies.[137]

The protagonists of bureaucratic elite theories often acknowledged implicitly that the extent of the changes in the civil service since 1918 had not been as great as they charged, for they looked to the bureaucracy as the guarantor of stability. Indeed, particularly toward the end of the Republic, homage to the bureaucracy was by no means confined to the political Right.[138]

Spengler absorbed many of the characteristic elements of the bureaucratic elite theories into his own conception of the ideal elite. "Free from the filthy craving for profits," the elite were to achieve the "common good."[139] The "high money-disdaining ethic" of the elite would create "a mighty politico-economic order which transcends all class interests."[140] Through "unselfishness," "self-sacrifice," and "self-renunciation," the elite was to serve the good of all.[141] The devotion to duty on the part of the elite, like that of the officer or bureaucrat of the Prussian myth, had to be unquestioning. A member of the elite "served" with his "whole self."[142]

parlamentarische Demokratie (Berlin, 1928). For Lent see his *Parlamentarismus und Führertum: Die Erneuerung des Führertums in der Gegenwart*, Schriften zur politischen Bildung, ed. Gesellschaft "Deutscher Staat," *Friedrich Mann's Pädagogisches Magazin*, Heft 1271 (Langensalza, 1929), esp. pp. 74–75.

[137] See Eberhard Pikart, "Preussische Beamtenpolitik 1918–1933," *Vierteljahrshefte für Zeitgeschichte*, VI (1958), 119–37; Bracher, *Die Auflösung der Weimarer Republik*, pp. 174–91; Hans-Karl Behrend, "Zur Personalpolitik des preussischen Ministeriums des Innern: Die Besetzung der Landratstellen in den östlichen Provinzen 1919–1933," *Jahrbuch für die Geschichte Mittel- und Ostdeutschlands*, VI (1957), 175–77, 186–87, 202, 205–06, 214; Wolfgang Runge, *Politik und Beamtentum im Parteienstaat: Die Demokratisierung der politischen Beamten in Preussen zwischen 1918 und 1933*, Industrielle Welt, V (Stuttgart, 1965).

[138] See, e.g., Alexander Rüstow's remarks at a roundtable discussion held during the summer of 1929 at the Hochschule für Politik in Berlin: "Wir wissen gar nicht, was wir in den zehn Jahren [of the Weimar Republic] unserer Bürokratie verdanken. Diese Bürokratie war das Element der Stabilität, das Element, *das überhaupt das Staatsschiff am Scheitern gehindert hat*." Waldemar Besson, ed., "Dokumentation zur Frage der Staatsführung in der Weimarer Republik," *Vierteljahrshefte für Zeitgeschichte*, VII (1959), 99. My italics.

[139] Preussentum," p. 47.

[140] *Untergang*, II, 583, 634.

[141] "Preussentum," pp. 45, 32, 35, 49, 63; *Untergang*, II, 454–55; "Neubau," p. 218; Aufgaben des Adels," pp. 91–92.

[142] It was indicative of the confusion over Spengler's views among his contemporaries that in 1925 a young political theorist, Otto Koellreutter, concluded approvingly that Spengler was a bureaucratic elite theorist. Drawing a sharp con-

This concept of "service" manifested, in an especially acute form, the tension in Spengler's thought between the obligation of the elite to achieve the common good and the obligation of the elite to give priority to its own development. Using the analogy of Hegel's great man, who furthered the "progress of reason" by pursuing his own goals, one might consider Spengler's elite as contributing indirectly to the common good by concentrating upon the accomplishment of its own goals. Spengler often implied such a convenient solution; and where the great man became involved, Spengler, as we have seen, adopted this solution explicitly.

Despite his concentration upon the development of the elite, he retained the conception of the state as an institution standing above both elite and nonelite. He still attributed to the state the function of fulfilling the "common good." Unlike Nietzsche, he did not therefore reject the state as just another device by which the nonelite sought to enslave the elite.

Spengler thought of service to the common good as a logical consequence of the elite's assertion of its "will to power." Although in prehistoric times the prototype of the elite individual had lost some of the freedom to assert his will by assuming a leadership position within a social group, this loss constituted a prerequisite for the organization of society. Rather than participating in a presocietal Hobbesian war of all against all, he now had greater opportunities to accomplish more through the assertion of his will. The resources provided to him by a society were far more abundant than those that had been available to his prehistoric prototype. The elite had to provide for the basic needs of the nonelite in order to have the full resources of society at its own disposal. As a result, the elite became the servant of the common good.[143]

One of the pressing tasks of Spengler's elite was to establish social harmony. Although he viewed conflict as "the original fact of life" and as "life itself," Spengler entrusted the elite with the task of abolishing all conflicts between itself and the nonelite. The only conflicts that he wished to continue were those between nations and between individuals. Like the Social Darwinists, he viewed these conflicts as essential to the selection of the elite.

---

trast between Spengler's and Weber's views on bureaucracy, Koellreutter overlooked many of the similarities in the two men's criticisms of the old state bureaucracy. See Otto Koellreutter, "Die staatspolitischen Anschauungen Max Webers und Oswald Spenglers," *Zeitschrift für Politik*, xiv (1925), 481–500. Koellreutter, who went on to become an important theorist and apologist for the bureaucracy during the early years of the Nazi period, had written his doctoral dissertation on Spengler.

[143] See *MuT*, pp. 52–53, 57–58, 63–64.

The concern of Spengler's elite for the common good and social harmony further obviated any need on the part of the nonelite to influence elite decisions. Well-protected from nonelite pressures, a highly cohesive elite formulated all significant decisions. It consisted of experts with great intuitive powers whose decisions were the only ones appropriate to Germany. The nonelite had no possibility or need to influence the elite's policies. An ideology of work kept the nonelite in check and permitted its mobilization for the goals of the elite.

SPENGLER AND NAZI GERMANY

Spengler appealed for undiscovered talent and scanned the horizon for a great leader. Contemplation of the potential achievements of new talent harnessed by a "Caesar" fascinated him. Often Spengler's rhapsodic discourses on Caesarism obscured his basic goal—the establishment of a single, stable elite upon much the same social basis as the Junker-bourgeois coalition in Wilhelminian Germany except that big businessmen would play an even more important role. A great leader was a critical instrument for the achievement of this goal. If not himself a true Caesar, this man would be his precursor.

Since Spengler never found the appropriate great leader, it would be tempting to interpret his reserve toward Nazi Germany as a consequence of his contempt for Hitler. Spengler probably clung until his death in 1936 to his private characterization of Hitler as a "dumbbell" who could never begin to act as a true Caesar.[144] Yet the general development of the Third Reich, at least until 1936, should have been pleasing to Spengler. The Nazis followed much the same course that he had outlined. They stressed the recruitment of a new, largely self-reproducing elite from all strata of German society. They established institutions such as the *Ordensburgen* and *National-politische Erziehungsanstalten* to train a new, highly cohesive elite. At the same time, they drew heavily upon the skills of the nobility, bourgeoisie, and administrative upper middle class. In June 1934, like Spengler's Caesar, Hitler turned against many of his followers. With much the same ambiguity as Spengler's ideal elite, the Nazis claimed to act in the interests of the German nation, while stressing an ethos which gave precedence to the presumed interests of the elite. The populace was manipulated and mobilized in the service of German expansion. Nazi propagandists exhorted Germans to follow blindly and work obediently.

[144] The reference to Hitler as a "dumbbell [*Dummkopf*]" is attributed to Spengler by his sister, Hildegard Kornhardt, who was in charge of his household, in a diary entry of Apr. 21, 1932. Koktanek, "Spenglers Verhältnis zum Nationalsozialismus," p. 50.

Or was Spengler correct in regarding National Socialism as, at best, a preliminary stage to true Caesarism? The Nazi system never functioned as smoothly as the Caesarism he had envisioned. Competing hierarchies existed, whether we consider them imperfections in the system, essential to it, or vestiges of a previous era. Although Hitler claimed to act according to an intuitive genius, he could never act as independently as one of Spengler's Caesars.

Yet these deviations from the pattern of true Caesarism do not adequately explain Spengler's coolness toward the Third Reich. Our understanding of this reserve is advanced if we distinguish two phases in his attitude toward the Nazis during the period from the early 1930's to his death. During the first phase, which extended at least until the latter part of 1933 and perhaps as late as the middle of 1934, his position toward the Nazis was similar to that which he had taken in 1923. He welcomed them, but he wished to see them used and held in check by those on the Right to whom he felt closer. During the second phase, which lasted until his death, he felt that the Nazis were contributing less than he had hoped to prepare the way for true Caesarism and that they might even be initiating developments that would interfere with its emergence. His basic position during the two phases was similar; what changed was his assessment of the consequences of Nazi tactics.

He was willing to be indulgent, if patronizing toward the Nazis during the first phase. As the largest group on the Right after the Reichstag elections of 1930, they probably appeared to him as an indispensable reservoir of strength for the Right. In the presidential election of 1932—or at least in the run-off election that became necessary when no candidate received a majority of the votes—he voted for Hitler.[145] A vote for Hitler would have made sense to Spengler since Hitler was the candidate of the Right and Hindenburg had to run as the candidate of the middle and Social Democrats. A vote for the Communist candidate, Ernst Thälmann, was obviously out of the question. Both before and after the presidential election Spengler complained to Reusch about Cossmann and the editorial policies of the *Münchner Neueste Nachrichten*. Foremost among Spengler's grievances was that the newspaper often made derogatory remarks about the Nazis, but did not immediately add similarly critical remarks about the Social Democrats.[146]

[145] See Koktanek, "Spenglers Verhältnis zum Nationalsozialismus," p. 50.
[146] Letter of May 9, 1932 from Spengler to Reusch in *Briefe*, p. 663. See also *Briefe*, pp. 647, 649, 663, 680–81. Samples of the findings of ongoing research into Reusch's activities during the early 1930's, including his forceful efforts to steer the policies of the *Münchner Neueste Nachrichten* and his pact with Hitler to secure more favorable press treatment of the Nazis, can be found in Henry A.

While cautiously welcoming the "National Revolution" in 1933, Spengler distrusted the National Socialists.[147] He withheld his blessing for the party, despite the public belief, widespread among both Nazis and others, that he not only belonged in its ranks but also was one of its most prominent mentors. Privately, he referred to the new cabinet as a Mardi Gras Ministry (*Faschingsministerium*). He expected that it would not last long, and he urged upon an acquaintance in the publishing industry the urgent need to consider how "the national movement as such," which Spengler did not identify simply with the Nazis, could be saved from going under despite "the grotesque incompetence of the leading cliques in the parties."[148] On more than one occasion, the Nazis attempted to convince him to make a public gesture of enthusiastic support for the new regime, and in the summer of 1933 he had a long private meeting with Hitler. But Spengler was willing to cooperate only on his own terms. He demanded the freedom to criticize the regime freely and the cessation of the growing attacks on him in the press. For a while he had reason to believe that he might be able to play the public role of a respected elder statesman and perhaps serve also as a private adviser to Hitler, but by the end of 1933 these hopes had largely evaporated.[149] While many of Spengler's friends and acquaintances on the Right began to move away from him, some went out of their way to indicate their appreciation of his courage.[150]

By 1934 Nazi publicists were removing the stops from their attacks on Spengler. Denounced for his "pessimism," he was denied the honor of a place among the prophets of national socialism.[151] In an unmistakable public reference to Spengler, Hitler himself joined the chorus of Spengler's detractors.[152] The major reason for the rising hostility of the Nazis toward Spengler is clear; he failed to cooperate with them. In the vituperativeness of their attacks, Spengler probably found con-

Turner, Jr., "The *Ruhrlade*, Secret Cabinet of Heavy Industry in the Weimar Republic," *Central European History*, III (1970), 217–18, and Kurt Koszyk, ed., "Paul Reusch und die 'Münchner Neuesten Nachrichten': Zum Problem Industrie und Presse in der Endphase der Weimarer Republik," *Vierteljahrshefte für Zeitgeschichte*, XX (1972), 75–103.

[147] See *JdE*, esp. the introduction (dated July 1933). Most of *JdE* had been written before Hitler became chancellor on January 30.

[148] Spengler to Dr. Alfred Knittel, Feb. 14, 1933 in *Briefe*, p. 682.

[149] See *Briefe*, pp. 698–99, 709–11; Koktanek, "Spenglers Verhältnis zum Nationalsozialismus," pp. 51–52.

[150] See Josef Maria Graf von Soden-Fraunhofen to Spengler, Sept. 22, 1933 in *Briefe*, pp. 705–06.

[151] See Stutz, *Oswald Spengler*, pp. 236–39; Hughes, *Oswald Spengler*, pp. 120–36.

[152] See the quotation from Hitler's speech of May 1, 1935 in Adolf Hitler, *Reden und Proklamationen 1932–1945*, ed. Max Domarus (Munich, [1965?]), I, 502.

firmation of the correctness of his aloofness. He may have drawn similar conclusions from the "Blood Purge" of June 1934, which struck down Gregor Strasser from whom Spengler probably still hoped for improvement within the Nazi party.[153]

What had begun seemingly as a quarrel among comrades-in-arms now assumed the character of a serious breach. We may have to know more than we do at present about the interplay between Nazi policy and big business, the relationship between competing big business interests jockeying for advantage, and the relations between Spengler and big businessmen during the early 1930's before his attitudes are fully explicable.[154] He may have shared the fears of state control common among big businessmen, especially those who believed that their competitors had closer ties to the Nazi party; or his old complaint that big businessmen did not know how best to pursue their own best interests may have taken on new meaning to him. There is little in the available evidence to permit us to go beyond such conjectures.

We are left, then, with more easily documented speculations. The demagogic exploitation of the elite concept by the Nazis repelled Spengler. He believed in German superiority, but not in the racial superiority of Germans. His concept of race contradicted that of the party's ideologists, and the experiences of the early years of the Nazi regime seem to have led him to clarify the concept a bit, if only to himself. In notes that he left among his papers he wrote: "There are no noble and ignoble races. There are only noble and ignoble types and specimens in *all* races."[155]

Perhaps he never forgave the Nazis for having seemed to "prolong" the life of the Weimar Republic. He had often made clear that he did not expect a mass party to provide reliable assistance for the creation of his elite. Certainly he viewed the leading Nazis, including Hitler, with a snobbish contempt that ill-befitted his own praise for an open elite. More importantly, Spengler never overcame his fear that the Nazis had no intention of creating an elite largely on the basis of the old social coalition. In his last major political work, published only months after the Nazis came to power, Spengler warned: "All really great leaders in history move to the Right, however low the depths

[153] See Koktanek, "Spenglers Verhältnis zum Nationalsozialismus," p. 49, n. 44.

[154] The most detailed study of big business during the early years of the Nazi regime, Arthur Schweitzer's *Big Business in the Third Reich* (Bloomington, Indiana, 1964), focuses on the defeat of *Mittelstand*-oriented corporatist measures and does not raise or pursue many issues about the in-fighting among big businessmen. For example, his index contains no mention of Reusch, Haniel, or the *Gutehoffnungshütte*.

[155] Hildegard Kornhardt, ed., " 'Deutschland in Gefahr:' Fragmente zum 2. Band der 'Jahre der Entscheidung' von Oswald Spengler," *Echo der Woche: Unabhängige Wochenzeitung* (Munich), Sept. 17, 1948, p. 6. Spengler's italics.

from which they have climbed. It is the mark of the *born* master and ruler. . . ."[156] The rhetoric as well as some of the actions of the Nazis misled him into believing that they favored the leveling and egalitarianism that he identified with the Left. In the notes found among his private papers, he complained that the Nazis did not know whether they stood on the Right or on the Left.[157] Like many other conservative Germans, Spengler was unwilling to accept the largely illusory concessions to the Left that his own works implied must be made. He shied away from the demagoguery that he himself had recommended. He shared the apprehensions about a Nazi-led social upheaval expressed by the conservative Hermann Rauschning after some years of working closely with the National Socialists.[158] Spengler wrote in his notes that the Nazis' hatred for the Bolsheviks was so great because the Nazis feared their competition, which was acute due to the similarity between the two parties in "origins, tendencies, methods, and capabilities. . . . It is painful to know," he continued, "that every step [taken by the Nazis] was taken fifteen years ago in Moscow."[159] Despite these reckless charges, Spengler was still willing to grant that national socialism might be a protoform of the coming Caesarism.

This concession suggests another, more elusive aspect of Spengler's attitude toward the Third Reich—his wish to be known by future generations as the master of historical metaphysics and the prophet of Caesarism. His hopes of playing an active political role had been checked, if only by his own vanity. He wanted to be remembered as a detached and unerring visionary. This reputation might best be enhanced if he did not publicly identify himself too closely with any contemporary cause or leader. After all, the true prophet looked to the future, and with luck his carping would be recalled later as profundity.

[156] *JdE*, p. 140. Spengler's italics.

[157] Kornhardt, " 'Deutschland in Gefahr,' " p. 6.

[158] See esp. Hermann Rauschning, *The Revolution of Nihilism: Warning to the West*, trans. E. W. Dickes (New York, 1939).

[159] Kornhardt, " 'Deutschland in Gefahr,' " p. 6.

CHAPTER NINE

Count Hermann Keyserling and His School of Wisdom: Grand Seigneurs, Sages, and Rulers

THE prevailing, usually unstated assumption in much of the scholarly literature on twentieth-century Europe and the United States is that the Right is nationalistic. The key to understanding the doctrines and activities of the Right is found in "nationalism," qualified perhaps by an adjective such as "extreme." Ignazio Silone's remark that "Fascism is exaggerated nationalism"[1] might well serve as the motto of most Western historical scholarship on the Right, particularly on German rightists and fascists. The subtitle of a major work on neoconservatism reads "The Political Ideas of German Nationalism between 1918 and 1933."[2] While "hypernationalism" is considered characteristic of the Right, internationalism and cosmopolitanism are seen as objects of the Right's distrust or scorn. Even a cursory inspection of the indexes in studies of the Right turns up numerous references to "nationalism," but a careful search through these indexes discloses few references to "cosmopolitanism" and "internationalism," and almost invariably these pertain to targets of the Right's hostility.

Yet the Right has endorsed many forms of internationalism during the twentieth century. More than half a century ago the bold generalizations of Lenin's *Imperialism* suggested that the institutions of monopoly capital are conducive to the development of bourgeois internationalism and cosmopolitanism as well as bourgeois nationalism.[3]

---

[1] Quoted in Angelo Del Boca and Mario Giovana, *Fascism Today: A World Survey*, trans. R. H. Boothroyd (New York, 1969), p. 441.

[2] Kurt Sontheimer, *Antidemokratisches Denken in der Weimarer Republik: Die politischen Ideen des deutschen Nationalismus zwischen 1918 und 1933* (Munich, 1962). Sontheimer's use of the phrase "des deutschen Nationalismus" is rooted in a usage—much more common in Germany than France and some other European countries—that tends to employ the terms "conservatives," "the Right," and "nationalists" interchangeably. This tendency was strengthened by the name of the major party of the Right during the Weimar Republic, the *Deutschnationale Volkspartei*. When Waldemar Gurian (using the pseudonym Walter Gerhart) wrote his pioneering study of German neoconservatism, *Um des Reiches Zukunft: Nationale Wiedergeburt oder politische Reaktion?* (Freiburg im Breisgau, 1932), he referred to his subject as "der neue Nationalismus."

[3] V. I. Lenin, *Imperialism: The Highest Stage of Capitalism* (New York, 1939), esp. pp. 74–75, 117–18. See also Lenin's "The United States of Europe Slogan"

Within a given nation state, apologists of imperialism appeal repeatedly to nationalist sentiments; the exploitation of nationalism and its use as an ideological screen play a major role in domestic politics, justifying imperialist structures and demanding, in the name of the nation, support for one or another rival international business venture. But the supranational character of monopoly capital compels the frequent intertwining of nationalism with internationalism. Both the ramifications of worldwide ties among monopoly capitalists and the domestic institutions of imperialist societies require at times the dissemination and cultivation of internationalist ideas. As Hannah Arendt has indicated, the development of imperialism undermines the historical foundations of the nation-state and fosters the growth of right-wing movements whose objectives are not merely nonnational, but antinational and international.[4]

Historians have long realized that nationalism means different things at different places and times; but particularly in the West, they and other scholars seem to forget some of the implications of this truism when they neglect to examine the diverse contexts in which internationalism and cosmopolitanism have developed during the twentieth century. Thus they treat the supranationalism of Nazi Pan-European doctrines during World War II either as a mere stratagem designed to enlist support for German expansion from the peoples of other nations, or as a racist product of the ideological mania of National Socialist organizations like the SS.[5] Scholars in the West are usually undiscriminating in their discussion of movements after World War II for Western European unity, failing, for example, to explore the class content and function of the internationalism of the Christian Democratic parties on the Continent. Although many of these scholars analyze the sectional interests served by various types of twentieth-century nationalism, they rarely look for the sectional interests advanced by any form of internationalism. The ease with which most Western historians have accepted the view that the investigation of the German Right during the Weimar Republic is a problem in the study of an aberrant nation-

---

(1915) in his *Marx, Engels, Marxism,* 5th English ed. (Moscow, 1953), pp. 359–64.

[4] Hannah Arendt, *The Origins of Totalitarianism* (New York: Meridian paperback, 1958), pp. 126, 131, 153–55, 226–27, 269–70, and passim.

[5] See, e.g., Hans-Dietrich Loock, "Zur 'grossgermanischen Politik' des dritten Reiches," *Vierteljahrshefte für Zeitgeschichte,* VIII (1960), 39–41, 49; Paul Kluke, "Nationalsozialistische Europaideologie," *ibid.,* III (1955), 240–75; Karl Dietrich Bracher, *Die deutsche Diktatur: Entstehung, Struktur, Folgen des Nationalsozialismus,* 2nd ed. (Cologne, 1969), p. 443. See the Bibliographical Essay, Section II, B for some specific suggestions about the type of research on internationalism that is needed.

alism poses a promising subject for a historical inquiry that will, hopefully, be undertaken someday.

No doubt the German Right during the Weimar Republic is properly associated with nationalistic ideas. On balance, the Right espoused nationalism more vigorously and persistently than internationalism; the latter was usually subordinated to the former. But in some rightist circles internationalist ideals were cherished. As in the commitment to Pan-Europeanism and Franco-German understanding by Stresemann's wing of the People's party (DVP), often the form of internationalism embraced served to foster the consolidation and extension of the institutions of monopoly capitalism. The articulation of other types of internationalism was less directly related to the consolidation and extension of these institutions, and was not primarily a reflex response to the transient tactical requirements of a section of the bourgeoisie.

Illustrative of one of these latter types of internationalism are the elitist views of Count Hermann Keyserling, whose cosmopolitan, internationalist ideals overshadowed his nationalism. A Baltic nobleman, he came from a background conducive to a cosmopolitanism often reminiscent of that of Metternich or of the Hungarian magnates during the nineteenth century. Many other Germans born and raised outside the boundaries of the Bismarckian Empire, including Keyserling's fellow Baltic Germans the historians Theodor Schiemann and Johannes Haller, became fervid nationalists. Keyserling identified himself with many of the internationalist themes sounded by the German Right when he made Germany his home after World War I. An examination of his elitism provides a good corrective to the caricature of conservatism drawn by those who stress unduly the nationalism of the Right.

His conservatism, although flexible and modernized, had much in common with the early nineteenth-century proponents of the nobility. The old conservative core of his elitism was masked both by his posture of indulgence toward the twentieth century and by his aversion to any simple restoration of the past. Like the conservative of the early nineteenth century, he postulated the need for passivity on the part of the populace. He hoped for the development of an elite whose rule would rest upon the recognition by the masses of their own inferiority and would not entail their permanent mobilization. Although he acknowledged some of the advantages that many neoconservative and new liberal elitists found in mass mobilization, his attitude toward it was scarcely equivocal, for example, as was that of Spengler. Keyserling even distrusted the notion, which, as we shall see in Chapter Ten, became common on the Right after 1918, of a final mobilization of the masses that would lead speedily to their permanent demobilization.

While placing him closer to traditionally minded conservatives, this distrust limited his ability to appeal successfully to a broad segment of the Right, as Spengler did. Far less systematic than Spengler—or, for that matter, than any other elitist to whom this study is devoted— he did not bother to try to work out a comprehensive, detailed political philosophy. His contempt for systematic thought contributed to this predisposition that brought him closer than Spengler to the suspicion of theory characteristic of nineteenth-century conservatism. But Keyserling's attractiveness to traditionally minded conservatives was diminished by his pointed criticisms of them. The sense of irony and flashes of humor that enlivened his work may have made it appear less dependable than Spengler's stolid prose, brightened only now and then by a clever turn of phrase. Thus Keyserling did not come to occupy a central position on the Right, as Spengler did after 1919. Keyserling became the gadfly of the Right. He sought to establish himself as a genial critic of all political camps, and he came to associate as much with men from the middle of the political spectrum as with those of the Right.

THE ODYSSEY OF A "BALTIC BARON"

As a cultivated aristocrat who traveled extensively, Keyserling viewed the world with an aloofness that facilitated the articulation of his conservative elitism while rarely tying him closely to specific political causes. He was nearly forty when he settled in Germany. Apparently he regarded political questions as of little consequence until World War I, and only at the end of the war did he become actively engaged politically, if at the periphery of formal political life. He was always somewhat of an outsider in Germany; he remained, as he had been since childhood, an aristocrat attempting the impossible task of straddling not simply two, but several lands in a period of nation-states. To the end of his life, he retained a strong sense of superiority and a feeling of "being above it all." The air of relaxation and detachment that he cultivated carefully was no mere pose, but an important facet of his personality and a key to his elitism. His elite theories owed much to his origins as a Baltic German nobleman, and not surprisingly in view of his enormous self-esteem, he regarded himself as an excellent model for the new aristocrats whom he hoped to see elevated to a position of power. Often, only his urbanity and his sensitivity to the general tasks of conservatism prevented his elitism from becoming merely an *apologia pro vita sua*.

Keyserling was born in 1880 in Könno, Livonia, in an area then belonging to the Russian Empire and subsequently included in the Latvian Republic. He spent his earliest years at the nearby family estate, Rayküll, in a section that later became part of the Estonian Republic. The small, closely knit group of Baltic Barons into which he was born occupied a position in Russia's Baltic provinces similar to that of the Junkers in East Elbian Prussia. Holding large estates worked by peasant labor, the German noblemen in the Baltic lands of Courland, Livonia, and Estonia had extensive prerogatives. Yet there were several important differences between the Junkers and the Baltic noblemen that fostered among the latter a greater sense of confidence and a more cosmopolitan outlook.[6] The Baltic Barons ruled over an almost exclusively non-German population. Their relationship both to their peasants and to the Tsarist autocracy did not permit them to identify themselves with nationalism.

Two other differences also set them apart from the Junkers. Not only did the estates in the Baltic provinces tend to be considerably larger, but also medieval institutions had undergone less change. As Keyserling noted with some hyperbole, he spent his early years in a semi-feudal atmosphere "the likes of which had not been seen elsewhere in Europe since the eighteenth century."[7] Through the provincial diets and similar corporative institutions, the noblemen governed the Baltic lands and held a tight rein on the countryside. Before the Russian Revolution of 1905, which involved the Baltic provinces as well as other parts of the Empire, the self-assurance of the Baltic nobility and its confidence in the indefinite perpetuation of its rule was unshaken. "A fossil in an age of industrialism and nationalism,"[8] the Baltic nobility as a group retained much of its aplomb until the end of World War I.

For many decades after the incorporation of the Baltic lands into the Russian Empire in the eighteenth century, the Baltic noblemen remained undisputed masters of their own territories. Until the middle of the nineteenth century, the Tsarist regime did not tamper with the institutions of the provinces. Many Baltic nobles served in high military and civil positions elsewhere in the Empire of the Tsars. Little wonder that the legend that Germans were the real rulers of Russia lingered well into the twentieth century. Although intermarriage led to the absorption of many Baltic families by the Russian aristocracy,

[6] See Georg Hermann Schlingensiepen, *Der Strukturwandel des baltischen Adels in der Zeit vor dem 1. Weltkrieg* (Marburg, 1959), esp. pp. 1–2, 5, 28, 80–81, 103–04, 113. The following paragraphs draw heavily upon this work, as well as Reinhard Wittram's *Baltische Geschichte: Die Ostseelande Livland, Estland, Kurland 1180–1918* (Munich, 1954).

[7] "Sinnbilder aus meinem Leben" in Otto Taube et al., *Das Buch der Keyserlinge: An der Grenze zweier Welten. Lebenserinnerungen aus einem Geschlecht* (Berlin, 1937), p. 401.

[8] Schlingensiepen, *Strukturwandel des baltischen Adels*, p. 1.

often this assimilation was not complete. Some Baltic noble families became intertwined with Russian families without resettling permanently outside the Baltic provinces and without undergoing complete Russification. With poetic license Keyserling referred to his father as a "typical Russian grand seigneur."[9] As a consequence of intermarriage with Russian aristocrats, one side of the family claimed to be descended from Genghis Khan, a relationship that Keyserling made much of until he discovered during the Nazi period that the legend was unfounded.[10]

After the middle of the nineteenth century, beginning notably with the reforms of Tsar Alexander II, the Tsarist regime attempted to introduce some Russian institutions into the Baltic provinces. The introduction of these institutions was not systematic, and there was no attempt to destroy the basic institutions through which the Baltic nobility exercised its hegemony.

The Russification policy initiated during the 1880's posed a more serious problem, for the perpetuation of this hegemony was, in the long run, incompatible with the transformation of the Empire of the Tsars into a nation-state. The allegiance of the Baltic nobleman was to the person of the Tsar and to the Tsarist Empire, not to a nation-state. The Baltic nobleman had a homeland, his province, but not a fatherland. The Tsarist policy of Russification deepened his commitment to German culture without making him into a German nationalist. For centuries he had ruled over a population consisting largely of Letts, Estonians, and Lithuanians, none of whose mother tongue was either a Germanic or a Slavic language. The population of the Baltic provinces, which had reached several million by 1914, included only about 160,000 Germans.[11] Division along nationality lines coincided with division along social lines more closely than perhaps anywhere else in Europe. Those German Balts who were not noblemen—and most German Balts were commoners—were, for the most part, businessmen, craftsmen, and professionals. The Germans had not pursued a policy of Germanization in the Baltic lands. German culture had been a mark

[9] "My Life and My Work as I See Them" in *The World in the Making*, trans. Maurice Samuel (New York, 1927), p. 13.
[10] See "Vorfahren" in his posthumously published autobiographical volume *Reise durch die Zeit, I: Ursprünge und Entfaltungen* (Vaduz, Liechtenstein, 1948), p. 38, n. 1. The second and third volumes of this work appeared as vols. 2 (Darmstadt and Baden-Baden, 1958) and 3 (Innsbruck, 1963) of Keyserling's *Die gesammelten Werke*, endgültige Neuausgabe. They will be cited as *Reise durch die Zeit*, II and III. To date, only three volumes of the *Gesammelte Werke* have appeared, although six are planned. Work on an edition of Keyserling's correspondence prepared by Professor Hans G. Wiebe of the University of Toronto has been underway for some years.
[11] Wittram, *Baltische Geschichte*, p. 234.

of social superiority. Although the non-German population was not attracted to Russification, resistance to Russification tended to pit the Baltic Germans against the other Baltic peoples. A common defense in the name of provincial liberties against Russification had become impossible with the rise of the Latvian, Estonian, and Lithuanian national movements. The Germans could not join the ranks of these national movements without giving up distinctions that had traditionally set them apart from the vast majority of the population and signified their superiority. The struggle against Russification thus accentuated both ethnic and social divisions. The national movements of the Letts, Estonians, and Lithuanians were directed against the cultural hegemony of the Germans as well as against a nobility and bourgeoisie that were stigmatized as consisting of foreigners. Until 1905 these national movements were confined largely to the towns, and hence the potential danger was easily underestimated by the nobility.

Closely related to the threat posed by the national movements were other new forces. By the late nineteenth century, industrialization and the working-class movement that accompanied its advance were beginning to develop rapidly. As in Germany, migration from countryside to town and the growth of the urban bourgeoisie threatened the hegemony of the landed nobility, but in the Baltic lands industrialization contributed also to the growth of divisive national movements. Industrialization drew non-Germans into the rapidly expanding, and once largely German, ports of Riga, Reval (Tallin), and Libau (Lepaya). The class struggles of the new industrial workers tended inevitably to assume a national character and to pit German against Lett or Estonian.

The placidity of the Baltic nobility in the face of the forces that were beginning to undermine its position seems remarkable. Even after the Revolution of 1905, the Baltic nobleman's belief in the legitimacy of his position persisted; he could scarcely conceive of a day when it would vanish. Keyserling grew up with a secure place in the commanding heights of a society that seemed to most of its lords destined to endure forever. He never experienced the panic that was to grip younger and less socially secure Baltic Germans like Alfred Rosenberg, an artisan's son who studied architecture in Riga and later became a prominent Nazi ideologist.

The self-assurance of the Baltic nobility was enhanced by the feeling of equality that prevailed in its ranks. As Keyserling pointed out with pride, there was no special caste or group of high nobles in the Baltic lands.[12] He regarded himself as the peer of any other member of the nobility and the superior of any commoner.

[12] "Vorfahren," pp. 44–49.

Keyserling also prided himself on not coming from a military family. Since the eighteenth century, he was fond of noting, no Keyserling of importance had been a professional soldier (*Krieger*).[13] He might have added that this absence of a family military tradition was more common among the Baltic Barons than among the Prussian Junkers. By the second half of the nineteenth century, the Baltic noblemen were usually not closely associated with the army, and the institution of the reserve officer never came to have the importance in Baltic society that it did in Prussia. Keyserling's paternal grandfather, Alexander Keyserling, was a famous educator who for many years was director (*Kurator*) of the Baltic university of Dorpat and whom Bismarck sought unsuccessfully to lure to the post of Prussian minister of education. Another close relative on his father's side, Eduard Keyserling, became well known in Germany as a philosopher. On his mother's side of the family, leaders of the nobility were prominent. His maternal grandfather occupied, as *Landesmarschall*, the highest elective office among the Livonian nobility.

Keyserling received his early education at home in the family circle. This instruction and his later schooling provided him with a broad, cosmopolitan culture.[14] After graduating from the Russian *Gymnasium* in the Baltic town of Pernau (Pärnu) in 1897, he studied at the University of Geneva for a year. Returning to the Baltic lands in 1898, he spent the next two years at the University of Dorpat. He appears to have been unperturbed by the Russification to which the university was then being subjected.[15] At Dorpat he became an *Urbursch*, a hard-drinking, raucous, cavorting "fraternity man." ". . . Without a doubt," he later commented, "I was the most unintellectual and most brutally animalistic of Dorpat's *Korpsstudenten*."[16] Like Max Weber, he soon passed beyond this stage in his life. After sustaining severe wounds in a duel, he underwent what he later denoted, without elaborating, an "inner change."[17] Taking up his studies more seriously, he went to Ger-

---

[13] *Ibid.*, p. 37.

[14] See the biographical sketch by his Baltic neighbor and *Jugendfreund* Otto Taube, "Aus Keyserlings Elternhaus und Erziehung" in *Graf Hermann Keyserling: Ein Gedächtnisbuch*, ed. Keyserling-Archiv, Innsbruck-Mühlau (Innsbruck, 1948), pp. 105–10.

[15] The Russification of Dorpat reached its high point while Keyserling was a student. See Wittram, *Baltische Geschichte*, pp. 180, 225, 232.

[16] Keyserling, "Graf Hermann Keyserling" in Raymund Schmidt, ed., *Philosophie der Gegenwart in Selbstdarstellungen*, IV (Leipzig, 1923), p. 102. Hereafter this essay will be cited simply as "Keyserling."

[17] *Ibid.* Although there were many similarities between the student *Korporationen* in Germany and in the Baltic lands, dueling was not a custom of the Baltic *Korporationen*. (See Wittram, *Baltische Geschichte*, pp. 178–79.) Hence there may have been no direct relationship between Keyserling's duel and his membership in a *Korporation*.

many. Following a short stay at Heidelberg, he moved on to Vienna, where he received a doctorate in geology in 1902.

Although he undertook another geological study after completing his doctoral dissertation, he soon wandered away from the natural sciences, and there is little trace in his subsequent writings of his early work in geology. The decisive change in his life seems to have occurred shortly after he obtained his doctorate. For a few years the predominant intellectual influence in his life became the expatriate Englishman Houston Stewart Chamberlain, whose popular philosophical writings were widely discussed in Wilhelminian Germany. Chamberlain's most famous work, *The Foundations of the Nineteenth Century*,[18] made a great impression upon Keyserling when he read—or reread—it in 1902.[19] Apparently the impact of Chamberlain's writings and personal contacts with the man himself turned Keyserling's attention to philosophy. He later asserted somewhat implausibly that he was never drawn to "Chamberlain's racism, Pan-Germanism, hostility to democracy and liberalism—the things that made Chamberlain a powerful political and intellectual influence."[20] Keyserling claimed that Chamberlain's "universality" had attracted him from afar.[21] However, Keyserling's admiration for the older man was probably at bottom due to Chamberlain's attack on democratic and liberal tendencies and his ability to express this dislike through a grandiose *Weltanschauung* that invoked the natural sciences while questioning their validity. For several years the two men were close friends. Keyserling visited Chamberlain's circle frequently, and they corresponded regularly. Chamberlain dedicated his book on Kant[22] to his young friend, and Keyserling reciprocated by dedicating his first philosophical work[23] to Chamberlain. Soon Keyserling began to move away from Chamberlain, and in 1910 an open break took place. Although continuing to admire Chamberlain as a "Renaissance man," Keyserling complained of his pettiness. The older man removed the dedication to Keyserling from subsequent editions of his book on Kant, although Keyserling left standing the reciprocal dedication in his own work.[24]

Much of Keyserling's time during the years of his friendship with

[18] H. S. Chamberlain, *Die Grundlagen des 19. Jahrhunderts*, 3rd ed. (2 vols., Munich, 1901). The first edition was published in 1899.

[19] "Keyserling," pp. 103–04.

[20] "Houston Stewart Chamberlain" in *Reise durch die Zeit*, I, 117.

[21] *Ibid.*, I, pp. 119, 134.

[22] H. S. Chamberlain, *Immanuel Kant: Die Persönlichkeit als Einfuhrüng in das Werk* (Munich, 1905).

[23] *Das Gefüge der Welt: Versuch einer kritischen Philosophie* (Munich, 1906).

[24] See "Houston Stewart Chamberlain," pp. 122–25, 128–34; "Keyserling," p. 104. In fairness to Chamberlain, it should be noted that his *Kant* was reprinted shortly, but Keyserling's book was not reprinted until after World War I.

Chamberlain was occupied with travels in Western Europe, Italy, and Greece. He wrote philosophical works for a broad audience and gave an occasional public lecture in Germany. In 1906 he attempted, how seriously is uncertain, to begin an academic career at the University of Berlin. According to his own account of the episode, the great philosopher Wilhelm Dilthey encouraged him, but the neo-Kantian Alois Riehl gently discouraged him.[25]

In Keyserling's earliest philosophical works, the basic approach that characterized his subsequent writings began to emerge clearly. He measured everything in accordance with its contribution to life. Like William James, he made "truth" dependent upon its usefulness. Keyserling's point of view has been described appropriately as one of the several types of "life-philosophy [*Lebensphilosophie*]" that began to become prominent in Germany at the end of the nineteenth century.[26] Drawing inspiration from Nietzsche's attack on traditional philosophies, the "life-philosophers" had much in common with the pragmatists in the United States and Henri Bergson in France. More obviously than all of our other elitists except Max Weber, Keyserling was concerned with establishing the importance of the irrational and the limitations of logical thought. He suggested, for example, that the world is probably neither finite nor infinite, even though logically a third possibility could not exist. Like Bergson with whom he became friendly,[27] he stressed the priority of movement and becoming.

[25] "Keyserling," pp. 109–10.

[26] I. M. Bocheński, *Contemporary European Philosophy*, trans. Donald Nicholl and Karl Aschenbrenner (Berkeley, 1957), pp. 101–02; Heinrich Adolph, *Die Philosophie des Grafen Keyserling* (Stuttgart, 1927), p. 4. Written by an admirer of Keyserling, the work by Adolph is one of the best of the numerous studies of Keyserling's philosophy, most of which were published during the 1920's. Three other works, all by Frenchmen, stand out: Maurice Boucher, *La philosophie de Hermann Keyserling*, 5th ed. (Paris, 1927); Louis Brun, "Hermann von Keyserling et son école de sagesse," *Revue germanique*, xviii (1927), 1–12, 103–13; xix (1928), 14–20, 117–25; Ernest Seillière, *La sagesse de Darmstadt* (Paris, 1929). Testifying to the lively interest in Keyserling in France, these three French studies alternate praise and criticism. Although perhaps the best of the three, Seillière's work abounds in reckless statements about Keyserling's intellectual debts. M. G. Parkes, *Introduction to Keyserling: An Account of the Man and His Work* (London, 1934) is the only extended study of Keyserling in English and deals with most of his career, but is uncritical. The chapter on Keyserling in Will Durant's *Adventures in Genius* (New York, 1931) is worthy of note only as an indication of Keyserling's popularity in the United States during the 1920's and 1930's. Adequate brief introductions to his philosophy can be found in *Friedrich Überwegs Grundriss der Geschichte der Philosophie*, Part 4: *Die deutsche Philosophie des 19. Jahrhunderts und der Gegenwart*, 12th ed., ed. T. K. Oesterreich (Berlin, 1923), pp. 478–79; and *The Encyclopedia of Philosophy*, ed. Paul Edwards (New York, 1967), iv.

[27] "Keyserling," p. 109.

Eschewing all traditional philosophical systems, Keyserling claimed that professional philosophers, with a few notable exceptions like Bergson and Georg Simmel, had played a small role in his life.[28]

In 1908, his *Wanderjahre* seemingly over, Keyserling took up permanent residence on his ancestral estate, Rayküll. For a while he apparently settled into a life of aristocratic leisure, punctuated by some writing, an occasional holiday, and correspondence with some of the brightest stars in the European intellectual firmament.[29] Yet he must have felt uncomfortable: he had not established himself in the academic, if bourgeois, intellectual world, and the life of a country gentleman did not satisfy him.

Soon he decided to set out on a trip around the world. From this journey, which began in 1911, emerged the book of random reflections that made him famous—*The Travel Diary of a Philosopher.*[30] Asking himself what drove him out into the wide world after the completion of his *Wanderjahre*, he replied: ". . . That which has driven so many into a cloister: the longing for self-realization."[31] The philosophies and religions of the Orient had begun to captivate him, and he used his journey, which took him through India, China, and Japan as well as North America, to intensify his pursuit of subjects such as Buddhism, occultism, and theosophy. Characteristic of his philosophy-of-life approach was his exploration of the value, for his own life, of any body of beliefs that seemed rewarding. It was probably to the period of his world journey that he referred when he wrote later that he had tried to become a "master in the oriental sense," but had abandoned the attempt after discovering that "this ideal required for its realization an intrinsic nature that I lack."[32] When he returned to his homeland, he found the atmosphere of Europe uncongenial. Until the outbreak of World War I, he toyed repeatedly with the idea of emigrating to Asia

[28] *Ibid.*

[29] He later claimed to have maintained a correspondence that included Bertrand Russell, Rathenau, Max and Alfred Weber, A. J. Balfour, R. B. Haldane, Benedetto Croce, Bergson, and Gustave Le Bon. See, e.g., "Keyserling," p. 111.

[30] *Das Reisetagebuch eines Philosophen,* 5th ed. (2 vols., Darmstadt, 1921). Hereafter cited as *Reisetagebuch.* The first edition appeared in 1918.

[31] *Ibid.*, I, 5. Where an English translation of one of Keyserling's works is available, I have often used it as the basis of my own translation. Keyserling knew English rather well and seems to have checked the English translations of his works carefully. However, as the British translator of the *Reisetagebuch* discovered, Keyserling's conception of translation was at times overly, and at other times underly, exacting. See J. Holroyd Reece's preface to *The Travel Diary of a Philosopher* (2 vols., New York and London, 1925). In general, the English translations of Keyserling's works are written in a more colloquial style than either the original or the French translations.

[32] *Menschen als Sinnbilder* (Darmstadt, 1926), p. 23.

and living out his days as a hermit.[33] He anticipated little success for his *Travel Diary*.

The outbreak of the war led to his virtual isolation on his estate in Rayküll and delayed the book's publication. When it finally appeared in 1918, it had, as Keyserling observed, a much better chance of success than it would have had a few years earlier since the atmosphere in Europe had changed so much during the war.[34] Like Spengler, he received the Nietzsche Archive prize in 1919.

Keyserling's alternation of pessimistic reflections on the course of history and the mass of mankind with optimistic reflections on the potential of the individual caught on with a substantial segment of the postwar reading public. His conservative, indeed, reactionary, impulses often appeared clearly in the *Travel Diary*:

> A feeling which resembles sorrow steals over me. It is explicable enough: no matter how much I may be an intellectual, I still feel the fundamental instincts of the knight very vitally in me, and they no longer fit into this age. The days of the nobleman are numbered. What folly to see in this fact a sign of unqualified progress! The typical traits of the nobleman do not, of course, imply absolute values, but absolute values are innate in no manifestation. . . . The knightly concept of honor is theoretically a prejudice, but so is the professional honor of the merchant, and what the freethinker proudly calls his lack of bias.[35]

During most of World War I, Keyserling seems to have done little writing other than revising the manuscript of his *Travel Diary* and preparing some somber reflections, published in British and American periodicals, on the significance of the war.[36] He later suggested that "the horror of the World War made clear to me for the first time that detachment in the sense in which I had attained it was by no means an ideal condition."[37] Despite his belief that the days of the old nobility were numbered, he did not foresee the abrupt changes that would compel him to reorient his life and that led to his adoption of a more articulate political position.

Like many other Baltic Germans, Keyserling probably welcomed the overrunning of the Baltic provinces by the imperial German army in 1917. The war had eroded the loyalty of the Baltic Germans to the Russian Empire, especially when the March Revolution in Russia en-

---

[33] *Ibid.*, p. 66.   [34] *Ibid.*

[35] *Reisetagebuch*, ɪɪ, 617.

[36] See "On the Meaning of the War," *Hibbert Journal*, xɪɪɪ (Apr. 1915), 533–45; "A Philosopher's View of the War," *Atlantic Monthly*, cxvɪɪ (Feb. 1916), 145–53.

[37] "Keyserling," p. 115.

couraged the forces of revolution and nationalism among the other Baltic peoples. Certainly the German occupation was important to him if only because it enabled him to go at last to Germany to facilitate the publication of his *Travel Diary*. The defeat of Germany in 1918 triggered a civil war in the Baltic provinces. The intervention of German, British, and White Russian military forces thwarted full-scale social revolution, but the newly founded Baltic republics expropriated almost all of the holdings of the Baltic Barons. Keyserling clung, although probably not as tenaciously as some of his peers,[38] to the hope that an alternative to the Baltic national states might be worked out. As late as 1920, he found attractive what he called a "Belgian" solution that would establish a multinational Baltic state in which the Baltic Germans and the other Baltic peoples would live together "within the framework of a higher synthesis."[39]

At the time, Keyserling regarded the expropriation of his lands as a horrendous injustice that had needlessly compelled him to make a new start in life. Yet he was better prepared for this blow than the Junkers were for the much milder shock that they received at the end of the war. During the Revolution of 1905, while he was traveling in Sicily, he believed for some time that he had lost his lands, and when he became reconciled to the actual loss of his estates after the war, he looked back on this misapprehension as having helped to prepare him for the future.[40] During the Russian Revolution of 1917, he later claimed, he decided that becoming a citizen of Monaco would be appropriate to his future life. As he observed playfully, the taxes in Monaco were the lowest in Europe, and the danger of war did not exist there.[41] Equally characteristically, but more revealingly he once explained that he went to Germany when "a lordly life in the homeland" became impossible.[42] At the end of his life, he offered still another perspective on his expropriation. In 1944 he wrote that he now realized that secretly "I experienced the end of my life as a seigneur in 1918 and 1919 as liberation from the chains that had prevented the unencumbered flight of my spirit."[43]

Not long after his arrival in Germany, he married in keeping with his social status. His bride was a Bismarck, a granddaughter of the Iron Chancellor. Soon Keyserling found a way of providing a material basis for his new life in Germany—through writing, lecturing, and,

---

[38] See J. W. Hiden, "The Baltic Germans and German Policy towards Latvia after 1918," *The Historical Journal*, xiii (1970), 295–317.

[39] "Sinnbilder aus meinem Leben," p. 405.

[40] *Ibid.*, p. 403; "Keyserling," p. 109.

[41] *Das Spektrum Europas*, 2nd ed. (Heidelberg, 1928), p. 377.

[42] "Sinnbilder aus meinem Leben," p. 405.

[43] "Besitzende und Besitzlose" in *Reise durch die Zeit*, ii, 337.

probably most important, his new School of Wisdom. Identifying himself more closely with Germany than earlier or later in his life, but assuming the posture of a somewhat detached dispenser of sorely needed advice, he published several political pamphlets and articles from 1918 to 1921. The themes of these writings, which will be discussed later, were often similar to those of Spengler's "Prussiandom and Socialism," and Keyserling began to be known as an undoctrinaire man of the Right. His political writings, his public lectures, and the fame brought him by his *Travel Diary* helped to attract the attention that enabled him to found his School of Wisdom. Regarding journalism as a distasteful profession, he listened intently when a former Protestant pastor related how he had been able to support himself by public speaking engagements.[44] Keyserling was searching for an undemeaning way to earn a living: ". . . It was physiologically beyond me to adapt myself to the earning of money. I had once for all [sic] been settled as the independent country gentleman: a circumstance which had been strongly ratified [sic] by my artistic nature."[45]

Toward the end of 1919, Otto Reichl, a Darmstadt publisher, brought out a programmatic pamphlet by Keyserling calling for a School of Wisdom.[46] Reichl, who during the next decade was to publish Keyserling's works as well as the publications of the School of Wisdom, played an important role in promoting the project and gained the support of Grand Duke Ernst Ludwig of Hesse.[47] By October 1920 the Keyserlings were moving into the house in Darmstadt that had once been the residence of the Grand Duke's court chaplain. The following month the School of Wisdom officially opened its doors.[48]

In his posthumously published memoirs, Keyserling complained that Darmstadt was a dull, provincial town, but publicly he seldom let slip an opportunity to glamorize the founding of the institution that played a key role in his elitist ideas. In an essay published during the late 1920's in honor of the sixtieth birthday of the School's patron, he offered a contrived explanation of how his own ancestry had drawn him

---

[44] "Die Schule der Weisheit" (written 1940) in *Reise durch die Zeit*, ii, 227. Hereafter this essay will be cited as "Schule" (2) to distinguish it from an earlier essay of the same title which will be cited as "Schule" (1). Keyserling wrote the earlier essay for the first issue of the School of Wisdom's bulletin: *Der Weg zur Vollendung: Mitteilungen der Gesellschaft für freie Philosophie*, Schule der Weisheit Darmstadt, ed. Graf Hermann Keyserling, i (1920), 5–23. Hereafter the *Weg zur Vollendung* will be cited as *WzV*.

[45] "My Life and My Work as I See Them," p. 57.

[46] *Was uns Not tut, was ich will*, 4th ed. (Darmstadt, 1922).

[47] "Schule" (2), p. 228.

[48] See *ibid.*, p. 234; Werner Kilian von Tryller, "Die Eröffnung der Schule der Weisheit," *WzV*, i (1920), 49.

to settle in charming Darmstadt.[49] While the School existed, Keyserling delighted in depicting its establishment as having entailed a titanic struggle within himself:

> By nature I am solitary and an artist. I lack all personal urge for external activity; I never felt the need of intercourse with my fellow men, nor did I ever have the wish to convince others of the truths I progressively recognized. . . . The founding of the School of Wisdom came about as an act of duty. . . . My superliminal consciousness was . . . little prepared for the new task. . . . During the first terms at Darmstadt I had to do constant violence to my nature. But it was only my superliminal consciousness that resisted: this was unmistakably proved by the inner growth manifesting itself with increasing strength, the more I gave myself up to my activities.[50]

With his usual aplomb, Keyserling went on to compare himself with Socrates, Jesus, Saint Francis, Luther, and Confucius.

The School of Wisdom contributed to the growth of Keyserling's fame and the sale of his works, but he certainly did not become rich from his activities in Darmstadt. His School provided him with a home and a base for his activities; it also gave employment to men sympathetic to his outlook, many of whom were noblemen like himself. Although he seems to have been tempted to seek once again to enter the academic world, by the time he received a definite offer of a professorship from Vienna in 1921, he was well settled in his new routine.[51] Able to make do financially without entering upon a university career and apparently still feeling rebuffed by his earlier experiences with academicians, he became even more disdainful of professional philosophers. Later he ascribed this attitude to his consciousness of being both an aristocrat and an "artist": "On the whole, my aversion to the scholar was closely related to the typical hatred of the artist for the bourgeois. Scholarship is an essentially bourgeois affair. The kind of exactitude that it demands is pyschologically almost identical to the ponderousness of the philistine, which the nobleman has despised from time immemorial."[52]

Until 1927 Keyserling spent much of his time in Darmstadt. This "Darmstadt period" of his life included frequent lecture tours, mostly in Germany. Later, when the school began to decline, he spent much of his time abroad. In the mid-1920's he classified himself in social,

---

[49] See *Darmstadt und Grossherzog Ernst Ludwig* (Darmstadt, [1928]), p. 6.
[50] *Creative Understanding*, tr. Teresa Duerr (London, 1929), p. 382. This work is the English edition of *Schöpferische Erkenntnis* (Darmstadt, 1922). I have modified Duerr's translation of this and subsequently quoted passages.
[51] See "Schule" (2), p. 227; "Keyserling," p. 110n.
[52] "Wolkoff" in *Reise durch die Zeit*, I, 196.

ethnic, national, and cultural terms. This self-classification, expressed with the bravura in which he delighted, displayed his pretentious cosmopolitanism. He described himself as: "1. myself, 2. an aristocrat, 3. a Keyserling, 4. a Westerner, 5. a European, 6. a Balt [i.e., a Baltic German], 7. a German, 8. a Russian, and 9. a Frenchman."[53]

SPIRITUAL RENEWAL AND THE ELITE

Keyserling's unsystematic philosophy emphasizing the importance of the irrational supplied him with ways of upholding positions that were difficult or impossible to support rationally. Regarding truth as pragmatic, he defended prejudices as often valuable: "Most of what intellect discards as mere prejudice is in its essence so deeply connected with the very basis of life that in the long run it always regains its validity."[54] Like other proponents of *Lebensphilosophie*, Keyserling would not permit his empiricism to be limited by scientific experimentation or rational analysis. Everything important to life had some validity, and mere reason and intellect were much poorer guides than intuition and immediate appreciation. In a work published toward the end of his Darmstadt period, he gave a succinct summary of his general approach:

If I had to summarize in one sentence the distinctive aspects of my philosophy as contrasted to other modern philosophies, I would answer: I begin with the living soul in contrast to the abstract man. The abstract man was an invention of the eighteenth century. As a working hypothesis it had certain advantages; but, for it, there is only the general, and not the particular. The moral and spiritual side of man remained outside the development of progress.[55]

Keyserling believed that the task of the contemporary philosopher was to help to restore the balance between spirit and intellect. The philosopher should accent man's soul, but not in a "regressive way." Keyserling criticized proponents of life philosophy and irrationalism who sought to negate the philosophical achievements of the past two centuries. The philosopher should not deny the abstract man, and suppress intellect, but rather relate the abstract man once again to the totality of the living man.[56] Keyserling was not prepared to abandon rationalism completely or to return to some past ideal. Yet his attitude toward the development of technology reflected his uneasiness about

[53] *Spektrum Europas*, p. 451.   [54] *Creative Understanding*, p. 114.
[55] *Menschen als Sinnbilder*, p. 9.
[56] See, e.g., *ibid.*, p. 10; *Reisetagebuch*, i, 285–86; *Creative Understanding*, p. 125.

bourgeois civilization. He did not have a deep commitment to modern technology as Spengler and the new liberal elitists did. With a strong touch of resignation, Keyserling suggested that the development of technology was necessary and could not be stopped. Without technological progress, he explained wistfully, no civilization could survive in the twentieth century: "There is . . . no question of halting or checking technological progress, as so many idealists hope for. Should a form of civilization, even the most beautiful, stand in the way . . . it will be destroyed, as indeed the Chinese, the Turks, and the Russians have already destroyed their own traditions."[57]

Keyserling referred to his personalism and pluralism as "polyphonic thinking." This unsystematic mode of thought afforded him great flexibility in explaining his judgments on social and political issues. He had no fear of contradicting himself. Inconsistencies and contradictions were essential to his general approach. In a book on the United States published in the late 1920's, he belittled the importance of factual accuracy and stressed rather the potential impact of his assertions on his readers:

> I am fundamentally indifferent to the question whether I am correct in all my statements of facts. Most probably on many occasions I am not. And this not only because, in order to act creatively, I had to simplify, to exaggerate, to caricature even, as the case may be; what may appear to be a lack of information, is very often an intentional artistic form. Nor do I want to convince intellectually: what I am [aiming] at in all cases is to start a process of "creative understanding" in my readers.[58]

Keyserling's pluralism and eclecticism appeared in his penchant for somewhat esoteric, if increasingly fashionable, subjects such as oriental philosophies and religions, parapsychic phenomena, yoga, Jungian psychoanalysis, theosophy, and expressionism. During the years from shortly before World War I through the early 1920's, his interest in Chinese and Indian practices and beliefs reached its peak. He discerned an urgent need for a synthesis of "Eastern" and "Western" modes of approaching life in order to cope with the grave situation faced by mankind. Later, he became less committed to an assertion of the importance of oriental ideas.

His conception of a worldwide crisis was not developed logically and consistently, but he frequently returned to the same, ultimately

---

[57] *America Set Free* (New York, 1929), p. 186. Hereafter cited as *America*. See also *Die neuentstehende Welt* (Darmstadt, 1926), pp. 98–100. Hereafter cited as *NeW*.

[58] *America*, p. xvi.

optimistic themes: despite the potentially catastrophic state of civilization, the displacement of old elites, and the current absence of true leaders in positions of authority, democracy was doing the spadework for the emergence of a new type of aristocratic leadership that would avert disaster. Occasionally, he traced the origins of the current crisis to the Renaissance; at other times, to the Reformation or the eighteenth century.[59] Although the crisis had cultural, political, and social manifestations, its roots were spiritual. Intellect and mind had been elevated above soul. All traditional civilizations were in decline, not simply, Keyserling emphasized in an implicit criticism of Spengler's views, Western civilization. Before the development of modern Western civilization, every culture had centered in "the irrational, the instinctive, the sensual, the alogical rooted in eros."[60] The crucial elements in a traditional civilization were "nontransferable." They were unique, irrational components of a culture that expressed directly a spiritual condition. The civilization of the modern West, on the other hand, was "transferable." Its component parts could be taken over by other civilizations.[61] For Keyserling the introduction of the characteristics of modern Western civilization into other cultures destroyed the spiritual harmony and integrity of these other cultures. He thus relied upon a basically idealistic explanation of the impact of imperialism upon non-Western societies.

One characteristic of modern Western civilization was, according to Keyserling, particularly disruptive, for it undermined the basis on which all political and spiritual leadership rested in other cultures, as well as formerly in Western civilization. Unlike any other civilization, the modern West had brought forth a "culture of ability," which had displaced the traditional "culture of being." The culture of being was static, whereas the culture of ability was dynamic. Under the former, men lived out their lives within fixed positions in the social order; social ascent was rare. Keyserling mentioned, as an extreme example, the Hindu caste system. Under a culture of being, a man expected at most to better himself in the next life or world. A culture of ability, however, rested on the assumption that anyone could do anything, regardless of his birth, social status, or spiritual condition. The masses rejected a static conception of their station in life. They no longer accepted unquestioningly the superior position of their betters. Men took progress for granted. They expected their own personal advancement, and they anticipated that civilization in general would rise. They defined progress in material, not spiritual terms. Even in the Orient, Keyserling explained, the old culture of being was giving way to a culture

[59] See, e.g., *Creative Understanding*, p. xii.
[60] *NeW*, pp. 19–20.   [61] *Ibid.*

of ability. Bolshevism had success in the Orient because it promoted the culture of ability. In the West, the United States represented an extreme expression of the new type of civilization.[62]

Keyserling denied that the culture of ability was bringing happiness —true happiness—to anyone. Materialism and social mobility made for a feeling of malaise. Men concentrated on their external lives, neglecting their inner lives.

He frequently compared the present crisis to that of fourth-century Greece or of the later Roman Empire. He found many signs of a deep illness especially in Europe: "The current era recalls the first centuries after Christ more than any has done since then. Modern Europe is swarming with founders of religion, magicians, and saviors. . . . Each one finds crowds of blindly believing followers."[63] Keyserling alluded ominously to the arrival of a new dark age that would this time envelop all of mankind. Yet he warned against the attempt to draw parallels with other great historical crises as deceptive. The present juncture, he implied, was not as severe as that which had led to the dark ages, and another descent into barbarism could be avoided. Unless a new barbarism triumphed, there was no need for a new religion, as there had once been a need for Christianity to aid in the restoration of civilization.[64]

He argued that the parallel with fourth-century Greece was similarly misleading. In ancient Greece knowledge had failed, but "what was then fate is no longer fate."[65] New possibilities now existed. Science, technology, the culture of ability—all of the components of modern Western civilization that had led thus far to a one-sided development—could contribute to the basis for an entirely new type of culture. A true synthesis of the culture of ability with the culture of being might be created—a synthesis in which the latter would receive its proper emphasis: "We are entering, first upon a phase of darkness; this is the period of conception, incubation, and gestation. The soul of man must reconstitute itself, and this cannot happen without a period of sickness, disorder, and disease. But the outcome may be such an Age of Light as the world has never seen before. . . . Today we are probably at the very climax of the crisis."[66]

Keyserling suggested confidently that the transition to the new

[62] *Creative Understanding*, pp. 160ff. Keyserling seems to have changed his mind more than once about the United States. For example, in the mid-1920's, he described the United States as an "obsolete remnant of the past." "Werden und Vergehen," *Der Leuchter: Weltanschauung und Lebensgestaltung. Jahrbuch der Schule der Weisheit*, vi (1925), 17.

[63] *Creative Understanding*, p. 38.

[64] See, e.g., *Reisetagebuch*, i, 178; *America*, p. 582.

[65] *Creative Understanding*, p. 237.

[66] *America*, p. 584.

aristocratic order was well underway. Fascism, bolshevism, and democracy were all moving, if by different paths, toward this new aristocratic order.[67] Although the masses still clung to the belief that external progress was possible, even this illusion and the contemporary "culture of making all things easy" were educating them to expect more from themselves than ever before in history. In the general leveling of men that had taken place, the masses had risen. Once they had been further schooled, the false belief in the equality of all would disappear. The masses would desire and accept the reconstruction of a hierarchical order, which Keyserling occasionally referred to as a new caste system. They would come to recognize their own inferiority; they would welcome a society in which everyone had his appropriate place.[68] Keyserling wrote optimistically that "the new aristocracy will be based on a higher level than was the old one, whose qualities will have become the inheritance of the masses."[69]

He was less specific than Spengler in describing the condition of the masses in the new order, but now and then he made a casual remark that helps to place in perspective his glowing reference to the possibility of creating the Kingdom of Heaven on earth.[70] For example, he believed that in the foreseeable future the material conditions of the work process would not change radically. After discussing the need for man to express his personality in his work, as the medieval artisan had presumably done, Keyserling went on to write: "But for centuries to come, repetitive labor will correspond so well to the inner state of development of the overwhelming majority that the question whether the worker's existence is worthy of a human being will not have to be posed."[71] Thus Keyserling justified implicitly the maintenance indefinitely of the class structure of bourgeois society. He assumed that transformations of mind and attitude must precede objective changes. Like Spengler, he relied heavily upon the manipulation of the masses, by means of ideas, to still discontent, avert revolution, and assure compliance with the dictates of an elite, but he was far less brutal and explicit.[72]

The major models on which Keyserling based his conception of the

[67] See, e.g., *NeW*, pp. 40, 68; "Werden und Vergehen," *Der Leuchter*, VI (1925), 17.

[68] *Reisetagebuch*, II, 733, 842–44; *Creative Understanding*, p. 81; *NeW*, pp. 68–69; *America*, p. 448.

[69] *Reisetagebuch*, II, 731.

[70] For the allusion to the Kingdom of Heaven see *ibid.*, II, 835.

[71] "Vom Beruf," *WzV*, II (1921), 23.

[72] Georg Lukács observes correctly that Spengler is much blunter than Keyserling, but Lukács asserts unconvincingly that since the views of the two men were so similar there is little value in examining Keyserling's. See Georg Lukács, *Die Zerstörung der Vernunft* (Neuwied am Rhein, 1962), pp. 16, 404.

future aristocracy were derived from his own Baltic homeland, from England, and from Asia. In his *Travel Diary* he sketched the outlines of the new type of aristocrat, which he subsequently repeated with few basic modifications. The spirit of the new aristocrat would be similar to that of the medieval knight. He would have abundant moral courage, idealism, self-denial, loyalty, nobility of outlook, and disdain for personal material advantages. But he would be superior to the knight because he would be able to give greater play to his individual temperament. He would need "an enormous innate culture which even the bearers of the greatest names do not possess in our days" and "a capacity for conscious self-limitation which is indirectly opposed to the ideal of the emancipated average." Such a man would be "the English gentleman made intellectual and universal."[73]

Keyserling conceived of the English aristocrat as perfectly suited to his environment. The versatile English aristocrat succeeded in realizing fully his possibilities. He knew how to organize his personal strengths so that every one of them was fully productive. He was not highly talented and lacked originality, but he was similar to an animal "who, furnished with a number of unerring instincts control[s] a certain sector of reality perfectly." Keyserling admitted that he was always shocked when he met an English aristocrat by the discrepancy between the dearth of his talents and the restriction of his horizons, and "the measure of recognition which every one of them exacts from me as from everyone else."[74] Although beginning with the French Revolution the Continent had become decadent politically, England had continued to produce true leaders. In an era of excessive emphasis upon intellect, English hostility to theory and systematic thought had stood the English aristocrat in good stead. Through the concept of the gentleman, England had managed to perpetuate an aristocratic ideal during an age of belief in equality. But even the English aristocrat had been unable to stave off indefinitely the political decline of England, and World War I, Keyserling felt, had accelerated this decline. The English aristocrat was dying out as a human type, and he could never be reproduced.[75]

In his works written after the war, Keyserling often discussed two types of men who stood above the general level of aristocracy and who provided models for the most vital type of leadership. The first was the grand seigneur, the second the sage. While the grand seigneur was an aristocrat of the highest type, the sage stood somewhat apart.

Keyserling's interest in the grand seigneur helps to explain the ad-

[73] *Reisetagebuch*, II, 618.   [74] *Ibid.*, I, 70, 72, 328.
[75] See *Spektrum Europas*, pp. 52, 239; *Südamerikanische Meditationen* (Stuttgart, 1932), pp. 185, 239.

miration that he often expressed for the Magyars. The Baltic Barons had long been fond of comparing themselves with Hungarian as well as English aristocrats. Keyserling regarded the Hungarians as the most aristocratic nation in Europe: as a people they were very similar to the Baltic Germans. The Hungarian grand seigneur was one of the highest expressions of mankind. The secret of his superiority was that any lack of personal talent could be compensated for by tradition. The Hungarian grand seigneur employed "the principle of distance," and rejected intimacy with his inferiors. He had mastered the rules that made leadership possible. On the other hand, "where democracy is understood literally in the sense of the agreement of men on a one-to-one basis at the level of mediocrity," no true leaders could exist. Keyserling treasured the Hungary of Admiral Horthy as a living musuem of Europe's former greatness, a museum now all the more important since the dispersal of the Baltic German aristocracy. Everything that had once made Europe great rested on the same aristocratic spirit that survived only in Hungary. This spirit prized freedom, if only for a few men. Where all men were oppressed, a "ghetto mentality" developed that Keyserling deprecated as "the dominant ideal of a sardine can."[76]

Seeking to promote a stable social order and passivity among the masses, Keyserling argued that only an aristocratic order could do the job without the application of counterproductive force. In an aristocratic order, he suggested, leadership would be accepted willingly: ". . . All *leadership* always depends on the state of being. Only he can rule others personally—personally as opposed to rule by brute force or impersonal machinery—whom others involuntarily follow or obey; and this they do in case their level of being is the lower one. . . . Aristocracy thus has a sound foundation."[77] The aristocrat could perceive more clearly than even a more talented commoner the needs of mankind. Lacking the resentments of the plebeian, the aristocrat was able better to comprehend human weaknesses since his position had shel-

[76] See *Spektrum Europas*, pp. 237, 243, 252–53, 265, 267, 379.

[77] *America*, p. 377. Italics Keyserling's. Compare "Von der Selbstführerschaft," *WzV*, II (1921), 25–27, where Keyserling states that everyone is capable of learning how to lead himself, and goes on to make two distinctions that appear to be incompatible with this statement. First, not everyone is capable of leading a nation; hence the "final decisions" must be made by those most qualified to do so. Second, the free man should select the man who will lead him: "The first, very tentative embodiment of this tendency is the democratic principle." Keyserling seems to say that although everyone is potentially capable of leading himself and hence selecting his leaders, not everyone has actualized this capability. Thus the basic difference between Keyserling's position here and in *America* may be a matter of emphasis: in the former, he leaves open the possibility that someday everyone may participate in the selection of leaders; in the latter, he implies that some men everywhere will never be capable of selecting their leaders. See also "Ansprache an die radikale Jugend," pp. 17–18.

tered him from their worst consequences.[78] Keyserling expected individual members of the old aristocracy who, like himself, had not degenerated to contribute greatly to the development of the new aristocracy.[79]

Keyserling's belief in the contributions that members of the old aristocracy could make to the new rested partly on his conception of heredity, race, and caste. His ideas were not consistently racist; many of his remarks reflected a form of racism similar to that of Rathenau and Spengler. Often Keyserling alluded to "blood" as an explanation for attitudes and characteristics. For example, in a passing reference to the Reformation he asserted that "the more Teutonic the blood, the more pronounced was the Protestant sentiment." Similarly, he attributed the superiority of the Magyars "to a very great extent to their Turanic blood admixture." Even a little bit of Turanic blood went a long way.[80]

He followed carefully the writings of the American Lothrop Stoddard and other well-known racists.[81] But despite the praise that Keyserling gave to some racist works, he rather consistently raised several objections, and these objections clarified his own point of view better than the passages on race in most of his other writings. First, he complained that racists underemphasized or ignored the great advantages that resulted from many racial mixtures. Second, he faulted racists with underplaying the importance of physical environment. Third, and most indicative of his basic point of view, he argued that race and blood were ultimately less significant than nonmaterial circumstances. Under primitive conditions, race and blood might be very important, but the more highly developed a culture, the less important they became. The decisive factor for both the individual and his society was what Keyserling referred to variously as "spirit [*Geist*]" and "psychic conditions."[82]

He used "blood" and "race" as loose explanatory concepts that revealed less racism than emphasis upon social background and origins. For example, he defined heredity as the "transmission of blood as well as tradition." In historical man, the synthesis of heredity and tradition constituted inheritance, "for the inherited spiritual attitudes and the

[78] *Reisetagebuch*, ɪ, 53.

[79] See, e.g., *Creative Understanding*, p. 121. For an earlier, similar statement see *Reisetagebuch*, ɪɪ, 559.

[80] *Reisetagebuch*, ɪ, 203; *Spektrum Europas*, pp. 274–75.

[81] See, e.g., the book reviews in *WzV*, ɪɪɪ (1922), 52; v; (1923), 74; xvɪ (1929), 48–49.

[82] See, e.g., "Bücherschau," *WzV*, xvɪ (1929), 48–49; *Reisetagebuch*, ɪ, 218–20; ɪɪ, 611; *NeW*, pp. 14–15, 51–52; *Spektrum Europas*, pp. 284–88, 452–57; *America*, pp. 23, 95, 99.

inherited level depends in good part on the nursery."[83] Keyserling's concepts of race, heredity, and blood served to justify his argument that the old aristocracy and upper classes in general had a substantial contribution to make to the new aristocracy: "Within the old cultural ranks, as far as they have not degenerated, nobler souls grow up than among the people at large (although the latter may often prove intellectually superior) because only tradition, imparted to the very atmosphere of the nursery and acting as a sovereign claim during the decisive years of development, achieves an organization of the psyche, making it beautiful in itself and, moreover, tending harmoniously to assimilate new spiritual contents."[84]

Yet Keyserling's descriptions of the recruitment of the new aristocracy were sufficiently varied to give much hope to men from the lower classes. For example, he suggested in one passage that the nobility and bourgeoisie could make only a minor contribution: "Please note that I am not arguing for any preference to be given to the higher classes [in the development of the new aristocracy]; rather I am arguing that a substantial percentage of them are racially at an end and that the new aristocracy, upon whose development the future of Europe depends, will create itself [*sich emporzüchten*] from previously insignificant families, as has again and again been the case in history due to the dead end created by inbreeding."[85]

Except when discussing the role of the School of Wisdom, Keyserling seldom became specific about the techniques through which the new aristocracy would be constituted. Rarely did he mention, as in the following passage, what he elsewhere took for granted—that the new aristocracy would be self-selecting and self-perpetuating: "I have no doubt that sooner or later the German people will produce a new recognized ruling stratum. Under the new conditions, the maintenance of this stratum will of course depend not upon inheritance, but upon cooptation. And this ruling stratum will govern Germany better than it has ever been governed."[86]

Keyserling's strictures on the necessity for the slow development of the new elite dovetailed neatly with his desire to avoid rapid, far-reaching social and institutional changes. He assumed that spiritual changes within the individual must precede changes in society. Like his old friend Gustave Le Bon,[87] he countered aspirations for radical changes by belittling the significance of institutions. Before any major

---

[83] *NeW*, p. 51. See also *Creative Understanding*, p. 121.

[84] *Creative Understanding*, p. 121. I have altered the English translation, which is unnecessarily ambiguous.

[85] "Zur Überwindung des Bösen durch Gutes," *WzV*, v (1923), 31.

[86] *Spektrum Europas*, p. 165.

[87] See "Um das Individuum" in *Reise durch die Zeit*, iii, 237–38.

new development could come about—whether socialism, a united Europe, or even substantial reforms in Germany—new types of men imbued with a new spirit must be ready: "Whoever wishes to improve external conditions must begin by improving the inner man."[88] The thrust of this statement was directed against Social Democrats and Communists. Socialism, he argued, could not come about until "true socialists" existed. Not everyone had to be altered inwardly; an elite of new men would suffice to initiate the decisive steps in building socialism: "If only a few thousand socialists were inwardly formed by their world-philosophy, then and only then, the predicted socialist era might be close at hand."[89] Although much more gently, Keyserling criticized, on similar grounds, the Pan-Europeanism of his friends the Austrian aristocrats Count Richard Coudenhove-Kalergi and Prince Karl Anton Rohan.[90]

The rhetoric of Keyserling's admonitions on the need for the precedence of spiritual changes seems occasionally to have gotten out of hand. For example, in a lecture in Berlin in 1920 he implied that little had changed in Germany since the war—a suggestion which, as we shall see, was incompatible with his basic views on postwar Germany: "The external is always only an expression of the internal. . . . Therefore external reforms as such never help. Today everything is being reformed in Germany: church, school, university, social structure, constitution, army! And even now we see that [these changes] amount to nothing; on the contrary, breaking through the ruts of habit deprives the German of his last bit of security. What is really important—that the Germans become different, deeper men—is left untouched."[91]

Keyserling's commitment to the need for spiritual change as a prerequisite to other changes appeared also in his conception of the highest exemplars of mankind. Spiritual leaders, or sages, would play a crucial role in the preparation of the new order. The sage influenced and inspired others by the force of his example and wisdom. He pointed the way to the future. His greatest impact was not on the masses, but on potential members of the elite: "How does the spiritual guide act? I have already said it. Not by suggestion, like the mass-leader, the lion-tamer, but like a model, a mold or a fruitful symbol.

[88] *Creative Understanding*, p. 203. Keyserling italicized this sentence.

[89] *Ibid.*, pp. 99, 170.

[90] *Ibid.*, p. 302; "Fruchtbare und unfruchtbare Diskussion," *Europäische Revue*, I (1925), 210.

[91] "Erscheinungswelt und Geistesmacht" in *Philosophie als Kunst*, 2nd ed. (Darmstadt, 1922), p. 220. This lecture was given on Jan. 8, 1920 at the University of Berlin under the auspices of the *Vereinigung für staatswissenschaftliche Fortbildung*.

He does not need the slightest material power."[92] Occasionally Keyserling spoke of a man who would be a spiritual as well as a political leader. The highest type of man, the "ruler-sage" had a direct effect upon the course of history. Although even he had to accept most events as "fate," he could steer in new directions. The mere sage also stood above destiny; events that overwhelmed other men did not shake him. But his impact on history was less than that of the ruler-sage, who was both a man of wisdom and a statesman.[93]

Like Hegel's great man, the ruler-sage was bound to a specific time and place. He had to appear at the appropriate moment in history; otherwise he could do nothing. Keyserling presented this Hegelian conception of a great man in the trappings of Jungian psychology. The ruler-sage had an insight into the collective unconscious. He made people aware of what they really wanted, but were scarcely conscious of desiring. Keyserling found only two men in recent years, Lenin and Mussolini, who began to measure up to the model of the ruler-sage.[94]

The Sage and His School

Keyserling denied that he sought a personal following,[95] but the major purpose of the School of Wisdom—aside from its usefulness in providing for his own physical existence—was to erect for himself, as a "sage," a platform from which to influence others and promote the formation of a new aristocracy. He does not appear to have seriously regarded himself as a potential "ruler-sage," although it would have been uncharacteristic of him not to entertain the possibility. Certainly he felt no great need to be modest about his abilities as a sage. He stood at the center of the School of Wisdom, helping others in their endeavors to reach his level: "Most men are different from me. By opening my soul to the man of a different nature and linking it with mine, I temporarily entered into his mind and potential, and [I] thereby grew beyond my previous state." Keyserling went on to describe his own historical task as "to prepare the way, through experimentation, for a new general condition [of man]." Anyone else in his place would soon have become "if not the founder of a religion, at least the father of a specific metaphysical system."[96]

The School of Wisdom was intended to give a decisive impetus to

---

[92] *Südamerikanische Meditationen*, p. 287.

[93] See *Creative Understanding*, pp. 345, 352, 357; *NeW*, p. 107.

[94] See, e.g., *Reisetagebuch*, II, 669–70; *Creative Understanding*, pp. 101, 273, 307–14; *NeW*, pp. 107–09, 115; *Menschen als Sinnbilder*, pp. 154–55, 267; *Spektrum Europas*, p. 222; *Südamerikanische Meditationen*, p. 127.

[95] See esp. "Von der Selbstführerschaft," *WzV*, II (1921), 25.

[96] *Wiedergeburt* (Darmstadt, 1927); pp. 544, 558–60.

the formation of the new aristocracy by providing a place where its potential members would meet each other under Keyserling's guidance. Stimulated by exchanges with each other, and especially by contact with Keyserling and his staff, some of the visitors would acquire a new, spiritual perspective on life. According to a brochure describing the methods and purposes of the School, and probably written by Keyserling himself, its primary objective was "to develop sages from fragments of men, from inwardly indecisive leaders, from men with [merely] theoretical knowledge."[97]

Although varying in degree of rodomontade, his other pleas for support expressed similar themes. Speaking in 1920 to a convention of the Free German Youth (*Freideutsche Jugend*) that was marked by a paralyzing split between the right and the left wings of the Youth Movement, he explained that the School of Wisdom was not a school in the traditional sense, but rather a center from which to influence men. It was designed to attract all those "who have gotten the impression from my accomplishments that I can assist them in their self-realization." The School of Wisdom would develop "the true leader of the future . . . , who, starting out from the heights of the old culture, will come to embody the highest ideals of the new era. To him and to him alone, belongs the leadership of the future."[98] Most men, Keyserling remarked in another description of the School, would not be able to become the type of leaders that he desired. At first, the new wisdom could be comprehended only by a few.[99] The School of Wisdom, he asserted, would assume a place beside—perhaps above—the historic institutions of church and university. Predictably, he once referred to his School as a "rebirth of Plato's Academy."[100] On another occasion, in a thinly veiled appeal in an American magazine to gain backing for the School and to save Europe from bolshevism, organized labor, and the stupidities of the Entente, he depicted Darmstadt as the coming center of the "Fourth International of the Best."[101]

The School had no fixed program of instruction. In its early years, several staff members, including Keyserling, when he was not away on a lecture tour, were in permanent residence. By giving prior notice, members of the association supporting the School could come to Darmstadt for short periods, usually lasting no longer than two weeks.[102] Through contemplation, yoga exercises, dialogues with staff

[97] From an undated brochure on the School of Wisdom found in a copy of *Was uns Not tut.*
[98] "Eine Ansprache an die radikale Jugend," *WzV*, II (1921), 17.
[99] *Creative Understanding*, pp. 148, 436.
[100] *Ibid.*, p. 143; *Was uns Not tut*, pp. 43–45.
[101] "Peace, or War Everlasting?" *Atlantic Monthly*, cxxv (Apr. 1920), 561–62.
[102] See "Schule" (1), p. 19; anon., "Geschäftliche Mitteilungen," *WzV*, xviii (1930), 51.

members, and other informal methods of instruction the individual would come to know himself better and to acquire new insight into his own personality and the world. The first series of "spiritual exercises," which seem to have drawn heavily upon oriental religions and philosophies, was attended by about thirty people.[103]

During the early years of the School, special convocations (*grosse Tagungen*) were held fairly regularly at yearly intervals. Keyserling, other staff members, and prominent guests spoke at these convocations, but the center of attention always came back to Keyserling, who delivered the concluding lecture. He fondly termed the method employed in the annual meetings "spiritual orchestration."[104] His function was not to synthesize the ideas of the lecturers or to reconcile the conflicting views expressed, but rather to respond to their ideas and the situation as seemed appropriate to him at the moment.

Most of the activities involved small groups. Keyserling prized the intimate character of the School. Although he once apologized that "for technical reasons" (such as limited space?) no more than thirty-five people could normally attend,[105] on a different occasion he attributed this restriction to other circumstances. Attempting perhaps to flatter prospective visitors to the School, he explained that only a few people were really suited to its character.[106]

He often took pains to emphasize that the School was open to all.[107] "Today, unlike antiquity," he wrote in an early description of the School, "wisdom is not the goal of small circles but of all of mankind. The symbol of the School of Wisdom is therefore not the closed circle but the open angle."[108] Several times the School's publications mentioned the possibility of providing financial assistance to those without adequate means to attend its functions,[109] but apparently the funds never became available, certainly not in any sizable amount. Keyserling rarely succeeded in inducing a worker to participate in any of the School's activities.[110] Neither the routines nor the organization of the

[103] Anon., "Geschäftliche Mitteilungen," *WzV*, III (1922), 73.
[104] See his Introduction to the English edition of *Creative Understanding*, p. xviii.
[105] "Von der Schülerschaft in der Schule der Weisheit," *WzV*, II, (1922), 11.
[106] *Creative Understanding*, pp. 435–37.
[107] See the previously cited undated brochure on the School. See also "Schule" (1), p. 13: "Die Schule der Weisheit kommt es nicht darauf an, woher einer stammt, wovon er ausgeht, was er gerade denkt, sondern einzig darauf, wer er werden kann."
[108] *Creative Understanding*, p. 263. In examining the School's publications, I have found no evidence that this symbol was actually used.
[109] See, e.g., anon., "Geschäftliche Mitteilungen," *WzV*, II (1921), 65.
[110] See Keyserling's Introduction to the *Leuchter*, v (1924), 3. According to Keyserling a worker named Artur Zickler spoke on "Die Welt des Arbeiters" at the School's convocation in 1923, but the lecture was not printed in the *Leuchter*

School was conducive to lower-class participation. Members (*geistig Verbundene*) were required to contribute at least a hundred marks annually—this was the amount requested before the great inflation of the early 1920's had reduced the mark to a small fraction of its previous value—and benefactors (*Förderer*) were asked to make even larger donations.[111]

In describing the School, Keyserling usually took for granted that its pupils and backers would be drawn mainly if not exclusively from the ranks of the bourgeoisie. For example, he mentioned theologians, philosophers, military officers, captains of industry, and businessmen as those who would be likely to become involved in the School.[112] In an early appeal for support he addressed himself pointedly to businessmen: "It is more important that one economic leader understands [Keyserling's appeal] in time than fifty politicians and ten thousand intellectuals."[113] Keyserling explained that he turned mainly to businessmen because of their importance in the contemporary world—an importance that was a consequence of the primacy of economics in the lives of modern nations.[114]

Despite this tribute to businessmen, most of the speakers at the School's annual convocations were scholars. These speakers and other special guests included: Ernst Troeltsch; Carl Gustav Jung; Martin Dibelius, one of the foremost German students of English life and letters; Hans von Raumer, the Reich minister of economics in 1923; Count Hugo Lerchenfeld, the Bavarian minister president in 1922–1923; Rabbi Leo Baeck, a prominent Jewish theologian; Friedrich Gogarten, a proponent of *Lebensphilosophie*; Leo Frobenius, an anthropologist close to Spengler during the early 1920's; and Leopold Ziegler, a Lutheran theologian who corresponded with Rathenau and later collaborated with Edgar Jung. In 1932 the School claimed as members literary, political, and academic figures such as Jakob Wassermann, Frank Thiess, Hans Luther (the German chancellor in 1925–

---

because Zickler never bothered to send in his manuscript. A subsequent volume of the *Leuchter*, VII (1926) included a contribution by a Friedrich Herfurth, who was identified as a *Tischlergeselle*. Herfurth's anti-Marxist essay was entitled "Die Beschränktheit des sozialistischen Freiheitsbegriffs." No other workers lectured at a convocation and the publications of the School do not contain any other contributions by workers. The 1926 issue of the *Leuchter* contained an essay by August Winnig, a former Social Democrat who became a ubiquitous exponent of neoconservatism. Winnig was expelled from the party after he supported the right-wing Kapp *Putsch* in 1920.

[111] See the previously cited brochure on the School of Wisdom.

[112] See *Creative Understanding*, p. 424.

[113] "Wirtschaft und Weisheit" (Nov. 1921) in *Politik, Wirtschaft, Weisheit* (Darmstadt, 1922), p. 189. Hereafter this collection of essays and articles will be cited as *PWW*.

[114] *Ibid.*, pp. 188–89. See also *America*, p. 447.

1926), and Alfred Weber. Walther Rathenau's mother and Georg Simmel's widow donated books to its library.[115]

Its yearbook, *Der Leuchter* (*The Beacon*), resembled, in its simple luxury and black binding, an expensive Bible or missal. The *Leuchter* contained the texts of lectures given at the annual convocation, as well as other essays, many written by prominent writers and scholars. Serving as a prestige publication for Reichl's publishing house, the yearbook never had a large circulation. Probably no more than 3,000 copies of any issue were printed. The circulation of the School's other publication, *Der Weg zur Vollendung* (*The Way to Perfection or Fulfillment*), was probably a better guide to the size of the group of men who followed sympathetically Keyserling's endeavors. This publication, which appeared at more frequent, if less regular, intervals than the yearbook, claimed a printing of 5,000 copies in 1923. Its circulation was always considerably less, certainly under 3,000 copies.[116]

In the late 1920's, Keyserling put forth a plan that reflected the importance he attached to the School in the formation of a new elite. The German copyright law protected material for only thirty years. Keyserling proposed that copyright protection be extended to fifty years and that a fixed proportion of all royalties be placed in a special fund. This fund was to support a new institution, analogous to the Church. The new "church of intellect [*Geisteskirche*]" would be organized "aristocratically and hierarchically." He claimed to have won support for his proposal from such luminaries as Frau Förster-Nietzsche, Hugo von Hofmannsthal, Thomas Mann, Richard Strauss, Romain Rolland, and Siegfried Wagner. Keyserling suggested that Prince Karl Anton Rohan's *Union Intellectuelle* might provide the core of the new church.[117] A prominent neoconservative, Rohan, edited the *Europäische Revue*, a periodical that succeeded in enlisting essays as well as support from a broad spectrum of prominent European writers. Rohan was a frequent guest at the School of Wisdom during the 1920's.[118] The proposed royalties' pool may well have been intended to provide a broader basis for the School and to capitalize on Rohan's prestige to improve its finances; but nothing seems to have eventuated from this proposal.

[115] Georg Seelbach, "Chronik der Schule der Weisheit," *WzV*, xx (Apr. 1932), 20; anon., "Geschäftliche Mitteilungen," *WzV*, v (1923), 111.

[116] See *Sperlings Zeitschriften-Adressbuch*, 50th ed. (Leipzig, 1923), pp. 138–39; *ibid.*, 51st ed. (Leipzig, 1925), pp. 149–50; *C. F. Müller Zeitschriften-Adressbuch 1927* (Leipzig, 1927), pp. 163, 289.

[117] "Der Peterspfennig der Literatur," *WzV*, xii (1927), 13–24.

[118] See *NeW*, p. 41n. On Rohan and the *Europäische Revue* see Klaus-Peter Hoepke, *Die deutsche Rechte und der italienische Faschismus: Ein Beitrag zum Selbstverständnis und zur Politik von Gruppen und Verbänden der deutschen Rechten* (Düsseldorf, 1968), pp. 43–64.

Keyserling was sensitive to the charge that he was a charlatan who exploited the cultural pretensions of the well-to-do. One of his friends sought to brush aside the more serious criticisms of his activities by conceding that Keyserling had given his detractors some grounds for complaint; excessive zeal in the pursuit of a noble cause had prompted him to lower his standards: in endeavoring to popularize his ideas he may have overly simplified his philosophy.[119] Keyserling's own defense of himself was more subtle. Without acknowledging any criticism of the School, he explained that only a few of the School's students might be capable of becoming members of the new aristocracy and that his methods were justified by expediency. According to Keyserling, the leadership exerted by the School depended upon spiritual influence. After receiving "living impulses" in Darmstadt, a man would return home, where he would, in turn, influence men in his own occupation or circle of friends. Even if only a few true leaders emerged from the School, "the fertilization of the majority" would be assured.[120] The School would gain wide influence and affect the masses through the men that it sent back to the outside world. Eventually, a "very unspiritual way which alone is open for the purpose" would have to be utilized. To ensure that the highest type of man received the most prestige—a prerequisite to the maximizing of his influence—his reputation would be enhanced by means of methods of suggestion akin to advertising techniques or those of political propaganda. In a passage that was rewritten after the appearance of Bruce Barton's best seller, *The Man Nobody Knows* (1925), in which this New York advertising man acclaimed Jesus Christ as the creator of a twelve-man sales organization that sold the world, Keyserling invoked a similar parallel: "There is nothing degrading or immoral in the technique of forming the masses independently of their personal understanding. There is no other way and will never be any other way. . . . What happens every Sunday in church is nothing but advertising; an incessantly repeated extolling of the person of Jesus is like the build-up for a new product. Thus Jesus became more fashionable than his rivals like Mithras. . . ."[121]

THE GERMAN PROBLEM

During the period from his arrival in Germany in 1918 through the early 1920's, Keyserling was more involved publicly with German

---

[119] Gerhard von Mutius, "Darmstadt," *Preussische Jahrbücher*, CXCI (1923), 275–76.

[120] *Creative Understanding*, pp. 438–39, 454.

[121] *Ibid.*, p. 434.

issues than at any subsequent time. He published more on Germany, particularly on German politics, than he was ever to do again. His advice was more explicit and detailed than his advice to any other country. In his direct responses to the German situation, we can see again both the concrete applications of many of his ideas and the conservative, counterrevolutionary thrust of his elitism.

For a brief period after the November Revolution of 1918, Keyserling probably cooperated closely with monarchist forces seeking a restoration—forces which had many ties to Baltic émigré groups.[122] But his own position was much too flexible and his attitude toward simple reactionary measures too skeptical to provide for a lasting association. He saw the major danger to Germany as stemming from Marxian socialism, not the introduction of political democracy. His dating of the derailment of Germany from its true course varied. Sometimes he mentioned 1870, other times 1890.[123] He dismissed the old order as "ready to go under."[124] Imperialism had been a mistaken policy because it was not in accordance with German needs and abilities.[125] The Entente had triumphed because it had a more attractive ideology for the masses. Germany had no ideology that could appeal to the masses in either the Central or the Allied Powers.

As long as there appeared to be some possibility that a successful social revolution might sweep Europe, Keyserling proclaimed that Germany's highest mission was the creation of socialism—not bolshevism or Marxian socialism, which did not deserve the name Socialist, but "true" socialism. Although some other anti-Marxist proponents of a "German socialism" presented consistent if muddled schemes designed to advance the interests of the *Mittelstand*,[126] Keyserling dissociated his concept of socialism from any specific content: "A man can be a Socialist and still be conservative, liberal, or radical; an orthodox believer or a member of no church; a historicist or a rationalist; a friend or an enemy of inheritable property." In the same article, Keyserling went on to explain that if everyone claimed to be a Socialist the Social Democratic party could not survive.[127] When Spengler's "Prussiandom and Socialism" appeared, he acclaimed its thesis that Marxism

---

[122] See "Vorfahren" in *Reise durch die Zeit*, I, 73.

[123] See, e.g.: "Deutsche Dämmerung" (1920) in *PWW*, p. 108; *Creative Understanding*, p. 330; "Geschichte als Tragödie," *Leuchter*, VI (1925), 66.

[124] "Deutsche Dämmerung," p. 106.

[125] *Deutschlands wahre politische Mission* (Darmstadt, 1919), pp. 4–5, 7.

[126] See Herman Lebovics, *Social Conservatism and the Middle Classes in Germany, 1914–1933* (Princeton, 1969).

[127] *Deutschlands wahre politische Mission*, pp. 45–47n. Keyserling is quoting an article that he published in the *Neue Europäische Zeitung*, Nov. 26, 1918, under the title "Der Sozialismus als allgemeine Lebensbasis."

was a falsification of the idea of socialism.[128] Keyserling related the building of socialism to the new aristocratic order of the future. Spiritual and moral incompetence would be swept aside by the replacement of the rule of the masses by the rule of "an aristocracy of the truly best." He coupled this hope to an urgent call for the full utilization of untapped leadership abilities: "Henceforth everyone should obtain the position for which he is inwardly suited. Never again should either mediocrity assume leadership or any talent for leadership remain unused."[129]

When he identified democracy with the beginnings of the coming aristocratic order, he defined democracy in such a way that the masses had little control over it. He claimed that a new "authoritarian state [*Obrigkeitsstaat*]" was developing in place of parliamentary government. This new, "basically neutral" state would be constituted so that class rule would be impossible. Impervious to the rapidly changing moods of the masses, the state would be

> an organization in which competence alone is accepted as proof of ability to govern. What is objectively correct and expedient will have acknowledged priority over [mere] hopes and wishes. In the division of powers along these lines [of an authoritarian state], American democracy has advanced the farthest; its central government rules autocratically during its term in office. French syndicalism has worked out the idea [of authoritarian democracy] the most clearly if rather one-sidedly. The abstract ideal is presumably along the lines of that system of national guilds under whose banner more and more English social reformers gather because it ensures the individual more freedom than would be possible in any other socialist form of state. But Germany is best suited to the full realization of the new idea of the state. . . .[130]

While increasingly distancing himself from most of the Right, Keyserling characterized Communists, Social Democrats, and liberals as hopelessly out of touch with reality. The farther to the left a man stood, the more likely he was to be a reactionary:

> Conservative Prussian circles often speak as if we stand today in the midst of an era of nationality struggles; in reality these struggles are leading us to a universalistic era. The liberal bourgeoisie is still fighting for a democracy which, at best, is lethal to a new aristocracy. The Socialists pursue a leveling that corresponds to the spirit of the

[128] "Die Zukunft des Preussentums" (1919) in *PWW*, pp. 99–100.
[129] "Deutschlands Aufgaben im Frieden" (1920) in *PWW*, pp. 103–04.
[130] *Deutschlands wahre politische Mission*, p. 20.

eighteenth, not the twentieth, century. And the Communists, despite their ideas, express a mentality whose most recent historical representatives appeared in the sixteenth and seventeenth centuries.[131]

By the middle of 1921, Keyserling was under severe attack by Count Kuno Westarp, the chairman of the prewar Conservative party and a leading member of the new Nationalist party. Keyserling responded by identifying Westarp and the Nationalists with the past, with a past that, despite its value, had led to the catastrophe of 1918. But Keyserling softened these harsh words by promising that if the nobility responded to the challenge of the present it might serve as a model for the new aristocracy. If the old nobility cultivated *noblesse oblige*, it could even maintain its inherited position without retaining special privileges.[132]

Although often expressing admiration for true conservatives, whom he did not identify by name, Keyserling tended to lump together both the new and the old Right as irrelevant to the German situation. Soon he was dismissing most of Spengler's prophecies as "absurd"; Spengler's early postwar political writings expressed "a reactionary mentality of the most hopeless kind." Keyserling belittled Spengler's followers as "Catos," "the historically dead," and "purely mechanical spirits of the type of the head chauffeur, the modern captains of industry." Those who shared Spengler's personal political views were, Keyserling asserted, becoming fewer every year; they consisted in good part of followers of Ludendorff, racists, and old Prussian monarchists who, however large their numbers, were now "only of archaeological interest."[133]

Keyserling believed that the traditional rulers of Germany had been tested and found inadequate. Militarists, princes, and scholars had all failed. In a general work on Europe written in the late 1920's, he playfully referred to scholars as the *de facto* rulers of Germany insofar as "other castes" did not play a role. Even the German aristocrat, he complained, had reverted to the type of the scholar in the course of his dis-

[131] "Volksbewusstsein und Weltbürgertum" (1920) in *PWW*, p. 122.

[132] See Keyserling's articles in the *Kreuzzeitung*, which are reproduced with addenda in *PWW*, pp. 138–39.

[133] *Menschen als Sinnbilder*, pp. 160–61. Although Keyserling took a lively interest in Spengler's works, Spengler did not return the compliment. The two men seem to have become acquainted in 1919. In 1922 Keyserling invited Spengler to speak at the next convocation of the School of Wisdom. Spengler declined. In an imperious reply he criticized Keyserling and the School of Wisdom as academically oriented and divorced from life. See Keyserling's letter of Dec. 14, 1922 to Spengler and Spengler's reply of December 30, 1922 in Oswald Spengler, *Briefe 1913–1936*, ed. A. M. Koktanek (Munich [1963?]), pp. 228–30; 232–33.

integration.[134] The scholar and the aristocrat were caught up in the ethos of work that permeated Germany. Unlike Spengler, who welcomed a work ethos for the bulk of the population, Keyserling regarded it as an obstacle to leadership. The Germans must give up their glorification of work. All work was subaltern. The ethos of work must be replaced by an aristocratic ethos.[135] Keyserling did not grapple with the possible contradiction between an entire people filled with an aristocratic disdain for work and the aristocratic organization of the new order that he wished to promote. This contradiction becomes more glaring when we note his repeated denunciation of imperialism, for unlike Spengler, he did not suggest that conquests abroad would enable the entire population to maintain an aristocratic attitude toward foreigners.

Keyserling's belief in the need for distance between the aristocrat and the masses, and his occasional references to the special position that the aristocrat must occupy reflected his assumption that in the good society there would be enormous differences between elite and nonelite. Each kind of organism, he once explained, must possess a different standard of living. Until men realized this necessity and acted on the basis of it, there would be "dissatisfaction, unrest, in extreme cases war or the equivalent of war."[136] In another connection, he remarked that "the higher man rises as man, the more privileges he requires in order to exist."[137] And in discussing his own life, he asserted that "it is simply unjust to mankind not to see to it that creative spirits focused solely on spiritual values shall not have to give thought to material things. They, on whom all human progress depends [sic], really have no time for private business."[138]

He chastised the Germans for their frenzied calls for a great man. Keyserling observed that the demand for a great man served partly as an excuse for people who did not want to demand much from themselves.[139] He also observed that the Germans were especially prone to misunderstand the true nature and role of great men.[140] Like many other German elite theorists, he felt that a great man could emerge only when the new elite had appeared.[141] His emphasis on the role of the new aristocracy may have reflected his suspicions about rule by one man. As he frequently pointed out, the true aristocrat was a republican, not a monarchist.

[134] Spektrum Europas, pp. 131–33.
[135] Ibid., p. 266; "Bücherschau," WzV, xiii (1927), 45.
[136] America, p. 190.   [137] Ibid., p. 207.
[138] "My Life and My Work, as I See Them" in World in the Making, p. 58.
[139] "Von der Bedeutung des Einzelnen" (1921) in PWW, pp. 118–19.
[140] Creative Understanding, p. 108.   [141] See, e.g., NeW, p. 137.

THE DECLINE OF THE SCHOOL OF WISDOM AND THE
TRIUMPH OF THE NAZIS

Keyserling's fame probably reached its zenith during the late 1920's. In a work published in 1929, he confidently pointed to some of the promising signs of the emergence of the new aristocracy:

> . . . The spiritually minded minorities are more spiritual today all over the world, and that in a deeper sense than ever before. . . . In the eighteenth century, the masses believed in everything, the *élite* in nothing; today, even those of the *élite* who twenty years ago were at best indifferent to spiritual questions are either grasping the reality of the spirit or groping for it. And from the point of view of the future, the spiritually minded minorities count more than any minorities have ever counted in the past.[142]

Ironically, when this passage appeared, the School of Wisdom, its task only begun, was disintegrating. Although in 1930, about three hundred people gathered for ceremonies marking its tenth anniversary,[143] the last great convocation took place in 1927. Keyserling spent much of his time after 1927 on lecture tours, frequently in foreign countries. Staff members who left or died were not replaced, and the yearbook was no longer issued. Now that there were no longer annual convocations the yearbook may well have lost its rationale. The School's newsletter often mentioned the possibility of holding another convocation,[144] but apparently the response was inadequate. The tone of appeals for support became desperate.[145]

Some of the School's problems can be traced to the withdrawal of Reichl's support. In 1927 Reichl ceased to publish the newsletter, as well as Keyserling's new works, and new editions of Keyserling's older works were often brought out by other publishers. Although a quarrel over royalties may have initiated friction between the two men, political issues appear shortly, if not from the outset, to have disrupted the relationship. Reichl began to publish many pro-Nazi works that Keyserling must have found uncongenial.

Yet the breach between Keyserling and Reichl cannot fully account for the fate of the School. The basic explanation must be sought in the changing political situation in Germany. During the period of political

[142] *America*, p. 582.

[143] O. A. H. Schmitz, "Die zehnjährige Jubiläumstagung der 'Schule der Weisheit,'" *WzV*, XIX (1931), 17.

[144] See, e.g., Georg Seelbach, "Chronik der Schule der Weisheit," *WzV*, XXI (Nov. 1932), 8.

[145] See, e.g., Georg Seelbach, "Chronik der Schule der Weisheit," *WzV*, XX (Apr. 1932), 20.

stabilization after 1924, the School probably appeared less deserving of assistance to many of its backers. As long as the future seemed doubtful, he had much to offer affluent conservatives and liberals concerned about ways of escaping from the dilemmas of the present. If nothing else, he could be regarded as a harmless concocter of comforting tonics. The political polarization that began in 1928 and was accelerated by the depression struck still another blow at the School. He could expect little help from the dwindling ranks of the moderates, and none from the Left. His cosmopolitanism isolated him from most of the Right when it became increasingly chauvinistic in the late 1920's. At worst, he appeared as a self-serving crank; at best, as an impractical dreamer. While he talked about providing a "lion-tamer" for the masses, many other men, among them Hitler, were vying for the opportunity of actually performing the role. Sages were expendable.

With the fading of his hope that the School of Wisdom would become the center of a new world, Keyserling might have emphasized the lengthiness of the road to a new elite, or he might have placed his trust in governmental changes to overcome the obstacles. He was perhaps too sanguine to accept the former alternative, and he committed himself implicitly to immediate political changes. In doing so, he revealed more clearly than before his failure to describe practicable methods for the realization of his ideas. He was more successful in offering fragmentary critiques of the present—the import of which was the need for true conservatives not to despair—than he was in detailing the measures necessary for the creation of a new elitist order.

His response to the protracted political crisis of the last years of the Weimar Republic demonstrated this inability to relate his elitism to a concrete political situation. He came to respect Heinrich Brüning, who was appointed chancellor in the early spring of 1930, lacked a majority in the Reichstag, and governed with the help of emergency powers granted by President Hindenburg. Like many other conservatives and some liberals, Keyserling believed for a while that Brüning could play the key role in establishing an enduring political regime. In an article published in late 1931 in the *Kölnische Zeitung*, a major newspaper close to the Stresemann wing of the People's party (DVP), Keyserling proposed the transformation of the Brüning cabinet into a "Directory."[146] Assuming that parliamentary government was undesirable and, in any event, no longer workable, he sought an authoritarian regime that would be established without an upheaval and without explicit constitutional changes. The members of the Directory would be selected as individuals, not as members of a party. They would prob-

[146] "Die 'psychologische Nuss,'" *Kölnische Zeitung*, Nov. 12. 1931.

ably, Keyserling explained, be drawn largely from the "middle parties" —the People's party, the Democrats, and other smaller parties, for "most of the best heads in Germany" were to be found in these "middle parties." He anticipated that the Social Democrats would offer no serious opposition to the development of this Directory as long as they were not needlessly provoked by identifying them with the Communists; the Social Democrats sought to preserve the existing order and were prepared to make far-reaching compromises in order to do so. The formation of a Directory would prevent the National Socialists from coming to power. Although the Nazi movement contained "the best raw material" in the younger generation, the assumption of power by the Nazi party would lead to a catastrophe. Only the existence of a Directory would bring the Nazis into a "fruitful relationship of polarity" to the state. To Keyserling the Nazis represented little more than *Stimmung*, a vague, excited mood of enthusiasm which, however necessary, had no positive policies to offer. Like Brüning, a Directory would display dispassionate, impartial expertise.

In this article in the *Kölnische Zeitung* and in several subsequent writings in 1932, Keyserling explained in some detail his objections to the Nazis. Despite his own emphasis upon the irrational, he found national socialism excessively irrational. The Nazis had neither a real program nor an effective leader; their notions of reform, insofar as practicable, were similar to those of the Communists. Like Spengler and many other conservatives, Keyserling found a dangerous affinity between nazism and communism: "Hitler will be able to maintain himself as dictator only to the extent that he proves himself a *socialist*. Only then will the masses continue to follow him, and Hitler has even said that to him his socialism is more important than anything else. Thus Hitler will proceed much more socialistically than the Marxist parties have. If he does not, Communism will bury him."[147]

Keyserling skillfully interwove his strictures on the resemblance of national socialism to bolshevism with somber warnings about the Nazis' racism and "lack of spirituality." Noting that the Germans were a racially mixed, largely nonnordic people, he claimed that this mixture was crucial to their very spirituality:

> . . . Germany's world significance rests solely upon the universalism of this spirituality. If the Germans want to be "only" German, they will renounce everything that has made Germany great. . . . Only a very small percentage of Germans, even among those who swear al-

---

[147] "Warum Hindenburg, nicht Hitler?" *Kölnische Zeitung*, Apr. 8, 1932. Keyserling's italics.

legiance to National Socialism, is nordic—except in the realm of fantasy. Simply for this reason, the present National Socialist program, if enacted, would lead inevitably to *civil war*, and, in the event of a National Socialist victory, to *an enslavement of the majority* similar to that imposed on Russia by the Communist party. Yet in the case of Germany the most spiritual individuals would be shut out—the very men who alone can save Germany . . . today.[148]

Unlike the national spirit of every other nation, the German spirit, Keyserling suggested, was all-embracing. Thus although there was a place for Nazi racism in the German spirit, people like the Nazis who opposed the universality of the German spirit were dangerously anti-German: "In Germany anyone who places the accent mark on blood rather than spirit is in the deepest sense of the word a racial alien [*artfremd*], and not the person in whose veins no nordic blood flows."[149] In a review of Alfred Rosenberg's *Mythos des 20. Jahrhunderts*, he attacked Rosenberg for serving up "warmed over" ideas of Houston Stewart Chamberlain and dismissed the work as "absolute nonsense": "Rosenberg's book has finally made clear to me that National Socialism is, in its present form, *basically hostile to the spirit*."[150]

The famous conductor Wilhelm Furtwängler wrote to Keyserling to deplore his condemnation of national socialism. Furtwängler distanced himself from the Nazis' emphasis on racism, but suggested that it be treated sympathetically: for the National Socialist, the concept of men with superior racial qualities served in part as a substitute for the old notion of nobility. Keyserling cavalierly deprecated Furtwängler's views by replying that of course Furtwängler was offering a valid explanation of "the deepest source of faith in the new movement," but anyone who believed in the supremacy of the spirit must take a stand against overemphasis on blood.[151]

After Hitler came to power, Keyserling encountered difficulties with the new regime. There soon began what Keyserling termed a "campaign of vilification" against him.[152] This campaign may not have begun as a concerted and coordinated endeavor, as Keyserling assumed, but his assumption is readily understandable. In March 1933 he was prevented from going to Spain to lecture. In July his citizenship was taken away under a new law that permitted the revocation of the citizenship of naturalized Germans, and his two sons were also deprived of their citizenship. Although soon the Prussian minister of the interior

---

[148] "Die 'psychologische Nuss.' " Keyserling's italics.
[149] "Warum Hindenburg, nicht Hitler?"
[150] "Bücherschau," *WzV*, xx (Apr. 1932), 13–14. Keyserling's italics.
[151] "Zum Problem von Blut und Geist," *WzV*, xxi (Nov. 1932), 5–6.
[152] "Chronik der Schule der Weisheit," *WzV*, xiii (Oct. 1934), 23.

reversed these decisions, a year later Keyserling was complaining in the School of Wisdom's newsletter that, as never before in his life, he had been forced to fight for his very existence since 1933.[153] He remarked to Rathenau's biographer, Count Harry Kessler, whom he met in Paris in May 1933, that his tribulations under the Nazi regime were even worse than his experiences during the Russian Revolution.[154]

Probably in an attempt to free himself from continued harassment Keyserling wrote a long article on the new regime for the School of Wisdom's bulletin in November 1933. As presented in this article, his basic opinion of national socialism had not changed, but he expressed himself circumspectly, going out of his way to make observations that might ingratiate him with the Nazis.[155] Indeed, the article may well have been a *quid pro quo* for the restoration of his citizenship. After seeking to discourage speculation about what might have happened had the Nazis not come to power, he suggested that people over twenty-five had more difficulty than their juniors in determining their relationship to the new regime. "What," he asked rhetorically, "should one do?" "He should by all means surrender himself inwardly to the colossal things that he is experiencing." Keyserling advised against criticisms that would serve no good end, but argued that *Gleichschaltung*, although essential due to Germany's present condition, was a "purely external affair." Taking a dig at the Nazis, he noted that the need for *Gleichschaltung* was also deeply embedded in the German national character: "It *seems* [Keyserling's italics] that military customs based on command and obedience—customs which most peoples cannot comprehend, least of all the essentially nordic peoples, who are extremely individualistic—lie deep in the blood of the Germans." Obviously alluding to men like himself, he went on to suggest that non-Nazis were more useful to the new regime than were sudden converts to national socialism. He admitted that many things had turned out differently than he had wished, but he claimed to have predicted the general lines of development. "The German Revolution" was merely "a particular expression of the current world revolution, the first act of which is a revolt of long-suppressed subterranean forces. . . ."[156]

In a work in French written about the same time, he described na-

---

[153] *Ibid.*, pp. 23–24.

[154] Harry Graf Kessler, *Tagebücher 1918–1937*, ed. Wolfgang Pfeiffer-Belli (Frankfurt am Main, 1961), p. 718.

[155] Circumstantial evidence to support this interpretation of Keyserling's attitude may be found in Kessler's *Tagebücher*, esp. pp. 726–27, 729, 733. In addition to meeting Keyserling in Paris in May 1933, Kessler saw him on several other occasions during the first year of Hitler's chancellorship.

[156] "Gleichschaltung und Zusammenklang," *WzV*, XIII (Nov. 1933), 3, 5–6, 15–16.

tional socialism as "pacific and nonimperialistic" and as "the first non-imperialistic movement in modern history."[157] Although this description of national socialism seems to be a prime example of Keyserling opportunistically taking his own advice about the usefulness of non-Nazis to the new regime,[158] his analysis of Nazi Germany in the book was generally in keeping with his previous statements. He depicted national socialism as the culmination of an age-old movement against privilege, a movement, which, according to de Tocqueville, had begun in the thirteenth century.[159]

In private, he made some observations along similar lines, but put them simply in negative terms. For example, he complained to Kessler in May of 1933 that the Nazi upheaval was a "total revolution" that was leveling society and eradicating every trace of class differences. Contradicting himself, Keyserling then said that only the peasant and the small shopkeeper carried any weight under national socialism; the petty bourgeoisie now ruled Germany.[160] In a conversation less than two months later, he predicted that in ten years Germany would be ruled by Jews as a consequence of the hostility of the Nazis toward commerce and industry. On the basis of some sort of minority statute, the Jews would obtain a monopoly of all business transactions, while other Germans would be degraded to the status of *muzhiks*.[161]

His public endorsement of the Third Reich probably helped to secure him freedom of movement for several years.[162] The confusion about the Nazi regime that he spread was no doubt welcome for a while to some German officials. Although some of his works were apparently suppressed,[163] he continued to go on travels abroad until 1936 or 1937. An admirer who interviewed him for a right-wing

[157] *La révolution mondiale et la responsibilité de l'esprit* (Paris, 1934), p. 136. The book seems to have been written in late 1933 (see p. 196). A prefatory letter by Paul Valéry is dated Jan. 12, 1934.

[158] He may have regarded the description of national socialism as "pacific and nonimperialistic" as accurate. In July 1933 he remarked to Kessler that the Nazis had no interest in foreign policy. Kessler, *Tagebücher*, p. 726. Both in Germany and in the West the regime's foreign policy during its first year was often regarded in a similar light.

[159] *La révolution mondiale et la responsibilité de l'esprit*, p. 148.

[160] Kessler, *Tagebücher*, p. 718. See also p. 726.

[161] *Ibid.*, p. 727.

[162] He was willing to go beyond general approval and pay obeisance to anti-Semitism. Thus a remark in an essay published in 1937 was probably intended as a concession to the Nazis. He claimed that the Jewish press throughout the world had maligned him systematically when he refused to see Emil Ludwig because Ludwig had slandered Keyserling's mother-in-law, Princess Herbert von Bismarck. "Sinnbilder aus meinem Leben," p. 407.

[163] According to the biographical notes in *Mensch und Kosmos: Jahrbuch der Keyserling-Gesellschaft für freie Philosophie 1949*, ed. Eleonore von Dungern (Düsseldorf, 1949), p. 247, his writings were suppressed.

French journal at the end of World War II asserted that Keyserling became a virtual prisoner upon his return to Darmstadt in 1937.[164] In 1939 a polemical German doctoral dissertation castigated him for failing to understand great men and racism. Using Alfred Rosenberg's *Mythos des 20. Jahrhunderts* as a standard, this dissertation found that Keyserling's view of history was, despite many deceptive similarities, "totally different politically."[165]

During the war Keyserling withdrew to a small Tyrolean village near the ski resort of Kitzbühl. In a posthumously published autobiographical work completed shortly before the defeat of the Third Reich, he portrayed himself as far in advance of his times: "In retrospect, I can see that down to the present day I had to come into conflict with the representatives of *every* expression of the times: at home, with the Baltic Germans; in Germany, at first with the German Nationalists, but then also with the liberals and left radicals because I instinctively advocated an extremely aristocratic and hierarchical world order; later [I had to come into conflict with] the Nationalists of the newest stripe [i.e., the Nazis]."[166] The sage of Darmstadt had become a seer. The experience of Nazi Germany compelled him to postpone to the distant future any possibility of realizing his cosmopolitan, aristocratic dreams.

He had long stood uneasily between the world of aristocracy and democracy. Despite, perhaps because of, this uneasiness, he adapted his aristocratic outlook to the twentieth century, thereby gaining for himself a congenial place in Germany during the first half of the Weimar Republic. Pertaining largely to the manipulation of ideas, his advice to the Right during the immediate postwar years was often shrewd. But with Darmstadt as his base, he became an itinerant peddler of nostrums, too clever to be dismissed as a fool, but too erratic to be taken seriously. Rather than fostering the detachment from which to develop a coherent, conservative position, his distance from the day-to-day struggles of politics permitted him to indulge many of his egotistic, self-serving fancies uninhibited by realistic social and political considerations. Even as a friendly critic of the Right, he had by the early 1930's little to contribute that was not being being said more

---

[164] Pierre Frédérix, "Un petit village d'Autriche" in *Graf Hermann Keyserling: Ein Gedächtnisbuch*, ed. Keyserling-Archiv, Innsbruck-Mühlau (Innsbruck, 1948), p. 45. The interview was first published in *Carrefour*, Aug. 24, 1945.

[165] Rudolf Röhr, *Graf Keyserlings magische Geschichtsphilosophie* (Leipzig, 1939), p. 73.

[166] "Wandel der Reiche" in *Reise durch die Zeit*, III, 89. Italics Keyserling's. For an attempt to pinpoint shifts of emphasis in Keyserling's philosophy after 1933 see Hermann Noack, "Sinn und Geist: Eine Studie zu Keyserlings Anthropologie," *Zeitschrift für philosophische Forschung*, VII (1953), esp. p. 592.

cogently, if often less flamboyantly, by others. Although he was too wary of mass mobilization to share the widespread belief on the Right that the Nazis might be enlisted for conservative purposes, this wariness reflected the ideological limits of his conservative elitism. His warnings about the Nazi movement were more a function of these limits than of a soberly conservative appraisal of its functions in German society. Other elitists on the Right such as Edgar Jung and Hans Zehrer were directly involved in the politics of the later years of the Weimar Republic; their desperate search for methods of implementing their elitist ideas led them to be less pessimistic about the opportunities afforded by a temporary mobilization of the masses. Although seemingly even fonder of the aristocratic past than Keyserling, Jung had a more positive relationship to the big bourgeoisie.

CHAPTER TEN

Edgar J. Jung:
The Quest for a New Nobility

Edgar J. Jung had little of Keyserling's patience with the Weimar Republic. He did not share the Baltic aristocrat's indulgent belief that even political democracy could make positive contributions to a future elitist order. Jung built his career as a neoconservative publicist and activist on determined opposition to the German Republic. His ideals were much more simply oriented toward the past than Keyserling's. Seldom were the yearnings for preindustrial institutions, and for the revival of Christianity, common in some neoconservative circles expressed as insistently as by Jung. His views were representative of important tendencies on the Right that drew heavily upon an idyllic version of the Middle Ages. Unlike the other major twentieth-century elitists examined in this study, he relied frequently upon concepts derived from Christian theology and doctrine. With the exception of the young Naumann, he was the only one who claimed to build his political ideas upon religious foundations. Although aware of Nietzsche's interpretation of Christianity as a weapon used by the weak, resentful masses against the few superior men, Jung failed to confront this interpretation and blithely contributed to the neoconservative admiration of Nietzsche. Jung assumed that true Christian beliefs demanded the establishment of a hierarchical order in which a "new nobility" would grow "organically." He devoted his short life to serving as the herald of this new nobility. His failure to explain how the necessary "conservative revolution" would develop organically and his restless wish for the rapid emergence of the new order helped him to become a pathetic victim of the Nazi regime.

The Making of a Young Neoconservative

The road that brought Jung to prominence on the new Right was a frequently traveled one. He was born into the educated middle class in the Bavarian Palatinate in 1894. An elementary school teacher, his father later moved up to the position of *Studienprofessor* at a *lycée* for girls.¹ In 1914 young Edgar Jung marched off anxious to do his part for the inevitable German victory. He later complained that volunteers like himself from the intelligentsia had little opportunity for advancement in the German army,² but he proudly looked back on his military experiences as a turning point in his life. He returned to a new Germany from which he found himself alienated.

An incident at the war's end contributed to his dismay. A persistent tale from postwar Italy relates the humiliation of a returning officer, or even enlisted man, who, believing his sacrifices could not have been in vain, encountered abuse from a crowd of civilians embittered by the war, the military, and anything identified with them. Similar cases were recounted more rarely by Germans, but according to Jung his officer's insignia were ripped off his shoulders in 1918. He found the experience particularly distressing, he later related, because he regarded himself not as a member of the military caste, but of a broad popular stratum.³

Like Hans Zehrer and Ernst Jünger, both of whom were to find even greater significance in their membership in the "front generation," Jung continued to be involved in military actions for some time after 1918. Although he resumed his interrupted university studies almost immediately after the armistice, he joined a Free Corps unit to participate in the liberation of Munich from the yoke of the Bavarian

---

¹ Friedrich Grass, "Edgar Julius Jung" in *Pfälzer Lebensbilder*, I, ed. Kurt Baumann (Speyer, 1964), p. 320. Hereafter cited as Grass, "Jung." This twenty-eight page biography is still the most important published source of information on Jung's life. Grass, an old friend of Jung, used Jung's *Nachlass*, as has Grass's son, K. M. Grass. Although the focus of K. M. Grass's "Edgar Jung, Papenkreis und Röhmkrise 1933–34" (Heidelberg diss., 1966) is on the last months of Jung's life, he presents some material not available elsewhere on Jung's earlier career. Bernhard Jenschke, *Zur Kritik der konservativ-revolutionären Ideologie in der Weimarer Republik: Weltanschauung und Politik bei Edgar Julius Jung* (Munich, [1971?]) is a generally reliable if judgmental and uninspired examination of Jung's life and thought. Two other works on Jung will be mentioned here because of the material they contain and points of view they represent. Chapter VI of George K. Romoser, "The Crisis of Political Direction in the German Resistance to Nazism: Its Nature, Origins, and Effects" (Chicago diss., 1958) is devoted to Jung. Hereafter cited as Romoser, "Crisis." Although brief and fragmentary, Romoser's account of Jung's career draws upon some information obtained from Jung's acquaintances. Leopold Ziegler, *Edgar Julius Jung: Denkmal und Vermächtnis* (Munich, 1955) is a brief biographical sketch written by another of Jung's friends. Hereafter cited as Ziegler, *Jung*. Ziegler, whom we have encountered also in connection with Rathenau and Keyserling, was encouraged by Jung's family to prepare a work dedicated to Jung's memory. Some of Ziegler's material on Jung's career before the late 1920's can not be found in other published works.

² "Die Tragik der Kriegsgeneration," *Süddeutsche Monatshefte*, XXVII (May 1930), 522–23.

³ *Ibid.*, p. 523.

Soviet Republic in the spring of 1919.[4] During the Franco-Belgian occupation of the Ruhr in 1923–1924, he was active in organizing ter-
rorist resistance activities. He played a central role in the successful
plot to assassinate the president of the newly proclaimed Autonomous
Republic of the Palatinate, a separatist state whose brief existence
owed much to French intrigues.[5] Like many of Jung's activities directed against the French, Palatine separatism, and the German Left,
the assassination may have received financial support from the Bavarian government.

Unlike many other middle-class members of the front generation
who became involved in the Free Corps and their successors, Jung
established himself in a respectable bourgeois occupation. Even before
the invasion of the Ruhr, he had completed his studies, obtained a doctorate in *Jura*, and begun to practice law in Zweibrücken. He entered
the law firm of *Geheimrat* Dr. Albert Zapf, who had close ties to regional business interests. Both men were active in the German People's
party (DVP). Zapf belonged to the Reichstag; Jung served on the directory of the local DVP.[6] A broad rightist coalition, the DVP in the
Bavarian Palatinate contained a wider range of conservative elements
than those predominant in the national organization of the party.
Groups like the League of Agriculturalists, which had been linked
closely to the former Conservative party and which elsewhere joined
the Nationalist party after the November Revolution, combined with
old National Liberals in the Palatine branch of the DVP.

Jung's activities during the time of the Ruhr occupation led to his
expulsion from the Palatinate by the French. After the passing of the
crisis of 1923–1924, he established himself as an attorney in Munich,
which remained his home until his death. We know little of Jung's

[4] "Aufstand der Rechten," *Deutsche Rundschau*, ccxxix (1931), 81; Grass,
"Jung," pp. 321–22.

[5] See Grass, "Jung," pp. 324–28; Romoser, "Crisis," p. 190; Robert G. L. Waite,
Vanguard of Nazism: The Free Corps Movement in Postwar Germany, 1918–1923
(New York: Norton paperback, 1969), pp. 234–35; Paul Fechter, *Menschen und
Zeiten: Begegnungen aus 5 Jahrzehnten*, 2nd ed. (Gütersloh, 1949), p. 358. See
also the account of the assassination by a British journalist, G.E.R. Gedye, *Die
Revolver-Republik: Frankreichs Werben um den Rhein*, trans. Hans Garduck
(Cologne, 1931), pp. 241–42. The German edition of this work is more detailed
than the English original entitled *The Revolver Republic: France's Bid for the
Rhine* (London, 1930).

[6] See Grass, "Jung," pp. 322–24; Karl Schwendt, *Bayern zwischen Monarchie
und Diktatur: Beiträge zur bayerischen Frage in der Zeit von 1918 bis 1933*
(Munich, 1954), p. 578; Romoser, "Crisis," p. 190. For some fragmentary information on Zapf's role as a representative of South German sugar processing
interests see Lothar Döhn, *Politik und Interesse: Die Interessenstruktur der
Deutschen Volkspartei* (Meisenheim am Glan, 1970), pp. 359, n. 1506, 410, 425.

career as a lawyer,[7] but obviously his political activities, which may often have been closely related, continued to make great demands upon his time and energy. Although he was drifting away from the DVP, he ran on its list for the Reichstag in both elections of 1924.[8] Through his political associations and his involvement with the *Juni-Klub* he came into contact with many of the writers subsequently known as neoconservatives. Throughout the remainder of the decade of the 1920's, Jung continued to be active in right-wing clubs, including the *Herrenklub*.[9]

During these same years, Jung made his name as a political writer. Since the time of the Ruhr invasion, he had been writing an occasional article for business-oriented and right-wing periodicals,[10] but once the stabilization of the Republic became apparent he seems to have felt the need to develop in depth both a conservative critique of democracy and an alternative to Weimar.[11] Many of his longer essays appeared in the *Deutsche Rundschau*, which, under the editorship of Rudolf Pechel, displayed strong neoconservative tendencies. Jung's major work, *Die Herrschaft der Minderwertigen* (*The Rule of the Inferior*), was published in late 1927 or early 1928 by the *Deutsche Rundschau*'s own press.[12] When a revised edition was issued two years later, the book's size had more than doubled. It had grown into a massive, meandering volume of almost seven hundred pages, which Jean

---

[7] The literature on Jung scarcely mentions it.

[8] Grass, "Jung," p. 324.

[9] See esp. *ibid.*, p. 332; Romoser, "Crisis," p. 193; Hans-Joachim Schwierskott, *Arthur Moeller van den Bruck und der revolutionäre Nationalismus in der Weimarer Republik* (Göttingen, [1962]), p. 20.

[10] Both K. M. Grass "Edgar Jung, Papenkreis und Röhmkrise" and Jenschke, *Zur Kritik der konservativ-revolutionären Ideologie* draw upon Jung's articles in such newspapers as the *Münchner Neueste Nachrichten*, the *Berliner Börsenzeitung*, and the *Rheinisch-Westfälische Zeitung*.

[11] Cf. his pretentious statement in a letter of Aug. 21, 1930 to Leopold Ziegler: ". . . ich bin aus der Praxis und aus der Politik zum Spekulativen gekommen. Weil meine zahlreichen Versuche politisch zu wirken, ob es nun mit der Pistole in der Hand oder als Reichstagskandidat war, einfach an dem Ungeist der Zeit und des Systems scheiterten, stellte ich mir die Aufgabe, dieses System aus seinen Wurzeln zu heben, weil alles andere nur Symptombekämpfung ist." Quoted in Grass, "Jung," p. 335.

[12] *Die Herrschaft der Minderwertigen: Ihr Zerfall und ihre Ablösung durch ein neues Reich* (Berlin, 1927). All references to this work will be to the second edition (Berlin, 1930) and will be cited as *HdM*. An important recent monograph on Pechel sheds little new light on Jung, but contributes generally to our knowledge of the relationship between neoconservative writers and big business. See Volker Mauersberger, *Rudolf Pechel und die "Deutsche Rundschau" 1919–1933: Eine Studie zur konservativ-revolutionären Publizistik in der Weimarer Republik* (Bremen, 1971).

Neurohr refers to as the bible of neoconservatism.[13] Both because of Jung's lack of intellectual rigor and his obvious preference for ambiguous formulations that would offend as few right-wingers as possible, the work was one that could appeal to many diverse tendencies. Yet a more fitting description might be the bible of "young conservatism," as the ideas of those neoconservatives have often been termed who looked for inspiration to early nineteenth-century conservatism and to the Middle Ages. Even this description is misleading, since Zehrer and Spengler have often been identified with the Young Conservatives, but many of Jung's political ideas were sharply at variance with those of both men. Almost invariably he invoked Spengler's authority as if there were no grounds for disagreement, although he once hinted at a pivotal difference. In the preface to the second edition of the *Herrschaft der Minderwertigen*, Jung noted that he dared to challenge the older man's "pessimism."[14] Jung may well have had in mind Spengler's refusal to grant the possibility of a new civilization that would be inspired by the Middle Ages. Spengler's concept of Caesarism seems to have struck Jung as a dangerous updating of an ancient institution.

Jung became deeply involved in the revival of corporatist doctrines during the Weimar Republic. Although conservative Roman Catholics exhibited a marked interest in corporatism, it colored the thought of many groups from the Right to the non-Marxist Left.[15] As a method of constructing a viable social order that would reduce social conflict and stabilize society without entailing a social revolution it had a broad appeal on the Right. Corporatism became very popular among neoconservatives. Young Conservatives who like Jung were Protestants often felt strongly attracted to Catholicism. Indeed, after 1918 many a devout Lutheran came to believe that the Catholic Church stood closer to the ideals of the Reformation than the Protestant sects and state churches.[16] An astute analyst of right-wing political thought has observed that it is difficult to distinguish the ideas of Protestant Young

---

[13] Jean F. Neurohr, *Der Mythos vom 3. Reich: Zur Geistesgeschichte des Nationalsozialismus* (Stuttgart, 1957), p. 187.

[14] *HdM*, p. 12. K. M. Grass, "Edgar Jung, Papenkreis und Röhmkrise," n. 49, writes that two men knew each other well, but does not elaborate.

[15] For a brief discussion of the attractions of corporatism see Heinrich Busshoff, "Berufständisches Gedankengut zu Beginn der 30er Jahre in Österreich und Deutschland," *Zeitschrift für Politik*, XII (1966), 451–63. For more detailed surveys see esp. Ralph H. Bowen, *German Theories of the Corporative State: With Special Reference to the Period 1870–1919* (New York, 1947), and Justus Beyer, *Die Ständeideologien der Systemzeit und ihre Überwindung*, Forschungen zum Staats- und Verwaltungsrecht, ed. Reinhard Höhn, Reihe A, VIII (Darmstadt, 1941).

[16] See Neurohr, *Der Mythos vom 3. Reich*, p. 186.

Conservatives from those of many Catholics on the Right.[17] Jung looked forward to the union of the Christian Churches in Germany, although he considered a formal act unnecessary.[18] He became so closely identified with neoconservative Catholic circles[19] that many of his contemporaries, including some personal acquaintances, believed that he was either a Catholic or a convert to Catholicism. Even recent historians have contributed to the confusion about Jung's religious affiliations.[20] In the late 1920's and early 1930's, he served as one of the most important spokesmen for a Christian-oriented neoconservatism that was espoused by a small but growing group of publicists in the Center

---

[17] See Klaus-Peter Hoepke, *Die deutsche Rechte und der italienische Faschismus: Ein Beitrag zum Selbstverständnis und zur Politik von Gruppen und Verbänden der deutschen Rechten* (Düsseldorf, 1968), pp. 69–77.

[18] See *HdM*, p. 85.

[19] See esp. Klaus Breuning, *Die Vision des Reiches: Deutscher Katholizismus zwischen Demokratie und Diktatur (1929–1934)* (Munich, 1969), pp. 107–08. Most of the studies of Catholic political thought and action at the end of the Weimar Republic and the beginning of the Third Reich have concentrated upon the relationship of the Church and the Center party to the Nazis. Although largely descriptive, Breuning's study contributes to the broadening of these questions by surveying the backward-looking views of Catholics who propagated the notion of a revival of the medieval Reich.

[20] Among Jung's contemporaries his admiring friend Hermann Rauschning was probably a major source of the belief that Jung was a Catholic. See Rauschning's *The Conservative Revolution* (New York, 1941), p. 51. Four examples will illustrate the continuing confusion. Fritz Stern's *The Politics of Cultural Despair: A Study in the Rise of the Germanic Ideology* (Berkeley, 1961), p. 296n. refers to Jung as "a leading conservative revolutionary among Catholics." A study of the Bavarian Right takes for granted that he was a Catholic: James Donohoe, *Hitler's Conservative Opponents in Bavaria, 1930–1945: A Study of Catholic, Monarchist, and Anti-Nazi Activities* (Leiden, 1961), p. 29, n. 15. A recently published short history of the Church by a Catholic historian, A. Franzen, *Kleine Kirchengeschichte* (Freiburg im Breisgau, 1965), p. 373 alludes to Jung as a "leader of the Catholic Church." (For this example I am indebted to Breuning, *Die Vision des Reiches*, p. 108, n. 68.) Eliot B. Wheaton, *The Nazi Revolution, 1933–1935: Prelude to Calamity* (Garden City, N.Y., 1969), p. 541, n. 221 describes Jung as a "Jewish lawyer who had been converted to Catholicism." I have found no tangible evidence to support the belief that Jung ever converted to Catholicism. His Catholic friend and political confidant Edmund Forschbach does not mention the possibility in a study in which the information would have been pertinent. See Edmund Forschbach, "Edgar Jung und der Widerstand gegen Hitler," *Civis: Zeitschrift für christlich-demokratische Politik*, VI (Nov. 11, 1959), 82-88. Hereafter this article will be cited as Forschbach, "Jung." The unfounded belief that Jung was born into a Jewish or partly Jewish family seems to have originated with his political opponents. This belief was promoted during the late 1920's by Nazis seeking to discredit Jung among right-wing students. In 1928 Baldur von Schirach, the head of the National Socialist Student Association, responded to an inquiry about Jung from a local chapter by warning that Jung was a *Halbjude*, whose frequent speeches to students were all the more insidious since they were often stolen, almost word for word, from Hitler's and therefore gave many unsuspecting people the erroneous impression that Hitler was a popularizer of Jung's ideas. The letter is reproduced in Harry Pross, ed., *Die Zerstörung der deutschen Politik: Dokumente 1871–1933* (Hamburg, 1959), p. 367.

party, by the circle around Martin Spahn, a leader of the Center party who joined the Nationalists in 1921, and by many Protestant neoconservatives close to, or members of, the parties of the Right.

A popularizer who drew his ideas from many sources, Jung found a major source of inspiration in the work of Othmar Spann, a Viennese sociologist and perhaps the most prominent theoretician of corporatism in the German-speaking lands during the twentieth century.[21] Spann's influence contributed to Jung's dependence upon the reverent view of medieval corporative institutions developed by the German Romantics of the early nineteenth century. He shared Spann's almost boundless admiration for Adam Müller, whom Spann depicted as the founder of his own school and as one of the greatest economists and political theorists of all times.[22] Due to the work of Jung and other German admirers, Spann's influence in Germany came to reach far into the ranks of Catholic intellectuals and the Center party by the time the Nazis came to power.[23]

The old middle class of artisans and small businessmen was the social group most strongly attracted to notions of reordering society through the establishment of corporative bodies based largely or entirely on occupational divisions and provided with broad self-regulating powers. To the old middle class the formation or consolidation of "estates" and other corporative institutions promised a secure status in society, as well as a halt to, or even reversal of, the development of industrial capitalism with its giant, monopolistic enterprises and massive, consolidated trade unions.

The interest taken by big business in corporatism was not as intense or widespread. Much less vulnerable than any other segment of big business to the threat of competition from rejuvenated small firms and artisan enterprises, heavy industry was the sector of big business that gave the most backing to corporative doctrines.[24] Corporatism offered

[21] Spann's most popular work, *Der wahre Staat: Vorlesungen über Abbruch und Neubau der Gesellschaft*, 3rd ed. (Jena, 1931), was first published in 1921. The excellent chapter on Spann in Herman Lebovics, *Social Conservatism and the Middle Classes in Germany, 1914–1933* (Princeton, 1969), includes a perceptive general discussion of the role of corporatism in Germany and Austria. See also the instructive analysis of Spann's thought in Alfred Diamant, *Austrian Catholics and the First Republic: Democracy, Capitalism, and the Social Order, 1918–1934* (Princeton, 1960), esp. pp. 131–40, 229–40. Martin Schneller, *Zwischen Romantik und Faschismus: Der Beitrag Othmar Spanns zum Konservatismus in der Weimarer Republik* (Stuttgart, 1970) is uninspired but useful.

[22] See Othmar Spann, *Die Haupttheorien der Volkswirtschaftslehre auf lehrgeschichtlicher Grundlage*, 24. Aufl. (Leipzig, 1936), pp. 103–04.

[23] For some indications of the growth of Spann's popularity among German Catholics see Breuning, *Die Vision des Reiches*, pp. 37–38, 76–77.

[24] For succinct general discussions of big business attitudes toward corporatism see Heinrich August Winkler, "Unternehmerverbände zwischen Ständeideologie und Nationalsozialismus," *Vierteljahrshefte für Zeitgeschichte*, xvii (1969), 341–

a way of bidding for support from the old middle class, while deflecting its frustrations away from big business. Perhaps more importantly, the monopolistic structure of big business, as we saw in discussing Rathenau, might be consolidated by the formation of self-policing economic associations. These associations, even if glamorously renamed "corporative bodies," could promote cooperation among industrial giants and increase their leverage in dealing with the state.

The political situation offered perhaps the strongest stimulus to the intensified interest in corporatism in big business circles during the last years of the Republic. The political strength of the working class rested directly on the role played by Social Democracy in government, particularly in Prussia, and this role made the drastic reduction of social welfare benefits difficult and their elimination impossible. By the late 1920's, some segments of big business were searching desperately for ways of bypassing or destroying the parliamentary bodies whose composition blocked the dismantling of welfare institutions and interfered with the realization of other business policies. More directly vulnerable to trade unionist pressures and more heavily burdened by mandatory contributions to welfare institutions, small and middle-sized businessmen were potential allies in these endeavors by big business. While commercial and banking circles exhibited much less interest in corporatism, by 1932 the major association representing their interests, the National Chamber of Industry and Commerce (*Deutscher Industrie- und Handelstag*), was calling privately for an upper house of parliament that would be appointed by the president of the Reich and governments of the states and that would be able to override the wishes of the Reichstag.[25] The consistent application of most versions of corporatism would have blocked the development of the strong state powers that many big businessmen had come to desire, but the piecemeal introduction of corporatist measures promised some immediate gains through the establishment of economic and political chambers that would assume powers still entrusted to parliaments and coalition governments.

Middle-class corporatists and other backward-looking right-wingers like Jung have often been depicted misleadingly as the purveyors of ideas serving past rather than present interests. The industrialization of Germany, it is argued, occurred with such rapidity that many Ger-

---

71; Ernst Lange, *Die politische Ideologie der deutschen industriellen Unternehmerschaft* (Greifswald diss., 1933), esp. pp. 67–70; Wilhelm Treue, "Der deutsche Unternehmer in der Weltwirtschaftskrise 1928 bis 1933" in Werner Conze and Hans Raupach, eds., *Die Staats- und Wirtschaftskrise des deutschen Reiches 1929–1933*, Industrielle Welt, viii (Stuttgart, 1967), esp. pp. 118–19.

[25] Treue, "Deutschlands Unternehmer in der Weltwirtschaftskrise," p. 119.

mans clung to preindustrial attitudes.[26] Even when this argument is modified to suggest that these attitudes were reinforced by the survival of many preindustrial institutions and were related to the discontents of the old middle class, the classic question that must be put to Jung's work—*cui bono?*—is only partly answered. Although many of his ideas may have spoken to the ills of the old middle class, he was not an ideologist for it. His enchantment with preindustrial institutions expressed not so much a desire to return to the past as an effort to highlight the ills of the present. Like T. S. Eliot, Jung and many other neoconservatives invoked the Romantic image of the Middle Ages as a harmonious society in which everyone had the security of knowing where he stood.[27] Jung's critique of the present served as the basis for demands for modifications in existing institutions, not for their wholesale destruction. Many of these demands were governed by the concerns of substantial segments of the middle class, but he tended to accommodate his ideas to the interests of big business.

We know much less about his personal relationships with big businessmen than we do about Spengler's. Through Jung's work for the DVP and in the right-wing clubs that he frequented after 1924 he certainly encountered big businessmen, as well as journalists, publishers, and politicians. It was probably in these circles that he became acquainted with Spengler's friend Paul Reusch and other prominent businessmen.[28] Although there are indications that the publication of Jung's works was assisted by financial support from Ruhr industrialists,[29] some of the more important of his associations with business circles may not have developed until after 1930.[30]

[26] The classic formulation of this thesis is still Helmut Plessner, *Schicksal des deutschen Geistes am Ausgang seiner bürgerlichen Epoche* (Zurich, 1935). A postwar edition of Plessner's work appeared under the title *Die verspätete Nation: Über die politische Verführbarkeit des bürgerlichen Geistes* (Stuttgart, 1959).

[27] We have already encountered similar allusions in Keyserling's work, but Keyserling did not use them to summarize an entire political program. It might be noted that while Jung and his intellectual compatriots blithely propagated their view of the Middle Ages, Marc Bloch was in the midst of working out a skillfully documented interpretation of medieval society that provided the starting point for a rewriting of medieval history incompatible with this Romantic view.

[28] Grass, "Jung," p. 333 states without elaborating that after 1924 Jung came into contact with big businessmen and was especially close to Reusch, Minoux, Karl Haniel, Duisberg, and Brandi. According to Henry A. Turner, Jr., "The Ruhrlade, Secret Cabinet of Heavy Industry in the Weimar Republic," *Central European History*, III (1970), p. 220, n. 91, Jung received a monthly subsidy of 2,000 marks (in 1931?) from an organization of Rhenish-Westphalian industrialists. After Jung's murder in 1934, Reusch provided funds for his family. K. M. Grass, "Edgar Jung, Papenkreis und Röhmkrise," n. 6.

[29] See Winkler, "Unternehmerverbände zwischen Ständeideologie und Nationalsozialismus," p. 346, n. 14.

[30] See Forschbach, "Jung," esp. p. 82. Cf. Grass, "Jung," pp. 343–44.

The basic reasons for his friendly relationships with big business must be sought both in the sympathy for corporatism present in industrial circles, as well as in the political objectives, such as the destruction of state social welfare agencies, that he shared with many businessmen. Both his *Herrschaft der Minderwertigen* and Spann's major treatise on corporatism were favorably reviewed in *Der Arbeitgeber*, one of the most important organs of German employers.[31] Jung left little doubt as to his general attitude toward organized labor. For example, in a series of reports on Germany written for a prestigious Swiss periodical, he often alluded to the deleterious consequences of the class consciousness and political power of the German worker. Among the more serious of these consequences were enormous business debts, excessive wages, and, most alarming, a threat to the capitalist system of the entire world.[32] On occasion, he went out of his way to praise heavy industry, as when he excepted Ruhr industry from his complaint about the unsympathetic attitude of businessmen toward war veterans seeking jobs. Outside the Ruhr, he asserted, members of the front generation were regarded with suspicion and the experience of age was preferred to the energy of youth.[33]

Yet there is little evidence that Jung came as close as Spengler to serving as a propagandist for heavy industry. Jung's attitude toward big business was often very critical, and, more important, the ramifications of some of his doctrines were at odds with the development and policies of German monopoly capital. He never clarified the role big business would have in a society modeled on preindustrial institutions. This failure may have bothered him. Certainly it contributed to his feeling of uneasiness when he dealt with economic issues; a close associate reports that Jung remarked that economics was "not his kettle of fish."[34]

[31] Winkler, "Unternehmerverbände zwischen Ständeideologie und Nationalsozialismus," p. 346.

[32] See, e.g., "Bericht aus dem Deutschen Reiche," *Schweizer[ische] Monatshefte*, x (Apr. 1930), 39 and xi (Aug.-Sept. 1931), 275–76. Jung began this series of articles for the *Schweizer Monatshefte* in 1927. Some contributions in the series were published under different titles.

[33] "Tragik der Kriegsgeneration," p. 529.

[34] Ziegler, *Jung*, p. 16. Ziegler (p. 17) states that Jung obtained advice on economic matters from "einem wirtschaftlichen Vertrauensmanne." It is unclear whether Ziegler means that Jung received advice from a representative of industry, as the passage implies, or simply from a man well versed in economics whom he respected, as Ziegler seems to indicate on the preceding page. In the preface to the second edition of the *Herrschaft der Minderwertigen*, Jung thanks three men for help in revising and expanding sections of the work, but fails to note any assistance with the sections on economics. One of these three was his law partner Otto Leibrecht. Another was Karl E. von Loesch of the *Deutscher Schutzbund*, an organization to which Jung acknowledged a substantial intellectual debt for ideas on foreign policy. Founded in 1919, the *Schutzbund* cooperated with

CHRISTIANITY VERSUS DEMOCRACY?

Jung's critique of democracy lacked originality. He rested the cornerstone of his case on the consequences of human inequality. His use of religious arguments gave his critique its distinctive appearance. But as compelling as he found concepts drawn from Christian theology and doctrine, he was never content to rely solely or even primarily upon them. Despite his often effusive religious sentiments, he was unable or unwilling to express his political and social views consistently through the medium of Christian doctrine.

His views were untouched by the revival of natural law concepts that began in some Catholic circles in Germany during the late nineteenth century and that inspired the corporatism of the Catholic "Solidarists," many of whom were close to the Christian trade-union wing of the Center party. Like Spann and like most German Catholic political thinkers, he accepted the struggle waged by Adam Müller and other theorists of the German Restoration against any form of secularized natural law. Thus Jung's repudiation of the theory of natural rights was in the mainstream of German Catholic, as well as Protestant, thought.[35]

Jung assailed democracy as a derivation from "that political plague of the Western World"—the notion of human equality.[36] The typical attitude of later Lutheran pessimism appeared in his relegation of the notion of equality to a realm where it did not even have the significance of a normative principle for social or political reality. He recognized equality only in a "metaphysical" sense: ". . . There is only one place where men . . . are equal—before God."[37] A religious ideal, he complained, was corrupted by its secularization. The application of a religious ideal to "this world" could never be complete and therefore "debased" the ideal itself.[38] Anyone who attempted to transfer the no-

---

the older and much better known VDA (*Verein für des Deutschtum im Ausland*), which claimed to confine itself to cultural matters. The *Schutzbund* seems to have been active particularly in Central Europe, becoming involved in political activities that the VDA, for tactical and other reasons, avoided. See Kurt Sontheimer, *Antidemokratisches Denken in der Weimarer Republik: Die politischen Ideen des deutschen Nationalismus zwischen 1918 und 1933* (Munich, 1962), p. 311; Hans-Adolf Jacobsen, *Nationalsozialistische Aussenpolitik 1933–1938* (Frankfurt am Main and Berlin, 1968), p. 165. See also the discussion of the *Schutzbund* in Mauersberger, *Rudolf Pechel und die "Deutsche Rundschau,"* pp. 41–46.

[35] On the weakness of natural law theory in German Catholic thought see Edgar Alexander, "Church and Society in Germany" in Joseph N. Moody, ed., *Catholic Social and Political Movements, 1789–1950* (New York, 1953), pp. 377, 497–98.

[36] *HdM*, p. 101.

[37] *Sinndeutung der deutschen Revolution* (Oldenburg, 1933), p. 103. Hereafter cited as *Sinndeutung*.

[38] *HdM*, pp. 95–96.

tion of equality to human affairs committed "a sin against nature and reality."[39]

Jung buttressed this theological line of thought with secular considerations. The granting of equal rights to everyone led inevitably to a war of all against all. The resulting anarchy would destroy any worthwhile society.[40] To Jung the primary goal of democracy lay in an "unnatural" endeavor to realize the ideal of equality. Since men were patently unequal, democracy permitted and furthered the rule of the mediocre. Citing Tocqueville and Nietzsche, Jung imputed to most men envy and resentment against anything superior. The majority tolerated nothing better than itself. In a democracy the masses had to be cajoled, and their fickleness precluded the emergence of capable leadership. Thus the German public permitted no outstanding individuals in leading positions.[41]

Stemming from democracy's emphasis upon equality, the majority principle, Jung suggested, encouraged everyone to seek merely his own self-interest. To most men self-interest indicated simply material interests. Economic values became predominant, and the strongest economic power, finance capital, exploited the "era of the masses." Making distinctions favored by heavy industry and employed by Spengler, Jung spoke contemptuously of the "financial pirates" who inevitably manipulated democracy and political parties to their own advantage.[42] Jung considered political parties as vital links in an unequal alliance between finance capital and the masses. The parties always duped the masses. "Private associations for the rule of money,"[43] they served to mask the pursuit of private interests, which were seldom more than those of the party leaders themselves and the finance capitalists. One of the main functions of the parties consisted in the organization of the masses in order that an oligarchy within each of them could maintain its power.[44] As instruments employed by the party faithful to advance themselves, the parties did not promote the ascent of the individual in accordance with his achievements and his ethical commitment to service.[45] Jung appealed to the authority of Robert Michels to substantiate this view of the workings of political parties.

During the Weimar Republic, Michels's "iron law of oligarchy" became a basic axiom for many political scientists from the moderate Left to the Right. While these men agreed in recognizing the accuracy

[39] *Sinndeutung*, p. 96. [40] *HdM*, pp. 47, 270.
[41] See, e.g., *ibid.*, pp. 22, 160, 237, 247, 260, 325.
[42] See, e.g., *ibid.*, pp. 96, 106, 172, 178–81.
[43] *Ibid.*, p. 231. [44] *Ibid.*, pp. 231, 249, 286.
[45] *Ibid.*, p. 344.

of the "iron law," they differed in their assessment of its significance, which they in turn viewed as an unfortunate inevitability, a desirable development, or the beginning of the self-destruction of the parties.[46] A second edition of Michels's *Political Parties* in 1925 formed the center of repeated discussions of the nature of modern parties. The reorganizations of the Social Democratic party in the early years of the Republic further accentuated the prewar tendencies analyzed by Michels, while the Communist party and later the National Socialist party, each in its own way, developed a hierarchical structure to a still greater extent.[47]

To Jung the differences between the theory and the practice of democracy did not resemble the "normal" tension between theory and practice. In most democracies, especially in England, an aristocracy actually ruled and prevented the "excesses" that had occurred in Germany. In the West, where democracy was not a "foreign import," the ideology of democracy had not gotten completely out of hand. In Germany, an unjustified and deceptive belief in democracy had become intoxicating. The least scrupulous and least capable leaders had triumphed. The notion of equality had prompted the naive Germans to believe in the possibility of a society without an elite.[48]

Despite his belief that the parliamentary system was decaying in the West, Jung marveled at the stability of English society. In the midst of the depression he observed wryly: "In England an unemployed man votes for the tail-coated lord; in Germany the tail-coated votes for the unemployed National Socialist."[49] In this passage, as in many others, Jung expressed the social concerns that shaped his attitude toward postwar Germany. Even more revealing was his description of a viable

[46] See, e.g., Herbert Sultan, "Zur Soziologie des modernen Parteisystems," *Archiv für Sozialwissenschaft und Sozialpolitik*, LV (1926), 109; Alfred Weber, *Die Krise des modernen Staatsgedankens in Europa* (Berlin, 1925), pp. 137–38; Heinrich Triepel, *Die Staatsverfassung und die politischen Parteien* (Berlin, 1928), p. 35.

[47] See Richard N. Hunt, *German Social Democracy, 1918–1933* (New Haven, 1964), esp. pp. 44–47, 70–74; Karl Dietrich Bracher, *Die Auflösung der Weimarer Republik: Eine Studie zum Problem des Machtverfalls in der Demokratie*, 3rd ed. (Villingen im Schwarzwald, 1960), pp. 74–79, 98, 112, 122.

[48] *HdM*, pp. 23–24, 69, 168, 238–39, 331; *Sinndeutung*, p. 44. Cf. the following statements by another Young Conservative, the classical scholar Hans Bogner, whose elite theory resembled Jung's rather closely: ". . . In der grossen modernen Nation regiert das Volk nicht unmittelbar, regieren vielmehr nur einzelne, konkrete Personen, eine Minderheit, die durch jeden wirklichen Regierungsakt der Ideologie, durch die sie allein legitimiert ist, zuwiderhandeln muss." "Die gedanklichen Voraussetzungen dieser [Weimarer] Verfassung sind einer politischen Führung aus Grundsatz feindlich und vielmehr dahin gerichtet, jede Möglichkeit einer Führung systematisch zu verbieten." Hans Bogner, *Die Bildung der politischen Elite* (Oldenburg, 1932), pp. 20, 21.

[49] "Aufstand der Rechten," *Deutsche Rundschau*, CCXXIX (1931), 87.

democracy as "the consequence of a social stratification that permits an upper class [*Oberschicht*] rich in tradition to rule with the consent of the masses, and in their name."[50] In another of his many definitions of true democracy, he referred to "trusting belief in the leadership of the Best, whom a people places above itself as a symbol."[51]

THE REICH OF THE NEW NOBILITY

Jung believed that only a "spiritual revival" would overcome the crisis provoked by democracy in Germany. He dated the beginnings of this revival with World War I. The most important consequences of the completion of the revival would consist in the final development of a new nobility in Germany and the resurgence of German power in Europe. Both consequences would be intricately intertwined.

Like Naumann, Weber, Rathenau, and Spengler, Jung adhered explicitly to the doctrine of the primacy of foreign policy. The effects of domestic policies had to be measured by their value for international politics. But Jung carried this doctrine a step farther than Naumann and Weber by making explicit an assumption that he shared with Rathenau and Spengler. The formulation of foreign policy should not in any way be dependent upon domestic politics, for "politics really exists only between states" since the term "assumes the existence of more than one group struggling for power."[52] Struggles over foreign policy were characteristic of the era of the rule of parties and the degeneration of parliament. Only an elite that was accepted unquestioningly by the people and whose foreign policy was in the interest of the entire nation could pursue foreign affairs successfully. Most men lacked the qualifications even to assess foreign affairs. Democracy therefore increased the role of chance and mass passions in the making of foreign policy. Since Germany no longer had a nobility capable of conducting foreign affairs, the proper formulation and execution of policies awaited the advent of the new nobility.[53]

Jung's strong emotional commitment to the notion of German superiority made the spiritual revival of Germany and the resulting emergence of a new nobility appear still more urgent. He argued vigorously for the inequality of nations. Nations were equal only in the sense that individuals were equal.[54] The equality of nations would al-

---

[50] "Deutschland und die konservative Revolution" in Edgar J. Jung, ed., *Deutsche über Deutschland: Die Stimme des unbekannten Politikers* (Munich, 1932), p. 372.

[51] "Bericht aus dem Deutschen Reiche," *Schweizer Monatshefte*, vii (1927), 464.

[52] *HdM*, p. 158. See also pp. 294, 454, 599.

[53] *Ibid.*, pp. 157, 266, 625.

[54] See *ibid.*, pp. 7, 96, 103, 113, 117; *Sinndeutung*, p. 96.

ways remain merely a metaphysical principle. In all essential respects, and especially "spiritually," the German nation was superior to all others.[55] It would perform the leading role in the "spiritual revival" of the West. "Europe's salvation" would be a "new Middle Ages" initiated by Germans.[56] "Fate" had entrusted the German nation, as the "prophet of a better Europe," with the "mission" of reordering the entire continent.[57]

Like many other neoconservatives, Jung hoped that Germany would initiate a "revolution" with "even more universal significance" than the French Revolution. The "German Revolution" would break the chains wrought by the Treaty of Versailles and establish a new European order, for "whoever introduces a new principle of order into social and political existence will lead for the coming centuries."[58] The Germans could transform their recent defeat into an overwhelming victory: "Every true revolution is a world revolution. If the German Revolution is to ascend to such heights, an idea conceived by Germans must redeem a tormented and fragmented continent."[59]

Jung did not specify the form that German leadership would assume, but like Moeller van den Bruck and other Young Conservatives, as well as a small group of right-wing Catholic politicians, publicists, historians, and poets,[60] he associated his plans with a revival of the medieval Empire.[61] Presumably, ethnic conflicts within the indefinite, but extensive boundaries of the new Reich would vanish. Jung relied upon the skills of the new German nobility and upon decentralized political institutions[62] to overcome ethnic tensions. The foremost mission of his new nobility would consist in erecting a Reich encompassing most of Europe and ensuring German predominance on the Continent. The accomplishment of this mission was predicated upon the destruction of the socialist movement. Jung noted pointedly that the old upper class had failed to avert the rise of socialism by leading the German worker in his "healthy longing for social justice."[63]

Jung took pains to disassociate the Reich of his dreams from colonial

---

[55] *HdM*, pp. 75–76, 120, 379, 627, 654.

[56] *Ibid.*, pp. 91–92.

[57] *Ibid.*, pp. 515, 629. See also pp. 26, 79, 371, 676; *Sinndeutung*, pp. 42–43; "Die Bedeutung des Faschismus für Europa," *Deutsche Rundschau*, ccxxvii (1931), 186; "Revolutionäre Aussenpolitik," *Deutsche Rundschau*, ccxxx (1932), 90.

[58] "Neubelebung von Weimar?" *Deutsche Rundschau*, ccxxxi (1932), 157.

[59] *Sinndeutung*, p. 96.

[60] See Breuning, *Die Vision des Reiches*, p. 151 and passim.

[61] See *HdM*, pp. 388, 629; *Sinndeutung*, p. 96; "Deutschland und die konservative Revolution," p. 96.

[62] See esp. "Die Föderalistische Staatsidee und ihre aussenpolitische Bedeutung," *Süddeutsche Monatshefte*, xxv (1928), 259–62.

[63] *HdM*, p. 446.

imperialism. He did not regard German expansion on the continent as imperialistic, and unlike Naumann, Weber, Rathenau, and Spengler he disclaimed any interest in the acquisition of colonies overseas.[64] He intoned internationalist, Pan-European notes, although not as loudly and frequently as Keyserling did.

THE ROOTS OF THE NEW NOBILITY

Jung's thought contained strong traces of the cult of great men, but an elite headed by a great man did not occupy a prominent place in his plans. He desired an elite which would preclude any need for great men: "A genius at the head of a nation is a rarity, and the lack of a successor equal in rank is a danger. It is therefore desirable that a stratum exist which can at any time replace a departing individual possessing leadership qualities with an individual equal in value and similar in tendencies."[65] Like so many other German elite theorists, Jung found in the British aristocracy a group worthy of imitation because it seemed to supply continuity without making the nation dependent upon great men.[66] Now that the monarchy had disappeared, it appeared all the more important to have an elite that would free Germany from dependence upon the fortuitous appearance of great men. Reaching a conclusion familiar to us by now, he attributed Germany's difficulties since the dismissal of Bismarck mainly to the absence of a true elite. The concern for a new nobility took precedence also over Jung's desire for a monarch. Despite a strong sympathy for monarchism, he placed his trust in the new nobility. Once the new nobility had come, a new monarchy might, he suggested, follow. The edifice of the Reich of the future would then receive its last, largely symbolic touch.[67]

In his justification for the necessity of an elite, Jung continued to employ many other arguments similar to those that we have encountered earlier. Like Treitschke, he sought to refute both Marxism and democracy by referring to human psychology: "According to a well-known law of economics even the most amazing inventions do not reduce the amount of toil and drudgery; at each ascending level, human demands increase. With each succeeding step, the external picture becomes more splendid, but the internal expenditure of toil, misery, and effort on the part of the great mass of men for their indispensable daily bread remains the same."[68]

Unless one took for granted the existing stratification of society, it

[64] See *ibid.*, p. 616.
[66] See *ibid.*, p. 170.
[68] *HdM*, p. 436. See also p. 382.

[65] *Ibid.*, p. 170.
[67] See, e.g., *Sinndeutung*, pp. 78–81.

would have been difficult to derive from this "law of economics" a principle indicating who should be relieved of "toil and drudgery." Jung's rejection of equality, combined with his "organic" conception of society, supplied him with the necessary principle. Without any detailed examination of the origins of human inequality, he accepted it as a dogma. He viewed functional differentiation of the members of a society as the inevitable consequence of inequality. Since he thought of society as analogous to a living organism, social differentiation had to depend upon the value of the individual for the whole.[69]

Jung appended a somewhat incongruous line of reasoning to the justification of his elite on the basis of an organic conception of society. Following the notion of creative contrasts, which later German idealism had canonized and which Treitschke had also used, Jung praised the presence of dissimilarities among human beings. Most of these dissimilarities eventually complemented each other. The tensions arising among individuals as a result of their differences induced cultural innovation.[70] But Jung felt reluctant to depend upon any sort of "preestablished harmony" and believed that the production of social tensions had to be restrained. Thus the "great task" of the new nobility was "to establish order among unequals."[71]

Lagarde's name appeared often in Jung's writings. Jung shared the desire of the reformist conservatives of the nineteenth century for a nobility with a diversified economic basis, but if we take Lagarde's proposals as a point of reference, we see clearly that Jung abandoned the concept, still central to Lagarde's thinking, of a landed nobility. Jung did not insist upon the possession of landed property as a prerequisite for admission to the new nobility. Businessmen would have played a far greater role in Jung's new nobility. Moreover, Jung rejected Lagarde's proposals for a nobility which would include a large portion of the higher state administrators. He shared the concern, manifested also by other twentieth-century German elitists and expressed most cogently by Weber, that the bureaucrat act simply as a tool of the elite.[72] Indeed, Jung was far more optimistic than Weber about the possibility of reducing the power of the bureaucracy. "Bureaucratization" represented the antithesis of the "organic growth" to which Jung had committed himself. Behind these slogans lay, as we shall see later, a program of "self-administration" that had many attractions for patricians, old aristocrats, and small businessmen seeking to reassert their vanishing prerogatives in the face of governmental

[69] See, e.g., *ibid.*, pp. 3, 20, 48, 101–02, 132; "Die Wirtschaft in der Zeitenwende," *Deutsche Rundschau*, ccxxiv (1930), 3–4.

[70] *HdM*, p. 47.   [71] *Sinndeutung*, p. 103.

[72] See *HdM*, pp. 245, 261, 345, 496; "Aufstand der Rechten," pp. 82–83.

bureaucracies controlled or influenced by representatives of the working-class movement, and the same slogans were attractive to big business interests concerned about the incursions of the state apparatus into their operations.

Although indicating that the new nobleman would normally possess substantial property, Jung insisted that property by itself would not enable anyone to enter the nobility. Perhaps this insistence derived partly from a fear that his new nobility might appear to be little more than a continuation of the prewar nobility with a large influx of wealthy industrialists and businessmen. He sought to make clear that certain ethical attitudes must be present before any man of wealth could qualify as a true leader:

> A businessman becomes a leader because he is driven by a higher calling, not because the power of money makes him capable [of leadership]. . . . Property and the personal independence derived from it have always been an appropriate basis for leadership. . . . Indeed, originally a position of leadership probably generated property. Only the era of civilization, the rule of the Third Estate, creates conditions in which property leads to a striving for power. History is not the history of class struggles . . . until power and leadership become merely instruments of property. . . . In no way does wealth conflict with the possibility of an inner commitment to leadership. The independence of the rich man may even divert his concern for his own person to a concern for the whole. The landed aristocracy [*der Grundbesitz*] developed such a feeling of leadership on the basis of its relationship to property. . . . With the increasing mobility of property, however, the feeling of responsibility for the whole disappears.[73]

In this circuitous passage, especially in its warning in the last sentence against the forms of property characteristic of twentieth-century monopoly capitalism, Jung revealed both his misgivings about the possible consequences of the creation of a new nobility as well as his ultimate faith in the power of the "conservative revolution" to promote values that would restrain egoism. He appealed vaguely to the need for a new ethic of property to check the concentration of capital and increase the number of property owners.[74]

Unlike Zehrer, he dismissed any suggestion that an intellectual or spiritual aristocracy could form the basis for the new elite. Jung criti-

[73] *HdM*, pp. 171–72.
[74] "Die deutsche Staatskrise als Ausdruck der abendländischen Kulturkrise" in Karl Haushofer and Kurt Trampler, eds., *Deutschlands Weg an der Zeitenwende* (Munich, 1931), p. 122.

cized his friend and fellow neoconservative Leopold Ziegler for believing in the "phantasmagoria" of a "spiritual and intellectual aristocracy of individuals."[75] According to Jung, Ziegler ignored the social
prerequisites for an aristocracy. Jung believed that the new nobility
must form a cohesive estate or stratum. He complained that an aristocracy of the type proposed by Ziegler would never be able to command and hence wealthy men without any vocation for leadership
would inevitably rule.[76] Similarly, Jung rejected the notion of an elite
whose function would be simply to provide political leadership. The
tasks of leadership could not be compartmentalized. Social, economic,
and intellectual leadership should precede political leadership. For
Jung the basis of a healthy upper class (*Oberschicht*) from which a
new nobility could arise were "inherited property," education, and
birth. He noted that the highly educated usually became hereditary
members of the upper class, and he defined birth as the "hereditary
factor."[77]

Although like Spengler and Keyserling Jung rejected racist and Social Darwinist notions of "breeding" an elite through social planning,[78]
he emphasized the role of heredity in perpetuating inequalities. His
conception of the accumulation of elite qualities over generations resembled that of the early conservatives. Nevertheless, his self-imposed
task of helping to lay the theoretical foundations for a new nobility led
him frequently to speak of the role of "breeding" in promoting the development of his new nobility: "Peoples with much experience and
ancient cultures, like the Indians, know full well that properly bred
[*gezüchtete*] families transmit leadership qualities hereditarily. . . ."[79]
The type of breeding which Jung had in mind had to take place slowly.
It could only occur "naturally" and "organically." In other words, a
social group had to develop cohesiveness before it could begin to relate the propagation of its progeny to the production or transmission
of desirable traits: "At first a nobility is always a social stratum, and
then, owing to its consciousness of its own status, it breeds itself." "A
race of human beings grows; an estate, on the other hand, can breed

[75] *HdM*, pp. 88, 331.   [76] *Ibid.*, p. 86.
[77] *Ibid.*, p. 328.
[78] Jung's view of race was similar to Spengler's and almost identical to Keyserling's. Jung warned against the belief in nordic superiority since all races were
mixed and little was really known about them. He assailed the interpretation of
history in racial terms as a "materialism of the blood" and a denial of the "spirit
[*Geist*]." "Man," he wrote, "is not a domestic animal that can be bred, least of
all the soulful [*der seelenhafte Mensch*]." *Ibid.*, pp. 120–21. In an apparent contradiction, Jung nevertheless favored measures to strengthen the valuable racial
elements in Germany and to reduce the immigration of undesirable elements. *Ibid.*,
p. 126.
[79] *Ibid.*, p. 331.

itself."[80] Like the nobility of the *ancien régime* the new nobility had to be "exclusive" and to maintain "distance" from the rest of society.[81]

According to Jung, the introduction of a thoroughgoing corporative organization of society was essential to the emergence of the new nobility.[82] A corporatively structured society with a formally recognized nobility would promote the development of true leadership at every level and the ascent of the best leaders. Jung believed that the basis for the corporative bodies of the future already existed in Germany. He regarded many of the established occupational and professional groups as providing promising beginnings. Although all of these groups would have to undergo a spiritual transformation before they would be ready, associations of engineers, teachers, and judges, as well as those of physicians, attorneys, and agriculturalists, provided a solid foundation. Jung suggested also that some trade unions on the Right like the German Nationalist Federation of Commercial Employees (DHV) had demonstrated much promise since the pursuit of wage struggles was not their primary objective. He was much more critical of the various artisan associations, which he criticized as narrow-minded and short-sighted.[83]

THE RELATIONSHIP OF THE NEW NOBILITY TO "THE PEOPLE"

In dealing with the problem of encouraging the growth and selection of the new nobility, Jung allotted a certain role to the evaluation of an individual's achievements by the remainder of the community. Despite his contempt for "mechanical methods of selection,"[84] he believed that communal "self-administration" based partly upon popular suffrage might hasten the formation of the new nobility. His plans for some direct local elections followed by a series of indirect elections leading up to the national level even manifested many similarities to the proposals of groups with a somewhat sympathetic attitude toward the Weimar Republic. For example, the manifesto of the *Jungdeutscher Orden* in 1927 advocated, as Jung himself noted,[85] a similar scheme in place of nationwide universal suffrage. Although less influenced by corporate doctrines than Jung, the *Jungdeutscher Orden* proposed a hierarchically constructed system of elections in which each leader would be elected by the individuals or leaders on the level immediately below him and in which his election would then be sub-

---

[80] *Ibid.*, pp. 597, 121. See also pp. 174, 260, 325–26, 330–31.
[81] *Ibid.*, p. 321; "Neubelebung von Weimar?" p. 158.
[82] *HdM*, p. 330.   [83] *Ibid.*, pp. 296–300.
[84] *Ibid.*, p. 325.   [85] See *ibid.*, p. 336.

ject to confirmation by the leader immediately above him.[86] Jung's friend Leopold Ziegler, who was fascinated by an elective system of this type, pointed to its appropriateness in an "organic" state: "The skipping over of levels [by an individual] is as impermissible in the organic state as in organic nature and in the biography of the individual."[87] Although Jung was more inclined to envision alterations in the boundaries of existing German states in order to bring them more in line with historic ethnic divisions, he shared Ziegler's commitment to federalism in the German sense—to an emphasis upon the powers of these states.[88] Jung's federalism provided a barrier, however ill-defined, to the power of the new nobility. He was the only one of our elitists who took a keen interest in federalism. But since a major source of his federalism, as indeed of much of the federalism on the Right during the Weimar Republic, was a desire to eliminate Social Democratic influence upon the Reich and Prussian governments, his commitment to "states' rights" was tenuous.

By permitting elections to play an indirect role in the selection of the elite, Jung indicated the appeal that the notion of communal democracy still exercised upon him. Elections, he argued, could only be of value if the elector knew personally the man whom he elected. The true leader emerged from the everyday affairs of the community. He was a leader in the daily life of his fellow citizens.[89] The selection of leaders had to be "transferred from the realm of the rational to that of the irrational, from collectivistic sociological [sic] structures to those which have grown up naturally."[90] Jung clung sentimentally to the concept of the political notable,[91] whose decline Weber and Naumann had found both inevitable and desirable. Symptomatic of Jung's hope that the professional politician would disappear was his commitment to the principle of nonremuneration for political leaders of the corporative bodies within the state: "True self-administration stands and falls with the principle of unpaid office holding."[92]

[86] See esp. Klaus Hornung, *Der Jungdeutsche Orden* (Düsseldorf, 1958). See also the appropriate section in Ernst H. Posse, *Die politischen Kamfbünde Deutschlands*, 2nd expanded ed. (Berlin, 1931); Ernst Maste, *Die Republik der Nachbarn: Die Nachbarschaft und der Staatsgedanke Artur Mahrauns* (Giessen, 1957).

[87] Leopold Ziegler, *25 Sätze vom deutschen Staat* (Darmstadt, 1931), p. 50.

[88] See HdM, pp. 351–61; "Die föderalistische Staatsidee und ihre aussenpolitische Bedeutung," *Süddeutsche Monatshefte*, xxv (1928), 259.

[89] HdM, pp. 234, 323, 329, 337, 344.

[90] *Sinndeutung*, p. 92.

[91] See, e.g., "Bericht aus dem Deutschen Reiche," *Schweizer Monatshefte*, xii (1932), 159.

[92] HdM, p. 345.

By introducing the principle of cooptation into all of the elections except those on the lowest level, Jung severely restricted their effect. The cooptative element predominated in the system that he proposed. He relied upon a "strong corrective will" from above.[93] Jung intended the elections, both the direct as well as the indirect ones, simply as a method of supplementing the "natural growth" of the new nobility. Although he believed that they would provide a channel to keep the elite open to suitable outsiders, he anticipated that only the men elected and coopted to the highest levels would belong to the new nobility.[94] Moreover, the bulk of the new nobility would seldom have had to enter the electoral process. Weber had viewed elections primarily as a device for establishing rapport between elite and nonelite by giving the latter a sense of participation in political affairs; but despite some reservations, he had also assigned to elections the function of assisting in the choice between competing elites. Of these two functions of elections, Jung accepted only the former.

Although he contemplated some external, institutional checks upon the composition of the elite at the lower levels of decision making, his conception of the relationship between the new nobility and the populace followed essentially the pattern of an unchecked elite. He entrusted the elite with the task of formulating and initiating all important policies. The doctrine of equality, he complained, degraded the leader into an agency for carrying out the orders of others,[95] for "even the master of mass psychology does not rule the people; he remains merely its exponent."[96] "If the rulers of [the] Weimar [Republic]," Jung charged in 1933, "had really ruled, instead of regarding themselves as the exponents of the masses, they would not have lost the people."[97]

Part of his position rested upon a polemical distinction between "the people" and "the masses." Out of the true leader's love for "his people" arose his contempt for the favor of "the masses."[98] But for all practical purposes Jung identified "the people" with "the masses" once the latter had been excluded from any direct control over the elite. Thus the true leader could never act as a mere representative, even of "the people."[99]

To Jung the relationship between leader and led consisted essentially in a one-way channel. Through this channel only the latter was affected.[100] Direct influence was to proceed from the top downward.

---

[93] *Sinndeutung*, p. 92.   [94] See *HdM*, pp. 329, 337.
[95] "Wirtschaft in der Zeitenwende," p. 3.
[96] *Sinndeutung*, p. 91.   [97] *Ibid.*, p. 20.
[98] *HdM*, p. 331.   [99] *HdM*, pp. 103, 236.
[100] "Reichsreform," *Deutsche Rundschau*, ccxvii (1928), 102.

Jung repeated the substance of an aphorism used by many a German elite theorist: "In the realm of the state a people has only one right— to be ruled well."[101]

He derived his conception of leadership largely from hierarchical organizations. Despite his praise for the "stratified," "hierarchical" social structure of the Middle Ages,[102] he identified good leadership with a modern military hierarchy: "Imagine to yourself a marching column in which the movements are led by a leader. The essential characteristic of this leadership is that the leader determines the actions of the led as well as those of his own."[103] The leader had to be able to count upon the "faith" of his followers without the "uninterrupted public demonstrations of confidence" which characterized democracy. Democratic elections merely indicated lack of confidence on the part of the led in their leaders.[104]

Other considerations also diminished any need for external checks upon the policies or activities of the elite. Jung explained that in the "organic" society there would be an "uninterrupted flow of fresh blood into the circle of leaders [Führerschicht]."[105] Capable individuals would rise "step by step" through the corporative bodies.[106] The normal path to political leadership would be through social and economic ascent, not through the "artificial" structure of a political party.[107] There would always be a possibility for an individual from any segment of society to become a leader: "Democracy does not consist in the existence of a right for the manual laborer to become a minister. . . . Throughout history great leaders have come from the lowest strata of the people without asking whether [there was] a democratic constitution [that] permitted them to do so."[108] Jung regarded a formally open elite as a method of utilizing any superior talent appearing in the nonelite and of ensuring rapport between the elite and the nonelite. A formally open elite sufficed, he believed, to reduce the possibility of tensions arising between the elite and the people. He tended to consider devices for keeping an elite open as effective checks upon it. Making the equation common among neoconservatives, he occasionally used the term "democracy" simply to indicate the absence of class restrictions upon elite recruitment.[109]

He accused the Socialists of having restricted opportunities for the worker to ascend in German society. The "socialization of wages," the equalization of output by means of false wage and social policies, and

[101] *HdM*, p. 344.
[102] *Ibid.*, p. 138.
[103] *Ibid.*, p. 169. See also p. 267.
[104] *Ibid.*, p. 287.
[105] "Volkserhaltung," p. 188.
[106] *HdM*, pp. 138, 329.
[107] See *ibid.*, p. 454.
[108] *Ibid.*, p. 340.
[109] See, e.g., *ibid.*, pp. 101, 340, 344.

the bureaucratization of economic and political activity had drastically reduced the chances for personal advancement: "It is German Socialism that has finally blocked a career open to talents. Of course, a few exceptionally agile demagogues rise through politics, especially when a bit of corruption can play its part. But this form of ascent is restricted to the area of politics and affects relatively few. Social and economic ascent, much more important because it encompasses a broader area, has become more difficult than ever before."[110] Attempting to demonstrate the vital stake of the worker in the expansion of German power, Jung related opportunities for social ascent to Germany's position in international politics: "The smaller the power of a nation and the weaker its position in foreign affairs, the fewer the number of leadership positions that it has to offer."[111]

In England he found some of the best examples of broad elite recruitment. For there "feudalism changed with the times without sacrificing its constructive force."[112] Like Weber, he compensated for his disappointment over German labor leaders by enthusiasm for their British counterparts: ". . . How skillfully England has renewed and supplemented its upper class through the Labor party! What a sense of superiority and mastery these labor leaders develop! . . ."[113]

The organization of the Roman Catholic Church also played an important role in influencing Jung's ideas. Like Nelson, he regarded the Church as one of the most successful applications of elitism. Jung admired the hierarchical structure of the Church as a "marvelous combination" of aristocratic, democratic, and monarchical principles. He noted that although every priest had the possibility of becoming pope, the power of the pope was "virtually unlimited."[114]

Jung's conception of the effects of an open elite recalled that of the reformist conservatives of the nineteenth century. His new nobility would mirror in miniature the "best" elements of the entire society.[115] As a result, most external checks would merely have restricted the representativeness of the new nobility.

The new nobility would receive its highest legitimation by embodying the "true will of the people." Jung's Rousseauian distinction between a valid, hypothetical general will and a "mechanically formed," empirical will of all appeared most clearly in another of his definitions of "true" democracy: "True democracy . . . is the rule of the *volonté générale*, which can only be conceived of in a metaphysical sense."[116]

---

[110] *Ibid.*, pp. 454–55. [111] *Ibid.*, p. 455.
[112] *Ibid.*, p. 177. [113] *Ibid.*, p. 287.
[114] *Ibid.*, p. 271. See also p. 336.
[115] See *ibid.*, p. 328; "Volkserhaltung," *Deutsche Rundschau*, ccxxii (1930), 188.
[116] *HdM*, p. 225.

One of the loftiest tasks of the new nobility thus lay in the achievement of the common good. In the new society, leadership would fall to "that history-making minority" which "even in the face of death, fuses its own existence with that of the community [*Gemeinschaft*]."[117]

What did Jung understand by a concept as difficult to define as the common good? His organic conception of society furnished the starting point. The specific content of his concept of the common good depended in large part upon the neo-Romantic notions that had become associated with the word *Gemeinschaft*, or "organic social unit."

As redefined at the end of the nineteenth century by the sociologist Ferdinand Tönnies, *Gemeinschaft* denoted an explicit contrast to *Gesellschaft* (society).[118] Even Tönnies based this contrast upon an idealized version of social relations in a preindustrial society. Relationships in a *Gesellschaft* had simply a contractual character. Each party pursued its own rational self-interest. Each party regarded the relationship as the most efficient means available for the pursuit of its own ends. Such a relationship presupposed autonomous social units or individuals, each of which possessed separate, distinct purposes and values. A *Gesellschaft* was an "artificial" group united, at least temporarily, in the pursuit of a common, conscious purpose.

For Tönnies and particularly for those Germans longing for the presumed certainties of life in a preindustrial society, *Gemeinschaft*, on the other hand, indicated a much broader relationship of solidarity over an ill-defined area of life and interests. Such a relationship had an involuntary character. The individuals involved in a *Gemeinschaft* possessed virtually identical value systems. These people acted and were treated as participants in a unit of solidarity. They shared benefits and misfortunes in common, but not necessarily equally. Similarly, each individual contributed to the relationship according to his abilities and resources. By the time of the Weimar Republic, the Youth Movement and a substantial portion of German social thought had become enchanted by the ideal of *Gemeinschaft*.

Jung combined an interest in developing organic, *Gemeinschaft* relationships with his own particular stress upon human inequality. His conception of the common good included the voluntary self-subordination of the majority of society to the new nobility. The main-

[117] *Ibid.*, p. 82.
[118] See Ferdinand Tönnies, *Gemeinschaft und Gesellschaft*, 8th ed. (Leipzig, 1935). My discussion of Tönnies follows Talcott Parsons, *The Structure of Social Action: A Study in Social Theory with Special Reference to a Group of Recent European Writers* (New York, 1937), pp. 687–92. On Tönnies see also Arthur Mitzman, "Tönnies and German Society, 1887–1914: From Cultural Pessimism to Celebration of the *Volksgemeinschaft*," *Journal of the History of Ideas*, xxxii (1971), 507–24.

tenance and supervision of this subordination depended upon the capabilities of the new nobility. The common good could be attained only "by permitting each of the parts as much right to self-development as the value of its contribution to the life of the community."[119] "There are individuals whose importance for the culture (in the broadest sense of the word) is nil, and those whose importance for the culture is everything."[120]

Jung's conception of the common good presupposed the existence of a common, coherent, and unified set of values. His view of the new society assumed the existence of an extensive set of values held in common by elite and nonelite. At bottom, Jung's attitude on this point led to his rejection of Pareto's elite theory.[121] He disagreed with Pareto's proposition that the maintenance of the rule of an elite was best ensured by the adherence of its members to a system of values markedly divergent from those of the nonelite. Jung's insistence upon a common set of values distinguished his position also from Spengler's ambiguity on the same point. Despite his frequent invocation of Spengler's authority, Jung did not call attention to the difference.

Jung relied upon the coming "Conservative Revolution" to create a single set of values valid for elite and nonelite alike. He looked forward to the creation and dissemination of values which would regulate the activities of the entire society: "Only the reawakening of a sense for the higher purposiveness of the national existence can ensure a steady course. . . . Leaders will arise who equate the popular will with their own."[122]

Only Jung's faith in the possibility of overcoming the tremendous social and ideological cleavages within German society can explain his ecstatic references to the ability of the new nobility to perceive the common good. A member of the new nobility, by carrying within himself "the experiences of the entire society,"[123] possessed sensitivities which might otherwise appear inexplicable: "He feels responsible for the entire community. Its cares are his cares. He becomes a carrier of the collectivity; he becomes the focus of the spiritual perceptions of the whole."[124] Jung's conception of the state as an abstract institution

---

[119] "Der Volksrechtsgedanke und die Rechtsvorstellungen von Versailles," *Deutsche Rundschau*, ccxxi (1929), 7.
[120] *Ibid.*
[121] See HdM, pp. 279, 326. Unlike most German elitists during the Weimar Republic, Jung had more than a superficial acquaintance with Pareto's work. Jung (*HdM*, p. 279n.) mentions that Pareto, who taught at Lausanne for many years, introduced him to the social sciences. Since Jung spent two semesters studying *Jura* at Lausanne before World War I (see Grass, "Jung," p. 321), this contact with Pareto probably took place in 1913–1914.
[122] *HdM*, p. 626.   [123] *Ibid.*, p. 287.   [124] *Ibid.*, p. 169.

standing above society reinforced his concern that the new nobility act in accordance with the common good. The state acted as the "highest harmonizing and directing power."[125] The Weimar Republic represented the last step in the conversion of the state into the "plaything of [selfish] interests."[126] Jung believed in the possibility of the elite identifying itself completely with the state, but he nevertheless maintained a theoretical distinction between state and elite: ". . . The state is the highest entity in the entire order. The state is itself devoid of specific content, and is enthroned above the substantive groups of society. Serving the entire society as a supreme judge, it [the state] guarantees the rights of all groups and associations."[127]

Jung envisioned only one effective check upon the elite. This check had to exist within every member of the elite. It resulted from the "voluntarily assumed responsibility to act in a leadership capacity for the whole."[128] By imparting this responsibility with the character of a duty, Jung treated the individual rather than the community as its source. The individual's own conscience acted as the primary restraint upon his actions. By stressing that leadership consisted essentially in "service," Jung also circumvented the problem of effective controls.[129] "An intensely moral willingness to serve" would characterize the new nobility.[130] Thus Jung, like Nelson and many other elitists, regarded controls over leadership largely as a problem of personal morality.

Jung anticipated that a collective concept of honor would help to ensure that the new nobility fulfilled its "duties." Like the nineteenth-century conservatives, he expected adherence to a rigid code of honor from an elite occupying the uppermost level in a highly stratified society.[131] Yet for Jung success in enforcing this code depended upon the degree to which its imperatives had been internalized within each individual. In addition, its imperatives could differ only in degree, not in substance, from the values of the entire society. Otherwise, the single system of values in the new society would have been undermined.

By attributing a pedagogical function to the new nobility, Jung added a final reason for prohibiting the nonelite from exercising direct control over the elite. At the same time, he manifested a deepseated pessimism about the prospects for the creation of a unified system of values. He compared the effect of the elite upon the people to the impression made by a seal on soft wax.[132] The elite had the "right and

---

[125] *Ibid.*, p. 96. See also p. 291.   [126] *Ibid.*, p. 154.
[127] *HdM*, p. 138.
[128] "Neubelebung von Weimar?" p. 158.
[129] See, e.g., *HdM*, pp. 321, 344, 368; "Deutschland und die konservative Revolution," p. 381.
[130] *HdM*, p. 344.   [131] *Ibid.*, p. 220.
[132] *Ibid.*, p. 169.

duty to lead and educate the less valuable members of society [*die Minderwertigen*]."[133] Individuals might rise into the elite, but the proportion of elite to nonelite would remain more or less stable, for the "superior individuals are always the few."[134]

Jung envisioned a society that fit in well with the desires of many of the more traditionally minded members of the middle class. He offered a world free from the insecurities of the Weimar Republic. He presented a refuge from the ills of industrial society. As before the war, there would be a nobility to provide protection against the lower classes, but the new nobility would be far more attractive than the Junkers. It would integrate the working class into the nation without recourse to civil war. Social mobility would be possible in an ordered fashion. Jung offered a dream to fill the void left by the collapse of the Bismarckian Empire.

His concept of a new nobility also revealed a faith, unmatched in its intensity among almost all other German elite theorists, that the prewar trend toward the development of a single, cohesive upper class in Germany could be brought to completion. Purged of the crassness injected by the newly ennobled of the Wilhelminian period, his new nobility could develop rapidly once political democracy had been dismantled and corporative institutions established.

THE "INEVITABLE TRIUMPH" OF THE NEW NOBILITY

In 1930 Jung anticipated that the rule of the new nobility would begin shortly. Of course, the process leading to its rule would have to be "organic." He found some of the most promising beginnings in the Youth Movement and in the paramilitary organizations on the Right.

As we saw in discussing Spengler, these paramilitary action leagues (*Kampfbünde*), although claiming to stand above political parties, often had close ties to the parties of the Right. With the stabilization of the economic and political situation in Germany after 1923, the largest of the surviving *Kampfbünde*, the *Stahlhelm*, lost its character as a nonpartisan organization of the Right and became an open, if unofficial auxiliary of the Nationalist party. By the end of the decade, most parties had paramilitary organizations openly associated with them. This tendency was promoted by the development of the *Reichsbanner*, founded in 1924 as a nonpartisan defensive association of all "Republicans," which soon became little more than an arm of the Social Democratic party. The smaller *Kampfbünde* on the Right, many

---

[133] *Ibid.*, p. 368.   [134] *Ibid.*, p. 104.

of which had collapsed after 1924, also felt the pull toward direct involvement in political parties.[135]

Both in ideas and organization many of the successors of the prewar Youth Movement merged with the *Kampfbünde*. Although the number of youth tutelage groups increased appreciably after the war, a small, but significant portion of the Youth Movement maintained its independence from adult-sponsored organizations. In the late 1920's, between 50,000 and 100,000 young people belonged to independent youth *Bünde*.[136] As compared to the prewar youth groups, these *Bünde* were no longer loosely organized. Although prizing the flexibility of their structure, they valued the role of organization in creating a cohesive, tightly knit group. The prewar belief that youth organizations had to emanate from youth itself remained, but the principles of the prewar movement underwent systematization. The youth *Bünde* contributed substantially to the glorification of a group of individuals united by common devotion to a set of rather unclear goals and to a single leader. They paid homage to leadership based on acclamation, a leader responsible only to himself, a hierarchical structure with discipline and authority flowing from the top downward, and unconditional obedience. Considering themselves as the vanguard of the future, they believed that they must be highly selective in choosing their members.

Although scattered over the entire political spectrum, the youth *Bünde* gravitated toward the Right, where they made a significant contribution to neoconservatism. The unsettled atmosphere of the Republic strengthened a growing conviction among the youth *Bünde* that they must take direct political action. In addition, an increasing number of older members, individuals over twenty-five, kept in close contact with them and contributed to the interest in political issues among the younger members.

Throughout most of the Weimar Republic, the youth and other *Bünde* generally congratulated themselves upon their position outside all parties. They frequently declared their hostility to all political parties—including those of the Right. In the last years of the Republic, several of them temporarily overcame their "uncompromising" attitude in order to participate as a group in elections or to form alliances with parties. Yet the proclaimed aims always included destruction of the "party system" itself.

[135] See Posse, *Die politischen Kampfbünde Deutschlands*; Bracher, *Die Auflösung der Weimarer Republik*, pp. 128–46.
[136] Karl O. Paetel, "Die deutsche Jugendbewegung als politisches Phänomen," *Politische Studien*, VIII, No. 86 (1957), 3; Felix Raabe, *Die bündische Jugend: Ein Beitrag zur Geschichte der Weimarer Republik* (Stuttgart, 1961), p. 66.

The appearance of "active" individuals, "ready and able to make sacrifices," in the *Bünde* made a great impression upon Jung.[137] He prized the informal, but hierarchical, structure of the *Bünde* and anticipated the emergence of true leaders from them.[138] At the same time, he had reservations about the *Bünde*. Even the best of them, he argued, had not fully grasped the essentials of the new "organic" *Weltanschauung*. In addition, he objected to the emphasis upon the younger generation manifested by many of the youth *Bünde*. Although arguing that a conflict of generations always existed and that the war had made it acute, he viewed the cleavages within Germany as basically ideological rather than generational. The war and postwar generations would play a vital role in the formation of the new society; the *Bünde* would furnish much of the "material" for the new nobility. But even if the *Bünde* succeeded in uniting, they could never by themselves constitute the new nobility.[139] All of the forces on the Right opposing the Weimar Republic would have to unite on the basis of the new organic philosophy, and largely from the midst of this united front the new nobility would arise.[140]

Searching for means to create the new society, Jung manifested a perceptible impatience with his own concept of organic growth. As a "mechanical," "unorganic" construction, the Weimar Republic had to be destroyed at almost any price; only its destruction would furnish the last precondition to the emergence of the new nobility. But in responding to his own question as to the means by which an organic society would be brought into being, Jung became evasive. He hesitated to place his trust solely in the success of a "spiritual revolution" to ensure the "inevitable" triumph of the new nobility. He admitted that there was no "scientifically certain method" to indicate where and how to begin building an organic society; indeed, the characteristics of an organic society would become clear only as it developed.[141]

He indicated three methods by which the success of the "spiritual revolution" could be accelerated. The first consisted in an extraparliamentary popular movement. Since Jung's primary goal always remained the establishment of the new nobility and its insulation from direct popular pressures, he preferred to avoid this method. He thus favored one of the other two: the temporary, autocratic rule of one man, or the formation of a cabinet without regard for the wishes of the Reichstag and furnished with extraordinary powers. Although leaving open the possibility of the dictatorship of an individual, Jung opted for

[137] *HdM*, p. 673.   [138] *Ibid.*, p. 416.

[139] See *ibid.*, pp. 17–19, 329–30, 680–81; "Tragik der Kriegsgeneration," pp. 520–21.

[140] *HdM*, pp. 674–75.   [141] *Ibid.*, pp. 128, 290–91.

a cabinet free from responsibility to the Reichstag. If properly constituted, such a cabinet would, he felt certain, initiate the "revolution"
and receive the applause of the nation.[142] Like many right-wingers Jung
hoped for a bloodless "revolution from above."

Although from 1930 to 1932 the Brüning cabinet governed without
a parliamentary majority, it still had to submit its laws to the Reichstag for approval or rejection. Neither the policies nor the prerogatives
of the Brüning government satisfied Jung's requirements. Jung never
seems to have been certain whether Brüning was fully devoted to the
destruction of the parliamentary system, or was hoping eventually to
restore parliamentary government, as Brüning himself was to intimate
after the war.[143] In Jung's eyes the greatest achievement of the Brüning
era was the neutralization of the Social Democratic party, but as Jung
realized this achievement was mainly a consequence of the rise of the
Nazi party. He gloated that the SPD had been undercut and checked
as it had not been since the outbreak of the war. The fear of fascism
had, he suggested, scared the Social Democrats into nationalism.[144]
Jung hoped that the Right would give conditional support to Brüning's
policies when they clearly led in an antiparliamentary direction and
began to lay the foundations for an organic development of German
institutions. Through a new right-wing splinter party, the *Volkskonservative Vereinigung*, Jung hoped both to encourage the acceptance
of his attitude toward Brüning and to create an organization that
would bring together the creative forces on the Right.

Jung's activities in this new "Popular Conservative" group were
characteristic of his hectic political involvements during the last four
years of his life. As his friend Paul Fechter suggests, Jung was a rest-

---

[142] *Ibid.*, pp. 275, 277–78, 334, 677–79.

[143] See Heinrich Brüning, "Ein Brief," *Deutsche Rundschau*, LXX (1947), 1–22.
Brüning's posthumously published memoirs, *Memoiren 1918–1934* (Stuttgart,
1970), give a different impression of his objectives, indicating that from the beginning of his chancellorship he was involved in a systematic attempt to establish
permanently an authoritarian right-wing regime independent of the Reichstag
and perhaps capped by a restoration of the monarchy. For Jung's shifting assessments of Brüning see esp. the following in his "Bericht aus dem Deutschen Reiche"
series in the *Schweizer Monatshefte*: X (Oct. 1930), 321–22; XI (Aug.-Sept., 1931),
276–77; XI (Feb.-Mar., 1932), 620; XII (June 1932), 159; XII (Nov. 1932), 371.
The last article appeared under the title "Zustand in Deutschland."

[144] *Schweizer Monatshefte*, XII (Feb.-Mar. 1932), 619. A similar evaluation
of the impact of the rise of the National Socialists was offered by Friedrich Meinecke after their electoral victory in 1930. He wrote in a letter that the Nazi victory
was compelling the Social Democrats to be "statesmanlike" and cooperate with
Brüning. See Peter Gay, *Weimar Culture: The Outsider as Insider* (New York,
1968), p. 25. It is unclear why Gay (p. 25, n. 5) regards this summary of a
sober view that was widely held at the time as a "fantastic estimation of German
politics."

less man who throve on adventure.[145] Political intrigue came to occupy much of the remainder of his short life. He played an important role in the founding of the *Volkskonservative Vereinigung* in January 1930. The core of this group came from the German Nationalist party. The DNVP Reichstag deputies who left the party with Walther Lambach and Gottfried Treviranus included most of the neoconservatives among the party's leaders. At the founding meeting of the *Volkskonservative Vereinigung*, Jung claimed to speak for those neoconservatives who stood outside all parties: "Many are, like me, politically homeless in domestic politics, moved solely by one thought: the renewal of German life. . . . We can only promise the cooperation of political forces which have had no previous [political] ties if the association [the *Volkskonservative Vereinigung*] breaks with paralyzed ways of thought. . . ."[146] In July 1930 twenty-five other deputies, under the leadership of Count Kuno Westarp, left the Nationalist party. Efforts to merge the Westarp group with the *Volkskonservative Vereinigung* resulted in the founding of the *Konservative Volkspartei*, but this union of the two groups was unsuccessful. The *Volkskonservative Vereinigung* was not dissolved and continued to exist beside the new party. The party was closely identified with the Brüning government. Treviranus served in Brüning's cabinet, and the chancellor could rely upon the support of the new Popular Conservatives in the Reichstag. But the party won only four seats in the elections of September 1930. Serving in the ten-man directory (*Führerring*) of the *Volkskonservative Vereinigung* elected in the winter of 1931, Jung seems consistently to have sought to apply pressure on Brüning by encouraging the Popular Conservative movement to disassociate itself from the government. Jung's efforts met with greater success in the South and West— especially in Munich, one of the centers of Popular Conservative strength—than in northern and eastern Germany.[147]

Although most of the leading Popular Conservatives were reserved in their attitude toward Franz von Papen's "cabinet of barons" that succeeded the Brüning government in June 1932,[148] Jung's response

[145] Fechter, *Menschen und Zeiten*, p. 359.

[146] *Deutsche Allgemeine Zeitung*, Jan. 30, 1930. Quoted in Romoser, "Crisis," p. 176, n. 2. I have altered Romoser's translation.

[147] See Erasmus Jonas, *Die Volkskonservativen 1928–1933: Entwicklung, Struktur, Standort und staatspolitische Zielsetzung* (Düsseldorf, 1965), pp. 100, 103, 138–40; Erwein von Aretin, *Krone und Ketten: Erinnerungen eins bayerischen Edelmannes*, ed. Karl Buchheim and Karl Otmar von Aretin (Munich, 1965), p. 45; Brüning, *Memoiren*, p. 214; Grass, "Jung," p. 336. For a general analysis of the Popular Conservatives see, in addition to the book by Jonas, an article by Ulrich Roeske, "Brüning und die Volkskonservativen 1930," *Zeitschrift für Geschichtswissenschaft*, xix (1971), 904–15.

[148] See Jonas, *Die Volkskonservativen*, pp. 125–26.

was more favorable. He was very impressed not only by Papen's *coup d'état* against the Social Democratic government of Prussia but also by "the determination with which he [Papen] promises the necessary reforms."[149] The hesitation of the Papen government to antagonize the party organizations of the Right was a great disappointment to Jung, but he seems to have believed that, with luck, Papen could have established the foundations for the new nobility. Looking back in 1933, Jung wrote: "Von Papen had the last opportunity to eliminate, from above, the pluralistic forces (the parties and the economic interests) and restore the purity of the state without mobilizing the masses."[150]

Shortly after the formation of the Hitler cabinet on January 30, 1933, Jung consented gladly to act as a personal secretary for Papen, who had become vice chancellor.[151] By assisting with the preparation of Papen's speeches, Jung gained an opportunity to promote the cause of the new nobility from a position near the summit of the Reich.[152]

Since 1930 Jung had watched the rapid rise of the National Socialists with mixed feelings, characteristic of many non-Nazis on the Right. Although he often viewed national socialism as a part of neoconservatism, he feared that a mass movement would pervert the ideas of neoconservatism. He argued that the mobilization of the masses on the Right against those on the Left was an understandable, but dangerous procedure: "A new culture never begins with the unleashing of mass instincts, but only with their suppression."[153] In his articles Jung was critical of Hitler, depicting him as a man of very limited horizons and as a crude demagogue whose success came from an appeal to the prim-

---

[149] "Zustand in Deutschland," *Schweizer Monatshefte*, xii (Nov. 1932), 373. See also "Verlustbilanz der Rechten," *Deutsche Rundschau*, cxxiv (Jan. 1933), 5.

[150] *Sinndeutung*, p. 29.

[151] The widespread belief that Jung began to advise Papen months before the formation of the Hitler cabinet was fostered by Rudolf Pechel's *Deutscher Widerstand* (Erlenbach-Zurich, 1947), p. 76. Papen denies, in both versions of his memoirs, having met Jung before early 1933: Franz von Papen, *Der Wahrheit eine Gasse* (Munich, 1952), pp. 363–65; *Vom Scheitern einer Demokratie 1930–1933* (Mainz, 1968), p. 401, n. 135. There is mounting evidence that Jung and Papen had come into contact, if only through intermediaries, by the end of the latter's chancellorship in November 1932, but no conclusive evidence that Jung actually served him as an adviser and speechwriter until February 1933. Cf. Grass, "Jung," pp. 339–41; K. M. Grass, "Edgar Jung, Papenkreis und Röhmkrise," p. 50.

[152] A collection of the speeches delivered by Papen during the campaign for the Reichstag elections of March 1933 manifests many similarities, both in style and content, to Jung's writings. Even the introduction may have been written largely by Jung: Franz von Papen, *Appell an das deutsche Gewissen: Reden zur nationalen Revolution* (Oldenburg, 1933). See also Jenschke, *Zur Kritik der konservativ-revolutionären Ideologie*, p. 166, n. 1.

[153] "Bericht aus dem Deutschen Reiche," *Schweizer Monatshefte*, x (Oct. 1930), 323. See also "Das eigenständige Volk: Bemerkungen zu Boehms Volkstheorie," *Deutsche Rundschau*, ccxxxii (Aug. 1932), 89; "Deutsche Unzulänglichkeiten," *Deutsche Rundschau*, ccxxxiii (Nov. 1932), 81–82.

itive instincts of the masses,[154] and privately Jung's distaste for Hitler may have been expressed more sharply.[155] Like Keyserling, Jung described national socialism as "the last wave of National Liberalism."[156] Jung shared the general concern among neoconservatives that the electoral successes of the National Socialists would result in their accommodation to the parliamentary system, and hence give the Republic a new lease on life.[157]

On the other hand, he found much to welcome in the growth of a strong new party on the Right. He regarded national socialism as a part of the popular ferment which would accompany the establishment of the new society. He thought of national socialism as one of the potentially most powerful agencies for the destruction of the old "decayed" world. The Nazi party could assist in the destruction of the Republic and thereby clear the way for his own new order. During the temporary prohibition of the SA in Prussia before the arrival of the Papen government, Jung, like so many other neoconservatives, viewed himself as a paternalistic guardian of the party: "National Socialism is *our* popular movement and must be protected by us. . . ."[158]

By the latter part of 1932 Jung's reservations about the Nazis had become more urgent. Perhaps in the hope of encouraging a split in the Nazi party that would lead to a regrouping of forces on the Right, Jung suggested that an acute conflict now existed between "revolutionary conservative forces and the mass beliefs of National Socialism."[159] He complained that the leaders of neoconservatism had been involuntarily excluded from the party, which had expanded in such a way that it was lacking in intellectual and spiritual qualities. Indicative

[154] See, e.g., "Bericht aus dem Deutschen Reiche," *Schweizer Monatshefte*, x (Oct. 1930), 323; "Aufstand der Rechten," *Deutsche Rundschau*, ccxxix (Nov. 1931), 84.

[155] Jung's friend Edmund Forschbach claims that at the meeting of Nazis, German Nationalists, and *Stahlhelm* representatives in October of 1931, which Jung attended and which resulted in the formation of the "Harzburg Front," Jung told a small group: "Ich kann mir nicht vorstellen, dass ein Mann mit einem solchen Verbrechergesicht in Deutschland Diktator wird." Forschbach, "Jung," p. 82.

[156] "Bericht aus dem Deutschen Reiche," *Schweizer Monatshefte*, x (Apr. 1930), 39. See also "Tragik der Kriegsgeneration," (May 1930), 529.

[157] "Neubelebung von Weimar?" (June 1932), p. 156; "Revolutionäre Staatsführung!" *Deutsche Rundschau*, ccxxxiii (Oct. 1932), 1–8.

[158] "Neubelebung von Weimar?" (June 1932), p. 160. Jung's italics. See also "Aufstand der Rechten" (Nov. 1931), p. 84; "Deutschland und die konservative Revolution," (1932), pp. 382–83. Cf. Hans Bogner, "Das Ende der aufgeklärten Demokratie," *Deutsche Rundschau*, ccxxxi (Apr. 1932), 13: "Grosse Gedanken werden nur dann zu geschichtlichen Mächten, wenn sie *Massenwahn* werden. . . . Dieser Massenwahn ist unser Kairos, unser Glücksaugenblick. . . ." Bogner's italics.

[159] "Zustand in Deutschland," *Schweizer Monatshefte*, xii (Nov. 1932), 374.

of Jung's distrust of the Nazis was his invocation of an argument inconsistent with his own conception of leadership.[160]

When Hitler came to power in January 1933, Jung tried to accommodate his thinking to the new situation. Without abandoning his most cherished dreams, he concluded that a mass movement in the form of the Nazi party offered the only hope for the establishment of the new society. The combination of a "plebiscitarian dictatorship" with a mass movement could provide a desirable preliminary stage. In a work published in the latter part of 1933 he wrote: ". . . The attempt of the von Papen cabinet to refound the Reich never gained momentum; a detour via the great popular movement had to be taken. In January of this year von Papen himself recognized the validity of this conclusion [by becoming vice chancellor under Hitler]."[161] Jung's reservations about this conclusion appeared clearly in his insistence that "the objective of the German Revolution must be the depoliticization of the masses, their exclusion from the *leadership* of the state."[162]

Throughout 1933 it probably became increasingly apparent to him that most National Socialists, and particularly Hitler, would refuse to consider their victory as merely a stage on the way to his own new society. With the destruction of the Left and the disintegration of the non-Nazi Right, no organized political counterweight to the Nazis existed. The regrouping of the Right that Jung and others had worked for tirelessly had led the National Socialists to become *the* party of the Right in Germany. Within the Nazi party itself, there gathered around Hitler many of the National Socialists whom Jung had felt were least promising. The beginnings of the totalitarian dictatorship of a single party distressed him. He was willing to recognize many National Socialists as entitled to become part of the core of the new nobility, but he refused to sanction the identification of the bulk of any party with *his* elite. He warned against a "dangerous exclusive tendency" among the National Socialists and pleaded for a more tolerant attitude on their part toward the remainder of the Right.[163] Above all, he returned to his earlier stress upon the organic development of the new nobility. The National Socialists, he argued, could not create the new nobility merely by identifying themselves with it or by contemplating measures to supervise the breeding of it. But he still believed that the "way to the nobility" was open.[164]

[160] *Ibid.*, p. 373.   [161] *Sinndeutung*, pp. 29, 48.

[162] *Ibid.*, p. 29. Jung's italics. See also "Deutschland ohne Europa," *Deutsche Rundschau*, ccxxxviii (Feb. 1934), 75, 78.

[163] "Einsatz der Nation," *Deutsche Rundschau*, ccxxxiv (Mar. 1933), 157, 159–60; *Sinndeutung*, pp. 50–53, 82–84.

[164] See esp. *Sinndeutung*, pp. 50–52.

At some point between the fall of 1933 and the early months of 1934, Jung changed his mind. The way to the new nobility was, for the moment, lost. Probably concluding that a *coup d'état* to unseat Hitler was necessary, he seems to have become deeply involved in some of the plans on the Right to rely upon support from the Reichswehr to remove Hitler. Indeed, Jung may even have considered personally assassinating Hitler, but there is no conclusive evidence to indicate that Jung's schemes had come to fruition or had any chance of success.[165]

Seeking to promote criticism of the Nazi regime, and perhaps to threaten Hitler with removal from office, he composed a public address that Papen, still holding the title of vice chancellor, presented in Marburg in June 1934.[166] The address reiterated all of the major complaints that Jung had been making about the Nazis during the past year and a half. Above all, Papen's speech contested Nazi claims to exclusive leadership of the "German Revolution" and expressed, if more subtly, fears of social instability engendered by the continuance of the demagogic mobilization of the masses by the new regime. The only clear answer to the pleas for moderation contained in the address came in the form of the arrest of Jung and others of Papen's associates. Several days later Jung was murdered in the course of the "Roehm Purge."

The formula for the organic process leading to the new nobility went to the grave with Jung. Later in 1934 a member of the old nobility, Franz Freiherr von Papen, now demoted, but quite alive, arrived in Vienna as the ambassador of the Third Reich.

According to Jung's elite theory, the new nobility could emerge only slowly, but the upheavals in the last years of the Republic prompted him to search for shortcuts. He greeted, if with some reluctance, the development of a mass movement of the type which he intended to eliminate from his new society. During the same years, other neoconservative elite theorists, less anchored to the past than Jung, concerned themselves especially with the relationship of the intellectual to mass movements.

[165] The only detailed study of Jung's activities and plans against the Nazi regime is K. M. Grass, "Edgar Jung, Papenkreis und Röhmkrise," but the account in Chapter Six of Romoser's "Crisis" is still worth consulting for its more critical approach.

[166] See Papen, *Der Wahrheit eine Gasse*, pp. 363–65, and "Rede des Vizekanzlers v. Papen vor dem Universitätsbund, Marburg, am 17. Juni 1934" in *Der Prozess gegen die Hauptkriegsverbrecher vor dem internationalen Militärgerichtshof*, xi (Nürnberg, 1949), 543–58.

Hans Zehrer and the *Tat* Circle: The *Révolution Manquée* of the Intelligentsia

Shortly before the collapse of the New York stock market in 1929, Hans Zehrer wrote an article that would, he hoped, become the manifesto of the German "intelligentsia." In a procedure unusual for a man who rejected Marxism, Zehrer cited a passage from the *Communist Manifesto* to support his position. After quoting the assertion that "all previous historical movements were movements of minorities or in the interests of minorities," he suggested a "more meaningful" formulation: ". . . All movements began as intellectual [*geistige*] movements of intelligent, well-qualified minorities which, because of the discrepancy between that which is and that which should be, seized the initiative."[1] Engels once remarked that he and Marx found Hegel "standing on his head" and put him back on his feet. Zehrer wanted to set Marx and Engels on their heads. Finding illusory the Marxist vision of a "self-conscious, independent movement of the immense majority in the interests of the immense majority," he believed that a self-conscious, intellectual minority was predestined to play the predominant role in creating and ruling a new Germany.

During the final years of the Weimar Republic, he and several of his friends used the pages of a monthly magazine *Die Tat* to stake out the future path of this minority. They participated prominently in the last, most turbulent phases of the widespread controversy about the type of leadership best suited to Germany since its defeat in World War I. Their efforts helped to make the *Tat* into one of the largest and most influential journals of German neoconservatism.[2]

---

[1] Hans Zehrer, "Die Revolution der Intelligenz," *Die Tat*, xxi (Oct. 1929), 488. Unless noted otherwise, all articles cited in this chapter are in the *Tat*. Thus, a mere volume number following the title of an article refers to the *Tat*. Since most of the articles cited were written by Zehrer, the author of an article will be indicated only when he is one of the other contributors to the periodical.

[2] The first extended study of the *Tat* circle appeared in Edmond Vermeil's *Doctrinaires de la Révolution allemande 1918–1938* (Paris, 1938), pp. 188–220. Vermeil misleadingly places the *Tat* circle directly in the tradition of Nazism. Kurt Sontheimer's pioneering article "Der Tat-Kreis," *Vierteljahrshefte für Zeitgeschichte*, vii (1959), 229–60, shares the major weaknesses of his book *Antidemokratisches Denken in der Weimarer Republik: Die politischen Ideen des deutschen Nationalis-*

Although the members of the *Tat* circle were almost alone on the Right in referring to the "intelligentsia" in a positive sense and depicting it as the core of the political elite of the future, their basic conception of this elite resembled closely that of most other neoconservatives. An authoritarian elite would select its own members and would not be subject to popular control. The *Tat* circle's belief that the emergence of such an elite could resolve the problems of the middle class revealed in a particularly striking form the concern among neoconservatives for the fate of that class. While receptive to the possibility of making significant changes in the social structure, the members of the *Tat* circle were concerned primarily with the frustrations encountered by young, well-educated intellectuals like themselves. In the admission to power of such men they found the solution to their own problems, those of the middle class in general, and those of the entire nation.

ORIGINS OF THE TAT CIRCLE

Born in Berlin in 1899, Zehrer volunteered for service in World War I when he was seventeen.[3] Much more emphatically than Edgar Jung he regarded himself as a representative of a new generation whose conflict with its elders had been expressed most dramatically in its enthusiastic response to the Youth Movement and the battlefield. His experiences during the early years of the Weimar Republic were similar to those of many other postwar students. He became a "short-term volunteer"[4] in the Reichswehr and fought against the Communists and left-wing Socialists in the disorders following the Kapp Putsch of 1920. After the inflation made difficult the continuation of his studies at the university, he obtained a position on the moderate, republican *Vossische Zeitung*. He was serving as the newspaper's foreign affairs editor when he began to contribute articles to the *Tat* in 1928.

---

mus zwischen 1918 und 1933 (Munich, 1962). Like many other recent students of neoconservatism, he fails to take seriously the ideas that he is treating; he tends to dismiss them as unrealistic without looking closely into their social origins. Also very judgmental in approach is the first political biography of Zehrer, Ebbo Demant's *Von Schleicher zu Springer: Hans Zehrer als politischer Publizist* (Mainz, [1971?]). The value of Demant's work rests primarily upon its use of much unpublished material and its attempt to deal with Zehrer's entire career from the 1920's to the 1960's.

[3] The biographical material in the following paragraphs is derived mainly from four sources: a letter of Jan. 29, 1964, from Zehrer to me; *Wer ist's?* ed. Herrmann A. L. Degener (Berlin, 1935); *Wer ist wer?* ed. Walter Habel (Berlin, 1962); and Sontheimer, "Der Tat-Kreis," pp. 231–33.

[4] *Zeitfreiwilliger.* I am following the translation of this expression suggested by Harold J. Gordon in his *The Reichswehr and the German Republic, 1919–1926* (Princeton, 1957), rather than the more common translation, "temporary volunteer."

Founded before the war, the *Tat* had long been under the control of Eugen Diederichs, the owner of a small, but well-known publishing house. Diederichs' dissatisfaction with the Weimar Republic and his interest in the Youth Movement contributed to his deep involvement in the development of neoconservatism.[5] He concerned himself particularly with the position in society of the more highly educated members of the middle class. He hoped for the formation of a stratum of intellectuals who, coming largely from the middle class, would "renew" German social and cultural life.[6] By opening the pages of the *Tat* to prospective members of this stratum, he sought to assist in the propagation of their ideas.

In the fall of 1929 Diederichs placed the *Tat* at Zehrer's disposal and permitted him to choose several co-workers.[7] Zehrer selected four young men who also had participated in the Youth Movement. They had recently begun, or were about to begin, careers in journalism or education. Horst Grüneberg taught in a secondary school. Like Zehrer, Ferdinand Fried[8] held a responsible position on a moderate newspaper; Fried wrote for the business section of the *Berliner Morgenpost*. Too young to have served in the war, Ernst Wilhelm Eschmann and Giselher Wirsing were still university students.

The members of the *Tat* circle had chosen occupations that became overcrowded long before the depression. Both journalism and education were particularly sensitive to the pressure from an expanding "academic proletariat" seeking suitable employment. Although in Germany journalism lacked much of the prestige associated with positions for which an academic degree was mandatory, the former student who became a journalist could regard himself as much more fortunate than many of his friends. From 1925 to 1931 the number of students enrolled in universities and technical colleges increased by more than 50 per cent. Much of the great increase in enrollments came from the middle class, especially from children of white-collar workers and lower ranking civil servants. These students expected that higher educa-

---

[5] Diederichs and the earlier phases of the magazine's history are discussed in Klemens von Klemperer, *Germany's New Conservatism: Its History and Dilemma in the Twentieth Century* (Princeton, 1957), pp. 97–99; Harry Pross, *Literatur und Politik: Geschichte und Programme der politisch-literarischen Zeitschriften im deutschen Sprachgebiet seit 1870* (Olten and Freiburg im Breisgau, 1963), pp. 94–96; George L. Mosse, *The Crisis of German Ideology: Intellectual Origins of the Third Reich* (New York, 1964), pp. 52–64.

[6] Eugen Diederichs, "Die neue Tat," xxi (Oct. 1929), 481-86.

[7] Beginning with the October issue Zehrer became the unofficial editor. When he finally resigned from the *Vossische Zeitung* two years later, he assumed the official editorship of the *Tat*.

[8] He was better known by this pseudonym rather than by his real name, Friedrich Zimmermann.

tion would furnish them with credentials guaranteeing their "right" to enter professions with a higher social status than those of their fathers. By the late 1920's an average of 25,000 students left German universities each year and competed with one another for less than half that number of available positions requiring academic training.[9] The shortage of jobs for former students contributed to the marked tendency among young university-trained Germans to repudiate democracy; they tended to hold the republic responsible for their insecurity. A similar lack of jobs in Italy after 1927 helped to alienate many Italian intellectuals from Fascism and fostered their acceptance of communism and other leftist doctrines identified with steadfast opposition to the regime.[10]

The members of the *Tat* circle worked together closely. They all had strong interests in economics, sociology, and politics, but with the exception of Zehrer each man concentrated upon a few special topics. Zehrer wrote the programmatic articles, as well as essays on his own favorite subjects. He sought to attract readers from all political camps. The impact of the economic and political upheavals after 1929 helped greatly to provide the new *Tat* with a receptive audience. The magazine's circulation increased rapidly from less than 3,000 in 1929 to 25,000 or more in 1933.[11] Many prominent scholars and writers,[12] not all of whom were identified with neoconservatism, contributed articles. But the most favorable responses to the new *Tat* came from the Right, especially the neoconservative Right. Hans Schwarz, the literary executor of Moeller van den Bruck, detected the spirit of his

[9] Svend Riemer, "Sozialer Aufstieg und Klassenschichtung," *Archiv für Sozialwissenschaft und Sozialpolitik*, LXVII (1932), 552–54; Robert Michels, *Umschichtungen in den herrschenden Klassen nach den Kriege* (Stuttgart, 1934), pp. 58–61; Walter M. Kotschnig, *Unemployment in the Learned Professions* (London, 1937), pp. 118–19. Among the general discussions of marginal intellectuals in modern society, see esp. William Kornhauser, *The Politics of Mass Society* (Glencoe, Ill., 1959), pp. 183–93, and Karl Mannheim, *Man and Society in an Age of Reconstruction: Studies in Modern Social Structure* (London, 1940), pp. 98–106. The latter work has an excellent bibliography which includes much of the basic material relevant to the Weimar Republic.

[10] H. Stuart Hughes, *The United States and Italy* (Cambridge, Mass., 1953), pp. 97–98.

[11] The increase in circulation was especially rapid after 1931. My estimates follow those in the annual editions of *Sperlings Zeitschriften- und Zeitungsadressbuch* (Leipzig, 1928–33). When Zehrer became unofficial editor of the *Tat*, its actual circulation may have been less than a thousand if the estimates given in the following are correct: [Zehrer?] "25 Jahre 'Tat,'" xxv (Apr. 1933), 85; Sontheimer, "Der Tat-Kreis," p. 232.

[12] Among them: Eugen Diesel, Paul Fechter, Friedrich Sieburg, Alfred Kantorowicz, Wichard von Moellendorff, Werner Sombart, and Ernst Graf Reventlow.

dead friend in its pages and bestowed his blessing upon Zehrer.[13] The *Tat* became a leading organ of neoconservatism.

THE INTELLIGENTSIA AS A CULTURAL AND POLITICAL ELITE

By the 1920's it had become fashionable in many quarters in Europe and America to speak of "the intelligentsia." Zehrer felt no need to supply a rigorous definition of the term. Implicit in his articles was the assumption that most intellectuals had attended a university, but he did not identify everyone who had acquired a higher education as a member of the intelligentsia.[14] In general, he regarded the intellectual as a well-educated individual involved in the production, transmission, or manipulation of "higher" cultural values. Without being bothered by the inconsistency, Zehrer occasionally restricted the intelligentsia to the more original creators of the "highest" cultural values.

Why did Zehrer refer to "the intelligentsia" despite the term's unfavorable connotations among right-wingers? First, it was less encumbered with such connotations than a possible synonym such as "the literati." Second, much more than "the intellectuals," another possible synonym, "the intelligentsia," implied the existence of a readily identifiable, rather cohesive group. Third, Zehrer could anticipate that many members of the audience that he wanted to reach would respond favorably to appeals to "the intelligentsia." In his campaign to attract readers from every political camp, he sought to demonstrate his magazine's independence. From the term's Russian origins, it carried revolutionary associations, and Zehrer was anxious to identify himself as an advocate of radical change. Like other neoconservatives, he wished to be thought of as a man who stood outside the conventional political spectrum. Indeed, he was much more receptive than most neoconservatives to views espoused by moderates and leftists. Unlike Jung and Spengler, whose sense of identification with the Right was much stronger, Zehrer took many of these views seriously; he rarely dismissed an idea out of hand simply because of its identification with the Left.

He derived many of his concepts from the work of Social Democrats and professional sociologists who employed terms such as "intellectuals" and "intelligentsia" as a part of their technical vocabulary. Zehrer integrated material derived from their work into his own elite theory. He used this material to support two basic propositions about

---

[13] Hans Schwarz, Preface (dated Nov. 1930) to his edition of Moeller's *Das 3. Reich* (Hamburg, n.d.), p. xvi.

[14] See "Revolution der Intelligenz," p. 500.

modern intellectuals: that an intelligentsia existed as a distinct social stratum; and that it performed crucial functions in society.

He found much support for both propositions in the work of Karl Mannheim, a young sociologist who rose to prominence during the last years of the Weimar Republic. Zehrer's programmatic article on the intelligentsia appeared in October 1929, shortly after the publication of Mannheim's *Ideology and Utopia*.[15] Perhaps the most searching and certainly the most discussed analysis of the "problem of the intelligentsia" published during the Weimar Republic, this book soon became the center of much controversy. Although Mannheim's political sympathies lay with Social Democracy, Zehrer had great respect for him and borrowed freely from his ideas.[16] Personal contacts may have increased this dependence upon Mannheim. When Zehrer's co-workers Eschmann and Wirsing began writing for the *Tat*, they were assistants at Heidelberg, the same university where Mannheim taught until 1930. Eschmann was a pupil of Alfred Weber, another sociologist who had devoted much attention to the intelligentsia and who had influenced Mannheim.[17]

Yet it would be incorrect to regard Zehrer's conception of the intelligentsia as derived primarily from Mannheim and Alfred Weber. The assumptions made by all three men reflected widespread images of the past, present, and future role of the intellectual in German society. Many of these images were accepted by the Right as well as the Left, but the belief that intellectuals should assume political leadership was confined almost entirely to non-Marxist leftists like Kurt Hiller of the *Weltbühne*, as we saw in Chapter Six. Zehrer appropriated this notion

[15] Karl Mannheim, *Ideologie und Utopie* (Bonn, 1929). The English translation by Louis Wirth and Edward Shils, *Ideology and Utopia: An Introduction to the Sociology of Knowledge* (London, 1936), is actually an expanded edition and contains an entire section written after 1933. Much of the secondary literature on Mannheim and the "sociology of knowledge" fails to distinguish clearly between his earlier works written in Germany and his later works written during his exile in Britain after 1933. For a brief summary of the major periods in his intellectual development, see Urs Jaeggi, *Die gesellschaftliche Elite: Eine Studie zum Problem der sozialen Macht* (Bern, 1960), pp. 73–80. H. Stuart Hughes, *Consciousness and Society: The Reorientation of European Social Thought, 1890–1930* (New York, 1958), pp. 418–27, provides a succinct analysis of the early Mannheim's place in German and European intellectual history.

[16] Zehrer acclaimed Mannheim as "einer der aktuellsten Denker unserer Zeit." "Revolution der Intelligenz," p. 498.

[17] Apparently Diederichs' son Peter, who was studying at Heidelberg, brought Zehrer into contact with Eschmann and Wirsing. Sontheimer, "Der Tat-Kreis," p. 232; Demant, *Von Schleicher zu Springer*, pp. 62–63. During the period of Zehrer's editorship, the *Tat* continued to maintain many contacts with Heidelberg. In a letter to me (Aug. 28, 1961) Professor Hajo Holborn, who was a lecturer at Heidelberg until 1930, writes: "One used to say in Heidelberg that the *Tat* was composed in the cellar of the Insosta (Institut für Sozial- und Staatswissenschaften). This was of course only metaphorically true."

for the Right. He developed it at great length with arguments that often paralleled those of Mannheim, who, however, was reluctant to identify himself with it.

Following a substantially modified Marxian analytical framework, Mannheim's *Ideology and Utopia* suggested that directly and indirectly the socioeconomic position of an individual affected the type of ideas that he expounded or adopted. But the thought of the intellectual, Mannheim argued, depended much less directly upon his position in society. Owing to the nature of the intellectual's activities, he could transcend many of the restrictions tending to limit the thought of other men. Unlike many German Social Democrats, Mannheim regarded the intellectual as occupying a largely "classless" position in society. Adapting a phrase coined by Alfred Weber, Mannheim referred to most intellectuals as constituting a "relatively socially unattached stratum."

According to Mannheim, the intellectual could perform one of two basic roles in society. He could place himself at the disposal of a single class and formulate ideas acceptable to it, or he could act as a mediator between classes and attempt to produce an intellectual synthesis for the entire society. While calling upon intellectuals to become fully aware of their unique position in society and the alternatives open to them, Mannheim often seemed to intimate that in the future the entire intelligentsia should concentrate merely upon one of these roles.

Yet he hesitated to choose between them.[18] At one point, he indicated that the intelligentsia should assist with the formulation of the demands of the most deprived strata of society—strata that he identified largely with the working class. He feared that "utopias," notions strongly at variance with the existing social order, were disappearing rapidly in the modern world. He was troubled by the belief that the process of "rationalization" analyzed by Max Weber was undercutting any faith in the possibility of substantial alterations in the existing order. Mannheim felt that dynamic elements in the historical process might vanish if the intellectual did not help the working class. On the other hand, he did not want the entire intelligentsia simply to renounce its "independence." He held forth the hope that the intelligentsia could create an intellectual synthesis with immediate validity for German society as a whole. The intelligentsia might work out the basis for a "scientific politics" geared to the existing order and designed to reduce progressively the role of "chance" in the formulation of political decisions.[19]

The initial stages of Zehrer's analysis differed little from Mann-

[18] Mannheim, *Ideologie und Utopie*, esp. pp. 122–34, 233–50.
[19] See *ibid.*, esp. pp. 155–69.

heim's. Beyond all social classes, Zehrer argued, there existed a stratum of intellectuals who were "innerly more independent of the actual conditions and values of the times" than other men. The intellectual could place ideas and events within a far broader context. But Zehrer believed more strongly than Mannheim that the intelligentsia would soon have to make fundamental choices affecting Germany's entire future. He distinguished sharply between the "normal" and "abnormal" situation of the intelligentsia. In normal times the intelligentsia constituted a stratum, although its members were dispersed throughout all social classes. A portion of the intelligentsia concerned itself with "things eternal." In abnormal times the intelligentsia drew together and almost formed a social class. Although it would never constitute a true social class, it might formulate the demands of a single class.[20] The intellectual, Zehrer felt, should not hesitate to devote his energies to finding solutions to the problems of the middle class.[21]

If Zehrer had concluded his recommendations at this point, his views would have had the advantage of clarity in comparison with Mannheim's. The intelligentsia's choice would have been clear. Rather than maintaining its independence or aiding the proletariat, it would have sided with the middle class. But Zehrer felt certain that intellectuals could devise a program for one class and simultaneously incorporate into this program values for German society as a whole. His position permitted him to stress the independence of the intelligentsia only to the point where what he regarded as its basic affiliation with the middle class did not become doubtful. The intelligentsia could be "objective" and "neutral," while at the same time it developed an intellectual synthesis in which his conception of the needs of the middle class would occupy a central place. The intelligentsia was the only social group that could "feel responsible for the totality."[22] Exposed to all the tensions within German society, it would forge a coherent system of values for the future.[23] Thus Zehrer's position became even more ambiguous than Mannheim's.

Zehrer's treatment of the aged Social Democratic theoretician Karl Kautsky revealed the carelessness with which he searched for support for his insistence upon the intellectual's independence. He seized gleefully upon discrepancies in Kautsky's writings: at the end of the nineteenth century, the young Kautsky had been willing to place sufficient emphasis upon the independence of the intelligentsia; later Kautsky had reversed his position. Zehrer accepted unquestioningly Kautsky's

[20] "Revolution der Intelligenz," pp. 489, 493–95, 503.
[21] Zehrer used the terms *Mittelstand* and *Mittelklassen* interchangeably.
[22] "Rechts oder links?" XXIII (Oct. 1931), 556.
[23] "Revolution der Intelligenz," p. 495.

own interpretation of his earlier work as having rested upon the assumption that intellectuals might form a distinct class in a society undergoing a severe crisis,[24] but a close examination of Kautsky's early work would hardly have supported this interpretation.[25] The young Kautsky contradicted himself; even on the same page, he referred interchangeably to some intellectuals as a class and a stratum.[26]

Zehrer found many justifications for his belief that the intelligentsia should aid the middle class. He felt that the middle class included the most underprivileged and oppressed segments of the population. Because most members of the intelligentsia originated in the middle class, the two groups, he reasoned, might be regarded as overlapping. Both occupied intermediate positions in society. Despite the intelligentsia's great capacity for independent thought, the fortunes of the middle class affected the intelligentsia directly.[27] Furthermore, both were victims of the "revolt of the masses," as Zehrer termed the advances made by working-class movements when a German translation of José Ortega y Gasset's now famous book supplied him with a catch phrase. The "masses"[28] wanted to derogate the "brain-worker" and place him on a level with the manual laborer. Zehrer decried the "senseless plague of leveling" spread by the "masses."[29]

The *Tat* devoted many articles to attempts at clarifying the position of the middle class in Germany and other countries.[30] Zehrer called attention to the jeopardy in which political and economic developments since 1918 had placed the German middle class. Two revolutions had collided in 1918. "The unfulfilled liberal revolution of the nineteenth century" had defeated "the antiliberal revolution of the early twentieth century," but without achieving a decisive victory. Big

[24] *Ibid.*, pp. 490–93.

[25] Cf. Karl Kautsky, *Die Klassengegensätze von 1789* (Stuttgart, 1889), pp. 39, 43–46, and *Die materialistische Geschichtsauffassung* (Berlin, 1927), II, 491.

[26] See Karl Kautsky, *Bernstein und das sozialdemokratische Programm: Eine Antikritik* (Stuttgart, 1899), p. 135. See also pp. 133–34.

[27] "Revolution der Intelligenz," pp. 496–500, 505–06.

[28] *Die Masse.* Zehrer tended to make an important distinction between *die Masse* and *die Massen.* He used the the former to refer primarily to the working class; he used the latter to refer to active or potential participants in any large organization or movement.

[29] "Revolution der Intelligenz," p. 502; "Die eigentliche Aufgabe," XXIII (Jan. 1932), 780–84, 795; "Deutschlands Weg in den Engpass," XXIII (Feb. 1932), 861. See also Leopold Dingräve [E. W. Eschmann], *Wo steht die junge Generation?* 3rd ed., Tat-Schriften (Jena, 1933), pp. 34–55. Zehrer and his friends frequently used pseudonyms in order to make their circle seem larger.

[30] See, e.g., E. W. Eschmann, "Der Faschismus und die Mittelschichten," XXI (Feb. 1930), esp. 858; Ferdinand Fried, "Die Spaltpilze," XXI (Oct. 1929), 520–28; Horst Grüneberg, "Mittelstandspolitik—Staatspolitik," XXIII (June 1931), 191–212; Hans Thomas [Zehrer], "Akademisches Proletariat," XXII (Jan. 1931), esp. 818.

business and Social Democrats had joined hands. The Social Democrats had become conservatives committed to the defense of the existing order.[31]

In 1928 and early 1929 Zehrer had perceived that substantial segments of big business were increasingly dissatisfied with the economic policies possible under the alignment of political forces in the Republic. He noted a growing trend within big business favoring "economic freedom." In events such as the great lockout in the iron and steel industry during the winter of 1928 and Alfred Hugenberg's rise to leadership of the Nationalist party in the same year, Zehrer saw indications of a demand by big business for laissez-faire policies. He found a struggle between proponents and opponents of laissez faire within each of the non-Socialist parties.[32]

In his view the middle class was caught between the threat of big business liberalism and proletarian socialism. He feared that in such a situation reactionary forces to the Right of big business or revolutionary forces to the Left of the Social Democrats might gain the upper hand. He predicted that either a restoration or a revolution would ruin the middle class. A restoration of the Empire, in itself disadvantageous to the middle class, would provoke revolution from the Left. Revolution from the Left, which like every revolution would be inimical to the interests of the middle class, would provoke a counter-revolutionary drive for a restoration. Despite these warnings, Zehrer repeatedly assured his readers that neither a revolution nor a restoration would occur.[33]

He took a special interest in the new middle class. In dramatic terms he described its plight: "There thus arises in all of these strata [of the new middle class] a deep revolutionary resentment, which, springing from a desire for culture and protection from economic misery, is reinforced by a desire for independence from the power of both capital [that is, big business] and the organizations of the masses [that is, working-class unions and parties]."[34] Zehrer's readers must frequently have received the impression that the primary task of the intelligentsia consisted in acting as the tribune of the new middle class.

The rapid increase in the number of white-collar workers during the past few decades had helped to provoke a heated controversy about

[31] "Rechts oder links?" p. 542.
[32] See "Der Abstieg des deutschen Parlaments," xx (June 1928), 201–06, and "Das Gewitter steigt auf," xx (Jan. 1929), 782–85.
[33] See, e.g., "Bürgerliche Mitte: Kompromiss oder Synthese?" xx (July 1928), 279–80; "Zwischen zwei Revolutionen," xx (Oct. 1928), 528–32; "Der Sinn der Krise," xxiii (Feb. 1932), 942–44; "Revolution oder Restauration?" xxiv (Aug. 1932), 393; "Worum geht es?" xxiv (Oct. 1932), 530.
[34] "Revolution der Intelligenz," p. 504.

the future of the new middle class. The controversy centered in the relationship of the new middle class to the working class. Most non-Socialists regarded the new middle class as a group closely linked to the old middle class. They predicted either that such ties would remain strong or that the new middle class would become an increasingly distinct status group. Sometimes they admitted that both wage worker and white-collar worker stood in a similar relationship to the means of production; neither of them owned or controlled the means of production. Non-Socialists also conceded, often bitterly, that income level did not provide a satisfactory yardstick by which to distinguish the two; many a white-collar worker earned less than a skilled worker. But non-Socialists pointed to other yardsticks. They stressed the white-collar worker's "closer" relationship to his employer, the nonmanual character of his work, and his strong feeling of superiority to the wage worker. They applauded the aversion of many an "underpaid" clerk to think of himself as a proletarian.[35]

Social Democratic writers generally regarded this aversion as an understandable, but temporary aberration. They emphasized the similarities in the economic position of the wage worker and the vast majority of salaried employees. They denied that the social consciousness of the white-collar worker corresponded to his actual position in society. Sooner or later, they declared, he would become aware of this discrepancy and cooperate with the proletariat.[36]

Thus most observers were struck by the refusal of the vast majority of white-collar workers to identify themselves with the working class.

[35] See, e.g., Joseph A. Schumpeter, "Das soziale Antlitz des Deutschen Reiches" (1929) in his *Aufsätze zur Soziologie* (Tübingen, 1953), p. 224. A good discussion of the literature that expressed the viewpoint of the non-Socialist unions on the white-collar worker is in Hans Speier's "The Salaried Employee in Modern Society," *Social Research*, I (1934), 125–26 and passim.

[36] Within the Social Democratic party there were two major tendencies in discussions of the new middle class. The first, more "orthodox" tendency regarded most white-collar workers simply as proletarians clinging to a "false consciousness." The second, "revisionist" tendency placed much more emphasis upon the "subjective" differences between the wage worker and the white-collar worker. Straddling these tendencies was the work of Emil Lederer, a Heidelberg sociologist whose renown rested largely on his studies of the new middle class. See the classic study which he did with Jakob Marschak, "Der neue Mittelstand" in *Grundriss der Sozialökonomik*, IX, Part 1 (Tübingen, 1926), esp. p. 141, and also Lederer's "Die Umschichtung des Proletariats," *Neue Rundschau*, XL, Band 2 (1929), esp. pp. 158–59. In an article in a trade-union periodical, Eschmann praised Lederer as a man who had undertaken a fundamental revision of Marxism. E. W. Eschmann, "Zur 'Krise' des Bürgertums," *Die Arbeit*, VIII (May 1931), 365, 367. For a brief analysis of the discussion among Social Democrats about their party's relationship to the middle class and an assessment of their failure to win and hold the allegiance of middle-class voters see Richard N. Hunt, *German Social Democracy, 1918–1933* (New Haven, 1964), pp. 134–41.

Neither the political behavior nor the self-image of the new middle class corresponded to those of the wage worker. During the Weimar Republic, membership in unions and similar organizations of public and private salaried employees swelled. The number of members may have been as large proportionally as among wage workers. But only one of the three major organizations was affiliated with the Free Trade Union Federation (ADGB), the unofficial labor organization of the Social Democrats. In 1928, the two federations that cultivated the white-collar worker's feelings of superiority toward the working class had a combined membership twice as large as that of the Free Federation of Salaried Employees.[37] By the depth of the depression only about 12 per cent of employed white-collar workers eligible for membership in this Social Democratic federation belonged to it.[38]

As we saw in discussing Nelson, bourgeois political and social thinkers often regarded the new middle class as simply one section within a middle class that shared common interests. Although Zehrer was particularly sensitive to the problems of the new middle class, he too assumed the existence of a cohesive middle class despite the contradictory interests and aspirations of groups as diverse as small manufacturers and white-collar workers. The *Tat* circle designed an economic program for the entire middle class. As early as 1928 and 1929, Zehrer outlined the basic planks upon which he and the other members of the circle elaborated during the depression.[39] Basic industries, big business, and large banks were to be nationalized. Heavy taxation would break up large concentrations of wealth in private hands. The circle soon adopted the slogan "national socialism" to characterize its economic demands. Despite the Nazis' use of the phrase, it had become increasingly popular in many other quarters during the last years of the Republic.

The *Tat*'s proposals suffered from the difficulties in formulating a coherent program that would take into consideration the diverse and often contradictory interests of the various strata of the middle class. Even in Zehrer's earlier articles the program was tailored more to the

[37] See the tables in Ludwig Preller, *Sozialpolitik in der Weimarer Republik* (Stuttgart, 1949), p. 204, and Gerhard Bry, *Wages in Germany, 1871–1945* (Princeton, 1960), p. 34. For a concise survey of the development of white-collar unions during the Weimar Republic, see Günter Hartfiel, *Angestellte und Angestelltengewerkschaften in Deutschland: Entwicklung und gegenwärtige Situation von beruflicher Tätigkeit, sozialer Stellung und Verbandswesen der Angestellten in der gewerblichen Wirtschaft* (Berlin, 1961), pp. 146–68.
[38] My computation for the period 1931 to 1932 from the tables in Wolfgang Hirsch-Weber, *Gewerkschaften in der Politik: Von der Massenstreikdebatte zum Kampf um das Mitbestimmungsrecht* (Cologne, 1959), p. 150.
[39] See esp. "Achtung, junge Front! Draussenbleiben!" xxi (Apr. 1929), 38–39, and "Die Situation der Innenpolitik," xxi (May 1929), 117–18.

grievances of the urban portions of the old middle class than to the no less anguished complaints of the peasantry and the new middle class.[40] This tendency became pronounced in the writings of Ferdinand Fried. Arguing that an era of technological innovation had closed, Fried devised schemes to assist small, unprofitable enterprises to expand their share of the national economy.[41] Always highly ambiguous, the "national socialism" of the *Tat* would have reversed the trend toward large-scale, private capitalism, without stipulating a definite return to early nineteenth-century conditions of small-scale production.

Zehrer believed even more fervently than Jung that history was approaching a decisive turning point. Using the clichés of the most ecstatic neoconservatives, he depicted the future. Of all the peoples of Europe, only "this murky German people still has a great task to fulfill —perhaps the greatest task of all." A "world-redeeming idea" would enable the revival of Germany as a Great Power.[42] Through cooperation with the smaller nations of Europe and peoples under colonial rule, a policy that Moeller van den Bruck had helped to popularize, Germany would outmaneuver the Western Powers and the United States. Under the ill-concealed guise of "good Central Europeans," the new Germany would have embarked upon a policy of systematic economic and political expansion in eastern and southeastern Europe.[43]

The possible consequences of this expansion were not stated clearly. In general, they would have reinforced the results of the *Tat's* domes-

---

[40] While praising the "bemerkenswerte Frische und Tatkraft" with which the *Tat* explored the problems of the *Mittelstand,* a German Communist criticized the circle for not recommending that white-collar workers strengthen their consciousness of their own status and renounce petty bourgeois ideology. Hans Günther, *Der Herren eigner Geist: Die Ideologie des Nationalsozialismus* (Moscow, 1935), pp. 443, 446.

[41] See Ferdinand Fried, *Das Ende des Kapitalismus,* Tat-Schriften (Jena, 1931), pp. 15–16, 82, 95–96. This book brought together many of the articles which Fried had published in the *Tat.* See also his later articles, esp.: "Wo stehen wir?" xxiii (Aug. 1931), 383–84; "Gestaltung des Zusammenbruchs," xxiii (Mar. 1932), 975–86; "Der Umbau der Wirtschaft," xxiv (Sept. 1932), 464–67. The chapter on the *Tat* circle in Herman Lebovics, *Social Conservatism and the Middle Classes in Germany, 1914–1933* (Princeton, 1969) is focused on Fried's economic program. See esp. pp. 184–98. Written from the point of view of contemporary West German neoliberal economics, Wolfgang Hock's *Deutscher Antikapitalismus: Der ideologische Kampf gegen die freie Wirtschaft im Zeichen der grossen Krise* (Frankfurt am Main, 1960) provides a brief, clear critique of the ideas of Fried and other proponents of a "national socialism," but unlike Lebovics, Hock does not attempt to examine the social origins of these ideas.

[42] "Achtung, junge Front! Draussenbleiben!" p. 40, and "Deutschlands Weg in den Engpass," p. 870.

[43] See esp. "Die 3. Front," xxiv (May 1932), 115. Giselher Wirsing supplied the most detailed proposals for a German-dominated area between Russia and France in his *Zwischeneuropa und die deutsche Zukunft,* Tat-Schriften (Jena, 1932).

tic economic program. If the state had already nationalized many large-scale enterprises, small business might gain reduced foreign competition, protected sources of raw materials, and increased opportunities to expand. For the new middle class, positions as administrators and technicians would have become available outside the boundaries of Germany under the Treaty of Versailles.

The execution of the future German foreign policy presupposed, Zehrer argued, a "revolution" much more far-reaching than the French Revolution.[44] Germany must undergo a complete intellectual and political transformation to prepare for its new role. Every step in "the German Revolution" would depend upon the activities of the intelligentsia.

OPPORTUNISM AND ORGANIZATION

Both during the Weimar Republic and more recently, Mannheim has been accused of developing an ideology—or, to use his own term, a "utopia"—for the intelligentsia.[45] Although that was certainly not his intention, the partial validity of the charge has to be recognized. What of Zehrer? His own place in society was less secure. He was both desperate and ambitious, and at times he was disarmingly frank. Zehrer's intelligentsia had to be prepared to utilize the distress of the middle class for its own purposes. The intelligentsia should develop values to justify its "rightful" place in German society. The application of these values necessitated an opportunistic attitude, for the intelligentsia had to command "battalions," as well as marshal ideas. In order to achieve a predominant position in Germany, it had to ally itself with a social class: "The causes of revolutions are initially and primarily intellectual, and only secondarily economic or political. If the reverse appears to be true, . . . it is only because even the mind does not get anywhere by demanding [as does the Marquis of Posa in Schiller's *Don Carlos*]: 'Sire, give us freedom of thought.' The mind has to have material power for the realization of its ideas."[46]

Directly and indirectly, the intelligentsia would have made all significant decisions affecting German society. By creating highly binding values for all Germans, it would have predetermined the most impor-

---

[44] "Die Ideen der Aussenpolitik," xxi (May 1929), 108–10.

[45] See, e.g., Hans Speier, "Zur Soziologie der bürgerlichen Intelligenz," *Die Gesellschaft*, ix (1929), Band 2, pp. 58–72; Theodor Geiger, *Aufgaben und Stellung der Intelligenz in der Gesellschaft* (Stuttgart, 1949), p. 64; Kurt Lenk, "Die Rolle der Intelligenzsoziologie in der Theorie Mannheims," *Kölner Zeitschrift für Soziologie und Sozialpsychologie*, xv (1963), 331.

[46] "Revolution der Intelligenz," p. 488. See also "Wohin treiben wir?" xxiii (Aug. 1931), 343, and "Rechts oder links?" p. 555.

tant decisions. As long as a regime desired to "justify its rule ideologically and to rely upon methods of persuasion," Zehrer believed, it needed the intelligentsia, for the intelligentsia always provided, "the material, the idea, and the tendency."[47]

He would also have ensured the predominance of the intelligentsia in the future by having it occupy the most important political positions. Partly because of German political experiences since the failure of the Revolution of 1848 and the feeling of political impotence common among German intellectuals, Mannheim had tended to follow Max Weber in drawing a clear line of demarcation between the political leader and the intellectual. Mannheim had restricted the involvement of the intellectual in the formulation of political decisions to an advisory function. Zehrer, on the other hand, wanted the intelligentsia itself to make political decisions.

His conception of modern political development encouraged his confidence in the possibilities for the intellectual to act as a political decision maker. He interpreted the Bolshevik revolution as the coming to power of a large part of the Russian intelligentsia.[48] Robert Michels's studies of socialism and syndicalism in France and Italy had contributed to the common German image of the prominence of intellectuals in Latin politics. Even more important for Zehrer was the belief, which indirectly Michels had helped to encourage, that the establishment of parliamentary democracy in Germany had been largely the work of intellectuals. Although this belief was strongest on the Right of the political spectrum and Spengler had presented one of the most ingenious versions of it, some Social Democrats also contributed to its diffusion. Thus Hendrik de Man, a Fleming who was closely associated with postwar German political life and whom Zehrer regarded highly, argued that in modern nations intellectuals were coming more and more to make the important decisions: "All movements which crystallize in the form of party organizations share . . . the fate of the state; their guidance passes into the hands of professional specialists who have either sprung from the class of intellectuals or will become members of that class as soon as they become political leaders."[49]

Unlike Jung, Zehrer was obsessed by the notion of a conflict of generations. Political analyses in the *Tat* often resembled a fusion of Pa-

[47] "Revolution der Intelligenz," pp. 493–95. Compare the even more explicit formulations in Leopold Dingräve [pseud. for E. W. Eschmann], "Eliten," xxii (Jan. 1931), 799–800.

[48] "Revolution der Intelligenz," p. 500.

[49] Hendrik de Man, *The Psychology of Socialism*, trans. from the 2nd German ed. by Eden and Cedar Paul (New York, 1928), p. 202. I have altered the English translation slightly. See also de Man's pamphlet *Die Intellektuellen und der Sozialismus* (Jena, 1926).

reto's elite theory with slogans from the Youth Movement. Despite the admiration that Zehrer and his friends had for Pareto,[50] they accused him of ignoring the obvious solution to one of the central issues raised by his sociology. They reduced the problem that Pareto had called the "circulation of elites" to the "circulation of generations." Zehrer thought that in normal times intellectuals had no difficulty in obtaining key political positions. Younger men gradually replaced older ones. He complained bitterly that the process of slow replacement had virtually ceased in Germany. Wars, he reasoned, destroyed the normal cycle by which younger men steadily replaced older ones, and lost wars had an especially disruptive effect. After the younger generation of German intellectuals had been decimated on the battlefield, the revolution of 1918 had served to prolong the careers of older leaders. The least worthy members of the old elites had remained in power and had been joined by men accustomed to viewing themselves as "exponents of the will of the masses." The new generation of intellectuals had been denied positions of power. As a result, the "best minds" in the intelligentsia had become alienated from the existing order and withheld their services from all political parties. But the members of the future elite could not be held down much longer by the "alliance of capital and the masses." When most of the intelligentsia became fully conscious of its plight, refused to support the Republic, and universalized the aspirations of the new middle class, the existing order would crumble. An entire generation of young intellectuals would replace party hacks and calcified bureaucrats.[51]

The impatience of the *Tat* reflected a tendency, especially pronounced among younger Germans, to reject political parties as ossified impediments to decisive action. Except for the Communists and the Nazis, the parties manifested marked signs of "aging" in their leadership and membership. Particularly in the Social Democratic party, the average age of members, Reichstag deputies, and executive committee members increased appreciably during most of the Weimar Republic.[52]

Echoing one of the major themes of the Youth Movement, Zehrer emphasized the need for a new elite to develop in temporary isolation

[50] See, e.g., E. W. Eschmann, "Moderne Soziologen: Vilfredo Pareto," xxi (Jan. 1930), 771–79. In this article Eschmann announced plans for a complete German edition of Pareto's *magnum opus*, the *Trattato di sociologia generale* (2 vols., Florence, 1916), to be published by Diederichs, but the translation did not appear. Germans had to wait until after World War II for a translation of Pareto's work.

[51] "Revolution der Intelligenz," pp. 495–503; "Deutschlands Weg in den Engpass," p. 861; "Wohin treiben wir?" p. 342; "Der Weg in das Chaos," xxi (Nov. 1929), 572–75; Hans Thomas [Zehrer], "Die zweite Welle," xxi, 577–82.

[52] See Hunt, *German Social Democracy*, pp. 71–72, 89–91, 106–11.

from the rest of society.[53] The new elite would begin in small, closely knit groups that would eventually fuse. Involvement in the existing political order might lead to acceptance of it. The *Tat* followed the predominant mood in the youth *Bünde*, the small organizations of teen-agers and young adults that remained independent of established institutions such as churches and political parties. In the late 1920's the total membership of the various youth *Bünde* was, as we saw in Chapter Ten, no more than 50,000 to 100,000—1 to 2 per cent of organized German youth.[54] While bemoaning the absence in Germany of a social type that every German could emulate and asserting the need for a cohesive ruling group that would create a unified national tradition, the *Tat* circle was more reserved than most German elitists in its admiration for the achievements of the English aristocracy.[55] This reserve was a function of the *Tat*'s identification with those younger and more ambitious members of the middle class who were suspicious of schemes that might serve to mask a revival of the German nobility.

Zehrer frequently announced that the final formation of the new elite would begin shortly. He drafted a succession of plans to draw together the intelligentsia. Common to all of these plans were organizational patterns drawn from the experiences of the youth *Bünde*. Within the Youth Movement the issue whether a *Bünd* or an order (*Orden*) was the superior form of organization was being debated acrimoniously. Zehrer incorporated both of these concepts into a synthesis that might be attractive to the feuding groups. The youth *Bünde* themselves were to form the lower levels of the new, "compact" "ruling stratum [*staatstragende Schicht*]" and supply a reservoir of leaders. Zehrer dreamed of a higher organization above the youth groups. It would consist of the men holding the most important political positions, as well as older members of the youth groups. Like the Teutonic Knights and similar medieval institutions, the models on which the neoconservative notion of an "order" was based, Zehrer's *Orden* was to have a special ethos for its members. This ethos would be predicated upon their moral superiority. It would entail self-denial and "complete dedication." Like most other German elitists, Zehrer refused to acknowledge the possibility of any conflict arising between the ethos of the elite and the values of the nonelite.[56]

[53] See "Rechts oder links?" pp. 555–60; "Der Sinn der Krise," xxiii (Mar. 1932), 953–54; "Die eigentliche Aufgabe," pp. 786, 796–99.

[54] Karl O. Paetel, "Die deutsche Jugendbewegung als politisches Phänomen," *Politische Studien*, viii, No. 86 (1957), p. 3; Felix Raabe, *Die bündische Jugend: Ein Beitrag zur Geschichte der Weimarer Republik* (Stuttgart, 1961), p. 66.

[55] See esp. "Die eigentliche Aufgabe," xxiii (Jan. 1932), 796; Leopold Dingräve [pseud. for E. W. Eschmann], "Eliten," xxii (Jan. 1931), 801–10.

[56] See, e.g., "Ende der Parteien," pp. 75, 79; "An der Wende der Innenpolitik?" xxiv (Jan. 1933), 826–27; "Die eigentliche Aufgabe," pp. 795–97.

He also proposed a special organization of the intelligentsia. This organization would overlap in part with the order and the *Bünde*. It too would be centrally organized in order to foster close contact among its members and to ensure its cohesiveness.[57] All three sections of the elite would thus be united by a common consciousness of their special position and responsibilities.

Plans for the corporative and regional organization of society served as a brake upon the power of the elite envisioned by neoconservatives like Jung. Although the *Tat* frequently discussed such plans, it never fully espoused the principles involved in them. Desiring a strongly unified elite, Zehrer stressed the centralizing possibilities of corporatism. He thought that the retention of some elections on the communal level might be desirable, but he assumed that they would have little if any effect upon the composition of the elite.[58]

Nothing was to interfere with what Zehrer described as a *carrière ouverte aux talents*. He contemplated no meaningful popular control over either the selection or the policies of the elite. Since the intelligentsia could presumably ascertain trends in all segments of society, any institutional controls at the disposal of the general public would have been superfluous. The synthesis created by the intelligentsia would have established a set of general values for the entire society. These values would have indicated clearly the decisions necessary for the "common good." The elite, technically open for membership to every German, would have been well insulated from popular pressures that might have tied its decisions simply to the particular interests of a single group. Consequently, the elite would have represented the "true will of the people."[59] "In the future," Zehrer predicted, "perhaps only a half or a quarter of the people who have been 'making policy' and adding their two bits will have a voice in decisions. But this smaller circle will determine developments more authoritatively and decisively than the masses do today."[60]

Zehrer's views were typical of those neoconservatives who placed the need for an elite over that for a "great man." The Germans might be fortunate enough, he felt, to receive a great man to lead the way to the future, but an elite would be far more important than any such "savior." Especially in the modern world, a great man could not do without an elite. If he did not appear, for after all, his appearance

---

[57] "Rechts oder links?" pp. 557–59; "Ende der Parteien," p. 68.

[58] "Frühjahrsoffensive," p. 13; "An der Wende!" xxiv (Sept. 1932), 451; "Ende der Parteien," p. 68.

[59] "Die 3. Front," pp. 109–10. See also "Hugenbergs Glück und Ende," xxi (June 1929), 208; "Deutschlands Weg in den Engpass," p. 861; "Die Revolution von rechts," xxv (Apr. 1933), 10.

[60] "Die Etappe Papen," xxiv (Nov. 1932), 632.

would be a "matter of fortune," then it would undertake the transformation of Germany by itself. The main burden would, in any event, fall upon the elite.[61]

THE INTELLIGENTSIA TO THE FORE!

While Zehrer was designing the system of the future, he watched current events closely. From 1928 to 1930 he took much interest in the formation of an outspokenly middle-class party.[62] But he labeled these attempts as temporary expedients, and he soon became hostile to any organization faintly resembling the existing parties. He became even more strongly convinced than earlier that the new elite could attain power only after the completion of the "intellectual revolution" and the elimination of "mass organizations." He assured his readers that both of these preconditions would be fulfilled shortly. Intermittently, he drafted plans for a "third front" between the parties of the Left and those of the Right. Despite the vagueness of many of these plans,[63] the *Tat* circle established ties with several prospective candidates for membership in it.

Especially through Eschmann, the circle had since its inception been linked to the German *Freischar*, one of the youth groups most severely torn between political activism and withdrawal.[64] By the middle of 1932 loose ties had also been established with some *Reichswehr* circles, Otto Strasser's "Black Front," Gregor Strasser's "left wing" of the Nazi

[61] "Rechts oder links?" xxiii (Oct. 1931), 556; "Die Frühjahrsoffensive," xxiv (Apr. 1932), 13; "Achtung, junge Front! Draussenbleiben!" xxi (Apr. 1929), 27; "Grundriss einer neuen Partei," xxi (Dec. 1929), 641–42; "Deutschland ohne Hindenburg," xxiv (Dec. 1932), 726; "Das Ende der Parteien," xxiv (Apr. 1932), 77–78.

[62] See "Der Fall Lambach," xx (Sept. 1928), 464; "Grundriss einer neuen Partei," xxi (Dec. 1929), 656–60. In 1930, from his desk on the *Vossische Zeitung*, Zehrer followed with sympathy the attempts of the *Staatspartei* (a new party formed in part by dissidents from the Democratic party) to establish a broader basis by cooperating with a section of the Youth Movement. See Klaus Hornung, *Der Jungdeutsche Orden* (Düsseldorf, 1958), p. 102.

[63] See, e.g., "Ende der Parteien," p. 75; "Die 3. Front," p. 108.

[64] See Hermann Seifert, "Politische Vorstellungen und Versuche der Deutschen Freischar" in *Lebendiger Geist: Hans Joachim Schoeps zum 50. Geburtstag*, ed. Hellmut Diwald, *Zeitschrift für Religions- und Geistesgeschichte*, Beiheft 4 (Leiden, 1959), pp. 191–95; Walter Z. Laqueur, *Young Germany: A History of the German Youth Movement* (New York, 1962), p. 148. Zehrer had been a member of the *Altwandervogel* according to his letter of Jan. 29, 1964 to me. This group was one of the two major youth *Bünde* which merged to form what would be called in 1927 the *Freischar*. In the late 1920's the *Freischar* had about ten to twelve thousand members, of whom roughly three quarters were less than eighteen years of age. Raabe, *Bündische Jugend*, pp. 67–69; Laqueur, *Young Germany*, p. 144.

party, the German Nationalist Federation of Commercial Employees (DHV), and several less prominent organizations.[65]

Time and again, Zehrer predicted the imminent disappearance of all political parties. In his more optimistic moments, he declared that the "masses" had begun to "demobilize" themselves.[66] In his less optimistic moments, he admitted that the electoral successes of the parties most strongly opposed to the Weimar Republic might delay its disintegration. Electoral successes might reconcile the National Socialists and the Communists to the "party system."[67] He implored the Nazis, whom he referred to as embodying "the first wave" of the "intellectual, cultural, and organizational heritage of the German Youth Movement," to renounce their pretensions to being a mass party. The Nazis, he argued, must return to the notion of the small, exclusive *Bund*.[68] His colleague Ferdinand Fried pointed to another danger: the Nazis might be bought off by subsidies from heavy industry.[69]

In 1932 the *Tat* opted for a "revolution from above" to clear the stage for the emergence of the new elite. As Jung placed his hopes in Papen, Zehrer and his friends turned to General Kurt von Schleicher to lead their version of this "revolution." First as "chief" of the army and then as Reichswehr minister in the von Papen cabinet, Schleicher had become deeply involved in the political intrigues of the last years of the Republic. His strategic position and his apparent sympathy for "radical" solutions recommended him to Zehrer. Early in 1932 the *Tat* established a close liaison with the general.[70] Throughout the next year, Zehrer pleaded for the destruction of the Republic by a coalition led by a "neutral" chancellor with the support of the president, the army, and the ministerial bureaucracy.[71] The hour of the intelligentsia

---

[65] See esp. Otto Ernst Schüddekopf, *Linke Leute von rechts: Die nationalrevolutionären Minderheiten und der Kommunismus in der Weimarer Republik* (Stuttgart, 1960), pp. 326–28, 340, 381; Demant, *Von Schleicher zu Springer*, pp. 87–88.

[66] "Die 3. Front," p. 101.

[67] See, e.g.: *ibid.*, pp. 97–98; "Ende der Parteien," p. 73; "Frühjahrsoffensive," pp. 10–11.

[68] "Ende der Parteien," p. 75. See also "Rechts oder links?" p. 547.

[69] Ferdinand Fried, "Kapital und Masse," xxii (Jan. 1931), 798.

[70] The initial contacts with Schleicher may have been made in 1930. See Demant, *Von Schleicher zu Springer*, p. 85. Demant's examination of the details of the *Tat*'s relationship to Schleicher (pp. 84ff.) is the best that we have to date, although many aspects of the subject merit further exploration. The account of this relationship in James H. Meisel, *Counterrevolution: How Revolutions Die* (New York, 1966), pp. 138–48 repeats some of the legends about it. Meisel's main sources appear to be his own recollections as a German newspaperman during the early 1930's and, more important, his conversations with his acquaintance Friedrich Wilhelm von Oertzen, a journalist close to the *Tat* circle.

[71] See "Die Entscheidung entgegen," xxiv (June 1932), 199; "Worum geht es?" p. 531; "An der Wende!" pp. 445, 447; "Die Etappe Papen," p. 632; "An der

and the *Bünde* would then have arrived. The "real revolution" would depend upon them.[72]

In the late summer of 1932, with some financial support from Reichswehr funds made available by Schleicher, the *Tat* circle expanded its journalistic activities by taking over the *Tägliche Rundschau*. This small Berlin daily newspaper had been a voice of the Nationalist Federation of Commercial Employees and the *Christlich-sozialer Volksdienst*, an organization founded in 1929 in part by dissidents from the German Nationalist party.[73] Under Zehrer's editorship, the newspaper assumed temporary importance as a semiofficial interpreter of Schleicher's intentions.[74]

During the last, hectic months of the Republic there were some signs that Schleicher might be willing and able to piece together a "third front." The prospect of a split in the Nazi party heartened Zehrer. He hoped to obtain middle and working class support from Gregor Strasser's Nazi faction and from the Social Democratic trade unions.[75] With elaborate if frequently shifting and contradictory social analyses, the *Tat* sought to demonstrate similarities in the situation of the middle class and the working class.

The coming "German Revolution" that the *Tat* repeatedly predicted was a vague concept dependent upon new divisions in the working-class movement as deep as those that had led to the schism in Social Democracy during World War I. A pamphlet written by Hans Freyer, a young sociologist, and published by Diederichs, the *Tat's* publisher, provides some of the clearest indications of what Zehrer and some other neoconservatives had in mind when they spoke of "revolution" affirmatively. Freyer argued that the working class was basically integrated into German society and that the revolutionary bourgeois and proletarian forces of the nineteenth century had exhausted themselves. In the future a revolution of the *Volk*, that is, essentially of the middle class and a part of the working class, would occur. This "revolution from the right" would not follow the pattern of either the French Revolution or the Russian Revolution. Rather than being captured by a social class, the state would become a "neutral" agency of the *Volk*.[76]

Wende der Innenpolitik?" pp. 822–23; Hans Thomas [Zehrer], "Der Mensch in dieser Zeit," xxiv (Jan. 1933), 821.

[72] See, e.g., "Ende der Parteien," p. 77; "Die eigentliche Not unserer Zeit," xxiv (Feb. 1933), 926.

[73] See Günter Opitz, *Der christlich-soziale Volksdienst: Versuch einer protestantischen Partei in der Weimarer Republik* (Düsseldorf, 1969), p. 281, n. 41.

[74] For this phase of the *Tat* circle's activities see Sontheimer, "Der Tat-Kreis," pp. 248–51; Demant, *Von Schleicher zu Springer*, esp. pp. 90–97.

[75] See, e.g., "Die Entscheidung entgegen," pp. 201–02; "Revolution oder Restauration?" xxiv (Aug. 1932), 389.

[76] Hans Freyer, *Revolution von rechts* (Jena, 1931), passim.

The opportunistic attitude that Zehrer deemed essential for the success of the intelligentsia led the *Tat* circle to reach out toward the Social Democratic unions. There is even some evidence that the circle had been sounding out the unions before 1932. In 1931 one of Zehrer's colleagues had written an article for a trade union journal edited by Theodor Leipart, the head of the Social Democratic federation of trade unions (ADGB). In this article, Eschmann praised attempts to revise Marxism, emphasized the common interest of the proletariat and the middle class in building socialism, and looked forward to increasing contacts between the youth of both classes.[77]

The Strasser wing of the Nazi party represented those National Socialists who feared that the "socialist" aspects of their movement were being jettisoned by Hitler's opportunistic dealings with the bourgeoisie. Although not explicitly, Strasser had developed a point of view which, like the *Tat's*, was concerned primarily with the interests of the middle class. By the late spring of 1932, there were many indications that he and the leadership of the Socialist unions were prepared to cooperate politically with each other.[78]

Throughout the summer and fall of 1932 the *Tat* circle continued to assist Schleicher's attempts to obtain a mass basis.[79] For a while his negotiations met with some success. Then both Gregor Strasser and the Social Democratic unions failed to deliver the support that had been anticipated from them. The political leaders of the Social Democrats blocked the projected entente with the unions,[80] and on December 8, Strasser resigned from his offices in the Nazi party without summoning his followers to join him.[81] Although in the meantime Schleicher became chancellor, the vision of a "third front" had become

---

[77] See E. W. Eschmann, "Zur 'Krise' des Bürgertums," *Die Arbeit*, VIII (May 1931), 362–71.

[78] According to Reinhard Kühnl, *Die nationalsozialistische Linke 1925–1930* (Meisenheim am Glan, 1966), pp. 83–84, Strasser and Theodor Leipart made very complimentary references to each other in speeches for several months after April 1932.

[79] Unfortunately, Thilo Vogelsang's careful analysis of Schleicher's plans and intentions in *Reichswehr, Staat und NSDAP: Beiträge zur deutschen Geschichte 1930–1932* (Stuttgart, 1962), esp. pp. 258, 269, 276–77, 328–29, 340–42, 367, leaves many important questions unanswered.

[80] For a detailed analysis of Schleicher's negotiations with union leaders see Gerard Braunthal, "The German Free Trade Unions during the Rise of Nazism," *Journal of Central European Affairs*, xv (1956), 343–47.

[81] See Gerd Schumann, *Nationalsozialismus und Gewerkschaftsbewegung: Die Vernichtung der deutschen Gewerkschaften und der Aufbau der "Deutschen Arbeitsfront"* (Hannover, 1958), pp. 45–46; Thilo Vogelsang, "Zur Politik Schleichers gegenüber der NSDAP 1932," *Vierteljahrshefte für Zeitgeschichte*, VI (1958) 105–06, 115–17; Dietrich Orlow, *A History of the Nazi Party, 1919–1933* (Pittsburgh, 1969), pp. 278, 290–91.

a mirage. The Nazis survived the brief Schleicher cabinet with their party still intact, and Hitler became chancellor.

Zehrer tried to salvage what he could from the debacle. With the cooperation of the Nazis, Germany might still, he felt, combine the "revolution from above" with the often-postponed "revolution of the intelligentsia." Like most neoconservatives, he accorded some Nazis the right to become members of the future elite, but he cautioned against the dictatorship of a political party.[82] While calling for national unity,[83] the *Tat* begged for the reorganization of the cabinet to include Schleicher and Gregor Strasser. The "national revolution" had begun; the "socialist" phase *must* follow shortly.[84] Even after the Reichstag fire and the March elections, Zehrer held forth the hope that the Nazis would accept the imminent emergence of *his* new elite.

Writing under one of his many pseudonyms in May of 1933, he expressed himself much more cautiously. He now presented his dream of the future in an essentially spiritual form. The intellegentsia, he suggested, might have to adopt a modern version of monastic withdrawal from society.[85] In his last article before his own withdrawal he welcomed the destruction of faith in human progress, renounced the world of men, and turned his gaze to another world. "The masses," he charged, had "seized the rudder" and would remain at the helm for the foreseeable future.[86] He spent most of the next five years leading a secluded life on the North Sea island of Sylt, where he could meditate upon the imperfections of "this world." His friends Eschmann and Wirsing assumed the editorship of the *Tat*. Like Fried, they became apologists for the Third Reich.[87] During the Nazi period Zehrer stayed out of political journalism, becoming eventually the chairman of the board of Gerhard Stalling,[88] a small publishing house that had been

[82] "Revolution von rechts," (Apr. 1933), pp. 15–16; "Der Umbau des deutschen Staates," xxv (May 1933), 103–04.

[83] *Ibid.*, pp. 104–05; Z. [Zehrer], "Aussenpolitik und nationaler Sozialismus," xxv (June 1933), 208.

[84] Anon. [Zehrer?], "Schleicher und Strasser," xxiv (Mar. 1933), 1067–68; Hans Thomas [Zehrer], "Der Weg der deutschen Revolution," xxv (May 1933), 124.

[85] *Ibid.*, esp. pp. 128–29.

[86] Hans Thomas [Zehrer], "Das Ende des 'Fortschritts,'" xxv (Aug. 1933), esp. 358–64. In two works published shortly after the end of World War II, Zehrer returned to the themes of his last articles in the *Tat*. See *Stille vor dem Sturm: Aufsätze zur Zeit* (Hamburg, 1949), and *Der Mensch in dieser Welt* (Hamburg, 1948).

[87] For brief descriptions of the careers of Fried, Eschmann, and Wirsing under the Nazis, see Lebovics, *Social Conservatism*, pp. 203–04; Léon Poliakov and Josef Wulf, eds., *Das Dritte Reich und seine Denker: Dokumente* (Berlin, [1959?]), pp. 141, 144, 368, 477–78; Demant, *Von Schleicher zu Springer*, esp. pp. 64–66.

[88] See *Wer ist wer?* (1962).

associated with the Right. He might have been able to continue his career as a political journalist, but his identification with Schleicher may have caused him some difficulties while his attitude toward the new regime seems to have remained reserved.[89] After World War II he served as the editor of one of West Germany's major daily newspapers until his death in 1966. With the exception of Grüneberg, whose association with the *Tat* seems to have come to an end before 1933, the other former members of the circle also came to hold important positions in West German journalism, and Eschmann finally succeeded in resuming his academic career.

The convincing assertion that Zehrer had "illusions about power"[90] should not obscure the major sources of these illusions. The *Tat* circle expressed on a highly articulate level the grievances of social strata to whom Germany's economic and political development offered few meaningful satisfactions, but who could not really accept a radical transformation of the existing social order. Zehrer's identification with the fears and ambitions of the middle class led him to expect salvation from an authoritarian elite whose rise was blocked by every other group in German society, as well as by conflicts within the middle class itself. His conception of a "Revolution of the Intelligentsia" exaggerated the role of generational conflicts and presupposed the simultaneous disintegration or destruction of big business and organized labor. The arrival of the depression, when many people believed in the imminent collapse of capitalism and when enmity between Communists and Social Democrats seriously curtailed the power of the working class, emboldened him to make further miscalculations. Similarly, the success of Nazi demagoguery in winning extensive middle-class support appeared to confirm his vast underestimation of the importance of conflicts between the diverse strata of the middle class. He failed to devise an effective method of utilizing the severe social conflicts within Germany to produce the rule of his intelligentsia. The contradictory policies that he wanted the future elite to pursue would have required a return, in part, to conditions existing a century earlier. Perhaps in some colonial and neocolonial areas many intellectuals may temporarily become leading members of a political elite similar in certain respects to the one envisioned by Zehrer. But in Germany intellectuals did not constitute a cohesive and potentially powerful stratum.

[89] See esp. Demant, *Von Schleicher zu Springer*, pp. 120–25 and passim. His vulnerability was increased by the fact that his wife had been born into a Jewish family.

[90] Sontheimer, "Der Tat-Kreis," p. 246.

CHAPTER TWELVE

Ernst Jünger: Warriors, Workers, and Elite

SEVERAL months before Hitler became chancellor, Ernst Jünger published the most important work that he wrote during the Weimar Republic. *Der Arbeiter*[1] (*The Worker*) became the literary sensation of the early fall of 1932.[2] A hero of World War I, a recipient of the highest Prussian award for bravery, the *pour le mérite*, Jünger had previously exploited his war experiences in several autobiographical works that had won him a measure of esteem, especially on the Right. By 1932 his first book, originally published in 1920,[3] had sold about 45,000 copies, and most of his other books had achieved comparable success.[4] Less well known were the many political articles that he had published, most of them in small right-wing periodicals. In his works prior to the *Arbeiter*, he asserted a claim to speak in the name of the combat veterans, both living and dead, of the war.[5]

The *Arbeiter* presented the culmination of Jünger's political ideas during the Weimar Republic, as well as perhaps the most extreme conception of an open-yet-authoritarian elite developed in twentieth-century Germany. Jünger depicted the emergence of a society that seemed to diverge radically from the existing social order. He indicated little desire to retain any aspect of Germany's past. The society of the *Arbeiter* was mobilized permanently for total war. An open elite, dominated by irrational values, would exploit highly efficient and rational aspects of modern industrial society to manipulate and mobilize a nonelite that would be powerless to challenge the elite. Indeed, the nonelite would happily accept its subordination.

The vision of a society mobilized permanently for total war was de-

---

[1] *Der Arbeiter: Herrschaft und Gestalt*, 2nd ed. (Hamburg, 1932). Hereafter cited as *DA*.

[2] Hans-Peter Schwarz, *Der konservative Anarchist: Politik und Zeitkritik Ernst Jüngers* (Freiburg im Breisgau, 1962), p. 12. Schwarz's book is by far the best study of Jünger's political ideas, although most of it is devoted to the period since 1933.

[3] *In Stahlgewittern: Aus dem Tagebuch eines Stosstruppführers*, 13th ed. (Berlin, 1931). Hereafter cited as *Stahlgewittern*.

[4] See Schwarz, *Konservativer Anarchist*, p. 278.

[5] For an elaborate justification of this claim see "Die totale Mobilmachung" in Ernst Jünger, ed., *Krieg und Krieger* (Berlin, 1930), pp. 29–30. Hereafter this essay will be cited as *TM*.

signed implicitly to appeal to several, largely middle-class groups in Germany. One group included part of the audience to which Jünger's early books was addressed: men still strongly under the influence of their military experiences during the World War and in the Free Corps—especially younger veterans, on whom, as we have seen, the war often had the greatest impact because they had not established a place for themselves in the prewar world. Many of them had become fascinated by war, neither knowing nor caring for any way of life other than war among nations, civil war, and preparation for future wars.

Jünger's early writings had reached also a broad segment of the reading public too young or too old to have participated in the war and the military actions following in its aftermath. The response from this segment of his potential audience had been reserved during the immediate postwar years. Until the late 1920's literary works on World War I were dominated by antiwar novels and other writings expressing disillusionment about the war.[6] Powerful artists like Leonhard Frank, Ludwig Renn, Arnold Zweig, Fritz von Unruh, Georg Kaiser, and Ernst Toller composed vivid tales that often linked the horrors of war to capitalism and the abuse of technology. Erich Maria Remarque's *All Quiet on the Western Front*, although restrained in its indictment and not published until the end of the decade, is probably the most famous example of this literature. Jünger's early writings belonged to the less popular body of prowar literature, but they were written in such a way that they would still have much appeal to an antiwar audience. They avoided the ostentatious sentimentality and the tawdry romanticization of German heroism that suffused most of the prowar literature.

Jünger's *Arbeiter* could appeal not only to the large audience for war literature, now grown much more responsive to prowar writings,[7] but also to several other, partly overlapping groups. He directed himself to all those who sought to preserve, refine, and extend to every aspect of German society the military spirit expressed in the war. He offered formulas for German success to everyone who either looked forward to or regarded as inevitable another great imperialist war. More broadly, he appealed to those, whether on the Right or the Left, who spoke of destroying the Weimar Republic and bourgeois society without returning to the past. He appealed to every German who, while rejecting communism as an international movement, was impressed by the successes of the Soviet Union's First Five-Year Plan of 1928 and who believed that comprehensive national planning was imperative.

[6] See Wilhelm K. Pfeiler, *War and the German Mind: The Testimony of Men of Fiction Who Fought at the Front* (New York, 1941), p. 193.
[7] For this change see *ibid.*

He called upon everyone with strong antibourgeois sentiments to expect a non-Marxist transcendence of bourgeois society and the ascent to unparalleled heights of a reinvigorated German nation. His appeal was directed at the same time to those concerned with the problem of integrating the working class into German society and manipulating it for nationalist or imperialist purposes within a rigidly hierarchical order. Finally, the *Arbeiter* contained a more subtly expressed appeal to people attracted to the notion of freedom of action for a heroic minority of adventurers, who, unlike most veterans of the World War and Free Corps, would be able to indulge a passionate longing for novelty and excitement without transgressing military and civilian codes of behavior. These adventurers would have both the security of a dominant place in society and the freedom to disregard the bourgeois conventions that they found stifling.

From his personal experiences Jünger was well acquainted with the dwindling opportunities in Germany for the former front soldier who wished to remain or become a professional military man. Probably because of his outstanding war record, he was admitted to the small postwar German army; he was one of the few officers who had served at the front throughout the war able to remain on active duty. The Treaty of Versailles, which limited the nation's army to 100,000 men, placed severe restrictions on the size of the officer corps, but German military leaders pursued policies that contributed greatly to the paucity of positions in the Reichswehr for former front officers. Most of the openings were filled by men who had been professional officers before the war. During the latter half of the war, the few professional officers remaining on frontline duty were reassigned to the General Staff or other staff positions; after the war the army command favored the admission to the Reichswehr of staff officers and higher ranking field commanders. The number of openings for officers was further depleted by the admission of several hundred former noncommissioned officers, the so-called Noske officers.[8] Despite the influx of these former noncommissioned officers, the officer corps came largely from the

---

[8] Only 12 to 18 per cent of the officers eligible for the Reichswehr had the opportunity to remain on active service or to enter the paramilitary state police forces. See Bavarian Statistisches Landesamt, *Sozialer Auf- und Abstieg im deutschen Volk* [by Josef Nothaas], Beiträge zur Statistik Bayerns, cxvii (Munich, 1930), p. 68; Harold J. Gordon, *The Reichswehr and the German Republic, 1919–1926* (Princeton, 1957), pp. 66–68; Karl Demeter, *Das deutsche Offizierkorps in Gesellschaft und Staat 1650–1945* (Frankfurt am Main, 1962), pp. 48–49. Demeter (p. 49) and Hans Mundt, "Das Offizierkorps des deutschen Heeres von 1918–1935" in *Führungsschicht und Eliteproblem*, Jahrbuch der Ranke-Gesellschaft, iii (1957), 117 give seemingly contradictory accounts of the number of former noncommissioned officers admitted to the officer corps of the Reichswehr. Mundt refers to 200; Demeter, to "almost 1,000."

same social strata that had supplied officers for the prewar Prussian army.[9] The trend toward a decline in the proportion of nobles that had begun in the nineteenth century continued,[10] but the decline did not become precipitous.

Although Jünger himself would eventually have been able to qualify as a reserve officer in the prewar army and might even have gained entry to the professional officer corps, he did not come from either the nobility or a nonnoble military family. His father was a well-to-do scientist who owned a small chemical factory. Ernst Jünger came from strata within the middle class for whom the war temporarily opened up much better prospects in the officer corps than had existed in peacetime, but whose newly found positions were adversely affected by demobilization. Young lieutenants and even captains discovered that the prestige and social status that they had acquired during the war were denied them as a consequence of the smallness of the Reichswehr and the policies governing its recruitment. Although the Free Corps provided many opportunities for an adventuresome young officer, these opportunities soon dwindled and seldom led to a professional career in the Reichswehr.

Even for the more fortunate young former front officers like Jünger, the Reichswehr often proved a great disappointment. They soon found life in the new army dull and disillusioning, and there were few promotions to console them. Despite Jünger's war record and the favorable attention received by his first book,[11] he left the army in 1923 still a lieutenant.

DER ARBEITER—DREAM OR NIGHTMARE?

His early writings revealed an intense preoccupation with precision in the selection of words. He wrote detailed, mostly dispassionate descriptions of events, scenes, and emotions. Only occasionally did his

[9] See Demeter, *Das deutsche Offizierkorps*, pp. 51–56; Gordon, *The Reichswehr and the German Republic*, pp. 197–202; Hans Ernest Fried, *The Guilt of the German Army* (New York, 1942), pp. 140–42; J. W. Wheeler-Bennett, *The Nemesis of Power: The German Army in Politics, 1918–1945* (New York, 1954), p. 99; F. L. Carsten, *The Reichswehr and Politics, 1918–1933* (Oxford, 1966), pp. 214–17.

[10] See Nikolaus von Preradovich, "Die soziale Herkunft der Reichswehr Generalität 1930," *Vierteljahrschrift für Sozial- und Wirtschaftsgeschichte*, LIV (1967), 482–86; Correlli Barnett, "The Education of Military Elites," *Journal of Contemporary History*, VI (1967), 27.

[11] His *Stahlgewittern* was recommended by the *Heeresverordnungsblatt* in 1921. Wolfgang Sauer, "Die Mobilmachung der Gewalt" in Karl Dietrich Bracher, Wolfgang Sauer, and Gerhard Schulz, *Die nationalsozialistische Machtergreifung: Studien zur Errichtung des totalitären Herrschaftssystems in Deutschland 1933/34*, 2nd ed. (Cologne, 1962), p. 812, n. 305.

war books include highly personal passages intended to convey the mood of a nationalistic young front soldiery contemptuous of civilian life and appreciative of the military prowess of the opponent on the battlefield. Already his work was marked by the literary and aesthetic concerns that would eventually win him recognition as one of the great German stylists of the twentieth century. His political articles, which began to appear in 1925, were usually brief, pointed, and specific. Although the style of the *Arbeiter* was similar to that of his previous writings, the content was opaque. In an essay entitled *Die totale Mobilmachung* (*Total Mobilization*), first published in 1930, Jünger gave a substantial foretaste of the *Arbeiter*, but even this essay still had much of the clarity of his earlier writings. It did not contain the sustained abstractions of the *Arbeiter*. The detachment with which he viewed his material, the matter-of-fact way in which he described a seemingly bleak world, and above all the enigmatic form in which he presented his subject reached their apex in the *Arbeiter*: "The task of total mobilization is the transformation of life into energy as manifested by the hum of wheels in business, technology, and transportation, or [as manifested by] fire and motion on the battlefield."[12]

In reading the *Arbeiter* one often feels that he is in the midst of a dream—or nightmare. Every image, every scene seems precise, but on reflection becomes obscure. What appears at first tangible dissolves as one approaches it. The reader thinks he has grasped Jünger's ideas until he begins to question their meaning. Much more seems to lurk behind every passage, behind every word than is printed. The book moves gracefully from one point to the next, but no point ever seems to be completed. A sarcastic remark that one of his collaborators on a political periodical during the late 1920's makes about Jünger's articles applies even more forcefully to the *Arbeiter*: "Doubtless it was Ernst Jünger who gave it quality and created esteem for it, through articles that were so ingenious and so crystal-clear in expression that our readers laid them down with great respect, with admiration and a feeling that everything was fine if Ernst Jünger himself was certain that he understood them."[13]

It is probably significant that there is neither an English translation of the *Arbeiter* nor an extended treatment in English of its political content. It is one of those works that seem to be inordinately difficult to deal with except when writing in the same language in which it is written. Yet, as Sibree's translation of Hegel and Carlyle's correspondence with Goethe indicate, the rewards of dealing with a "difficult"

[12] *DA*, p. 201.
[13] Ernst von Salomon, *Der Fragebogen* (Reinbek bei Hamburg: Rowohlt paperback, 1961), p. 243.

work in another language often outweigh the disadvantages. What might easily be passed over as a delightful play on words or an unusual use of a familiar term poses a problem in interpretation. A clever ambiguity becomes a revealing equivocation. What at first seems precise, because the words are familiar, becomes indistinct when another tongue has to be used to explain it. "Every translation is an interpretation," someone once said. He should have added: "And every interpretation is written in another language."[14]

One reason for the elusiveness of the *Arbeiter* is beyond dispute. Jünger wished to present his vision of the future in a way that would make it difficult for the reader to focus upon the familiar aspects of this vision and thereby fail to perceive its full dimensions. Although employing much of the conventional terminology of social and political thought, he made a concerted effort to divorce this terminology from its customary associations in both bourgeois and Marxist literature. In a radio talk at the time of the publication of the *Arbeiter*, he gave an excellent account of this effort: ". . . I have tried to avoid using those general catchwords as they are used today by all parties. For example: culture, soul, idea, idealism, personality, psychology, Goethe, Hegel, Shakespeare, and any other proper nouns. . . . I have attempted to describe our reality as if it had to be explained to a man from the moon who had never seen an automobile or read a page of modern literature. . . ."[15]

Although elucidating Jünger's conception of his technique, this statement does not adequately account for the elusiveness of the *Arbeiter*, and most other explanations that have been offered are unconvincing. For example, to imply that Jünger is a neo-Platonist who regards the world he depicts as an imperfect reflection of pure ideas[16] contributes little to an understanding of the work. The interpretation of other Platonist works in the utopian tradition does not pose a similar problem; the intentions of Campanella and Thomas More may often be baffling, but their descriptions of men, events, and institutions are not murky. Even less helpful is the suggestion that the world presented in the *Arbeiter* is a Sorelian "myth."[17] Georges Sorel's conception of the general strike and its revolutionary consequences is clear. For Sorel

---

[14] In translating passages from the *Arbeiter*, I have tried to resist the temptation to do justice to it as literature. Considering the importance of providing the reader with a taste of the precision of Jünger's style and the imprecision of its content, I have rendered the *Arbeiter* into rather prosaic English.

[15] Quoted in Karl O. Paetel, ed., *Ernst Jünger in Selbstzeugnissen und Bilddokumenten* (Hamburg, 1962), p. 51.

[16] Schwarz, *Konservativer Anarchist*, p. 90, seems to agree with this interpretation, which was suggested by Martin Heidegger.

[17] In the course of inconclusive speculations about the possible influence of Georges Sorel on Jünger, Schwarz advances this view. *Ibid.*, pp. 91–93.

the general strike is a "myth," not because the idea of the general strike is unclear, but because its consequence is perfectly clear—the defeat of the bourgeoisie. The threat of the general strike, the mere existence of the idea, may lead the bourgeoisie to capitulate and may thereby usher in the revolution.

The basic explanation for Jünger's elusiveness and obscurity must be sought elsewhere. Due especially to the absence of proper names, many of his allusions are incomprehensible to anyone not familiar with the political literature of the Right during the Weimar Republic. In 1932 his audience could be expected to recognize these allusions, but by not attaching labels to most of them, he avoided triggering many political reflexes that would respond immediately to a name with approbation or condemnation. At a sacrifice of instantaneous recognition, he might succeed in gaining a hearing for his ideas among many political sects. The *Arbeiter* is, probably intentionally, a cryptic and ambiguous work. This ambiguity was not primarily, as Hans-Peter Schwarz argues,[18] a consequence of Jünger's retreat from active participation in politics. Rather, it was a consequence of an attempt to produce a work that would strike responsive chords in an audience larger than that to which Jünger had previously had access. He may well have welcomed the confusion that soon prevailed among his readers.

The meaning of his book became the topic of much speculation and debate among both his admirers and critics. Many reviewers on the Left felt that his ideas expressed the quintessence of fascism. Although usually received more sympathetically on the Right, the *Arbeiter* was often cited as evidence that Jünger stood perilously close to the brink of communism. For example, Edgar Jung warned that Jünger's ideas belonged to one of the more sophisticated and insidious forms of the bolshevism that was spreading throughout Germany.[19] Even within the same political camp contradictory interpretations of Jünger's intentions appeared. Thus in the small "National Bolshevik" groups on the Right, circles with which Jünger had been closely identified and among which he might expect to find a favorable audience, the responses were mixed. Ernst Niekisch tried to invoke the *Arbeiter* in support of his own demand for an entente between Potsdam and Moscow, while Karl Paetel warned that Jünger's work could be misused by

[18] *Ibid.*, pp. 106–07.

[19] Edgar Jung, "Verlustbilanz der Rechten," *Deutsche Rundschau*, CCXXXIV (Jan. 1933), 5. For a good sampling of the responses to the *Arbeiter* see Schwarz, *Konservativer Anarchist*, pp. 78–79, 114, 260, 290, n. 53; Otto Ernst Schüddekopf, *Linke Leute von rechts: Die nationalrevolutionären Minderheiten und der Kommunismus in der Weimarer Republik* (Stuttgart, 1960), pp. 259–60.

proponents of both fascism and state capitalism.[20] The elusiveness of the *Arbeiter* led to needless misunderstandings, but nevertheless helped to win a hearing for Jünger's ideas in circles that might otherwise have been inaccessible to him. In the *Arbeiter* he presented a work that could appeal, if often with reservations, to many diverse, feuding groups on the Right seeking to find a common platform and willing to reach out toward the Left.

In 1932 Jünger claimed, as he did even more insistently after World War II, that the *Arbeiter* was a diagnostic, not a programmatic work. Indeed, he once implied that he was a mere seismograph or barometer of his times.[21] Despite these claims, which once served to sustain his image of himself as a dispassionate prognosticator and later served to dissociate him from the Nazi regime, the problem of separating program from prediction is not as difficult in the *Arbeiter* as it is in the case of Max Weber's work. The severity of the problem is similar to that which we encountered with Spengler. Jünger believed that most of what he depicted was both inevitable and desirable. The basic lines of future developments had already emerged and could hardly be altered.[22] With some hesitations he was committed to the realization of the world of the *Arbeiter*.

Although Jünger's perspectives underwent many important changes during the decade preceding the publication of the *Arbeiter*, his previous writings help greatly in explicating it. They supply many of the details absent from the *Arbeiter*; they reveal, often more openly, Jünger's basic intentions. In dealing with the *Arbeiter*, we shall of necessity refer frequently to these writings.[23]

WARRIOR VERSUS BOURGEOIS

The *Arbeiter* portrays the incipient triumph of a new hierarchical society. Jünger dismissed as a mere *Scheinsieg* the victory of the *Welt-*

[20] See Schüddekopf, *Linke Leute von rechts*, p. 259; Schwarz, *Konservativer Anarchist*, p. 290, n. 53.

[21] *Strahlungen*, 3rd ed. (Tübingen, 1949), p. 9.

[22] See esp. Jünger's radio talk on the *Arbeiter* in 1932 quoted in Paetel, *Ernst Jünger in Selbstzeugnissen*, pp. 51–52.

[23] As Schwarz points out, Jünger's interpreters have neglected to relate the *Arbeiter* to his often inaccessible articles in small periodicals. Schwarz, *Konservativer Anarchist*, pp. 19–20. An appendix to Gerhard Loose, *Ernst Jünger: Gestalt und Werk* (Frankfurt am Main, 1957) provides a summary of these articles, but Schwarz is the only scholar who has gone through all of them and attempted to relate them to Jünger's better known works. Unfortunately, Schwarz does not adequately explore the connections between the political articles and the *Arbeiter*. Since I have been unable to obtain some of these articles, my own endeavor to explain the *Arbeiter* is deeply indebted to both Schwarz and Loose.

bürgertum in all countries due to the war.[24] This victory was illusory because the war had promoted the development of a new order that would supersede that of the bourgeoisie. The outlines of the future were apparent in the throbbing energy that propelled whirring wheels in the economy and turned battlefields into moving infernos. The new order was reminiscent of a landscape crowded with Tibetan prayer wheels; it was based on rigid principles recalling those of the pyramids; it demanded sacrifices far greater than any inquisition or Moloch. Yet the model for this new order was a military organization.[25] Jünger compared the state of the future to a warship; on a warship, unlike a passenger liner or luxury vessel, everything had to be examined and reexamined in order to make certain that it was necessary.[26] Similarly, in *Totale Mobilmachung* Jünger described a society fully mobilized for total war, a society in which there was no longer any tangible distinction between soldier and civilian, between front line and home front, between war and peace. He noted, as he had frequently even in his earliest writings, the congruity of industrial work and modern warfare. War was becoming a "gigantic work process."[27]

Like many neoconservatives, Jünger did not dismiss liberalism, democracy, and the institutions associated with them simply as unnecessary or decadent. Rather, he suggested that political parties, the notion of equality, leveling tendencies, parliaments, and the like were necessary prerequisites to the new hierarchical order. They were all part of the transition from the absolute state of an earlier era to the world of the *Arbeiter*. The "anarchy" and destruction that Jünger saw everywhere in the postwar world were essential preludes to the sweeping away of everything antiquated and superfluous.[28]

Although Jünger's view of history has often been termed cyclical,[29] this description is misleading. He was one of the few Germans on the Right who overcame the identification of his views with the classical cyclical view of history in which with each turn of the wheel civilization rises or falls a degree. Edgar Jung looked back to the past and announced the rise of the new Middle Ages. Spengler found himself pursued doggedly by the not wholly unfounded belief that he saw ahead an era of decline. Zehrer's commitment to the middle class entrapped him in reactionary, if vague, projects that conflicted with his basically unilinear view of history. Only Keyserling's vision of the future begins

---

[24] *DA*, p. 156. Note the ambiguity of the term *Weltbürgertum*. Does it refer to cosmopolitanism or to the world bourgeoisie?

[25] *DA*, pp. 13, 45, 201.   [26] *DA*, p. 199.

[27] *TM*, p. 14.   [28] *DA*, pp. 68, 90, 148, 161–62.

[29] See esp. Armin Mohler, *Die konservative Revolution in Deutschland 1918–1932: Grundriss ihrer Weltanschauungen* (Stuttgart, 1950), pp. 106, 130.

to approach Jünger's in its liberation from the classic cycle, but even his is punctuated frequently by the bittersweet musings of an old aristocrat. There is rarely any trace of a longing for the past in the *Arbeiter*, a longing still evident in Jünger's earlier works. Jünger stood to most neoconservatives as Marx stood to the utopian socialists: both men demonstrated that a radically new future would emerge from the present and that this future could not be concocted from the best of past ages. To be sure, this analogy breaks down, for Jünger, as we shall see, had no brief for historical materialism.

Jünger warned conservatives and reactionaries against futile wishes to recapture the past. There was "no road back."[30] He implied that Young Conservatives like Jung who spoke of a revival of Christianity and of a corporative society dreamed of the impossible. Any temporary success that they had would only accelerate the changes that led farther and farther from these objectives by helping to create two identifiable sides opposing each other.[31] With his own preference undisguised Jünger discerned a growing division between two camps: ". . . The front of restoration, and another that is determined to continue the war with all means, not merely those [the means] of war. But we must recognize where true allies are to be found. They are not where people want to preserve, but rather where they want to attack; and we are approaching circumstances in which every conflict that breaks out anywhere in the world will strengthen *our* position."[32]

Whereas Jünger's earlier writings, with the notable exception of the *Totale Mobilmachung*, had dealt largely with Germany, the *Arbeiter* dealt with general trends throughout the world. The *Arbeiter* depicted a world arising in conjunction with industrialization and modern technology. In his early writings, Jünger conceived of a new era that was primarily a product of World War I;[33] by 1932 he regarded the war itself as a mere consequence of the same underlying forces that were forging the world of the *Arbeiter*. With an insistence and finality lacking in his early works, he announced the end of bourgeois society. Already a relic from the past, the bourgeois would soon vanish: "The still relatively intact bourgeois masses [*bürgerlichen Massen*] will disappear. To be sure, it looks as if, for a short while and above all in Ger-

[30] *DA*, p. 14.

[31] See *DA*, pp. 236–37. Although the wording of the passage makes clear the types of neoconservatives Jünger is criticizing, it is characteristic of the *Arbeiter* that he does not address them directly. As should be recalled, he avoided proper nouns in the *Arbeiter*.

[32] *DA*, pp. 157–58. Jünger's italics.

[33] See, e.g., *Der Kampf als inneres Erlebnis*, 1st ed. (Berlin, 1922), p. 82. Hereafter cited as *Kampf*. Even on the page cited, however, Jünger refers to the war as a "Werkzeug zu letzten Zielen."

many, these masses have been handed by the event [the sweeping away of the privileges of the aristocracy] a long overdue and conclusive victory."[34]

Jünger's use of the term "worker" to designate the new type of man who was succeeding the citizen (*Bürger*)[35] of bourgeois society encountered misunderstanding on the Right. This misunderstanding, largely a product of the tenseness of the social and political situation in Germany, was a tribute to the skill with which Jünger succeeded in freeing the word from its historical associations, especially in the vocabulary of socialism. His achievement, although similar to that of Spengler, Moeller van den Bruck, and others in giving the term socialism a new set of meanings, surpassed theirs in audacity. In Jünger's usage, the term "worker" designated a type of human being whose emergence accompanied that of the new order. The worker was neither a member of an estate (*Stand*) "in the old sense" nor a member of a class "in the sense of the revolutionary dialectic of the nineteenth century." He lacked class consciousness "in the old sense."[36] The citizen or bourgeois (*Bürger*) was "ready to negotiate at any price"; the worker was "ready to fight at any price."[37] Although less direct than Spengler's proclamation of a society without classes, Jünger's *Arbeiter* had no more resemblance to the Marxist vision of a classless society. In the world of the *Arbeiter*, everyone would be a "worker," as in bourgeois society everyone was a citizen. Jünger himself made clear why he was able to describe everyone as a worker: as every soldier, whatever his rank, is a soldier, every member of the new order, whatever his position in the hierarchy, would be a worker.[38] In one of the rare passages in which he used the word democracy in an unqualifiedly favorable way, he referred to the "dissolution of liberal or social democracy by work or state democracy."[39] All historical class divisions and social distinctions would disappear or become irrelevant. In his *Totale Mobilmachung*, Jünger wrote:

Thus, with the obliteration of estates [*Stände*] and the curtailment of the privileges of the nobility, the concept of a warrior caste disappears too; military service is no longer the duty and privilege simply of the professional soldier, but rather the task of everyone capa-

[34] *DA*, p. 153.

[35] In the *Arbeiter* Jünger plays upon the many associations of the noun *Bürger* and the adjective *bürgerlich*. Often he employs *Bürger* with both of the meanings most common in modern German prose: to denote a civilian or citizen, as well as a bourgeois or member of the middle class. But especially in his use of *bürgerlich* he suggests an outmoded longing for security, solidity, and homely virtues.

[36] *DA*, pp. 74, 88.　　　　[37] *DA*, p. 38.
[38] *DA*, p. 145.　　　　[39] *DA*, p. 255.

ble of bearing arms. . . . Similarly, the image of war as armed combat merges more and more with the vastly expanded image of a gigantic work process. Alongside the armies that meet each other on the battlefields, there arise the new armies of transportation, food production, and the armaments industry—the universal *army* of work.[40]

In view of Jünger's desire for a new hierarchy and his conception of the worker, Spengler's criticism of the *Arbeiter* misses the mark. After remarking that he had only had time to leaf through the copy that Jünger had sent, Spengler proceeded to chastise him:

Like many others you have not succeeded in freeing the concept of the worker from the phraseology of the Marxists. An official, a peasant, an entrepreneur, an officer is a worker just as much as the manual laborer is. Today the only person who works until he can no more is the peasant, and it is he who is disregarded by the division [of society] into bourgeoisie and proletariat. But precisely in Germany the peasantry is also still a force. Anyone who contrasts an allegedly dying peasantry to "the worker," i.e., the industrial worker as a new type, abandons reality, and thereby forfeits any influence on the future, which will move in entirely different directions.[41]

Despite Spengler's overhasty conclusion fostered by Jünger's ambiguity, Marxian socialism had no place in the world of the *Arbeiter*. In a remark obviously directed against the Marxist concept of the proletariat as the social force that would destroy bourgeois society and undertake the creation of socialism, Jünger wrote that the highest claim or aspiration of the worker was to be the "bearer of a new state, not a new society."[42] Lumping together socialism and liberalism as characteristic of the same style of thought, Jünger ironically criticized them on one of the same grounds that Marx and Engels had found fault with many nineteenth-century critics of capitalism. Jünger argued that private property was not to be accepted or rejected on ethical or moral grounds: "It is characteristic of the liberal style of thought that attacks on property as well as its justification are made on an ethical basis. In the world of the worker the issue is not whether the existence of property is moral or immoral, but merely whether it can

---

[40] *TM*, p. 14. Jünger's italics.

[41] Oswald Spengler, *Briefe 1913–1936*, ed. Anton M. Koktanek (Munich, [1963?]), pp. 667–68. The date of Spengler's letter to Jünger is not known, but as the editor notes, it must have been written not long after Sept. 5, 1932. Earlier, Jünger had sent Spengler a copy of at least one of his war books, which Spengler praised as an exemplary work. See Spengler's letter of Apr. 11, 1924 to Jünger, *ibid.*, p. 313.

[42] *DA*, p. 25.

be accommodated by the work plan."[43] In other words, Jünger found no necessity for the abolition of private property.

In his earlier writings he had distanced himself even more insistently from socialism. Both capitalism and socialism, he grumbled, belonged to "the great church of progress, which in some places get along well together and in other places are locked in bitter combat. But neither of them breaks through the limits of their common beliefs —the stream of completely unconnected masses of individuals and the stream of equally unconnected masses of money presuppose the same abstract posture."[44] Only a short time before the publication of this passage Jünger had been more blunt in a reference to the Communists: ". . . What the hell do we have to do with the dirty wash of the rabble? There is no community of the discontented, and every dissatisfaction is worth only as much as the object on which it is based. It is difficult to undertake adventures with those who have in mind only class barriers. A man of rank should prefer wicked to bad company. . . ."[45] While admiring from afar the Russian Bolsheviks as a "revolutionary aristocracy forged by exile to Siberia,"[46] Jünger had little patience with German Communists.

He sought not the destruction of class society, but the destruction of a political order that did not provide a suitable basis for the activities of a "heroic" minority. What he occasionally referred to as a "new aristocracy"[47] would, as we shall see later, dominate the world of the *Arbeiter*. The *sine qua non* for the full realization of this world was not the defeat of the bourgeoisie, but the demise of a certain type of bourgeois.

Jünger's works did not express the intense hostility, cultivated by some of his political acquaintances, toward the big bourgeoisie. Ernst Niekisch, who, like the Jünger of the *Arbeiter*, is often described as a "National Bolshevik" or "National Revolutionary," could argue plausibly after World War II that he had been a social revolutionary during the Weimar Republic. Niekisch insisted in his memoirs that he had sought to attract bourgeois youth to an antibourgeois position by extolling the virtues of the old military aristocracy and appealing to nationalist idealism.[48] His claim that he was a revolutionary Marxist is

[43] *DA*, p. 274.   [44] *TM*, p. 27.
[45] *Das abenteuerliche Herz: Aufzeichnungen bei Tag und Nacht*, 1st ed. (Berlin, 1929), p. 238. Hereafter cited as *AH*. See also p. 233, where Jünger explains that he prefers anarchists to communists because the former are crazy (*verrucht*) rather than despicable (*schändlich*).
[46] *TM*, p. 25.   [47] See, e.g., *DA*, p. 66.
[48] See Ernst Niekisch, *Gewagtes Leben: Begegnungen und Begebnisse* (Cologne and Berlin, 1958), p. 154 and passim. See also Ernst Niekisch, "Die Legende von der Weimarer Republik," *Konkret: Unabhängige Zeitschrift für Kultur und Politik,*

unconvincing, but there can be little doubt that his long-range objectives included the destruction of the German bourgeoisie, even though he temporarily subordinated this goal to the "external liberation" of Germany from the chains of the Treaty of Versailles through German cooperation with the Soviet Union and the colonial peoples against the West, the bastion of the world bourgeoisie. Despite the close association that developed between Niekisch and Jünger during the late 1920's and persisted into the early 1930's, Jünger seems never to have shared Niekisch's attitude toward the big bourgeoisie. Jünger, unlike some other "National Revolutionaries" including a few of his own close associates, never joined the Communist party or one of the several independent Communist groups that sprang up during the last years of the Weimar Republic.

The *Bürger* whom Jünger attacked was the preindustrial bourgeois and his contemporary counterpart, the member of the old middle class.[49] Like many other members of the Youth Movement and the Front Generation, Jünger never moved decisively beyond rejection of the middle-class milieu in which he was raised. His adolescence became a series of rebellions against the solid, comfortable environment of his family. Although an intelligent youth, he encountered endless difficulties with his teachers in the *Gymnasium*.[50] When he was seventeen, he ran away from home to join the French Foreign Legion. He had reached North Africa and was beginning to serve a five-year enlistment before his father succeeded in having him brought back to Hannover. The father exacted a promise from Ernst that he would finish secondary school before he left home again. The original model for Jünger's depiction of the detestable *Bürger* seems to have been provided by his father,[51] who, in the manner of an enlightened and

Jan. 1962, pp. 6–7. Niekisch's claims that he was a social revolutionary are accepted by Karl O. Paetel, *Versuchung oder Chance? Zur Geschichte des deutschen Nationalbolschewismus* (Göttingen, 1965), p. 80 and with reservations by Herman Lebovics, *Social Conservatism and the Middle Classes in Germany, 1914–1933* (Princeton, 1969), pp. 139ff. For a discussion of Niekisch that approaches his claims more sceptically, see Schüddekopf, *Linke Leute von rechts*, pp. 354–70.

[49] For this point I am indebted to Helmut Kaiser's often speculative and rather uneven polemic against Jünger. Helmut Kaiser, *Mythos, Rausch und Reaktion: Der Weg Gottfried Benns und Ernst Jüngers* (Berlin, 1962), p. 340.

[50] See the first volume of his brother's autobiography: Friedrich Georg Jünger, *Grüne Zweige: Ein Erinnerungsbuch* (Munich, 1951), pp. 119–20. The second volume, which deals with the period from roughly 1926 to 1945, is entitled *Spiegel der Jahre: Erinnerungen* (Munich, 1958). F. G. Jünger's reputation as a writer has been overshadowed by that of his older brother. Both during the Weimar Republic and subsequently the two were close intellectual and political associates. F. G. Jünger's memoirs contain some revealing material on the years before World War I, but are disappointing for the period thereafter.

[51] F. G. Jünger, *Grüne Zweige*, esp. pp. 17, 25, 245–49. F. G. Jünger reports (p. 261) that the father adopted a somewhat nonconformist posture toward the

sympathetic, but protective parent, was aiding his son's preparations for another, more easily controlled project when World War I began. After taking his *Abitur*, Ernst was to be permitted to participate in an expedition to Mt. Kilimanjaro in German East Africa.[52]

Always ambiguous, Jünger's estrangement from his own educated middle-class background was intensified by his experiences as a volunteer in the war. These experiences also broadened the focus of his animosity, making the *Bürger* as a social type Jünger's antagonist. The strength of aristocratic military traditions in Germany aggravated the tension ever present in bourgeois society between soldier and civilian. Jünger's early autobiographical works described a front soldiery whose experiences could never be comprehended by the civilian. Jünger developed the point, common to most of the literature of World War I, that war became a way of life for the front soldier: "The few at the front who realized this knew that those at home would never understand it."[53] Having discarded bourgeois conventions, the front soldier joyfully threw himself into the arms of death, either because of a sheer love for Germany unencrusted by ideology, or merely because he loved to fight.[54]

Jünger enjoyed war. He delighted both in its discipline and in the uncertainty of battle. As he perhaps realized, he had exchanged the dull certainties and uninspiring unpredictabilities of his comfortable life at home for the exciting unpredictabilities and awesome certainties of the front: "I have never had so carefree a life as at the front. Everything is clear and simple. My rights and duties are prescribed. I need earn no money. My food is provided me, and if things go badly with me, I have a thousand fellow-sufferers, and above all, the shadow of death reduces every problem to a pleasant insignificance."[55] Although in this passage Jünger was obviously generalizing—money and food had been no problem for him before the war—he was also expressing the satisfaction of the upper middle-class volunteer who found gratifying the belief that he was no longer dependent upon the bourgeois world identified with his family.

---

values of the upper middle class in his later years. Perhaps the son's message finally sank in.

[52] Wulf Dieter Müller, *Ernst Jünger: Ein Leben im Umbruch der Zeit* (Berlin, 1934), p. 21.

[53] *Kampf*, p. 42.

[54] *Ibid.*, pp. 32–33; Preface to the first edition of *Stahlgewittern* (Hannover, 1920), p. xi. This is the only reference in this chapter to the first edition. Over the years Jünger has made many changes in the various editions of his works.

[55] *Das Wäldchen 125: Eine Chronik aus den Grabenkämpfen 1918*, 1st ed. (Berlin, 1925), p. 6. Hereafter cited as *Wäldchen*. My translations of passages from this work rely heavily on the English edition, *Copse 125: A Chronicle from the Trench Warfare of 1918*, trans. Basil Creighton (London, 1930).

Trench warfare and what the Germans dubbed "the battle of matériel" destroyed the romantic conception of war as a heroic adventure
that Jünger and many others marched off with in 1914. The dreams of
enraptured youth, Jünger wrote, fell victim to the power of the machine.[56] In the days of the machine and the mass army, only the aviator
could still fight a duel and act with chivalry.[57] But Jünger found compensations for the new face of war. Often he pointed to examples of
man's mastery of the machine, and he derived exquisite satisfaction
from describing the mechanization of warfare: "Somewhere stood a
man with a face of granite above a red collar at a telephone and rat-
tled off the name of ruins that had once been a village. Then orders
clattered and steel armor and dark fever showered from a thousand
eyes."[58] Jünger savored the possibilities for hand-to-hand combat:
"There the select manhood of nations pursued each other in fighting
packs through the twilight, fearless assailants trained to plunge into
death at the sound of a whistle and a short exclamation. When two
squads of such warriors met in the narrow corridors of the flaming
wasteland, the embodiment of the most ruthless wills of two peoples
ran head on into each other. That was the highpoint of the war. . . ."[59]
Both the resilience and the malleability of men under the new conditions of battle gave Jünger cause for optimism. The war forged one of
the "hardest and most able races that has ever lived."[60] He delighted in
calling the front soldiers "day laborers of death."[61]

By the mid-1920's he was elaborating at length another notion that
gave meaning to the war: battle had rejuvenated the front soldiers. It
had led them to rediscover primordial forces; it had exposed the decadence of the modern world. The front soldiers of all nations were
not simply "day laborers of death," but also "day laborers for a better
day" who had smashed "the brittle shell of an entire world."[62]

Jünger developed a theme that served to set him apart from most of
his comrades and impart still more significance to his rebellion against
the *Bürger*. He contrasted two types of men at the front. Most front
soldiers were materialists and petty bourgeois who did not understand
the war.[63] They were not full-fledged members of the "new and iron
race tempered in every fiber" by the war.[64] Like a member of the postwar Free Corps, the true front soldier, Jünger suggested, was both a
volunteer and a mercenary.[65] One of Jünger's favorite expressions for

[56] *Feuer und Blut: Ein kleiner Ausschnitt aus einer grossen Schlacht*, 1st ed.
(Magdeburg, 1925), p. 22.
[57] *Wäldchen*, p. 62.
[58] *Kampf*, p. 20.
[59] *Ibid.*, pp. 28–29.
[60] *Wäldchen*, p. xi.
[61] See, e.g., *Kampf*, pp. 24–25.
[62] *Ibid.*, pp. 48, 54–55, 116.
[63] *Ibid.*, p. 85.
[64] *Wäldchen*, p. 254.
[65] See, e.g., *Kampf*, p. 56.

him was *Landsknecht*. Jünger found the genuine front soldier only in the small special units of storm or shock troops developed by all of the belligerents during the course of the war.

The German shock troops were widely organized beginning in the latter part of 1916. Wearing distinctive uniforms and given equipment previously issued only to officers, they were encouraged to regard themselves as members of elite units. Much friction developed between them and other soldiers. The shock troops were billeted in quarters of their own and brought by truck to the front for special actions. The discipline of the shock troops departed from traditional military norms. The relationship between officers and men was more intimate. In speaking to officers, the men often used the familiar *du* rather than formal modes of address. The officers had to meet unusual requirements. They had to be unmarried, under twenty-five, in excellent physical condition, and "ruthless."[66]

In 1918 Jünger was entrusted with the formation of a shock troop. He set about his task elatedly. In his first book, he explained that during the course of the war it had become clear that every success depended upon the actions of individuals, while "the mass of participants provide only impact and firepower. Better to be leader of a small resolute group than [leader of] a hesitant company."[67] In a subsequent work, Jünger made even more pointed claims: "The cowards do not stay in our ranks. We know our way to the enemy; they [the cowards] know how to find the safe ground of the hinterland. . . . To stand first in battle—that we still regard as an honor of which only the best are worthy."[68] The member of a shock troop was "the new man . . . the elite [*Auslese*] of Central Europe."[69]

During the early years of the Weimar Republic, Jünger looked to the spirit of the front soldier to deliver the Fatherland from its bondage to foreign powers. Although he remained in the Reichswehr, he apparently conceived of the Free Corps as a valuable repository of this spirit. Perhaps as was common in right-wing and military circles he considered the Reichswehr as the core around which the Free Corps and other contingents would gather to form the future army of liberation. In an autobiographical work that appeared after World War II, he described his initial conception of the Free Corps. He compared them to the volunteers who helped to liberate Prussia from Napoleon's yoke.[70] But a series of perturbing experiences during the middle years

[66] On the development of the shock troops see Robert G. L. Waite, *Vanguard of Nazism: The Free Corps Movement in Postwar Germany, 1918–1923* (New York: Norton paperback, 1969), pp. 24–27.

[67] *Stahlgewittern*, p. 268.　　　　[68] *Kampf*, p. 111.

[69] *Ibid.*, p. 74.

[70] *Jahre der Okkupation* (Stuttgart, 1958), pp. 245–46.

of the Republic made Jünger less sanguine about the potential of paramilitary organizations.

While studying at the University of Leipzig after his departure from the Reichswehr, he communicated with Captain Gerhard Rossbach, the leader of a group of right-wing activists that had grown out of one of the most famous Free Corps units. Jünger was entrusted with the task of serving as the group's representative for Saxony. After a month he resigned. He found little enthusiasm among Rossbach's followers and compared them with nihilistic conspirators described by Dostoevski: "Depressing is their absorption in the techniques of action, the lack of higher types as compared with the Decembrists or the romantic revolutionaries."[71]

In 1925 Jünger and some other young veterans who shared his general outlook on the war assumed the editorship of a literary supplement to the journal of the *Stahlhelm*. He and his friends sought to gain a hearing for their ideas among the members of this, the largest organization of German veterans.[72] Like most right-wing action leagues, the *Stahlhelm* was moving during the mid-1920's toward tacit acceptance of the Republic.[73] Although the basic objectives of these leagues presumably remained unaltered, they began to work openly within the framework of the Republic; the "system" would be destroyed by its own methods, by methods that it recognized as legitimate. The reaction within the action leagues against the new emphasis on legality would soon lead to splits and to the formation of new, more militant groups, but for the moment militants like Jünger and his friends could still hope to play a decisive role within the established organizations.

In the process of developing a comprehensive world view, at the center of which stood the experiences of World War I, the members of Jünger's circle sought to erect a common platform for a vanguard of "New Nationalists" drawn from the ranks of World War and Free Corps veterans, from the action leagues, from other right-wing groups, and from the Youth Movement. A *Stahlhelm* publication seemed to offer an excellent vehicle with which to gain access to a responsive audience. Jünger and his friends may well have come to expect that they and men sharing their outlook might be able to gain control of the *Stahlhelm* organization itself. The leaders of the *Stahlhelm* seem, for their part, to have hoped to make their organization more attractive to youthful militants. A sarcastic commentary by one of the young writers on a *Stahlhelm* encampment triggered the first in a series of

[71] *Ibid.*, p. 246.

[72] For Jünger's political contacts and journalism from 1925 to 1933 see esp. Schwarz, *Konservativer Anarchist*, pp. 97–107; Paetel, *Versuchung oder Chance?* pp. 54–71.

[73] See Schüddekopf, *Linke Leute von rechts*, pp. 204–05; Volker R. Berghahn, *Der Stahlhelm: Bund der Frontsoldaten 1918–1935* (Düsseldorf, 1966), pp. 64–91.

bitter conflicts between them and the leaders, aggravating the discord over the *Stahlhelm*'s policies. Among the underlying sources of conflict were the organization's tacit acceptance of the Republic and the *Stahlhelm*'s unofficial, but increasingly prominent ties to the Nationalist party. Another issue, already emerging during the struggle with the *Stahlhelm* leadership, was the belief of many right-wing activists that the action leagues had to break decisively with the widespread image of them as reactionary groups hostile to the working class.[74] There was much animated discussion, to which Jünger contributed, of how to gain a base in the working class.

After eliminating the literary supplement, the leadership of the *Stahlhelm* provided Jünger and his friends with an "independent" periodical, which unlike the literary supplement would not be distributed to the subscribers of the *Stahlhelm*'s journal. But this attempt to keep the young militants away from the rank-and-file was soon succeeded by the closing down of the new literary organ. For a while Jünger and some of his friends attempted to gain influence in the *Stahlhelm* through other publications, and with financial assistance from Captain Hermann Ehrhardt, a former Free Corps commander and the leader of an action league, they acquired another periodical of their own.[75] Although the leaders of the *Stahlhelm* appropriated, if in a watered-down form, the ideas of the "new nationalism" to supply the ideology that the organization had lacked,[76] the breach had become irreparable.

By the end of 1927 Jünger concluded that organizations of front soldiers were unsuited to his purposes: "During this year it has become certain that the leagues [*Bünde*] [of front soldiers], above all the *Stahlhelm*, have in no way become organs of a new warriordom, but rather have developed into protective associations of what are for the most part decaying interests and have become similar in structure to the parties, as whose guard troops they [the *Bünde*] already occupy the foyer of parliamentarism, from the right to the left wing."[77]

For a short while longer, Jünger seems to have felt, although some-

[74] See Schüddekopf, *Linke Leute von rechts*, p. 211. See also the description of the National Socialists' attempts in 1926–1927 to work out a position on trade unions in David Schoenbaum, *Hitler's Social Revolution: Class and Status in Nazi Germany, 1933–1939* (Garden City, N.Y., 1966), pp. 27–28. Cf. Max H. Kele, *Nazis and Workers: National Socialist Appeals to German Labor, 1919–1933* (Chapel Hill, 1972), pp. 122–23.

[75] Ironically, Ehrhardt, who was active in the *Stahlhelm*, had coined one of the slogans ("Hinein in den Staat!") used to justify the accommodation to the status quo of the *Stahlhelm* and other action leagues. See Berghahn, *Der Stahlhelm*, p. 103; Schüddekopf, *Linke Leute von rechts*, p. 206.

[76] See Berghahn, *Der Stahlhelm*, p. 99.

[77] "Zum Jahreswechsel," *Der Vormarsch: Blätter der nationalistischen Jugend*, I (Jan. 1928), 180–81. Hereafter this periodical will be cited as *Vormarsch*.

what resignedly, that the youth *Bünde* still offered a promising area to cultivate. With some of his friends he edited and wrote articles for periodicals, which although addressed to the entire Youth Movement, were most closely linked to the *Freischar Schill*. Like many other youth *Bünde*, the *Freischar Schill* was strongly under the influence of former Free Corps members.[78] The group moved toward what was often known as a "National Revolutionary" position; a belief in the need for Russo-German cooperation in international politics and an often hazy demand for revolutionary changes in Germany led some of these "National Bolsheviks" close to the German Communist party. Jünger never expressed a strong commitment to Soviet-German co-operation, and as we have seen, he was contemptuous of German Communists. But these differences in perspective were not prominent at the time and probably contributed little to his gradual withdrawal from active politics.

As the decade of the 1920's drew to a close, he found little hope in gaining a mass basis through any existing organization. He ruefully admitted that "the forces that have thus far represented nationalism did not know how to dissociate themselves clearly from legitimism, from the parties, from the resentment of a class whose claims are threatened, from the eternal bourgeois in general."[79] He seems to have concluded that the best hope for the future lay in tiny bands that would engage ruthlessly in "revolutionary" activities against the existing political order. He compared himself to a man cutting his way through a jungle with a machete, hoping eventually to find someone else also at work.[80] Symptomatically he entitled an article proclaiming the ultimate triumph of the New Nationalists "The Unseen Nucleus."[81]

During the years between the shattering of his hopes for influence within a mass movement and the publication of the *Arbeiter* in 1932, Jünger went through a phase characterized as "Prussian anarchism" by writers sympathetic to him.[82] He established contacts with the small group of bomb-throwing activists in the *Landvolk* movement in Schleswig-Holstein.[83] In a letter written in the latter part of 1929, he referred

[78] See Felix Raabe, *Die bündische Jugend: Ein Beitrag zur Geschichte der Weimarer Republik* (Stuttgart, 1961), pp. 75–76; Schüddekopf, *Linke Leute von rechts*, pp. 208–09.

[79] Preface to Ernst Jünger, ed., *Der Kampf um das Reich*, 2nd ed. (Berlin, [1930?]), p. 7. The first edition appeared in 1929.

[80] *AH*, p. 153.

[81] "Der unsichtbare Kern," *Vormarsch*, II (Apr. 1929), 329–31.

[82] This characterization has often served as a way of playing down the extent of Jünger's political involvement. See, e.g., Armin Mohler, ed., *Die Schleife: Dokumente zum Weg von Ernst Jünger* (Zurich, 1955), p. 84.

[83] On the *Landvolk* movement see Rudolf Heberle, *Landbevölkerung und Nationalsozialismus: Eine soziologische Untersuchung der politischen Willens-*

to the *Landvolk* as "the first practical movement that I have really sympathized with."[84] Intellectually, Jünger stood during this period closest to small, difficult to classify political groups such as Niekisch's *Widerstand* circle. Increasingly Jünger seems to have played the role of observer, rather than participant-observer.[85] Apparently he played no important active role in any group. Even in the small circles that he frequented, his posture was similar to his behavior in large groups: "Jünger was fond of taking part in big demonstrations as an observer. He enjoyed watching as the general excitement assumed turbulent forms."[86] Jünger glorified the activities of heroic individual "anarchists" in his writings of the period. In *Das abenteuerliche Herz* (*The Adventurous Heart*) of 1929, he looked down, as if from Olympus, on the scurrying mortals below. He expressed satisfaction in seeing "the towns begin to fill with armed men, and how even the dullest system, the most boring attitude can no longer do without armed representatives."[87]

Yet the concept of a phase of "Prussian anarchism" in Jünger's development is misleading. Only if we focus on his major work at the turn of the decade *Das abenteuerliche Herz* and ignore his other writings of the same period, does there appear to have been a distinct phase of "Prussian anarchism," for by 1930 he had developed all of the major themes that would be brought together in the *Arbeiter*. He had moved from the glorification of segments of front soldiery to the glorification of tiny groups dedicated to the destruction of "bourgeois" institutions; from contempt for the civilian and the *Bürger* to a general contempt for the institutions associated with them; from reliance pri-

bildung in Schleswig-Holstein 1918–1932 (Stuttgart, 1963); Gerhard Stoltenberg, *Politische Strömungen im schleswig-holsteinischen Landvolk 1918–1933: Ein Beitrag zur politischen Meinungsbildung in der Weimarer Republik* (Düsseldorf, 1962). There is also a compelling fictionalized account of the movement in Ernst von Salomon, *Die Stadt* (Berlin, 1932). On the relationship of Jünger and his friends to the *Landvolk*, see Stoltenberg, esp. pp. 136, 146, 161, 174; but Stoltenberg, who draws on some details provided by Schüddekopf's *Linke Leute von rechts*, may have overemphasized the extent of Jünger's role. See Reinhard Kühnl, *Die nationalsozialistische Linke 1925–1930* (Meisenheim am Glan, 1966), pp. 239–40.

[84] Letter of Sept. 10, 1929 to Bruno von Salomon. Quoted in Mohler, *Die Schleife*, pp. 85–86. The second clause of the quotation (". . . an der ich wirklich Anteil nahm") is ambiguous and might have been translated as "that I have really participated in."

[85] See, e.g., Ernst von Salomon's belief that Jünger regarded Salomon's deep involvement in the *Landvolk* movement with a bemused, patronizing attitude: ". . . Meine Betätigung bei der Landvolkbewegung jedenfalls schien er als das zwangsläufige Ergebnis einer Mischung aus Geltungstrieb und Beschäftigungsneurose zu betrachten. . . ." Ernst von Salomon, *Der Fragebogen*, p. 244.

[86] Niekisch, *Gewagtes Leben*, p. 189.

[87] *AH*, pp. 183–84.

marily on an elite of front soldiers to reliance on an elite still in the process of formation; from the glorification of mechanized war to the glorification of a society based on permanent mobilization for total war. As the mass of mostly mediocre front soldiers had once given rise to the shock troops, now a remorselessly mechanized society was giving rise to a new heroic elite, one of whose major goals was the resumption of the war that had come to a temporary halt in 1918.

Only one major shift in theme indicated a marked change in Jünger's approach, and this theme—his dependence upon basic, worldwide trends rather than upon the willful, concerted efforts of individuals to produce the new elite—was overshadowed until the publication of the *Arbeiter*. This shift appeared in his *Totale Mobilmachung* (1930), but in other works he gave priority to the self-creation of the elite. For example, in an essay similar in many respects to the *Totale Mobilmachung* and published during the same year, he did not view the emergence of the elite as the inevitable consequence of forces beyond its control:

> Above all, it [total mobilization for war] awaits the pressing forward into the decisive positions of a stratum that recognizes its responsibility to German destiny. Then the technical questions, which today, as always, are questions of the second order, will resolve themselves even more rapidly than they could be solved after 1806 [after the defeat of Prussia by Napoleon at the Battle of Jena]. For the power of the secret Germany is great, and after the Great War the anxiety of the world recognized this [power] much sooner than the German himself.[88]

As Jünger became less optimistic about the potential of small groups of activists, he fell back upon a belief in the inevitability of their eventual success due to the development of technology and the impact of other inexorable forces.

TOWARD THE ERA OF THE WORKER

In the *Arbeiter* there reappeared the three basic justifications for a new elite that Jünger had developed in his earlier writings: an inherent human need, determined by the laws of nature, for authoritarian leadership; general historical developments such as modern war, industrialization, and the growth of technology, all of which required a certain type of elite; the peculiar German situation that necessitated a distinctively German variant of this elite. Two of these justifications,

---

[88] "Das grosse Bild des Krieges" in Ernst Jünger, ed., *Das Antlitz des Weltkrieges: Fronterlebnisse deutscher Soldaten* (Berlin, 1930), p. 251.

the inherent nature of man and the German situation, received more attention in his earlier works than in the *Arbeiter*. He regarded war as a natural phenomenon, stemming from the natural order of which man was still a part: "War is as little a human contrivance as the sexual drive; it is a law of nature. Therefore we shall never extricate ourselves from its jurisdiction."[89] A part of man's animalistic nature, war put him to the supreme test in which Jünger discerned "an inner necessity that puts men in their proper places at the decisive moment."[90] As an integral and permanent part of the world, war and preparations for war acted to prevent the attainment of the equality sought by democrats. War shattered the belief in what Jünger contemptuously termed "our new idols"—"the masses and equality."[91]

In the *Arbeiter* Jünger placed arguments about the nature of man and the impact of World War I in a more elaborate historical framework. He found signs that a new era was beginning as the age of the Third Estate drew to a close. During the French Revolution, "the old masses," like the throng that stormed the Bastille, had come to the fore. The "old masses" now belonged to the past. Drawing upon his own experiences in the shock troops and in postwar politics, Jünger offered a conception of the new superiority of small groups of determined men[92] that was similar to if not dependent upon the views of the Italian theorist of the *coup d'état* Curzio Malaparte.[93] Believing that the execution of a successful *coup d'état* had become a science, Malaparte cautioned against the Bonapartist tactic of wrapping oneself in a cloak of legality and appealing to the masses. He argued that recent events such as the Bolshevik seizure of power in 1917 and Mussolini's March on Rome in 1922 demonstrated the superiority of small, highly skilled groups of political technicians who could capture the state, not through a frontal assault on the government, but rather by seizing strategic points such as power plants and communications centers. Sharing Malaparte's view of the vulnerability of the state to attack by a small contingent of activists, Jünger tended to consider the weakness of the masses and the resolution of the activists as equal in importance to technique: "Mass movements have lost their irresistible magic wherever a truly determined mien confronts them. . . . Today the

[89] *Kampf*, p. 36. See also pp. 7, 40, 114; *Wäldchen*, pp. 50–51.

[90] Preface to *Der Kampf um das Reich*, p. 5. See Helmut Kaiser's suggestion that Jünger isolates war from its social context. Kaiser, *Mythos, Rausch und Reaktion*, pp. 25–26.

[91] *Kampf*, p. 54.   [92] *DA*, pp. 110–12.

[93] See Curzio Malaparte [pseud. for Curzio Suckert], *Coup d'état: The Technique of Revolution*, trans. Sylvia Saunders (New York, 1932). The original Italian edition appeared in 1931. A German translation followed shortly: *Der Staatsstreich* (Vienna and Leipzig, 1932).

masses are no longer capable of attack; they are no longer able even to defend themselves."[94] Alluding obliquely to the irrelevance of the concepts of liberalism, socialism, and democracy to the newly emerging era, Jünger coined an aphorism to express the critical role of tiny groups: "The more the individual and the masses weary, the greater becomes the responsibility entrusted to the few."[95] Political parties, conventions, parliamentary debates, voluntary associations, and the individuality prized by the nineteenth-century liberal had all become outmoded.

Jünger referred to newly emerging "organic constructions," which, like Jung's concept of Gemeinschaft, were not based on individual free choice. But Jünger described these constructions using mechanistic analogies that imparted a contemporary rather than an archaic note to his use of the term organic. The elite forged on the battlefields of World War I both foreshadowed and fostered the new type of relationship: "One does not belong to an organic construction by virtue of individual decision, by an act of bourgeois freedom, but rather through a real involvement determined by the particular characteristics of the work. It is, to give a banal example, as simple to join or leave a [political] party as it is difficult to get out of the kinds of organizations to which one belongs as a recipient of electrical current."[96]

As the age of the Bürger came to an end, Germany had, according to Jünger, a great advantage over the Western democracies. The German had not been a good Bürger. Germany was not as affected by the age of the Third Estate as the Western Powers were.[97] Like most other neoconservatives, Jünger believed that Germany had unique characteristics that had prevented its development parallel to that of the Western democracies.[98]

With an insistence equaled only by Keyserling, he also argued that these unique characteristics had recently put Germany at a great disadvantage. The failure to participate fully in the age of the Third Estate had weakened Germany's international position, made adequate mobilization of the entire population for war impossible, and contributed to defeat in the World War. Perhaps because of his preoccupation with preparation for total war, Jünger was even more troubled than most other neoconservatives by the failure of Germany to mobilize fully the "Fourth Estate." The "progressive" characteristics of the Western Powers had facilitated their mobilization: "Thus mobilization in the United States, a country with a very democratic

94 DA, p. 110.   95 DA, p. 194.
96 DA, p. 114.   97 DA, pp. 11–12.
98 See DA, pp. 36–38. See also TM, pp. 13, 16–20, 25–26, 30; "Das grosse Bild des Krieges" in Der Antlitz des Weltkrieges, p. 239.

constitution, could be instituted with a severity that was impossible in the military-state Prussia, the land of the [three-]class electoral law."[99] The remnants of monarchical absolutism had made Germany very vulnerable in a war with the Western Powers: ". . . Late in the era of belief in the rights of man, monarchical structures are particularly vulnerable to the destruction of war."[100] German leaders had been "much too satisfied, much too convinced of the values of a world that unhesitatingly recognized in Germany its most dangerous adversary."[101] Insofar as the *Bürger* had ruled Germany, he had been incapable of drawing on the elementary forces of the nation. He could neither win the war through total mobilization nor lose it in a way that identified the highest form of freedom with ruin (*Untergang*).[102]

TOWARD AN ORDER OF WORKING WARRIORS AND WARRING WORKERS

The primary objective of all of Jünger's writings during the Weimar Republic was the reassertion of the German nation in a war or series of wars. He expressed this objective in a fairly conventional way in his earlier writings: "The incorporation of all Germans in the great future Reich of a hundred million—that is a goal worth dying for and smashing all resistance to."[103] In the *Arbeiter*, he alluded to similar objectives more calmly if less concretely. He referred to the colonial status imposed on Germany by the Treaty of Versailles and the shaking off of this bondage in the future.[104] Looking forward to an era of great empire building, he expected that Germany might win out in this competition.

Essential to the achievement of this vague, but insistent imperialistic objective was the full utilization of the abilities of Germans from every segment of society. The world of the worker would be highly stratified. Ranks would be "more sharply graduated" than they had been for centuries.[105] Jünger compared the structure of this world to a pyramid divided into three fundamental levels. The first—and to a lesser extent—the second level had already begun to take shape in a clear form. The first level comprised those engaged in routine activity, as well as the routine aspects of everyone's life. On the second level

[99] *TM*, p. 18. [100] *TM*, pp. 17–18. [101] *DA*, p. 36.
[102] *DA*, pp. 37–38. Cf. *Kampf*, p. 60: "Es ist von sehr tiefer Bedeutung, dass gerade das Kräftigste Leben sich am willigsten opfert. Besser ist es, unterzugehen wie ein zersprühender Meteor, als zitternd verlöschen."
[103] *Wäldchen*, p. 186. See also, e.g., *Stahlgewittern*, p. 283; *Kampf*, pp. 37, 89; Jünger's preface to Friedrich Georg Jünger, *Aufmarsch des Nationalismus* (Berlin, [1928?]), p. xii. The first edition appeared in 1926.
[104] *DA*, p. 39. [105] *DA*, p. 148.

stood "the active type" of the "worker." Not exercising decisive leader-ship functions, the active type was a specialist who was not in a posi-tion to see clearly beyond the limits of his specialization: ". . . Whether an economic functionary, a technician, a soldier, a nationalist, he needs integration, command that draws directly on the source giving mean-ing to the whole."[106] The third and highest level of the pyramid had not as yet emerged clearly. On this level, statecraft would be prac-ticed. Although in his earlier writings Jünger had committed himself to the necessity for a single great leader,[107] his position in the *Arbeiter* was ambiguous. At times he implied that a single man would stand at the apex of the pyramid;[108] at other times Jünger wrote as if he as-sumed that the third level would consist of a number of elite individ-uals.[109] Perhaps he was leaving open the possibility of a supreme lead-er, whose absence, as Jünger had suggested in his earlier writings, should not provide an excuse for inaction. In the *Arbeiter* he was more concerned with the development of "a unified stratum of leaders" than with a great man.[110]

The decisive criterion for the occupant of every position within each level of the pyramid was "mere suitability," or "capacity."[111] As we shall see, Jünger used these terms in a context that hinted at, but did not require radical changes in the existing social structure.

Jünger's concern for the elimination of privilege based on social status as a factor in elite recruitment appeared strongly in his early writings on the war. His complaints about the selection and promotion of officers were much more far-reaching than Edgar Jung's. Unlike Jung he did not confine his criticism mainly to the advantages ac-corded the nobleman in competition with a candidate from the edu-cated middle class. Jünger considered unjust the privileges of the one-year volunteer, as well as the entire system of the reserve officer, and he commented bitterly on the lack of mobility in German society: "Not enough room is made for the able—that is always our cancerous sore."[112] He complained of the barriers that made it impossible for a worker to become an officer. Asking himself whether he was not ex-pressing democratic ideas, Jünger replied: "I hate democracy as I do the plague—besides, the democratic ideal of an army would be one consisting entirely, not of cadets, but of officers, with lax discipline and great personal liberty. On the contrary, for me and the young German

[106] *Ibid.*

[107] See, e.g., "Die Grundlagen des Nationalismus" in *Stahlhelm Jahrbuch 1927*, ed. Franz Schauwecker (Magdeburg, 1927), pp. 82–83. Hereafter this essay will be cited as "Grundlagen." See also the brief discussion in Schwarz, *Konservativer Anarchist*, pp. 116–17.

[108] See *DA*, pp. 100, 147, 222, and, less clearly, 234.

[109] See *DA*, pp. 64–65, 257.

[110] *DA*, p. 63.   [111] *DA*, pp. 108, 145.   [112] *Wäldchen*, p. 72.

of today in general, affairs could not be conducted too severely, too dictatorially, and too absolutely—but this sort of conduct requires a system of selection that is not sheltered behind any kind of privilege, but rather opened up to keener competition."[113] Improving morale and establishing better relations between officers and men were crucial to Jünger's criticisms. He argued that even if a worker became an inferior officer, a possibility that he regarded as unlikely, "the ideal rewards" would compensate a thousand times over for "the material damage."[114]

Jünger's commitment to the principle of an open elite was only partly compromised by his notions of race and destiny (*Schicksal*). In the *Arbeiter* he did not allude as frequently as in his earlier writings to destiny as a determinant of the elite. He referred to the members of the elite as "decreed by destiny to rule."[115] He did not include a detailed discussion of the notion of destiny as he had done in an article published five years earlier. In this article, he identified destiny with an overriding historical necessity:

> We find nothing blind and accidental in destiny, but rather a creative force, the objectives of which we do not perceive. We do not even know whether it has any goals, or is simply a pure, divine will, as powerful and as consummate from one instant to the next. Yet we can recognize the pull of destiny, which is indicated by a feeling for the necessary, a compulsion that often leads us to act against our own interests, against tranquility, happiness, peace, even against life itself.[116]

As we have seen so often among other elite theorists, Jünger denied that his concept of race had a biological basis, but insisted that a member of the elite must have "more race" than other men.[117] In the *Arbeiter* he remarked that race would be the principle determining everyone's position in the new hierarchical order. Offering an analogy from physics, he compared race to a copper electrical conductor. Copper conducted better than any other metal, but copper was independent of electricity. What counted was copper's achievement (*Leistung*), its ability to conduct electricity, not the fact that it was copper.[118] With this neatly worked out play on words, he avoided a rational explanation of race. The concept had become even hazier than in his earlier works.[119]

[113] *Ibid.*, pp. 73–74. [114] *Wäldchen*, p. 73.

[115] *DA*, p. 65. [116] "Grundlagen," p. 77.

[117] For the concept of race in his earlier works see, e.g., *Kampf*, p. 50; *Wäldchen*, pp. 29, 229; "Grundlagen," pp. 68–71; *AH*, p. 128.

[118] *DA*, p. 145. See also p. 281.

[119] For vestiges in the *Arbeiter* of the notion of war as a force molding race see *DA*, p. 233.

There appeared prominently in Jünger's use of the concept of race a note that was struck much less frequently in the works of other elitists we have examined. An important function of the concept—and nowhere in Jünger's writings is this function more apparent than in the *Arbeiter*—was to support the claim to superiority by an elite whose members might lack socially prestigious origins. For example, claims to preference by men of noble birth or patrician background could be undercut by invoking a new standard—that of race. Since for Jünger race was more spiritual than biological and was manifested in ability and achievement, it could serve as a "democratic" weapon compelling the formation of an open elite. Writing of the war, he referred to the "proliferation of important new functions, the execution of which makes requisite a new sort of selection. Thus aviation, and especially aerial dogfighting, is an occupation that should be filled on the basis of racial, not social qualifications. The number of individuals in a nation who are at all capable of such accomplishments of the highest order is so limited that mere suitability must by itself suffice as a legitimation."[120] Among other elitists employing the concept of race, its "democratic" potential was usually counteracted by conservative or reactionary uses. Thus Rathenau, Spengler, Jung, and Keyserling tended to employ the concept to strengthen the claims of individuals from the old nobility and the bourgeoisie to join the new elite. In Jünger's work, at least through the *Arbeiter*, the reactionary potential of the concept is seldom exploited. The best known parallels in Germany to the function of Jünger's concept of race are to be found in much of National Socialist racism, as we shall see in Chapter Thirteen.

Although in the *Arbeiter* Jünger no longer made frequent references, as he had in his earlier writings, to inherent (*angeborene*) characteristics and other inscrutable factors that made rational education and training of no help in developing elite traits,[121] he continued to surround these traits with mystery. Indeed, the abstractions and ambiguities of the *Arbeiter* often made their origin appear even more difficult to ascertain. For example, Jünger referred to "a unique, neither inherited nor acquired consciousness of rank," that was the hallmark of the new aristocracy.[122]

He envisioned the use of training, not to create specialists, but to develop elite qualities. Jünger's conception of this training presup-

---

[120] *DA*, p. 108. Jünger may be restricting the application of this racial principle to selection for new occupations. Note esp. the wording at the beginning of the quotation: ". . . [es] mehren sich wichtige Funktionen, *deren* Besetzung eine neuartige Auslese erforderlich macht." My italics.

[121] See, e.g., "Grundlagen," pp. 77, 82, 86.

[122] *DA*, p. 80. Jünger uses the term "angenommenes," which I have translated as "acquired." It might also be translated as "assumed" or "fictitious."

posed the destruction of the educational institutions of the era of the *Bürger*.[123] Education, "in the usual sense of the term," was detrimental to the elite of the future. Jünger complained that universal education had robbed Germany of a "sound reserve of illiterates."[124] Comparing his ideas to those presented in the classics of the utopian tradition, he suggested that the state of the future could engage in the rearing of children, particularly illegitimate children. Although presumably some of the children would become members of the elite after they grew up, obviously many, perhaps most, would not. They would become technicians of the sort that Jünger associated with the second level of the pyramid in the new world:

> One of the loftiest tasks for its [the state's] educational designs is the devoted and meticulously thought-out raising of a particular race in special settlements located in coastal and mountainous regions or in broad belts of forest. There is the possibility of creating, from the ground up, a corps of officials, officers, captains, and other functionaries that would have all of the characteristics of an order [*Orden*], which can not be planned to be more homogeneous and more carefully fashioned. This, rather than the transplanting of big-city dwellers is also the surest way of developing a reliable reserve of settlers and their mates for use at home or abroad.[125]

Like some other neoconservatives, Jünger was intrigued by the notion of an order. He considered it a model for two reasons. First, he looked upon some postwar organizations, despite his often bitter criticisms of them, as harbingers of the future. Assuming some of the attributes of an order, these organizations fostered new relationships between men, relationships that were appropriate to the world of the *Arbeiter* and which had begun to develop in the armies of the World War. He contrasted such organizations favorably to political parties:

> A movement of war veterans, a social revolutionary party, an army transforms itself in this way [by becoming an organic construction and focusing upon the state] into a new aristocracy, which provides itself with the decisive intellectual [*geistigen*] and technical means. The difference between a power of this sort and a party of the old style is obvious. In the former there is training and selection [*Züchtung und Auslese*], while the endeavors of a party are directed toward attracting the masses [*Massenbildung*].
>
> Expressive of the differences in an organic construction is the fact, visible everywhere, that at a certain moment "the list is closed" and

[123] See *DA*, pp. 40, 203. [124] *DA*, p. 203. See also *AH*, p. 146.
[125] *DA*, p. 281.

that purges occur repeatedly—measures which a party, true to its nature, is incapable of. This leads to a reliability and homogeneity among the remaining members of which only the type [of the worker] is capable in the historical situation we find ourselves in. . . .[126]

The second reason why Jünger found an order attractive was his conception of the "monkish or soldierly" poverty in which the elite would live. In the emerging world of the *Arbeiter*, outward signs of differences between men were disappearing.[127] Jünger observed that World War I had provided a foretaste of this change; it had become increasingly difficult to distinguish officers from other soldiers.[128] His suggestion that the elite live a spartan life may have reflected a search for a method of forestalling the development of hostility by the non-elite. He hinted that the outward appearance of poverty could mask social differences: "Phenomena like the German knightly orders, the Prussian army, and the Society of Jesus are models, and it should be noted that soldiers, priests, scholars, and artists have a natural relationship to poverty. This relationship is not only possible, but even appropriate in the midst of a landscape dominated by workshops in which the figure [*Gestalt*] of the worker mobilizes the world."[129]

Drawing on the influential concept publicized by Stefan George's follower Friedrich Wolters, Jünger referred to domination and service (*Herrschaft und Dienst*) as identical. Jünger implied that since the elite served the state, as did everyone else, the state could not be explained in terms of contractual theories of government. Freedom would be a loan or fief granted by the state: "Everyone and everything stands within the system of tenure, and the leader can be recognized because he is the first servant, the first soldier, the first worker."[130]

Disciplined leaders would set the tone for everyone. Jünger defined work in such a way that the elite, while itself engaged directly in the work process, would control it. There was nothing that could not be conceived of as work: "Work is the tempo of the fist, of thought, of the heart; life at day and at night; science, love, art, faith, devotion, war; work is the oscillation of an atom and the force that moves stars and solar systems."[131]

Jünger derived his conception of discipline and the work-oriented attitude that accompanied it more from military than industrial discipline. A crucial characteristic would be the voluntary, but complete subordination of the inferior to the superior: "It is the secret of the true language of command that it makes demands, not promises. The

[126] *DA*, p. 259. See also p. 109.
[127] See *DA*, pp. 116–24.
[128] *DA*, p. 108.
[129] *DA*, pp. 201–02.
[130] *DA*, p. 130.
[131] *DA*, p. 65.

happiness of man comes when he is sacrificed, and the highest art of command consists in pointing to goals that are worthy of the sacrifice."[132] Universal military service had provided an important preparatory step in the development of a discipline adequate to this consummation of the art of command. The mobilization of the populace would be achieved through the regulation of all work.[133] Jünger described a style of leadership that depended upon a populace completely responsive to the demands of the elite:

> The masses and the constitutions that they have granted themselves are too ungainly to permit the execution of changes with the speed and certainty required by a dangerous situation. The masses are no longer the power that, for better or worse, makes the climate, but rather are themselves exposed mainly to storms. Therefore the language of agitation with its artificial storms is senseless; it must give way to a language of command similar to the one heard on the bridge of a ship.[134]

Why would men obey? What would keep them toiling? Jünger dealt impatiently with these issues. He made clear that material rewards were not the answer. Although the material existence of the nonelite would be made secure presumably through state economic planning,[135] he dismissed cavalierly the subject of the standard of living: "The issue is not to improve this way of life [the worker's, i.e., the way of life in the world of the *Arbeiter*], but rather to impart to it the highest, decisive meaning."[136] Satisfaction would come, not with the expression of individuality, but with the individual's identification with his task and the performance of it according to his station in life. Jünger described "the anonymous soldier" of World War I as a suitable symbolic hero of the enormous military-industrial process that he looked forward to: "His virtue is that he is replaceable and that behind everyone who falls, there stands a replacement. His standard is that of matter-of-fact achievement, taciturn achievement."[137]

In Jünger's early works, when he was still absorbed in the problem of counteracting the demoralizing impact of the West's political warfare against Germany, he suggested several methods of reinvigorating the German will to fight. He frequently discussed ways of manipulating "the masses," and especially the working class. "A sort of demagogy from above" must be employed, as well as nationalism, "Prussian drill," and hatred for the enemy.[138] But his impatience with ideology usually

---

[132] *DA*, p. 71.   [133] *DA*, pp. 288–89.   [134] *DA*, p. 278.

[135] *DA*, p. 233. See also "Untergang oder neue Ordnung?" *Deutsches Volkstum*, xv (May 1933), 418.

[136] *DA*, p. 201.   [137] *DA*, p. 147.

[138] See, e.g., *Stahlgewittern*, p. 268; *Wäldchen*, pp. 31, 62, 165.

prevented him from filling in these outlines. Often he indicated that a mere love of fighting would suffice. Even in his *Totale Mobilmachung* he contented himself with the suggestion that the simple faith of the volunteers in the war, their belief that "we are fighting 'for Germany,'" required only some embellishment in order to provide a satisfactory ideology.[139]

Preoccupation with war still stood at the center of the *Arbeiter*. Jünger's reluctance to work out the details of a new German ideology reflected his persistent suspicion toward ideas, as well as his failure to develop an overall view of society except by extrapolation from war. He dismissed ideology as unimportant as long as the populace could be effectively mobilized and manipulated: "The more cynically, spartanically, Prussian, or Bolshevistically life can be pursued the better it will be."[140] Less flippantly Jünger advocated forthright manipulation: "It is therefore absolutely necessary to free oneself from Machiavellian prejudices when one considers the conclusion that the type [of the *Arbeiter*] perceives of public opinion as a technical matter. The procedure derived from this perception is available, . . . not to every power. It is available only to the type [of the *Arbeiter*], to whom every instrument must appear simply as an instrument for his work, that is, as the tool of a certain feeling toward life."[141]

Jünger's conception of ideas to promote the work of the nonelite was much less rich in material from the past than was Spengler's work ideology. In the *Arbeiter* Jünger pointed to the Prussian conception of duty as the only significant element from the past capable of being adapted to the requirements of the new era.[142] Although sharing Jünger's concern for the mobilization and manipulation of the nonelite, Spengler clung to many of the historical justifications for work. Jünger's attitude revealed not only a more ingenuous manipulative intent but also a contempt for most work. Much more thoroughly than Spengler Jünger freed himself from traditional practices and institutions. Jünger's more flexible approach was better suited to the maintenance of monopoly capital than Spengler's more specific and historically encrusted proposals. Neither the way in which the new elite came to power nor the details of the methods used to manipulate the nonelite concerned Jünger. His prescriptions were open-ended:

[139] *TM*, pp. 21–22.

[140] *DA*, p. 201. In keeping with this same disregard for ideology is a remark that Jünger's acquaintance Karl Paetel reports having heard him make during the late 1920's or early 1930's: "They [isms] are omnibusses that one boards and can then leave at any stop he wishes." Karl O. Paetel, *Ernst Jünger: Die Wandlung eines deutschen Dichters und Patrioten*, vol. 2 of *Dokumente des anderen Deutschland*, ed. Friedrich Krause (New York, 1946), p. 40.

[141] *DA*, p. 260.   [142] *DA*, p. 66.

In point of fact there is no difference whether the type [of the *Arbeiter*] suddenly manifests itself in the appearance of a party leader, a minister, a general; or whether a party, a veterans' organization, a national or social revolutionary association, an army, a bureaucracy begins to constitute itself in accordance with the very different laws of an organic construction. It also makes no difference whether the "seizure of power" is accomplished on the barricades or in the form of a prosaic taking over of the existing apparatus. Finally, it is of no consequence whether the acclamation of the masses during this process is voiced under the impression of a victory for collectivist world views, or whether the acclamation of the individual finds in it [the seizure of power] the triumph of a person, of the "strong man."[143]

Jünger's elite was completely independent of any control by the nonelite. He recognized the usefulness of plebiscites as manipulative devices,[144] but he did not regard them as essential to the new authoritarian order. He denied that the new order would be a dictatorship even if no plebiscitarian means were employed. A dictatorship would be only a transitional stage. The new man "knows no dictatorship because for him freedom and obedience are identical."[145] Jünger assumed that "bourgeois" institutions of social discussion such as parliaments would become organs of the state; technical argumentation would replace social discussion. The constitution would be replaced by the work plan.[146] Although Jünger's concept of an *Orden* and of "organic constructions" contained elements of corporatism, he gave no hint of corporative institutions that would offer any check upon the elite. Thus he moved not only far beyond Jung, but even Zehrer and Spengler. There was no possibility for the nonelite to influence the elite. Jünger suggested that the more suited the elite to its task the greater would be its power.[147]

The role of the irrational in Jünger's vision of the future remained unclear. Rational techniques would be employed to mobilize the nonelite, but the purposes of this mobilization other than to control the nonelite, to pursue an ill-defined imperialistic foreign policy, and to provide an exciting life for the elite were vague. Jünger took delight in the thought of a society caught up in endless, frenetic activity. As one of his critics has pointed out, Jünger, like Nietzsche, frequently used the example of ants and other insects to indicate both the blind subordination and bustling activity of most men. Both Jünger and Nietzsche welcomed the simplification, standardization, and diminu-

---

[143] *DA*, p. 257.   [144] *DA*, p. 260.   [145] *DA*, p. 145.
[146] *DA*, pp. 260–61, 280.   [147] *DA*, p. 67.

tion in potential of the mass of men as a necessary foundation for a new, stronger kind of men, who would be only a tiny minority.[148] Jünger exalted the new possibilities for "a serene anarchy within the most rigid order." The motor was for him a symbol of the new era: "It [the motor] is the daring plaything of a race that has the ability to blow itself up with delight and to see in this act another confirmation of the order [to which this race is subject]."[149] As indicated by this passage, which Jünger seems to have regarded as applicable to everyone in the coming world of the *Arbeiter*, the life of the elite would be dangerous as well as adventurous. Despite all the talk among German elitists, especially on the Right, of the need for an elite capable of heroic sacrifice, perhaps no other elitist matched Jünger's glorification of the pursuit of hazardous activity and regarded this pursuit as its own reward.

In the future, then, Jünger hoped for the realization of his unfulfilled dreams from World War I. Now embodied in a panoramic vision of the future, these dreams expressed the egocentric longings for adventure of men who, while railing against the pacifism of the old *Bürger*, were being suffocated by the industrial order led by the new *Bürger*, the monopoly capitalist. The new *Bürger* directed the processes forging the instruments of death for the battles of matériel that had drastically restricted the opportunities for heroism and self-assertion. Stoically accepting this restriction, but still seeking to secure avenues for a heroic minority to indulge an omnivorous appetite for danger, Jünger did not challenge the new *Bürger*, whose instruments had now become, he assumed, essential to the self-realization of this heroic minority.

Although threatened with the prospect of becoming an economic functionary of the state, the monopoly capitalist might feel almost as secure in the world of the *Arbeiter* as the old *Bürger* once had in a very different world. Indeed, the monopolist might feel even more secure now that a working class no longer existed, everyone had become a "worker," some of these "workers" served as technocratically minded experts, every adventurous or heroic impulse among a tiny minority served to perpetuate a social order accepted unquestioningly by all, and state economic planning had replaced the uncertainties of the market.

THE DREAM FULFILLED?

Yet, in a sense, the *Arbeiter* was an incomplete work. Not only did Jünger's distaste for ideology lead him to omit critical details, but per-

[148] See Erich Brock, *Das Weltbild Ernst Jüngers: Darstellung und Deutung* (Zurich, 1945), pp. 188, 190.
[149] *DA*, p. 34.

haps more important his description of the elite was tentative and fragmentary. Jünger himself seems to have sensed this incompleteness, although his comment on it in a work published after World War II gives the false impression that the *Arbeiter* contained no conception of an elite: "The drawing [in the *Arbeiter*] is precise, yet it is like a sharply engraved medal without a reverse side. A second volume should delineate the subordination of the previously described dynamic principles to a serene order of higher rank. When the building is finished, the mechanics and electrical engineers leave. But who will be master of the house?"[150] In this comment, Jünger implies that the *Arbeiter* dealt only with the first and second level of the pyramid (note the reference to "mechanics and electrical engineers"). We have seen that Jünger had much to say, both implicitly and explicitly, about the third level, "the master of the house." In view of his own reticence to identify himself with any existing political group in the Germany of 1932, and in view of the unparalleled power that he granted to the future elite, it is hardly surprising that he did not have more to say. Never before or since has the notion of an open-yet-uncontrolled elite that would lead a rejuvenated German nation been developed with such relentless consistency and expressed with such literary force. Jünger anticipated better than any other German elitist the major configurations of a regime like the Third Reich.

Among the many explanations offered for his rejection of Nazi Germany, the most common among his critics has been that he reacted with an aristocratic contempt to its plebeian aspects.[151] Building upon this type of argument, which, as we have seen in previous chapters, has been invoked to explain the distaste of many neoconservatives for the Third Reich, Hans-Peter Schwarz has developed a more elaborate explanation. From a point in the mid-1920's at which Jünger felt very close to the Nazis, he gradually if erratically distanced himself, Schwarz suggests, from the bulk of the party and especially the Hitler wing. Anxious to guard the purity of the ideas of the new nationalism, Jünger saw in the National Socialist party the same danger of "party egoism" that he found in other groups and parties. Although Hitler's rejection of the *Landvolk* movement in 1929 led Jünger to write an article in the independent leftist periodical *Das Tagebuch* criticizing the National Socialists, and although he was increasingly wont to find fault with their legalism and their compromises with the Republic, he remained very sympathetic toward them as late as 1930. Schwarz finds

[150] Diary entry of March 17, 1943 in *Strahlungen*, 3rd ed. (Tübingen, 1949), p. 283.

[151] See, e.g., Niekisch, *Gewagtes Leben*, p. 189; J. P. Stern, *Ernst Jünger* (New Haven, 1953), p. 49.

the decisive reason for Jünger's break with the Nazis after 1933 in his individualism.[152] If we follow Schwarz's interpretation, it would be logical to conclude that the vision of the *Arbeiter* provided Jünger with a satisfactory explanation of his reluctance to endorse the Third Reich and his subsequent passive opposition to the regime[153]—an explanation similar to that employed by many other neoconservatives. He could regard the Nazi regime as transitional, as a transitional regime with many undesirable, although perhaps unavoidably undesirable, aspects.

While compelling, Schwarz's interpretation and this conclusion drawn from it do not touch directly on the crucial point. Intellectually and perhaps emotionally, the Third Reich was most deficient, from the point of view of the Jünger of the *Arbeiter*, in ideology. Jünger had not foreseen the need for the elaborate efforts to construct an ideology, which, however unsuccessful, characterized the Nazi period. Jünger's form of racism, while akin to some Nazi types of racism and serving the function of legitimizing the claim of a new elite to rule, did not predominate among Nazi ideologues. His racism lacked the biological pretensions of the prevailing racist theories of the Nazis. For example, despite his own occasionally expressed, vaguely nonracist anti-Semitism, Jünger ridiculed Nazi anti-Semitism as early as 1929: "It is not a major characteristic of the Nationalist that he gulps down three Jews at breakfast—for him anti-Semitism is not a significant issue."[154] Like the leaders of the Third Reich, Jünger was obsessed by the need for manipulating people, but he either pulled back at the logical consequences of his own ideas or failed to anticipate the lengths to which the Nazis would be driven in seeking success in a class-torn society in which the class-conscious worker had not been fully displaced by the *Arbeiter* of Jünger's dreams.[155]

Jünger's detachment from the regime was reinforced by his contacts in high places, especially with career officers who felt a strong

[152] Schwarz, *Konservativer Anarchist*, pp. 111–15, 120–21.

[153] For a discriminating analysis of Jünger's position during the Nazi period, see the chapter on him in George K. Romoser, "The Crisis of Political Direction in the German Resistance to Nazism: Its Nature, Origins, and Effects" (Chicago diss., 1958).

[154] "Nationalismus und Nationalismus," *Das Tagebuch*, Sept. 21, 1929, p. 1554.

[155] See Wolfgang Sauer's suggestion that Jünger refused to recognize the National Socialist *Weltanschauung* as a legitimate offspring of his concept of total mobilization because Nazism failed to measure up to his intellectual and aesthetic demands. Sauer concludes that Jünger was appalled by the consequences ensuing from the attempt to realize his own ideas. Wolfgang Sauer, "Die Mobilmachung der Gewalt" in Karl Dietrich Bracher, Wolfgang Sauer, and Gerhard Schulz, *Die nationalsozialistische Machtergreifung: Studien zur Errichtung des totalitären Herrschaftssystems in Deutschland 1933/34*, 2nd ed. (Cologne, 1962), p. 809.

antipathy toward the Nazis.[156] When he was reactivated during World War II, he served largely in Paris, where he broadened and deepened his contacts with the Junker and professional military element of the old ruling class. Ironically, these contacts and his attempt to justify the role of the old nobility led him close to a biological form of racism. In his diary he compared the English to the Prussians, noting with favor the

> often commented on superiority of the Norman inheritance, which is more conducive to the formation of a stratum of leaders than the ordinary Germanic [inheritance]. It is always better to stand back to back or even side by side with such cousins . . . than face to face. Indeed, that was always the endeavor of Prussian policy, which was good as long as large landlords, and not the elect of plebiscitarian democracy, conducted it. Naturally, the influence of land declines when the population increases and becomes concentrated in cities. . . .[157]

Suggestive of the reasons behind this expression of appreciation for the more reactionary elements in the German ruling class is Jünger's *roman à clef* first published in 1939 and entitled *On the Marble Cliffs*.[158] In this novel a chief forester, whose style of life recalls Hermann Goering's, begins to terrorize the inhabitants and devastate the environment in an area that two naturalists are studying. Jünger and his brother Friedrich Georg, thinly disguised as the naturalists, are offended by the injustice of the forester and bitterly resent his disruption of their idyllic life of seclusion. The brothers had once belonged to the Order of Mauretanians headed by the forester, but having come to realize that their membership in it was an expression of an illusory search for some way of avoiding the consequences of living in an era of decline, the brothers had decided to seek personal fulfillment in their devotion to botany. Now they find that their pursuit of botanical

---

[156] Cf. Helmut Kaiser's explanation of Jünger's attitude toward the Third Reich. By inexplicably identifying Jünger during the Weimar Republic and the Nazi era with a single group, Kaiser suddenly denies the broader significance of Jünger's work: ". . . Jünger ist ein Ideologe desselben Imperialismus, dessen Politik auch die NSDAP besorgt hat; nur gehört er einer anderen Fraktion an. Seine Gruppe stützt sich in erster Linie auf die Generalität, und die ist im Kampf um die Macht, der nicht nur gegen die revolutionäre Arbeiterklasse, sondern auch innerhalb der Reaktion geführt wurde, 1933 unterliegen." Kaiser, *Mythos, Rausch und Reaktion*, p. 199.

[157] Diary entry of Aug. 16, 1942 in *Strahlungen*, pp. 153–54.

[158] *Auf den Marmorklippen* (Erlenbach and Zurich, n. d.). The English edition is entitled *On the Marble Cliffs*, trans. Stuart Hood (London, 1947). On Jünger and his works since 1933, see esp. Schwarz, *Konservativer Anarchist*, chs. 4–9.

studies has become precarious. For no good reason the forester is determined to subject everything to his tyrannical control. The only prospect for deliverance is provided by some noblemen, but these leaders of the struggle against the forester are themselves caught up in the decadence and nihilism of the era.[159] Only a concern for personal autonomy still distinguishes clearly the leading nobleman from the forester. This identification of aristocracy with the preservation of personal autonomy suggests that Jünger's fondness for the nobility stemmed from his desire to continue to be a writer not subservient to the Nazi regime. He cultivated hopes that aristocratic circles would assume leadership in the struggle against the Third Reich.

But the *dénouement* of the novel indicates that Jünger was unwilling to merge his own destiny with that of the nobility. One of the brothers, Jünger himself, joins the final battle against the forester—a rout which, as soon becomes obvious, never had any chance for success. The leading nobleman commits suicide, but the brothers escape. Their unwillingness to die heroically and their headlong flight from the territory under the forester's immediate control suggest that Jünger had concluded that he could continue to assert his own autonomy only through "inner emigration." As *On the Marble Cliffs* ends, the brothers feel that they have returned to the tranquility and security of their father's home. Jünger seems to imply a rediscovery of some of the virtues of the once despised *Bürger*.

The man on the German Right who had previously manifested perhaps the greatest insistence upon coordination by the state of every aspect of life except the activities of a "heroic minority" of adventurers had, under the impact of demands for the regimentation of writers, decided that many of the old conservative and liberal values might not be as antiquated as he had once believed. He now rejected the concept of total mobilization that was as foreign to both the aristocrat and the *Bürger* of the nineteenth century as it was germane to the development of the monopolist bourgeoisie of the twentieth century. Or was Jünger simply modifying his concept of total mobilization in order to remove from its full jurisdiction the aloof observer that he wished to be known as after World War II?

---

[159] See *Auf den Marmorklippen*, pp. 101, 103.

CHAPTER THIRTEEN

The Sources of National Socialist Elitism

Nazi elite theories were mediocre in comparison with those of the other German elitists whom we have studied. Even the lesser of the latter appear in comparison rigorous, detailed, and consequential. It would be tempting to ascribe the low level of Nazi elite theories to the lack of quality among Nazi writers, or to suggest, in the manner of many conservative critics of national socialism, that the party's attempt to appeal to "the masses" dictated a lack of intellectual rigor.[1]

The basic explanation is, however, to be found elsewhere. The exigencies of gaining power in a society wracked by outbreaks of civil war determined the quality of Nazi elite theories before 1933. A movement that received support from groups whose immediate and long-range interests were irreconcilable—unemployed workers and big businessmen, white-collar workers and their employers, small businessmen and giant monopolies, independent peasants and large landowners—could not produce detailed and consistent elite theories without destroying the prospects for its success. Under the Tsarist regime, the Bolsheviks, pursuing forthrightly a clear sectional interest, found the public exposition and discussion of their theories limited by external censorship. Under the Weimar Republic, censorship was imposed from within the Nazi party. A classic instance is the treatment of the National Socialist program, which, after it was declared unalterable in 1926, could no longer be discussed freely by party members themselves. To cope with Tsarist censorship, Lenin found it necessary to employ "Aesopian language," but not to conceal his argument or re-

---

[1] There is no adequate study of National Socialist conceptions of an elite. Even Ernst Nolte's recent study of three types of European fascism lacks conceptual clarity in its brief discussion of Nazi elitism: Ernst Nolte, *Der Faschismus in seiner Epoche: Die Action française, der italienische Faschismus, der Nationalsozialismus* (Munich, 1963), esp. pp. 495–99. Joachim H. Knoll's *Führungsauslese in Liberalismus und Demokratie: Zur politischen Geistesgeschichte der letzten 100 Jahre* (Stuttgart, 1957), pp. 198–205 suffers from the same defect and finds little more than racism in Nazi elitist ideas. Perhaps the best beginnings of a survey of these ideas are to be found in David Schoenbaum, *Hitler's Social Revolution: Class and Status in Nazi Germany, 1933–1939* (Garden City, N.Y., 1966), pp. 59–76, 245–51, but Schoenbaum's main scholarly contribution is to German social history. A major weakness of his work is his undiscriminating application of the term "social revolution" to the Third Reich.

frain from developing it. Similarly, when Donoso Cortés presented the Spanish parliament with a frank program for the salvation of the ruling class in 1849, he pursued his argument to a logical conclusion.

After 1933 the requirement of consolidating and maintaining power prevented the thorough and consistent elaboration of Nazi elite theories. To be sure, during the first years of the Third Reich many former non-Nazis, especially on the Right, began to develop a coherent body of elite theories associated with the new regime, as, in the main, National Socialist political thought was now able to tap the rich resources of former opponents and critics who joined the Nazi camp.[2] Many able political theorists, of whom the best known is perhaps Carl Schmitt, contributed elaborate justifications for the emerging Third Reich. But after being welcomed to the fold, most of these political theorists soon found themselves under attack. As early as 1936, Schmitt was no longer accepted as an authoritative interpreter of the Third Reich.[3] There is much justification for the claims made after World War II by demoted theorists that they sought during the early years of the regime to guide it into safer, more traditional, and less violent channels. The apologetic intent behind these claims should not obscure the effect that the ideas they propounded during the honeymoon days of their relations with the regime had and, often, was intended to have. The formulations of a Carl Schmitt tended to box in the Nazis; when the authority of such political thinkers became less useful in justifying the regime both at home and abroad, and as the regime itself found its possibilities limited by their theories, these men lost their status as "crown jurists" and semiofficial interpreters of the Third Reich.

The rapid development of a dictatorial regime with powers unparalleled in German history complicated enormously the tasks of the Nazi elitist. Propaganda and terror did not remove the underlying conflicts within German society. Workers' pressures on profit margins remained, as did the contradiction between the productive potential of German industry and its underutilization or its subsequent operation at higher levels under the stimulus of the manufacture of military goods, which, in turn, aggravated tensions with other states and led to war. As long as the basic contradictions of German society remained unresolved, and as long as the Nazis made no concerted effort to resolve them, no rigorous, uniform National Socialist elitism could be articulated.

[2] See Karl Dietrich Bracher, Wolfgang Sauer, and Gerhard Schulz, *Die nationalsozialistische Machtergreifung: Studien zur Errichtung des totalitären Herrschaftssystems in Deutschland 1933/34*, 2nd ed. (Cologne, 1962), p. 268.

[3] See Hasso Hofmann, *Legitimität gegen Legalität: Der Weg der politischen Philosophie Carl Schmitts* (Neuwied, [1964?]), pp. 198–203.

It is thus easy to understand why many studies of Nazi Germany have reached the conclusion that no Nazi ideology existed.[4] Ideas were employed by the regime to manipulate the populace, but no systematic, coherent body of thought was developed to serve as a guide to and justification for policy. To deny that a Nazi ideology existed does not, of course, necessarily lead to a denial that any fixed, recurrent themes appeared in Nazi writings and propaganda or that the policies of the Third Reich contained no consistently pursued objectives.

THE ALLURES OF AN OPEN ELITE

A common finding among students of Nazi Germany has been that racism, and, in particular, anti-Semitism, was a consistent aspect of Nazi thought and policy. For example, Alan Bullock in his biography of Hitler argues that anti-Semitism provided one of the few, perhaps the only, constant elements in Hitler's thought.[5] Certainly a good case can be made for concluding that racism was a recurrent and central part of Nazi political thought, but one can make an equally good case for the suggestion that the concept of an open-yet-authoritarian elite was also recurrent and central. The easier part of the case can be made concerning the "open" half of this concept, which can be found in many diverse forms. In view of this multifariousness, it would be foolish to speak of a single Nazi elite theory; rather, we must use the plural and refer to Nazi elite theories. The existence of such diversity may appear less surprising if one recognizes, as is often ignored, that many disparate types of Nazi racism existed.[6]

The theme of an elite based upon merit or achievement recurs again and again in Nazi speeches and literature, whether we look at the writings and addresses of Hitler, Goebbels, Rosenberg, and other leading Nazis or examine the works of less well-known exponents of the party.[7]

[4] See, e.g., Franz Neumann, *Behemoth: The Structure and Practice of National Socialism, 1933–1944* (New York: Octagon Books, 1963), pp. 37–39 and passim. Both this edition of Neumann's book and the recent Harper paperback edition (New York, 1966) are unaltered reprints of the 1944 edition of Oxford University Press.

[5] Alan Bullock, *Hitler: A Study in Tyranny*, rev. ed. (New York: Harper paperback, 1964), pp. 406–07. See also Bullock's more pointed essay "The Political Ideas of Adolf Hitler" in Maurice Baumont et al., *The Third Reich* (New York, 1955).

[6] For some examples of the varieties of Nazi racist doctrines see Karl Saller, *Die Rassenlehre des Nationalsozialismus in Wissenschaft und Propaganda* (Darmstadt, 1961).

[7] The recurrence of this theme in the two major scholarly editions of selections from Hitler's speeches, those by Baynes and by Domarus, is all the more impressive since the bulk of both collections deal, in accordance with the intentions

The Nazi party program of 1920[8] deals with aspects of this theme in several passages. The primary reference appears in Point 20, which discusses education and its relationship to political leadership: "In order to enable every capable and industrious German to obtain higher education and thus to assume a position of leadership, the state must concern itself with a fundamental expansion of our entire educational system. . . . We demand the education, at state expense, of the gifted children of poor parents without regard for class [*Stand*] or occupation."[9]

Time and again in his speeches, writings, and private conversations Hitler dwelled upon similar ideas. Often, as in a speech in the *Sportpalast* in Berlin delivered in early 1942 to an audience consisting mainly of workers from the armaments industries, nurses from military hospitals, and wounded soldiers, he assumed that the expansion of educational opportunities led directly to the formation of an open elite. In this speech he claimed that national socialism had succeeded in developing "a school system on the basis of which a talented youth, no matter of what sort his parents are, can obtain only God knows how high a position. . . ."[10] The party program as well as this speech and many other Nazi statements suggest a marked affinity with liberal elite theories. In the same breath as Nazis denounced liberalism, they called for careers open to talents and for an elite based on ability or achievement.

How deep was this affinity with liberalism, and how can we account for it? As we have seen, neoconservative elitists criticized the Nazi party as caught up by liberalism, but by focusing upon the use of parliamentary methods and the development of a mass party, men like Jung, Spengler, and Jünger missed the deeper point, as indeed they had to if they were not to confront their own dependence upon liberal

---

of the editors, with foreign policy and military affairs: Norman H. Baynes, ed., *The Speeches of Adolf Hitler, April 1922–August 1939* (2 vols., London, 1942). Hereafter cited as Baynes, followed by the volume number. Max Domarus, ed., *Hitler: Reden und Proklamationen 1932–1945, kommentiert von einem deutschen Zeitgenossen*, 2nd ed. (2 vols. Munich, [1965?]). Hereafter cited as Domarus, followed by the volume number.

[8] Available in many editions. I have used the text in Walther Hofer, ed., *Der Nationalsozialismus: Dokumente 1933–1945* (Hamburg, 1957), pp. 28–31.

[9] The most widely circulated and reprinted English translation of this point, which was published in Raymond E. Murphy, et al., *National Socialism: Basic Principles . . .* (Washington, 1943), is very misleading. Indeed, the translation in Murphy's work of the other points of the party program contains serious errors that alter the meaning of entire passages. Unfortunately, most collections of historical documents for college students published in the United States have adoped, without change, the same garbled translation when selections from the Nazi program are included.

[10] Speech of Jan. 30, 1942. In Domarus, ii, 1827.

notions. During the dismantling of the parliamentary system of government after 1929 and its destruction with the coming to power of the Nazis, the call for democracy of personnel selection, the same appeal being made by their neoconservative critics, might well have appeared as a more important and enduring sign of National Socialist dependence upon liberalism. Like the neoconservatives, the Nazis were demanding a type of open elite that would, implicitly, remain within the confines of a capitalist society. Here then is the basic source of the affinity between Nazi and liberal elitism: both called for an elite which would ineluctably function within the parameters of bourgeois society and whose members would be selected in accordance with the basic values of that social order.

Significantly, the Nazi party was composed largely of men from social strata that had once supported liberalism, and the party's electoral gains before 1933 occurred partly at the expense of the liberal parties. Never securely within the fold of liberalism, as the course of the Revolution of 1848 demonstrated, the lower strata of the middle class gravitated more to the Right than to the Left during the latter half of the nineteenth and the early twentieth century. Although as we saw in Chapters Two and Three the left-liberal parties retained, and the Social Democrats gained, the allegiance of many small businessmen, lower-level officials, and artisan craftsmen, these groups supplied much of the mass basis for the parties of the Right. The ranks of these same social strata, swelled by the tremendous expansion of the white-collar working force, but dwarfed by the development of monopoly capital, predominated in the early Nazi party.[11] Even in some strongholds of the Catholic Center, the Nazis scored their greatest successes with the lower strata of the middle class. Later, but still before 1933, the party made substantial if less striking inroads into the upper strata of the middle class. Middle-sized businessmen, higher officials, and members of the free professions had been among the most faithful supporters of liberalism during the middle of the nineteenth century. Unlike the lower strata of the middle class, they were not attracted in large numbers to the Social Democrats by the end of the nineteenth century. When their political allegiances shifted, they almost invariably moved to the Right, but until 1930 most of them remained with

[11] See Michael H. Kater, "Zur Soziographie der frühen NSDAP," *Vierteljahrshefte für Zeitgeschichte*, xix (1971), 124–59 for a good discussion of the literature on the social composition of members and supporters of the party before 1933, as well as a detailed analysis of the party's membership in 1923. An important short study dealing with the relationship between liberalism and fascism, Reinhard Kühnl's *Formen bürgerlicher Herrschaft: Liberalismus—Faschismus* (Reinbek bei Hamburg: Rowohlt paperback, 1971), reached me too late to deal with in this chapter.

either the moderate parties or the Nationalists. Much of the attractiveness of the Nazis to both the lower and the upper strata of the middle class stemmed from the ability of National Socialist propagandists to exploit disillusionment with the liberals, while at the same time convincing middle-class groups of the sincerity of the party's commitment to the worthwhile, positive objectives of liberalism.

Have we looked only superficially at the question of the depth of the affinity between Nazi and liberal elitism? Did not Nazi concepts of an open elite diverge radically from those of the liberals? Certainly, if we compare nineteenth-century liberalism with Nazi ideas, there is a profound difference. The abandonment of the classic concepts of *Besitz* and *Bildung* and the introduction of racist criteria for elite selection are but two of the most important differences. On the other hand, since the latter part of the nineteenth century liberal theorists had abandoned *Besitz* and *Bildung* as slogans and had often introduced racist criteria. Liberal political thought was far along the road to scrapping nineteenth-century liberalism before the Nazi party was founded in 1919. To be sure, as we have seen in discussing the new liberal elitists Weber, Naumann, Rathenau, and Nelson, the concepts of *Besitz* and especially *Bildung* persisted, if under different labels. Although still employing criteria favoring the bourgeoisie and the middle class, most liberal elitists did not spell out the consequences of applying these criteria. Only Weber laid bare his social concerns, but it became increasingly difficult for him as well as other liberal elitists to reveal clearly the social consequences that would ensue from the realization of their elitism. Due to the social basis of the Nazi movement and the opportunism of its tactics, the Nazis presented criteria that were vaguer and more ambiguous. By 1930 what the Nazis chose to emphasize depended largely upon the audience being addressed at any given moment.

Racist concepts were well suited to Nazi tactics because racism could be used to suggest different, often contradictory demands that facilitated attempts to appeal to various audiences. The arbitrariness and inconsistency of Nazi racism corresponded to the tactical needs of the party before 1933; both before and after 1933 the invocation of racist criteria for elite selection often masked the social concerns involved in Nazi elitism. A few examples will serve to illustrate the versatility of racism. In a speech on culture delivered to the Party Congress at Nürnberg in September 1933, Hitler discussed methods of selecting leaders. As was his wont, he equated superior racial traits with manifest ability and with a positive response to national socialism. On the basis of these criteria, a potential member of the Nazi elite was any capable man who responded strongly to "the National Socialist idea": ". . . We could not reach a conclusion about ability from [a man's] race. Rather, we had to assess racial qualification on the basis of ability. And ability could be ascertained by the way in which the individual reacted to a newly proclaimed idea. This is the unerring method of looking for the men whom we want to find, for everyone responds only to the tone to which his innermost [nature] is attuned."[12] The conception of race that appears in this passage cannot be derived from physical anthropology. Hitler is, in effect, saying that the leaders of the Nazi party are, by virtue of their positions, men of good race. Thus the concept of race serves to legitimize the power of Nazi leaders without imposing any tangible restrictions upon their recruitment.

Hitler's impatience with the invocation of physical indices of race such as head measurements has often been commented upon. He discounted and privately even ridiculed the claims brought forward by many other Nazi racists, such as those current in SS circles. But he seems to have perceived the practical advantages of inconsistent racist criteria. By invoking an arbitrary concept of race, the Nazis questioned the legitimacy of the existing social order without entrapping themselves in categorical demands for its destruction. Those who cooperated with the regime or provided supposedly indispensable technical skills could be accepted as racial comrades; those who did not could be designated unacceptable because of race. In an extreme instance, Germany's Japanese allies became "honorary Aryans." During a private conversation, apparently in 1934, with Hermann Rauschning, Hitler commented on the usefulness of race doctrines to the new regime:

"I know perfectly well," he [Hitler] said, "just as well as all these tremendously clever intellectuals, that in the scientific sense there is no such thing as race. But you, as a farmer and cattle-breeder, cannot get your breeding successfully achieved without the conception of race. And I as a politician need a conception which enables the order which has hitherto existed on historic bases to be abolished and an entirely new and anti-historic order enforced and given an intellectual basis. Understand what I mean," he said, breaking off. "I have to liberate the world from dependence on its historic past. . . . The conception of race serves me well. It disposes of the old order and makes possible new associations."[13]

Although the general drift of these remarks is in keeping with Hitler's approach to racism, the wording of them presented by Rauschning

[12] Adolf Hitler, *Führung und Gefolgschaft* (Berlin, [1934]), p. 53.
[13] Quoted in Hermann Rauschning, *The Voice of Destruction* (New York, 1940), p. 232.

may be influenced by Rauschning's belief that the epitome of Nazism was nihilism. Hence his version of the conversation may make Hitler seem intent upon destroying bourgeois society, rather than simply inducing, through both threats and promises, the old ruling class to cooperate.

Especially in the early years of the Nazi movement, racism was often used to legitimize the resentment of the middle class against the bourgeoisie and nobility. Without calling into question the necessity of a nobility or bourgeoisie, without implying a rejection of class society, racist concepts were used to attack both groups in general, as well as individual members of them. In a speech in 1922, Hitler asserted that the leadership of the parties of the Right must be rejected, for Jews had systematically "bastardized" upper-class families through the marriage of Jewesses with Gentiles: "The result was that in a short time it was precisely the ruling class [*Schicht*] which became in its character completely estranged from its own people."[14] Similarly, in *Mein Kampf* Hitler described the nobility, especially the high nobility, as "Jewified" (*verjudet*), and he went on to lament that now the blood of the bourgeoisie was being poisoned as well and that the bourgeoisie was already on the same road to ruin gone down earlier by the nobility.[15] These attacks on the nobility and bourgeoisie left open the possibility that individual noblemen and bourgeois might be welcomed as members of the elite, and more importantly held forth the prospect of openings at the top for the largely middle-class members and supporters of the Nazi movement. At the same time, the attacks did not constitute a direct threat to the collective interests of the bourgeoisie or nobility.

The case of Erhard Milch is one of the best known of numerous others that might be selected to demonstrate the arbitrariness of racism in practice. A director of the Lufthansa during the Weimar Republic, Milch was named secretary of state in the Air Ministry under Goering in 1933. Probably under the criteria often employed by the Nazis and certainly under the clauses of the Nürnberg Racial Laws of 1935, both of Milch's parents were Jews. But despite some attempts to oust him, Milch stayed on in the Air Ministry, rising to the rank of *Generalfeldmarschall*, the highest rank in the German military forces below that of *Reichsmarschall*, a title originally created for Goering. Milch's mother testified that her son was the product of an extramarital relationship, and Goering, echoing the words of Karl Lueger, Vienna's anti-Semitic mayor of some four decades earlier, announced:

[14] Speech of July 28, 1922. In Baynes, I, 27.
[15] Adolf Hitler, *Mein Kampf*, 10. Aufl. of the Volksausgabe of the 2nd ed. (2 vols., Munich, 1933), I, 270, 346.

"I decide who's a Jew."[16] Wheeler-Bennett remarks that Goering "never took his anti-Semitism seriously when a case of technical ability was involved,"[17] a reasonable interpretation of the Milch case and others similar to it, but Goering's concern for the utilization of skills may have been fostered or even initiated by other considerations. In his position at the Lufthansa during the 1920's, Milch seems to have dipped into the airline's political slush fund to aid his spendthrift friend Goering, who, partly in exchange, pushed vigorously for larger appropriations for the Lufthansa when he entered the Reichstag.[18]

Although the application of anti-Semitic doctrines promoted the displacement of some members of the upper classes, the often seemingly arbitrary enforcement of them increased the political leverage of the Nazis as the guardians of these doctrines. Thus the second in command of the *Stahlhelm*, Theodor Düsterberg, a small manufacturer who ran against Hitler and Hindenburg in the first round of the presidential election of 1932, was discovered to have been, probably unknown to himself, the great grandson of a Jew. The Nazis discredited Düsterberg, and in 1933 they succeeded in forcing into political retirement a man whose presidential aspirations had been backed by most Junkers and most of the Hohenzollern princes.[19] Even in Himmler's SS, usually and properly regarded as the bastion of some of the most doctrinaire and fanatical racists during the Third Reich, so high an official as Reinhard Heydrich was known by some of his superiors to be burdened with a genealogy that probably made him a "quarter Jew" under the Nürnberg laws and could not measure up to the more demanding tests presumably applied to the SS.

But more significant than the presence of "non-Aryans" in high positions under the Third Reich is the way in which the racial standards of the SS were construed by its top leadership. During the first years of the regime many high party members, as well as prominent businessmen and other upper-class Germans, were made honorary SS leaders. There was little pretense of enrolling these men on the basis of their racial characteristics. In the selection of lower-ranking SS men ostensibly racial characteristics were extensively applied and proved helpful in checking the great influx into the SS during the early years of the regime.[20] As an historian of the SS has noted: "Under the ideo-

[16] "Wer Jude ist, bestimme ich."
[17] J. W. Wheeler-Bennett, *The Nemesis of Power: The German Army in Politics, 1918–1945* (New York, 1954), p. 342.
[18] See Konrad Heiden, *Der Fuehrer: Hitler's Rise to Power*, trans. Ralph Manheim (Boston, 1944), pp. 298–99, 640–41.
[19] See *ibid.*, p. 444; Volker R. Berghahn, *Der Stahlhelm, Bund der Frontsoldaten 1918–1935* (Düsseldorf, 1966), pp. 239–43, 246–63.
[20] Ermenhild Neusüss-Hunkel, *Die SS* (Hannover, 1956), p. 18.

logical cover of selecting those who measured up best to the ideal of the nordic man, the principle of biological selection was . . . applied at most to the broad mass of followers and was to this extent merely a technique for imbuing the followers with a contrived elitist mentality and *esprit de corps*."[21]

In a lecture delivered during a political instruction course for the armed services in 1937 and published in a volume for circulation among the military, Himmler provided some revealing glimpses into the use of racial characteristics in the selection of the SS.[22] Himmler found two possible methods of ascertaining "good blood." The first was the severe selection that occurs in a war: "In this process of selection good blood manifests itself through achievement [*Leistung*]." When he took charge of the SS in 1929, Himmler explained, there were in its ranks many former soldiers whose achievements at the front had demonstrated their "inner value," but other criteria had to be employed for peacetime, when the supreme test of bravery was not available. He had no choice except to go by a man's looks: "Many [of you] will immediately object: 'That is all very well, but if you start with height, blond hair, and blue eyes—and, for all I care, cranial measurements—then the whole business is very problematical.' I know all of this full well. We could never proceed in that way." Himmler went on to say that he had required applicants to be at least five feet six inches (one and seven tenths meters) tall. Men of this size would, "in some way," have the desired blood, although, he hastened to imply, no general standard should prevent exceptions. He also used photographs of the candidates. In looking at each picture he asked himself if the man's features betrayed highly visible indications of foreign blood. Inquiring rhetorically why he had done this, Himmler asked his listeners to recall the type of men who had been members of the Soldiers' Councils in 1918 and 1919:

> Every one of you who was an officer at the time knows a number of these people from personal experience. You can confirm that in general these were people who looked somehow peculiar to our German eyes, [people] who had some sort of odd feature, [people] in whom some sort of foreign blood had entered. This was the type of man who can certainly be restrained and who in untroubled times behaves properly, who in war is even brave, audacious, and determined, but who, at the very moment when the final test of character and nerves comes, must somehow fall down due to his blood.

21 *Ibid.*, pp. 67–68.
22 See the excerpts from this work in Léon Poliakov and Josef Wulf, eds., *Das Dritte Reich und seine Denker: Dokumente* (Berlin, [1959?]), pp. 24–26.

The examination of the photos of SS applicants, Himmler stated, had enabled him to avoid the most serious errors in choosing among the candidates. Concluding his description of the initial process of selection, he emphasized that the important test after the candidate had been selected was his performance or achievement (*Leistung*): "Achievement, how the man stood up in the ensuing months and years, was always decisive." As an example Himmler mentioned the high dues that had been required of the SS man, even during the worst days of the depression. Payment of the dues often constituted an enormous personal sacrifice for an SS man; if he paid them, he demonstrated his value.[23] In Himmler's lecture racial standards are established and upheld in a way that is, as generally during the Third Reich, capricious, arbitrary, and open ended. Few men are automatically excluded by these standards, and the possibility of exceptions is held forth.

Another instance of the open-endedness of the racial concepts of the SS can be found in a letter that Himmler wrote to a high subordinate during the early stages of the mass murder of Jews: "I urgently request that no decree concerning the concept 'Jew' be issued. We only tie our own hands with all these foolish undertakings [i.e., definitions]. The occupied eastern territories will be free of Jews."[24] As this letter indicates, mere expediency could become paramount in the avoidance of clear-cut racial criteria. Racism in the SS, as in other institutions and practices during the Third Reich, provided an often transparent veil for other standards, of which one of the most clearly stated was ability or achievement.

One of the keys to the success of the Nazis in gaining electoral support before 1933 and in consolidating the regime afterward was their ability to project a credible image of deep commitment to democracy of personnel selection. A consistent theme in surveys of German attitudes—of party members during the early years of the regime, of prisoners of war during World War II, and of the general populace after the war—is a widespread belief that the Third Reich undertook policies which opened up new possibilities for the lower classes and reduced the privileges of the upper classes. Often cited measures facilitated the higher education of bright children from poor families, diminished class differences, and enabled "the little man" to obtain justice through the courts,[25] all of which in some way identified the Nazi

---

[23] *Ibid.*

[24] Himmler to Gottlob Berger, July 28, 1942. The letter is reproduced in *ibid.*, p. 26.

[25] There is a large body of literature on this subject. See, e.g., Theodore Abel, *Why Hitler Came into Power: An Answer Based on the Original Life Stories of Six Hundred of His Followers* (New York, 1938), recently reissued in a new edition under the title *The Nazi Movement: Why Hitler Came to Power* (New York:

426—Conservatives in Search of Elites

movement both with an emphasis upon the selection of the able for high posts regardless of social position and with the closely related subject of fostering social mobility. Before as well as after coming to power, Nazi spokesmen often emphasized the unwillingness of their aristocratic and bourgeois competitors to renounce class privileges and accept the principle of ability as a criterion for elite selection.

This charge was misleading. As we have seen, even the more traditionally oriented conservatives were willing to commit themselves publicly to such a program after the defeat of 1918, and the neoconservatives were often as adamant as anyone in professing adherence to the principle of an open elite. Yet despite the changes in political ideas that occurred on the Right, many of these professions were hedged in by restrictions and vitiated by ambiguities, especially when the threat of revolution receded after 1919. Of course, the commitment of the Nazis to democracy of personnel selection was also restricted and ambiguous, but during the Weimar Republic the Nazis were neither a governmental party in the Reich nor identified with the upper classes in the existing social order, and these restrictions and ambiguities could be more easily passed over than they could in another party such as the Nationalists. Most Germans had repeated experiences that called attention to the gap between theory and practice among the Nationalists. The credibility of the commitment of the Nazis to an open elite depended partly upon the obvious weakness of their major competitors' commitment, for by 1929 there was abundant evidence of the failure of practice to live up to theory in the Nazi party. Ironically, "the party cadres all but duplicated the status divisions of German middle-class society. . . . Far from leveling the social divisions of Germany under the Kaiser the NSDAP [*Nationalsozialistische Deutsche Arbeiterpartei*] perpetuated them among party militants."[26] But as listeners to Hitler's speeches were often reminded, the *Führer* had been merely a common soldier during the war and was a man of the people. Certainly *Geheimrat* Hugenberg and other leaders of the non-Nazi Right could never claim to come from such a humble background. The shift to the *principle* of an open elite did not appear decisive in the other parties of the Right.

Moderates as well as the Right became dependent upon the Nazis to close a credibility gap in German society. The bourgeoisie had to rely upon the Nazis to foster a convincing illusion of vast opportunities

---

Atherton paperback, 1966); Heinz Ludwig Ansbacher, *Attitudes of German Prisoners of War: A Study of the Dynamics of National Socialist Followership*, Psychological Monographs, No. 288 (Washington, 1948); Milton Mayer, *They Thought They Were Free* (Chicago, 1955).

[26] Dietrich Orlow, *A History of the Nazi Party, 1919–1933* (Pittsburgh, 1969), p. 171.

for social ascent and of an earnest undertaking to create an open elite born aloof by the buoyant camaraderie of a *Volksgemeinschaft*. Although in his famous speech to industrialists at the *Industrieklub* in Düsseldorf on January 27, 1932, Hitler depicted the Nazis as the only party of political idealists in Germany, as the only group that could unite a nation divided equally into "Bolshevik" and "nationally oriented" camps by leading it away from material concerns and back to idealism,[27] even after he became chancellor the middle class probably found talk of creating an open elite more enticing and credible than did most of the working class. The establishment of full employment seems to have been more effective in manipulating much of the working class,[28] but to be plausible to the middle class and appear less specious to many workers, the principle of democracy of personnel selection, the Nazis had to claim, applied to everyone, including proletarians.

Leading Nazis, including Hitler himself, demonstrated an acute awareness of the importance of resolving what they often continued to call—in the euphemistic terminology of the nineteenth century— "the social question." Once in power, they realized that defusing this issue was a precondition to the continuance of the regime. Speaking before very different types of audiences, Hitler often returned, albeit with somewhat different emphasis, to the theme of the restoration of the people's faith in leadership as one of the supreme objectives of the Third Reich. Thus, in an address to the first Congress of the new German Labor Front in May of 1933, he told an audience that probably consisted largely of workers and Nazi labor officials: "The State must be led by a real authority and one which is not dependent on any one class. The leaders must be such that every citizen can trust them and be sure that they do not wish for anything but the happiness and the good of the German nation; they must be able to say with right that they are completely independent." Hitler went on to declare that millions of people had to be restored in the faith "that the State does not represent the interests of a single group or class, and that the Government is there to manage the concerns of the entire community."[29] Speaking privately to a group of leaders of the armaments industry in

[27] Domarus, I, 82, 84–85, 89.

[28] Cf. the provocative suggestions in two recent articles by T. W. Mason that even full employment could not gain the allegiance of most of the working class and that hence the regime had to fall back upon the precarious expedients of terror, war, and the militarization of the working force. T. W. Mason, "Labour in the Third Reich," *Past and Present*, No. 33 (Apr. 1966), pp. 131, 136, and his "Some Origins of the Second World War," *Past and Present*, No. 29 (Dec. 1964), pp. 86–87.

[29] Speech of May 10, 1933 in Berlin. In Baynes, I, 430–31.

mid-1944 he claimed: "I have succeeded so well that there is no strike in Germany, and no lockout. But that is only possible because even the worker has the conviction that he is treated fairly, that he is paid in accordance with what he achieves, that he can buy something with his money, and, above all and of course most importantly, that he is not a second-class citizen and that his child can become, just as yours can, anything of which he is capable. That is the decisive reason [for the absence of strikes]."[30] Here Hitler suggested that the worker will be satisfied with his lot if he believes that his children will have the opportunity, perhaps not granted him, of ascending socially. At the same time, Hitler implicitly reassured his audience that a worker's son would not be favored over an industrialist's.

This last theme, that favoritism would not be shown to the lower classes, appeared more clearly in other addresses and conversations. In the transcript of some of the most private of his conversations, in his "table talk," Hitler is reported as having remarked one day in early 1942: "There are three ways of settling the social question. The privileged class rules the people. The insurgent proletariat exterminates the possessing class. Or else a third formula gives each man the opportunity to develop himself according to his talents." Obviously Hitler was implying that Nazi Germany had put into practice the "third formula," for he went on: "When a man is competent, it matters little to me if he's the son of a caretaker. And, by the way, I'm not stopping the descendents of our military heroes from going once more through the same tests."[31] In these remarks and elsewhere, Hitler was careful to assert that men from prominent as well as obscure families would be able to rise as high as their abilities would carry them. Speaking to a broader audience several years earlier, he went out of his way to suggest that some members of the old upper class occupied their positions legitimately. In a public address on May 1, 1937, the new German national holiday, he reviewed the achievements of the past four years:

> We in Germany have really broken with a world of prejudices. I leave myself out of account. I, too, I am child of this people. . . . By my side stand Germans from all walks of life who today are among the leaders of the nation: Men who once were workers on the land

---

[30] Speech of early July 1944 at the Obersalzberg. The text, transcribed from a recording, is available in Hildegard von Kotze and Helmut Krausnick, eds., *"Es spricht der Führer:" 7 exemplarische Hitler-Reden* (Gütersloh, [1966?]), p. 353. Hereafter this collection of transcriptions of recorded speeches will be cited as Kotze and Krausnick. According to Domarus, II, 2113, about 200 "Mitarbeiter Speers und Fachleute aus der Rüstungsindustrie" were present for Hitler's address.

[31] Adolf Hitler, *Secret Conversations*, trans. Norman Cameron and R. H. Stevens (New York, 1961), p. 317. Hereafter this edition of Hitler's "Table Talk" will be cited as Hitler, *Secret Conversations*.

are now governing German States in the name of the Reich, former metal-workers are Governors of German shires [*Gauleiter*] and so on. It is true that men who came from the bourgeoisie and former aristocracy have their place in this Movement. But to us it matters nothing whence they come if only they can work to the profit of our people. That is the decisive test. . . . Is it not wonderful for every humble mother amongst our people and for every father to know that perhaps their boy may become anything—God knows what!— if only he has the necessary talent?[32]

In a speech containing similar passages and delivered two days earlier to a group of district party leaders (*Kreisleiter*), Hitler elaborated at length on the crisis of democracy and how it had been overcome in Germany. What had been necessary, he explained, was to attempt to obtain, through "natural selection," men from every sphere of life suited to be national leaders:

And that is also the most beautiful and in my eyes most Germanic democracy. For what can be more wonderful for a people than the conviction: "Without regard for origins or birth or anything else [like that] the most capable from our midst can move up to the highest position. He need only have the ability to do so." We are endeavoring to find able men. It is entirely irrelevant who they are, who their parents were, who their dear mothers are. If they [the able] are capable, every door stands open to them.[33]

AUTHORITARIAN FÜHRER AND ELITE

Both in theory and practice the Nazi authoritarian elite differed significantly from the patterns that we have found developing among liberals and conservatives. One of the most obvious differences was the insistence upon a supreme leader standing above the remainder of the elite or the elite proper. As expressed in what came to be known as the *Führerprinzip*, this insistence made a great leader appear far more important than he was to the other elitists whom we have studied. Although concern for a great man occupied a central place in the thought of men like Weber and Spengler, they wished to avoid what they regarded as unrealistic hopes for a situation in which a great leader would always be available. Convinced that the appearance of such a man could not be counted upon, they sought to construct systems which could function independently of him. By 1930, as we shall

[32] Baynes, I, 620–21.
[33] Speech of Apr. 29, 1937 at the Ordensburg Vogelsang, in Kotze and Krausnick, p. 140.

see, the Nazi movement was committed to the indispensability of a single leader. The Nazis extolled dependence upon Hitler. Of our elite theorists, only Nelson placed a similar emphasis upon the necessity of an authoritarian leader, but his theory of the "just" ruler was not as closely linked to Nelson's own person as the notion of the office of *Führer* was to Hitler's person. More importantly, the narrow social basis of Nelson's movement permitted his idiosyncratic logic with its immediate intellectual roots in the *Aufklärung* and German Idealism to be pursued without serious opposition. His views, restricted in their appeal mainly to small circles of students and university graduates, were elaborated in directions that brought his movement farther, in both theory and practice, from the abstract affinities that it had to the Nazi movement due to similarities in the political and social context in which Nelson had originally developed his ideas.

The failure of the Nazis to subordinate the concept of a single leader to that of an authoritarian elite was indicative of the middle-class origins of the movement. Feeding on discontent with monarchism, the concept of the supreme *Führer* developed during the early years of the party, although at first this concept did not play the prominent role that it would after the ascent of Hitler, the partial consolidation of his position before the abortive *Putsch* of 1923, and the final consolidation of his position after his release from prison in 1925. Until Hitler's victory over the forces in the party that gathered around the Strasser brothers, over the "North German" or "left-wing" Nazis, the adherents of two opposing concepts of the supreme *Führer* competed with each other in the NSDAP. In more subtle forms, this struggle was to continue after 1926 and even after 1933. Initially, Hitler identified himself with both concepts, although eventually he abandoned the one that potentially restricted his own powers. In one concept, espoused openly by Hitler in a passage in the second (1930) and subsequent editions of *Mein Kampf*, the *Führer* had unlimited authority. He appointed his immediate subordinates, who in turn appointed their subordinates. The powers of each subordinate leader were limited simply by the powers of the leader above him. Only the supreme leader was, Hitler stated evasively, "elected, *as stipulated by the* [German] *laws governing associations* [my italics], by the entire party in a general membership meeting."[34] In the phrase that I have italicized Hitler implied that the *Führer* was elected merely to avoid breaking the Reich laws governing associations; if these laws did not exist, no election would be

---

[34] *Mein Kampf*, 10. Aufl. of the Volksausgabe of the 2nd ed. (Munich, 1933), I, 378. With the exception of the English translation, this is the only edition of *Mein Kampf* that will be cited in this chapter.

necessary, for the *Führer* was simply the man who had become, and was generally recognized as, the *Führer*.[35]

Elsewhere in the second edition of *Mein Kampf*, Hitler continued, as in the first edition, to speak of "true Germanic democracy" as "the free election of the leader together with his obligation to assume full responsibility for his actions and omissions. In it [Germanic democracy] there is no majority vote on individual issues, but only the decision of one man who must answer with his fortune and life for his choice."[36] This passage, with its quaint final clause reminiscent of Max Weber's conversation with Ludendorff and similar remarks by Weber,[37] was in accordance with a widespread belief within the young Nazi movement that although the leader should have unlimited authority he should be subject to periodic reelection or removal by his followers. This more restrictive form of authoritarianism was espoused fairly consistently by the Strasser wing of the party during the mid-1920's and was one of the issues around which a vigorous factional conflict crystallized.

If Reinhard Kühnl's suggestive analysis of the Strasser wing of the party as marked by a consistent espousal of a *Mittelstand* program for the party is correct,[38] it would be logical to conclude that commitment to a restricted form of authoritarianism was more characteristic of much of the middle class than was acceptance of the unrestricted version of the *Führerprinzip* championed by Hitler during and after this factional conflict. The "little man," or member of the *Mittelstand*, tends to be attracted to the concept of a single leader, for he senses that he will seldom be able to join the elite. He would prefer to vest supreme power in the leader than in the elite as a whole; his distrust of big bosses, whether bourgeois or labor leaders (*Bonzen*), nourishes his realistic skepticism about the policies and behavior of any elite. He may prefer to entrust supreme power to a heroic, selfless individual who will check egocentrism even among the elite itself. The purity,

[35] In the first edition of *Mein Kampf* Hitler had noted matter-of-factly that "the chairman is elected." See *Mein Kampf*, trans. Ralph Manheim (Boston: Houghton Mifflin Sentry, n.d.), p. 345n. The alteration of this passage is probably the most important change made in *Mein Kampf* after the first edition. See Hermann Hammer, "Die deutschen Ausgaben von Hitlers 'Mein Kampf,'" *Vierteljahrshefte für Zeitgeschichte*, iv (1956), 165, 171.

[36] *Mein Kampf*, i, 99. In translating this passage I have found Ralph Manheim's rendition of it in the Sentry edition (p. 91) helpful, but my version differs at several critical points.

[37] See Chapter Four. In calling attention to the similarity with Weber's ideas, I am not implying that Hitler was in any way influenced directly by him.

[38] See Reinhard Kühnl, *Die nationalsozialistische Linke 1925–1930* (Meisenheim am Glan, 1966), esp. pp. 88–89.

first of the movement and then of the State, can be maintained by giving this man the authority to intervene wherever necessary. But will the great leader's own integrity endure indefinitely? The Strasser wing of the party implied that checks upon the actions of the great leader himself would be required and that he might have to be removed at some time. The opposition of the Strasser wing to a nonremovable leader seems to have reflected well-founded apprehensions on the part of the middle class about unrestricted leadership—apprehensions that were widespread even among those who subscribed to the *Führerprinzip* in one of the many versions of it then current.

How then can we explain the adoption of Hitler's view of "Germanic democracy" as the most authoritative Nazi one? There are two major reasons. First, Hitler's version was rarely offered in its more extreme forms. Even in the second edition of *Mein Kampf*, it was not, as we have seen, stated with complete candor. The second explanation is to be found in the broadening of the social sources of the Nazi movement, after 1925, again after 1928, and finally after 1933. Let us look at the second reason, and return later to the first.

One of the historical functions of monarchism, as well as of the dictatorship of a single man, has been to provide a scapegoat. If things go badly, the ruler can be blamed: let him abdicate, or if need be, behead him. The ruling class can say: "He's at fault; the social order is sound; the political system is basically good, although it may need some modifications." As the circle of the National Socialists' bourgeois backers expanded and deepened far beyond certain provincial Bavarians whose enterprises paled beside those of the great industrialists of the Ruhr and the commercial undertakings of North and Central Germany, beyond the prospect of an occasional foreign subsidy, beyond a rare Fritz Thyssen, emphasis upon an authoritarian leader subject only to vague and inconsistent checks became increasingly helpful in broadening the appeal of the party. The notion of the businessman-leader, as propagated by heavy industry in particular, also made Hitler's *Führerprinzip* serviceable, not only within the party, but also among those who, although they might never join the NSDAP, would contribute to its finances, petition the government on its behalf, and apply pressure on the other bourgeois parties to cooperate with it. By the late 1920's, as we saw in earlier chapters, critical sectors of big business were coming to the conclusion that only a dictatorial regime could push through domestic and foreign policies essential to the success of their ventures and the maintenance of capitalism in Germany. The requirements of German monopoly capital, reinforced by the traditional emphasis, especially in heavy industry, upon the authoritarian (*Herr-im-Hause*) firm directed by the family head contributed to the success of Hitler's version of democracy of personnel selection rather than decision making. Similarly, if less critically, the aristocratic segments of the ruling class found Hitler's "Germanic democracy" useful. Indeed, many a wistful monarchist, whether aristocrat or bourgeois, might harbor the sentimental dream that one day the "Drummer," as Hitler occasionally referred to himself during the early years of the Nazi movement, might relinquish his place to a monarch; of course, his bowing aside would be a voluntary act of deference unencumbered by a majority decision.

As might have been expected, even a *Führer* does not readily offer himself up as a scapegoat. The problem of the German upper class during the Nazi period was that neither the resolution nor the support to dump Hitler was forthcoming when, as in 1938 and 1944, some concluded that his removal would be advantageous. They may well have been wrong in their assessment of the situation. For many of them, Hitler's suicide under the pressure of advancing foreign armies may have turned out to be preferable to the need to find a replacement for the great "mesmerist" or an alternative to "his" system before both defeat in a devastating war and a full twelve years of misdeeds could be laid at the foot of his unmarked grave.

Perhaps the composition of the upper-class resistance circles is indicative of the extent to which the industrial and commercial bourgeoisie far more than the landed aristocracy or the core of the old officer corps had linked its fate to Hitler's *Führerprinzip.* Every major study of upper-class resistance to Hitler has confirmed that the overwhelming majority of those involved, especially in the more hazardous aspects of the conspiracies, came from the military and aristocracy. Of course, one might, modifying a familiar argument, suggest that big businessmen were not in as favorable a position to take direct action against Hitler as were officers. It might also be objected that the monopolists would always find someone else to do their dirty work for them. But both of these objections are unconvincing in the absence of substantial evidence to indicate widespread involvement by big businessmen in the search for an alternative to Hitler's leadership of the Third Reich. For example, one of the key figures in the conspiracy of the July 20, 1944, Carl Goerdeler, despite many ties to business circles, was a professional civil servant who after serving as mayor of Königsberg and Leipzig assumed the post of commissioner of price administration in the Brüning government and again in 1934–1935 under Hitler. During Goerdeler's extensive travels abroad and his discussions with foreign political and business leaders in 1937–1938, he may have served as a spokesman for some major German business leaders, but he seems to have had no clear mandate. During the war he belonged to a circle of businessmen and economists that included Spengler's old friend Paul Reusch of the *Gutehoffnungswerke* and several other leading businessmen such as Albert Vögler of United Steel. When Goerdeler was apprehended after the failure of July 20, he contended, with some success, that the other members of the so-called Reusch circle were not involved in the conspiracy and that the group had met merely to discuss technical economic questions. Although the businessmen in the circle were badly compromised by their association with Goerdeler, they were either not arrested or soon released. A Gestapo report argued that they were not true resistance fighters, and Hitler's "economic dictator" Albert Speer intervened to protect them and other businessmen with the plea that they were indispensable to the armaments industry.[39]

A discussion of the second reason for the success of Hitler's concept of the authoritarian leader, the broadening of the social basis of the Nazi movement, must deal with the limitations, in both theory and practice, to which this concept was subjected. Hitler's extreme version of it was rarely defended in public. Even in private, other ideas advanced by the Nazis frequently implied modifications of it, and it was never fully realized, either in the party before 1933 or, later, in the Third Reich itself.

Examples of several important variations of this version will serve to illustrate some of the contradictory notions identified with it. These contradictions are particularly noteworthy since all of the variations to be presented were offered by members of the Hitler wing of the party. Like other German elitists with the notable exception of men such as Spengler and Jünger, the Nazis often described measures that would potentially act as brakes upon authoritarianism.[40] In *Mein Kampf* Hitler proposed the establishment of a senate in the *völkisch* state of

---

[39] Gerhard Ritter, *Carl Goerdeler und die deutsche Widerstandsbewegung* (Munich: DTV, 1964), pp. 440–41, 519, n. 11, 534–35, n. 18; "Stellungnahme von Albert Speer für SS-Gruppenführer Hermann Fegelein, Vertreter Heinrich Himmlers im Führerhauptquartier, vom 20. August 1944 zur Beschuldung führender Monopolherren wegen ihrer Verbindung zu Verschwörerkreisen des 20. Juli 1944" in Dietrich Eichholtz and Wolfgang Schumann, eds. *Anatomie des Krieges: Neue Dokumente über die Rolle des deutschen Monopolkapitalismus bei der Vorbereitung und Durchführung des 2. Weltkrieges* (Berlin, 1969), pp. 458–59. Cf. the description of Goerdeler as the "Vertrauensmann führender Vertreter des Krupp-, des Bosch- und des Haniel-Konzerns" in Karl Drechsler, Hans Dress, and Gerhart Hass, "Europapläne des deutschen Imperialismus im 2. Weltkrieg," *Zeitschrift für Geschichtswissenschaft*, XIX (1971), 920.

[40] Of little consequence to these measures was the demagogic description of all Germans, the German *Volksgemeinschaft*, or the German racial community as an elite. The idea of belonging to a people that constituted an elite among nations performed important functions in facilitating the manipulation of even the lowliest members of this "elite," but posed no serious impediment to authoritarianism within Germany.

the future. Standing above a bicameral parliament, the senate would encourage fruitful cooperation between the two chambers. Neither the parliament nor the senate would have the power to make decisions, and no votes would ever be taken in any of the three bodies. All three would exercise simply an advisory function. Indeed, Hitler seems to have gone out of his way to note that this advisory function would be performed by their members as individuals. What then distinguished the senate from the parliament? One chamber of the parliament would be a "political chamber." This political chamber seems to have corresponded to the Reichstag, and although Hitler did not indicate how its members would be chosen, presumably they would continue to be elected by the populace. The second chamber would be an "occupational [*berufsständische*]," or corporatively constituted, body. Although Hitler did not explain how its members would be selected, they would presumably be appointed or elected by the corporative bodies that they in turn represented. Again, he failed to indicate the method by which the senate would be constituted. He implied that this "special senate" would constitute an "elite [*Auslese*]" drawn from both parliamentary bodies.[41] Throughout the passage in which he dealt with all three of these institutions, he insisted frequently upon the application of the *Persönlichkeitsprinzip*, or the need for one man to make all national decisions of consequence and for a single leader in every lesser organization to make all major decisions pertaining to it.

The notion of a senate cropped up repeatedly in Nazi speeches and writings. For example, a section of a pamphlet published by Goebbels in 1932[42] reads like a highly interpretative gloss on the senate proposed in *Mein Kampf*. Discussing the institutional changes that would occur when the Nazis came to power and initiated a "transitional period" of the dictatorship of the party, Goebbels mentioned the development of an economic parliament, which would be elected by everyone engaged in useful work on the basis of universal, equal suffrage. This parliament would be permitted to pursue only economic, not governmental policy. After the National Socialist state was secure, a senate would be set up. Goebbels discussed in detail its composition and functions: "[The senate] is composed of some 200 notable individuals, who are summoned, by the dictator, from all social strata and stations of life to direct the destiny of the state. These 200 will constitute the elite of the entire people. They [the 200] will assist the government by word and deed. They will be named for life. When one of them dies, they will select his successor." Although the senators would elect the

[41] *Mein Kampf*, II, 501–02.
[42] Joseph Goebbels, *Der Nazi-Sozi: Fragen und Antworten für den National-sozialisten*, 4. Aufl. (Munich, 1932), esp. p. 24.

chancellor, the chancellor himself would have the power to appoint his ministers and other governmental associates.[43]

In the *Mythus des 20. Jahrhunderts* (1930),[44] Alfred Rosenberg discussed an institution corresponding to the senate. In describing this institution, Rosenberg used terminology familiar to us from our examination of neoconservative elite theories. He referred to an order (*Orden*) that would be established after the "refounding" of the Reich. The members of this *Orden* would consist of every male who played a leading role in the renewal of the German nation. The criterion for selection would be "achievements in the service of the people," regardless of the sphere of activity in which these achievements had been made. The members of the *Orden*, or Council of the Order (*Ordensrat*), as Rosenberg now began to call the body, would be appointed for life by the head of state and would come from all strata of society. Comparing the *Ordensrat* to the organization of the Roman Catholic Church and the "nordic" ancient Roman Senate, Rosenberg explained that it would elect, from its ranks and by majority vote, the head of state, whether known as president, emperor, or king, who would serve a life term. In addition to the "directing" *Ordensrat*, there would, according to Rosenberg, be a parliament to advise the government. Apparently, this parliament would be elected by the chairmen or leaders of corporative bodies such as the army, peasants' associations, guilds, businessmen, universities, the state bureaucracy, and organizations of the liberal professions. Like Edgar Jung, Rosenberg derived many of his models from the Middle Ages, and among the leading Nazi theoreticians, he was one of those most concerned with permanently demobilizing the masses. Rosenberg envisioned vigorous communal elections that would contribute to the pool from which the top leaders would be chosen. These elections would be conducted on the basis of the selection of individuals, not lists or parties. The "principle of personality" would be decisive, although Rosenberg suggested that the local chapters of the German *Orden*, the guilds, and similar bodies would be able to nominate candidates. In the communal elections, women would be permitted to retain the right to vote. Rosenberg made clear that the major purpose of the institutions that he proposed was not to permit or encourage direct popular control, but rather to make possible the "unimpeded rise" of "creative individuals" whose talents would be further developed under the discipline of the *Orden*.[45]

Although during the Third Reich no senate or *Ordensrat* was estab-

[43] *Ibid.*

[44] Alfred Rosenberg, *Der Mythus des 20. Jahrhunderts: Eine Wertung der seelisch-geistigen Gestaltenkämpfe unserer Zeit*, 91.–94. Aufl. (Munich, 1936).

[45] *Ibid.*, pp. 546–48, 555–56.

lished, the notion was occasionally bandied about. For example, in a speech to high Nazi officials, *Reichsleiter* and *Gauleiter*, in August 1933, Hitler alluded to a senate that would consist of senior members of the party who had best demonstrated their loyalty and ability.[46] At the beginning of World War II, he announced a line of succession in the event that he should die. He intimated that he was planning, apparently soon, to summon a senate that would choose the most worthy successor if both Goering and Rudolf Hess, whom Hitler named as first and second in the line of succession, were dead.[47] In Hitler's "table talk" during the war, the by now elusive senate was occasionally discussed at length,[48] but no action on it ever seems to have been taken. After the Fascist Grand Council compelled Mussolini to resign in the wake of the Anglo-American invasion of Sicily in 1943, Hitler had every reason to be wary of the subject of a German senate.

It would be a mistake to dismiss as mere daydreaming Hitler's references to restrictions, however slight, upon authoritarianism. No more than his endless schemes for rebuilding Linz, the town of his boyhood—plans that have often been attributed to his personal idiosyncrasies—should these references be regarded as of little import. It would be an even graver error to view the public discussion of limits to authoritarianism as empty rhetoric, for this discussion assumed widely held reservations about the powers of any *Führer*. Of course, the devices to circumscribe his authority mentioned by the Nazis were inconsistent and conflicted with other themes of Nazi propaganda. Although these devices were characteristically opportunistic, they suggest an often overlooked possibility. To what extent was the authoritarianism of the Third Reich an unanticipated and unplanned product of the requirements of the regime to remain in power by consolidating and extending its position? Were the continuing divisions and contradictions within German society so great that in order to remain in power, the Nazis, in response to the situations they confronted, had to develop an authoritarian system that Spengler and Jünger anticipated, in detail as well as in sum, far better than any major Nazi spokesman? Indeed, did any prominent Nazi envision before 1933 the structure of the Third Reich? Given the general goals pursued by the regime and the exigencies of remaining in power, were not the National Socialists, or at least Hitler and some other high Nazis, compelled to discard, as mere daydreams of yesteryear, ideas that they had once toyed with,

[46] Speech of Aug. 6, 1933. Quoted in Domarus, i, 292.
[47] Speech to the Reichstag, Sept. 1, 1939. In Domarus, ii, 1316.
[48] See Hitler, *Secret Conversations*, pp. 369–70, 501. The last recorded mention of it seems to have been in June 1942, shortly before the "table talk" began to be recorded less frequently and, apparently, rather haphazardly.

438—Conservatives in Search of Elites

however opportunistically? Some tentative answers to these questions will emerge from the remainder of this chapter.

Although most of the restrictions upon authoritarianism discussed by the Nazis never amounted to anything, Hitler's power of decision making was in practice circumscribed. Both Trevor-Roper and Franz Neumann have explored some of the more important limitations. Trevor-Roper suggests that the primary restrictions were imposed consciously by Hitler himself: to prevent the rise of anyone to challenge his own powers, Hitler avoided clear decisions on many issues and left competing lines of authority; as a consequence, his subordinates became engaged in endless, exhausting rivalries with each other that averted the danger of a joint challenge to his authority.[49] Neumann argues that Hitler had no choice except to select from among the policies presented by competing if increasingly intertwined hierarchies, of which the most important were the leaders of big business, the high military leadership, the top echelons of the Nazi party, and the ministerial bureaucracy. "It is clear," Neumann wrote in 1944, "that only major decisions are made by Hitler, and even in those he merely expresses compromises made between different forces within the ruling class. Political decisions are made by contract. . . . It is doubtful whether Germany can be called a state. It is far more a gang, where the leaders are perpetually compelled to agree after disagreements. Indeed, innumerable agreements are made between the chiefs [below Hitler]."[50]

Although Trevor-Roper's conclusions, which have been supplemented by the bizarre, antihistorical view that Nazi Germany was in

[49] See H. R. Trevor-Roper, *The Last Days of Hitler* (New York: Berkeley paperback, [1958?]), pp. 5–6, 14–24, 32–38, and passim.

[50] Neumann, *Behemoth*, p. 522. Cf. the critique of Neumann's analysis by a prominent American elite theorist, Suzanne Keller, *Beyond the Ruling Class: Strategic Elites in Modern Society* (New York, 1963), pp. 116–18. Some penetrating criticisms of Neumann's methodology are coupled to a vigorous, but unconvincing attempt to provide an alternative in T. W. Mason, "The Primacy of Politics: Politics and Economics in National Socialist Germany" in S. J. Woolf, ed., *The Nature of Fascism* (London, [1968?]), pp. 165–95. Although based upon assumptions incompatible with those made by Neumann, Edward N. Peterson's *The Limits of Hitler's Power* (Princeton, 1969) concludes that Hitler was not involved in the formulation of most domestic policies other than setting the broad lines to be pursued in some instances. Unlike Trevor-Roper, Peterson sees Hitler's reluctance to make unequivocal decisions as a consequence of both his desire to conceal the ability of party and state bureaucracies to thwart his will and his disinterest in the details of most matters of government except the waging of war. Peterson has investigated in depth only aspects of Hitler's role in the governance of some parts of Bavaria, but relates this investigation effectively to broader issues about the Third Reich. Unfortunately, Peterson devotes little attention to economic affairs.

reality a feudal regime,[51] are useful in explaining the intended consequences of Hitler's policy of promoting friction between his subordinates, Neumann's theory explains more satisfactorily the basic limitations under which Hitler had to function as *Führer* and to which political decision making in Nazi Germany was subject. Distinguishing
threat from regret, or candid admission from subtle flattery, in Hitler's
recorded speeches and conversations may often be a futile task, but
the context usually provides abundant evidence of an awareness, at
least down to the last days of his life, of his acceptance of the circum-
scription of his powers by the basic framework of bourgeois society.
Or perhaps his famous "psychic powers" were busily at work when, in
the manner of Bismarck at the Congress of Berlin, he presented himself to the German nation in May 1933 as an "honest broker" seeking
to reconcile the divergent, but legitimate claims of conflicting interests
within Germany.[52] Despite his often extravagant rhetoric about the
disappearance of social classes and divisions under the Third Reich,[53]
he continued to refer, even in his public speeches, to the existence of
classes and other deep social and national divisions. For example, in
a speech broadcast by radio on the German Memorial Day in March
1940, he spoke as if class and status persisted in the Third Reich:
"Above and beyond all classes and estates, occupations, religions, and
every other confusion of life, the social unity of Germans without regard for status and birth asserts itself, [and this unity is] grounded in
blood, joined together by a thousand-year life, bound by destiny for
better or for worse."[54] The continuing divisions and contradictions of
German society at large, as well as the conflicts within the dominant
social groups, limited the potential range of Hitler's decisions.

Especially when speaking privately or before audiences composed
of big businessmen and other members of the ruling class, Hitler frequently called attention to the reassertion of faith in authoritarianism
that the Nazis promoted, the party's ability to mitigate social conflict,
and how the Third Reich could be created without any need to unleash
social revolution. In his speech to the *Industrieklub* in Düsseldorf in
1932, he suggested that the general acceptance of private property was

[51] An adroit attempt to present this view is Robert Koehl, "Feudal Aspects of
National Socialism," *American Political Science Review*, LIV (1960), 921–33.

[52] Speech of May 10, 1933. In Domarus, I, 267–68.

[53] See, e.g., his interview of early 1934 with the poet Hanns Johst, in which
Hitler maintained that in the National Socialist *Weltanschauung* a man was either
a "citizen" as well as a "worker," or neither a citizen nor a worker. "Gespräch mit
dem Dichter Hanns Johst über den Begriff des Bürgers" (first published on Jan.
27, 1934), now in Domarus, I, 351. See also Hitler's public proclamation of Nov.
12, 1944 (in Domarus, II, 2162), which is more cautiously worded.

[54] Speech of Mar. 10, 1940 in the Zeughaus in Berlin. In Domarus, II, 1479.

jeopardized by the revolutionary epoch that the world was experiencing; the beliefs and theories that had once aided in the acceptance of private property were being undermined. Although private property could be justified on the basis of differences in men's accomplishments, this justification was unconvincing, Hitler indicated, as long as both politics and economics were not based on the same authoritarian principles. What held for economic life must also hold for political life. Hitler implied that the mere belief in political democracy imperiled the existence of private property.[55] Somewhat later in the same speech he described the Nazi party as the only political organization in Germany that had successfully overcome democratic principles. The NSDAP was, he told his listeners, "based on the idea of the absolute authority of leadership in every area [of human existence], at every level—the only party that has remorselessly overcome, within its ranks, not only the international, but also the democratic idea, [the only party] that throughout its entire organization knows only responsibility, command, and obedience, and thus for the first time in the political life of Germany integrates an organization of millions that is grounded in the achievement principle."[56] Hitler went so far as to assert that if the Nazis did not exist there would no longer be any bourgeoisie in Germany, an assertion which, according to the official text of the address, provoked the exclamation "Very true!" from the audience.[57]

In his address to leaders of the armaments industries in 1944, he sought to present an encouraging view of the future to his audience. Seeking probably to dissipate resentment and undercut complaints about government restrictions upon business, he discussed the relationship of business activity to the state; as a general rule the state should not interfere with entrepreneural initiative and the selection of business leaders:

> And it is not the responsibility of the state to seek to prevent the
> lazy from finding a spot somewhere in a bureaucracy or the unrea-
> sonable from finding a niche in some agency and thereby regaining
> a position of leadership in business. Rather [the responsibility of the
> state is] only to be concerned with the ruthless elimination of the
> lazy, the incapable, and the less gifted, and their replacement by the
> gifted. The state has, then, only the task of calling upon the most
> gifted of the gifted men who are manifestly brought to the top by
> the natural economic process. [The state calls upon the most gifted
> of these men] in order to exercise leadership together with them,

[55] Speech of Jan. 27, 1932. In Domarus, I, 72–73.
[56] Domarus, I, 87.   [57] *Ibid.*

that is, to provide the stimuli, the orders [*Aufträge*], and, let us say, the changes in economic life that are necessary from the point of view of the state.[58]

If Germany won the war, Hitler said later in the same speech, "private initiative" would experience "its greatest flowering" in German history:

> There will be so much to do then [after the war]! Just don't think that I shall set up a couple of state construction offices or a couple of state economic offices. We shan't do that. . . . When the great era of the German peacetime economy resumes, I shall only be interested in letting the greatest geniuses of German business go to work. Of course I shall always be concerned that this [referent unclear] is not turned against the interests of the nation, but you have already perceived, gentlemen, that the interests of the whole are easily reconciled with the interests of the individual and that in the long run the interests of the individual can only be realized if they are not pursued to the detriment of the whole.[59]

Hitler presented in several forms the theme of the renewal of Germany and the formation of a new elite as having been possible without disorder or the destruction of the old upper class. At the Nürnberg Party Congress in 1937, he observed, somewhat vaguely, that the "development of a new elite [*Führungsauslese*] for our nation without the wasteful, chaotic destruction of existing conditions is one of the greatest deeds in the history of our people."[60] He was more explicit in a radio address during the war, and perhaps in view of the military reverses suffered by Germany and its allies he felt the need to emphasize the "socialist" aspects of the National Socialist "revolution." Claiming that over 60 per cent of the young officers in the armed forces "come from the lower ranks, therefore forming a bridge to hundreds of thousands of workers and members of the lower middle class [*des kleinen Mittelstandes*]," Hitler predicted: "Someday it will be described as one of the greatest achievements of history that in this way [such as through promotions from the ranks] it has been possible to introduce and carry through, in this great state, a socialist revolution which, without imposing any limitations on the creative powers of old social groups [*der alten Stände*], has nevertheless achieved full equality for all."[61]

[58] Speech to Leitern der Rüstungsindustrie, auf dem Obersalzberg, in early July 1944. In Kotze and Krausnick, p. 341.
[59] *Ibid.*, p. 352.
[60] Speech of Sept. 7, 1937. In Domarus, ɪ, 716.
[61] Speech from the Wolfschanze, Jan. 30, 1944. In Domarus, ɪɪ, 2085.

Even more revealing are some of Hitler's private remarks "at table." In early 1942 he explained how national socialism had "a calming effect" and reconciled men with one another; it "introduced into daily life the idea that one should choose an occupation because one is predisposed to it by his aptitudes, not because he is predestined for it by birth." A bit earlier in the same conversation Hitler had mused upon what might happen if the British Fascists under Sir Oswald Mosley were set free and how they could deal with "certain social problems which are ripe to be settled." With Germany's experiences of the past decade seemingly in mind, Hitler went on: "At present these problems can still be solved from above, in a reasonable manner. I tremble for them [the English] if they don't do it now. For if it's left to the people to take the initiative the road is open to madness and destruction. Men like Mosley would have had no difficulty in solving the problem, by finding a compromise between Conservatism and Socialism, by opening the road to the masses without depriving the elite of their rights."[62]

Yet even in private and before the assassination attempt of July 20, 1944, Hitler expressed much impatience with this old elite in Germany. Aristocrats he often found particularly exasperating. Contemptuous of the Italian court and high nobility, which he described as "fossilized" and an "aristocratic mafia," he sympathetically portrayed his friend Mussolini as hampered severely by these "cretins." Mussolini would not be able to ensure that a true elite occupied the most important positions in Italy until he got rid of them. Hitler expressed gratitude that the Social Democrats had swept away the German counterparts to the Italian fossils, although he implied that some remnants remained even in Germany.[63]

GERMANY'S BOURGEOIS REVOLUTION?

The animosity in many Nazi circles toward the aristocracy in particular, and more generally toward the old upper class, became especially marked toward the end of the war. Relating this attitude to the persistent theme of establishing an open elite during the Third Reich suggests the usefulness of Ralf Dahrendorf's thesis about the historical function of the Nazi regime. Dahrendorf argues that in order to remain in power and effect an aspiration to achieve total domination of Germany the Nazis had to foster modernization. Institutions that had impeded the development of liberalism and capitalism provided sources of resistance to the objective of total domination. Since the

[62] Hitler, *Secret Conversations*, pp. 255–56.
[63] *Ibid.*, pp. 266–68, 303.

Nazis, before coming to power, had seemed to be committed to a re-assertion of values derived from the German past, "the social revolution effected by National Socialism was an unintended, if inevitable result of its rule."[64]

Several untenable components of Dahrendorf's provocative thesis should be noted. His suggestion that "the entire cloudy National Socialist ideology seem[ed] to demand the recovery of values from the past" is erroneous on two counts. First, and this is admittedly a matter in part of terminology, it is doubtful, as we saw earlier, whether we can legitimately refer to a Nazi "ideology"; hedging by using the adjective "cloudy" makes little sense. Second, and much more importantly, we have found that both before and after 1933 Nazi propaganda and theories were not consistently oriented toward the past. Indeed, the very principle that Dahrendorf describes as the epitome of modernity, "autonomous equality of opportunity for all men,"[65] was, despite often "cloudy" racist restrictions, a constant Nazi theme. Dahrendorf seems to have overlooked the invocation by the Nazis of the concept of an open elite; perhaps the secondary emphasis upon authoritarianism by the Nazis misleads him into assuming that their elitism, like their hostility to the emancipation of women and many other Nazi notions oriented toward the past, called simply for turning back the clock. Also, as we shall see later, the demand for an authoritarian elite may be very much a part of modernity under the institutions of monopoly capitalism.

But Dahrendorf's basic point is well taken. The thrust of German policy under the Third Reich and the consequences of Nazi practices were to destroy impediments to the development of German capitalism and to promote the modernization of German society. Through an examination of the relationship between Nazi practices and the establishment of an open-yet-authoritarian elite, we shall explore the ramifications of the central proposition in Dahrendorf's thesis.

At the outset this proposition must be subjected to an important qualification. Even the cumulative effects of Nazi rule did not add up to a "social revolution," as Dahrendorf believes. Many of these effects accelerated the development of previous social tendencies, but did not bring about a radical transformation of German society. The requirements of remaining in power dictated that measures bearing on the creation of democracy of personnel selection be undertaken without promoting revolutionary changes and indeed that these measures be

[64] Ralf Dahrendorf, *Society and Democracy in Germany* (Garden City, N.Y.: Anchor, 1969), p. 382. See also Dahrendorf's essay "Demokratie und Sozialstruktur in Deutschland" in his *Gesellschaft und Freiheit: Zur soziologischen Analyse der Gegenwart* (Munich, 1962).

[65] Dahrendorf, *Society and Democracy in Germany*, p. 381. See also p. 31.

designed to modernize German institutions in such a way that an attractive façade of radical departures from the past was erected.

The great fanfare with which measures promoting an open elite were introduced and touted may indicate that they were often intended to reduce and thwart the revolutionary potential of the working, as well as the middle class. By suggesting the fulfillment of some of the radical aspirations of both groups, while denying more revolutionary urges, these measures may have contributed to the stability of German society and strengthened its resistance to revolution after World War II.

When we examine the substance behind Nazi rhetoric about instituting "careers open to talents" and democracy of personnel selection, we must keep in mind that many of the specific procedures undertaken had both a negative as well as a positive effect. Most of them can be considered under three headings: consequences of the struggle against domestic political opponents; consequences of racist practices, especially anti-Semitic measures; consequences of rearmament, the expansion of military forces, and the development of a continental German empire during World War II.

New opportunities appeared to open up especially for some men from the middle class. Of course, in comparison to those available to the big bourgeoisie, these opportunities may seem in retrospect less impressive, but they are difficult to belittle. Indeed, their importance was increased by the tremendous setback suffered by the middle class during the early years of the Nazi regime due to the defeat of corporatism.[66] Insofar as actions favoring increased social mobility, careers open to talent, and democracy of personnel selection offered tangible material and intangible psychological rewards to members of the middle class, these actions may well have been instituted or intensified in order to provide compensations for the failure to develop a corporate state, a failure that resulted from the opposition of big business. The significance of this failure can scarcely be underestimated: the very social strata that had provided much of the party hierarchy, its mass basis, and its chief source of electoral support found their characteristic version of the National Socialist "revolution" thwarted and "betrayed." The purging or departure, first of political opponents and then of "Jews," from political offices, from the state administration, the universities, the liberal professions, and business produced many va-

[66] See esp. chs. 1–3 ("Failure of Artisan Socialism," "Defeat of the Artisan Economy," "End of Middle-Class Socialism") in Arthur Schweitzer, *Big Business in the Third Reich* (Bloomington, Ind., 1964). See also Neumann, *Behemoth*, pp. 228–34, 270–75, and passim; Herman Lebovics, *Social Conservatism and the Middle Classes in Germany, 1914–1933* (Princeton, 1969), pp. 206–19.

cancies that fostered the notion of a vast increase in opportunities, especially for the middle class.

Although problematical in view of the methods and material employed, studies of the Nazi political elite are adequate to permit the conclusion that especially in the SS and in state and party administrative offices a substantial influx of men from the middle class occurred.[67] Of course, even after the assassination attempt of July 20, 1944, the higher positions in the old foreign office and some other state agencies continued to be staffed largely by men of social origins similar to those of the incumbents under the Weimar Republic, but in general the middle class made substantial inroads into types of offices that had seldom been available to its members previously. At least during the early years of the Nazi regime, the best opportunities for the sudden ascent of men from the lower classes probably occurred in the administrative apparatus of the party and its organizations and, to a lesser extent, in the state bureaucracy.[68] Within the party and its organizations, the SS provided exceptionally rapid advancement for younger men who were not *alte Kämpfer*, or early party members, but even in the SS almost all of the top leadership consisted of veteran party members.[69]

During the early years of the Nazi regime, Germany underwent what Himmler dubbed a "silent revolution." The leaders of the SS undertook a conscious infiltration of conservative, upperclass circles. At the same time, an influx into the SS of upperclass men, including many nobles, occurred. Both of these processes enhanced the status of the SS, especially of its top leadership, but almost invariably the upper-class entrants, many of whom may have been seeking to influence or even capture the SS for the objectives of their own class, were not able to rise into the highest positions in the SS.[70] Thus the substantial gains in status and power obtained by the older members of the SS were not offset. Rather, the influx of prestigious individuals worked somewhat one sidedly in favor of the largely plebeian leadership of the

[67] See Karl Dietrich Bracher, *Die deutsche Diktatur: Entstehung, Struktur, Folgen des Nationalsozialismus* (Cologne, 1969), pp. 299–303. Bracher's discussion relies heavily upon Daniel Lerner, *The Nazi Elite*, Hoover Institute Studies, Series B: Elite Studies, No. 3 (Stanford, 1951), which is now reprinted in Harold D. Lasswell and Daniel Lerner, eds., *World Revolutionary Elites: Studies in Coercive Ideological Movements* (Cambridge, Mass., [1965?]). See also Wolfgang Zapf, *Wandlungen der deutschen Elite: Ein Zirkulationsmodell deutscher Führungsgruppen 1919–1961* (Munich, [1965?]).

[68] On the state bureaucracy see Hans Mommsen, *Beamtentum im 3. Reich: Mit ausgewählten Quellen zur nationalsozialistischen Beamtenpolitik* (Stuttgart, 1966); Schoenbaum, *Hitler's Social Revolution*, pp. 243–44.

[69] See Neusüss-Hunkel, *Die SS*, pp. 16, 22–23.

[70] See *ibid.*, pp. 15–17; Heinz Höhne, *Der Orden unter dem Totenkopf: Die Geschichte der SS* (Gütersloh, 1967), pp. 125–33.

SS. Only, as we shall see later, in the continuation and expansion of the group of associate members (*Fördererkreis*) and the Friends of the SS (*Freundeskreis-SS*), both of which antedated 1933, was the relationship between the SS and the upper class rather different and largely reciprocal.

The territorial expansion of the Reich after 1937 and the administration of areas occupied by Germany during World War II increased greatly the availability of higher administrative offices, both private and public. We can infer that many of these positions, in organizations such as the SS and Rosenberg's Eastern Ministry, were obtained by members of the middle class. The proliferation of the administrative apparatus made for many new "careers open to talents"; this proliferation occurred at a time when the segments of the middle class involved in small and medium-sized business found opportunities contracting. Wartime economic policies had a detrimental effect upon many of the business activities of these segments of the *Mittelstand*,[71] and thus partly offset the gains in the administrative openings.

In the military forces, vigorous efforts were undertaken to promote what Franz Neumann, referring generally to German society under the Third Reich, calls "pseudoegalitarianism." Many of these efforts in the army and elsewhere can appropriately be regarded as pseudo-egalitarian, although they might more properly be described, in the words of the American radio correspondent William L. Shirer, as fostering a "spirit of camaraderie."[72] This camaraderie, which may often have been inordinately impressive to foreign journalists who arrived with archaic notions about Prusso-German military organization, entailed deemphasis upon the externals of rank, equalization of food rations, relaxation of traditional military discipline, and encouragement of personal relationships between officers and men. In view of the un-

[71] On the largely neglected topic of the fate of small and medium-sized business during the war see A.R.L. Gurland, Otto Kirchheimer, and Franz Neumann, *The Fate of Small Business in Nazi Germany* (Washington, D.C., 1943). (This pamphlet was issued by the U.S. Senate Special Committee to Study the Problems of American Small Business.) Other useful suggestions and pertinent material can be found in the "Kilgore Hearings" (U.S. Senate. Committee on Military Affairs, *Hearings on the Elimination of German Resources for War* [Washington, D.C., 1945–1946], esp. p. 165); Neumann, *Behemoth*, esp. pp. 282–84, 626–27; Heinz Boberach, ed., *Meldungen aus dem Reich: Auswahl aus den geheimen Lageberichten des Sicherheitsdienstes der SS 1939–1944* (Munich: DTV, 1968), esp. p. 311; Richard Grunberger, *The 12-Year Reich: A Social History of Nazi Germany, 1933–1945* (New York, 1971), pp. 167–81, 337. Although also bringing together a wealth of other information that might be employed to illustrate my basic theses on elitism in Germany, Grunberger's book is disappointing. Episodic and anecdotal, it fails to refine its generally meager conclusions.

[72] William L. Shirer, *Berlin Diary: The Journal of a Foreign Correspondent, 1934–1941* (New York, 1941), pp. 267, 440.

concealed racist structure of the military forces of some of Germany's international competitors such as the United States, much of the camaraderie and pseudoegalitarianism in the German military service may often have appeared boldly innovative. Some of the overt restrictions upon the new spirit, such as Hitler's decree during the later stages of the war excluding Jewish *Mischlinge* from consideration in the awarding of the Reich's highest medals, did not seriously affect this spirit, and there have apparently been no studies to determine whether the decree was implemented or how consistently it was followed.

The camaraderie and pseudoegalitarianism appear more significant when they are related to procedures for the selection and promotion of officers. As in many other facets of German life, an important social change occurred. With rare exceptions, such as the "Noske officers" after World War I, the officer corps had been drawn almost exclusively from the ranks of the upper class and the uppermost strata of the middle class. Although the stereotypical officer in the army was a nobleman, the effective cutoff point in recruitment ran through the middle class itself, as symbolized by the privileges accorded the one-year volunteer under the Second Empire. Largely a function of social status and intraclass position, education provided a criterion for a bourgeois to be admitted for consideration as an officer's candidate, as did social acceptability as measured by the father's occupation. During World War I, the device of the *Offiziersstellvertreter* was employed to maintain the barrier within the middle class. During another great expansion in the size of the army, beginning with German rearmament in the early years of the Third Reich and culminating in the creation of a force of some 12 million men under arms, this social barrier was relocated or partly removed. It no longer ran clearly through German society, and even as it had been pushed downward, it no longer appeared so distinctly as formerly. The exigencies of total war, social pressures from the lower classes, and the absence of sufficient numbers of officer candidates from the upper and upper middle class acted to enhance greatly the prospects for the lower strata of the middle class in the officer corps of the army. When Hitler introduced universal military service in 1935, he did not reestablish the institution of the "one-year volunteer."[73] As the army expanded, elaborate procedures were developed to select new junior officers. German psychologists worked out extensive batteries of tests designed to reveal capable candidates. Some of the situational tests were similar to, if not models for, those

[73] Hans Speier, "Ludendorff" in E. M. Earle, ed., *Makers of Modern Strategy: Military Thought from Machiavelli to Hitler* (New York: Atheneum paperback, 1966), p. 319.

subsequently employed in the selection of members of the United States Office of Strategic Services (OSS).[74] Whatever the abstract validity of the new screening methods used also by other armies during World War II, the German tests both accompanied and promoted the notion that the German army had now become for the first time in history an organization open to talents regardless of social origins. Since the German navy had, from its rise in the late nineteenth century, a substantial proportion of middle-class officers,[75] and since the expansion of the navy during the Third Reich was considerably smaller than that of the army, the alterations in the social composition of the naval officer corps were less dramatic.

Among the most heralded measures associated with the creation of an open elite in Nazi Germany was the founding of special boarding schools. In practice, these schools served to increase opportunities mainly for the same strata that benefited from changes in the recruitment of the officer corps. For the offspring of the upper class, these schools could scarcely have provided avenues of ascent; at best, the schools may have occasionally helped to maintain status by giving evidence of personal and family identification with the new political regime. Although in some of the schools a significant proportion of the students came from upper-class backgrounds, most came from the middle class.

Both during the Nazi regime and subsequently, the National Socialist boarding schools have been depicted as part of a comprehensive educational structure designed to produce a new elite. Thus the Napolas (*National-politische Erziehungsanstalten*, or National Political Training Institutes), attended by children ten to eighteen years of age, and the Adolf Hitler Schools (*Adolf-Hitler-Schulen*), attended by children twelve to eighteen, are depicted as the first rung on the ladder of ascent. The Castles of the Order (*Ordensburgen*) are described as the second rung, mounted by young adults after the completion of an intervening period with the military or with the labor service, and the projected High Party-School (*Hohe Schule der Partei*) is regarded as the uncompleted third and final rung. As a recent study of one of these types of schools suggests, there is no conclusive evidence to demonstrate that the four types of schools were designed to form an ascending hierarchy or were part of an overall plan.[76] Originating as parts of

[74] On the testomania in the German army see H. L. Ansbacher, "German Military Psychology," *Psychological Bulletin*, xxxviii (1941), 370–92.

[75] See Wahrhold Drascher, "Zur Soziologie des deutschen Seeoffizierkorps," *Wehrwissenschaftliche Rundschau*, xii (1962), 559–61.

[76] See Harald Scholtz, "Die 'NS-Ordensburgen,'" *Vierteljahrshefte für Zeitgeschichte*, xv (1967), esp. 268–69, 296–97.

the bureaucratic domains of high Nazi leaders who were engaged in bitter rivalries with each other, the schools tended to overlap, as did most obviously the Napolas and the Adolf Hitler Schools. Struggles for control of the schools impeded the thorough development of any one type and prevented the creation of a comprehensive party educational system.

Often neglected in references to a Nazi system of special education designed to produce an elite is the National Socialist German Secondary School (*Nationalsozialistische Deutsche Oberschule*) in Feldafing, Bavaria. Located some eighteen miles from Munich near the resort area on the *Starnberger See*, Feldafing, as this school commonly came to be known, seems to have suffered from its initial association with the SA (*Sturmabteilung*) and the ill-fated Ernst Röhm. Producing few graduates and favoring for entry the sons of old party members, Feldafing probably merits the obscurity into which it has fallen.[77]

The creation of the *Hohe Schule*, one of Alfred Rosenberg's pet projects, although perhaps originally proposed by Robert Ley, the leader of the German Labor Front, was authorized by Hitler in 1940, but conflicts among leading Nazis blocked its founding. Rosenberg succeeded in creating merely one section of the *Hohe Schule*, his Institute for the Study of the Jewish Question, and even this institute met with opposition in high party circles that eventually crippled its operations.[78]

The Napolas were founded in 1933.[79] Of all of the new Nazi schools they were probably the most attractive to traditionally oriented members of the upper class. Since three old Prussian cadet schools were converted into Napolas and the regimen was similar to that of the traditional cadet schools, the Napolas may appear representative of the meeting of the new and the old in the Third Reich as symbolized by the photographs of Hitler bowing deferentially before the aged Field Marshal and President Hindenburg in full military uniform during the ceremonies in the Garrison Church in Potsdam marking the opening of the Reichstag on March 21, 1933. The Napolas, numbering eventually over thirty, trained prospective officers for the SA, SS, police, Labor Service, and especially the army. With the acceleration of rearmament and the approach of World War II, the primary function became analogous to that of the old cadet schools, as the Napolas

[77] On Feldafing see Schoenbaum, *Hitler's Social Revolution*, pp. 278–79.

[78] On the *Hohe Schule* see Poliakov and Wulf, *Das Dritte Reich und seine Denker*, ch. 3; Reinhard Bollmus, *Das Amt Rosenberg und seine Gegner: Studien zum Machtkampf im nationalsozialistischen Herrschaftssystem* (Stuttgart, 1970), esp. pp. 134, 153.

[79] On the Napolas see Horst Ueberhorst, ed., *Elite für die Diktatur: Die Nationalpolitischen Erziehungsanstalten 1933–1945. Ein Dokumentarbericht* (Düsseldorf, 1969).

helped to meet the greatly increased demand for military officers. Although commanded by a high SS officer and run by SS and SA men, the Napolas were under the administrative control of the Reich Ministry of Education, and the curriculum was similar to that of other German secondary schools. Elementary school teachers throughout Germany could recommend candidates, who were supposed to belong to the Hitler Youth, as well as demonstrate prowess in sports, good health, and Aryan descent. The district party leader had to provide a recommendation. Since the Napolas were not tuition-free, there was a built-in tendency to prevent or render difficult the entry of lower-class children.[80] The costs were staggered partly in accordance with the ability of the parents to pay, but the minimum annual payment seems to have been 200 marks.[81]

Begun in 1937, the rival Adolf Hitler Schools were free. Much emphasis was placed upon their "Socialist" character; they were to be available to boys from any level of society. A notable step in the direction of equality was taken when applicants of illegitimate birth were explicitly placed on the same level as those of legitimate birth,[82] a stipulation that may not have applied previously to other special Nazi schools. The candidate's racial characteristics were presumably to be decisive. In practice a simple device helped to discourage applicants from the lower classes. In lieu of payments to the school, parents were "permitted" to contribute to a specially established "Adolf Hitler Fund." The overwhelming majority of the pupils came from the middle class, including a sizable proportion of youths from the more affluent and secure segments of the middle class. Higher party officials seem to have preferred to send their children to Adolf Hitler Schools rather than to Napolas.[83]

The founding and development of the Adolf Hitler Schools reflected the limited prestige of the Napolas. Robert Ley, the leader of the German Labor Front, and Baldur von Schirach, the leader of the Hitler Youth, cooperated in the early development of the Hitler Schools, thereby winning a substantial, but never fully consolidated victory over Bernhard Rust and the Reich Ministry of Education. Under the immediate control of the leadership of the Nazi youth organization,

---

[80] See the data on the occupations of the fathers of Napola pupils in 1940 in R. H. Samuel and R. Hinton Thomas, *Education and Society in Modern Germany* (London, 1949), pp. 52–53, n. 1.

[81] See Rolf Eilers, *Die nationalsozialistische Schulpolitik: Eine Studie zur Funktion der Erziehung im totalitären Staat* (Cologne and Opladen, 1963), p. 45.

[82] See Schoenbaum, *Hitler's Social Revolution*, p. 280.

[83] See Dietrich Orlow, "Die Adolf-Hitler-Schulen," *Vierteljahrshefte für Zeitgeschichte*, XIII (1965), 274–75, 277; Samuel and Thomas, *Education and Society in Modern Germany*, pp. 52–53, n. 1.

the Hitler Schools were clearly identified with the party and independent of state supervision of schools and the Ministry of Education. The methods of choosing candidates for the Hitler Schools were similar to those employed for the Napolas except that the German Youth organization played a direct role, and the Ministry of Education no role, in the selection. A Hitler School was supposed to be established eventually in every district (*Gau*); by 1943 only ten had been opened.[84] According to a quota system laid down for each *Gau* in 1937, about 300 pupils were to be accepted annually.[85]

Of the special Nazi schools, the *Ordensburgen* were probably the only ones that included a sizable proportion of students from the lower strata of the *Mittelstand*, as well as a significant if small proportion from the working class.[86] The *Ordensburgen* were designed for young adult males, most of whom were required to be married. The monthly support payments for dependents of the students, or cadets (*Junker*), were so low that many young men accustomed to middle-class living standards shied away from the *Ordensburgen*, while the entire institution seems to have been unattractive to the wealthy, who would have found the support payments unnecessary anyway.

Apparently the *Ordensburgen* as originally conceived in 1933 were intended to serve primarily as centers for the training of functionaries for the Labor Service and Labor Front. By 1937 Ley, his associates, and some of his allies sought to gain acceptance of them as part of a comprehensive educational system for developing a new elite. Ley and his co-workers often claimed that the *Ordensburgen* would supply the elite of the future. In the published text of a speech to a group of applicants in the mid-1930's he asserted that the *Ordensburgen* would "open the door to the highest positions in the party and the state. The humblest son of the people . . . has the possibility of reaching the most important posts in the party, the state, and every organization."[87] Lured by such promises, the students often seem to have expected that they would be able to advance rapidly after completing their three years in the *Ordensburgen*. According to Ley's plan, each student was to move occasionally from one *Ordensburg* to another during the three years, somewhat as German university students customarily attended

[84] Samuel and Thomas, *Education and Society in Modern Germany*, p. 52.
[85] Orlow, "Die Adolf-Hitler-Schulen," p. 275. Cf. Schoenbaum, *Hitler's Social Revolution*, p. 280, where the figure is given as 600.
[86] See Scholtz, "Die 'NS-Ordensburgen,'" pp. 278, 287; Schoenbaum, *Hitler's Social Revolution*, pp. 282–83. This statement is an inference from the somewhat meager information on the social composition of the student body of the *Ordensburgen* contained in these two studies. My discussion of the *Ordensburgen* is based largely on Scholtz's discriminating article.
[87] Quoted in Scholtz, "Die 'NS-Ordensburgen,'" p. 290.

several universities before completing their studies. The last year was to be spent in Marienburg, West Prussia, the seat of the Teutonic Knights during the Middle Ages. Only three *Ordensburgen* were actually built: Krössinsee in Pomerania; Vogelsang in the Rhineland; and Sonthofen in the Bavarian Alps. Ley hoped to admit a thousand students every year, but this objective was never achieved.

The pressures of war and, more important, rivalries with other Nazi organizations prevented the realization of Ley's grand scheme. Some academicians seem to have feared that the *Ordensburgen* would compete with or even supplant the universities. Both the National Socialist Student Association and a prominent professor of pedagogy, Ernst Krieck, criticized the *Ordensburgen*. Rosenberg, formerly one of Ley's allies, but unsuccessful in bringing into being most of his own educational projects, opposed Ley's plans, and without the fanfare and publicity that accompanied most of the new training institutions of the Third Reich, Himmler worked with increasing success after 1937 to establish still another system of education for potential members of the new elite.

With the exception of the system developed in the SS, all of the many attempts during the Third Reich to establish training centers for an elite fell prey to a similar unresolved contradiction. Even the SS system did not, as we shall see shortly, avoid a second contradiction. The first contradiction plagued all of the special new schools from their beginnings. On the one hand, the founders and administrators of each type of school claimed that their type of school was designed to produce a new elite or replacements for the Nazi elite and differed radically from other educational institutions. On the other hand, the training differed little from that provided by the other educational institutions; the new elite schools turned out men who became lower ranking civil or military administrators—or often simply common soldiers—all of whom had been equipped to act, not as formulators, but rather as blind executors of policy. For example, in the Adolf Hitler Schools, poetry depicting heroic soldierly death constituted a substantial part of the required reading.[88] The curricula of the elite schools tended to downgrade purely "intellectual" achievements and emphasize physical training, but the indoctrination was similar to that in other schools. To be sure, one reason for the founding of some of the schools was to provide a more extensive and militant indoctrination in "the Nazi *Weltanschauung*" than was possible in the state schools due to impediments such as those posed by the Concordat of 1933 with the Vatican.[89] The elite schools provided little specialized technical training that would

[88] Orlow, "Die Adolf-Hitler-Schulen," p. 281.
[89] See *ibid.*, p. 273.

set their graduates apart from the mass of the populace. That preparatory training for fields such as military aviation was available at some of the elite schools—hardly an esoteric skill by the late 1930's—does not undercut this generalization.

Was there to be a single ethos and *Weltanschauung* for all Germans, or would the elite have a special ethos of its own? Here was a basic issue that the elite schools never came to grips with, as, similarly, German elitists before 1933 had tended to leave the question unresolved. Only a few, like Ernst Jünger, had, following Nietzsche's lead, tackled the problem head on, and even Jünger became, as we have seen, entangled in ambiguities. Publicly, Nazi spokesmen usually denied that the elite had or should have a special ethos, but privately they seem occasionally to have taken the opposite position.

Of innumerable possible examples of this inconsistency, two might be cited. Privately Hitler told Rauschning in 1932:

> There must be only one possible education for each class, for each subdivision of a class. Complete freedom of choice in education is the privilege of the *élite* and of those whom they have specially admitted. . . . Knowledge is an aid to life, not its central aim. We must therefore be consistent, and allow the great mass of the lowest order the blessings of illiteracy. We ourselves, on the other hand, shall shake off all humane and scientific prejudices. This is why, in the *Junker* schools I shall found for the future members of our *Herren*-class, I shall allow the gospel of the free man to be preached—the man who is master of life and death, of human fear and superstition, who has learnt to control his body, his muscles and nerves, but remains at the same time impervious to the temptations of the mind and of sciences presumably free.[90]

Although shortly before making this statement Hitler had been speaking of Eastern Europe and had described it as the area in which the new order would first emerge clearly, he certainly had the entire Reich of the future in mind when he came to discuss education. The divisions that he established are not simply those between German and Slav, despite the resemblance of the passage both to many of his anti-Slav remarks at table during the war and to some of Himmler's wartime decrees for the East.

A striking contrast to Hitler's statement to Rauschning is provided by a passage in an address to the Reichstag in early 1939. In this speech, Hitler inveighed against any special elite ethos: "The present German people's state sanctions no social advantages [for any group].

[90] Quoted in Hermann Rauschning, *The Voice of Destruction* (New York, 1940), pp. 42–43.

It therefore recognizes no special social ethic [for any group]. It recognizes only laws and necessities of life derived from reason and human perception."[91]

The contradiction between elite and mass education under the Third Reich was aggravated by social and political institutions. Insofar as the *Führerprinzip* corresponded to reality in Nazi Germany, it described a situation in which the existence of an office of supreme *Führer* and its occupation by Hitler militated against the creation of an elite ethos. The highest office in the Reich was, for the indefinite future, occupied, and Nazi schemes for elite training were in effect required to produce, even on what were presumably the upper levels of the leadership hierarchy, executors of one man's will. Thus in a speech at Vogelsang, Hitler raised the question of whether there were any limits to discipline and obedience, and went on to reply in the negative by mentioning historical examples: "What would happen to an army that operated in these matters [of discipline and obedience] with the concept of limitations—if only because a Napoleon once lived and might live again."[92] Similarly, in his Reichstag address at the beginning of the war, Hitler noted that even if he died the Germans were obligated to behave with the same "blind loyalty and obedience" toward his successor that he now demanded toward himself.[93]

In his speech at Vogelsang, Hitler spoke about another consideration that he, the men involved in the development of the elite schools, and other prominent Nazis often raised: the belief that the National Socialist party's long struggle to power, commonly referred to as the *Kampfzeit*, had produced a "natural" elite through a process of selection in the arduous and dangerous battle against "the system."[94] The process of selection, he observed almost wistfully, had become more difficult since the assumption of power. As he explained in an earlier speech, the Nazis must accomplish through their own efforts, "durch eigene Harte," the task of selection, in which they had formerly been aided by battles with their domestic opponents.[95] Although these and similar references to the trials of the *Kampfzeit* served both to legitimize the new regime by portraying it as led by men who had endured the most rigorous tests and to flatter the old party members by romanticizing their now legendary response to the challenges of a bygone era, the point of view reflected in Hitler's statements complicated the tasks of educating an elite. The mechanisms of selection operative during the

[91] Speech of Jan. 30, 1939. In Domarus, II, 1051.
[92] Speech to Kreisleiter at the Ordensburg Vogelsang, Apr. 29, 1937. In Kotze and Krausnick, p. 146.
[93] Speech of Sept. 1, 1939. In Domarus, II, 1316.
[94] Kotze and Krausnick, p. 141.
[95] Hitler, *Führung und Gefolgschaft*, p. 59.

Kampfzeit could not be duplicated; references to replicating, if only in part, "the years of struggle" provided a rationalization for a system which, rather than producing independent leaders, turned out pliable and dedicated followers by submitting the students at the elite schools to a regimen resembling fraternity hazing more than a reenactment of the earlier history of the party.

The educational system developed by the SS managed to avoid many of the problems encountered by the other elite schools.[96] Emphasizing the preparation of men for specific tasks by having them participate in the regular activities of the SS, this system, especially after its enormous expansion beginning in the late 1930's, consisted of a progression of internships that involved the young man with the day-to-day operations of the SS in various types of tasks and at different levels of authority. Himmler's system imparted the rising SS man with the sense of acting according to a special ethos, but there was little pretense of making him into anything more than an obedient and skillful executor of the decisions of the supreme *Führer*. The uncertainty faced by the graduate of the other elite schools as to his next occupation and subsequent status scarcely existed for the SS man who, after passing through an SS cadet school and various branches of the SS, including a probationary period on the staff of a concentration camp, received a commission as an officer in the SS. Although never fully developed, an institution that was less threatening than the *Ordensburgen* toward the existing universities was projected. Special residence halls for the SS were erected in university towns. Enabling SS men to study at the universities was one of the consequences of Himmler's plan to provide the German Foreign Office with fifty SS second lieutenants (*Untersturmführer*) every year. By the time an SS officer reached his thirtieth birthday, he was to make the final decision about the branch of the SS to which he would devote the remainder of his life.

Yet the contrast between the SS training system and the elite schools should not be drawn too starkly. The SS system never operated as tidily as the preceding description may suggest. Like the other elite schools, it developed in response to an ever-changing situation and in conflict with alternatives which, while making many aspects of it distinctive, tended to blur other differences. Also, the SS itself was involved increasingly in the elite schools. In the late 1930's the Napolas seem to have become increasingly supplements to the SS's own cadet schools at Brunswick and Bad Tölz.

More important than these qualifications is another point. Neither the SS training system nor the elite schools could produce a political

---

[96] My discussion of the SS training system is greatly indebted to Scholtz, "Die 'NS-Ordensburgen,'" pp. 297–98.

elite as long as the Nazi party remained a coordinate power in German society, as long as the structure of bourgeois society in Germany remained intact. At most, the Nazis could provide some replacements for members of the ruling class that existed when Hitler became chancellor. The primary function of Nazi elite training was by necessity limited to producing reliable instruments to carry out policies formulated through the interplay between top Nazi leaders and the old ruling class. As we shall see, the merger of the two was well underway by the last years of the Third Reich; participation in the activities of big business provided a surer avenue to entry into the elite than the establishment of elite training schools.

In 1942 Franz Neumann described the Continental Oil Corporation as a possible "model for the new ruling class" in Germany.[97] This corporation was a holding company for oil interests outside Germany that were acquired or appropriated by German interests. The promoters included major German banks and oil companies, among them some state-owned undertakings. The promoters held shares with so much more voting power per share than the publicly sold shares that it was inconceivable that control of Continental Oil could ever have been wrested from them. Headed by the Reich minister of economics, the corporation's supervisory council was "an amalgamation of industrial leaders, high party leaders, representatives of the armed forces and of the ministerial bureaucracy."[98] Neumann thought that the formation of Continental Oil constituted part of an attempt to merge these four groups into "one integrated élite" held together not by common loyalty, but by "profits, power, prestige, and above all, fear."[99]

The type of study that Neumann undertook has not been pursued systematically since World War II. An obvious question that might be raised, now that historians have scrutinized many of the institutions of the Third Reich for over a quarter of a century in the light of material unavailable to Neumann, is whether, especially during the last years of the regime's existence, the SS did not assume for itself the role that the party played more generally in the Continental Oil Corporation, whether the SS did not perhaps go a step farther and begin to provide the basic framework within which Germany's ruling class was reintegrated and restructured. The issue becomes more pressing when we begin to examine the business undertakings in which the SS was involved by 1945 and discover that a corporation with the inauspicious name German Earth and Stone Works (*Deutsche Erd- und Steinwerke GmbH*), an "SS enterprise" that included extensive installations in the vicinity of concentration camps, was perhaps the largest German

[97] Neumann, *Behemoth*, p. 396.   [98] *Ibid.*, p. 276. See also pp. 356–58.
[99] *Ibid.*, pp. 396–97.

armaments firm by 1945 and one of the giants of German business ventures.[100] Unfortunately, "SS businesses" have been largely neglected in the research on Nazi Germany, and when not neglected, they have been studied mainly from two vantage points that do not lead to the kind of research necessary to pursue the question of the extension and modification of the Continental Oil model. One type of study has seen in the business activities of the SS a development, which, although begun somewhat haphazardly, came to provide levers by which private enterprise would eventually have been destroyed through a "totalitarian" organization of the economy. The other type of study has depicted these business activities as evidence of the exploitation and ultimate domination of the SS by German monopoly capital.[101]

Yet despite the research that must be conducted before some of the most intriguing questions about the Third Reich can be answered adequately, enough work has been done on the recent social history of Germany to enable some generalizations about the effects of developments under the Nazi regime on the German ruling class.

The final impact of the regime, its policies, and the consequences of the World War that it unleashed was the consolidation, in West Germany, of changes in the composition of the ruling class well under way before the Weimar Republic. The Junkers disappeared as a social stratum; more generally, members of the nobility retained or acquired positions within the ruling class only insofar as they became industrial or commercial capitalists. Although the social and economic policies of the Third Reich until late in the war enabled some noblemen to retain their positions in the ruling class, this was possible mainly through their occupation of high posts in the party, in business, in the state bureaucracy, and especially in the army. Increasingly, the retention of their social status became dependent upon their identification with the regime and their participation in the army or in business; and the wartime decimation of the nobility—through military casualties, through executions following the assassination plot of July 20, 1944 and through

---

[100] Alan S. Milward, *The German Economy at War* (London, 1965), p. 157. On the German Earth and Stone Works see Enno Georg, *Die wirtschaftlichen Unternehmungen der SS* (Stuttgart, [1963?]), esp. pp. 42–58.

[101] Enno Georg's valuable monograph is an excellent example of the first type of study. Illustrative of the second type is a popular Czech work focused on concentration camps and genocidal policies, which synthesizes much of the Eastern European literature on these subjects and exploits some of the relevant archival material in Eastern Europe: Ota Kraus and Erich Kulka, *Massenmord und Profit: Die faschistische Ausrottungspolitik und ihre ökonomischen Hintergründe*, trans. Hanna Tichy (Berlin, 1963). For the second type see also Klaus Drobisch, "Der Freundeskreis Himmler: Ein Beispiel für die Unterordnung der Nazipartei und des faschistischen Staatsapparats durch die Finanzoligarchie," *Zeitschrift für Geschichtswissenschaft*, VIII (1960), 304–28.

suicide—contributed to the actual physical destruction of the nobility. Merely in the wake of July 20, hundreds, perhaps thousands of noblemen died. No study of the number of noblemen who died in the aftermath of this attempt to remove Hitler has been made, but roughly five thousand executions were decreed by civilian courts in the wake of the conspiracy,[102] and this figure does not include either sentences imposed by military courts or the numerous suicides of men implicated in the conspiracy such as Field Marshal Günther von Kluge and Major General Henning von Tresckow. The flight of Germans from the eastern provinces before the advancing Soviet Army in 1944 and 1945, the incorporation of German territories east of the Oder-Neisse line into the Soviet Union and Poland, and the expropriation of large estates in what became the East German state completed the dissolution of the Junkers and thereby weakened greatly the remnants of the German nobility. Men from noble families originating both east and west of the Elbe might play important roles in West and, if less frequently, East Germany, but simply as individuals who accommodated themselves to the social and political changes that completed the ruin of the social stratum into which they had been born. As had been increasingly necessary for the past century, the nobleman had to make his peace with a highly bureaucratized bourgeois society in order to retain or regain a position in the ruling class. If only covertly, he had to enter the world of business and acquire commercial and industrial property; or he had to obtain a high position in the army or civil service; or he had to enter politics and exploit his connections, status, and skills.

As many students of contemporary Germany have emphasized, one consequence of the Third Reich and the postwar purges of former "Nazis" was to accelerate the frequency of professional political activity as a route to social ascent and possible entry into the ruling class.[103] In postwar West Germany political activity stood side by side with business activities as one of the two major routes to membership in the ruling class. Indeed, to observers who view the occupation of political offices as the decisive criterion of power in modern society, the political route has often appeared more important. The situation that developed in West Germany became similar to that in the United States, where the ruling class consists of big businessmen supplemented by some politicians, who, in turn, become, like Lyndon Johnson, big busi-

---

[102] Bracher, *Die deutsche Diktatur*, p. 498.

[103] See Wolfgang Zapf, *Wandlungen der deutschen Elite: Ein Zirkulationsmodell deutscher Führungsgruppen 1919–1961* (Munich, [1965?]), esp. pp. 45–54, 57–58; Schoenbaum, *Hitler's Social Revolution*, esp. pp. 266–70; Lewis J. Edinger, *Politics in Germany: Attitudes and Processes* (Boston, 1968), esp. p. 187.

nessmen, even if their fortunes appear modest alongside those of the Duponts or Rockefellers.[104]

Like the inflation of 1922, the currency reform of 1948 in the Western zones of occupation worked to the advantage of the holders of real and industrial properties. Once again large segments of the middle class found their assets expropriated in fact if not in law. Some remarkable success stories of the rise of new big businessmen, of which the meteoric career of Willi Schlieker in heavy industry is *sui generis,* confirmed rather than contradicted the structural changes within the ruling class, whereby industrial and commercial interests now predominated unchallenged except by the ingenious fantasies of social scientists determined to assert the priority of a compartmentalized notion of power as exercised primarily by the holders of formal political offices or as dispersed among "functional elites" operative in various spheres of society.[105] The hegemony of commercial and especially heavy industrial interests within the West German ruling class was consolidated and extended farther by the integration of the West German economy into the Western European sector of the U.S. *imperium.* Partly as a consequence of the commitment of the military governments of the western zones of occupation, especially in the United States zone, to private capitalist institutions,[106] and partly as a consequence of the power of United States economic interests in the postwar world, decartelization and other structural reforms in the West German economy were pursued only up to the point at which two major changes occurred: first, the basis was laid, through the modification, loosening up, and destruction of some of the previous forms of German business, for a West German national economy adapted to the requirements of efficiency, competition, and cooperation of the postwar capitalist world; second, United States economic interests were able to penetrate western Germany, develop holdings on a scale unprecedented in German-American economic relations, and become the senior partners in international syndicates involving both German and American business interests. Denazification, decartelization, and, more

[104] Cf. the somewhat different analysis in two works by G. William Domhoff, *Who Rules America?* (Englewood Cliffs, N.J., 1967) and *The Higher Circles: The Governing Class in America* (New York, [1970?]).

[105] See, e.g., Erwin K. Scheuch, "Abschied von den Eliten," *Die Zeit* (Hamburg), U.S. edition, Dec. 2, 1969. But cf. Scheuch's "Sichtbare und unsichtbare Macht: Establishment in der Bundesrepublik. Die Herrschaft von Wirtschaft und Wissenschaft," *ibid.,* Nov. 28, 1967.

[106] Some suggestive examples can be derived from John H. Gimbel, *The American Occupation of Germany: Politics and the Military, 1945–1949* (Stanford, 1968), esp. pp. 118, 128, 155–58, 165, 170, 229–30.

broadly, military government provided the levers through which these changes were accomplished. Much of the muscle to push these levers was supplied by men who did not anticipate, and subsequently contemplated with abhorrence, the net product of their efforts: trustbusters, who often set out for Germany in the hope of achieving the success that had been denied them in the United States; German émigrés and other specialists on German affairs seeking to contribute to the reassertion of "the other Germany"; professional military men intent upon demonstrating the tasks that their army could now achieve in peacetime; and an occasional Germanophobe inspired by the vision of a new Germany of potato fields and compulsory pacifists that would be created out of rubble, dismantled factories, and a severely, but justly punished nation.

German Elitism from Past to Present

After 1945 political thought in the areas of Germany occupied by the Western Powers was long in disarray. Under the stimulus of "reeducation" many younger journalists, academicians, and politicians endorsed enthusiastically the ideas of political democracy identified with the Western Powers, especially the United States. The notion of an authoritarian elite was rejected; the high degree of popular control over leadership that presumably existed in the West was held up as a goal, as was the open recruitment of political leadership. When it soon became clear that this image of Western democracy, projected by Western propagandists, education officers, and scholars, had little bearing on the reality of conditions in the West, some Germans began to complain that the Americans had done them a disservice by trying to commit them to a type of democracy that no longer existed: the image of political democracy that the Germans had accepted was a mirage reflecting the realities of the past, not the present.

Many of the disillusioned idealists joined the ranks of those Germans who, although now often speaking in the current jargon of American social science, continued to propagate the idea of democracy of personnel selection rather than decision making.[107] Foreign observers, in turn, pointed with dismay at the persistence of authoritarian attitudes in West Germany. This persistence was frequently taken as a function

---

[107] A short, often undiscriminating, but occasionally incisive critique of elite theories in West Germany is provided by Ernst Gottschling, *Herrschaft der Elite? Gegen eine reaktionäre Theorie* (Berlin, 1958). A broader Marxist view of contemporary bourgeois elitism can be found in the works of Leo Kofler. See, e.g., Leo Kofler, *Der asketische Eros: Industriekultur und Ideologie* (Vienna, [1967?]). Also worthy of note is Miroslav Jodl, *Teorie elity a problém Elity* (Prague, 1968), which has a long English summary.

of the unbroken strength of an authoritarian national character and the failure of reeducation and denazification due, lamentably, but perhaps unavoidably, to the Cold War.

Yet there is a very different way of looking at the persistence of authoritarianism and of answering the specific questions that are most relevant to a study of German elitism. Why did the concept of an open-yet-authoritarian elite become the prevailing pattern in political thought in Germany during the first half of the twentieth century, while the concept of an open, nonauthoritarian elite become the prevailing pattern in political thought in the Western Powers? Why did the idea of creating democracy of personnel selection rather than decision making become in Germany both the central tenet in justifying the perpetuation of bourgeois society and the cornerstone of programs to combat the advance of the working class and establish social and political stability? In the Western Powers the notion of an open nonauthoritarian elite performed such functions. Why not in Germany too?

The answer to these questions can be summed up in an expression from Nietzsche. Prior to 1945 Germany was *unzeitgemäss*; Germany was both behind and ahead of the Western Powers. Although the idea of German development as out of step with that of Western Europe and the United States has provided the effervescence for many a heady concoction brewed by Germanophobes and Germanophiles, whether German or foreign, it can also serve as a leavening in more satisfying fare.[108]

The absence of a successful bourgeois revolution permitted the lingering into the twentieth century of institutions and ideas associated with absolute monarchy. The fiction successful in the West, that democracy of personnel selection as well as of decision making was being realized or already existed, was difficult to sustain in Germany. Before 1917 most German conservatives had little interest in promoting such a fiction since it implied the acceptance of principles that they were determined not to endorse, even as a tactical maneuver; as long as their position seemed secure for the immediate future and German society stable, they had no compelling reason to flirt with dangerous ideas. Any inclination they had to adopt a longer range view was counteracted by the knowledge that both disgruntled liberals and most socialists would have refuted vigorously the suggestion that an open-yet-authoritarian elite had been established in Germany. One type of liberal would attack this fiction by simple comparison with the West;

---

[108] See, e.g., Helmut Plessner, *Schicksal des deutschen Geistes am Ausgang seiner bürgerlichen Epoche* (Zurich, 1935). This work has been reissued under the title *Die verspätete Nation: Über die politische Verführbarkeit bürgerlichen Geistes* (Stuttgart, [1959?]).

another type of liberal would attack it by demonstrating its hollowness even in the West. Socialists invoking the standard of a classless society and employing the methods of Marxian analysis could combine both of these points.

The conflict between Germany and the Western Powers also worked against the acceptance of the notion of an open, nonauthoritarian elite, even as an ideal. Reliance upon the concept of democracy of personnel selection rather than decision making became an attractive way of distinguishing Germany from the very countries with which it had so much in common, and thereby vindicating the failure to reach an accommodation with the Western Powers before World War I. During the war the concept of an open-yet-authoritarian elite came to excuse the prolongation of the slaughter and to counteract Western as well as Bolshevik political warfare against Germany. Indeed, only after 1917–1918 were much of the Right and many moderates willing to hold on high the "open" half of the equation. Since the war led to no resolution of the struggle with the West, and since for the purposes of domestic politics the Right and many moderates found it convenient to emphasize the failure to resolve this conflict, the concept of an open-yet-authoritarian elite justified its continuation, and, eventually, the resumption of armed hostilities in 1939.

Considerations geared to international politics would not have sufficed to sustain the effectiveness of the concept of an open-yet-authoritarian elite. Some German liberals and Social Democrats toyed with the tactic of claiming that after 1918 Germany had become one of the world's most advanced democracies, that the Weimar Republic had realized more fully than any other nation the political ideas associated with the Western democracy, and that political equality and popular control had advanced in Germany with a sudden leap beyond the realities of the West. Although a good case could be made for this argument, it did not become prevalent. Decisive in preventing its acceptance was its explosiveness during the revolutionary era initiated tentatively by the Russian Revolution of 1905 and decisively by the Bolshevik Revolution of 1917. In the West the concept of an open-nonauthoritarian elite had taken firm hold in a period when the possibility of proletarian revolution could be dismissed as a specter, which, however haunting, as in the Paris Commune of 1871, would never materialize. By 1917 it was too late to adopt in Germany the fiction that had served bourgeois society in the West so well. Even in the West, the renewed threat of social revolution led in some circles to the abandonment or virtual renunciation of the concept of an open-nonauthoritarian elite in favor of the pattern prevailing in German elite theories. Germany was still both behind and ahead of the West.

During the Nazi period the concept of democracy of personnel selection rather than decision making served to set Germany off from both the Western Powers and the Soviet Union. At the same time, this concept, combined with the notion of a supreme authoritarian leader, helped to legitimize changes in German society that eliminated the major structural differences between it and the West—changes that were pushed forward and consolidated by the political consequences of defeat in World War II. West Germany became the major European country most similar to the United States. No longer an *unzeitgemäss* bourgeois society, Germany's western half became one of the most *zeitgemäss* of bourgeois lands.

Little wonder that the notion of an authoritarian yet open elite persists, although not unchallenged, in West Germany. In the old democracies of the West, the same notion is on the rise. Perhaps it meets the real needs of the imperialist social orders of the West in the second half of the twentieth century. Fabian elitists like the Webbs and George Bernard Shaw may prove to have been among the true prophets of bourgeois society in the twentieth century. Whether in the prestigious technocratic version propounded by Jean Monnet in France and James Burnham in the United States four decades ago, or in the less respectable versions espoused by Jacques Doriot and Huey Long during the same period, the concept of an open-yet-authoritarian elite could still be dismissed as marginal in the West before 1945. Yet, to mention only a few examples, the technocrats of the French Fifth Republic, sophisticated Tory politicians like R. A. Butler and Ernest Marples in Britain, American social scientists like E. Digby Baltzell,[109] popular political theorists like Walter Lippmann,[110] and Robert Welch of the John Birch Society have moved tentatively or decisively in the direction of advocating an open-yet-authoritarian elite. As the institutions of the West become less democratic in response to the increasing needs for social control by its ruling class, and as the hunger for political participation and self-determination among its peoples grows, what better bourgeois solution could be devised than democracy of personnel selection rather than decision making?

[109] See E. Digby Baltzell, *The Protestant Establishment: Aristocracy and Caste in America* (New York, 1964). Although hedging his statements about the extent of the existing powers of "the establishment," Baltzell, who comes from a socially prominent Philadelphia family, assumes the necessity of the perpetuation of an establishment and its retention of crucial prerogatives. He complains that the upper class in the United States consists primarily of Protestant "Anglo-Saxons" and pleads that it become more representative by admitting larger numbers of Catholics and Jews. His quaint book, written during the early stages of the recent upsurge in the black rights movement, scarcely gives even perfunctory consideration to the desirability of admission of blacks to the establishment, a theme that other elitists had, by then, already taken up.

[110] Walter Lippmann, *Essays in the Public Philosophy* (New York: Mentor paperback, 1956), esp. pp. 18–19, 23, 27–29, 42–46, 52–53, 124.

The more important primary and secondary material on which this study is based has been cited in the footnotes, where much of it has been discussed and evaluated. The reader wishing to look further into any aspect of the life and thought of one of my nine elitists will find that in the footnotes I have frequently pointed to works on these men containing good bibliographies. These bibliographies list some primary and much secondary material that I have not mentioned. For example, a few secondary works cited frequently by other scholars are not alluded to in my footnotes, either because these studies are of no particular relevance to my work, or because they are of little intrinsic value. Calling attention to them would have served little purpose other than the performance of a scholarly ritual that sometimes enhances undeserved reputations.

In the footnotes to each chapter, I have sought to provide the general scholarly reader, to whom the historical literature on many of the topics discussed may be unfamiliar, with a brief survey or critique of pertinent monographs and other studies.

The basic purposes of this bibliographical essay are (1) to give the reader some general guidance in locating material important to the study of the development of elitism in Germany during the Wilhelminian era and the Weimar Republic, and (2) to indicate some subjects that warrant further investigation.

I. The Institutional Context of Elitism in Germany, from Bismarck through Weimar

The bibliographies in a number of readily accessible works dealing with German history during the past century offer good guides to the literature. Although most of these bibliographies concentrate upon published material, they also furnish some leads to unpublished sources. Klaus Epstein's revised edition of Koppel Pinson, *Modern Germany: Its History and Civilization* (New York, 1966) contains a serviceable general bibliography, but ignores works published in the German Democratic Republic (DDR). This failing, an extreme instance of a tendency characteristic until recently of most Western

465

scholarship on Germany, is best remedied by a perusal of the articles and bibliographies in the major historical journal published in the DDR, the *Zeitschrift für Geschichtswissenschaft* (1953–   ). Since Arnold Price assumed the responsibility some ten years ago for preparing the selected list of articles on Germany for the *American Historical Review*, this list has offered a useful sampling of East German periodical literature on German history. Occasionally of assistance in surveying East German contributions are the bibliographies published in the most important West German periodical devoted to twentieth-century history, the *Vierteljahrshefte für Zeitgeschichte* (1953–   ).

Helpful introductions to the literature on nineteenth-century political and social history are available in two works by Theodore S. Hamerow: *Restoration, Revolution, Reaction: Economics and Politics in Germany, 1815–1871* (Princeton, 1958); *The Social Foundations of German Unification, 1858–1871: Ideas and Institutions* (Princeton, 1969). The bibliographies in Hamerow's books can be supplemented by turning to two studies by Helmut Böhme: *Deutschlands Weg zur Grossmacht: Studien zum Verhältnis von Wirtschaft und Staat während der Reichsgründungszeit 1848–1881* (Cologne, 1966); *Prolegomena zu einer Sozial- und Wirtschaftsgeschichte Deutschlands im 19. und 20. Jahrhundert* (Frankfurt am Main: Suhrkamp paperback, 1968).

In addition to the second of Böhme's works, surveys of the literature on political and social development from the late nineteenth century through the Nazi era are contained in Dirk Stegmann, *Die Erben Bismarcks: Parteien und Verbände in der Spätphase des wilhelminischen Deutschlands. Sammlungspolitik 1897–1918* (Cologne, 1970); Herman Lebovics, *Social Conservatism and the Middle Classes in Germany, 1914–1933* (Princeton, 1969); and David Schoenbaum, *Hitler's Social Revolution: Class and Status in Nazi Germany, 1933–1939* (Garden City, 1966). Particularly relevant to the Weimar Republic and the Third Reich, but useful also for earlier decades are the major works of Karl Dietrich Bracher: *Die Auflösung der Weimarer Republik*, 4th ed. (Villingen im Schwarzwald, 1964); a study written jointly with Wolfgang Sauer and Gerhard Schulz, *Die nationalsozialistische Machtergreifung: Studien zur Errichtung des totalitären Herrschaftssystems in Deutschland 1933/34*, 2nd ed. (Cologne and Opladen, 1962); and *Die deutsche Diktatur: Entstehung, Struktur, Folgen des Nationalsozialismus*, 2nd ed. (Cologne, 1969). The last two books are available in English translations.

A bibliography for the period since 1914, Wolfgang Benz, *Quellen zur Zeitgeschichte*, will be the third and final volume of *Deutsche Geschichte seit dem 1. Weltkrieg* (Stuttgart, 1973–   ).

II. Suggestions for Further Studies in
German Elitism, 1890–1933

A. *The Role of Business, Government, Employee Organizations,
Political Parties, and Other Groups in the Development and
Propagation of Elite Theories and Elitist Notions.*

During the past decade the number of investigations of "interest
groups" in Germany has increased markedly. The publications resulting from these efforts are of great importance for our understanding of
the structure and dynamics of German society. But most such research
has dealt only tangentially with elitism and has devoted little attention
to the views of individual elite theorists. Thus far much of the value of
this research for the study of elitism has been to supply some information on aspects of the relationships—both personal and institutional—
of scholars, publicists, and other writers to government, as well as to
private and semipublic associations. References to personal contacts
and other meetings, to direct and indirect subsidies to elitists, and to
similar influences can often be found in publications resulting from recent research. To be sure, many of these references are tantalizingly
brief, or even inconclusive. But the attentive reader will discover
promising clues to the attitudes and objectives of the elitists, and those
of their patrons and audience.

In West Germany the students of Gerhard A. Ritter (of Berlin, and
not to be confused with the late Gerhard Ritter of Freiburg), of Fritz
Fischer (Hamburg), and Wolfgang Abendroth (Marburg) have been
notably active in studying political and economic organizations, often
on the basis of considerable research into archival material. The published dissertations of Abendroth's students usually appear in the
series *Marburger Abhandlungen zur Politischen Wissenschaft*; the
major publications of Ritter's and Fischer's students are not confined
largely to a single series. Some have been included in the *Beiträge zur
Geschichte des Parlamentarismus und der politischen Parteien*, which
contains many other important works and whose range is broader than
the title of the collection suggests. Among the major works by Ritter's
students not included in this series are Hans-Jürgen Puhle, *Agrarische
Interessenpolitik und preussischer Konservatismus im wilhelminischen
Reich (1893–1914): Ein Beitrag zur Analyse des Nationalismus in
Deutschland am Beispiel des Bundes der Landwirte und der Deutsch-
Konservativen Partei*, Schriftenreihe des Forschungsinstituts der
Friedrich-Ebert-Stiftung (Hannover, 1967); and Hartmut Kaelble,
*Industrielle Interessenpolitik in der wilhelminischen Gesellschaft:
Centralverband Deutscher Industrieller 1895–1914*, Veröffentlich-

ungen der Historischen Kommission zu Berlin beim Friedrich-Meinecke-Institut der Freien Universität Berlin, xxvii (Berlin, 1967).

A very important recent product of the Fischer school is Stegmann's *Erben Bismarcks* (see above), which should be read in conjunction with Fischer's own *Krieg der Illusionen: Die deutsche Politik von 1911 bis 1914* (Düsseldorf, 1969).

A characteristic of Stegmann's work, shared by much of the literature on political parties and interest groups published in both East and West Germany, is the lack of attention given to systematic political thought. An example will help to clarify my point. Focusing on the formulation of government policy, Fischer and most of his students have done little with the works of highly articulate elitists; thus Stegmann is on shaky ground when he discusses the published programmatic works of the Pan-German leader Heinrich Class. A useful supplement to Stegmann's book is a Cologne dissertation by Konrad Schilling, *Beiträge zu einer Geschichte des radikalen Nationalismus in der wilhelminischen Ära 1890–1909: Die Entstehung des radikalen Nationalismus, seine Einflussnahme auf die innere und äussere Politik des Deutschen Reiches und die Stellung von Regierung und Reichstag zu seiner politischen publizistischen Aktivität* (Cologne, 1968). Schilling's study is available both on microfilm and in a xeroxed edition.

Abendroth's students have, in general, been more interested in, and adept at, utilizing published primary material of a programmatic and theoretical nature. But even the invaluable monograph on the DVP by Lothar Döhn, *Politik und Interesse: Die Interessenstruktur der Deutschen Volkspartei* (Meisenheim am Glan, 1970), is of significance mainly for its examination of the structure of the party, and the social and economic determinants of the party's policies; Döhn does not explore in depth the ideology or elitist ideas of its leaders and others linked to it.

Still noteworthy for its methodology, as well as some of its material on organizations and their functions within the development of monopoly capitalism is a work first published a quarter century ago by Jürgen Kuczynski, *Studien zur Geschichte des deutschen Imperialismus*, i: *Monopole und Unternehmerverbände*, 2nd ed. (Berlin, 1952); ii: *Propagandaorganisationen des Monopolkapitalismus* (Berlin, 1950). Revising a customary remark made by reviewers in the United States about Marxist history, one can say that Kuczynski's work has worn so well because it is rooted in the fertile bed of Marxism. Although both these *Studien* and some of his other works contain an occasional and valuable discussion of the political ideas of some elitists, most work published in the DDR betrays an understandable, but regrettable impatience with the nuances of bourgeois thought in the twentieth century—or, much less frequently, a sentimental glorification of some upright bourgeois.

Among important East German works which, like those of some scholars living in the West, draw extensively upon archival material located in the DDR are Fritz Klein, ed., *Politik im Kriege 1914–1918: Studien zur Politik der deutschen herrschenden Klassen im 1. Weltkrieg* (Berlin, 1964); a Habilitationsschrift by Willibald Gutsche, *Die Beziehungen zwischen der Regierung Bethmann-Hollweg und dem Monopolkapital in den ersten Monaten des 1. Weltkrieges* (Berlin, 1967); Hellmuth Weber, *Ludendorff und die Monopole: Deutsche Kriegspolitik 1916–1918* (Berlin, 1966); Helga Nussbaum, *Unternehmer gegen Monopole: Über Struktur und Aktion antimonopolistischer bürgerlichen Gruppen zu Beginn des 20. Jahrhunderts* (Berlin, 1966); Kurt Gossweiler, *Grossbanken, Industriemonopole, Staat, Ökonomie und Politik des staatsmonopolistischen Kapitalismus in Deutschland 1914–1932* (Berlin, 1971). A sampling of current work in the DDR on social and economic history can be found in the pages of the *Jahrbuch für Wirtschaftsgeschichte* (1960–   ). A recent encyclopedic work published in the DDR on parties and interest groups was prepared by the Historisches Institut der Friedrich-Schiller-Universität Jena, *Die bürgerlichen Parteien in Deutschland: Handbuch der Geschichte der bürgerlichen Parteien und anderer bürgerlicher Interessenorganisationen vom Vormärz bis zum Jahre 1945* (2 vols., Berlin, 1968–1970).

Some scholars living in the United States, including Gerald D. Feldman and Henry A. Turner, Jr., have conducted noteworthy research in archival material pertaining to big business after 1914. But despite the contributions such scholars are making to our knowledge of the history of the relationship between politics and big business in Germany, they have not explored the subject of elitism, and the relevance of their works to this subject is similar to that of most of the German studies that have been mentioned. Of Turner's many recent articles see, for example: "Emil Kirdorf and the Nazi Party," *Central European History*, I (1968), 324–44; "The *Ruhrlade*, Secret Cabinet of Heavy Industry in the Weimar Republic," *ibid.*, III (1970), 195–228; "Big Business and the Rise of Hitler," *American Historical Review*, LXXV (1969), 56–70. Of Feldman's work see, for example: *Army, Industry, and Labor in Germany, 1914–1918* (Princeton, 1966); "The Social and Economic Policies of German Big Business, 1918–1929," *American Historical Review*, LXXV (1969), 47–55; "German Business between War and Revolution: The Origins of the Stinnes-Legien Agreement" in Gerhard A. Ritter, ed., *Entstehung und Wandel der modernen Gesellschaft: Festschrift für Hans Rosenberg zum 65. Geburtstag* (Berlin, 1970).

A review article on German economic history by Hans-Ulrich Wehler, "Theorieprobleme der modernen deutschen Wirtschaftsgeschichte (1800–1945)," can be found in this same *Festschrift*.

Both stringent analysis and much more research will be necessary before our understanding of crucial topics in the history of German capitalism is expanded sufficiently to permit the thorough exploration of the relationship between the development of elitism and that of the institutions of monopoly capital. In addition to the archival studies and other works noted above, an as yet scarcely tapped source is to be found in reports and periodicals issued by business associations, employee organizations, and similar groups. To date, this type of source has been used mostly by *Volkswirtschaftler* writing *Diplomarbeiten* or doctoral dissertations. Another rich, generally neglected body of material can be found, as many historians have remarked, in the published Nürnberg trial documents, of which the edition in German is to be preferred: *Der Prozess gegen die Hauptkriegsverbrecher vor dem internationalen Militärgerichtshof* (42 vols., Nürnberg, 1947–1949).

The use of archival and published primary material is likely to lead to penetrating and innovative research only if related to some of the major and often neglected works that have appeared during the past fifty years. For seldom have the suggestive insights and theories offered by these works been scrutinized systematically or followed up by other scholars on the basis of extensive research. Among those which must be consulted for their methodology, their formulation of problems, or for the documents and data that they contain—and which have not been mentioned above—are:

Das Argument: Zeitschrift für Philosophie und Sozialwissenschaften, especially some of the issues (nos. 32, 33, 41) during the 1960's devoted to fascism.

Charles Bettelheim, *L'Economie allemande sous le nazisme: Un aspect de la décadence du capitalisme* (Paris, 1946).

Robert A. Brady, *The Rationalization Movement in German Industry: A Study in the Evolution of Economic Planning* (Berkeley, 1933).

Costantino Bresciani-Turroni, *The Economics of Inflation: A Study of Currency Depreciation in Postwar Germany*, trans. Millicent E. Sayers (London, 1937).

Dietrich Eichholtz and Wolfgang Schumann, eds., *Anatomie des Krieges: Neue Dokumente über die Rolle des deutschen Monopolkapitalismus bei der Vorbereitung und Durchführung des 2. Weltkrieges* (Berlin, 1969).

George W. F. Hallgarten, *Imperialismus vor 1914: Die sozio-*

logischen Grundlagen der Aussenpolitik europäischer Gross-mächte vor dem ersten Weltkrieg, 2nd ed. (2 vols., Munich, 1963).

A. S. Jerussalimski, *Die Aussenpolitik und die Diplomatie des deutschen Imperialismus am Ende des 19. Jahrhunderts* (Berlin, 1954).

Jürgen Kuczynski, *Die Geschichte der Lage der Arbeiter unter dem Kapitalismus* (37 vols., Berlin, 1960–1969). Much more far-ranging than the title would indicate, this is actually an edition of Kuczynski's collected works.

Hermann Levy, *Industrial Germany: A Study of its Monopoly Organizations and their Control by the State* (Cambridge, 1935).

Franz Neumann, *Behemoth: The Structure and Practice of National Socialism, 1933–1944* (New York, 1963).

Helge Pross, *Manager und Aktionär in Deutschland: Untersuchungen zum Verhältnis von Eigentum und Verfügungsmacht* (Frankfurt am Main, 1965).

Arthur Schweitzer, *Big Business in the Third Reich* (Bloomington, Ind., 1964).

Fritz Sternberg, *Der Niedergang des deutschen Kapitalismus* (Berlin, 1932).

Eugene Varga, *Die historischen Wurzeln der Besonderheit des deutschen Imperialismus* (Berlin, 1946).

Wolfgang Zapf, *Wandlungen der deutschen Elite: Ein Zirkulations-modell deutscher Führungsgruppen 1919–1961* (Munich: Piper paperback, [1965?]).

Other promising topics dealing with the articulation and dissemination of elitism pertain to the role of periodicals, publishing houses, and "cultural" associations addressed to, or drawing upon, the middle class. One such organization is the DHV (*Deutschnationaler Handlungsgehilfenverband*). A short history of the DHV has been written by a student of Fritz Fischer, Iris Hamel, *Völkischer Verband und nationale Gewerkschaft: Der Deutschnationale Handlungsgehilfenverband 1893–1933* (Frankfurt am Main, 1967). Nelson Edmonson, "The Fichte Society: A Chapter in Germany's Conservative Revolution," *Journal of Modern History,* xxxviii (1966), 161–80 deals with aspects of an association that developed under the DHV's patronage. A monograph on a publicist who edited one of the periodicals issued by the DHV's publishing house, the *Hanseatische Verlagsanstalt,* has been done by Heinrich Kessler, *Wilhelm Stapel als politischer Publizist: Ein Beitrag zur Geschichte des konservativen Nationalismus zwischen den beiden Weltkriegen* (Nürnberg, 1967). I am currently engaged in a study of the politics and ideology of the DHV. See my research note in the American Philosophical Society *Year Book* (1969), pp. 466–67.

Also promising subjects are periodicals intended for a socially better-situated audience. Intensive research on some of these periodicals is still in its early stages. A good example is *Der Ring*, the organ of the *Herrenklub*. Hans-Joachim Schwierskott's *Arthur Moeller van den Bruck und der revolutionäre Nationalismus in der Weimarer Republik* (Göttingen, [1962?]) deals in large part with a precursor of the *Ring*.

B. Elitism and Internationalism

As I have indicated particularly in Chapter Nine, the subject of internationalist ideas espoused by the Right offers a number of seldom explored avenues for further research. Much the same can be said of the liberal Left. Unfortunately the common identification with anti-Semitism of the issue of international ties among both liberals and big businessmen has served to inhibit some potentially fruitful inquiry. Norman Cohn's *Warrant for Genocide: The Myth of the Jewish World-Conspiracy and the Protocols of the Elders of Zion* (New York: Harper paperback, 1969) exposes a number of the more preposterous versions of anti-Semitic myths, but the uses to which these absurdities have been put should not lead us to overlook the historical significance of the role of internationalism on either the Right or the liberal Left.

Now and then during the past fifty years the question of the relationship of the Nazi party to foreign political and business groups has attracted much attention. One of the most discussed—and most tangled —issues has been the part played by foreigners in financing the Nazi party during the 1920's and early 1930's. I recall hearing some years ago a prominent West German historian, who was seeking to impress upon his students that foreigners could not be blamed for Hitler's coming to power, assert that allegations about subsidies provided by big business abroad for the Nazis were untrue. This assertion was made shortly after the publication of an article by Herman Lutz, "Fälschungen zur Auslandsfinanzierung Hitlers," *Vierteljahrshefte für Zeitgeschichte*, ii (1954), 386–96.

Lutz's article was based on one section of a book that he subsequently published in English, *German-French Unity: Basis for European Peace* (Chicago, 1957). Despite its misleading title, this book contains a good introduction to the topic of foreign subsidies (see pp. 105–30, 179–200). His conclusions differ somewhat from those presented in his article. Although he produces some evidence discrediting claims about the role of United States businessmen and corporations, he sustains many similar charges about French, British, and other non-German businessmen. Much detailed and painstaking work will probably be necessary before we shall be in a position to arrive at solidly based conclusions. But the sensationalism that has frequently been identified with topics on the Nazis should not distract us from the task of undertaking broadly conceived investigations of the financing of other political organizations.

An old general work that has been largely forgotten is attentive to the functions of internationalism and internationalist groups: R. Palme Dutt, *World Politics, 1918–1936* (London, 1936). A typological analysis of the cooperation of rightwing movements across national boundaries can be found in Arno J. Mayer, *Dynamics of Counterrevolution in Europe, 1870–1956: An Analytic Framework* (New York: Harper paperback, 1971), which has an excellent brief bibliography. On the relationship between the German Right and the Italian Fascists before 1933, there is Klaus-Peter Hoepke, *Die deutsche Rechte und der italienische Faschismus: Ein Beitrag zum Selbstverständnis und zur Politik von Gruppen und Verbänden der deutschen Rechten* (Düsseldorf, 1968). Rich in suggestive allusions, Hoepke's work is of more general import than might be gathered from its title.

Hoepke devotes a section to Prince Karl Anton Rohan's *Europäische Revue*. Both this right-of-center periodical and Count Richard Coudenhove-Kalergi's left-of-center Pan-European movement are promising subjects for research that have been largely neglected.

A broadly conceived, if brief work on German-American relations employs some of the more barren catch phrases of the post-1945 Cold War, but is unusual for its attempt to deal systematically with its subject: Karl Obermann, *Die Beziehungen des amerikanischen Imperialismus zum deutschen Imperialismus in der Zeit der Weimarer Republik* (Berlin, 1952). See also a recent monograph by Werner Link, *Die amerikanische Stabilisierungspolitik in Deutschland 1921–32: Die Vereinigten Staaten von Amerika und der Wiederaufstieg nach dem 1. Weltkrieg* (Düsseldorf, 1970).

C. Political Biographies and Other Topics

In general, major German elitists of the liberal Left have been better provided with biographers and with studies of their political ideas than have those of the Right. But there are still a number of important German and German-Austrian liberals who have been given little monographic treatment. Research focused on them as elitists would close important gaps in biographical literature, as well as contribute to our knowledge of the development of German elitism. Candidates for study include: Gertrud Bäumer, the writer and politician, whose path from Naumann's National Socials, to prominence in the Demo-

474—Bibliographical Essay

cratic party during the Weimar Republic, and, later, to a positive assessment of the Third Reich, has not been scrutinized; Hans Kelsen, the German-Austrian legal positivist, who emigrated to the United States during the Nazi era; Hugo Preuss, whose interest to historians has generally been limited to his role as "father" of the Weimar Constitution, and whose development as a left liberal in Berlin has not been examined systematically; Alfred Weber, whose importance is still obscured by the fame of his brother Max Weber; Friedrich Wieser, the German-Austrian economist and sociologist, whose *Das Gesetz von der Macht* (Vienna, 1926) might, by itself merit a short monograph.

Among the elitists of the Right after World War I, the neoconservatives have attracted the greatest amount of scholarly attention. But a perusal of the extensive bibliography of neoconservative writings in Armin Mohler's *Die konservative Revolution in Deutschland 1918–1932: Grundriss ihrer Weltanschauungen* (Stuttgart, 1950) will turn up many men on whom there has been little or no research, even during the past quarter century. Also a helpful guide—in addition to the other general surveys of neoconservatism cited in the footnotes to Chapter Seven—is Aurel Kolnai, *The War against the West* (New York, 1938). Kolnai's book contains long excerpts from, and résumés of, a number of neoconservative works.

Among the hundreds of volumes published in a popularly written series issued by *Friedrich Mann's Pädagogisches Magazin* during the Wilhelminian era and the Weimar Republic, many reflect conservative and reactionary elitism. These volumes, as well as the growing body of secondary literature on the non-Nazi Right, should be consulted for further leads to elitists and elitist groups on the Right that can profitably be studied.

The examination of scholarly periodicals should be included in the investigation of the development of elitism in Germany. Periodicals in the social sciences, particularly during the Weimar Republic, contain much elitist literature that is well worth scrutinizing. One of the most promising is the *Kölner Vierteljahrshefte für Soziologie*. See also:

Archiv für Sozialwissenschaft und Sozialpolitik
Die Gesellschaft
Politische Wissenschaft
Zeitschrift für die gesamte Staatswissenschaft
Zeitschrift für pädagogische Psychologie
Zeitschrift für Politik
Zeitschrift für Völkerpsychologie

The pressing need for more research on elitism in Germany will, I hope, lead to investigations conducted in a way that facilitates comparison with the development of elitism in other countries. For too long, many historians of Germany have tended to indulge in the extravagant luxury of yielding to an understandable fascination for the unique and seemingly unparalleled. German history, they then assume, cannot be examined within a framework of comparative historical inquiry. Historians have left the study of elites and elitism largely to social scientists whose behaviorist orientation is often a function of their attentiveness to the manipulative and policy requirements of the U.S. *imperium*. Some of these social scientists have made valuable contributions to our understanding of history, particularly in their formulation of research designs and their use of statistical methods. But even the best works of such social scientists usually take for granted a view of history, society, and change similar to that of the German bourgeois elitists committed to the notion of an open-yet-authoritarian elite. The basic approach of these works is too symptomatic of antidemocratic trends of their own era, and too responsive to the situation of the class they serve, to provide us with much more than monographs that have to be dissected and subsumed by others. Perhaps historians, although not noted for audacity and creativity in the development of methodology, will be able to see beyond the few narrow tunnels of the human estate explored by this type of elitist.

Index

LIBRARY OF CONGRESS CATALOGING IN PUBLICATION DATA

Struve, Walter, 1935-
    Elites against democracy.

    Bibliography: p.
        1. Political science—History—Germany.
    2. Elite (Social sciences) I. Title.
    JA84.G3S77   320.5   72-14034
    ISBN 0-691-07555-7
    ISBN 0-691-10020-9 (pbk.)

8-401